'Todd has a good ear for tone and a deep understand~ ~-
ingly thorough book' Emma Donoghue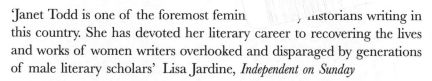

'A rip-roaring read' Michèle Roberts,

'Genuinely original' Antonia Fraser, T~

'Janet Todd is one of the foremost femin   ~~storians writing in
this country. She has devoted her literary career to recovering the lives
and works of women writers overlooked and disparaged by generations
of male literary scholars' Lisa Jardine, *Independent on Sunday*

'Janet Todd guides us with unfailing buoyancy and a wit all her own
through the intricacies of Restoration theatre and politics. [Behn's]
epitaph seems to suggest her wit is buried with her. Not at all; it is now
wondrously resurrected' Michael Foot, *Evening Standard*

'Thorough and stimulating....clear readable prose....a fascinating study
of the public face of Behn, of its shifting masks and modes'
Maureen Duffy, *Literary Review*

'A major new biography...Todd's rich biography will be of interest to
everyone who cares about the period or about women as writers'
Jane Spencer, *The Times Higher Education Supplement*

'Janet Todd, a feminist scholar, has done a great deal of ground-breaking
scholarship on women writers of the "long eighteenth century". The
book is certainly accessible for the lay historian—it reads quickly and
lightly...Even Todd's throwaway lines are steeped in learning and observation. Todd has documented so ably the daring attempt of a woman
to write, both for her daily bread and for immortal fame'
Ruth Perry, *Women's Review of Books*

'Todd is so scrupulous and educated an observer that one never has any
sense of being fobbed off with speculative fiction rather than well adduced
fact....Todd has shown that even determined secrecy and a series of
carefully shaped masks offer no protection against posterity. This is as
much of Aphra Behn as we are ever likely to know'
Brian Morton, *Scotland on Sunday*

'Janet Todd's brilliant biography of Aphra Behn weaves a story together
with precision, verve and confidence. Witty and pugnacious, Todd's book
is as much a window on the public cacophony of the era as it is a
portrait of a playwright' Melanie McGrath, *Independent*

Riley Pinx. R. W. fc.

Mrs Behn.

Aphra Behn, engraving by Robert White after a lost portrait by John Riley c. 1680

Aphra Behn
A SECRET LIFE

JANET TODD

**Fentum
Press**

Fentum Press, London

Sold and distributed by
Global Book Sales/Macmillan Distribution
and in North America by
Consortium Book Sales and Distribution, Inc.

An earlier edition of this book, *The Secret Life of Aphra Behn*,
was published in 1996 by André Deutsch Ltd/Rutgers University Press,
and in 2000 by Rivers Oram/Pandora.

A CIP catalogue record for this book is available from the British Library

ISBN (paperback) 978-1-909572-06-5

Printed and bound in Great Britain by CPI (CR0 4YY)

For Maureen Duffy

CONTENTS

ABOUT THE AUTHOR & AUTHOR'S PREVIOUS WORKS   IX

PREFACE   XI

ACKNOWLEDGEMENTS   XXI

INTRODUCTION TO THE 1996 VERSION   XXIII

1. Beginnings in Kent   1
2. Sir Thomas Colepeper and Lord Strangford   18
3. Voyage to Surinam   29
4. Colonial Politics: Willoughby and Byam   40
5. Surinam: African Slaves and Native Americans   51
6. Marriage and the Great Plague   63
7. On the King's Service   76
8. To Antwerp   85
9. Debts and Disappointment   100
10. In and Out of Prison   114
11. Theatrical Début: *The Forc'd Marriage*   134
12. *The Amorous Prince* and *Covent Garden Drolery*   146
13. *The Dutch Lover* and Theatrical Conflict   160
14. John Hoyle and *Abdelazer*   175
15. Poetry in a Theatrical World   194
16. *The Rover* and *Thomaso*   213
17. *Sir Patient Fancy* and City Whigs   227
18. The Popish Plot and *The Feign'd Curtizans*   240
19. Deaths of the Earl of Rochester and Viscount Stafford   255
20. *The Second Part of The Rover* and *The Roundheads*   274
21. Free-thinking in Politics and Religion   293

22. *Love-Letters between a Nobleman and his Sister*   307

23. The Great Frost and *Voyage to the Isle of Love*   321

24. Death of Charles II and Coronation of James II   343

25. Farewell to the Theatre: *The Luckey Chance*
    and *The Emperor of the Moon*   361

26. *Seneca Unmasqued* and *La Montre*   381

27. Part III of *Love-Letters* and Court Poetry   401

28. *A Discovery of New Worlds* and Poems for James II   412

29. *The Widdow Ranter* and *Oroonoko*   428

30. End of Stuart Dynasty and Death of Aphra Behn   442

NOTES   455

CHRONOLOGICAL LIST OF BEHN'S WORKS   545

BIBLIOGRAPHY OF WORKS WRITTEN BEFORE 1800   549

SELECTED WORKS PUBLISHED AFTER 1800   558

INDEX   569

Janet Todd was born in Wales and grew up in Britain, Bermuda and Sri Lanka. She has worked in Ghana, Puerto Rico, India, Scotland and England. In the US, at the University of Florida and Douglass College, Rutgers, she began the first journal devoted to women's writing. She has published on the novel and memoir and written biographies of Jane Austen, Mary Wollstonecraft, her daughters Fanny and Mary Shelley, and the Irish Lady Mount Cashell. A Professor Emerita at the University of Aberdeen and Honorary Fellow of Newnham College, Janet Todd is a former President of Lucy Cavendish College, Cambridge, where she established the Lucy Cavendish Fiction Prize. She has published two novels: *Lady Susan Plays the Game* and *A Man of Genius*. She lives in Cambridge and Venice.

JANET TODD'S PREVIOUS WORKS

Women's Friendship in Literature (New York: Columbia University Press, 1980, 1984, 1992)

English Congregational Hymns in the Eighteenth Century; their purpose and design (Watts to Cowper), co-authored with M. Marshall (Lexington: University of Kentucky Press, 1983)

Sensibility: an Introduction (London: Methuen, 1986)

Feminist Literary History (Cambridge: Polity Press and New York: Routledge, 1988)

The Sign of Angellica: Women, Writing and Fiction 1660–1800 (London: Virago, 1989; New York: Columbia University Press, 1990, 1992)

Gender, Art and Death (Cambridge: Polity Press, 1993)

The Secret Life of Aphra Behn (London: André Deutsch, 1996; New Brunswick: Rutgers University Press, 1997; London and New York: Pandora and New York University Press, 1999; London: Bloomsbury eBook, 2013)

The Critical Fortunes of Aphra Behn (London and New York: Boydell and Brewer, 1998)

The Revolutionary Life of Mary Wollstonecraft (London: Weidenfeld and Nicolson; New York: Columbia University Press, 2000; paperback London: Phoenix Press, 2001; London: Bloomsbury eBook, 2013)

Rebel Daughters: Ireland in Conflict (London: Viking, 2003; *Daughters of Ireland* New York: Ballantine Books, 2004)

The Cambridge Introduction to Jane Austen (Cambridge: Cambridge University Press, 2006)

Death and the Maidens: Fanny Wollstonecraft and the Shelley Circle (London: Profile Books; Berkeley: Counterpoint Press, 2007)

The Jane Austen Treasury: A Collection of Fascinating Insights into Her Life, Her Time and Her Novels (London: André Deutsch, 2014, 2017)

Lady Susan Plays the Game (London: Bloomsbury eBook, 2013; paperback, 2016)

A Man of Genius (London: Bitter Lemon Press, 2016; paperback, 2017)

Selected Editions since 1990

The Complete Works of Mary Wollstonecraft (7 vols., with Marilyn Butler) (London: Pickering and Chatto and New York: New York University Press, 1990)

Mary Wollstonecraft, *Mary, A Fiction and Maria*; Mary Shelley, *Matilda* (London: Pickering and Chatto, 1991; London: Penguin, 1992)

Oroonoko, The Rover and Other Works (London: Penguin, 1992)

The Complete Works of Aphra Behn (7 vols., London: Pickering and Chatto; Columbus: Ohio State University Press, 1992–6; London: Taylor and Francis ebook, 2017)

The Poetry of Aphra Behn (New York: New York University Press, 1996)

Aphra Behn, *Love-Letters between a Nobleman and his Sister* (London: Penguin, 1996)

The Political Writings of Mary Wollstonecraft (London: Pickering and Chatto; Toronto: University of Toronto Press, 1993; Oxford University Press, 1994)

Counterfeit Ladies: Mal Cutpurse and Mary Carleton (with Elizabeth Spearing) (London: Pickering and Chatto and New York University Press, 1994)

Charlotte Smith, *Desmond* (with Antje Blank) (London: Pickering and Chatto, 1997; Calgary: Broadview 2001).

The Complete Letters of Mary Wollstonecraft (New York: Columbia University Press, 2004; London: Penguin, 2003)

Aphra Behn, *Oroonoko* (London: Penguin, 2003)

The Cambridge Edition of the Works of Jane Austen (General Editor) (Cambridge, Cambridge University Press, 2005–8)

Selected Edited Collections

An Anthology of British Women Writers (with Dale Spender) (London: Pandora, 1989)

Aphra Behn Studies (Cambridge: Cambridge University Press, 1996)

Cambridge Companion to Aphra Behn (with Derek Hughes) (Cambridge: Cambridge University Press, 2004)

Jane Austen in Context (Cambridge: Cambridge University Press, 2008)

Cambridge Companion to Pride and Prejudice (Cambridge: Cambridge University Press, 2013)

PREFACE

Aphra Behn: A Secret Life tells the story of one of the most extraordinary writers in English literature. Behn was fortunate in her historical moment: the Restoration, that naughty period following the end of the Puritan republic and re-establishment of monarchy in 1660. It delighted in masks and self-fashioning as many people remade their pasts to fit new allegiances. Aphra Behn was a woman who wore masks. My biography tries to get behind as many as possible.

She was the first English woman to earn her living solely by her pen. The most prolific dramatist of her time, Behn was also an innovative writer of fiction and a translator of science and French romance. The novelist Virginia Woolf wrote, 'All women together ought to let flowers fall on the tomb of Aphra Behn...For it was she who earned them the right to speak their minds.' Minds *and* bodies. Behn was a lyrical and erotic poet, expressing a frank sexuality that addressed such subjects as male impotence, female orgasm, bisexuality and the indeterminacies of gender.

Despite Woolf's generous assessment, no woman would have such freedom again for many centuries. (And in our frank and feminist era Behn can still astonish with her mocking treatment of sexual and social subjects like amorphous desire, marriage and motherhood.) During the two more respectable or prudish centuries that followed her death in 1689 women were afraid of her toxic image and mostly unwilling to emulate her sexual frankness. In her day, Behn had the reputation of a respected professional writer and also of a 'punk-poetess'. For a long time after her death, she was allowed only to be the second.

Beyond her successes on the stage and in fiction, Aphra Behn was a Royalist spy in the Netherlands and South America. She also served as a political propagandist for the courts of Charles II and his unpopular brother James II. Thus her life has to be deeply embedded in the tumultuous seventeenth century, in conflict-ridden England and Continental Europe and in the mismanaged slave colonies of the Americas. Her necessarily furtive activities, along with her prolific literary output of acknowledged and anonymous works, make her a lethal combination of obscurity, secrecy and staginess, an uneasy fit for any biographical narrative, speculative or factual. Aphra Behn is not so much a woman to be unmasked as an unending combination of masks and intrigue, and her work delivers different images and sometimes contradictory views.

Much is secure about her professional career as dramatist, but there's a relative paucity of absolute facts about Aphra Behn's personal life. Coupled both with the sly suggestions she throws out and with her wonderfully inventive method of weaving experience and fancy with historical fact, this circumstance suggests that speculation and intuition are at times appropriate modes for her biographer. People of the Restoration made mirror and distorted mirror images of themselves. Fooling and deceit were art forms. So identifications in her life story are tentative, and the characters in her 'true' narratives and poems, relatives, friends and lovers, may be composite—or imaginary. I continue to see with varying degrees of clarity a 'real' human being and a protean author of protean works, a mainly independent woman who worked incredibly hard, often struggled with ill health, and was almost always short of money.

The Secret Life of Aphra Behn was originally published in 1996 following my edition of her complete works. Now, twenty years on, I find that much has been written about this marvellous writer, much that illuminates her rich oeuvre, but that nothing has significantly changed for me the overall picture of her and her tumultuous times.

Readers of today are more at home with speculative and experimental modes than they were two decades ago. We live in an age of information glut and the biographer is judged to be something close to a 'novelist' as well as an historian, writing and welcoming more fusion than was once acceptable. Lives can be brilliantly conveyed through words patched together from letters and comments, as if the author were writing his own diary, or the subject may be delivered less as a psychological whole than as a figment of the biographer's informed imagination. Or again the biographer may be almost entirely hidden or upfronted as questor of a strange life. The critic Frank Kermode once wrote, 'It is not that we are connoisseurs of chaos, but that we are surrounded by it, and equipped for co-existence with it only by our fictive powers.' If we want to live a while with Aphra Behn in the age of Charles II and Nell Gwyn, we have to use some imagination—and avoid imposing our present-day psychological and political views on a woman very much *not* of our time.

I remain convinced that imagination may complement careful

scholarship to illuminate an elusive biographical subject and an exotically strange period. My recent experience as an author of an historical novel probably has a bearing on my present attitude to biography. The need to decide what to include from the culture of a necessarily alien past, to provide a context either for the historical subject or for the invented story, brings the novelist close to the life-writer.

The extra twenty years of critical commentary since I wrote my biography tell me that, as an author, Aphra Behn is secure in the canon of English literature. She is taught in colleges and universities in English-speaking countries. Where Restoration drama is on the syllabus, she is there with the other great playwrights, William Wycherley and William Congreve. As author of some startling and innovative fictions, she enters as an originator or precursor of the modern English novel, along with Daniel Defoe and the trio of early women writers, Margaret Cavendish, Eliza Haywood and Delarivier Manley. Because of its setting in Surinam, her celebrated novella *Oroonoko* about a princely black slave is favoured in post-colonialist studies. Finally, in women's studies courses, Behn is hailed as the first thoroughly professional woman writer, concerned with her craft, with details of publication, and with her status in the literary world.

For all this critical activity, Aphra Behn is still not as high in appreciation and recognition as I believe she deserves to be—and as I expected her to be when I began thinking about her in the heady 1970s, that decade of rediscovery when so many past women writers were allowed out of the shadows. With her craft and experimental techniques, her exciting female perspective on everything from politics to domesticity and sex, I thought her on a level with Jane Austen in literary importance. I still do. And it's hard to imagine a more striking and adventurous life—even if a good deal of this life is and was intended to be secret!

Most of the articles and comments on Behn in the last two decades have been scholarly and subtle, some brilliant in their insights. They have responded to the changing fashions of the discipline of English and Cultural Studies. Second Wave Feminist criticism that brought her to greater notice in the 1960s and 1970s has given way to other 'Waves' much concerned with the performative and with amorphous and polymorphous desire, while the emphasis in post-colonialist studies, that other growth area within the discipline, is still overwhelmingly concerned with race and ethnicity. Aphra Behn as writer of sexually explicit poems and portrayer of England's early colonies has much to say in both areas of study.

Some work especially useful for a biographer has concerned Behn as dramatist and poet. It throws new light on her stagecraft, her shifting and often prominent position in the theatrical marketplace, as well as on her complex interactions with male colleagues and competitors. In her theatrical dedications Behn uses flattery in ways that both amuse and dismay present critics and, in her plays, she portrays rakes and whores with the kind of ambiguity that can be disturbing—as well as funny. Behn was fascinated by rank, by the notion of nobility, its honour and the manifold ways in which it could be dishonoured. She returned to the topic over and over again in her drama, investigating the allure and vulnerabilities of personal and political authority. Recent critics have applauded her lively enthusiasm for sexual games and her irreverence about the masculinity that dominated the age and which she expresses so well in her plays and in her frank and risqué poems. If her treatment of sex astonishes readers less than it did a century ago, Behn can still shock when she handles subjects such as rape and the seductions of power. In many areas of gender relationships, then, her drama, fiction and poetry are still capable of destabilising our own assumptions. So too can her utopian moral and political schemes, where desire and reality coalesce or clash, and where the body is left to subvert the mind.

However interesting and disturbing so many of her works can appear, overwhelmingly comment has settled on a single one, *Oroonoko*. This is usually delivered not in its historical or literary context but in terms of modern ideas of race, ethnicity and gender. Sometimes the novella is coupled with Behn's posthumously produced play, her 'American' work, *The Widdow Ranter*, set in the English colony of Virginia. Both novella and drama excite clashing interpretations.

For some contemporary readers *The Widdow Ranter* seems to advocate republican values against a stuffy, hierarchical and anachronistic world order that cannot easily adapt to a changed environment; the play discovers a superior cultural space that expresses America and a non-European future of freedom. For others, the work is staunchly and overtly monarchical, revealing the chaos of democracy that emerges when the 'people' are given power and allowed to decide; we may relish the Falstaffian carnival element of the play, but it remains a portrait of misrule in a disordered colony requiring noble English governance to restore order and prosperity.

Oroonoko provokes even greater interpretative divisions, especially in its depiction of slavery. This is an overwhelming interest of our own age and, inevitably, as with sex and gender, we look through our modern assumptions at a work written before the secure establishment of the dreadful trade of African and American slavery and when slaves included Englishmen caught by the French and Turks, as well as famous classical slaves like Aesop. Some readers find *Oroonoko* a roundly aristocratic text stressing nobility and rank beyond anything else. Nobility for Behn can be found in anyone regardless of the colour of his or her skin; conversely, the ignoble of whatever ethnicity deserve slavery. Ignoring the hero's own involvement in the trade in slaves, other readers see an abolitionist work, and they apply to this fiction of fluidity in types and ethnic groups such modern terms as 'miscegenation' and 'imperialism'. When *Oroonoko* and *The Widdow Ranter* are brought together, critics are more in agreement: for Behn may appear to combine humanism with an enthusiasm for noble honour, a comic understanding of life with a less characteristic tragic one.

If Aphra Behn's depiction of gender and race can be assimilated to our modern ideas or at least celebrated for its difference, her politics when separated from the moral and social results of Restoration government often remain troublesome. Many critics worry over the apparent conflict between her feminist understanding and her staunch Tory Royalist stance. Recent work has looked at her attitude to the various plots of the age, the Popish Plot and the Meal-Tub Plot and her mockery of fake kings like the would-be king Monmouth. The work sheds light on some of the difficulties in interpretation. In her plays and stories readers have found conflicting messages. Some see occasional critiques of the royal brothers Charles II and James II, others simply an exaggerated loyalty against apparent odds and the currents of history. Perhaps, as contemporary readers, we find splits between desire and hierarchy, between women and dominating monarchy, and between hedonism and loyalty where she and her age found no necessary distinctions. Behn lived through a time of immense political upheaval and we may be wrong to look for consistency. The Vicar of Bray is not the only person who had to move with changes in regimes.

Her literary milieu was quite different from our own. All educated men and many women were familiar with the classics and, although as a woman Behn would have been denied a university education, she reveals herself well aware of the literary culture of her time. Undoubtedly when reading her we miss many allusions that her original readers and auditors would have caught, both from the Greek and Roman authors and from her contemporaries: the dramatists, poets and romance-writers. *Aesop's Fables* which Behn rendered into English verse may leach into her narratives where animals may grow characteristics and show unstable identities. The romantic tales that filled the minds of her readers may enter a work like

The Fair Jilt far more than we now expect. What we might see as auto-biographical like 'Love-Letters to a Gentleman' may indeed reveal something of Behn's life and loves but also represent a pastiche of the fictional letters so popular at the time. And in this case, since they were published after her death by a notoriously unscrupulous publisher, there is always the possibility that they may be forgeries, so useful and lucrative was the name of the notorious and amorous Mrs Behn.

Claudine Van Hensbergen underlines this possibility when she reiterates the problematic nature of seeing the letters as Behn's subjective thoughts. After all, they were written in a period fascinated by the *Portuguese Letters,* supposed to have come from the pen of a despairing nun rather than, as is now thought, a male French diplomat. The Behn letters may be strategic constructions after her death to help make her an amorous bankable heroine, or, of course, Behn may be using a conventional form to express something both literary and experienced, distraught and manufactured. The many connections between the letters and Behn's secure works can reveal a hard-working ventriloquist or Behn often writing self-referentially.

Like so many authors of the age, Aphra Behn claimed much of her work was true. It was fact or history. In reality it might well have been all fiction or fact mixed with fiction. This is especially so of the writings based on her presumed periods abroad in Surinam and the Low Countries when she was a young woman in the 1660s. Any new information about this time is welcome indeed. One of my moments of greatest archival excitement in writing the biography in the 1990s was when, following leads from Maureen Duffy and Mary Ann O'Donnell, I found in the Cathedral records of Antwerp the statement of the wedding of the historical original of the protagonists from *The Fair Jilt*: Francois Louis Tarquini and Maria Theresia Van Mechelen. Later I opened the roll of dusty and decaying testimonies of the defendants and plaintiffs in the legal cases that followed. I worked with difficulty, having only a Dutch–English dictionary for help. So it is a pleasure to find Dutch and Belgian scholars now fleshing out and modifying this historical background and providing more of the detail of the events on which Aphra Behn may well have drawn. My other exciting moment was also archival, seeing the proof that William Scot, the agent she had come to bring back into the English fold and whom I speculated she had come to assume was in love with her, was in reality a triple agent— at least. Probably further material will emerge as Continental readers and scholars become more interested in the English émigrés of the

Restoration—their desperate political and economic expedients—and in Aphra Behn herself. So far nothing much alters the broad outline of what I wrote in the biography. But who knows what may yet be discovered? It was the business of spies to hide themselves.

Behn is a writer who has attracted misattributions: in her life as well as after her death. Indeed in the preface to *The Luckey Chance* she joked about the fact: people 'charge me with all the Plays that have ever been offensive; though I wish with all their Faults I had been the Author of some of those they have honour'd me with'. For us now, three and a half centuries later, attribution of anonymous or posthumous works is notoriously difficult in this period. Male authors may impersonate women to enter the female bedroom, just as women may make themselves at home in the masculine spaces of the battle ground and council chamber. Much present academic work is busy shearing off items from established writers such as Daniel Defoe and Henry Fielding

The long tripartite novel *Love-Letters between a Nobleman and His Sister* (1684–7) does not have Behn's name on the title page, simply the initials A.B. These of course could simply suggest anonymity—or they could indicate Aphra Behn. She was named as the author of the work soon after her death and her authorship was accepted by those who commented on or reprinted this famous novel. Anyone with a scholarly interest in Behn will, on occasion, have vacillated over this ascription. But on the whole I stay with the attribution in the absence of any better competitor. The subject matter—the progress of a woman from a sheltered aristocrat to a renowned courtesan and the oscillation in her character between noblewoman and whore, as well as the attractiveness, absurdity and ultimately social power of the rake—is close to Behn's concerns in all her genres, especially the plays and poems, where, too, she expresses enjoyment of energetic amorality. So too the politics, the Royalism that condemns the rebellion of the Duke of Monmouth against his uncle James II by trivialising the character and motives of the rebel. In addition, the work fits suitably into Behn's life, appearing just when income from the theatre was drying up and when she was seeking to diversify her literary output. Leah Orr charges me with relying on 'intuition and conjecture' in my (guarded) acceptance of the attribution. I must plead guilty. I do believe Aphra Behn the likeliest candidate for authorship. And, if she didn't write the novel, then there's another remarkable fictionist out there to be discovered.

Orr also accuses me of accepting the attribution to Behn of the posthumous short stories. Here I am *not* guilty. In the edition I included many works simply ascribed to Behn, so that scholars could make up their own mind. But I have never believed that all the posthumous short stories are by Behn, and I make this clear in the biography. As usual, I think the matter cannot be settled *conclusively* without some further exciting discovery, but I stay with my point, which many scholars have made and which Orr reiterates, that it is odd that Behn, with her chronic shortage of money, did not publish before her death so many stories later attributed to her.

For textual and historical scholars, there is still much work to be done on Restoration attributions. It is best done in a tolerant spirit, since no scholarly moment has complete purchase on the truth. And, to quote Germaine Greer's useful opinion: with Behn we have to be 'prepared to live with what [we] don't know'. Behn can be left a spectral presence, intentionally or unintentionally erased from literary history, or, from our own vantage and trapped in our own times, we can use what she left and make of her what we can through our (inevitably blinkered) eyes. In a note in *The Muses Mercury* of 1707 the suspicious reader is invited to 'inspect' Behn's manuscripts 'at the Booksellers' and, if secrets could be told, receive 'an unquestionable Proof of their being genuine'. I wish I could send out such an invitation.

In the last two decades, I have shaken off what many biographers feel when they are writing and when they have just finished their work, what A. S. Byatt described in *The Biographer's Tale*: a possessiveness about their subject. I have now become immersed in fiction far more than I had time to be in the 1990s and have grown 'perhaps' more indulgent to my earlier speculative, intuitive self.

In Muriel Spark's *Loitering With Intent* (1981), Fleur Talbot, an aspiring novelist, is employed by the Autobiographical Association to aid members in writing their memoirs: 'Now that I come to write biographically,' she remarks, 'I have to tell of whatever actually happened and whoever naturally turns up. The story of a life is a very informal party; there are no rules of precedence and hospitality, no invitations.' What and whoever turns up is a matter of chance, of literary fashion, and, yes, of pre-formed inclination and intuition. I tried to understand the phenomenon of Aphra Behn as best I could, and attempted to be as little blinkered as possible by the pride and prejudices of my own age. I am well aware that I trod in the steps of Aphra Behn's earliest biographers, who took many of their 'facts' from her writings, her own and other people's efforts at fashioning a saleable image. Fact and fiction are not easy to distinguish then or now, and Behn wrote faction long before the word was coined. I have given a possible narrative, while letting a reader see that other narratives are available. I doubt any one can do Behn 'justice' but all our biographies are, in their different ways, tributes.

So, in short, what has emerged for me from a brief look at the fascinating criticism of twenty years is a sense of a writer still seen to be destabilising, a shape-shifter, an author who allows no easy response. Aphra Behn appears not so much the self-fashioner we found in the 1970s as a fashioner of selves. Over the decades she has benefited from many subtle and probing studies that aim to tease out her connections and views. All help us to realise more and more the exciting ambiguities and bracingly divergent opinions of this still most secretive of women, counterfeiters, and authors.

For generous help with the revised edition, I should like to thank Katherine Bright-Holmes, Lisa Caprino, Maureen Duffy, Derek Hughes and Ken Moxham.

Janet Todd, October 2016

ACKNOWLEDGEMENTS

It is good to be able to say that Aphra Behn scholars are of a 'generous and open Temper' and 'very serviceable to their friends', like their subject. Among many, I am especially grateful to Elizabeth Spearing for her support, friendship and help through all stages of this book, to Mary Ann O'Donnell for her extensive and detailed bibliographical work generously shared, and to Germaine Greer, whose critical, stimulating and astringent comments have been unfailingly helpful. Anyone working biographically on Aphra Behn must owe a great debt to Maureen Duffy for her biography, *The Passionate Shepherdess* (1977), which has laid the foundation for future work on Aphra Behn.

I am deeply grateful to the following for their help: Jane Jones with Behn's Kentish years; Dawn Lewcock with the staging of Behn's plays; Sarah Barber with the background of George Marten; Sara Mendelson with Behn's lodgings; Robert Hume with the dating of plays; Hilde van den Hooff, Marysa Demoor and J. P. Vanden Motten for help with research in Belgium; Keith Davey with naval vessels; John Loftis with Colonel Bampfield; Paul Hopkins with the Roger Morrice entering book; Dame Eanswythe Edwards of Stanbrook Abbey with Interregnum convents; Sharon Valiant with the Sidneys; and Melinda Zook with the 1680 Whigs.

Over the years I have also benefited from conversations in person or by post with Jane Spencer, Ros Ballaster, Michael Harris, J. R. Jones, Cath Sharrock, Kathleen Lesko, Maureen Mulvihill, James Fitzmaurice, Virginia Crompton, Patricia Crawford, Alison Smith, Colin Davis, Francis McKee, Emma Rees, Lois Schwoerer, Deborah Payne, Margot Hendricks, Jessica Munns, Susan Hastings and Steven N. Zwicker, as well as the contributors to *Aphra Behn Studies*, Catherine Gallagher, Alison Shell, Susan J. Owen, Jacqueline Pearson, Joanna Lipking and Paul Salzman. In addition, I would like to thank James Lynn, Pamela Holt, Katherine Bright-Holmes and Diana Birchall for reading and commenting on parts of the manuscript.

ACKNOWLEDGEMENTS

Among librarians I am grateful to Laetitia Yaendel of the Folger Shakespeare Library, Washington, which provided me with a very timely fellowship, to Brian Jenkins at the Cambridge University Library Rare Books Room, to Virginia Renner at the Huntington Library, Pasadena, to Tania Styles of the Department of Manuscripts & Special Collections, University of Nottingham, and to the Librarians of the British Library, Dr Williams' Library, the Guildhall Library, the Corporation of London Records Office, the Public Record Office, the Westminster Abbey Library, the Victoria and Albert Museum, the Brotherton Library, Leeds, the Centre for Kentish Studies, Maidstone, the Canterbury Cathedral Archives, the Bodleian Library, the library of Worcester College Oxford, the William Andrews Clark Memorial Library, Los Angeles, the Library of Congress, Washington, the Manuscript Library, the Beinecke Library, Yale University, and the state and city archives of The Hague, Antwerp, and Ghent. I am grateful to Viscount De L'Isle for permission to inspect the Sidney family archives.

INTRODUCTION TO THE 1996 EDITION

'The writing a life is at all Times, and in all Circumstances the most difficult Task of an Historian....But if the Difficulty be so great, where the Materials are plentiful, and the Incidents extraordinary; what must it be when the Person that affords the Subject, denies Matter enough for a Page.'[1]

The playwright, poet, fictionist, propagandist and spy, Aphra Behn, born some time and somewhere before or during the Civil War and dying in 1689, has a lethal combination of obscurity, secrecy and staginess which makes her an uneasy fit for any narrative, speculative or factual. She is not so much a woman to be unmasked as an unending combination of masks. Secrecy is endemic to the Restoration, a period badly documented and given to covering traces when these traces hinted at complicated disloyalties; yet, for someone who became as famous as Aphra Behn, there is peculiarly little known. The secrecy conforms to her one certain activity: espionage.

For documented authors, it is thought vulgar and unscholarly to plunder literary works to make a tale. The story of Aphra Behn, Ann Behn as she is sometimes called by contemporaries, Mrs Bean or Behn, Astrea as she wished to be known, European or American, aristocrat or plebeian, wife or whore, Catholic, Protestant or atheist, *must*, however, be constructed from the works, for there is almost nowhere else to search. Women are excluded from most institutions that keep records; the lists of county gentlemen do not include Aphra Behn, nor do the rolls of Oxford and Cambridge or of the Inns of Court and the Middle Temple, which contain a hearty number of her playwright colleagues.

If she were firmly aristocratic, there would be a country seat to visit in hope of contemplating an oak which the child Aphra might have climbed, imagining long skirts rustling and dancing feet echoing. But she is not and there is no such house. Without it and without a great public school or college, or even a church or chapel fellowship, there is little chance that something startling will be found in an attic: a notebook or doodle that proves she was James II's mistress or the daughter of a pastry cook from Barbados. Upper-class women might record some seemingly trivial aspect of domestic life and let it survive, a Quaker woman might note a movement of the soul. There is nothing similar for Aphra Behn. If she visited her family, the visit went unnoticed; if she bared her 'soul', it was in code.

Since more conventional methods of characterisation are sparse—authenticated letters, diaries, other people's analyses—the construction of a life must rely on the more dubious questioning of the fictional narrators, the speakers of her many poems, the voices of the plays, the prologues and epilogues, the repeated characters, themes and expressions, accepting that autobiography may be diffused through them and that memory is a main imaginative resource for artists, exploited in oblique ways. All Aphra Behn's writings are rhetorical, all masks, all perspectives to be changed like clothes—but, like clothes, some were chosen, some inherited or given, some simply the fashion, and all may be expressive.

Aphra Behn did not share our own century's reverence for introspection. She regarded much talk of the inner life as a naïve Puritan habit followed by those of lower rank. As she did not see her general statements as universal truths, so her characterisations of her 'self' were never absolute but, rather, instrumental. For her, action and speech became a staging. The girl who grew up to be a spy, a playwright, political propagandist, and authority on love—when almost nothing is known for sure about her love life—and commentator on colonialism and race—when it remains uncertain whether or not she visited the colonies—must have had a sense of the self as performed, created, narrated and in writing. So a biography becomes another mask, inevitably formed in the culture of its moment from the writing of the past that has survived. Truth, as Behn came to think, was not necessarily empirical fact, but what was authorised by power, whether that power was divine, political, aesthetic or popular. She would expect to be what we make her, both out of what we take to be her writing and out of our desire to 'know' her. There can be many Aphra Behns, now as there probably were then.

For the centuries after her death, Aphra Behn was simply regarded as a smutty writer, worse for being a woman. 'Mrs Behn wrote foully; and this for most of us, and very properly, is an end of the whole discussion,' said the booklover William Henry Hudson in 1897.[2] Over a century of abuse and neglect prepared for this opinion; where, in different moods, her contemporaries Dryden, Rochester, Otway and Wycherley had appreciated her, the eighteenth-century fiction greats, Richardson and Fielding, vilified her as unwomanly. With this scorn, she shared the fate of the Restoration, or rather that small group of libertine and liberated courtiers and theatre people—never the majority of the population—who came to represent the Restoration for later ages. The group both scandalised its own times and sexually and politically haunted the next two centuries with its excess. Indeed Samuel Richardson might almost be seen as founding the eighteenth-century novel in horrified reaction to the Restoration and its corrupting theatre. As a woman, Behn was one of the scapegoats. 'The stage how loosely does Astrea tread, / Who fairly puts all characters to bed!' scoffed Alexander Pope in his *Epistle to Augustus* in 1735. Already in 1688 the conduct-book writer, the Marquis of Halifax, had remarked, 'the unjustifiable Freedom of some of your Sex have involved the rest in the penalty of being reduced'.[3] 'The disgrace of Aphra Behn,' declared the nineteenth-century critic Julia Kavanagh, 'is that, instead of raising man to woman's moral standard [she] sank woman to the level of man's coarseness.'[4] John Doran echoed the view: Behn dragged the Muses down to her level 'where the Nine and their unclean votary wallowed together in the mire'.[5]

In the early twentieth century, when woman's unique moral standard was doubted, other aspects of the 'ingenious Mrs. Behn' came to the fore: that she was the first professional woman writer in England and, for the twenty years of her writing life, the only female playwright.[6] Virginia Woolf understood the significance: 'All women together ought to let flowers fall upon the tomb of Aphra Behn, for it was she who earned them the right to speak their minds.' Unfortunately, the professional significance was so strong for Woolf that she lost sight of any literary merit. In this she was a woman of her time, for she wrote when literature was thought able to transcend its historical moment and when it had to refuse the contamination of politics. Romantic notions of art as self-expressing were not, however, current in the Restoration and men openly wrote for money and political purpose, as did Behn.

The woman Virginia Woolf praised in Aphra Behn's place was an invented one, a sister Judith for the great literary icon, the Renaissance William Shakespeare. Judith Shakespeare was a failed Romantic, a woman who grew suicidal under her injuries and did not even enter the stage door in her quest to write plays like her brother. Behn, who did enter, was reduced to a hack—her mind unfree because she wrote for money. She became a 'middle-class woman with all the plebeian virtues of humour, vitality and courage; a woman forced by the death of her husband and some unfortunate adventures of her own to make her living by her wits'. The fact of her writing 'outweighs anything that she actually wrote'.[7] Here the very professionalism which prevented Behn from ending up suicidal kept her from the ranks of the great artists. Woolf overlooked the motive that persuaded Judith's brother, William, to write.

Since Virginia Woolf's time, the Second Wave of feminism has washed over Aphra Behn. In this she became the subject of two full biographies.[8] Yet, in the 1970s, she was not much examined as a writer, for reasons clear in Woolf's remarks: she did not conform to the notion of what a woman author should be, a suffering soul working against patriarchal oppression, in deep conflict with men. Behn acknowledged the conflict between the sexes, but felt both sides were deeply implicated in it. Patriarchy was all-enveloping, but it was a cultural construction in which everyone had some stake and share. She depicted herself as confident, engaged and knowing. There was no panoply of feminine shame or modesty, no sense that she wrote because impelled to express her female predicament. She wrote because she was good at it and made money.

Nor did Aphra Behn fit in with the progressive sense of literature, the rise of the woman novelist, for example, in compensatory tandem with the rise of the male. Later eighteenth- and nineteenth-century fiction simply differed from Behn's supposed masterpiece, *Love-Letters between a Nobleman and His Sister*, a long work that had more in common with old historical romance and postmodern pastiche than with the realist novel—although, if one is searching for 'the first novel', it is hard to see why *Robinson Crusoe* or *Pamela* should be preferred to this. Her poetry too did not conform. It did not learn to express the woman in any absolute distinctive way. The French feminist writer Hélène Cixous wrote that 'Woman must write her self: must write about women and bring women to writing, from which they have been driven away as violently as from their bodies—for the same reasons....Woman must put herself into the text—as into the world and into history—by her own movement.'[9] Behn did not exactly do this, not in these terms, for she wrote in many respects identically to men. But she did do an equally revolutionary thing: she made a public space for women. All five of the female playwrights who suddenly flourished just after her death, 'Ariadne', Catherine Trotter, Mary Fix, Delarivier Manley and Susannah Centlivre, saw her as their most important precursor.

Now post-Restoration, post-Victorian and postmodern, we should be able to cope with Aphra Behn, for, although secretive, she has many advantages for her reader. She thought a good deal about images of women and the strategies they used to find their way through life. Her historical moment, buttressed by her own temperament, situated her in a place between two patriarchal concepts of woman, one biblical, the other secular: of woman seen through the misogyny of the Bible as the weaker vessel of sin and sex, and of woman as a physical, emotional and intellectual entity distinct from a man, ruled not by Eve's fault but by her oversensitive body. Behn was curiously, although not completely, free from the first, while her antipathy to the second fuelled many of her irritated generalisations about women; opposing both, she asserted female desires and appetites when the prevailing culture taught that God had ordained women to delegate most of these. She also thought about writing and the relation of writing to the self and to the state which was its context. Sexual politics was certainly her subject, but so was sexy politics and political sex—as it was for many in her circle who saw the entanglement of sex and power. She was fascinated by the interface between political and personal, the world and the word, culture and acts.

Here is another hurdle. We are used to seeing outspoken, ground-breaking women in a liberal mould, for feminism, liberalism and the rights of man (and woman) have become yoked. Behn, however, held to the very tradition that Milton and other icons of protest so ringingly deplored: that of divine-right monarchy and elitist aristocratic culture. In public pronouncements, she was a snobbish high Tory. For the people, slaves or the London rabble, and for democracy of any sort she expressed nothing but contempt. To her, the prerogative of a single distinctive man ensured freedom more satisfactorily than the will of a majority swayed by un-investigated desires and the loudest demagogues. She had grown up under Puritan rule and she associated any movement towards Parliamentary democracy with moral coercion, venality and vulgarity. From a modern point of view she was not even consistent in reaction: she was a patriarchalist in state politics, a Cartesian in psychology, and a contract theorist in family matters.

Now Aphra Behn has come into vogue, read and taught throughout the English-speaking world. Fittingly, her arrival has been due to the work that gave her currency after her death (albeit in another playwright's dramatisation), her short story of an African slave-prince, *Oroonoko*. This no longer seems, as it did in the eighteenth century, a sentimental romance in exotic setting, but, rather, the very model of twentieth-century interest in issues of gender, race and class. That Behn expressed none of these in an entirely palatable way makes her teasing and seductive. In fitting contemporary fashion, she renders them unsteady categories.

Behn wrote in almost all available genres—except the sermon. These demanded different poses, the pastoral lover, the appealing playwright, the prophetic singer, the bawdy actress, the humble admirer, and the supplicant. She is more than any one of these, but never less than their sum. Each genre demanded an audience to be seduced in distinct ways, through different voices displaying coyness, pathos or dignity. It was the repertoire of the whore, she knew. She also knew that all writing had its whorish element.

Aphra Behn was a professional spy, code-named Astrea and agent 160, before she became a professional writer. When she wrote her secret reports to London from Antwerp, she wrote partly in cypher. The habit persisted into her literary works, which also need decoding. In secret letters, one name may stand in for another, a commercial report be really a political one, an amorous encounter a treacherous one. In similar fashion, Behn's works transform and transmute their material so that they function on many levels. The black slave Oroonoko may stand in for the white British king, the male aristocrat for the female hack writer. A romantic novel may become a warning and a presentiment.

I have perhaps made a more political Behn than some would wish, fetishising this aspect as the central one of her story. All I can plead is that I did not start out with this conception. In his play *Volpone*, the Renaissance dramatist Ben Jonson created an English knight called Sir Politic Would-Be, who believed that meat could be cut in cyphers and coded messages delivered through cabbages and Colchester oysters. I would not like to be associating Behn with a butt of Ben Jonson, a playwright for whom she had most ambivalent feelings. Yet, coded state politics does seem to me to be at the heart of Behn's later professional life, however she may have struggled against it. She wrote in political modes; sometimes she assented to their assumptions, at other times not. In this biography, I have argued for a woman growing into Royalist politics, partly as the buttress of social coherence, partly as a grounding of personal identity, and partly as support for an aesthetic enterprise. I have accepted that Behn's public Royalist expression, so reiterated, must have had some authenticity beyond desire for financial reward. Yet she was a hack as well as an artist, needing to eat before she could write, and I have assumed that, while I am telling a primarily public tale of professional loyalties, other more scandalous tales might be told of hidden deviousness, of gutter politics and of writing sold to the highest bidder. There is much not entirely explained by the Royalist Behn—the persistent ascription to her of anti-Royalist works, her part in the compiling of anti-government satires for men who very definitely opposed what she overtly served, her involvement with turncoats, republicans and trimmers.

Inevitably there is instability in what follows, both in tone and material. There is much speculation, along with some scholarship. It is a curious venture to write the biography of a woman whose first twenty-six or twenty-seven years are not securely known. Michael Holroyd has said that biographies of writers are written in collaboration with the posthumous subject of the biography. I have to say that I have had less than perfect collaboration from dead agent 160.

For much of the time I have used the words 'perhaps' and 'possibly' and kept to the subjunctive. Sometimes, however, I have lapsed and left speculation in the declarative. Not everything here is 'true'; nor is it likely to be proven one way or the other, for the Restoration so shocked the English people that they were still mythologising its wickedness far into the next century, from which moment many of the stories of its actors derive. I can only hope that not too much flatly and absolutely contradicts what I have said. As a discerning reader will no doubt notice, the story of Aphra Behn in Kent as a child is corroborated only by a couple of jottings in private books and nothing links her incontrovertibly with Surinam or definitively explains why she should be there. What countries she visited except Flanders and when is not known and what propaganda she wrote and for whom is hidden. Whether or not she married is unclear, whether she had an abundance of lovers, male or female, whether she bore children as Wycherley said she did, whether she was a whore or just a scribbling woman, all this is opaque. All I can hope is that the reader, the one Aphra Behn cajoles as her 'Good, Sweet, Honey, Sugar-Candied Reader', will begin this biography with 'perhaps' and 'possibly', and end it murmuring 'probably'.

Yet I would not have attempted this biography if I had not thought that, through all the vagueness of historical fact and uncertainty of late twentieth-century opinion, there was some definite personality emerging, a woman who wrote, tried, yearned, changed a little and stayed much the same. Aphra Behn was a feminist in the sense that she thought as a woman and thought through being a woman, but she was an awkward one. She was not separatist or much involved in the modern feminist business of revising culture and reviewing experience, except in her laments for a mythical golden age of female education. Nor was she much interested in rights of any kind. Her feminism was interactive and dialectical, speaking in many voices, and it remains disturbing in its context of a cynicism so deep it undercuts all fixities. I am sympathetic to the image that has emerged to me from Aphra Behn's writings, but I have not tried to write what she was so well able to write for herself in her addresses to her readers: a polemical defence.

Behn is remarkable for keeping herself through her work. Since she did, she knew she wrote as well as anyone and, since popularity demands conventionality, she also knew she wrote like any appreciated man. With all her role-playing, her wheedling of the reader and the audience, her expressed contempt for the popular taste she so easily pleased, her staging of herself as a cozening whore, pathetic female, and unmerciful satirist, she emerges as a rare object indeed: a public female intellectual, a woman of supreme intelligence, a woman of letters.

In the 1670s and 1680s Behn surpassed even the Poet Laureate, John Dryden, in the number of plays performed, and she was courted by several factions as a political poet. Her works are topical, as fits with the times in which she wrote, but they are also, on occasion, subtle and complex, open to irony, ambiguity, and equivocation. At the end of her life, fatigued with pleasing and politics, she wanted literary fame—a shocking stance in the context of later women writers who came before the public in an attitude of profound apology and submission. She deserves this fame both for her cultural importance and because she wrote many competent, energetic works, some of the first order: a few plays like the two *The Rovers*, *Sir Patient Fancy* and *The Luckey Chance*, the prose *Love-Letters between a Nobleman and His Sister*, *Oroonoko* and *The Fair Jilt*, and the poems 'Desire', 'Love Arm'd' and 'The Golden Age'. They are a substantial achievement. For all her secrecy and obscurity, Behn deserves biography too, several biographies—as long as authors and readers share her sense of identity as masquerade and of fact as partly fictive, and accept her memoirist's humility before the 'ingenious' subject:

The reader must remember that there are few Astreas arise in our age, and till such an One does appear, all our Endeavours in Encomiums on the last, must be vain....

CHAPTER 1

✣

Beginnings in Kent

'a most beautifull woman, & a most Excellent Poet'

Aphra Behn's age was the Restoration, that vibrant, violent and shoddy period which began with the arrival in Kent of King Charles II in 1660 and ended with the flight of his brother, James II, in 1688. No one had quite anticipated its style. In 1654, under the rule of Oliver Cromwell, the Royalist gentlewoman Dorothy Osborne wrote of the 'folly that possesses young people of this age, and the liberties they take to themselves'; she concluded that 'the want of a Court to govern themselves by is in great part the cause of their ruin'.[1] She could hardly have been more wrong. When the Restoration came and the court returned to London, scarred by years of living in exiled hope and fantasy, it delivered a rude shock to the country, which did not easily recover its equilibrium. Gilbert Burnet, a chronicling Anglican cleric, saw 'a spirit of extravagant joy' overspreading the nation, causing people to turn from 'the very professions of virtue and piety: all ended in entertainments and drunkenness, which overrun the three kingdoms to such a degree, that it very much corrupted all their morals'.[2]

Burnet's assessment was in the future. At the time, the rejoicing was almost universal, as the nation responded to Charles II's desire to make his return a theatrical show. In style the Interregnum had not been the mass of unrelieved grey and black the Royalists liked to depict and the Oxford antiquarian, Anthony à Wood, had been appalled at the lavish dress of junior scholars, all Presbyterians and Independents, who sported ribboned hats, powdered hair, laced bands and tassels, snake-bow band-strings and long cuffs.[3] But the King and his courtiers brought with them far more extravagant French fashions, as well as some naughty ones: buttoned smocks for easy access were said to have been adopted by the King's current mistress.

King Charles II arrived in Dover, travelling across from the Continent on the *Naseby*, a name recording a Parliamentary victory—the ship was speedily renamed *The Royal Charles* and its sailors promised a month's extra pay. He journeyed from Dover to Canterbury where he attended Sunday service in the cathedral, met his new Privy Council, and gave the Order of the Garter to General Monck, soon to be the Duke of Albemarle, who had largely brought about the royal return by switching sides. He delayed his arrival in London to coincide with his thirtieth birthday on 29 May.

Eager to come to the attention of the restored King, the young Earl of Rochester hymned, 'loyall *Kent* renews her Arts agen, / Fencing her wayes with moving groves of men.' But it was in London that the initial enthusiasm grew hottest and even the usually dour diarist, John Evelyn, glowed,

> This day came in his Majestie *Charles* the 2d…to London after a sad, & long Exile, and Calamitous Suffering both of the King & Church: being 17 yeares: This was also his Birthday, and with a Triumph of above 20000 horse & foote, brandishing their swords and shouting with unexpressable joy: The wayes straw'd with flowers, the bells ringing, the streetes hung with Tapissry, fountaines running with wine: The Major, Aldermen, all the Companies in their liver[ie]s, Chaines of Gold, banners; Lords & nobles, Cloth of Silver, gold & vellvet every body clad in, the windos & balconies all set with Ladys, Trumpets, Musick & [myriads] of people flocking the streetes & was as far as *Rochester*, so as they were 7 houres in passing the Citty, even from 2 in the afternoone 'til nine at night: I stood in the strand, & beheld it, & blessed God.[4]

The revelry grew so intense that Charles had to make a proclamation against drinking, swearing and debauching in his honour. Yet he was not the man to dampen celebration and dissipation overmuch. He was already involved with the woman whom Gilbert Burnet called 'vicious and ravenous', she of the naughty unbuttoned smocks, Barbara Castlemaine, later Duchess of Cleveland. Under royal influence and patronage, brothels turned glamorous and theatres reopened. At both, Nell Gwyn, soon to supplant Lady Castlemaine, found her employment—although she insisted she had been a serving-maid in the former. At home in his rambling, dirty palace of Whitehall, Charles II seemed to be presiding over a perpetual masquerade party. It was soon too much for most people: just over a year after the Restoration, even the loyal diarist and civil servant Samuel Pepys was recording the 'lewdness and beggary of the Court'.[5]

None the less, this court had come to stay. Charles re-established the magical custom of touching for the King's Evil or scrofula and he declared himself in the twelfth year of a reign that had started with his father's death. There had been no Interregnum and all was as it had been in the Stuart past.

A few poets failed to join in the collective eulogy that greeted the accession and coronation. Andrew Marvell was silent, while his friend John Milton bitterly exclaimed: 'For this extolled and magnificent nation, regardless both of honour won, or deliverances vouchsafed from heaven, to fall back or rather *creep* back...to their once abjured and detested thraldom of kingship!' But Milton and Marvell were exceptions: Dryden, Edmund Waller, and Abraham Cowley all showered the King with complimentary verses, despite recent panegyrics to his foes. During the Interregnum Waller, for example, had been so terrified when caught plotting for the Royalists that he had thrown himself on to the other side with a fulsome poem to Oliver Cromwell. When the new King commented that the verses to him did not measure up to those for the Protector, Waller diplomatically replied, 'Sir, we poets never succeed so well in writing truth as fiction.'[6] Horribly aware that his last public poem had been 'Heroical Stanzas' on the death of Cromwell, Dryden rushed to make the very sun and thunder answer royal need.[7] His haste mirrored his anxiety: the King had arrived in London at the end of May and his *Astrea Redux* was in the shops by mid-June.

The eulogistic activity suited the Stuart concept of kingship, which demanded the almost manic interpreting of act and accident as providential. The King himself was quick to tell the story of his romantic escape after the defeat of Worcester in 1651, especially his seclusion in the Boscobel Oak, an adventure that cried out for symbolic interpretation, given the nation's patriotic link with oaks. Over the years he would tell it so often that the young Earl of Rochester yawned—despite his father's heroic role in the escapade. Less well-born poets gleefully leapt on the incidents, so avoiding entanglement with the immediate past and its murky collusions. Perhaps they privately marvelled at the Stuart ability to capitalise on failure.

In this festive time, young Aphra may have been one of the maidens who strewed herbs along the leisurely royal route through Kent and wondered at the height and swarthiness of the new King. Or she might have joined the perpetual party in London. In either case, she was transfixed in a posture of admiration she never publicly changed. Yet, with Pepys who, despite his enthusiasm, noted that the King's dog shat in the boat like other dogs, Aphra commented on the ordinariness of royalty for all its pomp: in a fictional Restoration in her first written play, *The Young King*, she makes the onlookers recognise the King only by the people kneeling to him; they cry in response, 'Good lack a day, 'tis as a Man may say—'tis just such another body as one of us, onely he looks a little more terrably.'

The story begins at the Restoration for Aphra Behn readers as well or, rather, with the shadow which the Restoration cast back on the past. All events before the 1660s Behn kept shrouded, although, like others needing to square a loyal present with a complicated or inadequate past, she threw out hints in her prefaces and short stories that fitted with her later image of court poet, dramatist to an aristocratic elite, and constant Royalist.

These hints were given substance by her first shadowy biographers who wrote after her death when, following a successful dramatisation of her famous short story, *Oroonoko*, she became current again in the late 1690s. It had become the fashion to inform the public about a writer's life before his or her works and a respectable picture was wanted which would not entirely obliterate the naughty image which Behn and her theatrical friends had earlier exploited. No one who knew Aphra Behn in childhood seems to have stepped forward at this juncture. So Charles Gildon, a young man who had known her only in her last years and was left with one of her plays to edit and publish, probably himself composed the short 'Account of the Life of the Incomparable Mrs. Behn' which he affixed to the play. It did not say much because, clearly, Gildon did not know much. Behn, so famous for her garrulity, had not chatted about her distant past. At the same moment, another possible acquaintance of the final years, a colleague of Gildon's called Samuel Briscoe, was eager to exploit and sensationalise the dead author. He wanted to publish a volume of the collected stories of which *Oroonoko* was the crown and he too needed a biography. So he commissioned 'The Life and Memoirs of Mrs. Behn. Written by One of the Fair Sex'. In the third edition this was expanded into a patchwork by the inclusion of some love letters, thought of originally as a short story, and some comic letters purportedly written when Aphra Behn was in Flanders.[8] Any one of Behn's female friends might have written the 'Memoirs' or the impecunious Sam Briscoe himself might have supplied it, or Gildon in less austere mood may have performed again. About Behn's early life, the 'Memoirs' like the 'Account' says almost nothing at all, except that she was the daughter of a gentleman from Kent. All the rest was lifted from *Oroonoko*.

Given her earliest alleged existence in hints within fiction, it is fitting that the Aphra Behn of *this* work should commence in marginalia and private jottings rather than in public disclosure of wills and banns. She begins, therefore, in a scribbled note of the aristocratic poet, Anne Finch, Countess of Winchilsea. After Aphra Behn's death, Finch had written a contest poem, called 'Circuit of Apollo', of the sort popular at the time. In this she imagined the god of poetry, Apollo, searching through Kent for a female poet to crown. Finding few candidates, he stood on the banks of the River Stour and

> ...lamented for Behn o're that place of her birth,
> And said amongst Femens was not on the earth
> Her superior in fancy, in language, or witt,
> Yett own'd that a little too loosly she writt....[9]

Aphra Behn would probably always have struck the exemplary wife Anne Finch as too frank and bawdy, but Finch may also have feared that the looseness would cause Behn's great contribution to letters to be forgotten, as it did for a while.

Whatever her true opinion of the poetry, Finch was piqued by the fabricated 'Memoirs', where Behn had become the child of a Kentish gentleman. 'Though the account of her life before her works pretends otherwise', Finch wrote, probably with some hauteur, Behn was 'Daughter to a Barber, who liv'd formerly at Wye a little market town (now much decay'd) in Kent'.[10] The information came from those in a position to know—quite a likely claim, since Anne Finch's husband had property round Kentish villages and Finch could easily have met acquaintances of Behn's parents.

Probably Anne Finch believed what she wrote, but she admitted she had it at second hand. More important is the testimony of Colonel Thomas Colepeper, the only person who claimed to *know* Aphra as a child. He declared that her mother had been his wet-nurse and that his foster-sister Aphra—as such suckling relationships were termed—was 'a most beautifull woman, & a most Excellent Poet'. Her father's name was Johnson, he said, and she had a 'fayer' sister called Frances. Aphra was born 'at Sturry or Canterbury'.[11]

Could Colepeper be telling the truth? Certainly he was a curious man. He had a passion for genealogy especially of the Colepepers, and for an idiosyncratic mix of magic, nature and science. In his later years, he grew litigious and pugnacious, even publicly assaulting the Duke of Devonshire in frustration over a lawsuit, and he spent much time composing eighteen volumes of an alphabetical 'Adversaria'. It was in this vast manuscript, much of it compiled in the late 1690s, that he recorded the details of the 'beautifull' Aphra Behn.

If he was a romancer of himself, a man of quaint theories and violent habits, brooder over lost inheritances, Colepeper was also a scientist and a fellow of the new Royal Society, founded on Baconian notions of empirical truth. He did experiments himself and took out patents with Samuel Morland, a projector who, despite a number of abortive inventions, did have some technical achievements to his credit.[12] Colepeper was not much interested in literary figures and few appear in his 'Adversaria'; so his recording of the life and death of Aphra Behn is strange if he were not connected with her. Given his obsession with rank and aristocracy, he is unlikely to have seen himself honoured by any tie to a literary lady, however 'Excellent'. Genealogy was his mania and he was making a sort of claim on Behn by mentioning her.

If Colepeper's memory is true, then it gives Aphra Behn an approximate birthdate, for he was born in Kent on Christmas Day, 1637, and his sister Roberta in 1639; in 1643 both Colepeper parents died. If Aphra's mother indeed gave him suck and if she herself were the original infant suckled by her mother, then this provides her with a birth between 1637 and 1643.

For Aphra, the daughter of Colepeper's wet-nurse and Finch's barber, a likely candidate is a child, Eaffrey Johnson, daughter of a Bartholomew Johnson of Canterbury, who was, among other functions, a barber. He became the father of a Frances as well as an Eaffrey.[13] He therefore accords with the Colonel's memories and the Countess's gossip. If Bartholomew Johnson was Aphra's father, then Elizabeth Johnson, née Denham, must be her mother and wet-nurse to the infant Colonel—a likely possibility since Elizabeth had lived close to Colepeper's mother during the latter's first, more elevated marriage to Lord Strangford.

According to the marriage register, Bartholomew was from Bishopsbourne and Elizabeth from Smeeth, both villages in Kent near Canterbury, and the wedding was at St Paul's, Canterbury, on 25 August 1638. Since Frances Johnson was baptised in Smeeth on 6 December, there had clearly been some urgency: the bride was five months pregnant.[14]

Two years later the Johnsons were at Harbledown, a village of under 200 inhabitants just outside Canterbury, known for its asylum for the disabled poor, when their next child, Eaffrey, was born on 14 December 1640. With its spelling variants of Affara and Affry, Afra, Eaffrey, Aphra was not uncommon in Kent; it was the name of a saint martyred under Diocletian, traditionally supposed to have been a Cypriot prostitute converted to Christianity. At least two other births followed, of George, buried at St Margaret's in 1656, and of an unnamed boy.[15]

So how could the baby Colonel Colepeper have sucked Aphra's mother's breast? Possibly Elizabeth had an earlier child out of wedlock, perhaps stillborn, so allowing her to suckle the baby Thomas eight months before her marriage. Possibly, since suckling went on for a long time and involved a succession of wet-nurses, Mrs Johnson might have taken on Thomas Colepeper after the birth of Frances, when an earlier wet-nurse died or went dry. When Aphra herself was born, the Colepeper infants were in London, but Mrs Johnson might still have fed the young Thomas when he was returned later to Kent. Colepeper does not say she was his first or only nurse, merely that she 'gave him suck for some-time'.[16]

Elizabeth herself had been born in 1613 at Faversham, a bustling and fairly prosperous Kentish town.[17] Her family seems to have attained at least a middling trade rank and her younger brother George, educated at Magdalen College, Oxford, became a doctor in Stamford, Lincolnshire, and claimed the status of a gentleman.[18] To appear in the *Lincolnshire Pedigrees* for 1666 he had to provide four generations of ancestors, but he omitted his sister Elizabeth—possibly she was only a half-sister and not to be counted or possibly her indiscretion out of wedlock or the poor marriage made him reluctant to acknowledge kin. If so, the adult Aphra may have returned the disdain: throughout her life she inveighed against the foolish arrogant students of Oxford who mistook a little learning for sense.[19]

If not a gentleman, Bartholomew Johnson did try to better himself and he was granted the freedom of Canterbury in 1648.[20] Little Eaffrey or Aphra would have been just eight. He was described as 'this city barber' and he was to pay an initial fee of £5 for the privilege. A few months later he was asked for a further £10.[21] Four months on he had failed to pay and should lose the 'benefit of the said order' unless he immediately found £7 'of lawful Englishe money'.[22] It sounds as though Bartholomew had ambitions but insufficient cash to support them. His daughter would follow in his steps.

In 1654, when Aphra would be thirteen, Bartholomew was appointed one of the Overseers of the Poor for St Margaret's, a parish in central Canterbury.[23] These officers had been created by the Poor Law of Elizabeth I to look after paupers, keep them from the affluent, and administer the monies levied from a reluctant parish. They had a shoddy reputation, but then they had much to fear: if they did not contain matters and cope with the poor relentlessly pushing in from the countryside, they themselves might become paupers rather than keepers. The post suggests that Bartholomew was a Protestant, although Catholics did surreptitiously hold offices, and that he could write.[24] The same could not be said of his wife Elizabeth, since she marked the marriage register with an E.

Such a background cuts a swathe through the social respectability of the 'Memoirs' and the grand claims of gentlemanly status for Behn in the fictions. The rank of gentleman was clearly outlined in *Britannia: or, a Geographical Description of the Kingdoms of England, Scotland, and Ireland...* (1673) by Richard Blome. To be a gentleman without title, a man had to have either good descent from an ancient family or, through education and estates, earn suitable respect. Blome listed the gentlemen of the English counties over the previous decades; there are many Colepepers but no Johnsons among those of Kent. Bartholomew Johnson was, then, not a gentleman. Indeed he was probably the son of another Bartholomew, buried in Smeeth near Wye in November 1617 and described as 'a poore man'. This makes amusing Aphra Behn's later sneer at people of whom not even 'a Parish Book makes mention or cou'd show there was any such Name or Family'.[25]

Confirmation of the lowly birth comes from a glancing remark of John Dryden, who certainly knew Aphra as an adult. Writing to an intended poet, Elizabeth Thomas, in 1699, he told her she was 'too well-born' to fall into the 'mire' of loose writing, into which Aphra Behn had tripped. Since Elizabeth Thomas was a lawyer's daughter and spent some years in prison for debt, Dryden cannot have located the presumably less well-born Behn far up the social scale.

Aphra, daughter of a barber and a wet-nurse, seems a surprising candidate for England's first all-round professional woman writer, author not only of numerous plays and stories but also of court pindarics, scientific translations and Latin paraphrases. Her background had some advantages, however.

First, George's snobbishness should not lower the status of Mrs Johnson too far. A wet-nurse was not of the highest order, but nor was she the lowly cow she would become in the eighteenth century. There are records of many middle-ranking women, even aldermen's wives, serving as wet-nurses and making on occasion a very good living. The tie between the suckled children and her own was honoured, especially if, as in the case of Thomas and Roberta Colepeper, the natural parents died so soon.[26] Sometimes the wet-nurse took her charge to her own home and both suckled and cared for it during the early years.

Second, although a barber—or barber-surgeon, as Bartholomew might have been—had little status, and was from what Robinson Crusoe's father called 'the Upper Station of *Low Life*' he did have interesting opportunities, whether in Canterbury or Seville. He met many people, could know the world, and might encounter the immigrants who came to and through Kent, the French Huguenots or Protestants who wove silk and made paper, the French-speaking Walloons from the Low Countries, and even the Dutch religious refugees who settled in nearby Sandwich. The daughter of such a man, if she had some linguistic talent, might gain a smattering of languages without stepping far from home. There was too always music around: a flageolet, gittern or lute was left out for waiting customers to play or accompany singing—as Behn mentioned in one of her early plays, *The Dutch Lover*. Like the narrator in *Oroonoko*, the child Aphra may have become adept at the flute; as a not-quite-elegant accomplishment (it drew attention to the mouth) it would not have formed part of a well-bred girl's education, but was acceptable for one of her rank.

Also something must be allowed to the times, when status was not as rigid as it had been or would be again. The 1640s and 1650s, the Interregnum between the fall and death of Charles I and the Restoration of his heir in 1660, formed one of the most turbulent periods of English history. Old boundaries were crossed and hierarchies overturned. Unlike earlier civil wars, the struggles were not between competing families or power groups of more or less similar composition, but between competing ideologies, ways of life and thinking. One group of Puritans, Roundheads, supporters of the 'Good Old Cause', saw law, Parliament and godly reformation as primary; the other, Royalists or Cavaliers, looked to the King and the ancient constitution as supreme. The conflict between these two threatened to overturn the whole traditional hierarchy of church and state, King, government and governed. When the country witnessed the executions of the Earl of Strafford, King Charles I's most trusted servant, the Archbishop of Canterbury and, finally, in 1649, the King himself, it knew that identity and rank were not secure. 'The English people are a sober people, however at present under some infatuation,' wrote the King to his son. When the father was beheaded, the son, now Charles II, became 'The poor King, who has nothing of it but the name...'.[27]

Further down the scale, too, times proved volatile. One gentleman was amazed to find that the mother of a servant and the grandmother of another were daughters of knights. Philip Skippon, the poet Katherine Philips's stepfather, rose from common pikesman to major-general under Cromwell. But great upward changes in status happened mainly when a family received sequestrated lands from the losing Royalist side. There appears no land in Aphra Behn's background and she would be very tart about those who gained from Royalist misery. None the less, in an unsettled time Bartholomew, with only a fraction of his daughter's proven energy and drive, may well have bettered himself. Or his widow may have done so. Or Aphra, twenty in the year of Restoration, may have done most of the bettering herself.

Aphra Behn's works suggest little sentiment about parents and home. Her mother outlived her father and was present in her adult years, but for some reason—drink perhaps or foolishness, even perhaps illiteracy— she was not entirely trusted by her daughter.[28] Certainly she was no financial support. As for fathers, Aphra seems pretty defiant of them, or indeed of anyone who would dictate to her, and she sounds an insubordinate child. Possibly Bartholomew unwisely tried to marry her off without proper consultation. Only royal parenthood appealed to her; then there entered a curious erotic quality, which just might echo some-thing in her relationship with her actual father.[29] Where she constantly mocked the sexual desires and designs of rich old age on youth, she found sexuality coupled with power a heady combination. As for barbers, Aphra tended in her works to mock them less than their customers; perhaps she remembered the comic vulnerability of the latter when soaped and ready for shaving by a man with a sharp knife.[30]

She was similarly unsentimental about Kent, its fertile hilly land, some suitable for fruit, grain and cattle, the occasional wooded parts round Canterbury and the waste and barren ground beyond. She was unmoved by its political traditions that made much of its settlement by Jutes rather than Saxons and of its independent history. Though it supposed itself to be full of heroic, liberty-loving people, it bred few important repub-licans of the sort Aphra Behn might have found heroic and it showed its libertarian spirit mostly by avoiding taxes and disobeying the Puritan injunctions to ignore Christmas and stop cock-fighting.[31] For most of the time, Kentish people were prepared to accept St Paul's useful injunction to obey 'the powers that be'. Consequently there was not much squealing as the 'Good Old Cause' of Parliament and Protestantism was overtaken in the late 1640s by the more radical and orderly power of the army dominated by Oliver Cromwell. What was left of Parliament after Cromwell's purges was a 'rump' of 240 members. In the future Behn would mercilessly mock this mutilated group, but she was never contemptuous of 'the great Oliver' from East Anglia.[32] She admired the politically tough just as much as she despised the weakly poor.

During the republican years, some Royalists compromised, wanting ease or losing patience with the young Charles II as he began dealing with Scots Presbyterians and other uncongenial groups. Few of his English followers wished to join an invasion from Scotland, and, when it began to happen, Cromwell easily crushed it. As a child of ten, Aphra would have heard of the disaster of the Battle of Worcester at which Cromwell thoroughly routed the Royalists and Scots, a major defeat which paradoxically became Charles II's most glamorous moment. Perhaps, in the duller years that followed, Bartholomew spiced his daughter's provincial life by a covert and not very strenuous Royalism. As a barber, he could pass messages to the few wandering spies and agents in England who had just arrived from the Continent and serve as a useful repository of information, without necessarily moving from Kent. Such activity would help make Aphra's childhood a suitable preparation for a life of counterfeiting and secrecy. Or, of course, he may have done nothing more than shave and trim customers. Or he may have worked for the other side—the county was riddled with government agents.

Whatever the paternal activities, until she reached her mid-teens at least, Aphra would have been caught in the female world. Despite the huge political events unfolding in the nation, the daily life for women inevitably went on as it always had, with the endless business of keeping the home, getting and preparing food, bearing and raising children. Canterbury was as fair a place to fulfil these tasks as anywhere. It was reasonably prosperous, with a good market-place and fairly well-ordered streets, though, like elsewhere, it lacked sanitation and a clean water supply and suffered from the frequent burnings of its wooden houses.

Perhaps in her early years, Aphra had her period of piety, as most children do who are raised on the edge of a religion. If she had, it was long passed by the time she wrote to publish, and in *Oroonoko* she conveyed two stages by portraying herself trying to teach the slaves about 'the true God' while making the hero Oroonoko 'jest' about the Trinity. In her works she showed no appreciation of the complex, beautiful devotional poetry of George Herbert or Henry Vaughan, and she made no mention of her contemporaries, Milton, Marvell or Bunyan. Later, in the Restoration, Edward Hyde, Charles II's Lord Chancellor, looked back at the generation of young people born during the troubled years and noted their spiritual damage: 'All Relations were confounded by the several Sects in Religion, which discountenanced all Forms of Reverence and Respect, as Reliques and Marks of Superstition....' He spoke mainly of men of course: few women dared break the seemingly natural link between femininity and piety.[33] Some managed to form the link into a kind of subverting force, but Behn was not among these; she disliked Puritans far too much to emulate or use them.[34] As a dissatisfied girl of independent habit and thought, she would have provoked homilies from moralistic men and she abhorred sermons in or out of church. Those in church had become dry discourses on speculative and national issues; talk had replaced ritual, which alone might have reconciled her to religion. Although she complained that Puritans aimed to squash the joy from life, like most Cavaliers Aphra also accepted that their joylessness coated lust. When in her play, *The Feign'd Curtizans*, she created a dissembling and lusty chaplain, aptly named Tickletext, she made Kent his home.

The signs of the Puritan ideal were all around her. In the 1650s the great cathedral of Canterbury appeared like a ruined monastery. The reformers had torn out the decoration left over from Henry VIII's earlier Reformation, desecrated many of the monuments, and stripped the choir of its hangings. They had left bare walls and roof, and even these had been neglected: the windows had been broken and the timber work had deteriorated. The organ had been damaged and the great library demolished, its books sold. So when Aphra visited as a child she could not have seen the once gilded shrine and tomb of Thomas à Becket, but she could have noticed the worn hollow made by the feet of the pilgrims who had once worshipped there. Roman Catholicism, the outward shows of which always attracted her, might have made its presence first felt as an emphatic absence.[35]

Throughout Behn's work, church-going is seen not as a chance for piety but as the only sexual resource for a girl in a repressive society, whether in Southern Europe, London or Kent. In one of her last plays a young woman exclaims characteristically:

I have been at the Chapel; and seen so many Beaus, such a Number of Plumeys, I cou'd not tell which I shou'd look on most, sometimes my heart was charm'd with the gay Blonding, then with the

Melancholy Noire, annon the amiable brunet, sometimes the bashful, then again the bold; the little now, anon the lovely tall! In fine, my Dear, I was embarrassed on all sides, I did nothing but deal my heart *tout au toore*.[36]

Beyond experience in family, shop, church or county, there was the world of literature and in this the young Aphra spent a large part of her time. If unmoved by Kent as countryside, she was inspirited by Arcadia, that mythical realm of pastoral literature existing in its peculiar Golden Age glow. The world she inhabited and which she herself later created so vividly was animated not by Nature or by God, but by human sexual desire and activity; it was not strange and sublime, simply responsive. Being pre-agricultural, this Arcadian world had no labourers or crops, only swains and untended fruit. These swains combined contented lower and upper classes without the economic realities of either. They inhabited a park of nobles, where nature simply supplied the necessary food and symbolic flowers twined themselves into bunches. No one had to struggle to town with produce or worry about price.[37]

In tune with this Arcadian pastoral world was French romance, that great love of bookish (and Royalist) girls.[38] Avidly they read the huge fantastic pseudo-historical works of Gauthier de La Calprenède and Madeleine de Scudéry, full of extreme and refined emotion, propriety and heroism, of derring-do carried out by both men and women, as well as women sold and exchanged as slaves between men. From 1652 to 1665, the many volumes of La Calprenède's *Cassandra* and *Cleopatra* came out in English. Dorothy Osborne, who chronicled a bright girl's reading in her letters to her fiancé, lapped the French versions up at once, seeing them as a fine test of her lover. She had, she exclaimed, 'six tomes' of *Cleopatra* and intended to lend them to him. When he was unresponsive, she wrote again, 'since you are at leisure to consider the moon, you may be enough to read *Cléopâtre*, therefore I have sent you three tomes…'. And again, 'I have sent you the rest of *Cléopâtre*….You will meet with a story in these parts of *Cléopâtre* that pleased me more than any I ever read in my life; 'tis of one Délie, pray give me your opinion of her and her prince.'[39]

Dorothy Osborne was not alone in her enthusiasm for this potent prose. Another contemporary, Mary North, 'diverted her sisters and all the female society at work together…with rehearsing by heart prolix romances, with the substance of speeches and letters as well as passages; and this with little or no hesitation but in a continual series of discourse'.[40]

Meanwhile the conduct- and cookery-book writer, Hannah Woolley, described a noble patroness making her read 'Poems of all sorts and plays, teaching me as I read, where to place my accents, how to raise and fall in my voice, where to lay emphasis on the expressions. Romances of the best sort she took great delight in.'[41] Aphra was similarly hooked. She read avidly—and listened too, for many of her later allusions to the great heroes of romance are spelt phonetically, as if from something heard, not read, long ago as a girl.

Since she had good clear handwriting, the kind from which the modern variety has derived, Aphra must also have spent some of her childhood copying the Royalist poems, which, along with romance, coloured her mind.[42] She had not so much money to lay out on printed works and, besides, many verses circulated only in manuscript. Girls spent much time on this activity, servicing quills, usually the second wings of geese or ravens, and licking them clean when greasy, ruling lines and rubbing them out with bread when the letters had been formed. The young Elizabeth Thomas, an admirer and imitator of Behn in the early years of the next century, remembered long hours of writing out chapters and compiling commonplace books. She also practised various scripts, as Aphra probably did. The skill Aphra acquired would have been useful in later life when she probably did copying for money. There was a huge industry of such work in London, since handwritten newsletters and poems were much in demand—as was the good-looking copying girl: rakish letters mention ambiguous visits to lady copyists in garrets.[43]

Aphra's background is not far from that of another Canterbury child, the sixteenth-century dramatist, Christopher Marlowe, son of a shoe-maker. The difference of course comes from his sex. As a clever boy, Marlowe had the advantage of formal education provided by the King's School. There were boarding schools for girls in Kent, but they were rather like finishing schools, fashionably aiming pupils towards marriage and the managing of a man in a domestic setting, although they could provide a start for an ambitious girl.[44] The poet Katherine Philips, Behn's most important literary predecessor, was largely self-educated and may have been influenced by her grandmother who wrote poetry, but she also attended a ladies' academy.

Some women wanted more. Hannah Woolley required girls to read edifying works and romances, but she also suggested that they learn Latin, so that they could go beyond reading Plutarch's *Lives* made English, the closest most girls came to classical learning. She did, however, recognise that men often mocked women's ambition and the smattering of knowledge to which it usually led. 'A learned woman is thought to be a comet that bodes mischief whenever it appears.'[45] Quite clever women still lamented their lack of formal schooling. The poet and science writer Margaret Cavendish, Duchess of Newcastle, never ceased to bewail her insufficient training, which revealed itself in both a beguiling spontaneity and an appalling spelling. She understood the tie of learning and power when she wrote of men, 'They hold books as their crown by which they rule and govern.' Behn's spelling, like her handwriting, was more ordered suggesting some training in script.

The extraordinary humanist education given to only a small group of aristocratic girls under the Tudors, with the notion that the classics combined with Christianity could breed virtue, was far in the past and the perennial dislike of intellectual women had intensified in the early seventeenth century. But, however illusory a past of general female achievement, thinking Englishwomen like Behn were irritated by a sense of increasing exclusion from male learning, at the very time when education in the classics and the new sciences was broadening to take in a far wider spectrum of young men than ever before—and for a long time after.[46] 'We are become like worms that only live in the dull earth of ignorance, winding ourselves sometimes out by the help of some refreshing rain of good educations, which seldom is given us,' wrote Margaret Cavendish bitterly.[47] Women yearned to be 'book-learned' and felt that their possible weakness by nature was being enhanced by nurture. Mary Astell, the major feminist thinker of the seventeenth century, roundly declared that female incapacity, 'if there be any, is acquired not natural'.[48]

All her life Behn felt, simultaneously, that she had missed something of importance in not knowing Latin and Greek well and that what she was missing was unnecessary, since its primary result seemed an unwonted sense of superiority in its owners. Perhaps Uncle George Denham had started her prejudice. Francis Kirkman, a contemporary writer and publisher, who, like Aphra, felt he had been deprived of the code of Latin that defined a gentleman, wrote defiantly in his autobiographical *The Unlucky Citizen* (1673):

you shall not find my *English*, *Greek*, here; nor hard *cramping Words*, such as will stop you in the middle of your Story to consider what is meant by them; you may read all that is here written without the use of a *Dictionary*; you shall need none, no not so much as an *English* one; and the Truth is, if I had a mind to confound you with hard Terms; I'le assure you I cannot, having not been bred so good a Scholar....

Aphra would later make this sort of truculent, envious gesture towards her absent formal education. That both she and Kirkman had to some extent to be autodidacts inevitably made them belligerent and resentful.

Years later, Behn spoke for many ambitious and intellectual girls when she claimed she had all her life 'curst' her '*Sex* and *Education*',

> And more the scanted Customs of the Nation,
> Permitting not the Female Sex to tread
> The Mighty Paths of Learned *Heroes* Dead.
> The Godlike *Virgil* and Great *Homers* Muse
> Like Divine Mysteries are conceal'd from us,
> We are forbid all grateful Theams,
> No ravishing Thoughts approach our Ear;
> The Fulsom Gingle of the Times
> Is all we are allow'd to Understand, or Hear.[49]

Sensibly, however, she let the 'Fulsom Gingle' resound in her mind. She later became adept at mimicking and mocking it.

If the male Christopher Marlowe is no real analogy, 'the German Princess', Mary Carleton, a great female 'rogue' who passed herself off as a German noblewoman, may be one. Mary Carleton was born about the same time in roughly the same place into roughly the same rank as Aphra Behn, and was one of those witty and pretty girls of the lower orders with some genteel manners who occasionally amused their betters.[50] All girls were raised to please men, a tendency exaggerated in themselves by the lowly-born who yearned to enter privileged educated ranks. The dual need produced a consummate ability to entertain—in Behn's case a play-writing career was pleasing on a large scale—and to counterfeit. Such quick, pretty and ambitious girls might be taken into grand homes for long periods where, as playmate or companion for the daughters, they could acquire a patina—or more than that—of education. In the words of Francis Kirkman, her biographer, Mary Carleton intruded herself

> into the company of the best Children in the City, with whose Relations, her winning Deportment, and ingenious answers on all occasions, soon did ingratiate her, insomuch that several persons of

good quality frequently took her home as a Play-mate for their little ones for a week together. Thus she learnt some genteel accomplishments such as singing and dancing and acquired an educated way of speaking above her station. She read English perfectly and played the virginal and violin at the age of five....

Inevitably, 'the meanness of her quality did not suit with her spirit' and she loathed the notion of 'laborious drudgery'.

Often the result of such patronage was that the girl, when grown and not as amusing, might make a modestly satisfactory marriage. Or, if less lucky, she might enter a life of dissatisfied upper service as a companion or lady's maid. Or she might fall into the ranks of the genteel courtesans, or, as in the case of Mary Carleton, a life of trickery and crime to procure those advantages seen at too close quarters when young. Or, if exceptionally intelligent, as Aphra certainly was, she might become a resourceful and witty woman of learning who had to earn a living and could not afford too many principles. There was no reason why, having survived such a background, a woman should discuss it.

After being accused of bigamy before the austere and stern justice, Sir Edmund Bury Godfrey, Mary Carleton awaited trial in prison. There she was visited by people of rank and position including, on 29 May 1663, the diarist Samuel Pepys, highly susceptible to the charm that had—so it later came out—procured three husbands, at least two of them living. He was 'high in the defence of her wit and spirit'. Aphra seems not to have shared the opinion. Years later, when Mary Carleton had made her 'untimely Exit' on the scaffold, a friend wrote an epilogue for one of Behn's plays which then flopped on the stage. It made a clever comparison between the playwright trying to cozen an audience and Mary Carleton, the 'German Princess', trying to cozen her husband, each being cheats in their own ways. Behn was clearly not amused and her reference to it was thoroughly ungracious. Was the comparison of the two upwardly mobile Canterbury girls too close?

CHAPTER 2

❧

Sir Thomas Colepeper and Lord Strangford

'born for greater things than her Fortune does now promise'

Something more than time and place was needed to transform Aphra
Johnson, daughter of a barber and wet-nurse, into the acquaintance
and entertainer of courtiers, some role that would bring her to the
attention of men she could hardly have met at home in Canterbury.
Beyond the obvious sexual one, functions available to a girl in restless
times were of messenger, courier and, just possibly, spy. These Thomas
Colepeper, her foster-brother, could have facilitated, for, as a well-off
young man with no parental constraint, he was soon deeply entangled
in Royalist activity. He may, also, have provided Aphra with some relations on whom to practise social and investigative skills.

The family of Thomas Colepeper was important in Kent, but not as
grand as the Sidney family—as the relatives of his mother, Lady Barbara,
noted when she proposed, after a whirlwind courtship of ten days, to
bestow herself on Sir Thomas Colepeper.[1] She was the daughter of
Robert Sidney, Earl of Leicester, and sister of the present Earl.[2] Their
son Thomas was, then, related through his mother to the Sidneys, one
of the most prominent families in the kingdom, in turn closely allied to
the great ducal family of the Howards.

The Howards included Protestants and Catholics, dukes and playwrights,
and for them Behn always had the greatest respect; indeed, in one of her
seemingly autobiographical remarks, she declared she had come 'into the
World with a Veneration for your Illustrious Family, and being brought up
with continual Praises of the Renowned Actions of your glorious Ancestors'.
Her first published poem was written to encourage a play-writing Howard;
fifteen years later she eulogised the Howard Duke of Norfolk as her patron.
After a Catholic Howard, Viscount Stafford, was executed during the
Popish Plot in 1680, she made him into an English saint and martyr.
Colepeper was impressed with the Howards too: in his 'Adversaria', their
family tree appears almost as frequently as his own.

Before her second marriage to Colepeper's father, Lady Barbara had been wife to the rich Lord Strangford. On his father's early death, their eldest son, Philip, became Lord Strangford, inherited a huge income of some £4,000 a year, and was made a ward of the crown. After much unseemly haggling, his maternal uncle, the Earl of Leicester, became his guardian and Strangford moved to the Sidney house of Penshurst.[3] At fifteen he had made a plausibly pleasant impression; only later did Dorothy Osborne, a close friend of the Sidney girls, term him 'the beast with…estates'. Soon the Earl regarded his nephew as extravagant and spoilt, while Strangford came to judge his uncle devious and greedy.[4]

Given the later closeness of the half-brothers, Thomas Colepeper is likely to have visited Strangford for considerable periods at Penshurst. Possibly he took with him the girl, Aphra, whose mother may have helped fill the gap of his own lost parent. If he did, Aphra would have encountered Literature there. The Sidneys were proud of their poetic traditions. The huge asymmetrical feudal square of Penshurst Place, with its chapel, towering hall, galleries and intricate rooms full of portraits, armour and aristocratic bric-à-brac, its jumbled splendour and vast uneven park, had been hymned by the dramatist, Ben Jonson, and the poet, Edmund Waller, as well as by its most famous son, Sir Philip Sidney. He had been the uncle of the present Earl and Colepeper's mother, the pattern of Protestant chivalry and author of the celebrated romance, *Arcadia*.

The Sidneys were also famous for literary women. The Sidney Countess of Pembroke had been a powerful patron under Elizabeth I, as well as an accomplished poet. Lady Mary Wroth, Colepeper's dead aunt, to whom Ben Jonson dedicated *The Alchemist*, could both inspire and warn an ambitious literary girl, for, notoriously, she had published a book.[5] This had been a *roman à clef* portraying herself and her family, as well as some of James I's courtiers. The latter were furious: one called Lady Mary an 'Hermaphrodite in show, in deed a monster' and ordered her to 'leave idle books alone' since 'wiser and worthyer women have writte none.'[6] After much furore, the work was withdrawn. If Mary Wroth's history was known to Aphra, it would have taught her, if not silence, then the need for circumspection in publishing under one's own name. Even codes must yield more than one possibility if they were to be used with impunity.[7]

Closer was Colepeper's much older cousin, the eldest daughter of the Earl of Leicester, Dorothy Sidney, Lady Sunderland. With her young son Robert, later the Earl of Sunderland, she lived at Penshurst until 1650, while her husband fought and died in the Royalist armies; thereafter she visited regularly. Before her marriage, Dorothy had become famous under the sugary name of 'Sacharissa' as the muse of her would-be lover, the poet Edmund Waller. He was one of the Cavalier writers Aphra began reading in her teens, valued throughout her life—indeed she called him the nurse of her 'Infant *Muse*', nourishing her with his 'soft *Food* of *Love*'—and elegised after his death. In his passion, Waller made Dorothy Sidney into the shepherdess of the aristocratic Arcadia of Penshurst. It was a vision that much appealed to young Aphra, growing up in what disgruntled Cavaliers deplored as 'verseless times'.

If Colepeper visited Penshurst, he is unlikely to have stayed there, for the Earl was determined not to take in stray children who could not handsomely pay their way—as Lord Strangford so palpably could.[8] In any case he had rather more elevated charges. For a short time there were in his nursery two of Charles I's children, who had been lodged there by Parliament to be taught with the Sidneys. One of them, Henry, Duke of Gloucester, lived just long enough to see the Restoration of his brother in 1660. Years later, Aphra would refer to this noble youth and his intended fate as a cobbler under the egalitarian protectorate: he was to have been 'bound Prentice to a Handy-Crafts Trade, but that our Lords could not spare Money to bind him out, and so they sent him to beg beyond the Sea'.[9] The good Cavalier, Loveless, roundly declared this 'Blasphemy against the Royal Youth'.

As half-Sidneys, Thomas Colepeper and his sister were allied to the numerous children of the Earl. They ranged from the eldest grown men and women—Philip, Algernon, and Dorothy—down to the young ones, Isabella and Henry. Despite the fact that Dorothy's husband died for the Royalist cause, the Sidneys largely accepted the Interregnum governments, though happily for their future none was involved in Charles I's death.

It is possible that, through Thomas Colepeper, young Aphra came into contact with one or two of these Sidneys. She was a friendly, clever girl with some beauty and much wit, and birth was less important in a pretty young person than in an older homelier one. Like Mary Carleton, she could entertain her betters, write appealing verses—her memoirist claims she composed poetry since 'the first use almost of reason in discourse'—and she was remembered as having 'agreeable repartees at hand', which she played off 'like winning cards'.[10] Perhaps she had use as a neat copyer, perhaps she dramatised short scenes from La Calprenède. In particular, she may have come to the attention of Philip, Lord L'Isle.

L'Isle, the tall, haughty, fair and heavy-featured heir, followed a cautious political path in the Interregnum, never being a 'fanatic' and pleading ill health when urged to undertake any dubious act. In this he contrasted with his bold and boisterous brother, the republican theorist, Algernon. In 1656, Philip accused Algernon of staging *Julius Caesar* (and himself playing Brutus) at Penshurst particularly to affront Cromwell.[11] On his side, Algernon described their father as demanding that Philip Lord L'Isle 'leave the lewd, infamous, and Atheisticall life that he led'. Though this report on a man who stood between him and the family title may be biased, L'Isle was, in the 1670s, a friend of the dissolute Earl of Rochester, so may have had some libertine and free-thinking inclinations.[12] A widower in his thirties in the 1650s, L'Isle was an aristocrat by birth, inclination and principle, with a high sense of rank and his own importance. He knew himself to have the right of primogeniture, supported patriarchal power, and, like his republican brother, despised the mob, the anarchic multitude. Perhaps this educated, disgruntled man gave some of his time and principles to his cousin Thomas's 'fayre' foster-sister and let her loose in the great Penshurst library of European and classical languages, history, philosophy and comparative religions. The adult Aphra Behn showed some surprising grasp of these.

In her late story, *The Lucky Mistake*, there is a character called Vernole, a learned older man from a great and noble house. This nobleman educates the twelve- or thirteen-year-old heroine, Atlante, speaking to her of philosophy and matters of state. Indeed he declares to her surprised father,

> I find the Seeds of great and profound Matter in the Soul of this Young Maid, which ought to be nourisht, now while she is Young, and they will grow up to very great Perfection; I find *Atlante* capable of all the Noble Vertues of the Mind, and am infinitely mistaken in my Observations, and *Act* of *Phisiognomy*, if *Atlante* be not born for greater things than her Fortune does now promise, she will be very Considerable in the World, believe me....[13]

The result of this praise, rather unusual for a heroine in the sort of romantic tale this purports to be, is that her father begins to value her more than he had. Vernole continues his efforts and

> as much of his Learning, as *Atlante* was capable of attaining to, he made her Mistress of, and that was no small Portion, for all his Discourse was fine and easily comprehended, his Notions of *Philosophy* fit for *Ladies*; and he took greater pains with Atlante, than

any Master wold have done with a Scholar; so that it was most certain, he added very great Accomplishments to her Natural Wit, and the more because she took a very great Delight in *Philosophy*.[14]

Aphra grew up to take considerable 'Delight in *Philosophy*' and to translate precisely the kind of books that communicated the knowledge of this man to discerning women. In the story, it does not follow from her admiration and gratitude that the heroine wants her teacher for a lover, but she deeply respects his learning and enjoys his influence over her. In the 'Memoirs', the young untouched Aphra leaves Kent, having provoked love in many. Could one of those provoked to a little flirtation have been Philip Lord L'Isle?[15]

Probably as fascinating to the lowly-born girl at this time was Colepeper's raffish elder brother, Lord Strangford. When Colepeper recorded Aphra's birth in his 'Adversaria', he gave as one of the possible places the small low-lying village of Sturry, just north of Canterbury on the River Stour. Possibly this was because he saw her there often: Sturry House, a grand brick manor, was the seat of his half-brother.

In 1653 Strangford marched out of Penshurst. He took with him his new young wife and cousin, Isabella Sidney. The Earl claimed distaste for the match since he disapproved cousin marriages, was not impressed with his still underaged nephew, and regarded him as after Isabella's portion which he resolutely refused to pay. Later Strangford declared that *he* had been bounced into marriage by the fortune-hunting Sidneys.

The new tie did not bind the families. Lord Strangford had acquired a sense of his own importance through easy money. He had been without parental control and, now married, he felt the smallest restraint a violation. According to the Earl, he had become wild and extravagant, gaining popularity with a set of people who fed on his wealth. On his side, the young man had had enough of his haughty relatives: Penshurst was a great house but not great fun, and he longed for freedom.

At Sturry, so short a distance from her Canterbury home, Aphra could have seen the epitome of the pleasure-loving, aristocratic lifestyle before the Restoration of Charles II. Strangford lived well and enjoyed himself, using his servants to collect money directly from the tenants on his estate. He ran through vast sums in drinking, eating and entertaining; Isabella, described by her family as 'soe unhappily married', seems to have enjoyed part of it too. No doubt there was music and all the pleasant graceful appendages of life that money could provide. Aphra would have been entranced by an existence of such intensity and luxury.

Inevitably the young man soon fell out with his new employees and blamed everyone but himself for his chaotic finances. He was in a 'low condition', he wailed, cheated and entrapped by the people around him. Soon he was broke and, according to Algernon Sidney, confessed he had long 'bin perpetually Drunck or out of his wits'. Promises were exacted that he should desist from 'the foolish courses he had taken, shewe him self kind unto his wife, live civilly, leaving the filthy company with which he conversed', and of course make peace with the Earl.[16]

At this point the Strangfords had 'a minde to goe into france'. So off they went with a retinue of ten servants and baggage on the *Yarmouth* for Dieppe.[17] They settled in a house in St Germain-en-Laye. Soon they were running up Parisian debts and shocking the Sidneys anew by their 'extravagant ways of liveing'. Algernon agreed, for £250 a year, to administer the Strangford estates and he moved into Sturry.[18] The good times at the Manor were definitely over.

Undoubtedly Strangford went to France because the Sidneys wanted to be rid of him, but he also went for *political* reasons. The Royalists were desperate for safe houses for their agents to stay in, since at public inns they could easily be apprehended by government agents. For a short period Lord Strangford seems to have provided one of these in St Germain. It was made especially secure by the frequent visits of the republican Algernon to discuss money with his feckless cousin.[19] Strangford may well have enjoyed acting against the political views of his overbearing relative.

Back in England, the half-brothers, Strangford and Colepeper, became involved with the loose Royalist organisation called the Sealed Knot. This had been formed to coordinate Royalist policy, liaise with the King and try to prevent premature effort. It was inefficient, however, and its control over plotting minimal. It failed to prevent several small useless uprisings which served only to create martyrs.

After years of inertia, the Sealed Knot was activated by the sudden death of Oliver Cromwell and the resulting turmoil as his heirs battled for the succession. A general Royalist uprising was projected—later known as Booth's rising because Sir George Booth's northern force was the only one remotely to succeed. Lord Willoughby of Parham, proprietor of the South American territory of Surinam and a distant connection of the Sidneys, was to possess King's Lynn in Norfolk; the eager brothers, Thomas Colepeper and Lord Strangford, were among those raising cavalry troops in Kent.

Then everything went wrong—as it usually did with events planned by the Sealed Knot. The able John Thurloe had built up a strong intelligence system under Cromwell and it was now run, as it had been before his tenure, by the equally able Thomas Scot. Scot was apprised of the details of the proposed insurrection, including a planning meeting near Gray's Inn in London, information of which was delivered by an alleged Catholic, Lady Willoughby, possibly a pseudonym or just possibly the wife of the Presbyterian Lord Willoughby himself—these were complicated times and the pair detested each other.[20] The London militia was readied and the City secured. The various rebels were then picked up before they could properly assemble—indeed there was so great a storm that a good many were simply lost before they could rendezvous.[21] Willoughby was taken and Booth defeated. About fifty Cavaliers were caught at Tonbridge, along with apprentices and local supporters. Lord Strangford was informed on and taken; Colepeper, loose for a little longer, followed him. By 11 August the brothers were together in prison—comfortably so, since Strangford did not stint himself and demanded that his servants attend him there. Soon, with the help of Isabella using her brother Algernon's name, he was bailed for £5,000. Colepeper put up £3,000. All was, in the words of the newssheet *Mercurius Politicus*, 'happily quelled'.[22]

In all these activities, it is possible that Colepeper's foster-sister Aphra had a role. She had been mixing with her betters and would have become adept at imitation and dissimulation. Women such as Lady Mary Howard were commonly used as messengers for the Sealed Knot to their colleagues abroad, while others like Lady Newport provided cover addresses for correspondence. Aphra Behn could easily have liaised with Lord Strangford in France, where Colepeper's journeys would be noted, as well as with other Royalist men. There is, however, no proof, for it is the nature of a secret service to remain secretive.[23]

If there is no *proof*, there is none the less a good deal of supporting evidence. In an early play, *The Dutch Lover*, Aphra Behn referred to a changeover of governors in Flanders in 1659, not a common detail for a provincial girl to give, and she set more than one play on the Continent in the charged time just prior to the Restoration. In the 1660s, she had some involvement with Lord Willoughby who was occasionally in Holland during these months, while later she showed considerable familiarity with the Cavalier Thomas Killigrew, in comfortable Dutch exile in the late 1650s, but still involved in intelligence. Earlier he had been a Gentleman of the Bedchamber to the young Duke of Gloucester when he had come to the Continent from Penshurst. Aphra is more likely to have made both acquaintances, with Thomas Killigrew and with Lord Willoughby, in their time of relative obscurity than when Willoughby was a courtier and confirmed owner of a goodly slice of English colonies and when Killigrew ran the King's theatre company, was Master of the Revels, politician and royal favourite.[24]

Through Killigrew, Aphra was later employed for a dangerous mission in the Low Countries at the height of war with Holland, which England was by no means winning. In such unfavourable circumstances, an attractive, youngish woman is unlikely to have been dispatched without any counterfeiting past, some proof that she would not spring a treacherous leak under pressure. She could have indicated this only through previous experience.

If she did act as agent and courier, primarily for the Royalists—although she may have picked up commissions where she could—Aphra would have joined a vast army of such people, answering loosely to the King's chancellor in exile, Edward Hyde. He had almost nothing but promises and honours to give out to his agents, but he was an astute man and the Stuarts always generated loyalty beyond self-interest. The service had to be vast since spies were needed to watch both the enemy and each other—a double agent could do more harm than a regiment of soldiers. So there was a veritable army involved in a potential infinity of spying. The movers of the game were the double and triple agents and the waverers.[25] One of these was Colonel Bampfield, who would loom large in Aphra's later spying life and is an example of the breed.

Bampfield had been a Royalist soldier serving in the early Civil War and intimate of the young James Duke of York, whom he had unwisely helped break his word to his Parliamentarian captors. With the aid of Anne Murry, a spirited young gentlewoman to whom the married Colonel was deceitfully paying court, Bampfield helped James escape in women's clothes from St James's Palace, Anne Murry providing a petticoat of mohair for the Duke and a 'Woodstreet cake' for his journey by barge from London.[26] In Holland, the fifteen-year-old James found some of the English fleet rebelling against Parliament. Without leave from his brother but with Bampfield's connivance, he set himself up as admiral, perhaps even fantasising a higher role. Charles had to intervene. James was removed and Prince Rupert put in his place to try to control the riotous sailors, now making drunken havoc in Rotterdam.

Before and after the incident, Bampfield appears on Scot's and Thurloe's payroll, giving information about the Sealed Knot and the

Booth uprising and sending information about Lord Strangford at St Germain-en-Laye. He would later appear on the books of the Dutch and of the Royalist English government after the Restoration, when Aphra Behn heard much of him and he of her. What was true of Bampfield could be true of any other agent: he or she was performing a function for whoever would pay.

On the Continent, the safest lodging for a *female*, primarily Royalist agent or courier was a convent of English nuns, and Aphra may have visited at least one of these. Many had sprung up in Flanders since the enthusiastic Mary Ward started the Institute of Mary in 1609, and they formed refuges for English women in exile, as well as for Catholic girls wanting a religious life or finishing touches to their education. The Benedictines had established themselves in Ghent in 1624 and later in Brussels, near Boulogne, and in Ypres. Many years on, Behn set a short story in a convent in Ypres, *The History of the Nun*, claiming that it was based on fact.[27]

In the Flemish city of Ghent, Mary Knatchbull, an acquaintance of Colepeper's, was abbess of the English Benedictines in Sint-Pietersnieuwstraat and a good friend to the Royalists.[28] Stationary and secure in her convent, Catholic and loyal to the Stuart kings who were ambiguously connected to her faith but certainly better than the Presbyterians and Independents who currently ruled her native land, Knatchbull had become a useful resource for the Cavaliers, for whom she acted as a kind of treasurer and counsellor. Possibly her covert activities were known to the Vatican, which would rather see Charles Stuart regain his kingdom than not, but felt no pressing need to provide funds.

Money laboriously raised by the King, his brother James and their courtiers from foreign princes, dukes and bishops needed to be held and distributed to the various Cavaliers and agents, complicatedly crossing and recrossing Europe on their undercover missions. Many were desperately poor. Thomas Killigrew described them as 'a race of men who have left praying, or hoping for daily bread; and only relye upon nightly drink'; they have 'no servants, no money, no clothes, no meat, and always afoot'.[29] The little money there was had to be carefully rationed from central sources. Mary Knatchbull's contribution can be illustrated by one itinerant nobleman who told Edward Hyde he was 'relying upon the promise, that of the first money returned into Flanders…there shall be put into my Lady Abbess's hands three thousand Florins for the clearing of me in Flanders'.[30]

If Aphra came here or to another intriguing convent, it would account for her extraordinary knowledge of Catholic institutions and ritual not easily explained by a Kentish childhood, as well as the claim before *The History of the Nun*, that she had once been tempted by the cloister but lacked the strength of character. Given the impecunious nature of the English convents in the Interregnum, when their usual supply of money from England had dried up, she would not have been much welcomed without a dowry.[31] None the less, Aphra may once or twice have thought about the matter while she was being made much of in a convent. In the same story she describes how a girl, a 'forward Pratler', acute and responsive, is patronised by cultured nuns: 'all joyn'd to compleat [her] Mind and Body' with dancing, singing, languages, manner and wit, in all of which she excelled.[32] For Aphra, the Benedictine nuns of Ghent may have helped the process of education that began with the Sidneys and Colepepers in Kent.

Aphra Behn knew little of the religious motives that might make girls want to devote their lives to God and their own sex or the piety that kept them serene under restrictions. But she was an enthralled spectator of the magnificence of Catholic ritual, ceremonial, erotic and aesthetic displays that led to ecstasy and tied her more to the theatrical arts of this world than to the mysteries of the other. As she later wrote of a fictional ceremony in Flanders:

> All I could see around me, all I heard, was ravishing and heavenly; the Scene of Glory, and the dazling Altar; the noble Paintings, and the numerous Lamps; the Awfulness, the Musick, and the Order, made me conceive myself above the Stars....[33]

The centre of the show in the novel is a young monk who 'bore new lustre in his Face and Eyes, Smiles on his Cheeks, and Dimples on his Lips... Ten thousand Sighs, from all sides, were sent to him, as he passed along, which, mix'd with the soft Musick, made such a murmuring as gentle Breezes moving yielding Boughs.'

Paintings, lamps, stars, and male charms—it was not exactly piety. Aphra loved the intrigue, the naughtiness, the finery, the ceremony, the sensual mystique, the scandal of what Puritanism had tried to eradicate in her home country. If she were on a spying mission, she would already have been showing her bent towards the unlawful in the terms of her own nation; she would have found Catholicism equally appealing because forbidden.

Aphra would have been struck, too, by the rivalry and envy that often fuelled the inmates of Catholic convents, some of whom were there for the convenience of their families and wanted for their dowries—she was definite that women should not be forced into convents or marriage before they knew what they were doing. None the less, she relished the gossip that excited and distracted the worldly nuns. The narrators in her stories are never nuns, although they often write of nuns and admit they have picked up details from convent gossip. They or their informers seem adept spies within the walls, images perhaps of the political activities of the Ghent convent.

CHAPTER 3

✤

Voyage to Surinam

'Men of Fortune seldom travell hither Sir'

Aphra may, then, have been an experienced spy at the Restoration. What could be more natural than that she should continue her activities, since the reign of Charles II did not relax surveillance?[1] The next place of her operations as secret agent might well have been the exotic colony of Surinam in South America, to which she journeyed in the early 1660s.

The seventeenth century was the age of the great English adventurer-trader colonists, who travelled the globe from the Moluccas to the coasts of South America, struggling with the Dutch and Spanish for trading supremacy and the chance to plant and form agricultural communities. They had little anxiety over impinging on other cultures, but they were curious about customs, when they had leisure from surviving and plundering.

Surinam, between the Orinoco and Amazon rivers, had not been truly conquered by the Spanish in the sixteenth and seventeenth centuries and was a target for colonial activity by many nations, especially French, Dutch and English. In the early 1630s, Thomas Howard, Earl of Berkshire, purchased a boat to send out settlers and published a prospectus in encouragement. He would, he said, dispatch honest and able men and artisans, 'besides women'; he even intended 'to goe with my wife & friends, to inhabit some part of that spacious & goodly countrie'.[2] None of his plans came to fruition, however. Other attempts were temporarily more successful, but all settlements foundered on quarrels with natives and alien colonising powers.

The Barbados patent, which covered Barbados and the Leeward Islands, was given by James I simultaneously to two favourites. After much wrangling, it fell to the Earl of Carlisle, from whose family in 1647 the turncoat Parliamentarian/Royalist, Lord Willoughby, received a twenty-one-year lease of property rights in the Caribee islands. He aimed at founding a new colony in Surinam, and a party of Royalists was sent out in 1651 from Barbados—the fourteenth attempt at settlement.[3] Plantations were begun along the Surinam River, with Willoughby, the proprietor and governor, investing over £20,000 in the enterprise. In the late 1650s Royalists were joined by failed settlers from Barbados, where Willoughby was having difficulty controlling the Parliamentarians. Amongst them came George Marten, brother of the famous Interregnum politician, the republican Henry Marten, who opposed both Cromwell and King Charles. Although the overwhelming motive of all the immigrants was financial, factional politics inevitably travelled with them. Presiding over this mixture of greed and grumbling was Willoughby's old political associate, William Byam, now Deputy Governor.[4]

The settlement of Surinam had been founded to cultivate sugar and tobacco. Cotton did not do as well as in Barbados, where the soil was less rich. Tobacco grew copiously, indeed better than in Virginia, but, because of the established success of the North American colony, the Surinam settlers never grew more than was needed for their own use—a substantial amount since all were addicted to the pipe. So Surinam became primarily a sugar domain. Potentially a profitable crop, sugar was difficult to exploit; it demanded expertise, large plantations, and considerable capital expenditure on equipment. Canes took twelve months to grow to six feet, but another three months before they were harvested, and it was some years before production justified investment. One might make a great deal of money or, equally, one might go broke.

Based on large plantations rather than small holdings, Surinam soon had a settler population of around 4,000. There were about 130 plantations, 40 or 50 profitably growing only sugar and owning their own sugar mills.[5] Others sometimes diversified with coffee, cotton or cacao. What the settlement lacked, it could get from the other colonies or from England; boats frequently went between Virginia, Barbados and Surinam, trading in meat and sugar. Sheep and pigs in particular were sent from Virginia, since they did not flourish in Surinam where they were irritated by bats biting off their teats.[6]

To develop Surinam through labour, Willoughby had urged settlers to come from Britain. In the troubled, impoverished and war-torn 1640s when prices rose steeply, it was easy to persuade poor people into migration from England and, increasingly, from an even more pauperised Ireland. By the 1650s, the economy in England had begun to pick up, food prices were more stable, and the government grew anxious about the out-flow of able-bodied men. By the late 1650s, emigration was discouraged.

In general, the colonies had difficulty attracting *bona fide* immigrants and there was suspicion that advertisements and favourable reports were simply 'decoys' to tempt the unwary. Colonists had, after all, to 'abandon the Land of [their] Nativity, and those comfortable outward Imployments and Accommodations which most of you had there, and to adventure [them] selves to the Hazards of a long Voyage at Sea, to come to this Remote part of the World'.[7] Others blamed the colonists: a Mr Hodges of Barbados said that 'It is grown a proverb with English merchants that, if a man goes over never so honest to the Plantations, yet the very air does change him in a short time. But it is not the air; it is the universal corruption of Justice'.[8]

To lure settlers, Willoughby issued a prospectus in 1655: 'Certain overtures made by the Lord Willoughby of Parham unto all such as shall incline to plant in the Colony of Surinam'.[9] But he himself was no advertisement: by 1663 he had not been near Surinam for nearly a decade. Colonists frequently seemed eager to reap the rewards of overseas proprietorship and grew energetic in persuading settlers to emigrate, while trying every possible means to avoid living in their violent and unhealthy possessions themselves. Indeed Lord Willoughby was so disastrous as a proprietor that he threw the whole system of proprietorship into disrepute; consequently he was the last of the individual colonial 'owners'.

The appalled response to Surinam society of one new arrival, after being persuaded to emigrate by Willoughby's propaganda, is caught in a letter of 10 December 1663. The Baptist pamphleteer, Henry Adis, had been deeply shocked by the brutish nature of the Surinam settlers, who displayed both debauchery and atheism and were, in his opinion, even worse than 'the very Heathens themselves, to the shame and stink of Christianity'. Collectively the Europeans were a 'rude rabble', given to drunkenness, blasphemous oaths and 'lascivious Abominations'.[10]

The 'Memoirs' declares that, through kinship with Lord Willoughby, Aphra's father went to Surinam as the designated 'lieutenant-general of six and thirty islands, besides the continent of Surinam' but died *en route*. The information was lifted straight from the short story that has given Behn posthumous fame, *Oroonoko*. This is a tragic tale of a princely black hero who is kidnapped from Africa, enslaved and taken to distant Surinam where, after trying to rebel, he is tricked into a gruesome death by the dishonourable white governor of the colony. The tale is told by a narrator, said to be the author, the writer Aphra Behn, who claims to have been his friend and companion and, to some extent, his keeper. The material was spiced in the 'Memoirs' with an allegedly false rumour that Behn had had an amorous affair with her black hero. This was of the exotic interracial sort that *Othello* and contemporary romantic fiction made glamorous, although, in lampoons, consorting with a black man rather signalled whorishness—no doubt this too enlivened the picture.[11] The 'Memoirs' was aimed at a sophisticated readership.

Something certainly happened to Bartholomew Johnson in the years after the Restoration: the Hearth Tax Returns for 1662 for his parish of St Margaret's appear to have been eaten by rodents, but in 1664 he should have featured in the extant Returns of Canterbury if he were still there, but he did not. The most likely explanation is that he died. Did he die at home in Canterbury or exotically at sea wrapped in a military uniform far beyond the aspirations of an average barber? The answer to this depends on the answer to the more basic questions: did Aphra go to Surinam at all?[12] Is it likely that she was the daughter of such an important man as the 'Memoirs' claimed?

To take the middle question: the main witness for Aphra's stay in Surinam is the story, *Oroonoko*, helped by a few supporting documents in manuscript collections and state archives. This story depicts the colony in some depth. It quotes odd words from the native Carib language of the sort an inquisitive visitor might have picked up during a stay and refers to the native habits of counting and healing that accord with detailed memories of others who indubitably visited the region, such as the traveller George Warren.[13] What Behn wrote may of course have taken details directly from Warren or from the Deputy Governor of Surinam, William Byam, whose observations were circulating in London in the 1660s. But why should she bother? When she set a story in Spain, she made little effort to provide local colour beyond reference to Spanish honour and the Prado; when she put it in the South of France the characters might as well be picnicking in Tunbridge Wells. Verisimilitude was not much prized by her audience.

The subsidiary Europeans in *Oroonoko* were all present in Surinam in the early 1660s, from Byam, made into the villain of the tale, with his sidekick, the crude and cruel James Banister, to the cultured young Cornishman, John Trefry, and the shrewd ex-Parliamentarian George Marten, now a colonel in the local militia. Indeed the fact that Behn's opinions of these men did not follow her later Royalist principles—she liked Marten, called a 'rational gentleman, and of loyalty and resolution' despite his Parliamentarian past, and disliked the Royalists, Byam and Banister— suggests personal experience.[14] Yes, she probably went to Surinam.

What then of her father, the alleged lieutenant-general? Would not someone have mentioned such an elevated background before Behn published *Oroonoko* during her last years of life? Wouldn't she herself?

Among vaguely maritime English functionaries, there is only a purser called Johnson and a storekeeper at Portsmouth. There are some Johnsons on both sides of the law in the West Indies, some being slavers, some pirates, and one becoming a lieutenant-governor of Nevil in the eighteenth century. But there is no Johnson intended for high office in Surinam in any of the records, nor any among Willoughby's known relatives.[15]

The biographical sketch which Charles Gildon wrote to preface her posthumous play, *The Younger Brother*, asserts that Aphra Behn went with her family merely to settle in Surinam. Yet there are no suitable Johnsons among the recorded settlers either. It is, too, an unlikely move for a man neither destitute nor equipped with money to trade or buy land. As a character enquires at the beginning of one of Behn's last plays, *The Widdow Ranter*, which calls on her Surinam memories, 'what Chance... drove thee to this part of the New World?' Another observes, 'Men of Fortune seldom travell hither Sir to see fashions.'[16]

Yet, if they do not endorse Aphra's *father*, Gildon's remarks may give some validity to the *daughter's* journey. *The Younger Brother* was dedicated by Gildon to Colonel Christopher Codrington. This young man, unborn when Behn allegedly visited Surinam, had a Caribbean past and his father, captain-general of the Leeward Islands, had sold property to George Marten in Barbados in the 1640s and 1650s, before the latter's financial collapse and removal to Surinam. In *Oroonoko*, Behn claimed she knew George Marten; his colourful family saga of dour Puritan father of two rakish sons, one flamboyant (Henry) and the other more secretive (George), forms part of the plot of her *Younger Brother*, a use suggesting some intimate talk between Aphra and George, whom, outside Surinam she could not have met. Also, a connection between Behn and Codrington seems possible, perhaps close enough to speculate that Gildon might have heard of Behn's Surinam past from the Colonel, who was probably known to them both. (Codrington could, of course, have refuted the claim to such a past if he had heard nothing of it.) Without such a connection, it seems strange that Gildon, a free-thinking man, should dedicate the amoral work of a woman often rebuked as an atheist to such a distinguished man; although a wit and patron of other playwrights, Codrington was also pious, and he left his Barbadian estates for the founding of a college to train medical missionaries who were to live obedient celibate lives.

Oroonoko and the 'Memoirs' have Aphra's father dying at sea, a claim which *The Younger Brother* sketch fails to make. As it happens, this was the fate of the real ruler and proprietor of Surinam, the Lord Willoughby, who was lost in a storm just after the time when Aphra must have travelled there. To make a good story, a transference would be easy. This is the more likely when one considers *Oroonoko* again. For what does it say about this important father? Nothing, except that he dies. His death seems to have had little impact on his daughter, who would be very noisy in her grief for patriarchal men in the future. It is also curious how little of her father's supposed importance rubs off on to his widow, as would be customary. Neither *Oroonoko* nor the 'Memoirs' nor any of the supporting records assign any particular status to Aphra's mother. It is Aphra alone who is prominent in Surinam.

A further transference may have been from Deputy Governor Byam to Aphra's father. Mr Johnson is said to have been given the position of lieutenant-general. This was, in fact, awarded to Byam through Willoughby at this time. Again it sounds as though Behn is organising matters fictionally, on this occasion to justify the attitude she provides for herself as fictional character in *Oroonoko*: of consuming hatred of Deputy Governor Byam. She could have been jealous of a man who had apparently taken her father's place.

As a voyager, then, Mr Johnson may well have been a fantasy or a displacement. And, if Aphra did indeed reach Surinam, it was more likely than not under her own sail. She was always adept at making necessary images of herself and, if one had the misfortune to go to the New World, one had to surround the event with as much respectability as possible.

This was partly because the West Indian colonies were desperate for European women, and everyone in England knew it. In 1655, Cromwell's Secretary of State, Thurloe, had responded to the pleas from men in Jamaica by dispatching to them a supply of Irish women, suitably outfitted at the state's expense. He was sorry that he had to use force to get the women on board, but he was determined none the less: he felt it was for their ultimate good.

Other women went out voluntarily, desperate for husbands. A typical ship-load of people bound for a colony such as Barbados consisted of a 'New-Exchange-Girl' who was leaving her husband for her lover, two 'Button-makers' who doubled as 'notorious Night-walkers and Pickpockets', an 'Orange-Wench' who was also a whore, bigamist and thief, 'two Crackt-Maiden-Servants', one of whom was pregnant by her master's son, and four 'Common Prostitutes'; the rest were transportable convicts.[17] Because of the female shortage, women who had failed to find a husband in England were said to have luck in the colonies, and those who had lost their reputations could pick up new ones. As the playwright, William Wycherley, wrote in his dedication to *The Plain-Dealer*, the plantations, like the stage and brothels, were 'propagated by the least nice Women'.

Aphra was well aware of the opprobrium and, in the dedication to her first written play, *The Young King*, which she said she had begun in Surinam, she declared she feared her Muse would be thought 'an *American*, whose Country rarely produces Beauties of this kind: The Muses seldom inhabit there; or if they do, they visit and away'.[18] This was a common anxiety in the colonies 'unrefined *from their* original Barbarisme', where people could not achieve 'polishings'.[19] There was no prestige in having been to America.

What then could she have been doing?

It is just possible that Aphra travelled to Surinam with more socially elevated ladies than herself, even in as lowly a capacity as a maid or companion. If the evidence of her status is doubted, she may have gone as an indentured servant like one of her last characters, the widow Ranter. But, although this Falstaffian woman, in whose description the ageing Aphra Behn may have put part of herself, is admirable and attractive in breeches, there is no suggestion that she could author plays, novels, poems and translations from French and Latin. No, whatever Aphra may have been born, it appears most likely that she went to Surinam as a 'lady'.

This does not preclude her going as a mistress. Possibly it was to hide the disgrace of being a kept woman that the author of the 'Memoirs' insisted on Aphra Behn's being too young for sexual activity when she left Canterbury for Surinam. Eaffry Johnson would have been twenty-two in 1663, several years older than the majority of pert young heroines in Restoration plays. Who then could have been a candidate as keeper?

Could it have been Lord Willoughby, expected daily in his neglected colony? Years before, he had been mocked for a fat mistress whom he transported overseas:

> an old *Mistris* and a yong *Saint*; one whose proportion puts us in mind of her *Excellencies*, and hee that meanes to board her, must put off his doublet and swim, it being of the same size with a *Fish-pond*; yet it is ten to one if he scape sinking, since shee is somwhat of kin to *Goodwin Sands*, having swallowed up many *Families*, many *Blew-Garters*, *Georges*, *Earls*, and *Baronies* innumerable; among them, as the latest

(though of a long continuance), is the Lord *Willoughby* of *Parham*; who hath now taken a journey to the *Barbados* and meanes to pipe her one way since hee cannot another; In Order wherunto he hath provided her a whole Plantation of Tobacco, it being her proper Element....[20]

But the slippery Lord Willoughby remained absent during Behn's stay and her reference to him in *Oroonoko* has a detachment that does not suggest sexual intimacy. No one else she mentions held the authority to give her the status she claims or to provide access to the best house in the colony.

It seems most plausible, then, that Aphra Behn went to Surinam as she would go to Antwerp and had probably been to Ghent, as a spy or agent. Many years later, Samuel Morland wrote a paper entitled 'A Brief Discourse Concerning the nature and Reason for Intelligence' in which he argued that the people were naturally vicious, looking always to their own advantage, and that any ruler should always mistrust them.[21] This was true of Restoration England and was also true of its outpost, Surinam, which was in need of controlling through secret agents. As the double-dealing Colonel Bampfield later remarked to the English government, 'you may come to the bottome of ill designes both at home and abroad, by throwing in fit persons amongst them, not suspected...'.[22] In *Oroonoko*, the narrator spies on the hero at the behest of the community; in real life the author might have had a wider remit. In contemporary accounts, Surinam was portrayed as riddled with spies and it was 'the grand complaint in that Colony that...no society or scarce family [was] found empty of an *Informer* or *Trapanner: one incitement* to many hot spirits to *speak* worse than they thought.'[23]

The writer of these words was a Lieutenant-Colonel Robert Sanford, a councillor and magistrate in Surinam. In theory, the colony had a fairly democratic form of government created through annual elections but, in 1661, Deputy Governor Byam announced he would retain supreme power. The following year Sanford wrote a petition blaming Byam for clinging to office through military force: 'The generality, thus robbed of their privileges, begin to mutter, and others better spirited openly deny his power; one of whom is kept prisoner in irons, and others are tried by a kind of military powers, where they are fined and banished.' Any who opposed his actions were seized when 'asleep in their beds'. Sanford ended his petition by complaining of how 'insecure their future life must be under an irritated authority' and begging 'those lawless rulers to be commanded home'. When petition led to opposition, Byam easily quelled it and he imprisoned, fined and banished Sanford. In the pamphlet war that ensued, Sanford was forced to prove his innocence *against* their no-proofs *of our guilt*, the very 'Grandeur of their oppression' giving them impunity.

Faced with conflicting accounts—since Byam also took the precaution of sending his version of events to London—someone in the government or with interest in the colonies might have wanted to send spies to filter out the truth.

The presence in Surinam of William, the son of the old secret service chief, Thomas Scot, could only mean trouble. He had already been suspected of playing a double game in Booth's uprising just before the Restoration and he was known to have ties with the Dutch, who coveted all England's precarious territories. Deputy Governor Byam had had Scot under surveillance for some time and had noticed how he consorted with the old Commonwealth faction in the colony. This inevitably made Byam jumpy, for dissidents were dangerous men.

Scot was now a middle-aged married man. He had used his father's position to gain an important place in the Post Office, which, given the link between espionage and the postal service, brought him very close to the work of intelligence—Aphra had probably come across the name if not the person before the Restoration. He may even have been known to Colepeper, whose distant relative he was. During Thurloe's tenure at the secret service office in the mid-1650s, Scot had gone to France, presumably as an agent of some sort, since he was given official passes. There he probably met Colonel Bampfield, by then another agent of Thurloe's and a former one of his father's. He took his wife Joanna and their child but, finding the child a burden, he dispatched it back to England, whence his wife also returned a month later. This domestic detail enforces William's reputation as a ne'er-do-well who had inherited his father's reputed susceptibility to women but not his professional abilities. In December 1656, Thomas Scot had the embarrassment of having to ask help from his successor, Thurloe, as a result of 'my improvident son in France and his only child here which his wife hath been pleased to send home to me'.[24]

With his father's resumption of power over the secret service after Cromwell's death, William returned to the Post Office. But his recklessness with money continued and, when the Restoration came in sight in

March 1660, two warrants were issued, the first for his arrest and the second for the requisition of £1000 from the Post Office.

As for Thomas, who had had 'little apprehension of his Majesty's probable accession to the Government', it must have been a miserable moment when it dawned on him that the son of the king whose death warrant he had signed was about to become supreme ruler of his country, worse when he learnt that his name had been omitted from the general pardon and Act of Oblivion that followed the Restoration. Belatedly, he disguised himself and escaped to Brussels. There he was recognised by English agents. Credulous to the end, he was persuaded to give himself up, apparently believing that he might save his life. In July he was in the Tower and his trial followed in October. Even at this juncture he hoped that 'his Majesty will not…Revenge as to blood.' During his trial Thomas Scot presented himself as a useful hack who could still be of some limited service to the new regime: 'some drudgery they might looke for from my knowne diligence & faithfulnesse.'[25] He gave much information on espionage, but declined to name all his sources, though he did mention Bampfield in Holland. Thomas Scot was executed on 17 October 1660, an exemplary lesson for his son William, who would try not to be as credulous and sincere.[26]

Thomas Scot's execution made hiding in England unwise for his son. Certainly William could not have gone near his family and he can have expected nothing from his father's property which was forfeited.[27] He had a brother, another Thomas, in Ireland who might have been useful, but this Thomas had, in the nick of time, moved over to the Royalist cause and could count himself among those who had forwarded 'the restitution of his Majesty'.[28] As a result, he was given a free pardon in January 1661.[29] He was not likely to have welcomed his less politically agile brother to his home.

The Continent would be the obvious place of escape, but his father's experiences in Brussels must have deterred the son. The far off colonies in America, full of criminals and fugitives, seemed good and distant places to hide, as many other dissidents who had failed to make satisfactory transitions had found. Major-General Whalley, a regicide, had, for example, fled to New England. Scot had the added incentive that another brother had settled in Surinam as one of Willoughby's planters. But, although it would take some time before the demand for the Post Office's £1000 arrived, he cannot have expected to be free from English agents who would watch him even there. Perhaps Scot did not entirely want to be. Possibly he had already approached Whitehall with some sort of complicated deal and needed someone to speak to and relay his message. Aphra might have been asked to make contact with William Scot in Surinam, as well as discovering the attitudes of his fellow dissidents.

If Aphra went as an agent, who would have sent her? Perhaps Hyde, now Earl of Clarendon, whose son Laurence was involved with Willoughby in the proprietorship of Surinam. Most likely it was in part Willoughby—or an agent of Willoughby's—who needed to know something independent of his Deputy Governor. Willoughby was a devious man; trusting no one and trusted by few, he may have been anxious about his own control over his colony now run by the autocratic Byam, a man who had, in the Sanford affair, shown signs of incompetence. At about the time of Aphra's visit, Willoughby had come from England to attend to his West Indian colonies and it is likely that he would dispatch agents to those he could not immediately visit, like Surinam. He himself concentrated on Barbados. Perhaps, too, the King himself heard of disputes and dangers in his territories and was interested. According to the 'Memoirs', when she returned, Aphra had an audience with Charles II to give him 'An Account of his Affairs there', not the usual consequence of a young woman's trip abroad.

It was never the policy in Whitehall to listen to only one agent or let anyone spy without being spied upon. At about the same time as Aphra went to Surinam, so did a Renatus Enys. He too was in touch with the authorities back in London. Since there are many records of spies wittingly or unwittingly travelling together, Aphra might actually have journeyed out with Enys from England. His ship arrived in Surinam on 27 August 1663.[30] It had taken nine weeks.

A person with such a purpose as Aphra's could not travel alone and she seems to have set off with her full family of mother, sister, younger brother and maids. They were useful in giving her respectability and covering her activities. The dead father could be lamented on arrival and a kinsman, mentioned in *Oroonoko*, perhaps a distant member of her family or, more likely, of the Colepepers, could be greeted as pretext for the outlandish journey.[31]

CHAPTER 4

✣

Colonial Politics: Willoughby and Byam

'a sympathetical passion of the Grand Shephead Celadon'

Aphra has left no description of her epic voyage in a wooden ship across the Atlantic to Surinam, but she does refer to the pains of sea travel. In an early play a character describes being becalmed during 'a long voyage to Sea, where after a while even the calms are distasteful, and the storm's dangerous: one seldom sees a new object, 'tis a deal of Sea, Sea'. Into a late translation she inserted a graphic description of a sea-storm, in which the sky grew black, 'The Billows all into Dis-order hurl'd, / As if they meant to bury all the World.'[1] The ship's passengers run to their cabins and distractedly try to repent to persuade Heaven to save them. Then the storm subsides, as do the fear and repentance, while each 'with still doubting Eyes looks round about'.[2] On more ordinary days she knew what it was to feel the ship dismantling about her as she lay confined in the small cabin on a damp mattress and to have her stomach 'wamble'—roll with nausea and sickness—from both the slurping sea and the mouldy meat.[3]

Aphra would have been on a smallish vessel, which would most likely have joined a convoy, since ships tended to congregate together to avoid privateers. The seas were violent places and it was always possible for a vessel to be captured by pirates and its passengers sold as slaves to the Turks—as she imagines in many of her later works.[4] There was also the fear of the Spanish who enslaved Europeans for their colonies in Peru and of the French who forced Protestants into their galleys. Then there was the conflicted interest of English authorities and colonists. The English authorities desired to control trade and shipping between its colonies and Europe; they were eager to prevent what the colonists especially wanted, direct communication between themselves and the Continent. Convoys prevented English ships from straying, or being lured, into strange ports.

No doubt at intervals Aphra witnessed the various rituals each ship followed, the 'baptising' of new travellers perhaps or the dousing of crew and passengers as they entered the tropics, the drinking to celebrate certain moments passed. Few long sea voyages could have occurred without a death, in which case the dead man would be thrown overboard and given a volley or two in respect.[5]

A typical few days from a seaman called Basil Ringrose suggests what Aphra endured. He described the food in some detail, how they made 'plumb Pudding of Salt-water and wine-Lees', how water, which quickly grew brackish and foul, had to be rationed once they were out to sea and beyond the rainy or drizzly climate. Towards the end of their voyage their food would be 'very scanty with us'. The live animals would have been slaughtered and eaten and the salted meat grown stinking. On the return route, there might have been oranges and lemons, but not on the voyage out (the use of fruit to prevent scurvy would not be common on sea voyages until the late eighteenth century). Ringrose also described the great winds and storms, the riggings giving way and the frantic and lengthy mendings, as well as the dull days hazy with rain. Huge tempestuous seas threatened the ship at one moment, while at another it was becalmed in fog and mist. A gale would make the crew take in the foresail and loosen the mizen which would be blown to pieces, while the sea splashed round them all a foam. His ship usually made about 32 or 35 leagues in a day, sometimes 42 in good weather, sometimes as low as 18 in the dark.[6]

The solvent passengers on the small ships had to travel light since there was not much room for baggage. When the useless young Tom Verney had been dispatched by his family to Virginia a couple of decades before to cultivate 'much tobacco', he had taken three servants, a featherbed, blankets and a pair of sheets. Aphra, her mother, sister and their maid would have had to carry along those necessary items to live in the tropics and to keep up appearances as ladies. No doubt they had brought pomanders and smelling salts. The lavatorial arrangements were crude for all, but, for menstruating women wearing multiple layers of clothing, they must have been particularly unsatisfactory. On such a long journey Aphra is likely to have had some ailment and she may thus have been wearing her hair unusually short; long hair was regarded as sapping to a woman's strength.

After many weeks of cold and damp, the travellers would spy the first land bird and know they would soon be seeing a coast. They would all begin 'to look out sharp on all sides for land, expecting to see it every minute'. Then at last there would be proof, that hazy line that could have been cloud, except that it was there in the morning as well as the evening: 'I cannot easily express the infinite joy we were possessed withal, this day to see our own country-men again.'

It is likely that these countrymen were first spied by Aphra in Virginia. This was an established settlement, and the wealth from tobacco allowed the planters and their wives flamboyantly to display new status unthinkable back in England. A person with a sense of the ridiculous would enjoy the sight of ex-criminals on the bench and of their ex-servant wives sporting expensive beaver hats. As in all the southern American colonies, the authorities had trouble with blasphemers, drunks and 'open scandalous livers', and the Governor had much ado to follow the orders of the English authorities, that he suppress vice and debauchery: it was, he had been told, especially important to keep up standards in 'plantations if far from their owne Country', for, without pleasing God and gaining his assistance, 'they are in dayly hazard of perishing.'[7] Laws were passed to keep the colonists in church or chapel on a Sunday—the fine for non-compliance being 50 pounds of tobacco.

Late in her life Aphra memorably portrayed the vulgar and ill-managed Virginian colony of ex-convicts and bankrupts in *The Widdow Ranter*, where one man is characteristically reminded, 'they say your Honour was but a broken Excise-man, who spent the King's money to buy your wife fine Petticoats, and at last not worth a Groat, you came over a poor Servant, though now a Justice of the Peace, and of the Honourable Council'. Already an inveterate snob, Aphra found such colonial rising vulgar and anarchic. She would be even more affronted by colonial Surinam, which she probably reached a few weeks later.

The coast of South America was swampy, but no doubt sweetly welcome as the end of a tedious voyage. It was made dazzling by the crowds of flamingoes. As the ship sailed close, the travellers would smell the balmy air, the scents of aromatic trees intensified by the new rains.

Although the English had established a small settler village near the mouth of the Surinam River, this was not the usual destination and ships tended to turn into the river. There was sand at the entrance, but the huge waterway was passable far into the land if they went carefully on the deeper east side. They continued to sail up its winding length, stopping for refreshments at various plantations where the inhabitants were mightily pleased to see new arrivals. Finally, they would reach the main town of the colony called Torarica, about thirty miles upstream, comprising around a hundred houses, a government building, a chapel and a harbour suitable for up to a hundred ships. Probably the passengers decanted themselves there into smaller boats to be rowed further up the river.[8]

Despite the sandy soil, the banks on both sides were sometimes thickly wooded by now, with the kind of denseness and luxuriance found in hot, wet places.[9] Elsewhere the ground was higher, with open fields and groves of trees full of monkeys and insects. Occasionally growth had been cleared to form settler plantations between the coast and the waterfalls, where boats were stopped. There the plantations petered out. The sandy ones farthest inland, together with those near the swampy mouth of the river which often flooded from inland streams during the rainy season, were owned by the poorer sort of settlers, who came without servants or capital; many of these were so monstrously troubled by ants and gnats that they gave up the whole attempt.

Aphra and her family would not have been heading for such impoverished terrain. Lord Willoughby had his main estate at Parham Hill on the Surinam River, but, though the new arrivals had access to the house, they did not stay there.[10] Instead, if *Oroonoko* is here to be credited, they lodged at the plantation of St John's Hill, one of three owned by the absentee landlord Sir Robert Harley, Willoughby's friend and now chancellor of Barbados. His agent reported to his employer that 'The Ladeyes that are heare live att St Johnes hill.'[11] Harley had bought the plantation from Deputy Governor Byam and it contained what Aphra declared 'the best house' in the colony. For an agent, its position was apt, since it was close to Parham Hill and adjoined the plantation of the former rebel councillor, Robert Sanford. If Willoughby were involved in Aphra's journey, he may well have arranged for her to stay in this house. Since little could be kept secret, it produced the immediate gossip that Willoughby had bought the plantation from Harley.[12]

Aphra never had a robust constitution and she would not have found it easy to adapt physically to the strange climate and food. She often fought off sickness and faintness; the narrator of *Oroonoko* described herself as 'but Sickly, and very apt to fall into Fits of dangerous Illness upon any extraordinary Melancholy'. In her quest for health, she probably tested the medical properties of the various new plants and roots. The vegetarian mystic, the 'mad hatter' Thomas Tryon, her acquaintance in later years and a visitor to the West Indies, was much concerned with tropical remedies in Barbados; 'bounanoes' he pronounced 'more venereal, and easier of concoction' than plantains and declared that they do 'gently loosen the Belly'. He also eulogised the 'very brave' potato. Regularity was what was needed, meals in early morning and then again at four rather than at noon as in England.[13]

The many stomach ailments afflicting Europeans in hot climates came in Tryon's view more from alcohol than from food: 'Now in these our *Western Plantations* all these tormenting Diseases are much encreased by the frequent Tippling of that pernicious Drink called *Punch*.' Along with drink, the other dietary evils were the very *raison d'être* of the Western colonies: 'poisonous Tobacco' and 'sweet Sugar'.

William Byam, Deputy Governor of Surinam under the absent Lord Willoughby, became the villain of *Oroonoko*. Aphra portrayed him as cowardly, treacherous and dishonourable. Yet Henry Adis, Willoughby's otherwise appalled settler, had nothing but praise for 'that worthy person, whom your Lordship hath lately honoured with the Title and Power of your Lieutenant General of this Continent of Guinah'.[14] A French visitor also regarded Byam as a brave gentleman of courage and honour, with a most beautiful and sympathetic wife—indeed the Byams were the only civilised couple encountered in the anarchic colony.[15] In the Frenchman's account there is no mention of the Indian mistress Behn gives Byam in *Oroonoko*. Why did Aphra Behn so dislike this man? Partly no doubt because he disliked her and had not welcomed her to his colony. For this he had several reasons, now difficult to disentangle.

Relations had become strained between Willoughby and his new chancellor in Barbados, Robert Harley. Harley had arrived from England in Willoughby's absence, and had swiftly antagonised the settlers—as indicated by one report: 'He stood up more like a comedian than a judge, and said, Gentlemen, now it is in my power to carry it which way I please, and which of you will give me the lustiest bribe shall have it.'[16] Some time in 1663, before Aphra arrived, Harley visited Surinam and cemented friendships with Byam and Banister, the two men most criticised in *Oroonoko*. He had also met Willoughby's agent, the young Cornishman John Trefry, whom he appears to have employed to manage his property at St John's Hill.

When Willoughby finally reached Barbados, matters came quickly to a head. Both men were hot-tempered and soon Harley was accusing Willoughby of luring him into bringing capital to the colonies with false promises. Willoughby grew furious and, in February 1664, he dismissed Harley. Harley refused to give up his seal of office. The council of the colony was convened and Harley was taken to prison. He was then banished.

Byam did not know this sorry outcome when Aphra and her party arrived in Surinam to stay at Harley's plantation, but he probably knew of the tension between Harley and Willoughby and of some sort of tie between Aphra and Willoughby. The arrangement whereby she stayed at St John's Hill, formerly Byam's plantation and now Harley's, had most likely been made before Harley fell from favour, and it had to be honoured. But, if Byam suspected Aphra as an agent of Willoughby's, he would not, now that his friend Harley was at odds with the Proprietor, wish to keep her for long on his territory.

He was made more uneasy at her speedy alliance with Trefry, the Proprietor's direct employee, which he saw as potentially undermining to his authority. Aphra found Trefry a gem; admiring his culture and education, she described him in *Oroonoko* as 'a man of great wit and learning'. From the young man's point of view, it was probably an unwise connection, since his partisanship with Aphra upset the Deputy Governor. Perhaps Aphra had promised Trefry some protection, in the manner of the narrator to Oroonoko. If she had done so, from a mistaken notion of her own importance, she could not deliver. Byam may well have complained to Willoughby about insubordination, and Willoughby had publicly to stand by Byam, whatever his collusion with Aphra. So, soon after she left Surinam, Willoughby sacked Trefry. The Proprietor was quite in the right according to the contrite letter the young man then wrote to Harley in Barbados. Not knowing of Harley's final disgrace, Trefry thanked him for preventing his 'utter deletion out of his Excellency's favour'.[17] When Aphra heard of this turn of events, it may well have soured her attitude to Willoughby, who is irritatingly missing from the Surinam of *Oroonoko*.

In Aphra's story, Trefry tries to fight Byam's law with law, or, rather, he fights Byam's civic law with an equivalent to the royal prerogative, Willoughby's superior authority in his directly ruled territory of Parham. His failure to get the better of the Deputy Governor no doubt fuelled Aphra's Royalist contempt for legal wrangling; the law seemed to her always to be serving dishonourable and violent men.

For Byam, Aphra's poking into his activities and her alliance with Trefry were as nothing to the affront of her growing intimacy with the treacherous William Scot. Byam's attitude is caught in a letter he wrote back to Harley in March 1664, when Aphra had left. In this he calls her 'Astrea', a name which denoted the goddess of Justice in the Golden Age, but, more aptly, was taken from a romance by Honoré d'Urfée, *L'Astrée*, where Astrea is a generous and jealous young virgin. Given his dislike of romance-reading, the reference suggests that Byam was hostile, as does the cause of his mention: a 'sympathetical passion of the Grand Shephead Celadon'. 'Celadon', the equally virginal shepherd of *L'Astrée*, was the lover of Astrea, and there is reason, despite discrepancies in image, to identify him with the middle-aged, married William Scot.

Perhaps Aphra became his mistress—Scot had after all been publicly promiscuous. But it is unlikely that she arrived so, since Scot, a wanted man, would not have been given the use of Harley's fine plantation, where Aphra and her family by implication stayed. Also Byam's remarks suggest a new flirtation rather than an established relationship, and he might have thought twice about using the names of the chaste Astrea and Celadon if the tie were openly sexual. Still, Aphra may not have acquitted herself so honourably as he would have wished; Byam was a pious as well as a violent man and he was disgusted by female impropriety.

Probably the relationship was mainly emotional and intellectual, and Scot may have made his mark mainly on Aphra's views of others. *Oroonoko* bears witness to her admiration of old enemies of the King like Henry Marten, described as the 'great Oliverian', though in fact the acerbically witty Henry Marten had been a famous and outspokenly republican opponent of Cromwell's dictatorship. As for his brother in Surinam, George Marten, he must have had some charm that appealed to Behn since she found she could imagine no treason in such a man, and, in her story of *Oroonoko*, she even lets him refuse to receive the quartered remains of the slave prince as if to redeem an anti-monarchical past. In contrast, Byam's critic, the rebellious Sanford, records Marten as the henchman of the Deputy Governor and involved with him in persecution.[18] Reading *Oroonoko* in the context of Sanford's truculent account, it seems that Aphra gave the ferocity, instability and blasphemy of Marten, 'who offered himself the Hangman of any at the Governours single command', to Banister whom she dismissed as a 'wild Irishman'.[19] In fact, Marten was probably between the extremes, a shrewd operator, much valued for his tie with his influential brother during the Interregnum. Perhaps it was not primarily his politics that Aphra admired. Marten was a hedonist like his brother, a high liver who was chronically in debt for fine wines. Both Aphra and William Scot may have drunk deeply of these.

Apart from any specific reasons arising out of her mission, the general cause of hostility between Deputy Governor Byam and his visitor Aphra was that the latter never appreciated the former's difficulties. Byam had helped establish and was now maintaining a colony in harsh circumstances for a demanding proprietor. He had to govern, keep peaceful and defend a mix of criminals, fugitives and settlers greedy for quick money and living outside the social constraints of Europe. The Jews, for example, brought in by Willoughby, planted at Savannah about thirty miles south of Paramaribo. They had been refugees from the Inquisition in Spain and Portugal who had found safety in Holland, helped the Dutch in their trade with their former compatriots, and involved themselves in sugar cultivation in Brazil. The enemy, in this heterogeneous colony, might be within of any colour, or without, materialising on the horizon under false flags. Aphra's incomprehension gives a modern tinge to her writings, for the enormity of colonisation has now overshadowed its audacity and difficulty.

In *Oroonoko*, Aphra judged Surinam as if it were a portion of the Home Counties, full of free men. Yet, apart from the few who arrived as planters with capital to invest and some political refugees, the majority came as transported convicts or indentured servants—their passages paid in return for their labour. These were a 'sort of loose vagrant people, vicious and destitute of means to live at home (being either unfit for labour, or such as could find none to employ themselves about, or had so misbehaved themselves by whoring, thieving or other debauchery, that none would set them to work) which merchants and masters of ships by their agents gathered up about the streets of London and other places, clothed and transported, to be employed upon plantations'.[20] The indentured labourers also included unfortunates, since the system was much abused and many of them had in fact come as involuntarily as the convicts. There was a brisk kidnapping business by agents or 'spirits' hired to take labour, especially young men and boys, forcibly from Britain to servitude in the colonial plantations. That they were often harshly treated when they arrived there can be gauged from the number of laws passed to prevent the settlers from 'Barbarous usage of some Servants'. This was important, since news of the fate of indentured labourers was putting off potential immigrants from England.

Behn's only depiction of the often cruel system of indenturing is in *The Widdow Ranter*, where she portrayed an indentured servant, the robust widow Ranter, who manages by adroit seduction to become an independent person of considerable means:

[she was] brought from the Ship by old Coll. *Ranter*, she serv'd him half a year, and then he Marry'd her, and dying in a year more, left her worth Fifty thousand Pounds Sterling, besides Plate and Jewells:

She's a great Gallant, But assuming the Humour of the Country Gentry, her Extravagancy is very Pleasant, she retains something of her Primitive Quallity still, but is good-natur'd and Generous.[21]

Of the majority of poor British male indentured labourers, with fewer physical attractions and far less luck, Aphra has little to say. She was silent about the many who sickened and died under the harsh treatment, but she mocked the few ex-labourers and criminals who, in the new air of the colonies, forgot their past and remade themselves in the powerful images of the old world: soldier, priest, justice, and politician. Crucially they lacked that patina of gentility and verbal dexterity she believed essential to any rise and to the holding of high rank.

What Aphra refused to see at any time was that the social hierarchy to which she was already so addicted, having made some headway in it herself, had to be modified where there was a shortage of upper-class men and where those without status in England needed to be given one fast. Otherwise, no one could ensure that they would become defenders rather than subverters and rebels. As one visitor pointed out, 'almost every considerable proprietor is a colonel, lieutenant-colonel, major, captain or lieutenant' in the West Indies, and new arrivals, both men and women, almost invariably invented kinship with illustrious people usefully absent, or with newly dead rich planters—as Aphra may herself have done in hindsight.[22] This social fluidity, in a context of violence and suffering, was the life blood of the colonies. It was, however, anathema to Behn, who saw it as sapping the little importance a woman might have from her rank. Indeed *Oroonoko* is at its most realistic as the lady-like narrator is made to learn, but never admit, that, in the colonial world, class and 'quality' might be less important than sex and force. So she insists on seeing an ill-bred rogue in Byam and a wild Irishman in Banister.

Despite all the colony's rifts and fissures, the agent, Renatus Enys, judged it in better shape than Aphra did. He found it fruitful and on the whole in good order under Deputy Governor Byam. He even suggested that some of the unfavourable reports reaching England had been due to the jealousy of the Barbados settlers. Like Aphra, however, he *did* regret the absence of Lord Willoughby and he believed that the want of royal authority 'has given encouragement to incendiaries, who have been seasonably suppressed and proscribed the country'.[23]

* * *

One of the 'incendiaries' on whom Enys was keeping an eye and who may also have come to Aphra's notice during her stay in Surinam was the troublesome Thomas Allin. A man of 'good natural parts', Allin had worked most diligently when he had first arrived in the colony to settle. But the heat and temper of the place got the better of him and he became notorious for his drunkenness. In this state he would curse and swear prodigiously. So blasphemous were some of his oaths that the superstitious Byam believed that, when recited in the court where his rumbunctious behaviour had landed him, they cracked the building's foundations with their force.

Something of Behn's memory of this man and his fate might have found its way into *Oroonoko*. At the end of the tale, the antagonism of slave to slave-owner becomes a personal obsessive hatred between the hero, Oroonoko, and Deputy Governor Byam, whom he desperately wishes but fails to kill. An analogue of this is the story told by Byam himself, of Allin's manic attempt on the life of the real Governor, the Proprietor Lord Willoughby.[24]

In November 1663, when Behn was still in Surinam, Allin fought a duel intending to kill his opponent, then kill himself, but he did neither. The event created enough stir for Byam to record it. Aphra may have met the man with whom she shared a passion for romantic tales and an admiration for heroic action. Worse followed after she left. Willoughby finally arrived in Surinam and arranged to meet the troublesome Allin who, fearing the Proprietor had designs on his property, secretly came to Parham, dressed in 'one of his Negroes" coats, and tried to assassinate his enemy. Despite his great plans, he managed only to wound Willoughby, although 'I came here to dye, to kill my Lord, and then my self.' Allin expected to be a kind of Ceasar in death, a character out of Plutarch's *Lives:* 'I have too much of a *Roman* in me to possess my own life, when I cannot enjoy it with freedom and honour,' he declared heroically.

For his murderous attempt, Allin was condemned to die ignominiously, a fate which he managed to pre-empt with 'Landocum'. But his corpse had the full treatment: it was

> dragged from the Gaol by the common Hangman, and Negroes, to the Pillory...where a Barbicue was erected; his Members cut off, and flung in his face, they and his Bowels burnt under the Barbicue... his Head to be cut off, and his Body to be quartered, and when dry-barbicued or dry-roasted, after the *Indian* manner, his Head to

be stuck on a pole at *Parham*, and his Quarters to be put up at the most eminent places of the Colony.[25]

Aphra Behn may well have read this gruesome account later in a small pamphlet that Deputy Governor Byam published on the affair. If so, the details remained with her and inspired some of the grimmer passages in *Oroonoko*. There the heroic slave, likewise fed on Plutarch's *Lives*, planned an heroic assassination of Byam followed by his own suicide. He, too, failed at both and was hacked to death.

CHAPTER 5

Surinam: African Slaves and Native Americans

'sure the whole Globe of the World cannot show so delightful a Place'

O n his third expedition to the New World in 1498, Columbus had arrived at the mouth of the Orinoco (or Oroonoko as it was often spelt) on the north coast of South America. He believed he had reached the river which led to the Earthly Paradise on the apex of the world, the nipple of the earth's female breast. Since Columbus logically concluded that he would need to travel uphill to follow the river, he turned back, declaring that it was God's will that he leave the Paradise untouched. This mixture of observation and fantasy can be traced in the work of many who actually stepped ashore in this region over the next two hundred years.[1]

If Aphra judged Surinam settlers as if they were Englishmen in England, she saw everything else, from St John's Hill and 'tigers' to slaves and Indian gold, through the lens of literature, much as Columbus had done. If not actually carrying with her the bulky romances of La Calprenède, she was certainly transporting them in her head. At the same time, such romantic looking could co-exist with down-to-earth calculations, both financial and political. In this again Aphra was far from unique.

Harley's plantation of St John's Hill appeared especially Arcadian; Aphra called it the most delightful place in 'the whole Globe of the World'. According to *Oroonoko*, in its groves it was 'Eternal Spring, always the very Months of *April, May*, and *June*'; the Shades are perpetual, the Trees bearing at once all degrees of Leaves and fruit, from blooming Buds to ripe Autumn'.[2] The land of alien abundance had become an idealised version of the seasonal north. Big colourful parrots screeched in the trees and the tiny hummingbird darted among the flowers. Black, saffron and wood-coloured butterflies flew about, as well as the 'Cammel-flye' with its wings like small leaves. The traveller George Warren wrote that, 'having lived a while, [this butterfly] at length lights upon the ground, takes Root, and is transformed into a Plant'. He had this 'Information of the Honourable *William Byam*, Lord General of *Guiana*, and Governour *of Surinam*, who, I am sure is too much a Gentleman to be the Author of a Lye'. For all her romance-reading Aphra was not so credulous.

The identification Aphra made of Surinam with Arcadia becomes even clearer in what she omitted from *Oroonoko*. Most settlers were forcefully struck by the mosquitoes, which could only be avoided by burning tobacco leaves, and by the heat. The colony was tropical, torrid, and always dank, and she had probably arrived towards the end of the hottest and most unhealthy season, when the climate was 'something violent'. Athough there were some cool places, the air was on the whole unhealthy, influenced by the marshes that surrounded the higher ground. It was only cooled by clouds, rains and the north east breezes which 'Refigerate the Aire'. These rains she could not have missed for, in the new year, they turned much of the land into muddy swamp. Warren thought the climate good for the old, but not for the young, who suffered often from fevers and agues. Many diseases awaited those who could not handle the climate or adapt to the diet, and yaws, dropsy and gout were common. Perhaps it was the memory of England that made it idyllic. In November and December, when she was in Surinam, England would have been suffering long dark nights and short days. The tropics, with almost equal days and nights, must have seemed a 'constant summer'.

With other travellers Aphra saw strange animals through the forms of those she already knew. Deer were like those in England, while native hares were as large as pigs. Porcupines she viewed as huge hedgehogs; the unfamilar 'cusharee' became a tiny lion; and the marmoset was the size of a rat, but with human hands and face. The big cats were labelled 'tigers', a word that included leopards, jaguars and panthers. Neither an eighteenth-century scientist listing types nor a Romantic seeing sublime vistas and energetic Nature, Aphra fitted things into her existing mental categories and perceived all in human terms.[3] Like John Evelyn, who noted it in his diary, she was, for example, astounded by the torpedo or electric eel that could deaden the feeling of any living thing it touched. As usual, however, she did not wonder long without bringing in its effect on humanity. It was dangerous since, in the temporary paralysed state it induced, a person swimming in the river might drown.[4] In her case the association was benign: she seems not to have been a swimmer and so had little to fear. Instead she records eating such an eel.

Inevitably, too, there was the vision of romance. In *Oroonoko*, the narrator goes with the hero on an expedition during which he single-handedly kills a tiger and presents it to her. It was the kind of valiant act that smattered the pages of La Calprenède. In Warren, the outcome of such a foolhardy encounter is less heroic: a man wanting very much to 'meet with a *Tyger*' does so and is killed by it.[5] Huge water snakes, not especially ferocious once they had eaten and grown unwieldy, were alarming in their bulk to many visitors, but Aphra had met such mythologically sized beasts before in the pages of La Calprenède, taking on the mighty Alexander.

Most visitors saw the 'primitive' native American Indians either as happy innocents to be taught or cannibalistic savages to be suppressed. Warren found them cowardly and treacherous, while, according to the traveller Esquemelin, before the European invasion of the region, they were barbarous, sensual, brutish, and idle, rousing themselves only to fight each other. It was generally agreed that the climate made them lazy and that they lacked northern shame, the women's 'Flap for Modesty' being thrown off once they had borne a child. Although they had an attractive initial bashfulness, they were labelled lascivious and addicted to caressing and kissing. (Yet, despite the attitude that they were 'a people bloody and Trecherous, and not to be conversed with', the natives were never so alien that the colonists could think of avoiding sexual contact with the women; consequently various sorts of venereal disease were rife among both natives and settlers.[6])

Although Warren had some hopes the Native Americans might be christianised, Aphra again saw through romance, outside the context of European religion. She relished the childlike frankness of the natives and had no interest in converting them from it, regarding them as inhabiting a Golden Age when words were 'simple' and souls 'sincere'. Her predecessor here is the sixteenth-century French essayist, Montaigne, who wrote in a tolerant essay about 'cannibals' on this coast: the South Americans are close to nature and without artifice, with 'no words for treachery, lying, cheating, envy, backbiting or forgiveness'.[7]

Despite this romantic image of Golden Age innocence, Aphra had no problem with England's imperial adventure. Years later in *The Widdow Ranter* she made her hero aware of injustice in conquest but also believe that the conqueror had the right to maintain what he had won by skill or force. The Native Americans were, indeed, innocent, and their innocence suggested their fate to her: since like children they would be controlled and disciplined and she expected the corrupt Europeans to dominate them where they could. The natives were there to be appreciated, to indicate where resources were located, and to be used.

As proprietor of Surinam, Willoughby had been instructed to trade and 'treat with the natives…or if injurious or contumacious, to persecute them with fire and sword'.[8] While Aphra was in Surinam, the natives had indeed proved troublesome and there was some fear of revolt from their combination with the slaves.[9] As an agent, she would need to find out about this possibility as well as about trading. On the evidence of *Oroonoko*, she made an interesting attempt.

Leaving her mother and sister in St John's Hill, Aphra went with her maid, 'a woman of good courage', probably the woman who remained with her for much of her life, and her brother, the kinsman, one or two others and a guide, to meet the natives. She was excited to come upon a group dancing and going about their household duties.

In most accounts, the Native Americans wear ornaments, mainly from the settlers, of glass or brass in their noses, lips and ears, and load their legs, necks and arms with beads and shells. To Aphra, bundled up in taffeta cap with black feathers, petticoats, shoes, stockings, and garters with silver lace at the edges, they appeared naked, however.[10] Her brother was no less resplendent in stuff suit, with silver loops and buttons and a quantity of green ribbon. It was a cross cultural moment to savour, as each group looked with amazement at the strangeness of the other, for these particular Native Americans had never seen white people before. The English were the greater spectacle: to find layered petticoats in tropical heat was certainly stranger than a discovery of nakedness.

The estrangement did not last long. Soon the natives were fingering her hair and Aphra was making a present of her garters, while retaining her shoes and stockings. Perhaps she was relieved to experience some slackness in her apparel at last. In exchange, she may at this juncture have received the full set of coloured head feathers which she took back to England as a novelty. Hospitality followed as she and her party ate venison and buffalo on top of broad leaves. It was a meal in Paradise, prelapsarian but too peppered.

In return, Aphra and her brother played flutes and the kinsman showed his scientific tricks—if a Colepeper relative, he here revealed a family resemblance with the Colonel, who was especially entranced by scientific experiments. The kinsman set fire to paper with a glass, thus turning himself into a powerful magician in the natives' eyes. It all helped to suggest the dominance of the Europeans, as Aphra noted.

But, when she met the young native medicine man, her understanding of how he worked, through tricks and cunning, became relevant to her own society of priests and quack doctors. It was perhaps no bad thing to cure patients more by 'fancy' than through medicines; the mystical vegetarian Thomas Tryon held the same view and accepted cures through the control of the mind.

Along with her perception of the country, its animals and people, Aphra also saw gold in a literary glow. The age was obsessed with gold and, in his 'Adversaria', Colepeper speculated endlessly about its creation from other metals. Much earlier, Columbus had assumed that El Dorado, the mythical Indian prince who was powdered in gold after his bath, lived in South America, while Sir Walter Ralegh in the late sixteenth and early seventeenth centuries had gone on futile quests for part mythical, part commercial gold in the very region Aphra was herself visiting. Only gold, natural it was thought to sunny lands, could originally have brought anyone to this steaming region.

Aphra, too, thought of gold as a kind of mystical money. Like Ralegh, she had bizarrely mingled the Golden Age myths with the stories of Indian gold; so, when she met some '*Indians* of strange Aspects', who 'brought along with 'em Bags of Gold Dust, which, as well as they cou'd give us to understand, came streaming in little small Chanels down the high Mountains, when the Rains fell', she transmuted their words into her myths. Indeed, in *Oroonoko*, even the effort to hold the 'Gold' drew on legends. In romance, guards are always placed on the golden river: something must stand between the adventurer and the realisation of the vision. In *Oroonoko* 'the Country was mad to be going on this Golden Adventure,' she wrote, but Lord Willoughby, having been sent a sample of the dust, relayed instructions that seekers should be restrained and that 'a Guard shou'd be set at the Mouth of the River of *Amazons*, (a River so call'd, almost as broad as the River of *Thames*) and prohibited all People from going up that River, it conducting to those Mountains of Gold.' Whatever Aphra had experienced in South America in the way of gold dust, she surely did not 'see' the Amazon.

The sceptical King Charles was probably less imposed on by legend. When, on her return, Aphra told him of the golden hope, she was aggrieved to find that, though his desire for new sources of wealth was mightily keen, he did not immediately try to develop Surinam gold. Spain had grown rich on American gold but, so far, the English had had nothing like such treasure from their outposts and the King was probably sick of legends of El Dorado. They had been around too long:

he knew how Ralegh had repeatedly been fooled by them and had irritated his grandfather, James I. Soon events overtook him:

> we going off for *England* before the Project was further prosecuted, and the Governour [Willoughby] being drown'd in a Hurricane, either the Design dy'd, or, the *Dutch* have the Advantage of it; And 'tis to be bemoan'd what his Majesty lost by loosing that part of *America*.[11]

The future was, however, with the King, though unbeknownst to any of the players, since he had by then exchanged Surinam for the colony of New York.

As she approached the Native Americans in Arcadia's light, so Aphra saw the African slaves through La Calprenède and a play which meant much to her as a young woman, *Othello*.[12] With her head full of the noble and passionate black hero of Shakespeare and the noble but barbarous Oroondates of La Calprenède's *Cassandra*, she may well have expected to see an African prince, a prince of Ethiop, such as Oroonoko in Surinam, where Warren anticipated only the 'naturally treacherous and bloody.'[13] Certainly her African Oroonoko would have much in common with Oroondates who, as prince of the Scythians, was simply a racial other for the Greeks.

The settlers had turned to African slaves when demand outstripped supply of indentured labourers in the 1650s, since sugar needed much cheap labour.[14] As neither white nor black managed to raise enough children in the unhealthy conditions of Surinam, a new supply of labourers was always wanted. Given the constant need, slavery proved a burgeoning trade for slave-merchants. In 1662 a charter was granted to a company headed by James, Duke of York, to supply 3,000 slaves per annum to the West Indies; soon the main source of labour in all the Caribbean colonies was slaves. Willoughby himself became a great slave-trader.

Slaves came from where they were available and where commercial contacts between European merchants and African slave traders existed. Some groups were more desirable than others. The Calabaries from the Niger delta, for instance, were not much in demand since they were regarded as poor workers and weaker people. The most desirable for both the Dutch and English came from the Slave Coast and Gold Coast, called Cormantin in some accounts after the much disputed English castle on the coast of modern Ghana, not far from Cape Coast; it was from this place that Behn's slave hero, Oroonoko, originated.[15] Although most slaves were obtained through African traders, European slave captains did sometimes capture their own cargo, as in her story and in an episode recorded by Anthony à Wood from 1678, when a 'Tall *Indian* King…was betrayed on Board of an English Interloper, and Barbarously abused'. (This man, Escelin, a chief from 'Guinny'—the word 'Indian' referred to any strange dark person—was redeemed from slavery by an English merchant and exhibited in Oxford for 3*d* a viewing.)[16]

Aphra had the prejudices and opinions of her nation and race, but she was also open to new customs and types, and she had no sense of absolute superiority of any group. She had grown up accepting that every race enslaved every other if it could and that no society existed entirely without this. Slavery as a trade by the English was not yet on a huge scale and, although she would have read of Nubian slaves, she would not have associated slavery exclusively with Africans. Indeed her romantic fictional reading would have acquainted her far more with Eastern slavery, especially of the Turks. Thus, although she had many blindspots and prejudices, the absolute distinction of race, so salient a feature of later imperialism, was not one of them. Nor was it likely to be when race was still considered not an absolute biological distinction but a behavioural and cultural one: one might become black by being too much in the sun.

Aphra was not alarmed by slavery as such. Some years later, Thomas Tryon discussed it in a book he wrote to give advice to West Indian planters. He made a rare anti-slavery case through an exemplary slave, provided with European rhetorical skill. Behn never shared Tryon's sentiments, and, although she warmed to his picture of an educated cultured slave who should never have been enslaved, she also thought some people, white or black, quite suited to slavery. People who could suffer slavery themselves and had a precarious hold on a tropical outpost far from any European centre of power could not assume the racial superiority of a nineteenth-century European in an established empire. Nor could they afford to be squeamish about slavery. In Surinam, Negro slaves were necessary because the natives were too numerous to be enslaved, she wrote.

In her attitude to culture and race, Behn was again close to the position of Montaigne, who wrote, 'every man calls barbarous anything he is not accustomed to; it is indeed the case that we have no other criterion of truth and right-reason than the example and form of the opinions and customs of our own country'.[17] When she came to write *Oroonoko* about an heroic black slave, Aphra made him distinct from everybody else in parts of her story, as a hero of romance should be, but perfect in the cultural terms of Europe—indeed he seems to have been given the learning of the Cornishman, Trefry, with whom Aphra always associated him in her mind, as well as the staunchness perceived in George Marten. Oroonoko differs from all other black slaves in his extreme blackness, his Roman nose, his straight hair, his European education, and the courtliness worthy of London society. He reads Roman history and appreciates mathematics and technological instruments. Behn knew what she was doing: Europeanising the exotic to make it perfection in her necessarily blinkered eye. She assumed that all found their standards of beauty in their own race, but did not therefore make value judgements about other people's beauty and their ideas of it: *'what we think a Deformity they may think a Perfection; as the Negroes of Guinney think us as ugly, as we think them.'*[18]

Records suggest no intended difference between the treatment of white and black workers in the western colonies, the main distinction between people being of religion rather than race. Both groups were simply seen as 'freight' by the shippers who brought them over, the indentured servants selling for about £10, the male slaves for £20–£30.[19] Both worked similarly in gangs and both were punished savagely. There was little subtlety in the punishments, which usually included the cutting off of parts of the body: a hand, an ear, or testicles. Both groups tried to rebel from time to time. Both could live with their families if they had any and cultivate little plots of land for their subsistence. The healthiest black women were chosen by white settlers as concubines, a fate that would no doubt have overtaken Oroonoko's bride, the beauteous Imoinda, in *Oroonoko*, had she not been in an heroic tale.

Although she was usually able to impose fiction on fact and conflate literature and life, Aphra may well have been struck by the predicament of a particularly sensitive slave. For, although the daily life of the Africans was no worse than that of the labouring Europeans, the fact of hopelessness separated them. The point was stressed by George Warren:

[The slaves'] wretched miseries not seldome drive them to desperate attempts for the Recovery of their Liberty, endevouring to escape, and, if like to be retaken, sometimes lay violent hands upon themselves; or if the hope of Pardon bring them again alive into their Masters power, they'l manifest their fortitude, or rather obstinacy in suffering the most exquisite tortures can be inflicted upon them, for a terrour and example to others without shrinking.

Such action would mark a hero and, whatever her tolerance of slavery, Behn was certain that heroes and people of 'Quality' should not be badly treated. About ordinary plebeians, black, brown or white, she was less concerned.

Despite her expeditions and observations, Aphra had much time on her hands in Surinam, and she used it in writing. Apart from the joy of creation, she must already have been considering literature as a possible source of income in the future when espionage failed. It was a strange idea since no previous woman had been known to make a *career* in such a way, but these were new times and something might be made of the role. Inevitably as she *looked* at the real world through romance, so she created a fantasy one in its style.

It was fittingly La Calprenède's *Cleopatra* which attracted her as the basis for her 'youthful sally', as she called her first play, and some of her lines are taken directly from this beguiling source.[20] To it she added incidents from older dramatists, especially from Fletcher's *Love's Cure; or, The Martial Maid* and from Calderón's *Life is a Dream* from the 1630s; Charles II was known to like Spanish drama. The result was *The Young King*, the sort of tragicomedy that was fashionable in the early 1660s, with heroic lovers speaking blank verse, passages of courtly dialogue, and a concoction of Arcadian shepherds, symbolic pastures, magic cures and absolute disguise.

As so often with first works which begin with accessories such as a title, Aphra may have started by thinking of a patron. This must of course be a nobleman. Even in her inexperienced eye, Lord Strangford was not a suitable one for a 'Virgin Muse'; besides, he was by now living an impoverished life.[21] But his kinsman, Philip Sidney, Lord L'Isle, a man who had satisfactorily negotiated the Restoration, who may have encouraged the sort of reading from which her play derived, and may even have seen a few hesitantly composed scenes, was a possible choice. When the dedication was finally printed two decades later it was to 'Philaster'. By then Philip had been elevated to the earldom of Leicester. He might, therefore, be Philaster, Leicester and lover of Astrea.[22]

The play was probably not staged until 1679 when its contemporary references indicate revision, but it retained enough of its early material to tie it firmly to Aphra's youth. There is, for example, more criticism of aristocracy and privilege than she would allow herself later. Probably Surinam had an effect here: absolute authority in the person of Charles II in London was one thing, authority embodied in the rogue Byam in a pugnacious colony was another. Stories from Surinam may also have urged her towards depicting an amazonian woman such as her heroine, for Columbus had reported warrior women in South America.

The play concerned a royal brother and sister, Orsames and Cleomena, the boy, because of an oracle, brought up in seclusion and ignorance of his birth, and the girl, in compensation, raised on manly pursuits and prepared for rule. Puritan fanatics were much given to belief in signs and portents, and Behn is here mocking this propensity, as she will do again many years later when it emerges in the rebellious and super-stitious Duke of Monmouth. In the play, gender will out for both boy and girl, and, at the opening, the princess is feeling a sexy dreaminess which makes her retreat from the hunt, while the prince, with an onrush of masculinity, rails against his passive life of musical idleness. At this interesting juncture, Cleomena falls in love and, feeling jealousy and feminine tenderness, concludes she is a woman. She, therefore, proposes that she should step aside for her brother. Orsames' first sortie into the outside world is not encouraging, since he confuses gods and kings and tends to want all who cross him thrown into the sea, but he is later presumed to have learnt some sense and civility. Brother and sister assume their gendered 'natural' roles and throw off the disguise of nurture. Cleomena declares, 'I am a perfect Woman now, / And have my Fears, and fits of Cowardice.'[23]

Despite the strident assertion of gender, there are some odd depictions in the play. When the soldier, who 'abhor[s] the feeble Reign of Women', thinks of the super-masculine lover of Cleomena, he exclaims, 'how soft and wanton I could grow in the Description I could make of him,' odd vocabulary in the circumstances. The play is certain that woman is 'no natural *Amazon* and that the martial attitude of the princess is to be laid to the 'faults of Education, / That cozening Form that veils the Face of Nature, / But does not see what's hid within'; yet Cleomena is given some perceptive remarks about the sword itself creating the martial arm. Underneath the deceiving veneer, she has 'a Heart all soft…all Woman', first touched by the sight of the sleeping hero, but she controls this hero in an unfeminine gaze—she even has his hair pushed back from his face to get a better look. And Love is not only feminine but triumphant, natural against the aberrance of masculine War.

Orsames' crude notion of kingship resembles the Parliamentary caricature of Stuart 'divine right' doctrine, the kind of attitude the Marten brothers once had towards the Stuart kings. He wishes 'To have Dominion o'er the lesser World' governing 'A sort of Men with low submissive Souls, / That barely shou'd content themselves with Life'. When his tutor argues that these humble men might 'Refuse Obedience to the mighty few', Orsames waves the notion aside; in that case he would destroy them. Even after he is restored, Orsames actually has little sense of kingship except as immense self-gratification, and he asks of the rival king, 'Dost see no marks of Grandure in my Face? / Nothing that speaks the King?' Yet, for all his palpable unsuitableness for rule, it remains axiomatic for Aphra that a nation will never be happy till it has a legitimate prince at its head.

Aphra had been too young in the civil turmoil of the 1640s to gain much impression of war and she had not yet had experience of international conflict. So she could follow romance in portraying war as a game in which a hero could fight on either side at romantic whim. A stupid populace simply moves in response to the moods and mistakes of its self-absorbed rulers.

The Young King has the kind of set pieces that would be rare in Behn's later works, but one in particular seems to draw on her own feelings. In later life she shared the age's love of alcohol. In the play the ignorant Orsames, describing his first taste of wine, finds it heightens the attractions of women as well as pleasure, and leads to 'strange uneasy Joys'. He also discovers that, like wine, language increases sexual feeling; the telling of passion arouses passion. Both would be themes of Aphra Behn's love poetry.

In the new year, while Aphra was still in Surinam, Deputy Governor Byam took a trip to Barbados to visit his employer Lord Willoughby, to see to lands he held there, and no doubt confer with disgruntled Chancellor Robert Harley. Perhaps he had confirmed what he had suspected, that Aphra was indeed a secret agent. So he grew determined to rid himself of his unwelcome guests and bundle Aphra and her entourage on to the next available boat. He would make no concessions to her charm, nor play the kind of flirtatious games which she enjoyed and regarded as part of her function.

After a voyage of seven days, Byam arrived back in Surinam in February or early March 1664. He found, he wrote to Harley, a ship 'full freighted' and ready to depart for London, with room for a few more passengers. So on it he dispatched 'the faire shouperdess and

Devouring Gorge…but with what reluctancy and regritt you may well Conjecture.'[24]

Gorges, a man Byam liked no better than Astrea and whom he assumed Harley would not like, was probably Captain Ferdinando Gorges, relative of the famous colonist Ferdinando Gorges of Maine in North America. He had been bred in Barbados among Puritans and was later suspected of harbouring 'fanatic' sympathies.[25] He might have gone to Surinam from the chronically mismanaged Barbados—which had in addition been plagued by caterpillars in 1663—in the hope of finding an alternative or additional place to plant.[26] At the end of March he was one of the Council in Barbados involved in the proceedings with Willoughby against Harley, and so he had presumably been hostile to Harley for some time. Neither Harley nor Byam would have reason to like Gorges much, while both might be inclined to call him by the inevitable nickname of 'Devouring Gorge', especially suitable since Ferdinando had grown very rich. If he was Aphra's co-passenger he was presumably returning to Barbados, at which a ship travelling from South America to England would naturally call.[27]

Aphra had to comply with Byam's demand, although she may not have wished to leave Surinam so abruptly, and her heart must have sunk as she saw the salted tortoises loaded on to the ship, a staple at sea despite the unpleasant taste.[28] She had not yet forgotten the rigours of the previous journey. She packed up various curiosities which she had acquired, including some remarkable dead butterflies and her set of Indian feathers; she also carried her various manuscripts and notes.

In the final encounter with Aphra, Byam remained on the ascendant, officiously seeing her from the colony he was pleased to have again to himself. But a quarter of a century later, with the publication of *Oroonoko*, in which the harsh, superstitious governor became the self-indulgent and dishonourable villain, the 'faire shouperdess' very much had the last word.

CHAPTER 6
✤

Marriage and the Great Plague

'a merchant of Dutch extraction'

The voyage from Surinam to London was long. At the end of it Aphra may have achieved something important if not much valued, for, between her arrival back in London and her leaving it again in 1666, she had become Mrs Behn. Who was her husband? She gave few hints.

In his 'Adversaria', Thomas Colepeper records a marriage between Aphra's sister Frances and a man whose name is obscurely written but might be Wrils or Write or even Wrede and who was a captain. In the same paragraph, he notes the marriage between Aphra and 'Mr Beene'. The 'Memoirs' adds the information that Mr Behn was a Londoner, a 'merchant of Dutch extraction'. The word 'Dutch' implies that he might be of Dutch or German lineage, since it covered many nationalities from German to Flemish. 'Behn' is a north German rather than a Dutch name.

A hint of Mr Behn's immediate provenance occurs in the dedication to *The Young King*—if this was completed just after the return from Surinam. There Aphra refers to her Muse if not to herself as 'an American'. Possibly Mr Behn was an 'American', that is, a frequent trader with the New World colonies.[1] So, a certain Johan Behn comes into prominence. He was one of the forty-odd crew serving on an Atlantic vessel called the *King David* in May 1655 when the ship was seized by the English settlers in Barbados. The Captain, who owned the ship, was a Captain Wrede—close enough to Colepeper's illegible word for Frances Johnson's husband. Johan Behn was a merchant sailing with him. The two men might have been together again sailing home to London from Surinam. If so, they may have coincided with Aphra and Frances Johnson and, especially before the cold began to dominate their lives as they pushed north, have wiled away time together. It is of course all speculation.

Aphra would have been considering her options. There was the possibility of a professional literary life, although there was no precedent for it, or there was the chance of future espionage. Or, more commonly, there was marriage since she was now at the usual age for it, the mid-twenties. Having passed as a lady, she would probably have wished to have a gentleman, but for this a woman needed a portion of about £1000, which Aphra clearly did not have. The life of a mistress was open to her, but it was precarious and, although the King elevated some women, not many achieved wealth and security. Unlike in Venice, where pretty, witty girls were provided with silks, pearls and high-heeled red shoes and fruitfully managed by their mothers, England had little of the tradition of clever respected courtesans. For a portionless young woman there rested only a union within the middling ranks.

After weeks of easy male companionship and debilitating travel, the wonderful idea of earning her own living by writing or spying might have palled. Both needed health and ebullience. So Aphra may well have accepted and been urged to accept the proposal of the merchant sailor, Johan Behn. With little respect for matrimony, she yet saw its necessity once. Perhaps it was some advantage that her elder sister may have been given a similar option with Captain Wrede.

No wedding of a Behn is recorded in London, but records are incomplete and it might have taken place elsewhere in Britain or on the Continent. Nor is the texture of the marriage known. Aphra Behn would write about miserable arranged and forced unions from her first staged play, *The Forc'd Marriage*, to one of her last, *The Luckey Chance*, providing in each case an escape. Usually this occurred through an earlier oral promise to marry which could be considered binding, especially if consummation had followed. It sounds like the personal fantasy of an unwilling wife.

Equally salient in Aphra's work will be the horrid coupling of an old man with a fresh young woman. In her final years when she returned to her earlier days for material, she combined the two themes very thoroughly:

> ...how fatal are forc'd Marriages!
> How many Ruines one such Match pulls on—
> Had I but kept my Sacred Vows to *Gayman*
> How happy had I been—how prosperous he!
> Whilst now I languish in a loath'd Embrace,
> Pine out my Life with Age—Consumptions Coughs.[2]

In the same play, one of the young women who has made a marriage for money pleads, 'remember I was poor and helpless, / And much reduc'd, and much impos'd upon.'

And yet, except for this first staged play, set in a mythical land of absolute kings who can cause anything, none of the marriages is 'forced', although Aphra notably downplays the collusion of the woman in the matches. Within her class in particular, a marriage might have been pressured; it is unlikely to have been precisely 'forced'.

Johan Behn had probably been a slaver since at least 1655. Aphra enjoyed adventurers and he may, like her admired Othello, have had some sea stories to tell which amused her at first. He may even have told her tales of his West African cargo, the slaves he had transported across the Atlantic. Whatever his initial attractions, however, they seem quickly to have worn off. One of the most villainous of the white men in *Oroonoko* is the slave captain who deceives Oroonoko on to his ship before carrying him to Surinam. Perhaps Aphra had learnt of some such action from her husband.

Johan Behn's *King David* is an elusive vessel. Probably a slaver, it might have been freighted with sugar for the Atlantic crossing from Surinam. Slave ships were no different from other wooden ships, and, with a few modifications, a predominantly cargo ship could house slaves between its decks, while a slaver could pack away sugar.[3] To make identification more problematic, ships could be rented and then fly the flag of the renting group; they might even assume a different name. The real slipperiness of vessels came, however, from politics: ships frequently changed their flags to hide their business and ownership. This might be due to state piracy or war—a Dutch *King David* was captured by the English and rechristened *The Good Intent*—but, most often, it responded to commercial needs. The English authorities were constantly suspicious that more tobacco and sugar were exported than ever reached England. The new Navigation Act ordered that Dutch-built ships were to be barred from trading directly with English colonies and, to keep tabs on trade, all ships and masters were to be listed. Naturally this situation bred subterfuge, for there was obvious reason for the Dutch ships to hide their provenance.[4]

Because of this elusiveness and the multiplication and subtraction of ships' names, it is a hard job indeed to follow either Mr Behn or his *King David* for long. So his identification is problematic as seafarer and husband. In the period when Aphra sailed home to England, there were possibly up to seven vessels called the *King David*—or there may be only two or three. There is of course no way to direct Mr Behn's *King David* to and from Surinam in the early months of 1664.[5]

Probably the Barbados ship owned by Erick Wrede was not the *King*

David or *King Davids* trading between London and Boston in New England in 1653 and 4 and between London and Virginia in 1666 and 7.[6] Happily not, since this London *King David* later had an unpleasant time with Native Americans who killed its passengers. Nor is it likely to have been the galliot of the same name which, in the winter of 1668, was commissioned to carry goods for Queen Henrietta Maria, the King's mother, to Rouen. Nor is it very likely to have been the Scandinavian *King David* from Druntheim in Norway owned entirely by the inhabitants of this town, but bought in Holland where it was built in 1655.[7] Mr Behn may, however, have served on the *King David* associated with the imperial free city of Hamburg—there is a Johan Behn born in Hanover in 1611.[8] In this case the ship, if calling at English ports, was probably doing so under false colours.

Of whatever nationality and whether legal or illegal, the ship on which Aphra and her party travelled arrived in London around the middle of May 1664 (according to the London Port Books a *King David* was in London in August and this may have been the vessel). Her marriage to Mr Behn followed sharply.

His absence from mercantile records suggest that he was no great merchant, but Mr Behn may well have had some business as secret if less legal than his new wife's. The risks of shipping were great and, to spread them, ships of the sort that travelled long distances were often owned by consortia like the West Indies Companies of England and Holland. They also relied on a rudimentary system of insurance, centred on Amsterdam or London. The captains could be shareholders or they could get a salary.[9] The financial accounts for all involved would be settled at the end of the voyage. It was important that ventures withstand the political hostilities of trading nations and that all concerned do what was necessary to contribute to free trade. The masters might avail themselves of a variety of flags, the owners might rely on some subterfuge, as can be seen from the records kept by one of King Charles's most efficient agents, William Blathwayt. He claimed that, in a dispute in a particular jurisdiction, it was common for a local person to pretend a part of a ship's cargo was his or hers, so that the true foreign owners could be obscured. Judging from an implied reference to him in the case of another ship called *The Abraham's Sacrifice*, it is likely that the otherwise largely unsuccessful Mr Behn lent out his services as a useful London resident to declare goods his when there was a dispute about the Dutch infringement of English navigation laws. Perhaps, then, husband and wife came together in their dissembling activities.

If so, this seems the extent of their compatibility. On board ship Mr Behn may have had some attractions, for Aphra admired a show of mastery, but on land he lost glamour. She had been too close to Colepeper's grand relatives to be happy with any family her new husband produced for her and her persistent mockery of bourgeois pretensions and vulgarity suggests an unpleasant period of adjustment to middling-rank home life. She never ceased to denigrate the money-grubbing merchants of the City and, in her play *Sir Patient Fancy*, she ferociously depicted a merchant family as combining self-indulgence with censure. Always she scorned the merchant virtues of thrift, sobriety, moderation and wifeliness.

Preceding many of her characters, Aphra probably married partly for money. Her irritation when she discovered there was not as much as she had hoped and that Mr Behn's property was shares in ships which it was impossible to realise may have fuelled her contemptuous descriptions of wedded sex. Having avoided earlier parental pressure, she had herself made the wrong choice. In later years Behn seems to have had no income except that which she procured for herself, and her husband appears not to have been an adequate provider. Pepys records the confusion which a merchant could leave: 'it seems that nobody can make anything of his estate, whether he be dead worth anything or no, he having dealt in so many things, public and private, as nobody can understand whereabouts his estate is—which is the fate of those great dealers in everything'.[10] It was fortunate that the Behns apparently had no living children.

Probably as agent 'Astrea' rather than the newly wed Mrs Behn, Aphra had an audience with the King after her return, to report on Surinam. No doubt she announced the shortcomings of Deputy Governor Byam and the ill-prepared defences of the colony. From her little experience of commerce, she could affirm that the natives were ready to be traded with and much to European advantage. Surinam, she insisted, was a colony to be kept safe, for it was more than itself—it was the gateway (England's only one) to the rest of South America.

She was already an accomplished talker and the King enjoyed curiosities. Perhaps he liked the dried butterflies she showed him or the head of feathers. Or perhaps Aphra had already strung together the story of the slave prince, darker even than the 'black' Stuart king, and amused him with the first telling.

He may have been called Oroonoko already, after the mighty river

Orinoco close to Surinam, a name that recalled one source of her inspiration.[11] Like another source, La Calprenède's princely Scythian, who saw the woman he loved, the black-haired and white-skinned Statira, 'the most perfect workmanship of the Gods…Ivory and Ebony', grabbed by an older king, Oroonoko becomes the victim of kingly concupiscence. Considering her audience, Behn may have included this part only when she came to publish, after the predatory King Charles's death.

His Majesty no doubt listened to tales and observations with the attention he gave to many of his subjects when earnestly conversing with him, especially if they were, if not in the first youth, still plump and fair. But his span was short and perhaps she felt her hold slipping. Behn would have few other occasions to see Charles II, but she would speak loyally, if not reverentially, of him as a man throughout her life.[12]

After her royal audience she considered how best to lay out the curiosities she had brought. The dried butterflies and snakeskin probably went to the newly organised museum of the Royal Society, which collected such artefacts.[13] The feathers went to Thomas Killigrew. So, with her gifts, Behn may have ingratiated herself with two of the most important institutions of the Restoration, the Royal Society and the theatre. Although excluded from one and embraced by the other, both would be important to her in providing her with many of her friends. With each group she would in time feel intellectually equal to arguing and debating.

If Behn had divulged her theatrical ambitions to the King, she may have been directed to Killigrew as the chief of the King's Company of actors, or she may have been invoking a shared Interregnum past when she approached him. During the time of her possible visit to the Low Countries in the 1650s, the Cavalier Killigrew had been in Maastricht, having reneged on his debts in England, made a shrewd second marriage to a wealthy Dutch lady, and obtained a Dutch military appointment. As a young man about Europe before the Civil War he had been judged a perpetual adolescent, playing 'the foole allwayes through the streets Like a Schoole-boy', while shocking his elders with his 'profaine and irreligious discourses'.[14] His ten-act play *Thomaso* suggested he had not much changed, for in it he revealed his egocentric dreams of being beloved by many women, as well as his sufferings as an exile.[15]

Killigrew had a strain of melancholy, which often adheres to arrogant people who feel they have something to write but are blocked in expression. He had had little formal education and described himself as an 'illiterate Courtier'. This usually meant unversed in the classics, but, in his case, it may have signified more. He was a great wheeler and dealer but he had trouble with writing; he could not spell or easily read 'his own hand'; more unkindly his writing was called 'Gibring'.[16] It is just possible that, if he had met young Aphra with her clear handwriting on the Continent, he had found in her a useful amanuensis. Perhaps she had even helped put *Thomaso* in order in the way Dryden would help William Cavendish, Duke of Newcastle, tidy up a play for performance. In the process she would have learnt the possibility of making good theatre from other people's inchoate material.[17]

In his forties, Killigrew was a man of some talents, 'a gentleman of great esteem with the King' according to Pepys, politically slippery, and deeply cynical. With little qualification for it, he had been given charge of one of the two patent theatrical companies. Perhaps with his rather erratic career in the Interregnum, this had been less reward for loyalty than bribe to ensure it, for he had had complicated dealings.[18] He remained a political force and dabbled in state affairs and in the secret service. Indeed Killigrew was possibly in part responsible for Aphra's mission to Surinam. He had plantations in the West Indies and might have been eager to know how combustible the colonies were and whether William Scot, whom he knew to be there, might be the tinder.[19]

As head of the King's Company of actors, Killigrew was a good recipient for Aphra Behn's feathers, which proved to be a very opportune present. Depending on when she returned, Killigrew used them for the first production of Dryden's and Robert Howard's *The Indian Queen*, which began his theatre's vogue for heroic dramas with exotic settings and elaborate props. Or they may have been first used for a revival towards the end of the 1660s. At either of these 'speckled plumes brought such an audience'.[20] The 'plumes' were used again for the sequel, *The Indian Emperor*. Presumably Behn hoped that she might benefit from her gift, perhaps by finding a home for her play, *The Young King*, and please the King and Killigrew all at once. Maybe she would have done so if the plague had not unluckily closed the theatres.

Soon after Behn returned from Surinam, news came to London that the plague had struck in Yarmouth on the Norfolk coast. By the winter of 1664 it had reached London and, by the summer of 1665, it was raging there. On 7 June, Pepys recorded 'the hottest day that I have ever felt in my life': this was just the condition in which the disease could flourish and, walking in Drury Lane, he had the shock of seeing for the first time 'a red cross painted on the doors of several houses'. Three days earlier, an edict had been signed closing all theatres and places of public entertainment. On 14 June, the actors left town.

Deaths mounted from hundreds to over a thousand a day by September. The weather remained hot and the unsanitary nature of the capital, with its open sewers and contaminated rivers, made conditions almost intolerable. Many who could left and grass grew in the deserted streets, unflattened by dogs and cats who had been destroyed by the authorities in an attempt to prevent the disease spreading. The air was made thick by fires to burn off plague vapours.

By many, the plague was seen as an act of God, not so much aimed at themselves as at the licentious court. The plague was mainly confined to London and the Home Counties, so Puritans of other regions could denounce courtly lewdness and ungodliness. In which case, it was sadly unfair that, like the theatrical people with whom they were so associated, the King and his court had quitted London for Oxford—where Charles's principal mistress, Lady Castlemaine, gave birth to her third royal bastard—thus leaving the less culpable inhabitants to bear the brunt of divine disfavour.

Perhaps Aphra Behn fled with many others to Kent down the Medway to stay with any of her family or friends left there; she had insufficient goods to worry about looters, who had a free hand during the exodus. Or perhaps she stayed and used the available remedies. A Constance Hall made plague water of woodsorrell, rosemary, sage, mint, wormwood, angelica, scabious, pimpernel, sundew, motherwort, snake wood and liquorice.[21] Others indicated further combinations of roots and herbs simmered in vinegar. Still others suggested lancing the buboes, as they did in the Middle East. Since many of the more reputable physicians had quitted the city, there were a good number of charlatans and mystical medics around. Reports claimed that excess of eating and drinking brought on and brought out the plague. There was even a notion that venereal disease prevented it and the bawds of London were said to be seeking poxed whores for prophylactic duty.

There was commonsense too and some heroism. One doctor, Thomas O'Dowd, who ministered to the sick, died for his pains. Behn would have approved his rejection of the Puritan notion of illness as a divine chastising rod. Inevitably everyone must occasionally have felt the pestilence providential and taken comfort from the idea—even the pragmatic Pepys does—but, if the plague were seen as God's hand, there was still no need to suffer without struggling. O'Dowd took the line that, if the disease was divine, so was his skill at healing. Perhaps like O'Dowd's daughter, his memoirist Mary Trye, Behn had the plague and, taking sensible advice, recovered.

In November, the heat ended in a severe frost, which did more than all the tracts and fanciful remedies to hinder the disease. Deaths started to taper off. Hardly a doctor or chemist remained in the city, and the survivors had largely depended on their own resources. Quickly the living overcame their gratitude for survival and began to repine at the lack of entertainment. Not a play or puppet show was on offer. Taverns and inns had mostly closed and fuel had reached an exorbitant price. The court had decamped without paying its debts and there was hardship for those dependent on the desires and needs of this large parasitical body.

By January of 1666 deaths had declined to such an extent that the King could return to Whitehall. Oxford was as glad to be rid of its demanding, expensive and dirty tenants as London was to receive them back. But, despite the decreasing deaths, the theatres were not allowed to reopen until the summer, when they began a lengthy process of refurbishment.

One of the casualties of the plague might have been Mr Behn for, if the marriage was not successful, it seems at least to have been short—Mr Behn disappeared between the return from Surinam and the summer of 1666.[22] His demise was happy for literature, since a seventeenth-century husband is unlikely to have accepted a commercially play-writing wife.

It is of course just possible that Mr Behn simply tired of matrimony: Aphra had a quick and busy tongue and the contemporary conduct-book writer, Lord Halifax, warned against marriage to talkative women. Also, as Mary Carleton proved, it was easy to lose a spouse in these scantily recorded times.[23] From her later *plays* it is clear that Aphra Behn felt that mistaken marriages had better be ended quickly, although her *fiction* was not so sanguine about the possibilities. Most likely, however, Mr Behn's disappearance was less colourfully caused and he simply died. He could, then, have perished in any of the many encounters a merchant-mariner would face at sea, but the plague is as good a termination as any.

After his 'death', the widow Aphra Behn was in need of money. She had to keep herself well dressed, for a bedraggled woman had little worth and little chance to use others to promote her interests, the only way to flourish. Thus she could not afford any lengthy period without income. Her immediate family were not of much assistance. After Behn had returned from Surinam, her brother had entered the Duke of Albemarle's regiment, the Coldstream Guards (the only Cromwellian regiment not to be disbanded). This was probably with the help of Colepeper, for his Sidney relatives had acted as Albemarle's patrons in

his extraordinarily successful career. The young man's love of finery
could be indulged in this regiment but, since he is not listed among the
officers, he probably held a lowly position, far from lucrative. Aphra
Behn must help herself. The theatre on which she might have had
designs remained firmly closed.

When in 1665 the plague had emptied the playhouses, the process had
been aided by the growing hostility between the Dutch and the English,
which had flared up into the Second Dutch War. The gallants who
frequented the theatre were signing up for naval service and the prudent
were leaving London for country estates. In June, the Duke of York
sailed his fleet up the English coast to Lowestoft where he engaged with
the Dutch in a battle which cost both sides a great deal in men and
ships. The English victory was much celebrated in London and Behn
would later write of her hero:

> Behold His *single* wonders of that Day,
> When o're the liquid Plain He cut His way;
> Through show'rs of *Death* and Clouds of dark'ning smoke,
> Like fatal *Lightening* the fierce *Victor* broke,
> And *kill'd*, where e're he dasht th' *unerring stroke*.[24]

Unfortunately, the English failed to follow up the victory and the
remainder of the Dutch fleet escaped. Unfortunately, too, the English
sailors were not paid for their efforts and, to the satisfaction of the Dutch
who knew of most English affairs through their spies, the victory of
Lowestoft was succeeded by a mutiny. By the time London had begun
to recover from the plague, the war with Holland had hotted up again.

In many ways, the Dutch and English should have been natural allies.
Helped by England in their struggle for independence from Catholic
Spain, the Dutch were appreciated as strong Protestants, potential victims
of the expansionist French Catholics under the most powerful ruler in
Europe, Louis XIV. With Holland the royal family had close ties, since
the young William, Prince of Orange, was a nephew of Charles through
his sister, Mary. Because of its wealth, status and connections, the House
of Orange tended to provide the *stadholder* or ruler for the whole country,
although this was in fact an elected rather than an hereditary position.
The Cromwellian government had heartily disliked the royal link and
had made it a condition of peace after the First Dutch War in the 1650s
that the Prince of Orange should never again be the *stadholder*. Naturally

the new English government removed this element from the treaty, but there were many in Holland who favoured the prohibition; they considered that the overweening House of Orange made their republic a monarchy in all but name. At the time of the Restoration, the young William of Orange was ten. He had little significance in England, since the virility of his uncles, Charles II and James Duke of York, was proven. No one could know that the royal brothers would produce a great many more healthy children out of wedlock than within.

Politically, Holland appeared more stable than the country that had recently changed from a monarchy into a commonwealth, then into a protectorship, then back into a monarchy, but it had its own factions and parties, and the various provinces were often at odds. Wealthy Amsterdam, for example, with its resolute interest in trade above politics and prestige, was often out of step with the other towns and provinces. Since 1654, Holland had been ruled by the astute statesman and anti-Orangist, John de Witt, who, with the help of his brother Cornelius and Admiral de Ruyter, did much to advance the country's commercial and military power.

Despite the obvious ties between the two nations there was a great deal of cultural contempt, probably in part due to the similarities. The Dutch, living in the 'Bogg of *Europe*', were regarded by the English as vulgar, ill-bred, and mercenary—though many a travelling Englishman took advantage of their probity in money matters. They were also seen as gluttonous and lewd—though much of the pornography the Dutch printed after the Restoration was for the English market.

Perhaps the most famous insult to the Dutch was penned by Andrew Marvell, a man probably in Dutch pay for a large portion of his life. In 'The Character of Holland' (1653), he wrote:

> *Holland*, that scarce deserves the name of *Land*,
> As but th'Off-scouring of the *Brittish Sand*...
> This indigested vomit of the Sea,
> Fell to the *Dutch* by Just Propriety.

In 1664 a pamphlet, ingratiatingly called *Dutch Boare Dissected; or, a Description of Hogg-land* (1664), described him thus: 'A Dutchman is a lusty Fat two-legged Cheeseworm. A Creature that is so addicted to eating Butter, drinking Fat Drink and Sliding that all the world knows him for a slippery fellow.'[25]

Beyond culture, there was much tension and rivalry between the two countries as commercial entities. Both were founding their prosperity on foreign trade, and, as one Englishman put it, 'the trade of the world is too little for us two, therefore one must down.'[26] The rivalry was enacted on a large stage, spreading from the East to the West Indies and stretching down into Africa. It involved the seizing of each other's colonies and ships, as the records of the *King David* amply indicate. On occasion throughout the seventeenth century, this rivalry erupted into full-scale war, but these wars were never fought to a conclusion. This time the immediate cause of open hostility between the two seafaring nations was as symbolic as absurd: the English demanded that the Dutch salute their flag when sailing in what they insisted were English waters; the Dutch refused. Beneath such niceties was of course the question of who ruled what waves and who controlled the lucrative Atlantic trade. There was, too, a further cause of English irritation. Because they shared the Protestant religion and republican ideals of the leaders in the Interregnum Commonwealth, the Dutch had become hosts to those who avoided the reprisals of the new Royalist regime in England. Some of these were working for the Dutch directly as spies, agents, advisors, and mercenaries. The expatriate dissidents, old Puritans and new opponents of the royal government, troubled Charles II, who feared their plotting, knowing that he owed his throne to English internal politics rather than to his own conquest by arms. He, and no doubt many of his courtiers, worried that, if these dissidents were armed and aided by the Dutch, his restoration might simply be an interruption in a long exile.

The English fixed on an incident in history to blacken their enemies. The massacre of Amboyna, a clove island of the East Indies, was never forgotten or forgiven. In a century of multiple atrocities, this stood out and it was mentioned whenever anti-Dutch feeling arose.

It had happened in 1623. The Dutch had incited the local population against the English merchants and factors and had then stretched these men out and strung them up, binding their faces with cloth into which they dripped water. Soon the English had to breathe water, which, 'with long continuance, forced all their inward parts out of their Nose, Ears, and Eyes, till they were almost stifled and choaked; then would they take them down till they vomited the water, and hoyse them up again, till their bodies swelled, to double their own proportion, their eyes stand out of their heads'. The Dutch also set candles on various parts of the English men 'till their very Inwards might be seen...'. It was, claimed the author of this account, 'A cruelty unparalleled among Christians'.[27] So struck were the English by the incident that, in 1673, during the

Third Dutch War, Dryden helped the patriotic effort by staging a play entitled *Amboyna: or, the Cruelties of the Dutch to the English Merchants.* The prologue urged the English to forget the compatibility of religion and prosecute the war vigorously, since 'Interest's the God [the Dutch] worship in their State'.

When the Second Dutch War broke out in December 1664, a large supply of money was granted to the King, but it was ill-managed. Soon the war effort was stymied for want of funds to such an extent that Pepys saw nothing but 'distraction and confusion' in the affairs of the navy and misery for the 'poor seamen that lie starving in the streets for lack of money'. On one occasion, he had been so discommoded by the pleas of the seamen's wives that he had been frightened to send out his venison pasty to be cooked 'for fear of their offering violence to it…'.[28] Behn was never much attuned to the sufferings of the poor, although she would note the menace in their complaints, but she cannot have failed to worry over the effect of such widespread dissatisfaction on a government she supported. The fear of Puritan return was still very present.

Apprehensive of further Dutch incursions and the subversive activities of dissidents, the English government needed reliable agents and some useful moles. The Dutch themselves were adept at espionage and prov-ocation, and their agents were busy assuring the English 'that the Dutch will land, headed by the old English officers in the States's [i.e. Holland's] service'. This information was in the domestic state papers of England, so must have been taken from an intercepted letter. Since the re-estab-lishment of the old English republic was never on the Dutch agenda, the information was surely disinformation, written to be intercepted. The English were conscious that their government was not well served in spying: 'how bad we are at intelligence,' exclaimed Pepys.

So they needed more agents. At this juncture, Thomas Killigrew turned to Aphra Behn with a proposal not for the theatre but for more espionage. He had heard from William Scot, Behn's old friend from Surinam, now in Holland, and he needed someone to liaise with the man. The proposal was that Behn should go to meet Scot in Flanders or Holland and, with bribes, secure him as an English informant. As she later wrote, it was a mission 'Unusual with my Sex, or to my Years'.[29]

CHAPTER 7

❧

On the King's Service

'Memorialls for Mrs Affora'

What was Aphra Behn like at this point when she clearly entered recorded history? All those who have left any clue speak of her as beautiful and witty. She was tall, well-built, even chubby perhaps, full-breasted, with bright eyes, flowing brown hair, well-shaped mouth, and a small neck.[1] In character she was gregarious, enjoying an evening of sociability; with the practised female ability to work and converse simultaneously, she was rarely alone. She liked a drink, aware that it made one both witty and susceptible to wit in others. To some, her tippling would seem immoderate but, in the circles in which she moved, it was common enough for a woman to 'drink her bottle'. Competitions in rhyme amused her and, humorous, quick and clever at mimicry, she turned out some respectable verse in company. She played the flute, sometimes with her brother, and was susceptible to music. Probably amorous, she was sensual as much as sexual, interested both in men and women and appreciating beauty in both. She appears to have had intense relationships but mainly to have accepted sexuality as a matter of flirtation and repartee, a sort of excited fencing which had the advantage of avoiding venereal disease and pregnancy.

Although she was adept at role-playing, Aphra Behn was not entirely astute in judging others' roles. She could be devious herself both about facts and about her attitudes; as a result, she admired openness and tended to be fooled by apparent sincerity more than she ought. In money matters, she could be feckless. As a pretty and clever child, she had probably often been the object of generosity and become generous herself. Indeed she rated generosity highly and was over scornful of the other virtues of thrift and care. She despised mercenariness but she did not despise money. Critical of others, she did not relish criticism of herself and she responded to rejection and withdrawal by falling ill, with the undefined psychosomatic ailments given to her narrator in *Oroonoko*.

With all her abilities, she was inevitably naïve and frequently unaware of her ignorance. Although she had gained the social confidence that comes of being admired when young, she did not have that absolute assurance she would ascribe to the nobly born who did not need to please and counterfeit. It was with this combination of strengths and weaknesses that Aphra Behn proposed again to deal with William Scot, in a far more dangerous environment than Surinam.

Shortly after Aphra and her party left Surinam for London, Scot had himself embarked on another ship for Holland. Mockingly Byam described him to Robert Harley as flying after his 'faire shoupherdess', 'being resolved to espouse all distress or felicities of fortune with her'.

Scot was probably decamping for motives other than love, however. As Byam sarcastically noted, 'the more certain cause of his flight…was a regimen of protests to the number of 1000 of pounds.' Since this was the sum owed in England, the warrant must finally have caught up with him, although it is possible that he had run up new debts in the colony and it was to these that Byam was referring. Of Puritan stock, William Scot was none the less as free with other people's money as any Cavalier.

Whatever the debts in Surinam, the £1000 was still outstanding in England, and Scot needed to avoid his native land. Though he probably made secret visits over the next months, he went first to Rotterdam, travelling in one of those ambiguously flagged ships that brought valued sugar and tobacco directly to the Dutch, without the payment of English duty. Scot had gone to Surinam partly because he had a relative there. He had the same motive in Holland, where a Richard Sykes had married his sister. Sykes's brother, William, was a merchant and a spy for the Dutch and the English dissidents, as well as being a friend of Scot's old associate, Bampfield. Like Scot in Surinam, Sykes was watched by Royalist agents.

Scot arrived in Rotterdam in May or June of 1665 when relations between England and Holland were especially fraught. Immediately he wrote to Bampfield, who had come to Holland just after the Restoration, having been released from the Tower to spy on the Dutch. He was now juggling roles; not only was he a Royalist spy but also a colonel of an English regiment in Dutch pay and an informer for the Dutch leader, De Witt, who had been warned against him but had use for him none the less, partly as spy among the English exiles. For each of these roles, Bampfield had to provide a special biography, explaining to the Dutch, for example, his known approaches to Whitehall as a necessary manoeuvre in their service. (Presumably Bampfield was ignorant that Scot was treading the same shady path and that he had already made it known to the Secretary of State, Lord Arlington, that he could give information about a plot for an English rising in Yorkshire aided by the Dutch.[2] Scot probably obtained this information from Sykes in an unguarded moment, since Sykes was liaising between the Dutch and the would-be English rebels.) Bampfield replied to Scot at once. He also brought him to the attention of the Dutch as the son of an old Parliamentary politician: Scot was an able man, he wrote to De Witt, 'esteemed as much for the memory of his father as for his own merit, and I think there is no need to suspect a man whose father was executed and the son deprived his possessions'.[3] He also had up-to-date information about the defences of the English colony of Surinam, of some interest to the Dutch.

Bampfield himself had immediate use for Scot: as *agent provocateur*, since several Royalist agents were ripe for picking. The first of these was William Corney, a merchant of Amsterdam employed indirectly by Arlington to give intelligence. Like the dissidents' agent, Sykes, he was a merchant in his own right and could be seen to be following business. He traded in 'sail duck', popular in England, and in tobacco, using the ports of Ostend and London. During the Civil War, Corney had been a supplier of arms to the Royalist forces and had held high office in the army, leaving England only when Parliament had seized his estate. He had settled in Holland but kept his Royalist loyalty, revealing it in intelligence reports on the Dutch navy. He loathed both the 'Phanaticks' and the disillusioned dissidents.

On 4 June 1665, Bampfield had had news for De Witt. In Amsterdam the agent Corney had been corresponding with a Nicholas Oudart, one of the council of the Prince of Orange in The Hague; he too turned out to be doing Arlington's business. Together they had penetrated the East India Company and were intending to send much useful information back to the authorities in Whitehall.[4] Bampfield's plan was now to plant Scot among these men to 'entertain' them, 'the better to penetrate the depths of their intrigues and practices and to engage them in a correspondence which would prove this'. Oudart was known to be a timid man and, since his acts were treasonable, he would be a fine example to others when caught. But Scot must be careful not to give himself away or intercept letters until he was sure he had the two men fast.

The naïve Corney was pleased to make the acquaintance of William Scot, a well-known exile in the 'discontented party', and excited to learn that Scot was, as he said, eager to come over and serve the King. Indeed Arlington had written to Corney already, suggesting he try to bring in

Scot for the royal service. Corney had little time to try his hand, however, for, by 17 July, Scot and Bampfield had enough information to strike. Corney and Oudart were betrayed to the Dutch, who arrested them and seized their papers. According to an unknown correspondent, 'the latter will die but Corney will be spared'.[5]

The English quickly realised the truth and, writing back to Whitehall, the ambassador declared that Scot had been working for De Witt all along. Indeed there was not much effort to hide the treachery since 'John [De Witt] has given Wm. Scott a place of 1,000 rixdollars' in Bampfield's regiment. The victims themselves were appalled, and Corney, in particular, had the outrage of a once naïve man suffering betrayal. He was stung hard and never forgot the pain and fright.

In October 1665, Bampfield and Scot made an undercover visit to England, from where Bampfield sent information back to the Dutch, along with an anti-Dutch pamphlet written by Thomas Killigrew. The pair were up to something because Bampfield reported that he 'spoke to Scot and have given him the necessary directions, which he will soon carry out'. Bampfield had had a lot of close shaves and had grown skilled at counterfeiting, but he was glad to be back in Holland by the beginning of November. Scot was less keen. He was lonely by now— especially since his brother-in-law Sykes had died and he and Bampfield, ostensibly friends and living together, were growing wary of each other. They talked much, probably without listening since both were garrulous. Each suspected the other of being treacherous and Scot was afraid that, when drunk, as he more and more often was, he might be too frank. Without enough money, he could not attract women and, unlike Bampfield, but like his father before him, he could not speak foreign languages. So he was cut off from many of the Dutch.

In January 1666, Corney and Oudart were unexpectedly released. Corney was fined heavily and told to leave the Dutch Republic at once; Oudart had a little longer. Corney left for Flanders, his mind filled with loathing for William Scot.

To control his dissident subjects during a difficult war, Charles II issued a stern proclamation demanding the surrender of those who had

> not only remained beyond the seas contrary to former proclamations but have treasonably served in the wars against their native country, to undergo their legal trial under pain of being attainted and forfeited for high treason.[6]

It was not a tempting invitation. Included in the list of twelve wanted men was William Scot whose father, readers of the proclamation were reminded, was 'lately executed for high treason'. Bampfield's name did not appear, although he had been proscribed the year before. Perhaps he was more credible in his double-dealings.

The additional threat concentrated Scot's mind. He could not be protected from English anger by the Dutch authorities, for English agents were everywhere, and the proclamation implied that he could be executed without trial if captured by any of these agents.[7] He responded by approaching Whitehall with greater vigour, indicating that he had a great deal to tell if he would.

The news of Scot's desire to engage in double-dealing again was welcomed in London, but it was difficult to know quite what he could tell. At one time De Witt had seemed to value him—he had given useful information about Surinam's weak fortifications and had helped capture English agents—but his regimental position was not high, and De Witt had not followed through with intimacy; by late 1666 Scot was clearly not in the Dutch leader's confidence. Perhaps the men in Whitehall did not know of this. In any event Scot could be most useful with the English and Scottish exiles who, under cover of war, might well be hatching plots. Since his betrayal of Corney and Oudart, he would seem trustworthy and he could easily inform on his friends. He could, for example, tell who was genuinely sick of expatriate life and eager to come home.

Mindful of his father's fate, Scot was cautious in his dealings, intending to save his skin at any price. To the authorities he let it be known that he would provide information both about the Dutch and about the English and Scots in the regiments, but he would not give it away all at once. He had already managed to indicate what his price was for cooperation: money and a complete pardon, which would allow him to return and live in England. He had to be careful: there were not only his fellow dissidents to fear but also their agents whom he did not always know.

Since spies and agents tended to exaggerate their own knowledge when negotiating for payment, someone was needed to go over to the Low Countries to meet with Scot, filter the material and assess his usefulness.[8] The charming young woman who had attracted Scot in Surinam, and had possibly already dealt with him, seemed the ideal agent for a man notorious for his 'lewdness'.

Byam's words in his letter about 'Astrea' had probably been read by Killigrew and Arlington through their recipient, Sir Robert Harley, now in England and himself much involved in 'intelligence'. They indicated a flirtation rather than a fully blown sexual affair. If it had been a matter of love, Killigrew and Arlington might have feared that Behn would put Scot's welfare before her duty. Seduction was no doubt part of the plan and Killigrew thought, along with Behn, that it could happen only once.

If the idea of Behn's mission was superficially a good one, it did not reveal Killigrew as a shrewd judge of character. Although she was witty and charming as everyone testified, and although she could be suitably dissembling and secretive about her past, all useful qualities for a secret agent, Aphra Behn would not strike others with her discretion. Such a character would invite confidence, but not necessarily keep it. She had little experience in handling money and the Low Countries were expensive. Above all, she had no experience in so dangerous a mission. She was not simply going to observe and report in relatively safe territory as in Surinam or take unread messages between one agent and another, as she may have done before the Restoration. Instead she was planning to enter enemy terrain and bring in a man who was already proving a double agent and might well be a triple one.

After the initial talk with Killigrew, Behn probably consulted her foster-brother, Thomas Colepeper, especially concerning Lord Arlington, her highest employer, whom she probably did not know personally. A relative of Killigrew's by marriage, Arlington was a cultured, courtly, and unprincipled man, who kept his Cavalier past current by wearing a distinctive patch on his nose to hide a sword cut gained in the Royalist cause.[9] Colepeper had had dealings with him: indeed he had sent Arlington a mare from Lord Strangford's Sturry house where he now lived, in the hope that he would obtain command of the King's militia in Kent.[10] He could assure Aphra Behn of the Secretary of State's worthiness and of her own abilities. He knew she needed money and had to consider even dangerous (and disreputable) plans seriously.[11] She agreed and accepted.

It was decided that Aphra Behn should initially go to Spanish Flanders rather than to Holland. Flanders was governed by the Marquis of Castel Rodrigo who, feeling vulnerable both to belligerent Holland to the north and aggressive France to the south, was friendly to England. He had already expressed his feelings through the half-English Royalist, Sir Mark Ogniate (Don Marcos Alberto de Oñate) a kinsman of his and Spanish envoy extraordinary living in Bruges, who had acquired an English wife and friendship with Lord Arlington. In March, Castel Rodrigo sent Ogniate to England to discuss tactics with Arlington.[12] The two men got on well and each felt he might ask favours of the other. Ogniate would be a useful contact for the female spy.

The brief was that Behn should meet with William Scot and, through providing him with a little ready money and tempting him with a pardon, find out everything he knew. The authorities were especially interested in Dutch movements of ships and troops and any plans they had for penetrating England. She would then relay this information in code to Major Halsall, an old Interregnum plotter, spy, and intended assassin of Cromwell. She would also write down anything Scot said and she herself might pick up concerning the exiled English and Scots.

For her work, Behn would be provided with instructions, a pass, a code and sufficient money to keep herself and pay Scot. She may also have been equipped with some of the paraphernalia of espionage, the recipe for invisible ink and lemon juice for writing. Killigrew had seen the letters between Byam and Harley and her code name was again to be 'Astrea'. Scot was of course 'Celadon'.

Presumably Aphra Behn did not know much of the record of royal non-payment, since, whoever had funded the trip to Surinam, it was probably not the crown alone. Although no one had much expected to be paid for Royalist service before the Restoration, there must have been some expectation after, which she shared. Unlike most other minor spies and informers who desired a pardon or the repeal of an exclusion order, she appeared to have no motive for her work beyond money.[13] There may of course have been unfinished business with William Scot, but, if so, she kept the matter out of her reports and it does not seem that, at this stage, he held much fascination for her.

As well as a name and code, Behn needed a chaperone; otherwise her purpose in a foreign city might have been misunderstood. Her mother and brother seem to have survived the plague and either could provide respectability. She had some problems with her mother and may have preferred to take her younger, more tractable brother on her dangerous mission. A man would also be a useful messenger. It was a relatively easy matter for Arlington or Halsall to get her brother released from Albemarle's regiment for a few months.

Behn also took with her someone called Cheney. Like her, he was probably from Kent, perhaps one of the Cranbrook Cheneys such as Thomas, relative of Thomas Colepeper.[14] Or he could be the Charles Cheney who, on 18 August 1665, had a commission erased to be ensign in a company of foot soldiers; this would make him free at the correct time and suitably impecunious to relish being kept.[15] Behn also had her elderly maid, perhaps the doughty lady who had travelled to Surinam and faced the Native Americans without fear, as well as a Mr Piers, whom she may have inherited from her dead husband and who would try to look after the muddled shipping affairs she had been bequeathed. Possibly he thought something might be done in the Low Countries.[16]

Before she set out, Behn worked at remembering her code. Some agents took a book as their source—known only to them and their control. Halsall had, however, given her a comparatively simply one in which numbers stood for names. Amsterdam was 26 for example, Scot's colleague Colonel Bampfield was 38, the 'Fanatics' or dissidents 60, and herself and Scot 160 and 159 respectively. She memorised the cyphers speedily, but found the system cumbersome. Would it not be better to make a single character stand for a single letter?

Code was of course not enough. No thinking person who had lived through the previous twenty years could have been unaware of the malleability of writing. Through the various changes of government and their different styles, he or she would have learnt an undercover sort of expression, a habit of casuistry which would allow multiple meanings to be squeezed from superficially clear words. Words were deeds in their own right and a person could be destroyed by an unguarded phrase.

'Memorialls for Mrs Affora' had been drawn up at the end of July 1666 by Arlington's secretary, Joseph Williamson, a fanatical enthusiast for intelligence throughout these years. They were to be handed to her just before she set out. The name suggests that either Behn or Killigrew was keeping silent about her marriage since 'Mrs Affora' was not a usual way to address a married woman. Perhaps she was practising secrecy or perhaps, since she was to be used partly as bait, none of the participants wished to know of any marriage. Most likely, it was just policy not to mention last names; none of Behn's relations is clearly identified with a surname in her reports.

There were fourteen 'Memorialls' and they give no very favourable picture of the mental order of Williamson's clerk who put them together both as instructions and as certification. Weaving backwards and forwards, they instructed Mrs Affora to find out whether 'Mr. S.' resolves to come over and serve the King and, if so, to promise him a royal pardon and a reward which, according to 'Memoriall' number 3, would 'punctually be perfformed'. The last item, no. 14, returned to the refrain, declaring that the agent could assure Scot that this reward would be considerable, such indeed that it 'may make him to live plentifully, with out depending on any forraigne state'. Behn herself had to work out how to hold frequent oral or written conversations with Scot and to give him directions about her method. She should also provide him with names and locations for meetings, using 'all secresy imaginable'.

From 'Mr. S.', she was to discover what loss the Dutch had sustained in the last encounter with the English at the end of July; how many ships they now had; whether they would join forces with their allies, the French, and if so where; whether they expected their East India fleet back in the near future and, if they did, where they would expect to meet it; and anything about the movements of other merchant fleets— when they had been sent out, to what destination, and when expected to return. She was also to ascertain from Scot whether there was any basis for the constant English fear of invasion and, if there were, where an enemy force might wish to land. The danger of internal sympathisers aiding external invaders terrified the authorities, and Behn was to discover all Scot knew about any English, Scottish and Irish correspondents the Dutch might have within the kingdoms.[17]

The instructions were daunting, both for Behn and for Scot whose ears would have to have been remarkably keen for him to have given satisfaction. Nothing was said of Behn's companions or of her cover story. Probably these matters were left to her; the presence of Piers, her factor, suggests that part of the cover was that she was trying to sort out Mr Behn's financial affairs. Introductions to Dutch merchants in Flanders through his connections could well be intended to assist her primary purpose.

CHAPTER 8

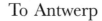

To Antwerp

'the shee spy'

Arlington knew that Corney and Oudart had been betrayed and imprisoned and that the latter had only just escaped with his life. Scot was recognised as treacherous and, if he did not like the offered terms or if he were attracted to even more complicated dealings, he could betray the new agent to his Dutch employers. He might indeed be forced to do so to save himself. Behn's assignment was therefore a dangerous one and Arlington needed to know how competent she really was. She would have to be seen in action.

The first decision was whether she should go to The Hague, where she could easily meet up with Scot and find out information on her own account, or whether she should stay in neutral Flanders, partly protected by Arlington's friends. If she went far into Holland, she risked capture, but she would be of greater use to her masters. There were English women in Rotterdam, The Hague, Amsterdam and all other major Dutch towns and, with her quickness at picking up smatterings of a language and her familial party, she would not seem out of place. But England and Holland were at war; she had documents that proved her an enemy agent and, if she were unguarded, she could easily betray herself. Perhaps a base in Flanders or near the border would be better. This decision Arlington prudently put into the hands of someone he could trust.

Sir Antony Desmarches was an old espionage hand, known to both Killigrew and Arlington. In the Interregnum he had infiltrated the French Post Office and had, through reading the English ambassador's mail, given valuable information to the Royalists about schemes between the English government and the French. Since he was going to the Continent and already doing an errand for Arlington—he was helping Sir Mark Ogniate in the export of horses from England for the Marquis of Castel Rodrigo—Sir Antony could easily arrange to be on the same boat crossing the Channel as Aphra Behn.[1] Without clarifying his own

85

relationship with Whitehall, he could casually engage her in conversation and judge whether he thought her capable of going far into enemy territory or safer doing her spying from a distance.

In such dangerous times, boats did not singly cross the Channel, unless their own business was secret. Packets were routinely stopped and plundered by the Dutch and the passengers ill treated. So vessels waited until they formed a substantial convoy to make the crossing as a fleet—just as they had assembled in the Americas to cross the Atlantic.

In July, the fleet of two small frigates and ninety merchantmen was held up while Sir Antony Desmarches fetched an export pass for the horses; Ogniate had left the pass at the wrong port. Once all the paperwork was in order, he, Aphra Behn, and other passengers, who included Viscount Stafford and his son John Howard, relatives of the Sidneys, embarked on the boat named for the Spanish governor, *The Castel Rodrigo*. When the wind was right, the fleet set out for Ostend.[2] While on board, Sir Antony no doubt spoke a little to Lord Stafford who, as a Catholic, often went to Flanders to visit his relatives in the convent at Louvain.[3] He also made certain he met Aphra Behn. Flattered, she was eager to tell him some of her business.

The Castel Rodrigo docked briefly at Ostend, but the plague, now abating in London, was raging there and, instead of disembarking its passengers, it left quickly for Paschendaele. There Sir Antony quitted the boat, along with Behn and her party, and probably Stafford. They took another vessel bound for Bruges, a town associated with Charles II in his years of exile: he had found it too quiet, but he had pleased people by visiting the English convent. Nine or ten miles from the sea, it was full of canals and pleasant gabled houses. Here Behn probably presented her letter of introduction to Sir Mark Ogniate, a sophisticated man of the sort she liked.[4]

In all this time, Behn may have had some slight connection with Lord Stafford, helped by her tangential tie to the Penshurst Sidneys, although, as a sober devout man in his fifties, he probably found little to admire in the independent young woman. She too might have been put off; his character was not to the taste of everyone—he disliked the admired affability of the King—and he was irascible and regarded as proud by many. But he was also of the class she approved and she may have been impressed that he was a member of the Royal Society.

In early August, Aphra Behn and her party moved from Bruges to Antwerp, along with Sir Antony Desmarches, Lord Stafford, and his son. Stafford knew the place well having lived there before the Restoration and his daughter, educated at St Monica's convent in Louvain, had just become a nun there. Behn was glad to have their company. She had grown used to Sir Antony in particular.

Antwerp was very different from Bruges. It was a large fortified international town—though not on the overcrowded scale of London—joined to the sea by the wide Schelde River, close to the border of Holland and Flanders. A rich and striking place of Flemish baroque, a centre for arts, music, painting and consumer luxury, it had a skyline of windmills, churches, towers, spires, gilded weathervanes, tall step-fronted houses, and masts of anchored merchantmen. Its greatest time was past, since the war of Dutch independence had elevated Amsterdam to preeminence, and its hinterland was constantly threatened by the French. But, though much bruised, Antwerp had, by the 1660s, regained some of its former prosperity and, when the diarist John Evelyn stayed there, he was pleased with its handsome and convenient lodgings. Now it was, *par excellence*, a city of informers: everyone seemed to be watching everyone else—it was a suitable but tricky place to start a mission.[5]

Already Aphra Behn was worrying about money. Antwerp was too expensive a town for an extended period, but she did not intend to stay long. She settled herself and her party at an inn called the Rosa Noble, a middling sort of place, not too extravagant she thought, but not the cheapest. It was in a street called Katelynevest and was owned by a Dutch couple Jacomyna and Joanna Huyckx.[6] In this immediate anxiety about money, Behn was echoing a whole line of government spies sent to the costly Low Countries without sufficient means for proper lodgings—and in some cases food and clothes. At once, she dispatched a message to Scot in Holland, inviting him to meet her. He had been waiting impatiently through the delays and was now keen for an encounter. Possibly he entertained the naïve hope that she had the pardon about her, but he could not have been surprised when this proved false. As with the Dutch, so with the English, he would have to sing for his supper. He probably hoped for some amusement with Aphra Behn, as well as some advantage with so inexperienced an agent.

When he received the message, Behn's suggestion that they meet in Antwerp rather than a Dutch city appalled Scot: in Flanders he would have neither the status nor the immunity he enjoyed in Holland. He had grown fearful through the years of double-dealing and remembered his father's fate in Brussels. Besides, his Dutch masters would wonder what he was doing in a country more or less allied to its enemy and rightly suspect treachery. His main reason for terror must, however, have been his discovery that his victim, Thomas Corney, was in Flanders and looking for him. He knew that Corney was aware of his movements and he feared that, if Behn waited for him in Antwerp, Corney would wait with her.[7] Neither Arlington not Halsall had mentioned Corney to Aphra Behn.

Despite his reluctance, Scot had in the end no alternative but to meet Behn in Antwerp. So, on a Sunday morning in early August, he came to the Rosa Noble oozing terror. Behn was not impressed, although she must have exulted that her charms or skill had brought him this far.[8]

Scot had sunk from his role as the dashing shepherd lover of Surinam, and the first meeting was far from the pastoral encounters of romance. If ever love had tied the pair, little remained. Scot had been drinking heavily over the months and the dangers of his situation told on his nerves.[9] On her side, Behn must have made some not very flattering comparisons between William and his father, who went to execution with conspicuous bravery. The nervousness was off-putting and made her anxious about a mission which depended so heavily on her handling of Scot. Would she be able to win his confidence? When he did open up to her, would she be able to discriminate between the useful and the trivial?

After less than an hour, Scot's terror got the better of him and he insisted they talk further in a coach travelling swiftly out of the town. So they went into the flat, featureless countryside round Antwerp, into a landscape of poplars, reeds and willow trees, where they could easily notice anyone following them. Such countryside held scant interest for one who liked her landscape Arcadian, but probably Behn had little opportunity to look abroad. Scot would have wanted the shutters closed. On the journey Behn began to understand the full cost of espionage: Scot expected her to pay his expenses as well as the hire of the coach, and the trip was costing at least £10. She had not budgeted for this outlay, which came on top of the unexpected cost of messengers, essential since she had no 'settled way of correspondence' between herself in Flanders and Scot in Holland.

During the first part of the journey, Scot still appeared reticent and Behn had to use all her reputed charm, stopping short, she implied in her report to Halsall, of actual seduction. The charm offensive worked, and, from being shy, Scot became 'so extreamly willing to under take the service that he saide more to conferme me then I could expect'. Indeed he grew positively expansive, 'seemingly passionate in the busen'. Perhaps there were frequent stops at inns.

Despite his growing cooperativeness, however, Scot remained insistent that for further information she, not he, should put herself in jeopardy by coming to Holland. He returned to the point at intervals throughout the long day and night of talk. It was, he urged, easier for Behn to travel. Scot did not mention his terror of the angry Corney, for the situation of Corney was rather too close to Behn's. Instead, he told her only of his anxiety about Colonel Bampfield, his 'ally' and commander, who, he claimed, was horribly possessive and watched his every move. Scot was greatly afraid of giving any cause for suspicion.

As it turned out, what he claimed was right: he should indeed have feared Bampfield. To Aphra Behn, however, it must have seemed that the Colonel was Scot's obsession, an obsession to which he would return in every communication. Not only did Bampfield appal Scot with his baseness but he rebuked him with his social skills—Bampfield was so ingratiating he had even been entertained by the young Prince of Orange at his country house in Scheveningen. What also irked Scot was his inferior position in Bampfield's regiment. He disliked soldiering and intended to leave it soon after his return to Holland. Fearing the change would make him less useful, he added that he would settle in The Hague, offer his services directly to the Dutch, and relay information to the English. To justify his envious obsession with Bampfield, Scot implicated Behn: the Colonel knew of her coming and had received a description; indeed he, Scot, had had to deny it when Bampfield accosted him with the news.

The result of the night's conference was that Behn agreed to move her party to The Hague. Despite her initial poor impression of him, she had been convinced that Scot was indeed a sincere man—although he had a discomfiting verbal habit of speaking of himself as 'another person'— while, on his side, Scot declared himself willing to answer all the questions in her 'Memorialls'. They parted amicably, Scot dashing off to Arnhem where he was to receive his Dutch pay. He expected to meet up with Behn again in Holland.

When he had gone Behn learnt in dismay that both Sir Antony and Lord Stafford had observed the meeting. She would not tell Scot, nor ask them to be discreet. She was supposed to be on a *secret* mission. In a slightly dissatisfied mood she sat down to write her first report. She had little time to complete it and was worried how to express herself. As all the spies knew, it was important to gain the attention and approval of the spy-masters in London and appropriate style was essential. She began by telling Halsall of her plan to go to Holland which she believed he 'would have me to do'; so she would not be in Antwerp to await an answer. She tried to be complacent about her performance and her ability to manipulate Scot for their ends; yet she sensed that her information was more gossip and narrative interest than hard fact.[10] Like Scot, she was eager to promise better in the future: 'by the next post you may expect som thing of me & from us.' The more detailed report, probably dispatched the next day, may have miscarried, since it is not in the records.

As Sir Antony had now confided in her that he served the King and was himself bound on business to enemy Holland, Behn felt justified in telling him more of her affairs. He had seen her with the jumpy Scot and she might just as well be 'ffree' with him, although, in telling Halsall this, she revealed some uneasiness. It was pleasant to have such a man to talk to. He quickly made himself invaluable by showing her a secret way to send and receive letters from Whitehall.

On his side, Sir Antony had by now formed his opinion. However compelling Scot might be in his demand that she come to The Hague, he advised Behn not to go. If she entered Holland at all, she should stay nearer the border. He suggested Dordrecht close to Rotterdam as a suitable place, less hostile to the English since it was at odds with the Dutch leader, De Witt. She agreed to follow this advice, especially since her conversations with Sir Antony had made her aware of receiving more protestations than intelligence from Scot, who had been concerned with his own skin rather than hers. She would, she told Halsall, change her plans again and go to Dordrecht in three days' time. The advice was probably right, since the Dutch authorities were now vigilant. Lord Stafford tried to cross the border in early September and was questioned rigorously, suspected as an adroit operator. At the end of September he was still detained, humbly apologising for an out-of-date passport, reminding the Dutch of his past services and asking permission to travel through Holland for his health.

Apart from espionage advice, Sir Antony provided a useful ear for Behn's money worries. She had set off from England with a bill for £50, given to her by Halsall. When this was changed into Flemish money, it yielded only £40 for, England being at war, the rate of exchange was not in its favour. With this deflated sum, she had to keep herself, her brother and the rest of her party.

Beyond the sum from Halsall, Behn had no private resources, except for a few personal jewels; if the elusive Mr Behn had left her anything, it was certainly not cash. She could not borrow money from Sir Antony, but he comforted her when she asked in despair what more she could do. He assured her that she was indeed being as 'ffrugal' as possible.

This may have been the case, although frugality and thrift were never virtues Behn much praised; £40 was not a great deal for several people in an expensive city, but it was a considerable sum to have spent in a few days. Whether extravagantly or thriftily, the money had gone and Behn desperately needed more. Yet she was uneasily aware, when she asked for it, that she had sent nothing of value back to Whitehall. Still, funds were a necessity if they wanted her to go to Dordrecht.

After concluding her letter to Halsall, Behn sat down again to write to Scot to change the place of assignation. She sensed that she had been a little gullible. She now wanted 'better sattisffection', more in deeds than words.

Having dispatched this note, she relaxed. There was company enough; she had met a merchant whose wife was in Amsterdam and with whom she had struck up a friendship—perhaps an old associate of her husband's, perhaps a contact through Scot. She continued also to discuss matters with Sir Antony, soon to leave Antwerp. Happily she had found a successor as confidant in Hieronymous or Jerome Nipho, who lived in Flanders but had often visited England and had, indeed, just returned from there. Although Behn seems unaware of it, Nipho was in fact one of the three main agents of the English government in Flanders, the principal one in Antwerp, retained at a fee of £100 a year to spy on the navy. He was a fund of ideas on secret strategies and he suggested that she receive letters from Halsall through him, since he would be far less suspect than she—this was indeed one of his functions for all the agents. Nipho was also useful to moan to, since he had much experience in trying to prise money out of Whitehall. With such men Behn set up a sort of court, in which they became her advisers, enjoying her conversation and perhaps keeping an eye on her. Rather ingenuously, when she next wrote to Halsall she mentioned these gentlemen as assisting her with council in her discouragement.

By now, events themselves were unhelpful. In early August, under Albemarle's and Prince Rupert's orders, an English fleet commanded by Sir Robert Holmes had sailed into the sheltered Vlie Channel off the island of Schelling, where about 150 Dutch merchant ships were lying at anchor, with only two men-of-war as guard. With the help of fire ships, the English managed to destroy and burn a large number, gleefully referring to the event as 'Holmes's Bonfire'. They then went ashore on the island of Schelling and burnt Brandaris, a town of about a thousand houses which contained stores for the East Indies fleet. Estimates of the number of Dutch vessels sunk varied, but all reports to England agreed it was a spectacular and treacherous exploit. Pamphlets were celebratory, and poets sprang into action: *Joyfull News for England, or, a Congratulatory Verse upon our late happy Success in Firing 150 Dutch Ships in their own Harbours* told the Dutch to 'Draw up your Sluces, ye may quench a flame / But never hope to wash away the Shame.'[11]

Despite the English claim that the inhabitants of Brandaris had escaped except for the old who 'were used with all gentleness and humanity', the whole Dutch nation regarded the sacking as wanton cruelty, quite beyond the proper prosecution of war. Anti-English feeling grew intense. Troops were recalled from Germany to help prosecute the war with England and an admiral and some statesmen were dismissed as scapegoats.[12] The merchant whom Behn had come to know was summoned by his worried wife back to a volatile Amsterdam, where there was much disordered anger against the English.

In such a climate, the rendezvous planned between Behn and Scot in Dordrecht became perilous, and her advisers were adamant that she should now not go to Holland at all. So she sent again to Scot cancelling the meeting and making another in a house two miles outside Antwerp on a Saturday in nine days' time. 'I daere as well be hanged as go,' she said of Holland. It was a prudent decision, but not very daring espionage. Possibly Behn could not have left even if she wished. By now her money had quite disappeared and she could not settle the bills at the inn and other eating-places, which amounted to over £35. She and her party together were costing some £10 a week, with another £2 or £3 going on expenses necessary for her mission. She had pawned a ring at one of the many pawnshops of Antwerp, but it had not yielded much. She had also tried to slow the growth of her enormous debt by skimping on her own food—indeed hardly any of the money had been spent on herself—but she could not skimp for others. Her friends were sympathetic and reassuring, but they offered no loans.

While Behn was awaiting Scot's inevitably disgruntled answer to the change of plan, she sat down again to write to Whitehall. She began apologetically, with a sinking feeling about her mission. She had nothing from Scot to send and was worried that she would be regarded as negligent. As she went on with her letter, the sense of inadequacy increased, until by the end she admitted herself 'really sick till I give you som good accompt'. Her decision not to pursue Scot to Holland was correct and Antwerp was, she assured Halsall, 'the nerest part of Flanders to him'. Yet it made her dissatisfied with herself and she expressed this by distancing herself from Scot, calling him a 'Rogue' and declaring that she would be warier of him in future. Her main burden was, however, money. She was in the costly town for London's benefit, not her own, 'it being no delight at all for me...but much the contrary'. Possibly she could have found cheaper lodging, but there was little suitable around and it would now be difficult to extricate herself from the Rosa Noble where she owed so large a sum. Since she had to stay in Antwerp or nearby, she could not 'flit', as so many of the Cavaliers had done; if she tried to do so, she would probably end in debtors' prison.

To improve her situation, Behn hit on the plan of sending Piers to London to fetch funds. This had the advantage of giving her one less mouth to feed and ensuring safe delivery of the money she trusted would be forthcoming. She could have sent her brother, but was keeping him to carry Scot's pardon when it was agreed.

The day after Behn dispatched her letter had been appointed for the meeting with Scot. Despite misgivings, he was at the designated place outside Antwerp, eager to show good faith by answering the questions in the 'Memorialls'. He and Behn discussed each point; then Scot wrote his answers in his own hand—she thought this might impress Whitehall since it necessarily placed him in some danger. As for himself, he claimed he was awaiting only the royal pardon before openly espousing the English cause; he reverenced Charles II as 'his Lawfull Soveraigne' and would do all to serve him within his 'slender capacity, & possibly mean opportunities'.

Scot estimated that probably five men-of-war had been destroyed in the encounter on the Vlie, though some claimed only two or three. The whole Dutch fleet was now mutinous and in disarray, as was the army, several companies of which had been reorganised to prevent plotting. The towns were in a similar state: law and order had broken down and people were openly murdering each other on the streets. So much for Holland. When he turned to the dissidents, Scot was more detailed and less apocalyptic. He was aware of the English obsession about a land invasion, but downplayed it, rightly believing that there was no such design. Although there was not much actual plotting, however, there was much incipient treachery, most laid at the door of Scot's grand obsession, Colonel Bampfield, 'the most dexterous & perniciously malicious enemy' and 'the most desperate and inveterate villain of all'.

Bampfield was, declared the incensed Scot, a spider in the web of intrigue emanating from Holland. Among his agents was Sands Temple, a lieutenant in the English navy prepared to bring over to the Dutch any ship he might command—in her next letter to Halsall, Behn relayed

Scot's warning not to let Temple, then in prison in England, know that he had been discovered; otherwise when he came out he would suspect Scot and herself and deliver both to the Dutch.[13] Scot also mentioned Joseph Hill, an agent of Bampfield's and probably of the Dutch, on whom he later blamed his necessary treachery to Corney. (Hill, he claimed, had been about to betray him, Corney and Oudart when he, Scot, had minimised the damage by betraying Corney and Oudart, thus saving his useful self.) Joseph Hill had agreed to go over to England for Bampfield, to help the dissidents, but Bampfield was being very close with Scot, who thus did not know whether or not Hill had left. Finally, Scot named Colepeper's cousin, Algernon Sidney. Whitehall had some interest in him since he was known to be writing a 'Treatise in defence of a Republique, & ag.st Monarchy'.[14] There was no mention of Stafford.

When Scot had finished, Behn noticed that he had tried to write his report in formal third-person style but failed. It was all due to 'want of time', she explained. Again Behn had been won over. In Scot's absence, she doubted, but when she met him she was converted: 'I beleeve him in all things,' she wrote of the man she had recently called 'Rogue'. No doubt their joint experience of debt pulled them together, but at times her gullibility seems extreme: for instance, she believed Scot would leave his military post solely to become a royal agent. So won over was she that again she promised to come to The Hague and even judged Scot delicate on the subject of money. She, however, had no such delicacy, and she reminded her employers once more of their responsibilities. Money was needed for herself and for Scot, now doubly disadvantaged since the Dutch had not paid him either. News was mainly available in Amsterdam, but Scot had debts there and must pay them if he wanted to visit. He also needed money for information: 'pray Sir think with all speede of thes things,' she begged Halsall.

By now, the intimacy of Surinam was re-established. Aphra Behn hardly imagined relationships between men and women that were not charged with sexuality. So Scot and she, both excited by secrecy, might well have come together for more than business, although she never wrote of Scot as inspiring love. She believed that he was bargaining for his life or at least for life in England, but she may also have thought herself chosen for the mission at his request: he was acting for her, out of a passion kindled in Surinam.

The tie grew emotional: together Scot and Behn formed an island of loyalty in a sea of corruption. Scot had said he would trust none but her and, warmed by his flattery, Behn was convinced of his truth. Indeed she was now feeling uneasy that he had had to give so much with no other surety than her word—an anxiety she would convey in *Oroonoko*, when the narrator worries over her unfulfillable commitments to the slave-prince. In the muddled politics of Surinam, the narrator made inappropriate political promises and played an intimate role that was half sincere and half calculating. As the narrator to Oroonoko, so she to Scot was promising liberty or pardon in the name of a foreign power which in the end she knew she could not control. And, like in *Oroonoko*, she herself might always be betrayed by that power or by the man she was dealing with but never quite knew or trusted.

Behn's intimacy with William Scot was doomed not to develop and this was probably the last meeting the pair would have. Although Scot stayed for three days in Antwerp, Behn had now learnt of Corney's murderous designs and was afraid to endanger Scot by visiting him. As for Scot, he did not care to wait any longer—it was pleasant to eat at someone else's expense, but he was heartily glad to leave Flanders.

By this stage Behn too was finding Corney troublesome. Though accustomed to using churches for assignations, she was surprised to be insistently accosted there in mid-August by a man who turned out to be Thomas Corney. He knew, he said, that she had had dealings with Scot and wished to warn her that Scot was a rogue, traitor, and drunk. He had learnt of part of Behn's purposes through informers, but he did not know of her directly from Whitehall and could thus hardly credit that she had come purposely to deal with Scot. He thought he would be harming both by telling the authorities of their intimacy, sure it would lead to Behn's being 'clapt up' when she returned to London. Perhaps, like Byam, he was also irked by a relationship in which he did not share.

From then on Corney trailed Aphra Behn. In the last original play staged in her lifetime, *The Luckey Chance*, she remembered Antwerp as she invented an intercepted letter from the Low Countries, and a man's plan to be another's 'evil Genius': he would 'haunt him at Bed and Board, he shall not sleep nor eat—disturb him at his Prayers, in his Embraces; and teaz him into Madness'.[15] She probably had Corney in mind.

Corney did not justify his attendance with any entertaining talk; he had little of the wit Behn sought in men, being merely garrulous and inquisitive. She was bored by his constant maligning of the lowly 'Trooper' Scot who, he claimed, was scorned by Dutch and English alike. Yet she could not herself keep silent and she matched Corney's boastfulness with her own. Soon she was displaying her papers as proof of her position. What he learnt shocked Corney profoundly, for she had indeed been sent to treat with Scot and offer a pardon to an habitual traitor, son of a regicide. It was all Halsall's doing, he surmised: he had never liked the man. On top of this, Corney regarded himself as a *professional* agent and in Behn he saw a rank amateur. He enjoyed name-dropping and was irritated to hear her prating of Lord Arlington. It was all a 'Cheat' and he would alert Arlington of the fact that she had even managed to settle in an inn swarming with Dutch spies; they knew her business quite as well as she did.

Meanwhile, Behn's money troubles inexorably grew. Having written three letters to Halsall in quick time, she was aware that she had received no answers and no supplies—she may have forgotten her instruction to Halsall not to write to Antwerp when she had intended to move to Holland. She could not have known of the Fire of London which broke out on 2 September in Pudding Lane and consumed the City, including the great cathedral of St Paul's—'during which Calamity', according to Arlington, 'we did not think it fit to let any Letters go abroad.'[16] Why had Halsall not written to her, not sent any word of any sort? Was she doing something wrong? Were her letters arriving? In desperation, she decided to go direct to Killigrew—perhaps Corney's opinion of Halsall was impinging on her. With Killigrew she could be franker and sharper.[17] He had landed her in this mess and should extricate her. It was awkward to be going behind the back of her control, but she had begun to suspect that Halsall had lost faith in her and she needed Killigrew to win him round.

To Killigrew, Behn could dispense with the conventional reverence for the King appropriate with Halsall, for she would 'presume to take a ffreedom with you more then any', and she blurted out what she knew probably from Nipho: that 'his Majestys friends heare do all complaine upon the slenderness of their rewards'. Perhaps recalling the past, she could even indulge in a little sarcasm: 'I suppose it may not be all together Unknowne to you Sir, the Charge of these places' and 'you Understand this place better than I.' The stay of the King and his courtiers including Killigrew in the Low Countries just before the Restoration had been famously extravagant, and the Dutch merchants were still trying to call in the debts. A King, even in exile, had more credit than a 'shee spy', however.

It was costing Behn ten gilders or just over £1 a day to live with her entourage. She was going to economise further she declared, without indicating why she had not taken this course sooner. Since her next messenger was to be her brother, presumably this would take his upkeep off her hands, although she would still have to find money for his passage. Her whole purpose would founder if money were unforthcoming: Scot could not send letters directly because it was too dangerous and he had to correspond with her through expensive private messengers. Without money, as she reiterated, there was absolutely no point in her going to Holland: indeed she could not do so if she did not first settle her debts. Halsall should be badgered into sending at least another £50—a mere £40 after the exchange had taken its cut. Actually, she needed more than that since, in waiting for the money, she would run up additional debts: 'I think you can not do less now then let me have a hundred pownds,' she concluded.[18]

For a few days, Behn nerved herself to the wait. She walked around Antwerp, fearing always to meet the ubiquitous Corney. Her brother was impatient to be gone but could not start until his passage was paid. After four days of silence, she could stand it no longer and took up her pen again to address Killigrew—she had quite given up on Halsall.

Her desperation is there in her repetition. She went over the old ground: her necessities, her frugality, her depleted money, her need to borrow to pay Scot's expenses for travel—her going to him being now quite out of the question given her debts—and her pawning of her rings to keep herself and her party. The desired £50 had earlier become £100 to cover all expenses; now she needed almost £100 simply for the debts. She was desperate to economise by leaving the Rosa Noble but, as she droningly repeated, she could not leave without paying the bill. Scot was waiting for her in The Hague, eager to set off for Amsterdam to spy in earnest. Yet nobody could move: 'be speedy I pray Sir in what you do for every bodyes good.' Killigrew and Halsall must have been amused at the audacity of the request. No one had any intention of sending so much. If they paid agents at that rate, the government would be even closer to bankruptcy than it was. Neither were they pleased at her approach to Killigrew. She had been diminished in all their eyes.

When Behn opened the next packet from Scot, her heart sank further, for there again was the old refrain: lack of money, desire for the pardon and fear of Bampfield. There was a little attempt at gallantry—he 'can deny Astrea nothing'—but it was jarring in the context of money and treachery. The letters were so disappointing that, rather than send them directly on to Whitehall and thus risk discrediting Scot, she made excerpts of their hearsay and speculation. It was the sort of information Arlington could have gained from foreign newsletters which came in to Whitehall, and indeed Scot actually referred him to these: a few titbits about the 'universal disorder' in the States, the readiness of the Prince of Orange, waiting at his uncle's in Cleve, to assume command, and a little about the dissidents, including the Quaker, Benjamin Furley, said to be plotting against England with his friend, Algernon Sidney. Nothing more.

Meanwhile, of course, Thomas Corney had been writing as furiously and frankly as Aphra Behn. Not only did he endeavour to assassinate her character, but he also gave bits of information which made her suspect. For example, he knew, but should not have known, that Scot had impudently met Behn outside the city and been closeted with '*this lady* to whom hee promises to doe much as I am informed'. He also knew that Scot had talked with a man who had since returned to Holland to consult with De Witt—something Behn had not mentioned, probably because she did not know it.[19]

Corney was anxious to undo any favourable effect Scot had made on the gullible 'shee spy' and, in contrast to Behn's reports, associate him firmly with Bampfield:

> Bampfield & hee are both alike, and both in the like Capacity & willingness to serve their King & Country, when upon my very contience they both hate the King...and would upon occation rally up that little couardly couradge they have left to doe a mischief to him or any of his.

He had heard that Behn still intended going into Holland. Given her ineptitude, Corney was sure she would soon be caught. In which case the Dutch would laugh that 'the Kings Officers can bee soe indiscreet as to send such people about a business they soe little understand which will redound much to the dishonour of his Ma[jes]tie.' As Corney brooded over Scot, he tried out various scenarios to explain his success, forgetting that he himself had been taken in only a short while ago. He pitched again on 'stout' Major Halsall, who must somehow have persuaded Lord Arlington that Scot could be useful. In fact he was 'noe more able to serve him...than the Dogg'.[20]

Still Corney continued to haunt Aphra Behn. As the days passed, she began to engage him against his will. She remained foolish and vain, was far too leaky a vessel for a secret agent, but she did have 'a great deale of witt'. He wanted her to be discredited in London, but he hoped she would not be stupid enough to destroy herself by going into Holland.

He had become a little sorry for her. She was in a desperate plight, one shared at some time by all Royalist agents: 'she hath been wind bound 3 weeks at the Roosa noble in Antwerp for want of money.'

For Corney, Behn showed no sympathy at all. With her own reverential attitude to royalty, she found it galling that he boasted intimacy with King Charles. Surely such a 'prating ffellow' could not really be employed by London, could not really be familiar with Arlington and 'the Ladyes at court'! She was especially angry that he had been doing her 'great hurt by writing in to Holland'. With such slanders, any possibility of slipping there inconspicuously had vanished. Happily, she had Nipho to grumble to: he had much the same opinion of Corney as she had, and both agreed the 'rogue' should be silenced.

The clerks in Whitehall who decoded and copied parts of letters must have marvelled at the bilious correspondence of Behn, Corney and Scot. All were so eager to destroy the others, while gaining so little credibility themselves, and they each made such parallel accusations. Behn's opinion of Corney—'ever body dreads him & none abids him, he is so insufferable a scandalous Lying prating ffellow: & I am sure they do not Love his Majesty intrest that trust him with the least of secreitt'—was uncannily close to Corney's description of Scot.[21] None of the trio fully realised the damage the others were doing. Corney, who presented himself as a discreet professional, was being written as a braggart; Scot, eager to paint himself as an invaluable double agent, appeared as a drunken rogue; Behn, regarding herself as a clever operator, was being portrayed as a naïve fool.

CHAPTER 9

Debts and Disappointment

'for christ his sake Sir let me receave no ill opinion from his Majesty'

Shortly before 7 September, Aphra Behn received letters from her mother—presumably through an amanuensis—and from 'Sir Thomas'. His last name, like her own and those of people related to her, was not given, probably for security reasons. So, although Behn's foster-brother, Thomas Colepeper, was not titled, it remains possible that the reference is to him under his dead father's name.[1] The letters confirmed Behn's worst fears. Marooned in Antwerp, she was being assassinated in London by 'pregudice'. The complaints spurred her to pick up her pen and address Killigrew, yet again.

It seems that both he and Sir Thomas had been irritated that she had sent Piers to Halsall for money. He was not the sort of man to have entrusted with her secrets, they said. Why not? He was her companion and trusted servant and she was convinced of his honesty. Besides, Halsall had sent the original £50 to her by one of *his* servants. It was unclear whom else Behn could have sent. Her brother was being reserved for the pardon and she had no one even in England suitable to go for the money and bring or dispatch it.[2] She could, she supposed, have asked 'Sir Thomas' or her mother. But she had been reluctant to use her mother and she was not sure Killigrew and his colleagues would have approved Sir Thomas, who was anyhow not often in London.

Behn was hurt that Killigrew and Halsall had seen fit to show Sir Thomas a supposedly secret letter, in which she had justified her choice of Piers by claiming he was the only man she could trust. Even more, she was stung by their need to inform the King of her ineptitude and so destroy His Majesty's good opinion. How could they believe her to have been boasting foolishly of her mission? She was, of course, unaware of what Corney had been writing: that everyone around knew her business.

When her irritation at Killigrew had subsided, Behn again felt exposed—however annoyed, she could not afford to upset the men in Whitehall further. Some humility was needed:

> you shall find still this that how great a Child soever I am in other matters: I shall mind dilligently what I am now about: & doubt not but to aquitt my self as becoms me, & is my duty.

Behn even conceded that, perhaps, she had 'not posibly heather too dun so much as might be expected'. Quickly reading over this letter, she noticed the changes in mood. Yet she had no time to rewrite it. Then, suddenly struck by the enormity of losing the King's confidence, she added an emotional postscript: 'for christ his sake Sir let me receave no Ill opinion from his Majesty who would give my poor life to serve him in never so little a degree: & really Sir in this I have not merritted it.'

The next day, another rambling demoralised letter came from Scot, still in Rotterdam and unable to get to The Hague. He now saw what Aphra Behn could not: that the pardon would always be in the future, while information had to come in the present. He was as financially desperate as she and breaking under the strain of the cat-and-mouse surveillance with Bampfield. Yet he claimed he was as eager as ever to serve the English—'provided I do it not as a foole'. Rightly Scot said that he had little news to give, at one point admitting that Behn and the Whitehall authorities might already know more than he about such naval matters as the engagement of the Dutch and English forces in the Channel. About merchant fleets he had nothing at all to say, they being 'a thing so utterly out of my way'. So again he padded out his report with the sort of general information about civil unrest that could have been gained from the Dutch newspapers. A few more bits on Furley and Bampfield closed the letter: he would do better in the future when he did not have 'difficulties to strugell with', in other words when he had some money.

It was a jumpy, self-absorbed letter. Perhaps it was due to fear of Furley, she thought, but more likely of Joseph Hill, whom Scot had identified as Bampfield's agent. If his dealings with Behn came to their knowledge, Scot would be exposed and at least exiled from Holland. Where would he go without his English pardon?

One piece of information that must momentarily have troubled Behn was that a letter in a woman's handwriting had been intercepted at The Hague. Could it be hers? Scot asked nervously. If so, it would put him in extreme danger, since Bampfield would recognise it and assume it was destined for Scot. She may have wondered how this could be since she had not corresponded with Colonel Bampfield, who did not know her personally. Had Scot been showing him her letters? Happily this particular letter was not hers.

When she had finished reading, Behn copied out Scot's missive, so that it would be in her handwriting and not endanger him. She wrote quickly, sensing that she was making silly mistakes. The messages from Scot came only a quarter of an hour before her letters were due to Nipho, and she had to catch the post, so desperate was she for money. Once she had sent the letter, however, she regretted it and later apologised: she did not wish to seem illiterate as well as incompetent.

At this point a bill of £50 appears to have arrived in Antwerp for her, perhaps with Killigrew's help, but, when she wrote again to Halsall in mid-September, Behn grumbled at its inadequacy. The exchange had cost £4 and she had borrowed this sum to make up £50, perhaps from her Dutch merchant, now returned from his wife in Amsterdam, or from Nipho who was—though she did not know it—dealing in hefty English sums.[3] Unhappily, the £50 had to be handed over to the innkeeper in its entirety—it was not even half of the £120 she now owed.

Although she moaned that she was 'wors then dead till I am out of this expensiue hous wheare I vow to god I do not rest with continuall thoughts of my debts...', the money seems to have cheered both Behn and Scot, who was writing regularly from Rotterdam. It was three weeks since she had seen him, although his renewed belief in the pardon suggests there might have been a fleeting encounter. Mostly, he grumbled about his fellow dissidents, exposing again his consuming jealousy of Bampfield.[4] In passing, he mentioned an ex-Parliamentary sea captain who was undertaking to block the Thames for the Dutch and so make the English sailors mutiny. This sort of plan—of attacking the English fleet in its home waters of the Thames and the Medway—the authorities heard a good deal of from their agents, but never quite took seriously. Although the copying of the information to Halsall was the closest Behn came to mentioning the future Dutch triumph, she made it into something of a story when she was snugly back in England.[5] As time went by, it was hard to remember much about the Second Dutch War except the Medway fiasco and a good raconteur would want to include it.

A few days on and Scot reported that the English dissidents were assembling in Utrecht—he did not know the reason, nor why a tall young man with straight black hair was travelling to England. With money he might be able to find out. Meanwhile the great Dutch admiral,

De Ruyter, was ill, probably with the plague now raging in the fleet. When she copied this out for Halsall, Behn added her own view, that this was therefore a good time to attack the ships, advice that must have given her a surge of importance. The decoder in Williamson's office underlined her point.

The next letter of five days later—about 30 September—revealed that news of the great Fire of London, occurring in early September, had reached Holland. It led to general rejoicing, many seeing it as a divine punishment for English treachery in the Vlie. Perhaps this supposed divine support heartened the Dutch, for Scot's next letter described an upsurge of national spirits. The English dissidents were also heartened. Algernon Sidney had gone to England to reconnoitre and was expected back in ten days. There was general belief that the country was in disorder and the dissidents would exploit this when they heard from Sidney. Scot ended his dispatch with some more names of agents and seditious correspondents, as well as some advice on whose messengers to intercept.[6]

Then the sudden run of letters dried up. Behn was alarmed. Given the frantic calls for money and her own predicament, she at once suspected that Scot had been taken for debt. She felt horribly guilty, sure it was her promises of reward that had 'ffoold him with vaine expectation'. Yet she need not have worried. Instead, the event Scot had feared for so long had happened: Bampfield had betrayed him to the Dutch. Scot had probably been planning to betray Bampfield, for he had learnt that his 'friend' was also having dealings with the English: to pre-empt this move Bampfield sensibly betrayed Scot.

As so often, a church had staged the crucial encounter: Scot was apprehended on a Sunday in early October and dragged to The Hague, to which he and Behn had so fervently wished to go only a month before. When he heard the news, Corney was delighted—though disappointed that he had not been the agent: '…[it] is sum satisfaction that that Rogue Scott is catched at last…'. He put the capture down not to Bampfield, but to the trips to the Rosa Noble, the inn full of Dutch spies.

With Scot silenced, Behn's own position came to the fore. The well-informed innkeeper grew openly insolent; instead of trying to keep her close so that she would not skip the country, he now thought it best to cut his losses and be rid of her and her party. She had already given over all her possessions to him as surety for her bill, but they were worth little. The smug Corney was on hand to depict the scene and sneer at 'the shee spy as they call her there, where there is allways hollanders, besides the man of the house a great friend to holland; & hath affronted her severall tymes to gitt her out, but she will not goe'.

By the end of the month, the innkeeper was threatening prison. Behn's desperation demanded desperate measures and, having tried Halsall and Killigrew, she now addressed the powerful Lord Arlington directly.

She began more humbly than to either Killigrew or Halsall but, as she went on, she grew emboldened. Of necessity she had to recapitulate the whole sorry history of the last two months, pointing out how regularly she had written, 'not missing a Post'. '[T]was all in Vaine,' however; both she and Scot had been hobbled by Whitehall. Because of debts, Scot could not enter The Hague, nor pick up crucial documents; now he was imprisoned and could be of little use to them. So what had been gained by allowing him to go there? Meanwhile, what was *she* supposed to do? She had been forced to run up debts which she could not pay. When owing £120, she had been sent £50. Now she was suffering constant abuse from the people at the inn—'I am in extreame want & nessesity,' she wailed. If she were sent to prison, what would other potential agents think?

By the end of her letter Behn was almost weeping on to the paper, begging Arlington not to 'let me be disgraced & ruend in a straing place where I have none to pity or help me'. Daringly she tried to shame him into action: she would rather starve than not keep *her* word to Scot, while Arlington was breaking *his* to her. She ended, 'take som Pitty on a poore strainger.' She then signed off as his 'afflicted servant Astrea'.

The letter, with its pathetic appeal, must have had some effect, for Arlington replied and authorised money to be paid to her to settle the most urgent debts. He also told her what she must have guessed from the moment she heard of Scot's imprisonment: that her mission was terminated. She should return to London.

Immediately Behn wrote to Scot in prison. She had now to tell him the worst: that nothing would come for him from Whitehall. Scot, who had long suspected as much, was now in desperate straits and he managed at once to get a message to her, for it was too dangerous to write. He begged her to have faith in him and not to go back until he was released and they could meet. Playing on her presumed affection, he assured her he would give 'more sattisfaction then ever yet I gave you'. Behn might be pardoned for wondering why he had not provided this when at liberty.[7] Having digested the appeal, she wrote to Halsall.[8] By now she had greater confidence in Lord Arlington than in his underlings and she also wrote directly to him with Scot's message, enclosed in a long letter. It was only nine days before Christmas and she was facing the festival in an alien country. Like Bampfield, Scot, and Corney, all lonely, desperate men abroad, she wrote too much for busy statesmen, but the letter movingly summarised her mission:

> I have troubld every body so offten wth my complaints, & to so little purpose that weare I not confident of the Justness of my cause (which I can make as cleere as day.) I think I should be wild wth my hard treatment: Pardon me Sir that I aply myself to your Lordship: as the ffountaine from whence all the marcy I can expect (it seemes) must spring: it is to your Lordship as to my last hopes: which I adress myself: & how Justly god of heaven knows: since the delays which my little merritts have causd you to put on me have bin the only occation of above twice as much expence to you: as I might other wise have chargd you with: all which your Lordship may please to remember I offten said: & with all tould mr Hallsall; I knew that in the end this would be my reward: I can Justly say: that if I have not servd him as was expected: it was because I wanted what he promisd: but I have allready saide so much of that: tis true I am sent for home: but tis as true that they knew well I had not money enough to com withall: I could not Beg nor starve heare: & I was keepd so long without money that I was glad at any rate allmost to get Creditt: & what I had was spent before it came: but every on[e] complaines of such usage that are any ways imployd by them: Pardon me my Lord for I do not study comply[me]nts but with abundance of sincerity would speake my griefe & misfortune but since I dare not venture upon too long a relation of it to your Lordship: I only do most humbly Pitition: that your Lordship would be pleasd out of your goodness alone to let me com home with creditt & hansomness for magre [despite] all those excuses which others make for my stay (as if I had a mind to do so) I do protest to your Lordship: I desire nothing so much as to come hom & wheare as tis thought my little Services are at an end: I am of another opinion & am very confident that I shall in a very ffew weeks or days be able to do more then ever: for, had I had those supplys for him which weare from Post to Post Promisd your Lordship [had] had a better proofe of my will & his abillity: I do expect him to have liberty in a ffew days if he have it not by this time: & I heare trouble your Lordship with a little part

of on[e] of his too long letters to me: however I do humbly beg to com home: & if your Lordship will be pleasd to lett me have a Bill upon mr shaw for on[e] 100 pound more, of which my friend shall have part: I will heare promise your Lordship: if when I com home I can not give you absolute sattisfection I will Justly returne it againe. which I hope I am able to do when at home & your Lordship shall be gratiously pleasd only to lend it me for that time: without which I vow to god I can not com home: & the longer I stay the worse it will be: for god sake my Lord consider me a poore strainger & farr from ffriends: & do not denye what my life depends on: & your Lordship shall see how I will indeavor to merrit it: & what a Just & good accoumpt I shall give of what I am now so Ill thought on ffor: I neither petitiond ffor nor desird the place I now have nor voyage I have taken: nor have I in the least bin prodigall more than what your delays have occationd: & I am all most killd with the griefe I have to be so Ill though[t] on; & if I com not now by this convoy I must stay this too months or more: for god of heavens sake Sir take Pity on me; let me be usd like a Christian & on[e] who would venture her life to gaine your ffavorable opinion & to be permitted amongst the number of my Lord your Lordships most ffaithfull & humble servant: A. Behne.[9]

She signed herself Behn: the spy Astrea was for the moment forgotten. Perhaps she felt the letter not desperate enough and a postscript was added: 'for god sake Sir: do not ffor gett me: & I am sure your Lordship will not repent your goodness & I humbly beg your Lordship to be speedy least I eate out my head.'[10]

She did not make the convoy, but neither did she 'eate out' her head.

There were quite a few actions Behn probably took. Over the months she may have tried to salvage something from her dead husband's shipping interests, with the help of Piers. She probably had another try now. Also, in moments of utter desperation, she might have yearned for the Abbess Mary Knatchbull and a quiet convent life. In Antwerp, she had visited the great seven-naved cathedral with its lacy stonework and its tinselled Catholicism. She was temperamentally drawn to it as a sort of religious version of aristocratic excess and the doctrines which so disturbed her compatriots hardly troubled her. She loved the sensuous drench of this alien faith, its heady amalgamation of candles, flowers and incense and, when she came to use the setting of Antwerp in her fiction, the location seemed to trigger memory of religious spectacle. Conceivably she might become a nun; she had been made much of in the convent if her *History of the Nun* may be credited as experience, and it was a common retreat for worried widows. She could have contacted the Ghent Abbess or the convent relatives of her travelling companion, Lord Stafford, in Louvain and Antwerp. But, if she thought of the notion, she soon dismissed it. If she could not pay the innkeeper, she could not muster a dowry for a convent. Besides, she had few religious feelings.

She may have entertained another idea more seriously. In her long novel, *Love-Letters*, the maid of the heroine Silvia, in similarly desperate straits in the Low Countries, tells her mistress not to despair while she has youth and beauty. Aphra Behn was still young and enjoyed amorous as well as political intrigue. Money had to come from somewhere. Her old companion, who had not been paid for many months, might, in the closeness of a night when they shared a bed, have suggested discreetly that, for a woman, there was an easier way of making a living than espionage, where the financial rewards could be achieved before the services had been rendered. Like Silvia, Behn never regarded herself as a whore, but she did see old rich men as fair financial game for attractive younger women and she did not condemn such women for giving sex for money in or out of marriage.

Scot's last letter to Behn from prison suggested that there was something beyond spying between the pair and the letters within the 'Memoirs' strengthen the suggestion that Behn might have been fooled by Scot's role of loving swain. These letters are fictionalised but, despite an anachronistic reference to the dismemberment of the Dutch leader, De Witt, well after Behn's stay in Antwerp, they may be by Behn and enclose some genuine happenings.[11] So, given her penchant for rearranging life and amalgamating real-life people into fiction, she might in part have used Scot for her 'character' of the suitor, Vander Albert, a man who had been in love with her 'before the War, in her Husband's time'. Curiously, though, Albert is said to have supported Astrea in Antwerp, a neat reversal of the real case, but a more usual one when sex rather than information is the commodity. After much merriment and swapping of bodies in bed, Astrea agrees to marry Albert, on whose love 'she grounded the Success of her Negotiations'. Then Albert 'dy'd', as Scot may have done.[12]

If authentic, the comic letters suggest how much Behn had changed since Surinam. Perhaps her marriage had been the catalyst. She no longer fantasised heroines from La Calprenède, chaste princesses awaiting their prince. She had too much humour for romance and may have begun to fear her own love life would be in comic mode. Her other possible encounter in Antwerp bears this out. The Dutch and Flemings were famous for being drunk rather than amorous, and for aiming at a quick fix more than erotic foreplay. Albert's fat friend, the old merchant Van Bruin, was in the mode; his letters might have drawn on the Amsterdam merchant Behn came to know, perhaps on the persistent Thomas Corney, perhaps on someone who had offered love but advanced no money, or perhaps, since he was a nautical man, on the dead and seemingly unlamented Mr Behn.[13] In the letters he is an 'old piece of worm-eaten Touchwood'.

To Van Bruin's nautical missive offering love, Astrea makes a spirited reply, describing to the old man the cost of keeping:

> have you set before the Eyes of your Understanding, the charge of fitting out such a Vessel (as you have made me) for the *Indies* of Love....There are Ribbonds and Hoods for my Pennons; Diamond Rings, Lockets, and Pearl-Necklaces for my Guns of Offence and Defence; Silks, Holland, Lawn, Cambrick, &c. for Rigging; Gold and Silver Laces, Imbroideries and Fringes fore and aft for my Stern and for my Prow; rich Perfumes, Paint and Powder, for my Ammunition; Treats, rich Wines, expensive Collations, Gaming Money, Pin-Money, with a long *Et cetera* for my Cargo; and Balls, Masks Plays, Walks. Airing in the Country, and a Coach and Six for my fair Wind.[14]

Whether written by Behn or not, the list gives a vivid sense not only of what a man set on keeping a mistress would have to expend, but also what an independent woman needed if she wished to make a show in the world.

It is entirely fitting that the one piece of prose *definitely* written by Aphra Behn and set in Antwerp should concern a woman's obsession with money. After relating the comic incidents of the suitors, the letters in the 'Memoirs' mention a tale Behn is supposedly not yet ready to write. Two decades later this became *The Fair Jilt*, concerning a Prince Tarquin and the fair, rich and treacherous beguine, Miranda. The pair had featured in a curious item Behn had noticed in the *London Gazette* for 28–31 May 1666, not long before she left London:

The Prince Tarquino being condemned at Antwerp to be beheaded, for endeavouring the death of his sister-in-law: being on the scaffold, the executioner tied a handkerchief about his head and by great accident his blow lighted upon the knot, giving him only a slight wound. Upon which, the people being in a tumult, he was carried back to the Town-house, and is in hopes both of his pardon and his recovery.

A subsequent issue of the *Gazette* noted his pardon by the Marquis of Castel Rodrigo, the Governor. It was the kind of heroic and grotesque story that Behn would store in her mind.

In the dedication to *The Fair Jilt*, Behn claimed she had actually spoken to Tarquin and been 'an Eye-Witness' of some of the events she related. This is unlikely given her probable presence in Surinam at the time of the earlier events and the later dates of her sojourn in Antwerp. She may, however, have had many details second-hand from eyewitnesses and she could have been made aware of the contents of Dutch year-books and newspapers as well as the pamphlet written or most likely commissioned by Maria Theresia (Miranda) in self-justification. Detail of the main sensational events which she later related were probably among the 'Journal Observations' in which, according to *The Fair Jilt*, she wrote of things 'curious to retain'. Also, in this city of baroque Catholicism, Behn might have seen indelible sights which could easily be assimilated into her tale, such as the rich show of a supposed penitent:

> [Miranda] was dress'd in a black Velvet Gown, with a rich Row of Diamonds at the Peak behind; and a petty-coat of flower'd Gold, very rich, and lac'd; with all things else suitable: A Gentleman carry'd her great Velvet Cushion before her, on which her Prayer-Book, embroider'd, was laid; her Train was born up by a Page....[15]

The historical events behind *The Fair Jilt* concerned two sisters, Maria Theresia (Miranda in Behn's story) and Anna Louisa (Alcidiana) van Mechelen, of an ancient and well-respected Antwerp family.[16] They were the nieces of a rich man, Caspar Oosterlincx, with a house in the Reyndersstraat in Antwerp. On 10 November 1656 in the magnificent cathedral of the Blessed Virgin Mary—where Behn was probably accosted by Corney—Maria Theresia married Francisco de Tarquini, with her uncle Caspar as witness. Anna Louisa settled down to keep house for her uncle.

Worried about the welfare of Anna Louisa, Caspar Oosterlincx made a will in which he left his substantial goods of gold, silver and diamonds, as well as his property, to the two nieces, provided that they inhabited the house in the Reyndersstraat. It was a disastrous arrangement and, when he died, it was not long before the two sisters were at each other's throats, Maria Theresia spurred on by her husband.[17] In Behn's story, *The Fair Jilt*, Tarquin is an infatuated malleable man, while Miranda is a ruthless dominant woman. In history, Tarquini seems to have been the harshest and most violent of the trio.[18]

Tension was high and, after much quarrelling, Anna Louisa left the house and sued Tarquini and her sister for her inheritance. A long legal wrangle followed, in which her witnesses described a frightful regime of cruelty. The young girl had been constantly mocked, called fool, whore, and pig by her savage brother-in-law, who also battered her and pinched her. She was not allowed to eat with the couple: sometimes she was given sticks to chew, sometimes food without implements, and sometimes she was starved. One of Tarquini's servants testified to the many death threats she endured and to an incident when, after a dispute between the two sisters, Tarquini had tried to run Anna Louisa through with his sword; failing that, he had thrown things after her as she fled.

Tarquini and Maria Theresia denied the charges, claiming the head-strong young woman had left the house capriciously. To prove her extravagance, they produced an account of her expenditure. On clothes and shoes alone she had used 467 gilders (a good craftsman would earn one gilder a day and a high official one thousand a year, so it was a substantial sum). One witness testified that, when Anna Louisa had left the house, the couple tried to make peace and went to a lawyer to that end, but that Anna Louisa refused ever to live under their roof again. Showing a flash of that character Behn would so flamboyantly give to Miranda, Maria Theresia declared it was never too late to improve matters, but by then Anna Louisa wanted only justice.[19]

The Tarquinis' murderous designs on Anna Louisa did not abate. Two shooting attempts were made on her life. In the first in 1662, Maria Theresia's coachman shot at her sister as she left the Carmelite church (close to Behn's future lodgings in the Rosa Noble). Bullets missed her body but pierced her clothes. As instigator of the crime, Maria Theresia was arrested. Under torture she refused to confess and, instead of being executed, she was publicly humiliated, then banished. The second attempt in early 1666 was by Tarquini himself, again by the Carmelite convent and again bullets tore only Anna Louisa's clothes. Caught with the pistol about him and known to feel murderous towards the victim, Tarquini was sentenced to death in May, with a sword rather than an axe, a privilege of nobility. The sentence was to be carried out the next day. The execution was bungled so badly that the authorities halted proceedings. Tarquini was then reprieved by the new Spanish governor, Castel Rodrigo, as Behn would have read in the *Gazette*.[20]

For a fiction she needed only a prelude, and the spacious and ancient beguinage on the outskirts of Antwerp, coupled with the great new Jesuit church near her lodgings, would provide it. Her heroine Miranda, based on Maria Theresia, would be a beguine and her amorous career would start with the attempted seduction of a friar as she knelt at the sort of sensuously decorated confessional Behn herself had seen in the Jesuit church. There the priest was divided from the penitent by carved angel's wings.

That the story of *The Fair Jilt* disturbed Behn was apparent from the joltingly strange morality she gave it when she came to write it up twenty years later. There the abused and mutilated Alcidiana, whose money Miranda squanders, is made to ask forgiveness of her manipulating and vicious sister, and the deceived and condemned servant (based on Maria Theresia's coachman) to beg pardon of the mistress who is causing his death. The glamorised Tarquin is largely forgiven by public opinion, which stands in for the morality of the tale, all because he behaves well on the scaffold and has sumptuous accessories. Perhaps in the clever, ambitious, and literate Miranda who never quite gets her comeuppance, Behn may have indulged in a little fantasy of how a woman might do what she pleased if she could only handle men and write engagingly— Miranda tries to seduce through letters.[21]

In the new year of 1667, William Scot was released from prison and promptly banished from Holland. He went to Antwerp but, despite his former pleas, he probably did not risk another meeting with Aphra Behn, nor inform her how little she need have worried about his debts, or indeed about his treatment from the Dutch. In all the time of his dealings with her, he had never broken his contact with them and, despite her belief in his affection for her, she did not figure at all in the story he told to them.

This formed a long letter in which, far from being contrite, Scot actually took the Dutch to task for ever doubting his loyalty to them. He demanded a repeal of the banishment that had taken him to Antwerp where he was 'abandoned to death by the vengeance of the king of

England'. His magnificent obsession with Bampfield continued, but Furley, against whom Scot had been informing to Behn, now appeared to have been his close friend all along, and Scot asked that Furley be given his papers in Holland. All in all, it was a cringing, lying letter, which Behn ought to have seen.[22]

Meanwhile, having offended Arlington, Behn and Corney were desperate to get to England to tell their version of events. Also, Behn was running up more debts. Fortunately she managed to leave first by borrowing £150 from an Edward Butler, possibly in Flanders, possibly from London.[23] So, after missing the Christmas convoy she'd been so eager to catch, she was enabled to take one many expensive months later.

Behn set off home as she had come, via Ostend, but then she journeyed on to Dunkirk, where she met Sir Bernard Gascoigne. He had obtained a pass to cross to England and he left in a fleet of sixty vessels on 1 May. Since she travelled with him, this was also her date of leaving the Continent. Despite his anglicised name, Sir Bernard was formerly Bernardo Guasconi, a Florentine merchant and financier, a flexible man of refined taste and few scruples. He had also been a Royalist soldier and spy and had been richly rewarded by Charles II with a fat pension— though, as usual, it tended to be in arrears. He was now returning from Italy, where he had gone to arrange for intelligence to be gathered from Venice and Vienna for Lord Arlington, since there were no English functionaries there. At the same time, he had ministered to other English needs and had written back about buying and dispatching a eunuch.[24] As well as being connected with Arlington, he was a friend of Lord Stafford's and, if she had not much appreciated that nobleman already, Sir Bernard's praise now recommended him to her.[25]

Later, according to the 'Memoirs', Behn told a tale of this voyage, of an apparition which both she and Sir Bernard looked at through the new 'Telescopes and Prospective Glasses' brought from Italy. At first, they assumed the glasses had painted scenes on the end, but then they realised the apparition was really there: a floating floor of marble, supporting fluted and twisted pillars with vines, flowers and streamers entwined and a hundred little fluttering cupids. Behn was not given to magical imaginings or to omens, and the most likely explanation of this is that they were seeing the Fata Morgana, an effect of wind and light in stormy weather in the Channel, apprehended by some as castles and battlements, but by a reader of romance as flowers and cupids.[26]

Behn herself did not write of the phenomenon, tending to be wary of telescopes as revealers of what their users wanted to see, but her memoirist clearly saw in the incident some expression of the romantic and amorous nature of Behn's future life. For the allegory, it was a pity that, as usual, the Fata Morgana preceded a great storm. This drove many of the ships on to the coast of England and wrecked them, with great loss of canary wine, as well as of the fancy goods Sir Bernard was trying to bring back to England. Some ships floundering in the sea became prey for French marauders, but, happily, the passengers and crew of Behn's vessel were saved by small boats that came from England to row them ashore.[27]

Soon Sir Bernard was in London; so probably was his fellow-passenger. '*Astrea* arriv'd safe, tho' tired, to *London*, from a Voyage that gain'd her more Reputation than Profit. The Rest of her Life was entirely dedicated to Pleasure and Poetry,' so concluded the memoirist. There was some truth in these statements. Behn was weary when she arrived and she had gained no more reputation than profit from her trip to Antwerp. Her life would have its 'Pleasure and Poetry', but above all it had to be dedicated to the getting of money. She would be helped in this by some of the psychological and literary skills of telling a convincing story, interpreting people, and investigating conflicting motives, which she had honed during her time as a government spy.

As for Scot, he was not heard of again. Perhaps he 'dy'd at *Amsterdam* of a Fever,' as the 'Memoirs' reported of Albert; perhaps Corney succeeded in murdering him.

CHAPTER 10

❧

In and Out of Prison

*'I would break through all, get to the King,
and never rise till he had paid the money.'*

The London to which agent 160 returned in the spring of 1667 was
not a happy place. Its population thinned by between seventy and
a hundred thousand from the plague, it lay charred and black from the
Great Fire, with some of its debris still smouldering. Dryden had imaged
the conflagration as Virgil's burning of Troy, with 'wond'ring fish' gazing
'in shining waters', but the ashes were beyond poetry. The fire had been
so ferocious it had obliterated streets, and rebuilding was a mammoth
task. Abused in Antwerp, Behn had at least avoided life in the tents and
temporary sheds in the fields of Islington and Hampstead, as well as
the hysteria that blamed the calamities now on a sinful court, now on
the Dutch, but mostly on the Catholics.

Low-spirited, people longed for peace, for the war drained resources
needed for rebuilding and destabilised the country. London and the southern
ports were made dismal by the unpaid, wounded soldiers whom Evelyn
saw trudging from Deptford to Chatham to Gravesend, finding no refuge
in the towns, so that the villages were 'peopled with the poor miserable
creatures'. Perhaps Aphra Behn, poor but not destitute, had now some
fellow feeling for them. Or perhaps she took the robust line on mutilation
seen in so many jokes. In one, a captain has both arms blown off three
inches below the shoulders; as his wounds are dressed, he laughs heartily:
he used, he explains, to want 'his P—' as long as his arm and now it was.[1]

Soon after Behn arrived in London, Atlantic ships came with news
that, back in February, a Dutch fleet had easily captured Surinam.
Writing dejectedly to Robert Harley, Deputy Governor Byam knew
exactly whom to blame: 'In February following arrived a Dutch fleet
from Zealand, by the advice of Scott, to take the colony.'[2] Through
Scot, the Dutch had known the place was 'ill armed, and our fort not
half built, but one bastion perfected'. Even more fortunate for the Dutch

had been the outbreak of fever that carried off half the inhabitants, including Behn's friend George Marten; the rest remained 'in a most weak condition... miserably weak'. The loss of Surinam did not much trouble the English government, but Behn lamented it.[3] She heard of Banister's efforts to negotiate for the remaining English settlers abandoned by the crown, but she did not change her opinion of him.

After more mishaps and military mistakes, feelers for peace were extended and accepted. In mid-May, Dutch and English assembled at Breda, wrangling over precedence so intensely that a room with two separate doors was provided for the ambassadors to arrive simultaneously, as well as an Arthurian round table with no one at its head. During these political skirmishings, the Royal Navy, already dilapidated, gently decayed. In Holland, however, where Holmes's bonfire burnt in the mind, shipyards and dockyards hummed with activity. A spectacular revenge was planned to strike at England's naval heart. Echoing many earlier, vaguer informants, including Behn, an agent now warned Arlington specifically of the plan, but he regarded the show as bravado.[4]

The Dutch raid on the Medway was meticulously designed by De Witt and carried out by his admirals. Dutch ships were to sail to England, enter the Thames estuary, then the Medway, capture and burn the vessels at anchor and destroy the military installations at Chatham. As peace negotiations grew irritating, it was added that the men-of-war should be *captured* rather than burnt, so that the English would be thoroughly humiliated.

Even when the raid started, few feared its success. Behn's brother had probably returned to his post and may have been dispatched with the Duke of Albemarle to Chatham. Things were moving, but 'backwardly', as Pepys put it. Then, suddenly, the raid *did* become real, and panic and flight ensued as the inhabitants of Chatham and Gravesend rushed their belongings and themselves into small boats to escape. From the Dutch perspective, all went brilliantly and a large portion of the English fleet was burnt or taken. Albemarle tried unsuccessfully to save the ships further up the river but did manage to fortify Chatham, mainly because the Dutch, having used up their fire ships and blocked the river with sunk vessels, had begun to withdraw. As they left the Thames, they cheekily dragged with them the *Royal Charles*, on which the King had returned to England in 1660.

As intended, it was a national disaster for the English. The *London Gazette* tried to play it down by claiming that 'the loss we have received has been hitherto so fully returned on [the Dutch], that they can have but little reason to Brag of their Success' and there was an attempt to write off the great flagship as unlucky and expendable because it had been built by Cromwell.[5] None the less, most people were appalled, and both court and city betrayed 'Distraction and Consternation'.[6] Pepys's diary expressed the general feeling, 'all our hearts do now ake' (12 June): he had joined the rush in getting his money together and sending his wife and his diary out of London. It would not, said many, have happened in Cromwell's day.[7]

The disaster did not benefit the secret agents, who, despite their warnings, became scapegoats, and a committee set up to inquire into the miscarriages of the war included discussion of faulty intelligence.[8] In such an atmosphere, neither Behn nor Corney found much joy in England. Corney complained that he had 'not received the least recompense for my charge, services, or sufferings'.[9] His dreary experience over the next months is fully documented. His trade in ruins, his banishment from Holland unrepealed, and his estates gone, he needed a paying post quickly. So he tried to make Williamson persuade Arlington to give him the modest one of storekeeper in the ordnance office in Chatham, now the previous incumbent was in Newgate prison for embezzlement. He was due for a long wait. One year and many self-pitying petitions later, he was still trying to flatter Williamson into action. Like Behn before him, Corney proceeded from lesser men to Arlington, urging him to 'move his Majesty to establish me' in the office which his Lordship had 'so frankly' promised and without which he would be 'completely ruined'. The final misfortune occurred when Corney was robbed of all his clothes and grew 'ashamed to stir abroad'.

Only the possibility of the ordnance post, open of course solely to men, separated Corney's debt-ridden plight from Aphra Behn's. Mr Butler now wanted the repayment of his loan and he was implacable.[10] No doubt she tried her dead husband's friends, her mother, 'Sir Thomas', everyone she knew. Since superficial charm and civility were much prized, probably no one repulsed her with hard words, but those to whom she appealed were unforthcoming. As in Flanders, probably many friends sympathised and entertained her to a meal.

Behn's main hopes had to be her old employers. Convinced that Killigrew's silence had been an error or a fault of the post, she may have promised speedy repayment to Butler primarily on his credit. Her new letter to him, kept among the state papers, suggests that he tried to do something through official channels, but he had nothing to offer personally. £150 was a large sum and Killigrew, though possessed of a fat income, was always in debt. Behn also petitioned Lord Arlington and even suggested that Butler apply directly to him. Arlington did not have personal ties to her, however, and he roundly told her creditor that no money would come from him. The expenses of Aphra Behn were not in the secret service budget and no one had given him orders to pay her more. Since, apart from the King, he was the highest authority to whom she could appeal, she must have found this hypocrisy galling, and her petition was probably her last direct application.[11] In the comic letters quoted in the 'Memoirs', there are hints that Behn suspected Arlington of treachery during the Dutch War; perhaps she got her own back by spreading rumours.[12]

With this absolute refusal, Behn grew desperate. She composed a further, more pathetic letter to Killigrew, declaring she would be dragged to prison on the very next day if no one helped her. Only the physical debility that dogged her at times of crisis kept her from dramatically dashing to Whitehall: 'I could find it in my heart to break through all & get to the King & never rise, till he weare pleased to pay this [money]; but I am sick & weake & unfitt for yt.' Failing strength to enact this fantasy, she would send her mother with a petition. She hoped the threat would bring Killigrew to his senses.[13] The letter was as unstable as Behn's mood. Now she saw herself as a poor victim brought low by the machinations of wicked men, now as a strong woman who would not, whatever men did to her, 'perish in a prison' or 'starve'. Butler was indeed demanding 'the uttermost farthing'. She had heard this kind of threat at least once before: from the innkeeper at the Rosa Noble. This was more serious.

When Arlington declared he had no money to give, Butler carried out his threat and Aphra Behn went to prison. There she needed money even more urgently if she was not to 'starve'. The 'common' side was dismal and cold, much of it ventilated directly through glass-less windows. Prisoners had to sleep on boards and the company could be seriously mad and dangerous. To avoid this, Behn would have tried for the 'state' side where, for payment, she could have had a bed and possibly a chamber. She would have needed more money for any legal writs necessary to her case and the paying would continue throughout the stay. If matters were sorted out, she would have to pay for her own discharge. Certainly it was as possible to end up with new debts from a stint in debtors' prison as it was from the King's service in Flanders.

Behn was, however, not witless and may well have stayed in prison for only a short time. Possibly she came to some compromise with the persecuting Butler, or the King, who would have done nothing directly for her, may have received her petition and jolted Killigrew into acting on her behalf and paying off Butler after she had served some time in prison. In which case, there is one other possibility: that, in return for money from Killigrew extricating her from debts and prison, she was persuaded to go to Italy, particularly to Venice, on a further mission. The suggestion is speculative but, like the secret Interregnum trip, it has some features in its favour.

When he met Behn, Sir Bernard Gascoigne, her fellow-passenger from Flanders, had been returning from Venice, where he had been setting up channels of intelligence for Whitehall. Now he went back to the Continent, and 'Mrs Affora', the agent, may have travelled some of the way with him. Killigrew was interested in events in Venice, where he had been the King's Resident in the Interregnum. Venice was fighting the Turks, in Crete and asking other Europeans to help— Arlington was prepared to give aid but only covertly since he feared to displease the Turks who would retaliate by seizing the considerable holdings of English merchants in their territories. Negotiations with Venice had, therefore, to be hidden and any aid provided 'with Secresie'. Agents would be needed for such a delicate operation. In addition, the government suspected the French of reneging on their promise to disarm in the recent peace by pretending to send a force of soldiers to the help of Venice. The English would like to know the truth.[14]

Years later, dedicating a work to Henry Howard, Earl of Arundel, later Duke of Norfolk, Behn mentioned that she had seen 'with what Transports of Joy, with what unusual Respect and Ceremony, above what we pay to Mankind, the very Name of the Great *Howards* of *Norfolk* and *Arundel*, have been celebrated on Foreign Shores!'[15] Arundel's father, another Henry Howard, had spent much time in Venice and, after the Restoration, had been eager to become the British ambassador there, but was prevented by his Catholicism. He was much appreciated for his 'passionate devotion' to the republic and Behn may have heard his praises in Venice.[16]

In a posthumous short story, 'The Dumb Virgin', the narrator, iden-tified with Aphra Behn the dramatist, liked Venice as she had liked Surinam, for its 'benign climate'. She made no great claims for her status there: wanting to take her to a ball her young friends thoughtfully provide her with a costly masquerade costume and carry her along in their own coach. She had, she said, been living three doors down from a wealthy Turkey merchant's family in Venice when the grotesque tragedy of trauma and incest took place. In the story, the narrator made a point of knowing some Italian, for, as she listened to a man believed to be English, she was struck by his 'pure *Italian*' and realised he could not be her countryman.[17] This knowledge was used again in the play *The Feign'd Curtizans* where, amongst the cacophony of foreign languages, one or two words of Venetian dialect unexpectedly appear.[18]

Such hints remain hints, but, if Behn did have an acquaintance with Venice, the late 1660s is the best moment for her to have made it. Later mentions of Venetians refer to this time: her second performed play, *The Amorous Prince*, and the short story set in Ghent, *The History of the Nun*, both allude to struggles of Venice against the Ottoman Turks which occurred then. That no record exists of Behn's activity proves little; reports from missions where no follow-up was needed were usually oral.[19]

Behn had, too, another cause that might have led her to Italy, as it may have helped justify her presence in Flanders. Widows of men in the business of shipping often retained their interest after their husband's death; so the mention of a 'Widow Behn' in connection with her dead husband's involvement is not unusual.[20] The ship at issue was the *Abraham's Sacrifice*.

It had been sailing past Galway in Ireland when it had been seized by men who assumed that, since England and Holland were at war and since the ship looked Dutch, it was a proper prize and they were acting as patriots not pirates. In the summer of 1667, some months after Behn had returned from Antwerp and was in the thick of her money troubles with Butler, the captain of the *Abraham's Sacrifice*, a Genoese called Anthony Basso, petitioned the English authorities to remove the soldiers from his ship and return it to him. The seizure, he claimed, had been quite illegal: both vessel and goods were Genoese rather than Dutch. This claim was some embarrassment to the authorities since the ship with its cargo had been sold off in Ireland at a fraction of their value, an action for which the Governor of Galway and others found themselves 'upon the carpet'; indeed Basso accused the Lord Lieutenant of Ireland of actually delaying an order from the King that the ship should not be sold. The Governor and others were therefore expected 'to come but blewlly off'. In fact, as so often in these cases, nothing much happened.

William Blathwayt, an official in the King's Hague embassy, was put in charge of the case to represent the English interest and, in April 1669 when the Anglo-Dutch War was over, to defend it in the Dutch admiralty courts, to which Basso had now appealed. The sum involved was large—about £80,000—and Arlington himself had written to the English ambassador in Holland urging him to 'apply all your Care and Diligence' to prevent the goods being taken back on the pretext that they were Genoese, 'for if it should prove so, His Majesty would be obliged to refund a great Sum of Money to them'.[21] As ever, His Majesty had little spare cash.[22]

For his case, Blathwayt was very eager to know if there were any insurers of the ship or its cargo. If these could be named or produced and if they were Dutch or in any way connected with Holland, it would go far to establishing his case: that the ship and cargo were legal prizes for the English in time of war. Even if not personally involved, Aphra Behn or her factor, Piers, could, Blathwayt had learnt, tell him something about the insurers of the vessel.[23] So Piers was visited by the English authorities in an undercover operation. He prevaricated: he could not at present give the name of the insurers, he explained, but he left his visitors in no doubt that it was a matter of 'would not tell'.[24] He did, however, declare that the cargo was insured by several people. In Holland, poor Blathwayt had even less success, being denied access to the Dutch records, and he abandoned his efforts, thoroughly frustrated. Of course he went unrewarded for his trouble. The only clarity in the whole business, which Behn could have foreseen, was that the King did not propose to pay anyone for anything.

Evidently Blathwayt and his agents did not find the widow Behn. If this widow is indeed Aphra Behn, she would be the spy Blathwayt probably knew about in Antwerp since he too dealt in espionage for Joseph Williamson. Undoubtedly she would be wary of anything involving payment or potential legal trouble: after all she had just been freed from prison for debt. Either she made herself unavailable in England or she had left the country, possibly *en route* for Italy, since it is conceivable that Mr Behn *did* have some financial involvement in the *Abraham's Sacrifice*. Either he had commissioned goods to be loaded in Genoa or, as Blathwayt presumably suspected, was a launderer rather than an insurer, acting as cover in England for an essentially Dutch venture. In either case, his widow might have wished to pursue claims with merchants in Italy. If she did, she got little out of the enterprise, for the Genoese remained unhappy and continued to complain. By 1669, Aphra Behn was certainly in England ready to try a new venture.[25]

She was sure that London should remain her arena of activity. It was an unhealthy choice. The 'fumes, steams and stenches', especially from the burning of 'sea-cole', stank the air.[26] The Fleet River had become fetid; a new canal was finished in 1674, but, not being used by ships as expected, the river soon reverted to a rubbish dump and sewer. Alcohol was drunk everywhere and the diet was poor. Ailing children had a hard time of it—but there was no abundance of these for, though the town was regarded as licentious, there were fewer births than in the country.[27] All the problems derived from the huge size of the population, now swelled by immigrants like Aphra Behn. Despite the depredations of the plague, London easily remained the largest city in the kingdom, with about one in fourteen or fifteen living there. Most dwelt in tenements, often carved out of once grand houses.

The city was also bustling, stimulating and transforming and Behn would have found more congenial men and women in London than anywhere else. Colepeper's wild half-brother Lord Strangford was only one of the many bored provincials who had longed to experience metropolitan diversions. The standard of literacy was higher than in the country and even maids, like their ladies, habitually read romances. In decorous City circles women would be excluded from intellectual or free conversations, but, in the more advanced and risqué ones around the court and theatre, a ready wit such as Behn's would be prized.[28] She was already a political animal and she could see that the court and its hinterland in the town offered more scope for spirited women than the bourgeois world into which she had probably married and which kept its coffee-houses, clubs and stock exchanges exclusively for men.

Behn likely settled in an area between the City of London and Westminster, her constant references being to Covent Garden and the Temple. She may have lived in Whitefriars or St Bride's, mixed bohemian areas, part down-at-heel and part respectable, with colourful acting and writing inhabitants, bookshops and taverns. The young Earl of Rochester, who had already made a name for himself by kidnapping the woman he was shortly to marry, occasionally lodged there and a medical man who, according to his advertisement, could cure all ailments from sciatica to 'Tortions in the Bowels' made it his home. The area also housed actors and musicians, as well as clubs for sodomists, Catholics, and other 'undesirables'; there were low dives in Fulwood's Rents in Holborn nearby and, with its warren of tenements and passages, Alsatia was a sanctuary for debtors.

Behn would have lodged, possibly still with her mother, rather than owned or occupied a whole house; it was a respectable enough action since professional men like lawyers did the same. The government listed Londoners who were houseowners or heads of households, so as to levy a hearth tax. Widows and spinsters were often amongst these; indeed some, such as the early seventeenth-century cross-dresser and confidence trickster, Mal Cutpurse, were eager to claim the status. Behn does not appear on the ten lists that are extant, however, and, throughout her life, seems to have been content or obliged to be a lodger. As such, she probably had enough room for herself and two or three servants, the elderly maid and a boy at least. She could write in shared space and a room of her own was not necessary.

The closeness of her lodgings to the Inns of Court suited Behn. She liked young lawyers, witty not overly serious men. They drank and gossiped, went to the theatre, 'adorn[ed] all their studies with the poets, and fill[ed] their heads with Lampoons, Songs, and Burlesque'.[29] They were away from their roots, often adopting a libertine lifestyle, in stark contrast to Puritan fathers, and were usually unencumbered with wives or had wives safely tucked away in the country. Fancying themselves as a rival society to the courtiers, they occasionally tried to overtop them in misbehaving, especially in the theatre pit, and even Rochester called them 'rakehells'.

Behn had been out of the country much in recent years and could fashion what identity she liked. Rochester described the demeanour of 'a waiting gentlewoman' who, to prove her descent from 'Sir Humphry' her great uncle, had to affect high spirits and an inclination 'towards a gentile convers'. There were many lampoons on the town miss who 'talks high of her *Family*, and tells a large story how they were Ruined by the late *Wars*. But the true History of her Life, is generally to this Effect: She is only the *Cub* of a *Bumpkin*, lickt into a Genteel form by Town Conversation' and now living 'with a maid in noble rooms in Covent Garden'.[30] No doubt Aphra Behn already knew that spiritedness was her way forward, and it was sensible to combine unshockability and gentility.

There was scope at court for a woman with beauty, wit and some means. Rochester's friend, the courtier Sir Charles Sedley, is supposed to have asked a new arrival among the Maids of Honour whether she intended to set up as 'a Beauty, a Miss, a Wit or a Politician'. Aphra Behn apparently had some beauty but perhaps not enough now to capture and captivate usefully. A wit she might have been or a she-politician, but both roles required money—it was costly to be seen at court.[31] But she could enter the alternative court of the theatre and town tavern, that louche, frank society in which transvestism and buggery were openly mentioned and people could become what they would.

In the gap between her return to England and her entry into recorded literature, Aphra Behn probably copied for money, helping to fulfil the huge demand for manuscript lampoons, political libels and any other material that people wanted to read but the government did not wish published. Throughout her life, she would be aware of this scribbling underworld, and many of her friends and enemies would emanate from it. She may also have done some legal copying since her addresses to the King suggested she knew the form of petitions, as well as some copying for the theatre.

But copying alone would not have kept her in suitable style, and it is hard to imagine a woman's finding time to write her own verses, as Behn did, without her being partly kept by a man or at least receiving substantial gifts. One 'keeper' or admirer from these years may be hidden in the name Amyntas which crops up in Behn's early poems for a promiscuous worldly man. On his behalf, Behn showed some possessiveness in 'To Mrs Harsenet. On the Report of a Beauty, Which she went to see at Church'.

The verses were printed in two versions in 1684 and 1707 but were probably composed now since the lady to whom they were addressed, Carola, daughter of Sir Roger Harsnett, appears in the 1707 version under her maiden name, changed in 1670.[32] In the poem Behn and Carola Harsnett are visitors to the fashionable and scandalous watering place of Tunbridge Wells in Kent, Behn accompanied by Amyntas. The place had come some way since 1606 when the ailing Lord North had drunk from the springs and found himself rejuvenated. The springs or wells had been fenced in and paved round, and bowling-greens and houses for coffee-drinking, pipe-smoking and gaming had been established. When Charles II and his court arrived in 1663, the King occupied a house on Mount Ephraim, but his retinue was forced to encamp on the common. By the 1670s there were still few permanent houses, although visitors could stay in surrounding villages, as Behn and Amyntas might have done. Anthony Hamilton described Tunbridge Wells as 'the most simple and rustic place in Europe, but the most delightful and entertaining'.[33] The social constraint of London was laid aside and all was fresh flowers, fruit, love and dancing on the soft grass. It was Arcadia moved to England, the pastoral made actual, sophistication in an organised rural setting. Some took a more jaundiced view. The Earl of Rochester said it was full of the most ridiculous and unpleasant people imaginable and he preferred his horse.[34] Others mentioned the fashionable ennui, the rampant envy and crime. Since she enjoyed artifice it was probably Behn's kind of place.

Behn had heard much of Carola Harsnett, the resplendent young woman who was a natural conqueror: 'How many Slaves your Conqu'ring Eyes had won, / And how the gazing Crowd admiring throng.' She was almost as susceptible to women as men and always paid tribute to female beauty: inevitably, she 'a lover grew / Of so much Beauty'. Characteristically Behn was smitten in church, spying Carola 'at the Altar' where she had put the old minister off his duty. More significant for Behn was Amyntas's stance of rapt adoration.

Behn's response was a tense verse letter mingling flattery and pique. It echoed the Shakespeare of the sonnets, when he cast himself as the ageing lover in a triangle with a flirtatious beloved and lovely rival. It sounds as though Carola (called Cloris in the poem) had got under Behn's skin, both disturbing her into erotic feelings for another woman and attracting her male lover away from her. So she warned her off, telling her she was too remarkable a person to bother to entrap such a man as Amyntas. Youth and beauty deserved an exclusive 'Virgin-Heart', not that of a roué.

Since Carola married Sir Samuel Morland in 1670, it is conceivable that Behn's keeping friend or admirer was in fact Morland, whom she was afraid of losing to the younger woman. Sir Samuel was an old Royalist acquaintance of Colepeper's, whom Behn may have met before the Restoration when, as Thurloe's secretary and plain Sam Morland, he acted as an agent for the Royalists. After 1660, he was knighted and pleased the King by inventing instruments for opening and resealing letters so skilfully that no one could notice they had been tampered with. For this he received a pension from the Post Office, which had trouble convincing people that its service was confidential.[35] In his private life, Sir Samuel had a penchant for pretty young wives (who tended to die young) and it is possible that he met Carola in Tunbridge Wells where he had gone with Behn. However, there are many other men who might have been keeping Behn and letting their eyes rove on to new beauties, and, for all his inventiveness, Morland was notoriously impecunious— indeed he had to sell his pension to pay his debts. The Amyntas of Behn's poem, who 'oft has Fetters worn', sounds altogether more solvent and rakish.

A more likely identification is, therefore, Jeffrey Boys, a law student from Gray's Inn and distant relative of Thomas Colepeper. With Algernon Sidney, his father had taken Sir Thomas Colepeper's place as lieutenant of Dover Castle in the Interregnum. Young Boys may have been acquainted with Behn from their shared past in Kent although, unlike Behn's father, his was listed among the 'Nobility and Gentrey' of Kent along with Colepeper's.[36] He was probably now keeping his Kentish connections warm by meeting Thomas Colepeper and other compatriots at the Kentish Club in London. Jeffrey Boys had thrown off some of the cultural traditions of a Parliamentary family and was playing the Restoration gentleman in laced cuffs, ribboned hat, silk stockings and wig of fashionable light hair.[37] That one version of Behn's literary lover Amyntas can be identified with Jeffrey Boys is made plain in a long poem she finished later, some of which may date from this time. Called 'Our Cabal' and associating Amyntas with Je.B, it again tells Cloris to guard her heart against a man who is not free. Neither 'To Mrs Harsenet' nor 'Our Cabal' suggests very deep engagement on Behn's side, but clearly Amyntas has had an amorous effect on the narrator and may have had a financial one as well.

Rather more feeling emerges from another poem that may date from this time, 'On the first discovery of falseness in *Amintas*', in which Behn either transposed her urban misery into a pastoral retreat or was writing again of the miserable time at Tunbridge Wells. Although so gregarious, when miserable she longed for solitude, a place where she could grieve, 'Where no dissembl'd complisance may veil / The griefes with which, my soul, thou art opprest'. The writer was aware that she was not being cunning and was too openly revealing jealousy, that infallible test of love. So she imagined herself fading out as Amintas courted another. Possibly it was Carola again, since the rival seems to be a younger woman: for, as Behn lay in the fallen leaves, she saw 'springing beautyes' on the boughs.[38] Apart from a therapeutic writing of it, the way to combat this sort of melancholy and suspicious mood was through work.

With her interest in poetry and drama, Behn had known of the early opening of the theatre in London and of the King's enthusiasm. Within the palace of Whitehall, the Cockpit had been fitted out even before the royal bedroom—while the coronation robes had gone from Westminster Abbey direct to the theatre. After some quarrelling over patents and power, Killigrew had obtained the King's Company and the playwright and impresario Sir William Davenant, the Duke's; with hindsight, it is comic that they were enjoined to 'Expunge all prophaneness and scurrility' from the old plays performed. These works were divided between the two patent companies and, because it was technically the heir to an old Elizabethan troupe, Killigrew's company had the rights to a good many of the best early dramas, such as those by

Ben Jonson, Shakespeare and Beaumont and Fletcher. The Duke's Company would have to be more aggressive in finding *new* plays.

Both companies had introduced a new sort of stage to the London public, with a backstage, proscenium arch and a platform jutting into the audience. Both provided scenery of backcloth and shutters which allowed 'discoveries' when these shutters were removed. Many of the discoveries were of the alluring female body, for both troupes innovated by allowing women to act on the public stage. Whatever new plays came forward, they would need to take account of all these changes.

Growing up in Kent, Behn had had only a few chances of watching plays. Theatricals in the Interregnum included the notorious production of *Julius Caesar* at Penshurst by Algernon Sidney, to which a large audience had been invited. In Ghent, while swooning over Catholic ritual, she might also have laughed at the itinerant English actors who came to the city and played first at the Town Hall before the councillors and then in rooms in inns or taverns.[39] In London after the Restoration, she would have had opportunities as long as she had money—or charm enough to have herself treated.

Could a woman *write* for the commercial stage? Behn knew that she could when she heard of the staging of a translation of the French dramatist, Corneille, by the poet, Katherine Philips. Philips had been born a decade before Behn into the family of a London Puritan merchant. She had had some education at a girls' school in Hackney, where she made intense friendships with other pupils, which survived her marriage at sixteen to a Parliamentary man much her senior. Over the next years, Katherine Philips remained quietly at home in Cardigan in Wales, writing poetry, ardently Royalist and ardent in friendship. In these verses, she preserved some of the ideals of the court of Charles I's queen, Henrietta Maria, which proclaimed a 'love abstracted from all corporeal gross impressions and sensual Appetite', consisting rather 'in Contemplations and ideas of the Mind, not in carnal Fruition'.[40] When her poems were published, the image which they and Philips (now called 'Orinda') conveyed had considerable influence, for she made the woman poet into a sensitive lady, writing of refined unphysical emotions in clear, elegant English. Praised by such poetic greats as Abraham Cowley, Philips became a modest corrective to the passionate and ambiguous Greek Sappho, the only other widely known female poet before her, and to the much scorned Margaret Cavendish, Duchess of Newcastle, who had published her verses herself and been mocked for her pretension.[41] Philips achieved this feat by accommodating herself to her readers' desires and displaying an elaborate feminine modesty: despite pleasure in publication, she insisted that she 'never writ a Line...with an Intention to have it printed'.

While pursuing a court case and visiting one of her women friends in Ireland after the Restoration, Katherine Philips had translated Corneille's *Death of Pompey*, which, with the help of influential friends, was staged in Dublin in 1663. Subsequently it was printed in London. Later, in February 1668, the London court witnessed a lavish production of a further translation from Corneille, *Horace*. But Philips had not completed this, for she had died of smallpox in 1664 at the age of thirty-three.

As a young married lady living a sheltered respectable life, Katherine Philips would be no real role model for Aphra Behn working for 'Bread' and negotiating the sexuality of the Restoration. Her platonics were not inspiring, although the two women would share some of the pastoral vocabulary and habit of pseudonyms: Behn's Muse was, from the start, more down-to-earth. At the same time, Philips must have been real encouragement to print and Behn must have thought a good deal about the woman with whom all her life she would be compared if praised, and contrasted if denigrated. Already aware of the intermingling of sex and politics, as her recent friendships with George Marten and William Scot showed, she would not wish immediately to write the sort of heroic political play Philips had created from Corneille. Nor did she have the clear status of Philips or the help of influential patrons. Without them, it was not easy to associate with the theatre and retain the modest reputation of 'Orinda'. But perhaps it was unnecessary. In some contexts, Behn's unstable status might be a different kind of asset. So, also, with her experience. To work as a spy and to ascend the social scale, to acquire education informally and through the good will of others, Behn had had to live much on the surface of life, ventriloquising, imitating, and always playing a part. Indeed she may well have concluded that this role-playing was what life was about and that there was only a surface. The theatre displayed surface.

Professionally, it was a good moment for a theatrical début. The two companies were in intense competition and anything from twelve to twenty-five new plays a year were becoming necessary. Thomas Shadwell started just before Behn, William Wycherley and Elkanah Settle about the same time, Edward Ravenscroft, Henry Nevil Payne, and Nathaniel Lee just after. Culturally, however, it was an ambiguous moment. Evelyn had found the playhouse immoral almost from the start and, by 1665, he was very seldom at any time 'going to the publique *Theaters*', claiming they were marked by 'atheisticall liberty, fowle & undecent'.[42] Others had found little risqué in the 1660s when plays were mainly revamped old ones with thumping morals or new ones very much in their mould. As the 1660s closed, however, there was a sense that the court and its shadow, the theatre, were changing. The glamour of Restoration had dimmed with royal penury and losses in war, and the supporters of the Interregnum regimes, the old republicans and Parliamentarians, as well as the poor and unrewarded Cavaliers, felt a malaise. This was often expressed in gendered terms, as when the misanthropical Anthony à Wood described 'A strang effeminate age when men strive to imitate women in their apparell', bedecking themselves in ribbons, scent and breeches like petticoats, while women strived 'to be like men, viz., when they rode on horseback or in coaches weare plush caps like monteros, either full of ribbons or feathers, long periwigs which men use to weare, and riding coats'.[43] According to Gilbert Burnet, the change came about 1668 when 'the court fell into much extravagance in masquerading', frolicking about the town in disguise. Rochester thought the three businesses were now 'Woemen, Polliticks & drinking'.[44]

Sexuality was always a political factor, and the influence or assumed influence of the most notorious of the royal mistresses gave new vigour to the tradition of castrating female power. In the first decade of his reign, Charles had not been outrageously promiscuous, largely confining himself to the voracious Barbara Lady Castlemaine. Then in 1669 Nell Gwyn was installed as mistress and was pregnant by 1670; meanwhile the plump, pretty, baby-faced Louise de Kérouaille, the most expensive and influential of Charles's mistresses, hated agent of the French Louis XIV, was awaiting her public bedding at Lord Arlington's country house in Euston near Thetford. The King's sexual desires were openly more rampant and many nocturnal visitors were conducted up the back stairs to his apartments.

Royal promiscuity in sex was matched by promiscuity in politics. Disheartened by the Dutch War and his inability to control Parliament and gain enough money, the King turned to Louis XIV, who was only too pleased to subsidise his cousin's independence from his people. The duplicitous Treaty of Dover, signed in 1670, whereby the King agreed to reintroduce Catholicism 'as soon as the welfare of his kingdome will permit' in exchange for a handsome subsidy, was known in its murky detail only to a few people, including Arlington. Yet the atmosphere of dissembling was sensed. Marvell declared the times bewitched.

Still on the periphery of events, Behn could not fully experience the corrosive and liberating effect of royal cynicism which blasted through the theatre, allowing plays to grow more bawdy, more sexually exploitative, and also freer to explore the vagaries of sex and gender. Although not yet aware how to capture its texture in words, Behn was intrigued by her society. In common with Rochester and the King himself, she relished scandal and gossip and enjoyed the major genres of the age: libel and satire.

Behn's first concern had to be pay and conditions in the theatre. She saw under what pressure playwrights often had to work if they were true professionals. A play might be demanded in great haste for a particular event or date, giving the writer only a week or two to compose, sometimes even less. Behn believed she had fluency and facility, however, and would not require the luxury of time to deliver. She was fairly confident of her talents, while knowing that self-confidence did not guarantee success. As for pay, it did not seem too low to her. She had not yet come to know Dryden, now Poet Laureate, although she probably met him casually—theatrical society was fairly small—and she certainly knew and greatly admired his work. Dryden was contracted to supply Killigrew with three new plays each year—he rarely managed it—in return for a portion of the company's profits, but no one else could have expected such terms. Some may have received a set amount in return for giving first right of refusal: Elkanah Settle was supposed to have had £50 a year from 1673, as long as he offered his plays to one company. But most playwrights subsisted on the revenue of the third night's performance. This meant that a writer must maximise profits by puffing the play between first and third nights.

Behn was not put off by anything she saw or learnt and she resolved to make the spy Astrea into the playwright Astrea. The pseudonym was a fashionable device, but it also separated the image from some more private self, as it had no doubt done for Orinda. So she would be less vulnerable to the inevitable comments made about a publicly writing woman.

For Aphra Behn, the most important development in the theatre was the arrival of the female body. It was not a neutral or 'natural' body, but a highly sexualised one. A decade of actresses had cemented the initial association of actress and prostitute, which Evelyn had quickly apprehended, and no one could be more aware of this than Behn. The first prologue to a play—*Othello*—known to include an actress on the public stage assumed that men would titter and, astounded by the female body, confuse the woman and the role. Decades later, the satirist Tom Brown summed up the tie of actress and whore from the male perspective: "Tis as hard a matter for a pretty Woman to keep herself honest in a Theatre, as 'tis for an Apothecary to keep his Treacle from the Flies in Hot Weather; for every Libertine in the Audience will be buzzing about her Honey-Pot.' The imagery is characteristic of this sort of comment, but it did not much bother Behn, who could see the commercial possibilities of the tie.

Actresses had to provide part of their costumes themselves. Since everyone knew that they must have acquired their rich garments from admirers and keepers, there would be some amusement when they were worn. Similarly, they might borrow their acting costumes for society occasions, muddying the distinction between life and stage. Men could and did go to the tiring-room to watch actresses dressing, although the King, who had other opportunities for voyeurism himself, tried to stop the practice. Royal disapproval did not prevent Pepys, who went to the tiring-room to be shocked by pretty Nell Gwyn and her bawdy talk.

When she first attended the theatre after her travels, Behn must have been out of touch, not one of the coterie that picked up the scandalous allusions and swipes at rival dramatists. The core of the small audience of under a thousand people consisted of regular theatre-goers, a few hundreds in number, including the courtiers who formed an identifiable group. In the early 1660s, Pepys was already grumbling at the citizenry coming to the theatre and even apprentices, but it was not they who counted. Indeed conduct manuals informed the lower-ranked spectators to watch 'Quality' and applaud only after aristocratic hands had clapped.

With its diverse components, the audience was vibrant, often uncontrollable and smelly—the heat from candles mingled with the odour of unwashed bodies, which even powerful nosegays could not mitigate. In George Etherege's play, *She Wou'd if She Cou'd* (1668), a character describes young sparks rambling 'from one Play-house to the other Play-house, and if they like neither the Play nor the Women, they seldom stay any longer than the combing of their Perriwigs, or a whisper or two with a Friend; and then cock their Caps, and out they strut again'. Gallants 'enjoyed the prettiest creature, just now, in a room behind the scenes' or at least 'toused and moused' naughty ladies, laughed at tragedy, faulted the music and whistled at the songs.[45] As for women, they might go to be seen, as Hannah Woolley described: after making up her face, a lady sends out to find out the name of the play and resolves to see it 'that she may be seen; being in the Pit or Box, she minds not how little she observeth it, as how much to be observed at it'.[46] As Wycherley put it, the theatre was a place where 'Widows and Maydes are exposed'. Meanwhile, the vulgar watched the 'fine Folks': 'men that comb their *Perriwigs*, and women that looking on their little Looking Glasses, did set their *locks* and *Countenances*'. They noted hair and clothes, the physique of the actors, and a saying of the clown, 'but few of the *Vulgar* understand the cheifest Part, the end of the *Play*, the *Soul* and *Plot* of it.'[47]

There were some people who *did* understand, however, the regular spectators who could weigh one play against another because they saw a whole series. This was an easy business when plays had small runs— eight to ten consecutive performances being an exceptional success for a new drama. Many lasted only the necessary three days for the author to have his money from the third night's takings, and few were revived after the initial season. The intimate knowledge of plays allowed barbs across works and among playwrights whose style the audience knew; soon Behn would be picking up such allusions and experiencing a heady sense of belonging. She would then relish the prologues and epilogues that began and ended plays.

These were a peculiar Restoration form, spoken by actors or actresses though written by the playwrights or their friends. They were recited on the forestage in front of the proscenium arch and allowed a special intimacy between actor and audience. Often separated from the play and lengthened and published independently, they could also be a communication between playwright and public, dealing with topical issues in politics and the theatre. Traditionally the prologue railed at groups in the audience, mainly men, although women were also addressed, usually in categories of ladies, citizens (cits) or whores. The tone was bantering, thoroughly aware of the listening men. Often the relationship of men and women imaged that of playwright to audience: the latter would become male, wheedled into being pleased by a play, or spectators would be flirtatious females whom the playwright-lover cannot quite please. Meanwhile, playwrights could be virgins, frightened of the first night's ordeal. Ladies tended to sit more in the boxes and men more in the pit; so arose a fantasy of a senate of ladies and a lower house of men. Pepys concluded that 'the upper bench' of the pit 'next the boxes' was the best place to be: 'I find I do pretty well and have the advantage of seeing and hearing the great people, which may be pleasant when there is good store.'

Epilogues punctured any illusion of realism a play might have created— theatricality was very much the mode. They were often spoken by the actress, to whose sexual peccadilloes they sometimes drew attention, and her charms could be used to plead for the play now over. If the men were not kind and did not applaud, she could threaten to withdraw her services. (The fact that she was sometimes rendering services offstage added piquancy.) She could also draw attention to her physical attributes beyond the part and mock a playwright who had given her a role that ignored them. Some epilogues ridiculed the very play that had just been performed and negatively drew attention to the presumably male play-wright behind the coquettish teasing actress. There was no reason why a female playwright as well as an actress should not try to titillate with her femininity. But it would be a risk if the play were disliked.

It is difficult to assess the effect of women spectators on theatrical fare. From the comments of ladies to gentlemen which she overheard, Aphra Behn understood why it was assumed that women sanitised plays: they objected to indecency and bawdry. But these comments were, she noted, made in a fluttering voice to gentlemen against whom they leaned: were women acting out the natural feminine characteristic of modesty or were they playing a sexual game? What was the mandatory blush that accompanied the comment? Did it indicate real innocence or igno-rance or, more rationally, did it mean that the sexual innuendo had been understood? Was it, in Wycherley's phrase, 'a conscious blush'? Was femininity a mask? Behn was not sure.

The uncertainty was aided by the habit of masking, which had caught on in London in the early 1660s. To keep in fashion, Pepys had bought a mask for his wife and, in 1663, he noted of Lady Falconbridge that, 'when the House begun to fill, she put on her vizard and so kept it on all the play—which is of late become a great fashion among the ladies, which hides their whole face.'[48] Masking was a fashion accessory, not only obscuring tired or over-emotional eyes and other blemishes, but also enhancing the face through mystery. There was much ambiguity in the fashion since it was adopted by whores as well as ladies. Pinchwife in Wycherley's *Country Wife* prefers to let his wife cross dress as a boy rather than wear a mask, since he believes it 'makes people but the more inquisitive...masks have made more cuckolds than the best faces that ever were known'. On the stage, play would be made of the mask as sign at once of modesty and of immodesty. Aphra Behn probably had her mask or vizard: she might even have worn it in witty allusion to what she was about to do and what she had done. Both the spy and the playwright were kinds of masked woman.

During the last months of the decade and into 1670, Aphra Behn must have haunted the theatre, both the Duke's and the King's, seeing the old plays of Ben Jonson, Fletcher and Shakespeare, as well as new ones by Etherege, Shadwell and Dryden. She would have known of further plays through announcements in earlier ones and through bills stuck on walls near the theatre or distributed directly to potential spectators. These bills gave the name of the work but not the author; since he or she was so much part of the production and the actors so much part of the final creation, there was no reason to puff one over the other.

To see a play, Behn would have set out in the afternoon with or without company, to be in her seat by about 3.30 when the play was put on. This afternoon performance allowed as much natural light as possible through the windows to supplement the candles. Given her recent money troubles, she probably paid half a crown and sat in the mixed seating in the pit, so scandalous to foreigners, on one of the backless benches with the 'sparks', 'fops', fashionable men of wit, some ladies, courtesans and the more expensive prostitutes touting for business. If she had a paying escort, she might have been in one of the boxes forming a U round the pit, where seats cost four shillings.[49] Having arrived early, she could pay a person to sit and save her seat while she went out for a few minutes or she could stay put, eat an orange bought from an orange-seller, and banter with the men. Then the curtain rose and the play began.[50]

CHAPTER 11

❧

Theatrical Début: *The Forc'd Marriage*

'The Poetess too, they say, has Spies abroad'

In January 1669 Walter Aston entertained his young cousin, Elizabeth Cottington, from the country. After explaining in a letter to her uncle that 'Wee are in expectatin still of Mr Draidens play,' Elizabeth announced:

> Ther is a bowld woman hath oferd one: my cosen Aston can give you a better account of her then I can. Some verses I have seen which ar not ill; that is commentation enouf: she will thnk so too, I believe, when it comes upon the stage. I shall tremble for the poor woman exposed among the critticks. She stands need to be strongly fortified agenst them.

Elizabeth could not banish the woman from her head and, in her post-script, added: 'I can not but tell you, I think my self more bowld then the wooman I have named, when I wright to you. For yr sensure is to me what all is to her.'[1]

While not referring to her, Miss Cottington's apprehension was appropriate for Aphra Behn as she determined to present her work on the stage. One needed to be thick-skinned for public display: the female playwright could combine the opprobrium felt for the professional writer with the scorn directed at the oldest female profession, and she could quickly be seen as a new-fangled whore. Or she could simply be regarded as absurd, 'A woman write a Play! Out upon it, out upon it, for it cannot be good, besides you say she is a lady, which is the likelyer to make the Play worse, a woman and a Lady to write a Play; fye, fye.'[2]

In her period of intense theatre-going, Behn made new, play-writing friends, but few could have been women. Katherine Philips was dead. Frances Boothby, to whom Elizabeth Cottington had been referring, had put on *Marcelia* to little acclaim and then, along with the shadowy Elizabeth Polwhele who wrote *The Faithful Virgins*, died or simply disappeared. If, as seems unlikely—the idea comes from a probable error of Samuel Pepys—Margaret Cavendish *had* written the play performed under her husband's name in 1667, she did not repeat the experiment; she held back from trying to get her acknowledged plays revised, made theatrical and performable with the help of a jobbing playwright, as she might have done. Perhaps she was reluctant to compete with a husband, who, after her first excursion alone into print in the early 1650s, had been publicly supportive of her unprecedented publishing. Or perhaps she was deterred by comments of a theatre manager, however obsequiously ventured: the accusation she quoted, that her plays were too serious and had no plots, sounds like a *theatrical* judgement.[3] For one reason or another, Behn had no female fellows.

Inevitably, the playwrights Behn came to know were men, highly educated ones, some with titles and many related to each other and connected closely to the court. As a woman without formal training Behn was therefore unusual in sex and status. With her propensity to admire the well-born and her special respect for the Howards, she was pleased to meet the arrogant, touchy Edward Howard, son of the first Earl of Berkshire and brother-in-law of Dryden. Mocked for having literary ambitions beyond his talents, he had been labelled 'Poet Ninny' by the new playwright at the Duke's, Thomas Shadwell.[4] Behn was probably more intimate with Edward Ravenscroft, a young gentleman of the Middle Temple who was hanging round the theatre wanting to make his mark. The two got on well and helped each other—although, inevitably, it was said that *he* helped *her*.[5]

In such company, Behn pondered the purpose of plays. In his 1671 preface to *Evening's Love*, Dryden claimed that audience reaction was no test of dramatic worth; pandering to public humour left him embarrassed. 'I confess I have given too much to the people in [the play], and am ashamed for them as well as for myself, that I have pleased them at so cheap a rate.' Such posturing annoyed Behn, who wondered what a play was for if not to please. She was even more irritated by the pronouncements of Shadwell, who, in his preface to *The Sullen Lovers* (1668), claimed that all dramatists should imitate the learned (and misogynous) Ben Jonson, 'he being the onely person that appears to me to have made perfect Representations of Humane Life'; Jonson was to Shadwell 'the man, of all the World, I most passionately admire for his Excellency in Drammatick Poetry'. Despite her friend Howard's admiration and despite the useful play some of her eulogists could make on her two names of Behn and Johnson, Behn was far from thinking Jonson perfection, either in his humour plays or in his insistence on rules in drama.[6] At this stage in her life she greatly preferred Shakespeare, of whose lack of learning much was made—to her great comfort.[7]

Behn was also heartened by the boast of another playwright, Thomas Randolph, who declared, 'I speak the language of the people.'[8] For play-writing she needed knowledge not of the classics but of society. It was no doubt irritating that women could not frequent coffee houses like men, but perhaps this was no great loss. In Thomas Sydserff's *Tarugo's Wiles: or, the Coffee-House. A Comedy*, coffee vapour mounts to men's heads, turning them into politicians and critics. In the midst of the discourse, a woman enters to drag out her husband, complaining he has left her to run their bakery and look after the children; coffee houses should be called the 'Prating-houses', she declares. In 'The Women's Petition against Coffee' (1674), the drink makes men unfruitful—it is a 'Ninny-broth' and 'Turkey-gruel'. True, news sheets were distributed or sold at coffee houses, but nothing prevented Behn from sending a servant to pick them up. In any case, she could sit in taverns and drink her bottle with whomever she wished, hear the gossip, and learn the intonation of the rake and fop.

Killigrew may have wanted to do something for his old colleague, but perhaps both he and Behn were wary of further collaboration. Also his company at the King's had the bulk of the old plays to perform and had less need of new ones than its rival, the Duke's. Possibly, then, Killigrew introduced Behn to Thomas Betterton, the manager of the Duke's, thus missing the opportunity of employing one of the most skilled and prolific playwrights of the era. Presumably Behn was unafraid of Betterton's reputation: as a lampoon put it, 'being cheif, each playing Drab to swive / He takes it as his Just Prerogative'.

Sir William Davenant had been the original theatre manager of the Duke's Company. His connections with the old pre-Interregnum theatre being stronger than Killigrew's, he had made sure these were known by encouraging the rumour that he was Shakespeare's natural son. Davenant remembered the dramatic ways of acting at the Blackfriars Company and, since he was a masterly teacher, his influence on his troupe was great. He died in 1668, leaving it to the management of his widow as guardian for their young son. Mary Lady Davenant was now the ruler of the Company at Lincoln's Inn Fields, and this fact may initially have attracted Behn to it. Under her, the actors Thomas Betterton and Henry Harris actually managed the day-to-day operations of the theatre, with some help in stage-managing from John Downes, the prompter. Downes wrote out the individual parts in each new play, along with the cues for the actors to learn; then he controlled and ordered rehearsals with his bell and whistle.

The actors of the Duke's Company had to be versatile. Harris himself was a singer, possibly a scene painter, a stage manager and an actor— he also had several places at court such as Engraver of Seals and Yeoman in the Revels Office. As well as managing the theatre, the 'brawny' and uneducated Betterton acted constantly, establishing the major tragic roles of Shakespeare on the new stage. He presided over a troupe that included his wife Mary, an accomplished actress of Shakespearean tragic roles and a good teacher, although never as famous as her husband; the rumbunctious William Smith, who, like Betterton, had been playing since the reopening of the theatre; Mary Lee, who had just joined the company, full of potential though none as yet knew for what; and, above all, the comic actors, James Nokes, Edward Angel, and Cave Underhill.

The later critic and actor, Colley Cibber, rhapsodised about Nokes (known to lampooners as 'Buggering Nokes' and famed for pursuit of 'smock fac'd lads' with 'gentle Bums'[9]): 'his general Excellence may be comprehended in one Article, viz a plain and palpable Simplicity of Nature.' Nokes could provoke laughter simply by appearing gravely on the stage, and many playwrights such as Dryden wrote parts directly for him.[10] Indeed Dryden's success was once rudely explained as due to 'old *Nokes* that humours it so well', for the audience 'bravely Clap the *Actor* not the Act'.[11] Nokes often played with Angel, who specialised in low comedy and farce, and Dryden called the pair together 'the best Comedians of the Age'. Meanwhile, Davenant named Underhill, who played lugubrious rustics, 'the truest Comedian in his Company'. According to Cibber he gave to the stiff and stupid 'the exactest and most expressive colours, and in some of them look'd as if it were not in the power of human passions to alter a feature of him....[He was] the most lumpish, moping mortal that ever made beholders merry.'[12]

What the Duke's Company lacked was a gifted comic woman. Nell Gwyn, whom the King's Company was about to lose, had formed the 'gay couple' with her first lover, Charles Hart, a spirited and witty pair who avoided sentiment and caught the exciting hostility of sex as they bargained over terms. Their roots were in Shakespeare's *Much Ado About Nothing*, with Beatrice and Benedick, but the pair predominated only in the Restoration. In young George Etherege, the Duke's Company had a playwright to do justice to the roles, but their possible actress, Moll

Davis, had been removed from the stage to the King's bed some time before Nell followed a similar route.

It was customary to bring a play to the theatre with some sort of reference.[13] Behn probably had three plays in draft, the early *Young King* and two new ones, *The Forc'd Marriage* and *The Amorous Prince*. She may have tried them all out on theatrical friends, perhaps Ravenscroft, who had not yet staged a play himself, or, more likely, Howard or Killigrew, who could have presented the chosen one, *The Forc'd Marriage*. The first reading was crucial; Behn hoped desperately that Betterton was in a receptive mood.

All three plays were in the mode of tragicomedy, as popular in the 1660s with Dryden as in the Jacobean era with Beaumont and Fletcher. Tragicomedy was an odd segmented form, in which melodrama was followed by romance. Suitably, it was a Royalist genre, since it fed off the political drama of the death of Charles I, followed by the restoration of his son:

> Our King return'd, and banish'd Peace restor'd,
> The Muse ran mad to see her exil'd Lord;
> On the crack'd Stage the Bedlam Heroes roar'd,
> And scarce could speak one reasonable Word...[14]

Increasingly aware that it was the going, not the coming style, Behn wrote in this mode. She was wary of the comedians, irritated by their tendency to intrude their developed stage characters into whatever they acted and to extend their fooling tiresomely. So she had not had them much in mind when she wrote her first plays.

The story of *The Forc'd Marriage* was not complicated but, like other dramas of the time, it had multiple pairings. There were mistakes and night encounters but little intrigue in the play, which was rather lacking in tension. Yet the sex struggle was there in embryo, and a shrewd reader might have discerned Behn's future preoccupation.

In *The Forc'd Marriage*, an old king rewards a young warrior, Alcippus, with the hand of the beautiful Erminia, who is privately betrothed to his son, Prince Phillander. Erminia refuses consummation and, maddened by jealousy, Alcippus tries to strangle her, leaving her for dead. (The influence of *Othello* was here so strong that Behn even gave the option of suffocating in the first printed edition of the play.) Still alive, however— for this is tragicomedy not tragedy—Erminia disguises herself as a ghost in a plot to persuade Alcippus that he is penitent, that he will be less violent, and that he really loves the tolerant princess Galatea, who loves him and whom he rather ungraciously comes to accept. The old king is happy to agree to whatever the headstrong young people want and soon all correct couples are joined. The theme of forced marriage outwitted, both a conventional concern and an idiosyncratic obsession, will run throughout Behn's dramatic career. It provided alternatives to the single legal marriage supported by parental power, which so many of her audience had complacently experienced. In the later plays, consummation might occur in the unwanted marriage to complicate the issue but, in the earlier one, it is not countenanced.

The instability of heroic romance within tragicomedy is caught in the character of Phillander, who postures like the heroes of the French dramatist, Corneille, laboriously deciding whether to kill themselves or their rivals, betray a woman or the state. Part of the absurdity is that the heroics are all in words. The martial drama has happened before the play begins, and the scene of the hectoring is the bedroom rather than the battlefield; despite a movement towards spectacle, this was still very much an oral theatre. The most compelling male lead is the strange Alcippus, who, like Erminia herself, at times seems to desire the abasement of the royal pair, Phillander and Galatea, on whom he feeds. He represents bullying male force, which his friend Pisaro constantly begs him to control, as if he were a mad bear who would destroy himself if let loose.

As for the women characters, they function both as simple pawns of war and as the main subjectivity of the play. Erminia, whose beauty, we learn, has caused the whole family to be raised in status, has a high sense of her 'Quality', and there is some tart dialogue between her and the elevated princess whose beloved has just chosen Erminia. Princess Galatea has her admirers, but all of them, including Erminia herself, agree that the greatest beauty is Erminia. Thus, when Galatea reminds her proud friend of what she was before Phillander's love raised her, Erminia points Galatea towards her beloved's passion for another. In other scenes, Erminia seems to relish her influence over the two powerful young men, while routinely lamenting the confusion she has caused. Yet she *does* share with all the women the sense of sexual warfare and, after her enforced wedding to Alcippus, she imagines the pastoral world which Behn's female characters would so frequently fantasise. This is a realm of softness, gentleness and love, without the noise of masculine jealousy and pride or the male ideologies of honour and courage.

Perhaps the strangest aspect of *The Forc'd Marriage* is the political.

Considering that the disasters result from an arbitrary decree and the exaggerated advancement of favourites, the play might have been used to assault autocratic rule of the sort the Stuarts approved. There is no suggestion of this, however, and the patriarchal power simply becomes paternal and puts all right. The old king, who needs to be a tyrant to prevent anyone speaking out at the start of the play, appears in the last act as a kindly father figure, eager to leave his children happy, however far down the social scale they wish to marry.[15] Although the play turns on patriarchal monarchical power, however, it fails to embody it satisfactorily. The kingdom in which the proud Erminia and Alcippus exist can have no very great hope of peace. There is even mention of the envy of the soldiers for the much rewarded Alcippus, suggesting that Behn was already aware of the dangers of men promoted too far or favoured too hugely at the expense of legitimate privilege and power. Alcippus is blustery and rude to his prince, a man whom he has thoroughly wronged. It is rather startling then when, towards the end, the old king pronounces good Stuart doctrine, saying of his son to Alcippus: 'Who dares gaze on him with irreverend eye? / ...all his evills 'tis the Gods must punish, / Who made no Laws for Princes.'[16]

There may be one or two precise if coded political allusions in *The Forc'd Marriage*. To the embarrassment of her father, the fury of the old queen Henrietta Maria, and the dismay of most of the court, Clarendon's daughter Anne had persuaded the King that her impregnation by the Duke of York, heir to the throne, should result in marriage. Behn may have intended a *frisson* in the audience with a play that closed with two royals marrying two commoners. In her play such unions are desirable if their common elements are worthy or beautiful; so Behn might have been trying for a compliment to the Duke of York and his wife. As for Lord Arlington, still chief minister of state, she cannot have harboured pleasant feelings towards him. In her play, the cowardly Falatius tries to persuade his doubting friends that he has been in the wars by wearing patches on his face. Could she have hazarded a dig at the man who had left her so coldly in the lurch, by jesting at the display of his Civil War wound?

Behn was not eager to put her own life and personality on the stage, but the minor character, the wild Aminta of 'fickle humour', is the nearest she came to the witty, comic heroine and perhaps to a self-portrait. Aware of the constructed nature of femininity and romance, Aminta advises the lovelorn Princess not to die but to scheme for what she wants—or, in the absence of male constancy, to appreciate a brisk young husband.[17] Her own taste is singular: as Falatius declares, '*Aminta*

/ Is a wit, and your Wits care not how ill-favour'd / Their men be'. Love comes, is pleasant while it lasts, and then declines; characteristically Aminta expresses her philosophy in verse:

> *I will not purchase slavery*
> *At such a dangerous rate.*
> *But glory at my liberty,*
> *And laugh at love and fate.*[18]

Since Aminta was a name Behn often took for self-images in her pastoral poetry, she may, through the character, have expressed something of her post-Antwerp feelings about love and its perversities, as well as her dissatisfaction with her Amyntases, including Jeffrey Boys.

The waiting must have been as tense as anything Aphra Behn had experienced. But, when he saw her again, Betterton told her he approved *The Forc'd Marriage* and would proceed. The drinks for her sponsors and friends that evening, for Ravenscroft, Howard and perhaps some of the Colepeper relatives, would only be the first of the expenses Behn would incur in her career. But money on entertaining and good cheer was never wasted. She enjoyed an evening of drink and talk, but she also knew it was the only way theatrical business was transacted.

Betterton always retained the right to ask for major alterations even at the stage of rehearsal, although as both actor and theatre manager, he was eager to keep the playwright as a partner. He declared it his practice 'to consult e'en the most indifferent Poet in any Part [he had] thought fit to accept of'.[19] Behn made no mention of changes to *The Forc'd Marriage*, but Shadwell, whose dramatic career got under way just before hers, 'was forc'd...to blot out the main design' of *The Humorists* before it could be acted, and Dryden claimed of one play that Betterton had 'judiciously lopt' it.[20] In such a milieu it was not possible to become snobbish about authorship: plays came from a social communion as much as from an individual head.

After the excitement of acceptance the real work began. The weeks spent in the audience were a necessary prelude, for the playwright had input in the choice of actors and needed to know the members of the company intimately, their talents and faults. Mostly Behn used seasoned players for her début: Betterton himself as the hectoring Alcippus, with his wife as Erminia—indeed she may have tailored the parts to the couple: Mrs Jennings, coming to the end of her acting career as Galatea, and the comic Angel as Falatius 'a Phantastick Courtier', but without Nokes to encourage his foolery. The small part of Olinda provided the début for Mary Lee, who would go on to far greater things, though, as a primarily tragic actress, she was never a major inspiration for Behn. By 1670 the majority of the actors in the Duke's Company had worked together for some years and they often irritated authors by insisting on knowing how things should be done. No doubt they had considerable influence on the prompt copy which was now made, laying out scenes and effects, and instructions for actors.

At rehearsals the author was frequently in charge of the actors. How far this would be true of Behn as a novice and a woman is difficult to gauge, but she must have played some part, although not always directly. Perhaps the copious stage directions in printed versions of her plays, indicating gestures and attitudes for the characters, as well as locations, to some extent compensated for her not being present to rehearse stage hands and actors.[21] In the next century, when *The Female Tatler* commented on the duties of a playwright, it was after Aphra Behn had dominated the stage for twenty years; there the intending female dramatist is warned 'that no woman ever turned poetess but lost her reputation by appearing at rehearsals, and conversing with Imoinda [a character originally created by Behn in *Oroonoko*]…[the] treatment authors meet with from the players is too gross for a woman to bear.'[22]

Just before the staging, a prologue and epilogue would be written either by Behn herself or by a friend. On this occasion the prologue must have been concocted to amuse those in the know, perhaps by Behn and Ravenscroft together. Seemingly escaping the control of the playwright, the actor creates the author as a new kind of potent female and, pointing to the whores and masked ladies in the audience, suggests both are spies or secret agents for the female playwright. A sense of slightly threatening feminine collectivity is created: 'The Poetess too, they say, has Spies abroad.' Jealousy becomes like a 'cunning Spy [which] brought in intelligence / From every eye less wary than it's own'. (Did any in the audience know the author's past or guess it from persistent mention of spies within the play? The prowling Pisaro grows 'wiser…by observation' and 'the King has many spies about the Prince', an unusual detail between father and son.) The actress who follows to conclude the prologue denies the female collectivity, however, as well as the stratagems it implies; she firmly separates the playwright and actress from the whore and reduces women from agents and manipulators to sexualised bodies with amorous power but no threat—since these bodies exist only 'to pleasure you'. The epilogue, spoken by 'a Woman', continues this gender reassertion, by giving wit to men and beauty to women. Female political agency is seductive, not assertive.

Despite this apparent obeisance to stereotypes, Behn (or her friend) is subtly innovative in prologue and epilogue. There is no pathetic appeal from a feeble woman to her audience: by now, Behn knew how much pathos depended on the erotic female form. Also, despite wit's resting with men, a witty seduction by a female is planned and expected. The image of the female playwright contrasts with that created much later in the dedication to *The Young King*, where Behn called herself or her play a 'Dowdy Lass'. She had learned that such conventional feminine modesty was not seductive within the theatre.

The Forc'd Marriage, or The Jealous Bridegroom: A Tragi-Comedy opened the season of the Duke's Company on Tuesday, 20 September 1670. There was excitement behind and in front of the proscenium arch, but in one breast there was more than usual first-night nerves. Behn had come to know a youth of nineteen, who shared her admiration for Shakespeare. His name was Thomas Otway and he was the son of a country rector and, although he was disorganised, rather feckless, and not very cleanly in his habits, she had warmed to him. He had been at Oxford for a time but had left, possibly beause the death of his father had halted his flow of money. Before that he had been at Winchester where, like Behn, he had felt what it was to be near a class of people to which he himself did not belong. Now he was stage-struck and, in a rash moment excited by her own power in the matter, Behn followed her feelings and gave in to his pleas to have a small part in her play. He was to be the old King, an odd choice for a youth; perhaps it was the only small role still on offer or perhaps the regular actor, Westwood, was unwell. It did not seem a great risk, for the King was silent through all the middle acts, but he did have an important function in opening the play.

Otway was a highly-strung young man, the extent of whose nervousness Behn did not anticipate. As she waited to see the effect of her first staged play on what she saw, with both trepidation and joy, was a full house, her own tension must have been heightened by awareness of Otway's mounting hysteria. She was used by now to actors' nerves, however, and like many people who have withstood difficult moments themselves, she probably presumed that the young man would manage at the crucial time to control himself; indeed the anxiety might well contribute to the conviction of the playing. With such ideas she must have argued against the evidence of Otway's sweating body and agonised moans.

In the event he could control nothing. The prompter, John Downes, completes the story: 'he being not us'd to the Stage; the full House put him to...a Sweat and Tremendous Agony'. He was, added Downes laconically, 'spoilt...for an Actor'.[23] (That Downes rescued this incident from oblivion was perhaps because he remembered his own début in the summer of 1661, when he too was 'spoilt...for an Actor' by the sight of the King and Duke of York seated in the royal box at the première of *The Siege of Rhodes*. On that occasion he played a eunuch so disastrously that he was hissed off the stage, and his prompting career began.)

As for Otway, he retained Behn's friendship despite this fiasco, but he never again tried to act. He went on his unkempt way, until, with his own play, *Don Carlos*, a few years later, he had so great a success that even he felt the need to clean and tidy himself up. Or, as a satire of the time put it: 'Don Carlos his Pockets so amply has fill'd / That his mange was quite curd, and his lice were all kill'd.'[24] Yet, despite his later writing success, his one stage appearance still haunted him and his acquaintances, for, in the same poem, he was not chosen as the greatest poet by Apollo because he 'had seen his face on the stage'. Behn no doubt also remembered the incident.

When she watched her play, she felt she had some reason to be pleased. Her couplets were ragged in places but surprisingly powerful and she approved her attempts at rhyming across speeches in the French manner. The music of the King's composer, John Banister, complemented the words and was well liked, a little ditty about Amintas and Silvia using the echo motif being especially popular. The stagecraft was competent, too, though Behn sensed she was not using all the resources available, happily so according to some of the elderly who deplored the theatrical changes as detracting from the words. At the beginning of Act II, she made quite an effective tableau of marriage, which alerted the audience to the lines of desire connecting the various mismatched lovers, and she conveyed, as she had intended, the power of state ceremony. Her scenes of discovery worked: the audience was slightly shocked to see Erminia in undress, so momentarily wondering if the improper marriage had been consummated. She saw as well where she might have done more: in the final act she had simply left reported speech to carry events that could have been enacted.

Behn watched anxiously the 'fop corner', where critics and beaux in fashionable blond wigs sat and talked, often loudly, to the more prosperous prostitutes in masks. She had learnt by now the power of ridicule, the effect of a shouted witticism from a self-regarding spectator. She desperately hoped no one would joke tonight or declare his half-crown admission wasted. She need not have feared. According to Downes, Behn's play was a good one and it had a good run for a first effort, 'lasting all of six Days'. It was taken off for the staging of 'a greater, *The Tempest*'.

Given this happy reception, Behn may have expected ample reward; if so she would have been disappointed. Every stage of putting on a play was expensive. In the anonymous *Comparison between the Two Stages* (1702), a would-be playwright describes the process. He began by entertaining ten or so judges to a tavern dinner, after which all except himself and a friend disappeared, leaving him with a bill of £2. Another £2 went on licensing the play with the Master of Revels—a process Behn too had undergone, although, with some exceptions such as the luckless Edward Howard's *The Change of Crownes*, suppressed because it satirised the sale of government offices, this was largely an expensive formality in these years.[25] Then the actors had to be treated to keep them rehearsing; otherwise they lost interest. Together with their coach hire and wine, this cost nearly £10. When the play was performed, the author had more expenses: gloves, chocolate, snuff and presents. Then came the third day and, with a good house, the author totted up the takings, subtracted house charges, and anticipated a reward of about £70.[26] He got £15. Looking into the matter, he discovered he had lost one half of the takings 'by the roguery of the Doorkeepers, and others concern'd in the receipt'.

After her death, the editor of Behn's posthumous play, *The Younger Brother*, Charles Gildon, wrote about the iniquities of theatrical payment in the Restoration, and complained that, while actors and managers made considerable profits from playwrights, Otway, Lee, and Dryden got little in their turn: 'Otway had but a hundred pounds a piece for his *Orphan* and *Venice Preserv'd*, tho' the players, reckoning down to this time, have got no less than twenty thousand pounds by them.'[27]

Behn may have made between £15 and £25 for *The Forc'd Marriage*, not a lot but enough to persuade her to continue play-writing. With it she could support herself and a few servants. There was no further mention of a brother, still living when she went to Antwerp. From now onwards, Behn appeared before the public as Astrea, a woman without male protection of father, brother or husband.[28]

CHAPTER 12

✣

The Amorous Prince and *Covent Garden Drolery*

'I have a thousand little Stratagems / In my Head'

...as 'tis my interest to please my audiences, so 'tis my ambition to
be read: that I am sure is the more lasting and the nobler design:
for the propriety of thoughts and words, which are the hidden beauties of a play, are but confusedly judged in the vehemence of action:
all things are there beheld as in a hasty motion, where the objects
only glide before the eye and disappear...those very words and
thoughts, which cannot be changed, but for the worse, must of necessity escape our transient view upon the theatre.

So wrote Dryden and Behn agreed.[1] Not for her Betterton's casual
attitude to literary ownership; she was eager to get her play into
print. She also wanted the fee: after the Restoration, playwrights could
dispose of their plays instead of finding them owned by the theatrical
companies as in the past, and publication was a useful if not substantial
source of income.[2]

As a woman, Behn might have felt the stigma of print, remembering
Lady Mary Wroth's experience of abuse, Katherine Philips's outrage
at finding herself piratically published, and a general male attitude that
women should have nothing to do with the Muses. Dorothy Osborne
had remarked of the publishing Cavendish, 'Sure the poor woman is
a little distracted, she could never be so ridiculous else as to venture at
writing books and in verse too. If I could not sleep this fortnight I
should not come to that,' and she later added, 'there are certain things
that custom has made almost of absolute necessity, and reputation I
take to be one of those.'[3] (It was as well that she remained unaware
that many of the romances in which she delighted had in fact been
written by Madeleine de Scudéry rather than her brother Georges,
under whose name they had been published.) Evidently Behn was
unmoved by such attitudes.

Several playwrights never made it into print, but almost all of Behn's plays were published, a considerable achievement.[4] The first, *The Forc'd Marriage*, came out with James Magnes, a predominantly literary publisher who also worked with Dryden. Behn and he were to continue their association until 1679 when Magnes died; then she was taken on by others of his family and by his partner Richard Bentley.[5] Together Magnes and Bentley formed her longest collaboration, appearing individually on her first and final published works. When she had secured Magnes, Behn either sent round the original unmodified version of her play, a modified one, or the theatre's copy, a prompt book, which could be returned after printing. Then, as a written text, the play had to pass the censor.

The notion that language had been debased by the endless quarrels of the Civil War and needed purifying allowed censorship of books and pamphlets to return after the Restoration, although it was somewhat relaxed around the early 1670s. Theoretically, all books had to be licensed by a Secretary of State, the Archbishop of Canterbury, the Bishop of London or a Vice Chancellor of Oxford or Cambridge; in reality 'seditious' authors continued to publish through various stratagems or circulate work in manuscript. Behn's play was innocuous enough and must have passed without comment.

Since prestige and patronage might be gained with a dedicatee, Behn considered the option. She had not yet courage to approach a suitable nobleman, however, whatever her imagined audacity in distant Surinam. So her first published play came unpartnered and she was left to face the incivilities of 'this loose Age' alone.[6] She added only the playful French tag, 'Va mon enfant, prend ta fortune.'

Printed quickly to take advantage of the publicity of performance, *The Forc'd Marriage* was a careless job, probably abandoned to more than one compositor.[7] The epilogue was placed next to the prologue in the beginning of the volume and the latter was squashed into two pages by changing the type size halfway through the second page. The page numbering was often awry. Typographical errors like upside down letters abounded. Characters were variously named. Nothing else of Behn's printed in her lifetime would arrive quite so shoddily on to the public scene.[8] Unlike many of her fellows, she would in time realise the power of print and try to look after her texts as she looked after her productions, but, as yet, she did not have the confidence and authority to insist on stop-press changes.

* * *

By the time Behn saw *The Forc'd Marriage* in print, her main care was for her next 'child', her second performed work, *The Amorous Prince, Or The Curious Husband*. It was already in rehearsal at the end of the year and it was staged in the beginning of the next, in 1671, only five months after her first play.

The Amorous Prince must have been written early since, like older works, it relies more on costume and disguise than on staging. In some touches it seems later than *The Forc'd Marriage*, however: although no sexual activity occurs on the stage, it is an oddly sexy play for a woman author to own. It is hard to imagine that Behn could have opened her very first work with a scene of two lovers whose undress indicates sexual activity and whose dialogue declares it extra-marital, or that she would have presented so easy an acceptance of homosexual or paedophiliac desire: a pretty plump white boy would ruin the market for women, one character points out.

When Gerard Langbaine was compiling his list of Restoration plagiarists in the 1690s, he was flattering to 'Mrs Astraea Behn', whose many plagiarisms he put down to haste. *The Amorous Prince* was the first of her plays to be noted, the subplot being based on an episode called 'The Curious Impertinent' from Cervantes' *Don Quixote*.[9] Behn was fascinated by Spanish intrigue plots and rigid misogynous Spanish or Italian society, which she tended to see as essentially comic material. The contemptuous fascination with Mediterranean culture had been inherited from the Elizabethan and Jacobean dramatists who had used the South for revenge plays and as a cover for comment on English matters. Behn's setting allowed her to exaggerate the social distinction of the sexes and point to the absurdity of cloistering women from the world and then expecting morals higher than those in men. The point was as true for England as for Southern Europe, despite Englishmen's complacency about the freedom of their women.

In Cervantes, a man asks his best friend to test the fidelity of his wife; the trial backfires and all ends tragically. Behn converts this ending into an absurd orgy of marriages. There need be no tragedy because the tested woman, Clarina, is knowing and does not fall. The threatening maid of Cervantes' story is replaced by a sister-in-law and a maid, both assiduously husband-hunting, and they enter spiritedly into the intrigue, so that the trio easily outwits the husband, Antonio, and his friends. Although the plotting of women had been in Cervantes, Behn greatly expands the motif. As one woman says,

...I have a thousand little stratagems
In my head, which give me as many hopes:
This unlucky restraint upon our Sex,
Makes us all cunning.[10]

The need for female virtue to be bolstered by cleverness is also stressed in the other plot, in which young Cloris is the victim of the male obsession with female sexuality: men think to control this aspect of women by raising girls in complete sexual and social ignorance. But, when such girls are exposed to marauding men, tragedy or near tragedy follows, for they mistakenly believe they can hold rakish gentlemen in their rankless, feminine realm.

Easily seduced by the amorous Prince Frederick, poor Cloris is rescued by other women and her own realisation that she must learn to scheme. She is even persuaded to cross-dress—although she regards this transvestism more as transgression than opportunity. None the less, she cannot avoid noticing that she arouses interest in men when dressed as a boy and her education in the fluidity of gender has begun. In the epilogue which she speaks, Cloris touches on the female predicament, declaring herself saved simply because 'the Prince was kind at last.' In the comic allusion to her creator, she claims her fall was 'want of art, not virtue' and she blames this on the author. Yet, all the author has done is allow Cloris to express 'simple nature'. Behn's belief in natural gender seems to have been dented since she created the naturally feminine Cleomena.

Like its predecessor, *The Amorous Prince* has divergent political messages. Prince Frederick embodies the Stuart doctrine of the divinity of kings, in which the king is responsible to God alone. Articulated by James I, the conception had survived the execution of Charles I and was held discreetly by Charles II and overtly by his less flexible and duplicitous brother James. But, since Frederick was also a rake who must be reformed, reverence was coupled with criticism of royal gallantry, which might just have arisen from Behn's irritation with a king who had abandoned her penniless, whilst wasting the nation's substance on expensive mistresses. Nearest to Frederick's pursuit of his friend's lady was Charles's public pursuit of the beautiful Frances Stewart, who incensed her monarch by refusing his overtures and eloping with the Duke of Richmond. The King responded with something like the amazed rage of Frederick in the face of sexual rejection.

In Behn's play, the figure of Frederick, like that of Orsames in *The Young King*, is disturbing in its abuse of power and hereditary privilege—Frederick is supposed to be a Duke's son but no father appears and, for most of the time, he acts as absolute monarch. A prince ruled by sex becomes a danger to his subjects, and, whatever his initial good qualities, turns injudicious and intemperate. The amours of Frederick even provoke a normally faithful subject to plot his death.

It is this sense of the arbitrariness of rank and power, far more than Antonio's trial of his wife, which makes the play a tragicomedy. Curtius, the abused friend of the prince, sounds decidedly republican as he muses on royal authority:

> —And he who injures me, has power to do so;
> —But why, where lies this Power about this Man?
> Is it his Charmes of Beauty, or of Wit?
> Or that great Name he has acquir'd in War?
> Is it the Majesty, that holy something
> That guards the Person of this Demi-god?

With this reproach goes a contrast between a dissembling courtier and an honest countryman. As times changed and Behn with them, these were the sorts of political statement she no longer felt inclined to make in public.

The prologue was the usual mixture of petition and seduction, rallying the audience for its confused desire for flattery and satire, regulated theatre and farce. Since *The Forc'd Marriage* was separated from *The Amorous Prince* only by a few months, Behn could still declare herself a novice and allude to the novelty of her sex. Yet she now had the assurance of a theatrical insider and she made in-jokes about the comedians, Nokes and Angel, and the broad-brimmed, cartwheel hat worn by tiny Nell Gwyn in one of her last acting appearances at the première of Dryden's *Conquest of Granada* in the rival theatre. Only those in the know recognised the allusion and were aware that the hat was parodying one worn by Nokes; he had been caricaturing the French entourage of Charles II's sister, Henriette, on her visit to England.

Behn also showed herself much aware of her form: she was on the side of the 'natural' not of the regulated playwrights. This division, sometimes expressed as the contrast of Ancients and Moderns, pitted those who believed that plays should be regulated by classical rules and by what she later called the 'learned Cant of Action, Time and Place' (the demand that a play have a single tone and take place in a single location and during one day), and those who could regard their works, in the prologue's words, as 'Th'imperfect issue of a lukewarm Brain', not 'serious, nor yet comick'. She joined the mockery of 'Grave *Dons*, who love no Play / But what is regular', despising 'Farce and Droll'.

The Amorous Prince still had many elements of the old theatre. The masque, so much a feature of Charles I's court drama and more recently used by Dryden, was employed here to unravel plot, not for the audience but for the actors. It was a device for which Behn never lost her fondness. In addition, there were too many asides and some of the verse was so irregular that later editors suspected it to be prose.[11] Yet, although the play had some old-fashioned facets and awkward parts, it had few longueurs, and it displayed the quick pace for which Behn was becoming known.

It was speedily printed, this time for Thomas Dring, possibly collaborating with Magnes as J.M., although the carelessness of *The Forc'd Marriage* may have caused a temporary breach with Magnes. Edward Howard, whose publisher Dring was, probably made the introduction. The result was a better job than the first play, but not perfect.[12]

The Forc'd Marriage was staged again on 9 January and Jeffrey Boys was in the audience. Clearly Behn and he were still close friends, perhaps sharing evenings after the tavern or outings in Hyde Park. Probably they went to the theatre together and took the rare opportunity of visiting the Continental puppets, which could teach Behn how much timing was the essence of good slapstick and how versatile slapstick could be. Together they survived the hot June when audiences forsook the stuffy theatre and the court left town. In the beginning of July, when Behn had a copy of her second play in her hands, she sent her boy with it to Jeffrey Boys. He probably dashed off one of those gallant notes that convention demanded.

If Behn had any complacency about her dramatic achievements she was jolted out of it by a wicked burlesque called *The Rehearsal*. This was ascribed to the witty politician, playwright and critic, the Duke of Buckingham, with the help of several other theatre-goers including the cleric and scientist, Thomas Sprat, whom Behn may have known by this time. Although, in Evelyn's words, it was 'buffooning all Plays', it was primarily aimed at Dryden, called here Mr Bays, mocked for his heroic drama and tragicomedy. It also ridiculed lesser writers, including Aphra Behn—probably seen as connected with Dryden because of her association with his brother-in-law, Edward Howard. It was gleeful over the more ludicrous moments in *The Forc'd Marriage*, such as the scene where the overwrought Prince Phillander is grimly serenading his beloved but married Erminia outside the bedroom. It also mocked the echo song—mockery Behn ignored since she later reprinted it in her collection of poems—as well as the funeral scene for the living Erminia: in *The Rehearsal* the dead Lardella's coffin is opened 'and a Banquet is discover'd'. Buckingham may have had the huffing and puffing Alcippus partly in mind, as well as Dryden's Almanzor from *The Conquest of Granada*, when he made his hero declaim: 'I huff, I strut, look big and stare; / And all this I can do, because I dare.'

More than *The Forc'd Marriage*, *The Amorous Prince* was ridiculed for pretentiousness, its use of 'in a cloud' to mean 'veiled'. It was also mocked for its scene in which, according to the 'key' to *The Rehearsal*, 'you will find all the chief Commands and Directions are given in Whispers': Mr Bays was made to begin his play with similar whispers. In Act V the mockery of Behn's copious and narrative stage directions grew even more wicked: Behn had the despairing Cloris leap into the river and be taken for dead: *The Rehearsal* rendered this:

> *The Argument of the Fifth Act.*
> *Cloris*, at length, being sensible of Prince *Pretty-mans* passion, consents to marry him; but, just as they are going to Church, Prince *Pretty-man* meeting, by chance, with old *Joan* the Chandlers widdow, and remembring it was she that first brought him acquainted with *Cloris*: out of a high point of honour, breaks off his match with *Cloris*, and marries old *Joan*. Upon which, *Cloris*, in despair, drowns her self: and Prince *Pretty-man*, discontentedly, walkes by the River side.[13]

When the epilogue to *The Rehearsal* begged that 'this prodigious way of writing cease', it must have given Behn some pause and perhaps decided her not to risk *The Young King* at this moment. Although she had declared *The Amorous Prince* a comedy in her prologue, she was aware it was a tragicomedy of the sort that made people 'laugh at Tragedy and cry with comedy' as *The Rehearsal* put it. Clearly fashion had moved from her practice.[14]

She was probably not devastated by the mockery. It was something to have been satirised in so famous a play as *The Rehearsal*; one might have felt worse by being left out. Besides, Behn was not the first female playwright to be ridiculed: the respectable Katherine Philips had been burlesqued for her *Pompey* by Davenant in his *Play-house To Be Lett* in 1663. Probably the publicity helped rather than hindered sales.

Far more upset by mockery was her friend Edward Howard, whose play, *The Six Days Adventure, or the New Utopia*, produced in the same season as Behn's *Amorous Prince*, had been thoroughly trounced by the critics. Although she disliked the influence of Ben Jonson, on whose plays Howard's was partly based, Behn was interested in Howard's fantasies of strong women ruling and fighting. The women were tamed at the end of the play, as Cleomena would be in Behn's *Young King*, so as not to disrupt the social order, but they were not destroyed, and they made some telling feminist points against male misogyny.

Howard blamed everyone but himself that his play was, in the witty Earl of Dorset's words, 'Laugh'd at by box, pit, gallery, nay stage'. Howard faulted the actors; then he suspected concerted malice in the audience, some cabal of the influential Earls of Rochester and Dorset.[15] Finally he blamed the vogue for 'Drums, Trumpets, Battels', by which he probably meant Dryden's *Conquest of Granada* and other heroic tragedies. To get his own back, he wrote a preface designed to irritate Dryden and Dorset. It was overkill: twenty-four pages with Latin quotations on the qualities of good drama, contemptuously dismissing farce and eulogising the comedies of Ben Jonson. Drama was serious and must delight and correct; comedy was for 'the reformation of Fopps and Knaves'. Since he himself would quit the stage, the advice was presumably for others. Howard did not rest here, but supplied poetic testimonials for his play from his friends, 'several persons of ingenuity, and worth... impartial and knowing apprehensions'. The first of these ingenious people was Aphra Behn, the next Ravenscroft.

Commendatory verse was usually paid for and it was wise to pick up a few pounds where one could. There was, however, much in Behn's poem that suggested more than a commission—something of a warning and pep talk for any writer, including herself. Howard should, Behn counselled, rise above the abuse. Other now-famous authors had been unpopular too: the ancient poets 'found small applause' and 'still were poor', and even Ben Jonson in his time displeased the public. Like these illustrious forebears, Howard would probably have to wait for 'Ages more refin'd' to esteem him at his true worth. This warning was especially apt for a well-connected playwright who might not be rich but did not have Behn's own desperate need for money.

For the purpose of the poem, Behn decided to accept Howard's estimate of 'mighty *Ben*' although she could not bring herself to see audience reform as the purpose of drama. So she associated Howard and Jonson in their supposed effect on the stage: bringing crude and rude farce to 'Comick order'. Indeed, in the customary fulsome rhetoric with which poets addressed each other, she saw Jonson and even Thomas More, author of the original fantasy *Utopia*, being surpassed by Edward Howard:

> This *New Utopia* rais'd by thee
> Shall stand a Structure to be wonder'd at,
> And men shall say this! this is he
> Who that Poetick City did create,
> Of which *Moor* only did the Model draw.
> You did compleat that little world, and gave it Law.

It is an interesting convention. Both Behn and Howard knew by now that the play had failed, and yet one could give and the other gratefully receive overblown and hyperbolic rhetoric having almost no connection with their shared reality.

At the same time Behn pointed out that no amount of justifying would change public opinion: 'Dull souls' could not be brought to sense 'By Satyre' any more than the stage could be reformed by 'wholesome precepts'. There was no point in writing to revenge oneself on 'the multitude, / Whose ignorance only make them rude'. If one were sucked into disputing with critics, there was an end to art. Behn's advice was to ignore them and get on with writing:

> Write on, and let not after Ages say
> The *Whistle*, and rude *Hiss* could lay,
> Thy mighty Sprite of Poetry,
> Which but the Fools and guilty fly;
> Who dare not in thy Mirror see,
> Their own deformitie.[16]

More persuasively, she argued that 'Silence will like submission show / And give advantage to the foe.'

Behn's poem was in the 'pindaric' mode, a form of public praise made popular by the poet Abraham Cowley before the Restoration. With Waller, Cowley was one of Behn's poetic models, for, following her age, she had turned from the obscure and rough metaphysical writers like John Donne to embrace the smooth Cavaliers, whose flowery, pastoral and courtly works she found invitingly erotic. Cowley had treated the Greek poet Pindar 'cavalierly' and he made direct imitation seem pedantic, associated with Puritans. The free pindaric was a useful form for the unlearned Behn, who was excited by its combination of poetic liberty and authority, as well as by its ability to express anything from desire to grief.

Yet, although the Pindaric was not a strict form for anyone, Behn's use of it was castigated. In *The Battle of the Books* (1697) Swift imagined a contest between Behn ('*Afra the Amazon* light of foot') and Pindar himself in which, as one might expect, Behn was thoroughly routed, while the editor of *The Muses Mercury*, when he reprinted the poem to Howard in the early eighteenth century, airily declared: 'The Reader will perceive, that Mrs. Behn had no Notion of a Pindarick Poem, any farther than it consisted of irregular Numbers, and sav'd the Writer the Trouble of even Measure; which indeed is all our common Pindarick Poets know of the Matter.' Had she been alive to read this comment, Behn would have recognised the common elitist abuse to which her sex and lack of education exposed her and against which her pep talk could have functioned.

Only partly pleased with her response, Howard replied in a rather confused poem.[17] Although he declared Behn's wit gave him fame, he also suggested that wit needed luck more than skill. Perhaps he expressed some ill-concealed resentment at his friend's greater theatrical success, a success that, Howard implied, she needed more than he. He also seemed slightly stung by her notion that he might be stopped from writing by public disfavour. If he had offered such a view, he had now forgotten it.

Having backed up her colleague, Behn returned to her own career. She had produced her two plays, was holding back on the third, and now needed time to create others. So she may have approached Killigrew again for some suggestion on how to augment her income while she worked. One or both came up with the idea of compiling a theatrical anthology, which would consist primarily of unpublished songs, prologues and epilogues from plays of the King's Company, given or sold to Behn by Killigrew. (No one thought twice of lifting songs from *published* works for, as a character in Behn's later play, *Sir Patient Fancy*, remarked concerning the search for a poem, ''tis but rummaging the Play-Books, stealing thence is lawful Prize'.) Since the King's Theatre had just burnt down and the company was in financial difficulties, the volume might have had some benefit for Killigrew as well, not least as part of an advertising campaign for his troupe and its plays. The volume needed a catchy title; one of them hit on *The Covent Garden Drolery*, 'Written by the refin'd Witts of the Age'.[18]

In the Interregnum, the form of the 'drolery', a fashionable collection of light verse, had occasionally been used for protest: Cromwell had ordered the *Choice Drollery* of 1656 to be burnt. So, after the Restoration, the term had a good Royalist ring, as well as a touch of naughtiness. Covent Garden, a London square like an Italian piazza, had been fashionable at least from the 1630s, when plays described the gentry and aristocracy mingling there. More importantly it was, in the 1670s, the theatrical area and most of the pieces were theatrical, fourteen out of the original seventy-five coming from John Dryden.

If Killigrew collaborated with Behn, he did not want his name on the work: it might displease the King and irritate the authors. Perhaps Behn too did not want more than her anonymous initials on a collection which included several salacious poems. These came from the King's Company's all-female productions, where Killigrew, who had at first resisted the introduction of female players, used the titillating device of putting the shapelier women into breeches. In Dryden's prologue to *The Maiden Queen*, printed in *Covent Garden Drolery*, men were expected to lust after the actresses in drag, while women were assured that they had all male advantages except one. In the epilogue spoken by Mrs Reeves, reputed to be Dryden's mistress, actresses boasted that they could be 'To the Men Women, to the Women Men' and that 'In Dream's both Sexes may their passions ease...'. The smuttiest prologue and epilogue Behn used were to Killigrew's own *Parson's Wedding*: here it was declared that the theatre, even of Shakespeare and Jonson, had always been lubricious:

> When boys play'd women's parts, you'd think the Stage,
> Was innocent in that untempting Age.
> No: for your amorous Fathers then, like you,
> Amongst those Boys had play-house Misses too:
> They set those bearded Beauties on their laps,
> Men gave 'em Kisses, and the Ladies Claps.

So the theatre had better be turned there and then into a brothel. Another saucy piece came from Dryden's *Marriage A-la-Mode* in which the aroused woman, foreseeing her lover's premature ejaculation, slows him down until she cries 'Now dye my *Alexis*, and I will dye too.' When the lovers wish to repeat the success, the imbalance returns: 'The Nymph di'd more quick, and the shepherd more slow.' Behn also included chaste fare, such as the prologue to Katherine Philips's unfinished *Horace*, spoken at court—perhaps a tribute to Philips or perhaps simply an opportunistic taking of a free poem, the writer of which was dead.

Behn's use of so much salacious material suggests that her own fairly innocuous early plays were somewhat behind her present taste. The collection in general breathed of easy morals—tolerant copulation without pregnancy and much disease, though there was reference to the fiery pox—and it celebrated the Restoration mania for masquerade and disguise. The few political poems assured the reader that the compiler was a firm supporter of the King, an enemy to 'Fanaticks', and those who killed in defence of law.

By now Behn herself was a known poet, with her manuscripts circulating to friends, and she included four of her own works in *Covent Garden Drolery*. She did not, however, use the verses already published in her plays: again this suggests she may not have wanted to make publicly clear her involvement. One of the four included poems proved immensely versatile. A description of love-making in the pastoral world, it was used by Behn repeatedly, with variously sexed protagonists and different seductive inflections:

> I led my *Silvia* to a Grove,
> Where all the Boughs did shade us
> The Sun it self, though it had strove
> It could not have betray'd us.
> The place secur'd from humane eyes
> No other fear alows,
> But when the Winds do gently rise;
> And kiss the yeilding Boughs.
>
> Down there we sate upon the Moss,
> And did begin to play,
> A thousand wanton tricks to pass,
> The heat of all the day.
> And many kisses I did give,
> And she returned the same,
> Which made her willing to receive;
> That which I dare not name.
>
> My greedy eyes no ayds requir'd,
> To tell their amorous Tale,

On her that was already fir'd:
'Twas easie to prevail.
I did but kiss and claspe her round,
[Whilst] they my thoughts exprest,
And laid her gently on the ground:
Oh! who can guess the rest.[19]

After Aphra Behn's death, the dubious *Muses Mercury* reprinted this poem, claiming it was from a manuscript. At the end the editor wrote: 'As Amorous as these Verses may be thought, they have been reduc'd to bring them within the Rules of Decency, which all Writers ought to observe, so instead of a Diversion they will become a Nuisance.' Since there is nothing indecent in the earlier versions, this seems journalistic puffing to make the verses appear more scandalous in a less frank age.

In fact 'I led my *Silvia* to a Grove', like Behn's other slight songs, was conventional enough, the sort of mildly risqué pastoral ditty being written by a host of literate men and women. In his *Essay on Poetry*, the Earl of Mulgrave described the form as a song with 'expression easy, and the fancy high', formally perfect and informal in style. The danger was that it could become insipid. Parodically Etherege summed up much of the sentiment: 'How charming Phyllis is! how fair! / Ah, that she were as willing…'.[20]

The *Covent Garden Drolery* came out in 1672 from James Magnes. It was a success and inspired a Bristol imitation, the editor of which advised his muse 'Humbly to cast herself on Madam *Bhen*.' In his play *The Country Wife*, Wycherley included it in the choice of reading-matter for his unsophisticated country heroine, Margery Pinchwife.

Behn and Dryden were of the new breed of men and women of letters. Before them authors had been aristocrats, actors or court officials, or they had had some other source of income or function. In this generation, however, a few began to make a living solely from writing. Such authors had to be flexible and write in whatever genre was required or fashionable. Most began in the theatre, the most lucrative place, and thus they gained a sense of audience at the outset. They also relied on patronage, but, so far, Behn had showed that this was not essential.

Later in the century, when Behn's and Dryden's careers had indelibly made their mark, a character in *A Comparison between Two Stages* grumbled:

I am an Enemy to those mercenary Scriblers who get their Bread
by [writing]: I have always thought it a pity that the *Muses* shou'd
be prostituted to every wretched Fellow, that because he lies in a
Garret, fancies himself on the top of *Parnassus*; 'Twas never any
where thus but in *England*. The *Greek* and *Latin* Poets were Men of
Figure in their Country, of Wealth and Reputation; ours, for the
most part, the Dregs of the People; some of 'em bred at School upon
publick Charity; who proving Rebellious to their Parents and Masters,
escape from their Discipline, and for a shift betake themselves to this
Trade: No wonder Poetry lies under such a scandal, to such a degree,
that it's become proverbial to say—*As poor as a Poet*—when indeed
some of 'em were Beggars before they began, and their cursed Poetry
serves but to keep 'em poorer.

To which another replied, 'the Trade of Play-writing is now (as we say)
one of *Jack's* last Shifts.'

It was not an uncommon view. Behn herself was caught in this
rhetoric, which even Dryden could not escape. As a woman she was of
course more vulnerable, for, as a typical disgruntled critic of *A Comparison
between Two Stages* exclaimed, 'What a Pox have Women to do with the
Muses? I grant you the Poets call the Nine Muses by the names of
Women, but why so? not because the Sex has anything to do with Poetry,
but because in that Sex they're much fitter for prostitutes.'[21] But it was
the vulgarity of writing itself that was most often attacked, and, if
Dryden was not quite seen as prostituting himself like Behn, he was
found pimping for his 'Young, plump and Buxsome' Muse, whom he
made into a '*Hackney-Whore*' for vile-Pence...*Against the Laws* of Art'.[22]

Whatever the scoffing élite might think, however, Aphra Behn knew
her writing to have been quite popular and this was its most salient
attribute. With two successful plays and an anthology under her belt,
she could pride herself on having launched her career. The money she
had earned, somewhat diminished by payment of debts, could procure
her the kind of wardrobe that allowed her to mix with people of 'Quality'
in the town and on the periphery of the court, and afford the chairs,
hackney coaches and link boys needed to keep herself fine. Her society
may have been a little louche like her poetry, but so was a large proportion of the court.

CHAPTER 13

❧

The Dutch Lover and Theatrical Conflict

'delicious whoring, drinking and fighting'

In the 1670s London was being rebuilt fast, although selfish competing interests prevented it from conforming to any one conception. Emphasising the need to rid the town of 'horrid smoke', Evelyn had imagined public buildings by the side of the river, while Christopher Wren visualised them fronting wide streets. The King ordered new houses to be of brick and stone, to have drainage pipes on the sides and to have flat facades. Some people complied, some did not. St James's Park was transformed for public use, part of it being drained, and a pattern of ornamental water and avenues in the French manner imposed. On the new lake there was skating—or 'sliding'. The Duke of York was especially adept. The Fire had emphasised the trend, also influenced by the court at Westminster, of fashion's moving westward. In the narrow dirty streets of the walled City, coaches could not easily be manoeuvred, but, in the growing West End, fashionable equipages could be seen to advantage in the wider streets. Entrepreneurs made vast fortunes through land speculation in the new suburbs, while sellers prospered by following their customers. London Bridge and the New Exchange in the Strand, consisting of about a hundred small shops on ground and upper floors, were the main attractions for trade to remain east at all.

As long as Behn had money, her domestic needs could easily be met in or near the old City. She could get her maid to buy food from street markets or barrows and she herself could obtain what she needed on London Bridge or hunt and haggle for cloth and accessories in the New Exchange. She could browse in book shops on the lower floor or go to Paternoster Row, where publishers had re-established themselves after being horribly decimated by the Fire (they had sought to save their wares by depositing them in old St Paul's, in the event the greatest bonfire of all). Unbound sheets were set out on tables and Behn could choose which she wanted to be bound or, more economically, read them in the shop to see if they were worth the considerable purchase price. As a good customer, she was probably able to borrow sheets and use shops rather like lending libraries.

If she could work partly by candlelight, Behn would have been free much of the day, breakfasting on cheese and toast, often softened in a mug of ale either in her lodgings or in a tavern. These taverns were usually converted private houses and consisted of several small rooms where friends could assemble. They were open all day and a patron could expect food or drink at whatever time it was wished. For lunch she could have meat: pigeon, mutton steak, or Westphalian ham. A fancy meal could cost as much as two guineas, but, at a lesser inn or 'ordinary', she could get a reasonable dinner for 3d. Probably she attended the expensive eating establishment called Lockets only when treated.

In the capital, Behn's social life flourished. Believing that politics and sex were not distinct, she caught her shifting, amorous society in a poem called 'Our Cabal' after the governing political group around Lord Arlington. In pastoral mode, always an easier literary realm for a woman to enter and describe than the coarse, violent, urban one of so much male verse, the poem described a sunny picnic to celebrate the newly restored May Day. Music played, bagpipes blew and the crowd talked and danced. As in her secret letters, Behn hid her friends, this time under pseudonyms. Some may be guessed, but not yet 'Urania' and 'Alexis'. Urania was dressed in white, adorned with spring flowers, her black curling hair blowing seductively in the wind; her beau was diffident and foppish: 'The price of Flocks h'has made a Prey / To th'Usual Vanity of this day.' (Behn was not commonly worried about the economic costs of display; so the young man must have had more than usual on his back.) As hidden now are 'Martillo' and 'Phyllis', glossed by contemporaries as Edward Butler and Ms Masters. If this was the Mr Butler who had threatened Behn with prison, it suggests how necessary it was in the small society of London to control feeling and superficially observe good manners. Perhaps she would need his services again.

Then there were the unattached young men, John Cooper, yearning to be a writer, whom Behn flattered by addressing as 'My dear Brother'. Later he became a translator and may have helped her with Latin. He was so young he still declared he despised sex, but his frank demeanour and lack of concern to impress, his vivacity and verve in throwing himself into any pastime of dancing, singing or playing, made him attractive. He already had many conquests. As had 'Ed.Bed.', possibly Edward Bedingfeild, a fellow Gray's Inn lawyer to whom Hoyle left £50 in his will.[1] His conquests tended to be men. Erotic feeling between men had always been a part of the pastoral world and, as her plays showed, Behn had little problem with it. She always found androgynous people especially seductive: 'A softer Youth was never seen, / His Beauty Maid; but Man, his Mein.' Ed. Bed. was dressed fashionably but less foppishly than 'Alexis'.

Among the young women was 'Amoret', sighing for N.V. Amoret may be the teenaged Elizabeth Barry who would become the most celebrated actress of her age. Already Behn had come to admire her forceful character, although Barry still had the acting craft to learn. She had a background almost as obscure as Behn's and the same habits of secrecy. The famously unreliable Edmund Curll later did for her what the memoirist did for Behn: gave her respectable antecedents, declaring her father a Cavalier barrister and colonel who ruined himself in the royal cause. Others, however, claimed that she had been a servant in Norfolk. Whatever her provenance, Barry was a quick and clever girl; she had come into the care of Lady Davenant, who had educated her and introduced her to society. Davenant himself was said to have tried and failed to train her for the stage. If so, and if her birth date is correct at 1658, then she would have been branded a failure before the age of ten (Davenant died in 1668). The date may be wrong however: by the time Barry was famous enough for anyone to care about it, she had reason to falsify it, like Behn with hers.[2]

On this particular May Day, Elizabeth Barry (if it were she) was apparently unhappy because she loved someone whose 'Amorous Heat was laid' and she was feeling both lovelorn and angry. Her young man might have been the pale Nick Vernatty, an acquaintance of Jeffrey Boys, something of a Don Juan figure despite his shyness. He had the unnerving habit of sympathising with those he harmed, declaring he had not expected them to love him. He must have had an uncomfortable time with the glowering Amoret.

The most interesting couple of the group should have been Behn herself and Jeffrey Boys, 'Amyntas', seductive in body and mind, 'Author of my Sighs and Flame', to whom Behn revealed her love with every glance. Although Amyntas had 'Majesty above his years' and the androgynous qualities of sweetness, wit and vigour, combined with a 'lovely Shape', he did not dominate the poem. This was left to Lycidas or Lysidas, the learned and tough lawyer John Hoyle, to whom Jeffrey Boys may have introduced Behn, since both were at Gray's Inn.[3]

Hoyle was the son of a Parliamentarian alderman from Yorkshire who had been so distressed by Charles I's execution that he hanged himself on the first anniversary of the event.[4] The son had become the sort of ex-Puritan that, in Burnet's words, had embraced the Restoration 'by going into the stream, and laughing at all religion'. In politics, however, he was reputed still to be a republican. In 'Our Cabal', Hoyle was an arrogant dark man with fierce black eyes, who trifled with women. Unlike the other men in the group, he was silent, and his taciturnity was curiously alluring. Not boasting of his amorous success, he indicated it with his self-confidence and contempt. He enjoyed power over others and himself, feeling it weakness to show response to or interest in anyone else's feelings. That Hoyle's disdain for women was connected with his homosexual desires was made clear in the poem, for it was on Hoyle that the young 'Ed. Bed.' bestowed his love; Hoyle 'pays his Tenderness again, / Too Amorous for a Swain to a Swain'. The amorous looks between the two men made a circle of desire which attracted voyeurs.[5]

Periods of carefree enjoyment of urban living must have been short for Behn. Her writing breathes of pleasure and anxiety, each with its distinct time, for she considered that it was Puritans or Dissenters who poisoned their days with agonising over the past and future. Being highly gregarious and garrulous, Behn threw herself into the delights of the present as if there were no tomorrow. When tomorrow came, she stirred herself and wrote furiously, so that she could procure another short period of ease. It was a see-sawing sort of existence that seems to have suited her temperament, if not perhaps her health. A perennial anxiety was money, for Behn was never financially secure, her expenditure frequently outstripping her earnings. On one occasion Jeffrey Boys declared that he gave 'astrea 5s for a Guiny if she live half a year'. Perhaps she was ill and he thought she might not last six months. Perhaps, since the words come from his account book, he records a bit of exor-bitant usury, whereby, for the loan of an immediate five shillings, Behn was to return over four times the amount in six months' time. It was presumably some while ago since she had needed 'keeping' by any man. The transaction might have been a step in a process of disengagement. Jeffrey Boys sinks out of Behn's amorous life.[6]

He was not replaced at once, although she may have suffered pretenders, each perhaps a little worried about addressing an emanci-pated theatrical woman who seemed to want the freedoms of a man within the sexual game, while needing the homage due to the feminine woman. Probably she refused to understand that few men could accept such a being. One uneasy man, whom she herself admired for a time, was hidden as Lysander in 'To *Lysander*, on some Verses he writ, and asking more for his Heart than 'twas worth'. He was apparently a married man since his other lady is Behn's 'happy licenc'd Thief' and he had offered intimacy far too cautiously:

> Take back that Heart, you with such Caution give,
>   Take the fond valu'd Trifle back;
> I hate Love-Merchants that a Trade wou'd drive;
>   And meanly cunning Bargains make.[7]

Like other men later, he was critical of Behn for assuming a masculine demeanour and freedom, but she protested: 'Be just, my lovely *Swain*, and do not take / Freedoms you'll not to me allow.' If they tried a relationship, they should do so 'upon the honest Square'. Probably Lysander failed the challenge.

Out of necessity, Behn began another play, this time for the grand, new, purpose-built theatre at Dorset Garden, into which Betterton and Harris had, after much preparation, just moved the Duke's Company.[8] How should she write for this exciting location? While she had been composing heroic tragicomedies in the late 1660s, Etherege and Dryden had been putting on frolicking plays which included libertines and sceptical witty couples. Indeed she had used their epilogues and prologues in her *Covent Garden Drolery*. With their libertine views, the plays were thoroughly of the town and in the tone of court culture, presenting rakish men both exploitative of and attractive to women, men so witty that by the end of the play the audience is satisfied to see them catch the rich virginal prize. The tendency to infidelity for which the 'amorous prince' had been so severely reprimanded was not punished and the rake's final marriage was not prefaced by repentance. Should Behn move in this direction?

Another new mode was influenced by the French dramatist, Molière, himself influenced by Italian *commedia dell'arte*, with its stock characters, stylised acting, improvisation, and transformation. Behn's friend Ravenscroft had adopted the mode, and his *Citizen Turn'd Gentleman* was an enormous success, pleasing both King and court. His *Careless Lovers* became an equal hit and much impressed Aphra Behn with its picture of the brisk young girl engaging the rake. In Ravenscroft's play, the former announces that women are no longer 'poor sneaking sheepish Creatures' for, 'in this Age, we know our own strength, and have wit enough to make use of our Talents'. If chaste, the heroine is 'a little waggish' in thoughts and, should a husband not suit, she resolves to 'swear my self a Virgin, and consequently, Sue a Divorce against him for Impotency'. The proviso scene, in which a couple bargain over behaviour rather than the conventional money and property, includes a demand for complete sexual liberty after marriage for both partners.[9]

Unlike the anxious Edward Howard, Ravenscroft accepted the easy mockery of playwrights. Like Behn he composed quickly, being irritated at those who made a fetish of writing and saw it as more than the trade he felt it to be. He was secure in his status of gentleman and confident enough to approach a 'Person of Quality' for a dedicatee. Behn noted the swagger with which he declared his impertinent address excusable in 'them that Write for *Bread*, and Live by *Dedications*, and *Third-Dayes*'. Like Howard, Ravenscroft had the easy confidence to let off theatrical steam by addressing the reader directly in his printed text.

Behn had experienced the elation of pleasing an audience, enjoying the crowd's laughter and rapt involvement with her creation. In her new play, she wanted to follow Ravenscroft and please more, but he was not yet her model and change was not sudden. Although she had exhausted much of her early material, she was still attached to the form of tragi-comedy. She always accepted Dryden as the foremost dramatist of her time and his play, *Marriage A-la-Mode*, pointed a way forwards to a combination of her old heroic and romantic mode with modern rakish intrigue, not using the second as comic relief or subplot, but rather keeping the two equal. Perhaps she might be even more successful than Dryden in connecting the disparate elements, by allowing her rake hero to enter both strands.

In addition to her artistic aims, Behn required her new play to exploit a political moment. In March 1672, the Third Dutch War had broken out between England and Holland. Various wrongs were cited, including the treatment of English planters after the ceding of Surinam, but many regarded the war as absurd. To encourage this opinion and detach England from French interest, William of Orange, now the power in Holland since the assassination of De Witt, used spies and agents, smuggled in pamphlets, and sponsored propaganda such as *England's Appeal*, which tried to whip up fear of Catholics from outside and within. There was a need to counter the effort, and the King urged Dryden to write *Amboyna* with an 'English heart' concerning the old Dutch massacre. Behn had no love for the Dutch who, apart from any unkindness on her Antwerp mission, stood for what she most deplored in society: mercenariness, acquisitiveness and vulgarity. A comic and cloddish

Dutchman might do well on the stage. So she created Haunce, a typical English country bumpkin marked as usual by his lack of metropolitan delicacy; decorated with anti-Dutch prejudice, he could also express the national contempt for the mercantile and unromantic enemy.

Behn had probably written part of *The Dutch Lover* before seeing *The Rehearsal*, since two of her characters are snatched away when young in the manner mocked in Buckingham's play, while Silvio, the change-ling, blusters through a Jacobean plot of incestuous passion, his story at times fitting awkwardly with that of the modish lover Alonzo, who speaks the bantering language of Etherege, Ravenscroft, and Dryden in worldly mode. In much the same way, Cleonte and Clarinda, who continue the innocence as ignorance theme of Cloris in *The Amorous Prince*, contrast with the sprightly Euphemia, who has long since conquered such naiveté.

Set in Madrid, the story, like that of *The Amorous Prince*, drew on Spanish prose: a collection of linked and embedded short stories by Francisco de Quintana called *The History of Don Fenise* (1651). Behn amalgamated several of these so intricately it suggests she worked from memory of something read in her youth. In one strand a man out of revenge seduces a woman and turns her into a courtesan. In another, the brother going to kill his fallen sister, meets a lady who persuades him to marry her to outwit a 'beastly' suitor; in the last, a bastard tries to kill the real son of the family. It was unpromising material for a comedy, except that Behn had the idea of making the beastly suitor into her comic Dutchman.

The play turns on much mistaking of veiled ladies in the dark and of armed gentlemen entering the wrong houses, as the over-protected daughters of Spain take to the streets to throw themselves on the aston-ished but always gallant Alonzo, a Flemish colonel of unknown parentage who draws the plots together. Thus, despite his sudden promise of marriage to the veiled Euphemia, Alonzo finds himself in a compro-mising position with Clarinda, which, since she turns out to be his sister, he happily fails to exploit. The opposite good fortune attends Silvio, who learns that his father is in fact the great Spanish minister, Count d'Olivarez: thus he and his seeming sister Cleonte can now indulge their passion with propriety: 'I must own a joy greater than is fit for a virgin to express,' says Cleonte, who, earlier on, had provoked fury in her lover when he had mistakenly thought her returning his passion. Less easy to resolve is the predicament of Hippolyta. Having been seduced by Antonio and placed against her knowledge in a brothel, she grows tired of playing the victim, assumes male dress and intends to fight and kill Antonio in a duel. In male attire she tries to suppress her residual femininity, destroy 'the feeble woman', and assume masculine qualities. Men and women are still psychologically distinct in this play then, but, more than in *The Young King*, the distinction is social rather than biological. (Since a cross-dressed woman can only become a *young* man and a pretty young man is almost as much a sex object to older men as a beautiful woman, transvestism is not a manoeuvre of great use to the serious heroine. It will, however, become a suitable ploy for the sprightly one with too sure an identity as a woman to begin to believe she can take on a man's role.) After the fight, Antonio proposes to compensate for his sadistic treatment of Hippolyta by marriage, transforming the woman he had humiliated as a whore into his wife.[10] Only a dance and comic masque, in which everyone, even the 'beastly' Haunce, gets coupled, can end such a play.

Despite her flirting with tragic themes, Behn was here allowing space for the rational and ridiculous: she avoided the magical in the Spanish source—an enchantress dwindles into a single reference to a beautiful woman as a 'fair Inchantress'—and some of what might earlier have become courtly discourse becomes brisk badinage. Probably it was from Dryden, but more from the satirical *The Rehearsal*, that Behn learnt to present and undercut simultaneously:

> ALONZO:...Her veil fell off and she appeare'd to me,
>   Like unexpected day, from out a cloud;
>   The lost benighted traveller
>   Sees not th'approach of the next mornings sun
>   With more transported joy
>   Than I this ravishing and unknown beauty.
> LOVIS: Hey day! What stuffs here?[11]

Behn's most successful element is her new depiction of the rake, Alonzo, the 'brisk young Lover', to match the pert girl, a minor character in her earlier plays. Alonzo is captivated, but declares no constancy, prepared to take adventures and couplings where he can. Unlike Behn's former heroes, he desires 'Sweets' of love without the ceremonious ties of marriage. There may be a hint of morality in the fact that, had he been successful on his second adventure, he would have committed incest, but, if so, it is slight. Alonzo's closeness to the Cavalier exile, that most romantic of figures, coming like Killigrew's hero, Thomaso, from a time before the sordid money-grubbing present, is marked when he calls himself 'a Wanderer'.

The brisk heroine, Euphemia, anticipates Behn's later ones in responding to control with cunning, but she cannot take the 'Sweets' without marriage; this remains an option only for men. Yet her *desire* for them attracts the rake: claiming he has seen the world and can allow women freedoms forbidden in Spain, Alonzo is cajoled into matrimony through her trick, but he enjoys the joke and humorously threatens:

> What shall I come to? all on the sudden to leave delicious whoring, drinking and fighting, and be condemned to a dull honest Wife. Well, if it be my ill fortune, may this curse light on thee that has brought me to't: may I love thee even after we are married to that troublesome degree, that I may grow most damnable jealous of thee, and keep thee from the Sight of all mankind, but thy own natural husband, that so thou mayst be depriv'd of the greatest pleasure of this life, the blessing of change.

To which Euphemia reasonably replies, 'would you have the conscience to tye me to harder conditions than I would you?'[12]

Behn was excited about the new theatre in Dorset Garden and intended to use it fully for her new complicated play. Meetings set in the dark would remain tricky, since both stage and auditorium were brightly lit, with hoops of candles in chandeliers hanging above the forestage and footlights of candles or lamps flickering at the edge. Some might be extinguished but real darkness took too much bustle to create. So a 'dark' scene had to persuade spectators that actors in full view of them and each other were in fact in pitch-blackness. Other scenes might be easier, now that more shutters could probably be opened and closed to create multiple locations on the single deeper stage. Behn liked the sense of people walking along streets and being followed; this she could now enact.[13]

Despite the instability and creakiness of *The Dutch Lover*, Behn knew her play was better than anything she had yet presented, close to Dryden's successful *Marriage A-la-Mode* and even improving on it in the interweaving of disparate sections. Her friends, probably Ravenscroft, Otway and possibly Wycherley, had read and listened to it before she gave it to Betterton, and their response had been encouraging. Much depended on the performance, however. Appreciating the popularity of the Duke's Company comics, she had written the farcical parts of Haunce and his cash-keeper Gload to exploit their talents. The roles were potentially very funny, but the actions needed to be slick, and the confusion between Alonzo and Haunce maintained by careful attention to costume and gesture. The part of Haunce might have been intended for Angel whom she knew as a crowd-puller since she had used him as Fallatius in *The Forc'd Marriage*. However, she feared his propensity to develop his own buffoonery.[14]

Once rehearsals began, Behn's heart sank. Perhaps no one at the Duke's could really animate her gay couple, although the actress, Jane Long, played sprightly girls reasonably well, was appreciated by Betterton, and may have played Euphemia. The real horror was the comic who was clearly not learning his lines. She was angry but kept strategically quiet. Then she suffered another setback. Ravenscroft had apparently promised a prologue and gone off to write it, or so he said. In fact, as she discovered later, he had contracted a bout of venereal disease and was taking the cure of sweating and mercury. The pain of both affliction and cure banished his promise from his head and no prologue arrived. As for the epilogue, this was hurriedly supplied from another unknown source. Despite her usual concern to keep everyone as favourable to her as possible, Behn could not express gratitude. This was strange since the epilogue was no better or worse than others of the time. Perhaps the problems were its mockery of Dryden whom she admired and the comparison it made between her and her famous compatriot, Mary Carleton, the 'German Princess'. Carleton had just been hanged for pilfering, and pamphlets were tumbling from the presses describing her career from her early days in Canterbury to her last years of roguery. Behn was uneasy at her art's being compared with this counterfeiting:

> Hiss 'em and cry 'em down, 'tis all in vain,
> Incorrigible Sciblers can't abstain…
> …sad experience our eyes convinces,
> That damn's their Playes which hang'd the German Princess.

The Dutch Lover was performed in February, with the King in the audience. Behn too was there and she distinctly heard a man mock the play before it began—because it was by a woman. The remark stung her, especially as she enjoyed using her sex to advantage: it was a novelty still and made the prologue and epilogue more piquant when spoken by a pretty actress. But, between prologue and epilogue, her sex was immaterial and this prejudiced damning irritated her profoundly. Then misery joined irritation when Behn realised that the play itself was undoubtedly a flop. She felt bitter towards the audience but, like Edward Howard and Ravenscroft, she mainly blamed the actors. She had reason. The actor playing Haunce, probably Angel, was adlibbing 'with a great deal of idle stuff, which I was wholly unacquainted with'.

The complaint that actors strayed too far from the written part out of 'Pitiful Ambition' had been most famously made in Hamlet's advice to the clowns to 'speak no more, than is set down'. In his *Life of Mr. Thomas Betterton* (1710), Charles Gildon claimed that extemporising was 'too frequently done by some of our popular but half Comedians'. Behn was in good company in her criticism, but, since she would have to go on working with the actors, she did not make it too stern, and she did not name and shame when she came to lament in print. To add insult to Behn's injury, some Jonsonian, probably Shadwell, though it might even have been Howard, dared to suggest that it was the crowded, unregulated nature of *The Dutch Lover* that made it fail. She knew exactly what she thought of men's obsession with dramatic rules and with Ben Jonson. She had also been insulted as uneducated. This made her furious. Here Shakespeare was again a comfort: his lack of training made him a good ally.

Despite its failure on the stage, Behn published the play in the following year. Anti-Dutch feeling was strong and satiric works such as *Hogan-Moganides: Or, The Dutch Hudibras* were encouraging the mood. But, if she had some slight propagandist aim, her main one, beyond money, was to respond to her self-appointed critics and the actors who had combined to render her best-written play a flop. So, like Ravenscroft (and Ben Jonson, though she did not make the parallel), Behn argued her case to the reader in an epistle. Realising that the pique displayed by Edward Howard and mocked by Shadwell and by *The Rehearsal*—'the vulgar never understand us,' says Mr. Bays—was not the best defence, she wrote in burlesque mode, using the abusive prologue style. Her butt was the absurd intellectual pretension of men and its connection with dramatic rules.

It was common enough to denigrate one's own work in prefaces: Dryden was always doing it when he addressed the great. Fewer play-wrights had the temerity to denigrate the actual business of play-writing, as Behn proceeded to do. Indeed she was one of the very few writers to dare to undermine the basic classical assumption that art should instruct and delight. Throughout the century the stage had been attacked by Puritans as a pernicious influence on the morals of spectators. Playwrights like Jonson had sought to counter this by urging the ethical and moral base of their work—certainly Dryden did so, but even Thomas Sydserff in his dedication of the light confection, *Tarugo's Wiles*, claimed that his 'Comical Trifle' had 'like most other Plays…its useful moralities'. Behn disagreed, and she regarded the attitude as a dangerous holdover from the time leading up to Civil War, when politics and theatre were defined by religion. She did not share the desire for drama or politics to be primarily ethical, for she saw this desire as coercive to others. She herself was writing to make money by pleasing those who paid for their seats; she suspected others of doing the same. Spectators came to the theatre from idleness and desire for amusement, not for edification.[15]

Behn was especially annoyed by the complacency of the bulky, arrogant, and dull Shadwell, avatar of the huge Ben Jonson. His plays were as naughty as anyone else's but he prated constantly of moral purpose.[16] He also boasted of his learning. Perhaps the tedium of sermons heard during her childhood fuelled Behn's contempt for the learned fools 'pestering' their hearers, but she was also in fashion. Her acquaintance, the cleric Thomas Sprat, had negotiated the Restoration for himself and the new Royal Society by setting science on a firm apolitical and utilitarian basis. It had to be apolitical since the pursuit of science was tainted by its use in Interregnum political agendas of recreating society and it needed to be utilitarian in the Baconian mode to separate its business from sterile speculation and silly empiricism. In his *History of the Royal Society*, which created the image that body wanted of itself, Sprat described fanaticism and pedantry as the enemies of knowledge. In similar vein, John Eachard mocked the custom of forcing a classical education on boys, 'let their parts be never so low and pitiful'.[17] He asked 'whether it be unavoidably necessary to keep Lads to sixteen or seventeen years of Age, in pure slavery to a few *Latin* and *Greek* words' instead of letting them read English authors, and he commented, 'you shall have Lads that are arch knaves at the Nominative Case, and that have a notable quick Eye at spying out the Verb, who for want of reading such common and familiar books, shall understand no more of what is very plain and easie, than a well educated Dog or Horse.'[18] Behn did not despise classical education, but she did take Eachard's attitude, that knowing 'how many Nuts and Apples *Tityrus* had for his Supper' was less important than commonsense. Memory was not knowledge.[19]

Despite such contempt and despite admission of her own lack of letters, however, Behn was eager to show she was able in her epistle to mock attacks on Hobbes such as Alexander Ross's criticism of *Leviathan* (Hobbes had a similar scathing attitude to wordy philosophers and so-called learned men) and with Henry More to attack Philostratus' *Life of Apollonius*, a Greek Pythagorean philosopher. Hobbes and Apollonius were interesting examples since both represented alternatives to orthodox Christianity, so Behn was lightly suggesting that her thoughts were not quite as conventional and simple as was expected from a female. 'Women were not born to read authors and censure the learned,' remarked the wife of the diarist Evelyn.[20]

Male addiction to sterile learning led to an absurd drama of rules which delighted no one. Despite her sympathy with Edward Howard, Behn had already rejected the doctrine of the unities of time, place and action, as well as the necessary imitation of Ben Jonson, which Shadwell, crowing over the success of his play, *The Sullen Lovers*, insisted should be the practice of *all* playwrights. Shadwell disliked the witty couple which Behn realised was her forte; he declared the hero-rake a drinking, swearing ruffian, with an impudent 'tomrig' for a mistress, whose bawdy conversation only the author thought 'brisk writing'.[21] Behn was further riled by Shadwell's division of writers into those composing for pleasure and those scribbling 'for profit' and by his opinion that a 'Correct Play' took a year at least to write, even for the 'Wittiest Man of the Nation'. Plays such as Behn's did not take a year to write, although they were not thereby contemptible in her view. Nor were they the most important productions of human endeavour, as some absurdly claimed, being rather 'among the middle if not the better sort of Books'. Over a century later, Jane Austen would bemoan the fact that the umpteenth male adapter of history was more valued than the sensitive woman novelist. Behn anticipates her by implying that the crudest male pedant is preferred to one who, like herself, briskly 'inscrib'd Comedy on the beginning of my Book'.

In this criticism of pretension, Shadwell was certainly a target. So, possibly, was Dryden, despite her probable indebtedness to his work. Behn seems to be mocking the smug prologue Dryden wrote to the University of Oxford in 1673, in which he described dramatists coming there to be taught literary precepts. In Oxford, poetry was an 'Art', Dryden declared, where in London it was merely a 'Trade'. There followed an implied attack on the unlearned who could 'ne'er Spell Grammar' and who 'made plays 'the *Lucretian* way' out of 'so many Huddled Atoms', then dignified their ignorance as following nature.[22]

If Behn did have Dryden in mind, however, she was not foolish enough openly to include him in any attack and, at the appropriate moment in her epistle, she excluded him from her statement that no man of today was writing beyond the scope of a woman. Dryden was, in her eyes, still the best dramatist around.

The 'Epistle to the Reader' gives an impression of a lively gossipy, rowdy, abusive and vociferous theatre. Plays were not greeted with a reverential hush; authors were not transcendental dramatists, on a plane above ordinary life, but jobbing playwrights who collaborated with many others to realise their work. Not isolated artists, they inhabited an ordinary economic and contingent world, fighting to be heard for money above the din of seducing and selling.

One man who well realised that art could not be separated from ordinary life was Edward Ravenscroft. When Behn knew that his defection over the prologue was not due to carelessness but sickness, she rallied him in a comic verse epistle. Their relationship was based on the theatre; so fittingly she wrote in different characters, at one point a conventional lyric poet, interrupted by the sudden vision of the tub, at another, a forthright friend speaking in man-to-man tones of venereal disease, tumescence and prostitution.

Behn's 'Letter to a Brother of the Pen in Tribulation' wittily parallels Ravenscroft's compulsory withdrawal for treatment with the religious self-mortification of Lent. The parallel was apt, for the cure involved fasting and avoiding meat. Syphilis had moist issue; so, following the notion of humours, to counteract it the patient had to eat dry biscuit, almonds and currants. Savile complained to Rochester that he was once confined to 'dry mutton & dyett drinke', while Ravenscroft's hard, dry food should mortify 'Soul and Body'.[23] Since the condition was rampant, there were many potions around for venereal disease. Physicians prescribed china, sassafras and sasparilla root, antimony, coriander, raisins and liquorice, all to be drunk instead of beer. Some such potion had been given to Ravenscroft, a 'Damn'd Penetential Drink, that will infuse / Dull Principles into thy Grateful Muse'. He was now sitting in a sweating tub to sweat out the disease, counterfeiting summer as Behn whimsically put it: 'Much good may't do thee; but 'tis thought thy Brain / E'er long will wish for cooler Days again.'

Now she knew the truth, she could mock Ravenscroft for his modest pretence that he had been away writing plays. Since the disease must have been contracted through copulation, his predicament revealed what he had in fact been doing:

who thought thy Wit
An Interlude of Whoring would admit?
To Poetry no more thou'lt be inclin'd,
Unless in Verse to damn all Woman-kind:
And 'tis but Just thou shouldst in Rancor grow
Against that Sex that has Confin'd thee so....
      ...ev'ry Grove does in its Pride appear:
Whilst thou poor *Damon* in close Rooms art pent,
Where hardly thy own Breath can find a vent.
Yet that too is a Heaven, compar'd to th'Task
Of Codling every Morning in a Cask.
   Now I could curse this Female, but I know,
She needs it not, that thus cou'd handle you.
Besides, that Vengeance does to thee belong,
And 'twere Injustice to disarm thy Tongue.
Curse then, dear Swain, that all the Youth may hear,
And from thy dire Mishap be taught to fear.
Curse till thou hast undone the Race, and all
That did contribute to thy Spring and Fall.[24]

Aphra Behn would not always be so light-hearted with men.

CHAPTER 14

❧

John Hoyle and *Abdelazer*

'mischievous usurper of my Peace'

Those friends who had read 'Our Cabal' and noted the powerful portrait of John Hoyle may have anticipated Aphra Behn's fate. Hoyle was a pitiless and violent man who, when still a student at Gray's Inn in August 1663, had been on a capital charge for stabbing an unarmed watchmaker in the street, then fleeing from the scene. He left his victim to die over six painful days. Perhaps bribery made the jury bring in a verdict of 'Ignoramus' despite the number of hostile witnesses: lawyer Hoyle was frequently lucky in his brushes with the law. Behn may have been unaware of this incident, for Hoyle was taciturn when he wanted to be and neither he nor she was frank about the past. Her outline in 'Our Cabal' indicates that she apprehended the authority and violence of Hoyle's character, as well as his sexual bent; yet she did not keep her distance, and soon she was infatuated with a man whose attraction partly lay in his self-absorption.

The catalyst was music, which always aroused Behn. John Banister, the King's musician, had instituted public concerts or music meetings in his house in Whitefriars near where she lodged.[1] They were mainly of new music, sometimes his own compositions, sometimes the popular songs and airs of the day. On payment of a shilling each, the audience assembled at five or seven in the evening in a room with seats and tables, where they could purchase refreshment of wine, cake and ale. The musicians sat in a box behind a curtain.[2]

On one occasion Behn heard passionate songs sung by a Mr P, possibly Henry Purcell or his brother, so powerful that she could declare, 'If I can live, and hear you sing, / No other Forces can my Soul subdue.'[3] On another, she encountered John Hoyle and was overwhelmed by the unison of sweet sound and male attraction. 'One Charme might have secur'd a Victory, / Both, rais'd the Pleasure even to Extasie /... Beauty and *Musick* must the Soul disarme.'[4]

Music turned admiration into love. Since Hoyle too was responding to the singing, it was a fine opportunity for voyeurism: his 'Body easey and all tempting lay, / Inspiring wishes which the Eyes betray' in anyone like herself gazing too much. The image is sensuous and baroque, as the object of Behn's gaze turns into a young angel listening raptly to the music of the spheres, while lying 'Charmingly Extended on a Cloud'.

The courtship was only partly amusing if her poetry can be credited. When Hoyle as Amyntas sent Behn some verses written as if made in a dream, she replied in poetry herself. The result was an intimate portrait. She had been awakened by a page, either hers (the same, perhaps, who had run to Jeffrey Boys with a copy of her second play) or more likely Hoyle's, perhaps a Benjamin Bourne but here called Bellario after a woman disguised as a page and causing a jealous stabbing in Fletcher's famous play *Philaster*. In this allusion to a beloved of indeterminate gender, Behn may be allowing herself a dig at Hoyle's other proclivities. The page brought a verse message from Hoyle: 'Thy Name to my glad Ear was brought: / *Amyntas*! cry'd the Page.' Behn broke the seal with trembling hands and let the amorous words wash over her as she tried to conceal her smiles and blushes. Of course she failed and the boy may have made a saucy remark. In her response, Behn praised Hoyle's eloquence—he wrote, she assured him, 'beyond the *Sence*... / Of ev'ry scribling Lovers common Art'. Hoyle had power whether he rallied or retreated, which suggested that he alternated the two. He was not a comfortable man to love.

A similar impression comes from verses entitled 'The Return' which caught the arrogance of the seducer and accused him of seeking 'Glory... when you rifle the Spoil'. It was not sex but conquest Hoyle desired, as Behn had remarked as early as 'Our Cabal'. His enjoyment was in the humbling of female pride. A 'Tyrant was never secure in his Throne' and he might one day be served as he was serving—perhaps Behn imagined herself turning the tables. Mostly, however, she felt the victim of love, the duped of Cupid.

Having given herself up completely to a relationship at last, Behn hoped for some satisfaction from it even if, as seems likely, she had to be the more forward in love-making. In 'Our Cabal', she had noted Hoyle's love of young men, but had grumbled only as it removed an eligible man from female grasp. Although there exists a letter purport-edly blaming Hoyle for his sexual preference, it is probably bogus since, in her published works, Behn easily (in theory) accepted homosexuality for men or women as part of sexual life—although, like others, she was easier with the classically sanctioned love of youths than with adult male love.[5] Yet, she clearly *did* have sexual problems with Hoyle, which may or may not have been connected with his bisexuality. There are simply too many descriptions both of male impotence and of male retreat from sex for there not to have been some autobiographical resonance, and Hoyle was Aphra Behn's main lover.

Most of the time she knew her hold tenuous. Hoyle dominated her thoughts but she did not dominate his. She responded more quickly than he and could not hold back. Here Behn was falling into conventional gender stereotypes and she knew it: the loving female and the self-reliant male.

She could not hide her uneasiness from her friends. 'Amoret', whom Behn had herself tried to console on the May Day picnic, asked why she had lost her sparkle. Behn replied in the pastoral verse with which she so often masked her vulnerability and which converted feelings into something manageable. She imagined Hoyle adorned with tributes from women, expecting further conquest. He pretended insouciance but was all calculation and desire for sexual power. Again she told of his silences, his moodiness, the harshness that her infatuation modified, his magnetism and male allure. In the dance in Arcadia into which this complex relationship had been translated, Behn was his partner:

> To whom much Passion he did Vow,
> And much his Eyes and Sighs did show;
> And both imploy'd with so much Art,
> I strove in vain to guard my Heart;
> And ere the Night our Revels crost,
> I was intirely won and lost.

Like Carola Harsnett with Boys, Elizabeth Barry was warned not to fall for Hoyle herself. Yet Behn must not have feared this much, for Barry had more important men in her sight. Rather, Behn was ending with a graceful compliment to the irresistible ones, Elizabeth Barry and John Hoyle. She loved both in different ways.

The relationship of Aphra Behn and Jack Hoyle was fraught. Behn was an outgoing, talkative woman; Hoyle was moody and self-centred. Both were used to freedom. Soon Hoyle found Behn overwhelming, too talkative, too demanding. She suggested they moderate their relationship by not being together all the time, hoping he would not agree, though,

JANET TODD

like most using the ploy, she knew he would. She also realised that, if she saw less of him, she should also avoid writing.

Hoyle's absence prevented her sexual advances, and yet Behn was more than ever in thrall to him, more than ever desiring. Even when he was ill she wrote of him as an exotic potentate, an 'Eastern Monarch'. It was a figure that fascinated the Restoration, but Behn turned it into an image of female masochism. If he died, women would live melancholy and lovesick, but she, 'Astrea', who had the happiness 'To be ador'd by thee, and to adore thee most' would die with him. Had he lived in ancient times, in the world of Plutarch's *Lives*, he would have changed the course of history, since Cleopatra *and* Caesar would both have fallen for him.

Possibly at this point Behn wrote a series of self-revealing and cajoling letters, catching the taste of sweet honey that held a sting. After her death, the letters were published, first as a separate short story and then as a part of her biography. It is never easy to separate fact and fiction in Behn and these writings are no exception, but, while conforming to a male stereotype of romantic woman lamenting her cruel treatment and propensity to love, they may also have served as personal letters sent to the arrogant Jack Hoyle.[6] If so—and I am tentatively accepting them as such—Behn probably sent them off through her boy and Hoyle replied through his, perhaps the child Benjamin Bourne, who may have brought the verses at the start of the affair.

Behn began by explaining her desire for a separation. Because he was tired of her talkativeness, probably her sexual demands, and certainly her flirtatious, flighty behaviour in public, Hoyle had grown cold and even more taciturn. Cruelly, he had obeyed her request for distance and Behn was now writing after a period of silence to complain of his neglect. He had let her know that he was going to have a life apart from her from now on, intending to take up public dancing. Inevitably she wanted his partners to be 'Ill-natur'd, Ill-dress'd, Ill-fashion'd, and Unconversable'. She also forlornly hoped that his time would be ruined by thoughts of her. She could not pretend that she was not more miserable than he, however, that she was not 'profoundly Melancholy'. Her sprightly heroine Euphemia from *The Dutch Lover* would not have given so much away.

Then out of the blue Hoyle did come to her, bringing with him a coveted letter. Behn had a crowd of other visitors and, since Hoyle did not want it known that he now had a relationship with her, she did not run to embrace him as she wanted to do. But she could not refrain from

178

signing to him how much she desired him to stay. Indeed she may have 'acted even imprudently to make my Soul be understood'. Hoyle was unimpressed, irritated no doubt at finding her yet again in company; he took umbrage, ignored her frantic efforts to detain him, and left with his letter, even though he knew that she 'burst to speak' with him. It was a little miming drama that could have taken place on the stage as well as in a private room.

Inevitably Behn wanted Hoyle to come again but in a better temper. She had yet to learn that, contrary to what French romances indicated, women could not easily affect male temperament. Perhaps he did come, for the next letter referred to some discussion of their relationship. This time she was constrained by his presence, having to prevent herself from saying what she would have been pained to see taken amiss. What then was she doing writing now?

> though I scorn to guard my Tongue, as hoping 'twill never offend willingly, yet I can, with much adoe, hold it, when I have a great mind to say a Thousand Things, I know will be taken in an ill sense. Possibly you will wonder what compels me to write, what moves me to send where I find so little Welcome; nay, where I meet with such Returns, it may be I wonder too.

Since she had last written, Hoyle had seemingly continued his tormenting of her in public. Banister's music meetings were inextricably bound up with her lover in her mind. So it was especially cruel when, at a recent one of these, he had refused to sit next to her. It was hardly the action of a friend and fitted oddly with his statement that it was *she* who had changed: 'You say I am chang'd... [but] whatever I was since you knew me, believe I am still the same in Soul and Thought.'[7]

When Behn took up her pen again after some time of silence, she found, as many writers of love letters before her, that she was becoming interested in her own psychology. Since Hoyle had always set up for 'Prudence and Discretion', she had been typed, femininely, as indiscreet and impetuous. So she found risible Hoyle's urging her not to deceive him: 'you need not have caution'd me, who so naturally hate those little Arts of my Sex, that I often run on freedoms, that may well enough bear a Censure from People so scrupulous as *Lycidas*.' She was a gambler, venturing against the odds, hazarding all while he chanced little. Uselessly she blamed Hoyle for the inequality of love, in a way revelling in her own feelings as inherently superior:

you woud have me give, and you, like a Miser, wou'd distribute nothing. Greedy *Lycidas*! Unconscionable! and Ungenerous! You wou'd not be in Love for all the World, yet wish I were so, Uncharitable!—Wou'd my Fever cure you? Or a Curse on me make you Bless'd?[8]

Then Hoyle visited again and was so unexpectedly kind and tender he caught Behn off her guard. He now became her 'Soul's Delight', while she would be his, 'befal me what will'. The evening was wonderful. He indulged in those intimacies and caresses that she so much wanted from him. There had been no attempt at sexual intercourse and so there was nothing for him to be disturbed about, but she was pleased to know that he could be 'soft and dear when he please, to put off his haughty Pride'. So she could see not a fundamentally self-centred man, intent on his own pleasure, but a basically kind one, hiding his true nature, his 'native sweet Temper'. It was a myth into which she vigorously threw herself. If he continued to show love as now and if, as he assured her, he did indeed love her despite all appearances to the contrary, she begged him to continue in his 'plain-dealing', for she could be 'purchased with Softness, and dear Words, and kind Expressions, sweet Eyes, and a low Voice'. The evening was so heady that Behn simply could not go to bed, but stayed up to write to Hoyle. She finished her letter with no shred of the caution she knew she should show, but against which her whole being revolted: 'I love thee dearly, passionately, and tenderly, and am resolv'd to be eternally. *My only dear Delight, and Joy of my Life*, thy *Astrea*.'

As the next letter showed, the moment did not last. The pair had been in a tavern or at a friend's house and, after Hoyle had gone, Behn stayed on for supper, reading out an act of her new play to a common friend. She was pleased to receive compliments for her depiction of the hero, who was, it was said, the image of Hoyle. The friend was a gallant man, Aphra Behn was known to love gallantry, and he did not quite comprehend the depth of her present infatuation. Thus he thought, after they had all supped together and grown mellow, that there might be room for another man in her life. So he began 'some rallying Love-discourse', to which he found her unresponsive—or so Behn assured Hoyle. The friend perceived that Hoyle's image still dominated her mind and he teased her by saying that Hoyle was not a handsome man. Another man was called over to confirm the opinion, but he agreed with Behn, that Hoyle was indeed handsome. This third man was named 'Philly' in the letter and it is just possible that this is a reference to Lord

L'Isle, the 'Philaster' of the dedication to *The Young King*. More likely, however, it was simply another playwright or lawyer of middling status.

The habit in the upper orders of drawing up marriage contracts making provision for both husband and wife necessarily influenced the commitments people made to each other outside matrimony. Restoration comedy is full of proviso scenes like the one Behn had just written in *The Dutch Lover*, in which the witty pair of lovers try to regulate intimate behaviour, agreeing, for example, not to invade privacy or not to humiliate or caress the other in public. Hoyle, the lawyer, had that evening whispered a set of rules to Behn to govern their future relationship: she was not to lie and dissemble, for he recognised her proclivity, nor was she to write often, lest she grow tedious. He intended to preserve love without letting it grow possessive, but, as so often in his demands, he overdid it with his 'Niceties and Scruples' and Behn was stung enough to tell him that the 'Articles' almost seemed to her a recipe for ending their complicated love. Beside, as she pointed out, Hoyle had already broken one of them in the act of composing, since 'They are writ with Reserves'. She was now breaking another by writing for no reason but to assure him of her 'Eternal Love'. Perhaps she needed to disobey to keep a shred of self-esteem.

One of the areas that clearly needed regulation was the sexual. Behn's love for Hoyle was overwhelmingly so, but he had grown weary of importunity. She agreed to scale down her demands, though, under the influence of wine and music, it was not always easy. She begged him not to misinterpret 'my Excess of Fondness'. If she did break the agreement, it would surely be enough to let the 'Check' she would be given make her desist. In any case, Behn knew the score and, if she did make sexual advances, he must know it was 'more out of Humour and Jest, than any Inclination on my side'. For, as she assured him, 'I could sit eternall with you, without part of disturbance: Fear me not, for you are (from that) as safe as in Heaven it self.'

Behn was probably deceiving herself. Her longing went on, translated simply into desire for Hoyle's presence, for some revelation of his 'heart', and for some proof that she influenced him in any way. Neither admitted they were in a power struggle, but both made it abundantly clear. Her pretences at resistance were forlorn indeed: it was so easy to declare she would 'march off' if Hoyle did not use her 'well', so difficult to carry out her threat when he continued simply to be himself. Inevitably she was enthralled to the bad usage—'I grow desperate fond of you.'

To erase the effect of the Articles, Behn begged Hoyle to visit again.

If she were not at home, he should try 'over the way, where I have ingaged to Dine, there being an Entertainment on purpose to Morrow for me'. When she read over her letter, she was worried that it revealed too much of a life outside her relationship, as well as representing her as too clinging and dependent. In fact it showed her almost afraid to go out in case Hoyle happened to call. She wanted to mitigate the effect and tagged on a postscript denying that she was the sort of person the letter was portraying. She was not demanding and insistent—Hoyle far surpassed her in 'that unnecessary Fault'.

By the next letter, Behn was again moaning about Hoyle's coldness. Although his love was 'the only Blessing I ask on Earth', his manner of leaving on the last occasion argued his 'No Love'. The result was the usual confusion of affection and mortified self-esteem: 'My Soul is ready to burst with Pride and Indignation; and at the same time, Love, with all his Softness assails me, and will make me write; so that, between one and the other, I can express neither as I ought.' She knew Hoyle was embarrassed by her expressions of passion: he found them artificial and sentimental, and Behn too promiscuous with her words. Full of resentment, she responded, 'what shall I do to make you know I do not use to condescend to so much Submission, nor to tell my Heart so freely?' She had never loved or talked 'at the rate I do to you, since I was born'. Infatuation and resentment jostled each other: 'You ought, Oh Faithless, and infinitely Adorable *Lycidas*! to know and guess my Tenderness; you ought to see it grow, and daily increase upon your Hands.' Somewhere, Behn realised that such a man as Hoyle would not brook so many 'oughts'. Deep down, she knew the truth: if her expressions of love were troublesome to Hoyle, it was 'because I fancy you lessen, whilst I encrease, in Passion'.

By now a curious comfort was appearing between the self-abasement and pride: of expression itself. It did not tend towards Behn's greater understanding of her predicament but, in its histrionics, was therapeutic and comforting. The pride is located in Hoyle's question, why she should express herself more than other women. Why should she not, she replied, for she knew herself more skilled with words? The writing of literary complaint pulled Behn on to the stage and made her predicament theatrical and more bearable: acting, she gained some control over her self and thus over herself in the relationship. She could be Dido or Sappho lamenting their faithless lovers:

oh! you went to Joys, and left me to Torments! You went to Love alone, and left me Love and Rage, Fevers and Calentures [delirium], even Madness it self! Indeed, indeed, my Soul! I know not to what degree I love you; let it suffice I do most passionately, and can have no Thoughts of any other Man, whilst I have Life. No! Reproach me, Defame me, Lampoon me, Curse me, and Kill me when I do, and let Heaven do so too.[9]

The final letter of the series came after an interval during which Behn had stopped writing, according to Hoyle's wish; yet it was he who broke the silence. Although she was still in love, accepting that 'whatever Resolutions I make in the absence of my lovely Friend, one single sight turns me all Woman, and all his,' she could now contain desire, while lightly expressing her refusal to control it or to abide by articles: 'I will henceforth never be wise more; never make any Vows against my Inclinations, or the little-wing'd Deity. I do not only see 'tis all in vain, but I really believe they serve only to augment my passion.' Yet she knew, ''Tis only the vanity of being belov'd by me can make you countenance softness so displeasing to you.' She saw that Hoyle had colluded in her infatuation, fanning flames whenever they appeared to be dying down, retreating when they flared up. Their relationship had been a power struggle for him from the start, hence the speed with which he jumped on any incipient bid for power on her side. He had, too, tormented her with failings he paradoxically wanted to reveal in himself: so he rebuked her for loving other men when it was he who had been unfaithful or cold.

Hoyle had also been wilfully cruel. Knowing she wanted to see him, he had yet passed by the end of her street without calling. He had been seen—for Behn spied on him though she knew he disliked it—in any number of coffee houses, 'squandering away' his time. When he did come, he was dull and melancholy because he resented her and could not be merry before her oppressive affection. She imagined him saying he was 'a Fellow that do not desire to be pleas'd'. Then, the moment she stopped trying to please him, he was back demanding to know where her 'Good-Nature' had gone.[10]

The relationship with Hoyle seems the dominating one of Behn's life, exploited by her and others when they wanted to make amorous images for good or ill. Ironically, it may not have been consummated or at least have been always sexually unsatisfactory. Yet it was not the less intense for that. As a bisexually inclined woman, Behn wanted sexual closeness but may not have longed for penetration by a man. What she clearly desired was emotional security, the very security against which her personality seemed to rebel. Behn had pointed out in one letter that she had no domestic ties, no parents or siblings who would care what she did, nobody to fear. So she could make choice of (and needed) an emotional tie, take someone to love without any family pressure for marriage. Yet, such apparently desirable freedom brought greater problems than anyone caught in family and marriage could appreciate. The failures of love, perhaps inevitable in so unconventional a person, could in the end be blamed only on oneself. *She* had chosen ill.

Roger Morrice, a Presbyterian cleric ejected from his living after the Restoration, kept a register of events from 1677 to 1691. In 1687 he had occasion to mention Hoyle and he noted that it was 'too publickly known that Mr Hoyle 10. or 12. yeares since kept *Mrs. Beane*—'. This was probably the time. Behn's failure with *The Dutch Lover* perhaps made a keeping arrangement desirable and it may have lasted for a few months, maybe longer. Friends were no doubt amused at the pair and their efforts to modify their strong and independent personalities, for Aphra Behn could not have been the easiest woman to 'keep'. But to be part of a recognised couple, even an unconventional one, had some sweet social aspects and, for a public woman, be she actress or writer, to be kept was acceptable. Although both might have gained respectability from a match, Aphra Behn as a wife and Hoyle as a married man less open to charges of buggery, they did not marry. A lampoonist suggested he, like Ravenscroft, helped her with plays instead of marrying her, implying that Hoyle was the one to hold back from commitment, but perhaps both were idealistic, hoping for a relationship of love and affection without external ties. Perhaps neither wanted to be trapped in the familial vortex of domestic needs.

Roger Morrice ended his comment on Behn and Hoyle by mentioning a 'difference between them'. He supposed that 'they two had interrupted all acquaintance many yeares since.' He was mistaken. Behn did not interrupt acquaintance with anyone if she could help it and, if she had to relieve herself of malice or resentment, it was better to do it in private to a few chosen listeners. There was no sense for a public woman to open herself to the malignancy of men—in her penultimate letter Behn had imagined Hoyle 'Lampooning' her. Also, she never 'interrupted all acquaintance' with Hoyle. Indeed, for all the unsatisfactory nature of the tie, perhaps because of it, he remained a potent force in her life. Intellectually exciting, controlled when it came to giving affection or pity, uncontrolled in anger and resentment, potential and enigmatic in his silences, Hoyle persisted as an object of fascination even when the sexual longing for him began to subside. Behn would desire other men sexually, but no one rivalled Jack Hoyle in her imaginative and emotional life.

As her works tumbled out over the next years, it starts to seem as though the beloved Hoyle were both lamented and used. Without such obsessive love, Behn probably would not have written much of what she did write and without the freedom he forced on her she may not have continued writing at all. As it was, her bonding with such a man and the fact that she had no family to 'fear' meant that she could mount in her work the sort of criticism of the family and of family values, of Christian, social and economic marriage and any legalised bonds, that few women could begin to make in the centuries to come.

In political terms, Hoyle probably intensified Behn's Royalism. He was an open republican, far more opinionated than Scot had been, and someone to react against rather than follow, when, much later, Behn did come close to investigating aspects of the relationship: in her first attributed prose fiction, *Love-Letters*, she made the heroine into a staunch Royalist and the seductive man into an opponent of any authority except his own. Republicanism was thus a sort of egomania, a ludicrous sense of one's own importance that could not brook any hierarchy without the self on top. Democracy became synonymous with brutal control of others, rather than with the freedom to which it was erroneously linked, while monarchy, by providing a single overarching relationship, freed people in all other respects and relations. If Behn could not control her feelings for a man whom she ought not to love at such a rate, she could at least show some independence by opposing his psychologically suspect political views.

As the affair concluded its infatuated phase, Behn needed some immediate relief. This might be gained through histrionics, through writing words that such a man as Hoyle might have spoken but which she, Behn, could control. She could imagine what it was like *being* Hoyle, imitate to gain a little of his authority and to distance him. The friend with whom she had had supper after Hoyle's departure and to whom she had read out part of her new play considered the main character like Hoyle. Some readers assume this refers to Willmore, the hero of Behn's most famous play, *The Rover*. But Willmore is talkative, good natured and securely Royalist and the author laughs at and with him. She was not yet ready to laugh at Hoyle. More likely, the reference is to the hero of the next play Behn wrote, the exotic and arrogant potentate, Abdelazer.

Love in Fantastique Triumph satt
Whilst Bleeding Hearts a round him flow'd,
For whom Fresh paines he did Create,
And strange Tyranick power he show'd;
From thy Bright Eyes he took his fire,
Which round about in sport he hurl'd;
But 'twas from mine, he took desire,
Enough to undo the Amorous World.

From me he took his sighs and tears,
From thee his Pride and Crueltie;
From me his Languishments and Feares,
And every Killing Dart from thee;
Thus thou and I, the God have arm'd,
And sett him up a Deity;
But my poor Heart alone is harm'd,
Whilst thine the Victor is, and free.[11]

When Aphra Behn published these powerful verses in her collection of poetry in 1684 as 'Song. Love Arm'd', she placed them next to 'Our Cabal' which, starting light-heartedly enough in the May Day party, ended with contemplating the enigmatic and compelling character of Lycidas, the 'haughty Swain' whose eyes killed with 'Fierceness, not with Love'. It cannot have been accidental that 'Love Arm'd', her most ferocious depiction of desire, was brought into such close contact with the main pseudonym of Hoyle.[12] If she had ever thought that she or anyone else could tame or domesticate a libertine, Behn had changed her mind. The truly selfish man in sex or ambition was beyond female sway. 'Love Arm'd' had been written for her relentless tragedy, *Abdelazer*, ordered by the enthralled Queen to be sung at the beginning of the play for the cruel Moorish general, Abdelazer. It makes him the embodiment of obsessive female love or lust in a work that circles round the themes of sexual submission and domination.

Apart from her sexual longings for Hoyle, Behn, ever the professional, was inspired in *Abdelazer* by the new fashion for extreme tragedy. It was a curious mode, since audiences simultaneously admired and mocked it and since it co-existed with a liking for cynical dramas which more obviously reflected the spectators' own compromised principles and political manoeuvrings. In May 1674, the young Nathaniel Lee had had an interesting failure with his first play *Nero*, an intense depiction of the psychology of power, in which the central character represented motive-less evil and expanding energy within a plot of family murder. There had been power-hungry men in plenty on the Restoration stage—Dryden's Almanzor in *The Conquest of Granada* being one of the most famous—but they were usually reconciled or tamed at the end. Lee's Nero was neither. A similar extreme play, put on at the Duke's in the summer of 1673, was Elkanah Settle's *Empress of Morocco*, where a mother poisons her son so as to put her lover on the throne. Dryden was incensed at the immoderation, perhaps because it exaggerated tendencies in his own work.

Christendom used alien Islam for a variety of purposes, from erotic titillation to religious historiography, but, in the seventeenth century, there was a growing scholarly interest in the social and ideological aspects of the faith. In the early years, high churchmen had studied Arabic scholarship as part of the search for pure biblical texts.[13] In the later, Islamic doctrine was used to bolster up Unitarian arguments about the Christian God and to challenge orthodox theology. Behn fitted this tradition, revealing again the scepticism she had felt in Surinam and suggested in her address before *The Dutch Lover*. The 'case of Sanctity was first ordain'd, / To cheat the honest world', she wrote, and she expressed Abdelazer's scorn for the mob in religious terms: 'The giddy Rout are guided by Religion, / More than by Justice, Reason, or Allegiance.' The religion she had in mind was probably Protestant Dissent, now becoming increasingly vocal: for James, Duke of York, the heir to the throne, had openly embraced Roman Catholicism and England was feeling very Protestant indeed.

Islam and exotic southern Europe could also be used politically to comment on the northern Christian world, mainly because it was assumed that, in Muslim countries, power was not constrained by moral considerations but could course through individuals in a pure way. So, within Islam or a single Muslim, the political philosophies that fascinated the English could be embodied. This was not only hereditary kingship, seemingly both natural and biblical, but also the rule of the most masterful male, utterly dominating both women and weak or morally bound men.

Like Dryden's great political drama, *The Conquest of Granada*, Behn's tragedy was set in Spain and turned on the hatred of Muslim and Christian. It had, however, a very tenuous connection with history, converting as it did the excessively pious fifteenth-century Queen Isabella into a lust-crazed murderer. Far more it drew on literature, and Behn's

Moor came from a Renaissance theatrical tradition of rationally villainous Muslims. Such men cannot blush, because of their swarthy skin, are faithless, fearless, contemptuous of women and adept at plotting. Given her interest in comparative religion, Behn may also have drawn on Alexander Ross's translation of the Koran from French, which depicted a cunning and sensual Mohammed establishing a religion not of conscience but of power.[14]

The story of Abdelazer centres on the Moor, Abdelazer, whose dark skin represents the devilish compact of Lee's *Nero*. Wanting to revenge the ousting of his father by the Spanish, he destroys most of the royal Spanish family and much of their court. His instrument is the equally cruel Spanish Queen, who kills her husband, connives in the murder of one son and declares the other, Philip, a bastard, all through infatuation with Abdelazer. She is an ageing beauty, however, and, though she can still work magic on others including a cardinal, she is no longer loved by the Moor. When she has served her turn, he treats her as he has persuaded her to treat so many of her family: he has her murdered.

For her previous works, Behn had either invented her plot, albeit on conventional lines, or taken it loosely from books. Considering the scorn felt for those who borrowed by those who did not have to write for money, she must have had some trepidation when, for *Abdelazer*, she set about turning another person's play into her own. *The Rehearsal* cannot have helped: one joke on Mr Bays the playwright was that he simply cribbed from other men's works. In fact, Dryden made no bones about his practice and explained how hard-pressed dramatists were forced to borrow, usually from French plots.[15] Shadwell too borrowed a good deal and was careful to name his sources and collaborators. In his 1675 version of *Psyche*, for example, he acknowledged not only French originals of Molière, Corneille and Quinault, but also the contribution of the composer, Matthew Locke, and the producer Thomas Betterton. Aphra Behn was secretive, however; so she opened herself to charges of plagiarism which the form of adaptation did not deserve.

In his *English Dramatick Poets*, Langbaine wrote of *Abdelazer* that it was 'originally an old Play of *Marloes*, call'd *Lusts Dominion*, or *The Lascivious Queen*, a Tragedy written about Forty years ago, tho' printed in octavo, Lond., 1661'. But, as well as accusing, Langbaine compliments: Behn 'has much improv'd it throughout'.[16] He was right. In spite of following the old play closely, her version has more speedy and shorter speeches, although occasionally this makes the devilish Abdelazer a slightly comic villain in the lively mode of Richard III. It was also more dramatic, with juxtapositions far more stylish than anything in the source.[17] Crowded public scenes follow private ones, formal speeches soliloquies; rhetoric changes in a line. Kneeling by the dying Queen whom he has ordered killed, Abdelazer gives a moving performance of a man in grief, only to term her his greatest plague immediately she dies. Behn had not entirely abandoned her device of whispering, so mocked by *The Rehearsal*, but she did not make it so central to this play, which is full of sounds, from songs to the clanking of swords, from whispers to declamations. So an essentially monothematic work is given some variety.[18]

Abdelazer retains the monstrousness of his source, Eleazer in *Lusts Dominion*, and his strangeness is stressed, his wearing of exotic clothes and his faked profession of Christianity, but Behn invites her audience to give him a little sympathy, especially in his love for his wife, Florella. Although she emphasises difference, she downplays references to his actual appearance. The seventeenth century confused Moor and Negro, frequently combining their physical characteristics: the Moor in *Lusts Dominion* had been more Negro than Moor, but in Behn's play it is the reverse. Abdelazer is conscious, even touchy about his race and colour. So he immediately takes disbelief in the Queen's adultery as a slighting of himself: 'what is there here, / Or in my Soul, or Person, may not be belov'd?' When the Queen's daughter declares her long-standing love for the handsome Alonzo, Abdelazer ascribes it again to his appearance, to 'Nature', that has 'dy'd my skin / With this ungrateful colour' and insists on an aesthetic of blackness, in which he is 'soft and smooth as polisht Ebony' in the dark.

The greatest change Behn made was in the ending. The original play presented a vision of overweening lust for power, finally caught in its own illusion. Philip is crowned and the wicked Queen takes the unlikely step of retiring to a life of penitence. In Behn's play, Abdelazer is destroyed by his own follower and the Queen, after wishing for more sons to kill for her lover, dies a dramatically amorous death, fitting end to a career which in both plays mixed extravagant savagery and farce.

Immediately after the Restoration, plays were political in a Royalist way, avoiding many of the awkward questions avidly discussed during the previous twenty years. By the early 1670s, however, Dryden, Lee, Settle and Otway were interrogating state and church in their heroic plays, as well as power, its potential obscenity, the violence and destruction it could imply. Although *Abdelazer* seems in this mould and suggests a new departure for Behn, the play was not primarily theoretical, and it does not investigate the possible questions of usurpation, right to rule, political morality and law.[19] (She was of course working with an old Renaissance play and some of its conceptions remained: one was Abdelazer's notion of a king as a kind of god, the apex of earthly glory, rather a different notion from the Stuart sense of divine right depicted in *The Amorous Prince* and *The Young King*. There the concept shored up a human weakness and seemed, above all, a prerequisite of social order.) Despite regarding themselves as good monarchists, Otway and others portrayed monstrous regal tyrants who seemed to undermine the patriarchal theory of kingship on which their Royalism was based.[20] Their violent chaotic tragedies had no convincing Shakespearean restoration of order and were quite unlike *Hamlet* or *Macbeth*. Behn might have realised how easy it was to slip from this position into the republicanism of Hoyle or Algernon Sidney, who ridiculed the idea that a trivial and dissipated monarch could be the father of a nation. Perhaps for this reason she saw to it that the most monstrous acts in *Abdelazer* were carried out by the Queen, who breaks sexual and maternal ties. An unmaternal mother is horrific, but not necessarily politically troubling.

In any case, Behn was more interested in the psychological than the political side of the story, the impossibility of fulfilling human desire. Spurred on by experience, she could in heroic tragedy resume the interest she had shown in *The Forc'd Marriage* in violent and uncontrollable men. In that play, Alcippus almost upset the state as well as everyone around him by his tendency to vast rages leading to violence. The women scuttled about him, forced in the end to a masquerade of ghosts to get his attention. It may have been the picture of extreme masculinity that attracted Behn when she read *Lusts Dominion* and saw what it might become. The man under the influence of such a concept was unable to respect women whom he could so easily hurt and murder, while simultaneously idealising a single woman for the purity and honour which she was somehow supposed to hold for his benefit.

Behn rightly saw that such a man could not be satisfied by any woman, since none would ever be pure enough. The Queen in her play, a kind of mother to the court, must prove her love to Abdelazer alone by killing husband and sons. She becomes then a mother only for the Moor, who wishes to placate her because she still has power at court. But she is not fitting as his sexual object; he is bored by her demands, for the woman he will desire sexually will not display *her* sexuality. The Queen killed Abdelazer's desire when she revealed her own, so becoming for him the ultimate whore and threatening an effeminising in himself. His most satisfying act in the play is her murder when she expects sex. It is how men deal with female passion.[21]

By now, Behn probably had considerable control over casting her plays. Although *Abdelazer* was staged at the unusual time of 3 July, when in most years hirelings rather than the regular cast were left to act in London, she was pleased that Betterton wanted to depict the Moor and she gave the major female role of the Queen to Mary Lee, converted since *The Forc'd Marriage* into a leading tragedienne.[22] The play probably had a prologue, but it was not printed with the play, and an epilogue 'Written by a Friend', possibly Ravenscroft or even Otway.[23] It was spoken by a child 'Miss Ariell' from the Nursery (perhaps the future star, Anne Bracegirdle, being raised in the Betterton household). Saucily she imagined herself growing into a woman through applause, each session adding an inch to her height and increasing her budding charms.[24]

Abdelazer was a moderate success, providing a dividend for shareholders of £25, a quarter of that earned by an opera spectacle like Charles Davenant's *Circe* but a great deal more than Elkanah Settle's *Conquest of China* for example.[25] It was seen by Nell Gwyn who had long given up her acting career for establishment as a royal mistress, and by her friend Otway, who probably introduced her to Behn. Flushed with his triumph with *Don Carlos*, Otway was in an expansive mood and he gushed over the play to its author afterwards in a tavern. Yet Behn was not satisfied with her play. Years later in 1687, when she wrote a poem to her friend Sir Francis Fane, eulogising his new tragedy *The Sacrifice*, she remarked:

> I Read with Pleasure, tho I Read with Shame.
> The tender Lawrels which my Brows had drest,
> Flag'd like young Flowers by too much Heat opprest:
> The Generous Fire I felt in every Line,
> Show'd me the cold, the feeble Force of mine.

Behn never tried the experiment of dramatic tragedy again. Perhaps she had no emotional need.[26]

Aphra Behn was back in the theatre, but her spirits did not improve at once. She was upset by her failure to please others with *The Dutch Lover* and herself with *Abdelazer*, which, with its intense portrait of erotic female obsession, may have struck too close to an aspect of her life. She did not like the fervour of her feeling for Hoyle, knowing what a drug obsessive love could become. Her safety valve, besides writing and humour, was, perhaps, emotional promiscuity.

This she may have indulged with the pretty young Emily Price, who was probably a new actress with the Duke's and may have been the daughter of a Captain Warcup, circulator of scurrilous works, a man perhaps known to Behn through her copying activity.[27] Behn had exhausted her confessional strain with Ravenscroft and Elizabeth Barry; they knew too much about her and she needed to steady her mind with a new object. Emily Price was flattered at her confidences. Behn was somebody in the theatre.

The lesbian interest, if there were one, would not have shocked the demi-mondaine circles in which she moved. Indeed, the lesbian and the female transvestite were never as unsettling for society as the male 'molly'—partly because of an inveterate male habit of seeing all sexual activity in terms of its attraction to men and of not regarding anything as sexual that did not include penetration. A woman loving a woman was not masculinised and was often seen in training for or stimulating male love. Such lore could be entertained in the theatre and, in an anonymous play staged in 1677 called *The Constant Nymph*, Elizabeth Barry acted a pastoral hero pretending to be a shepherdess so as to woo a nymph called 'Astrea' who has declared she will never marry. Behn may have had a hand in this work or it may teasingly allude to her; it plays with the lightly erotic tie of women so common in romance, including *L'Astrée*, from which Behn derived her *nom de plume*. If not shocking in the theatre and theatrical society, however, the new feeling for Emily Price may have been unsettling for Behn. After her death, three poems implying an anxious lesbian love were published; they may have been genuine or perhaps forgeries based on her known proclivities. The last two were addressed directly to Price, the first may have been to her as well.[28]

'Verses design'd by Mrs. A. Behn, to be sent to a fair Lady, that desir'd she would absent herself, to cure her Love' describes Behn's visit to the country. A friend or relative suggested she stay for a few weeks in the little village of Dorchester close to Oxford and she had agreed.[29] She might even get on with the 'drudge' of writing, as Dryden did when he retired from London. But, as usual, Behn found solitude and distance little help in combating 'bright Eyes': love was a disease that sufferers took with them.

The second and third poems accompanied the supposed letter to Emily Price. The young woman had been teasing Behn about her retreat, knowing that, for both of them, the bustle of the town was the life's blood. It was summer, however, and the countryside looked enchanting. Behn put on her pastoral spectacles and, ignoring signs of labouring hardship, resolutely saw nymphs and swains in 'rural sports'. Even the rivers joining near Oxford became not just a useful confluence for traffic but a bride and bridegroom uniting for content. As for herself, she was enjoying 'Calm...Day, and peaceful...Night' and she reprimanded Price for her 'deprav'd' preference for 'that hated Town, / Where's not a Moment thou canst call thy own'. Either the words were forged or Behn was showing herself a mistress of styles and opinions. Or they caught a momentary mood. The third poem, a postscript to the letter, was a love song to Price from whom the poet begged affectionate acts not words; if Behn's love is not reciprocated, she will 'cease to live'. The peaceful nights and calm days were only relative it seems.

Apparently, Emily Price wrote briskly back to her friend. After some pleasantries she gave unwelcome news: that Behn's failure to declare the source of *Abdelazer* had backfired and the adaptation had been labelled plagiarism. Even Otway had been heard maligning her, giving his opinion that the critics would not forgive her just because she was a woman. Behn replied at once. She was hurt by the allegations and by the tone of young Emily's letter. Of course she had taken *Abdelazer* from *Lusts Dominion*: she did not hide it. And she was stung by Otway's reported words. She knew she used her sex in a coy way to puff her work, but that her sex really had any meaning in the critical reception of her plays she disputed. Otway's damaging remarks were strange since she had so recently been listening to his rhapsodic praise. She put it down to natural hypocrisy—good-natured young men always wanted to please company. As for her play, she would explain matters when she took 'the pains next to appear in print'; she hoped she could get *Lusts Dominion* republished, so that her 'theft' could be the more public. Since it was Emily Price's opinion she was anxious about, she immediately sent her a copy of the source play, so that she could agree that Behn had indeed 'weeded and improv'd it'. She ended coldly—Emily had obviously not responded in that partly genuine, partly sophisticated way Behn had hoped. She would not be seeing her now until mid-September, she said.[30]

Certainly the news from the town was not inviting, but Behn had to conquer her pique. Since her next play was due on at the beginning of the Autumn season, she could not really afford to stay in the country until September. Rehearsals took a month. So, sensibly, she returned to London.

CHAPTER 15

❧

Poetry in a Theatrical World

'his pleasing Extravagance encreasing with his Liquor'

By the mid-1670s Aphra Behn had thoroughly contracted court cynicism. Her ambiguous status as widow of an obscure man and one-time kept mistress of a bisexual libertine allowed her a latitude unavailable to the respectable woman, married or unmarried. She was no longer young but still attractive, and she relished the sexual electricity in talk between men and women.

With her indifferent health, she would have been wary of bouts of the venereal diseases circulating among her friends; she may have been 'chaste' or she may have enjoyed a kind of safe sex or sexual foreplay, so avoiding the danger and disappointment of more. In a poem entitled 'The Platonick Lady', the Earl of Rochester describes what must often have happened between highly sexed men and women who feared pregnancy or pox. The old platonics of Henrietta Maria's court and Katherine Philips's verses are rejected for something more erotic: the woman wants to retain desire not ruin it with fulfilment, to enjoy the man in her arms, to cuddle and kiss him, to stare in his eyes, to be toyed with and ruffled, to be petted and squeezed, enjoying everything except 'the feate'. These are the 'sweets of Love', affirms the lady. Foreplay was the writer's business. Words replaced or endlessly delayed consummation.

Rochester's own 'sweets' were rather different, for they were now embodied in sex with Behn's friend Elizabeth Barry. She had been a flop in her stage début, probably as Draxilla in Otway's *Alcibiades*. The story goes that Rochester and his cronies saw a performance and found it so appalling that the Earl, a natural actor and steeped in the theatre, struck an improbable wager: that he would in six months make Barry the most convincing actress in the theatre. He then set about training her, making her rehearse repeatedly on stage and in costume. Although she had no talent for mimicry, the usual basis of acting, Barry was intelligent and, where she could not learn lines and remember how to say them, she could enter into feelings, becoming another person when inspired. Rochester developed her potential power from September until July of the next year, when Behn was flattered to be asked to give her friend the small part of Leonora in *Abdelazer*; her first starring role was, however, Queen Isabella in the Earl of Orrery's *Mustapha*.

If letters published after his death are genuine, Thomas Otway had become passionately devoted to Barry from the moment he first saw her.[1] Now he watched in agony as Rochester's care for her acting changed into love. Soon the Earl was begging Barry to 'Leave this gawdy gilded stage… / Where fooles of either sex and age / Crowd to see themselves presented.' He began to measure time by his sightings of her and fall into 'transports' when he received a letter. Like Behn with Hoyle, Rochester could not simply wallow in the 'soft' phrases of their love, but needed constantly to interrogate Barry's words. Which were authentic, which stagey and conventional? He did not know at the beginning and would not at the end. Barry was later accused of ambition and avarice, and called a 'mercenary prostituting Dame'; so perhaps the famous Earl, who termed himself the 'most fantastical odd man alive', was something of a career move for her.[2] Although perpetually broke and no great catch as a keeper, Rochester was a nobleman and a potent influence in the theatre. Like Behn, Barry knew herself to be a professional from a young age, a woman who had to be competitive to make her way in the world alone. She allured men despite her lack of conventional beauty, and she had few moral scruples about bedding them when she wished or when it was expedient.

The affair of Rochester and Barry was racked with jealousy on both sides and, on one occasion, Rochester feared his beloved was being advised by a lean lady and a fat one. When he returned to London and hurried to see her, he was immediately put on guard by the interruption of a neighbouring woman, presumably one of these advisors. He suspected the visitor of being a 'shee Spy', coming 'to solicit your love or constancy'—probably on behalf of a man, perhaps on her own. Could this neighbour, the fat one, have been Aphra Behn? Rochester probably knew something of Behn's past, so this might just have been a private joke.

In due course the relationship resulted in pregnancy and, in December 1677, Barry bore Rochester a child, a girl she named Hesther or Esther. Rochester was absent and Nell Gwyn was 'not without some gentle reflexions on your Lordships want either of generosity or bowells toward a lady who had not refused you the full enjoyment of all her charmes'.[3]

'[P]issing....blood' in the country, Rochester apologised for sending only 'Trifles', since he 'could come at no more', and he wrote to congratulate Barry on her delivery, hoping 'in a little while to look on you with all your beauty about you'. Obviously the 'great-belly' had not much excited him. He was glad 'the child is of the soft sex I love'—it was just as well for a bastard.[4]

'Anger, spleen, revenge, and shame' followed, although Rochester still declared he loved Barry above all things.[5] Perhaps she was not a good mother, perhaps, for all his unconventionality, the Earl had old-fashioned ideas of child-raising, or perhaps he feared her affairs with other men. For whatever reason, he threatened to seize the infant.[6]

Behn may have come to Rochester through Elizabeth Barry in the mid-1670s, although it is possible that he knew her before and helped the reception of her early plays; later, she claimed that he first praised her verses, 'School'd' her 'loose Neglect', and 'rais'd' her 'fame'.[7] She was enormously impressed by him, a young man of poetic gifts, Continental knowledge, glamorous alcoholic style, and aristocratic insouciance. He could afford to scorn fame and money and yet his work, even when it stung as well as mocked, won admiration from everyone of taste. To Aphra Behn he presented ease, charm, power, and effortless skill.

Although not from the major nobility or extremely rich, Rochester came of an exotic father, Lord Wilmot, who had died in exile and had accompanied the King in his escape from Worcester. Memorably he had refused to put on a disguise 'saying that he should look frightfully in it'.[8] This was the sort of panache the son emulated and then surpassed. Clarendon claimed that Lord Wilmot's wit was inspired when 'in the very exercise of debauchery'. The son could have said the same.

Behn was not repulsed by Rochester's seamier side, his drunkenness, his bullying violence, the story of cowardice put about by his enemy, the Earl of Mulgrave, and his comic but menacing exploits of spying on others. Behn, too, liked gossip and scandal and the sense of people's being looked at without their knowledge. Perhaps Killigrew had told her of Corney's surveillance; if so, it did not wean her from fascination with the power of the unknown gaze. The stories of Rochester posting his spies disguised as sentries at the bedroom doors of those he wished to lampoon did not shock her and she appreciated that, as a sympathetic memoirist wrote, 'never did he stab into the Wounds of fallen Virtue, with a base and cowardly Insult'.[9] Nor did he with his mimicry and his practical jokes. They placed him in her world of the theatre.

More surprisingly, Behn was not deterred by Rochester's misogyny, seeing his comic, almost manic, version as usefully moderating the more sinister sort in the general Christian culture. In this, as so often, she showed herself athwart later feminism and femininity. With Rochester, as with Ravenscroft, Behn became not so much a sex object or an asserter of feminism as one of the boys, using male language with a freedom no proper lady could have allowed herself. At the same time, she remained a woman of her time and culture, enjoying gender play and demanding and receiving the attention of gallantry. Rochester, misogynist as he so often sounded, made sex funny.

The Earl was one of a coterie who 'reverence bottle & bold Truth', part of what the Parliamentarian poet, Andrew Marvell, called the 'merry gang' and Dryden 'men of pleasant conversation...ambitious to distinguish themselves from the herd of gentlemen'.[10] They were on the whole sceptical young courtiers, like their King enjoying masquerade and frequenting brothels and the theatre. They scandalised the citizens with their pranks and crimes—as they fully intended to do.

The shifting and quarrelsome group—which at different times included Rochester, the gentlemanly playwrights, Etherege and Wycherley, the later Whig, the Earl of Dorset, Sir Charles Sedley, Henry Savile, the Earl of Mulgrave (before he became Rochester's ferocious enemy), and Killigrew's son, Henry—had enormous power within the theatre and inevitably attracted other playwrights to them.[11] Even if they were not actual patrons, the nobles in this group could pre-engage an audience and direct response. Dorset, an elegant and witty poet whose short satirical songs were in the patrician pastoral style Behn herself sometimes affected, was a generous supporter of Dryden, Otway and Wycherley. In 1685 Behn herself wrote a pindaric for Dorset's wedding to Mary Compton; in it she used her invented character 'Damon' to lament her own lack of riches. Yet she seems not to have appealed to Dorset in the 1670s. He did not like Hoyle, so perhaps that was a deterrent.

Rochester surpassed others of this glittering group, becoming almost mythological in his own time. His wit and his activities were not just idiosyncratic; rather, they appeared as an extreme form of what others might say and do. But what *he* said and did became definitive and fixed in the imagination, and anecdotes and sayings naturally stuck to him. His closest friend was Henry Savile, a little older, Groom of the Bedchamber and man about town, from a prominent Royalist family. Behn might have heard of him from his European tour as a young man in 1661 with the Earl of Sunderland and Henry Sidney, the younger brother of Algernon and Philip. Fat and bibulous (Pepys used him as a touchstone of lewdness), Savile juggled, as Rochester never quite did, politics and pleasure, giving up neither.

With Savile, Rochester, who famously declared his preference for 'a sweet, soft page' to 'forty wenches', may have been physically intimate, and he appears to have dispatched one or two possible lovers to his friend. One of these was James Paisible the French musician, sent as a 'present' from the 'tired bugger' Rochester. By 1677 Paisible was in favour at court and the King was hearing his compositions 'with very great delight'.[12] Aphra Behn wrote a poem to go with one of his tunes, in which a despairing lover threatens to haunt his unfaithful mistress as a ghost.[13]

Rochester's fatherless and shifting background was like that of many of the witty young men at court, as well as some lawyers like Hoyle. Deracinated, they were attracted to a popular version of the individualistic and materialistic philosophy of Thomas Hobbes, bugbear of the orthodox and tutor for a time of the King himself; his *Leviathan* (1651) caused him to be denounced as an 'atheist'. Hobbesianism, with its foreshadowings in the classical philosophies of Epicurus and Lucretius, dominated court culture: indeed Hobbes was said to have 'corrupted half the gentry of the nation'.[14] Even the members of the Royal Society had found his materialism too extreme to countenance and he had been refused membership.

For Thomas Hobbes, the spring of human motivation was the desire for self-gratification; the desirable was the state of ease, so action sprang from fear. In the absence of any compelling spiritual reality, reason served animal appetite. Since humanity was a mass of shifting atoms, the 'present only has a being in nature. Things past have a being in the memory, only. But things to come have no being at all, the future being but a fiction of the mind.'[15] This implied no care for an afterlife. In fact, Hobbes thought knowledge of the past could develop prudence and foresight, but Rochester reinterpreted the notion as a justification for refusing constraint and any notion of consistency or fidelity: "Tis Nature's Law to Change, / Constancy alone is strange.'[16] For Rochester, brought up in a pious household, it was perhaps the shocking reversal of Christianity implied in so much of Hobbes and the old philosophers that attracted him. For Charles Blount and others of Rochester's later circle, it was simply the thoroughgoing scepticism.

Hoyle had been a follower of Hobbes, but, in Rochester, Behn found the philosophy combined with wit and nobility more seductive. She had scanty religious grounding: her poetry reveals few echoes of liturgy or scripture and her inevitable years of churchgoing seem to have left little residue. Hobbes was not an atheist in the modern sense, but he did dislike doctrinal religion, and his mechanistic, materialist philosophy, if carefully cherry-picked, could be made to support libertinism amd allow a freedom from shame and corruption that attracted Behn as much as it did Rochester. People were free and noble until they became wretched through concepts of law and sin, both inventions of the human mind.

One element of the libertine philosophy that amused Behn was the notion of the critical moment. If atoms were shifting, they were in conjunction only once. Translated, this became the critical sexual moment at which orgasm had to happen. In *The Man of Mode*, Dorimant told Harriet that they should use 'the lucky Minute' and Rochester's Cloris, refusing princes, found her 'lucky minute' with a swain.

In his dedication to Rochester of *Marriage A-la-Mode* in 1672, Dryden wrote that, if the play were raised above the common rank, it was because he had been 'admitted to your Lordship's Conversation'. This was flattery, but it seems that easy aristocratic wit could affect the style of less privileged and more professional writers. In a curious way, the groups may slightly have envied each other. People like Dryden, and even more so Behn, coveted the status of the nobly born and gifted, while admiring their confidence and haughty disdain for mercenary scribblers. At the same time, someone like Rochester, without much political ambition, had no very clear function, and some of his manic escapades suggest a vast energy with no necessary channels such as the earning of a living would have provided.

Aphra Behn could write easily and fluently. This was just the skill for an amusing evening of the sort that the ageing expatriate French nobleman, Saint-Évremond, later described nostalgically to the Duchess of Mazarine: 'those sprightly Hours of Lord ROCHESTER's Life, when he fired the Breasts of Ladies with Love, and wounded those of Men with Envy'.[17]

Behn seems to have been part of various coteries of rhyming wits and she probably came to Rochester's attention at this time. The atmosphere he created round him was inspiring to Behn, who liked company and sparkle. Sometimes many were too drunk to sparkle much, although alcohol tended to inspire Rochester to his greatest flights, 'his pleasing Extravagance encreasing with his Liquor' as Saint-Évremond elegantly expressed it.

Drink also inspired the playwright Nat Lee, although it made his face erupt in carbuncles. He, too, was wittier drunk than sober and, since he was often drunk, he was often witty. Although he had a chequered relationship with Rochester and even moved over to his arch rival, Mulgrave, when Rochester dismissed a play of his as sentimental 'fustian', Behn liked Lee and they became friends. He may possibly have loved her, for the writer of the 'Memoirs' claimed that Behn had the acquaintance and friendship of 'the most sensible Men of the Age; and the Love of not a few of different Characters; for tho' a Sot have a Portion of Wit of his own, he yet like Old Age, covets what he cannot enjoy'. After her death, Lee claimed, 'I lov'd thee inward, and my Thoughts were true / ...Thou hadst my Soul in Secret, and I swear / I found it not, till though resolv'dst to Air.'[18] With his wit, drunken jollity and irascibility, Lee was not an easy man to know well but Behn was used to moody, violent men. Although she did not care for his virulent anti-Catholicism, she never let difference of opinion obscure friendship or interest.

Rochester's poems provided grim pictures of women's sexuality, but these pictures, Behn saw, sprang from anxiety as much as hate. Sexual feelings in women were accepted and sometimes women might imitate the frankness of men. Restoration culture exploited the female body, but it allowed women to exploit the exploitation, in the process giving a space to the unfeminine female for a kind of expression not allowed before in English culture. Behn's plays had already suggested some frankness on sexual matters, but, within the coterie of the Earl of Rochester, she saw 'looser Songs, and Pieces, too obscene for the Ladies Eyes'. She may even have read the scandalous play, *Sodom, Or, The Triumph of Debauchery*; since it had an uncharacteristically awkward style, this was perhaps attributed to Rochester primarily because of his wicked reputation. In the louche atmosphere, Behn began to write poetry even more risqué than she had already done and to mitigate her own sexual grief over Hoyle by seeing sex in comic mode. Burlesque was a good weapon with which to recover self-esteem. She was not too old or too unappealing and need not despair; besides, she had not the temperament for too long aching.

Behn had already adopted a masculine, hearty voice in her poem to Ravenscroft. Now, in the sessions of drink and talk, she heard the real accent: 'Much wine had passed, with grave discourse / Of who fucks who and who does worse...'. In one evening, the company took up Ovid; perhaps someone had read a French poem based on his famous depiction of impotence in *Amores*, and brought a copy along. They decided to write on the theme which had, with venereal disease so rampant, become literally a burning issue. Etherege may have proposed it, for he had, in the less explicit days of the early 1660s, already written his own 'Imperfect Enjoyment', where the man's failure was laid to the door of female modesty or prudery—in this drunken gathering there was no mention of 'brewer's droop'. The men were interested to see what a woman would write, and urged Behn on.

The poem she wrote, perhaps collaboratively, was called 'The Disappointment', and it was a second translation of a French poem. It had a pastoral form and was set in the dry and sunny land of Arcadia, where the ground was never damp. The amorous Lysander surprises fair Cloris when her few defences are down. The pair repair to a lone thicket 'made for Love', where Cloris permits his 'Force' with 'a Charming Languishment'. Soon she is taking the initiative.

At first Lysander gains fresh vigour from her desire and her muted and whispered protestations that she will cry out if he goes on. He 'Kisses her Mouth, her Neck, her Hair' and presses his burning and trembling hand on her 'swelling Snowy Brest'. Cloris is now at his disposal; all her 'Unguarded Beauties lie / The Spoils and Trophies of the Enemy'. He moves swiftly and soon reaches

> That Paradice
> Where Rage is calm'd, and Anger pleas'd,
> That Fountain where Delight still flows,
> And gives the Universal World Repose.[19]

'Repose' is not what Lysander achieves, however. They are now 'joyn'd' on the moss, Cloris in a swoon of desire, her bosom bare and herself 'half dead and breathless', when it becomes apparent that the 'O'er-Ravish'd Shepherd' is 'unable to perform the Sacrifice'. Indeed, as he parts Cloris's clothes, he realises that his pleasure has become pain, and that he now has desire but no erection. He tries a little masturbation to right matters, but 'No motion 'twill from Motion take' and he works away too vigorously or in vain: 'The Insensible fell weeping in his Hand.' Cloris is not pleased. She tries with 'Her timerous Hand' to feel for his penis but, finding it limp, draws back in horror. As Behn expresses it candidly, 'The *Nymph's* Resentment none but I / Can well Imagine or Condole.' She does go on to detail the misery of Lysander as well; yet, with some irony, she portrays the swain cursing his birth, fate and stars, but most of all Cloris, whose

Charms,
Whose soft bewitching Influence
Had Damn'd him to the *Hell* of Impotence.

The woman is at fault through her eagerness and desirability. Presumably Behn knew this scenario well.[20]

When Rochester put his Cloris in a pig sty and watched her masturbate there, he created a counter pastoral and broke the pastoral scene. Behn resists this level of polarising, but she does make Cloris run out of the pastoral world in comic parody of Daphne fleeing to safeguard her virginity from the amorous and ravishing god Apollo. After this, the euphemisms of the pastoral collapse and the word 'impotence' starkly appears.

Although 'The Disappointment' follows the French source closely at first, it veers off in the conclusion. The French poet had set his encounter in the world of domestic adultery, not pastoral love and, after Behn concluded, he proceeded for another thirty-six stanzas, of which the deficient lover used five for excited protestation. He was then hustled out of the window before the approaching husband. There was nothing about the woman's feelings, but a great deal about the shame and misery of Lysandre who, on the next evening, crept back to the lady, found her sleeping in appealing disarray, leapt on her 'Like a hawk on its prey' and recovered his manhood. Behn concludes her poem in the fourteenth stanza of the French original. The shock of her 'Disappointment' is that it is the *woman's*.

The seventeenth century believed in female pleasure, if few thought it as important as the male's. With a view of the body based on the four humours, the male was better than but not different from the female, being simply more hot and dry. The male semen was of course what mattered. It made the sex act complete, in many views it begot the child. But female orgasm was also thought necessary for reproduction; so the woman had to be considered and, as the famous sex manual of the time declared it, clitoral excitement 'is that which gives a Woman Delight in Copulation: For without this a Woman hath neither a Desire to Copulation, and Delight in it…'.[21]

Probably 'The Disappointment' had to be written in a social setting; it is a leap from plays about love and intrigue to poetry about sex, and no English woman before Behn is known to have been so explicit. Still, she was restrained even here, letting the mockery inhere in what she omitted. Rochester did not follow her restraint and, like Etherege and Ovid before him, in his poem of 'disappointment' he displayed his man railing against his penis for its failing. For Rochester, the realisation of impotence provoked mock shame and then blind rage in his hero who, however, managed to remember that 'This dart of love... / With virgin blood the thousand maids have dyed.'

In contrast, Nat Lee provided a pathetic variation, 'Love's Opportunity Neglected', in which the willing mistress was played with until her desire was heightened and 'her Passion was done'. This gallantry serves the man ill, for he has 'slighted the Critical Minute of Love'. As for Wycherley, he put his impotence poem on the stage as *The Country Wife*, making the man in control of his body by feigning impotence. He could thus become a rake by pretending to be a eunuch, or perhaps he merely became what Behn feared men could become: tradesmen with their sperm.

When she went home after her composition, much amused by what she had read and no doubt giving amusement by what she had written, Behn left a copy with Rochester or another in his circle. When he died a few years later, it was published as his, in the pirated *Poems by the Right Honourable the E. or R.*[22] She made no protest but quietly printed it again under her own name. It was a compliment to have her verses taken for his. After her death, it entered a new context: Sam Briscoe published it in 1718 within a letter supposedly to Hoyle, blaming him for his homo-sexuality. Whether this is genuine or not—and it seems unlikely given her views—'The Disappointment' may have been in part intended for Hoyle, a comic assault where he was most vulnerable. Throughout her works, male failure in performance with women would be in a context of men's relations with each other, as if she suspected homosexuality as the foe to fulfilment of her heterosexual desires.

Another poem of Behn's that passed for Rochester's, possibly because it began life in a poetic evening, was the sensuous and steamy 'On a Juniper-Tree, cut down to make Busks'. Busks are strips of wood used to stiffen the front of corsets; so they were intimate with the female breasts. The poem describes a voyeuristic tree, the evergreen juniper, leaning over and leering at a shepherdess, again called Cloris, in the throes of love. Like Behn before she met Hoyle, the tree had been self-sufficient, but it was now much aroused by the coupling. The encounter it witnessed was ambiguous: the woman had led the man on by her 'Languishment', but, none the less, the shepherd 'waits no consent', sex needing that little violence to make it piquant. In this, Behn echoes Rochester, who, likewise, implicates women in rape. But it is no matter in the pastoral world for, unlike in the real, there is no consequence: the woman is pleased to be forced and the man's love 'Before and after was the same'. In this happy state, the pair could eroticise the very landscape, including the juniper tree: 'The Shepherdess my Bark carest, / Whilst he my Root, Love's Pillow, kist.' Having been so aroused, the tree could not give up voyeurism or bear to be 'No more a joyous looker on'. In pity—but with overtones of a more violent and sexually aggressive act—Cloris cut the tree down and turned it into busks of a female corset. The corset became the mask of the female body and its guardian in the *real* world. In Arcadia there was no need for corsetry.

By the third quarter of the 1670s, Behn had a wide circle of artistic and intellectual friends, although she was probably never an *intimate* of Rochester's aristocratic circle or more than an occasional entertainer of the great.[23] More appropriate to her rank and business, she was now close to painters and writers, some met through the theatre, some through her legal friends. She had, for example, become a 'Mate' of Thomas Flatman, formerly of the Inner Temple and now a slightly melancholic poet and miniaturist.[24] It was easy to grow close to a man who tended to the confessional. Flatman shared Behn's admiration for Cowley and his Pindarics, though, like her, he had been mocked for his imitations, one of which had been a tribute to Katherine Philips. Rochester labelled them indiscriminately the result of 'a jaded muse whipt with loose reins'.

Flatman, in turn, was connected to the portrait painter Mary Beale, to whom he taught the art of miniature painting. Mary Beale moved to Pall Mall in 1670 and became moderately well known as a portraitist, especially of children. Yet, although the publication of Behn's racier works was in the future, and Beale possibly did paint Rochester (or at least his image, after Lely), the kindly, pious and married daughter of a Puritan clergyman is unlikely ever to have been intimate with such a woman as Behn. Perhaps, however, she painted Behn and the portrait now hanging in St Hilda's College, Oxford, is hers. Unfortunately the work, which appears to date from the Interregnum or early Restoration and to be of a generic Cavalier lady, looks like no other portrait of Beale's, being closer to the hard lines of the Flemish–Dutch school than to the soft focus Beale usually adopted. Nor does it look like any other alleged picture of Aphra Behn. Still, it is a nice idea that the only professional female portraitist of the later Restoration painted the only female playwright.[25]

More likely, though again neither artist nor sitter is authenticated, is the portrait allegedly by the luscious court artist, the Dutch Sir Peter Lely, who moved in the sort of literary circles of which Behn inhabited the fringe. In the Interregnum Lely had painted portraits of the Sealed Knot conspirators, with whom her foster-brother Thomas Colepeper and his half-brother had been associated, but his great success came later, when his languishing portraits of the nobility did so much to fix the Restoration's erotic gaze. The picture of Behn, a standard oval with cartouche, must be dated through the hairstyle to the 1670s. Quite likely it was ordered by the theatre since it was apparently the practice at Dorset Garden to hang up 'the poets' pictures'. The portrait is labelled 'Mrs Behn. The Poetess' and later was said to have come into the possession of Betterton's 'machinist', the playwright Tom Wright, a move quite feasible if it had been hanging in a dilapidated theatre for some years.[26] Despite stressing a solid self-assertion in the face, Lely gave his sitter the conventional soft clothes and skin, the plump chin and lips that were the hallmark of his lazily 'animated Canvas'.[27] This was inevitably so, especially for the drapery, since people of Behn's status tended to get mass treatment from Lely; that is, they chose a numbered pose which was then executed by artists in the studio, with the master doing the face alone from life. Aphra Behn appears in the fashion of the 1670s from the thick curls down to the full mouth.

Probably Behn's closest artist friend was John Greenhill, originally from Salisbury, who may also have known Mary Beale since he lodged with a dealer in her pictures. A former pupil of Lely's, Greenhill had, by the late 1660s, also become a successful portrait painter with his own practice and he was much in demand by aristocrats and celebrities. He provided likenesses of poets such as Cowley and Davenant, as well as of the Duke of York and the King. He probably also painted Aphra Behn or at least drew her, although no suitable picture has been identified.[28] Greenhill liked the bohemian society of literary and theatrical people, and soon his life became dominated by the heavy drinking and irregular hours that were taking their toll on Rochester, Lee and Otway. Like them, he had not the physique for debauchery. In 1676 he died, still in his early thirties, having supposedly got so drunk that he fell into a gutter in Long Acre near Dryden's home. He shared his mode of death with Nell Gwyn's mother.

When Behn wrote his elegy, she saw Greenhill not as a drunk, but as an equivocally erotic man, the sort to whom she was so frequently attracted. He was a person who could, in his painting, copy his own perfections, 'For he had all that cou'd adorn a Face, / All that cou'd either Sex subdue'—a conventional enough androgynous description, but Behn was especially prone to make it. She remembered him 'warm'd with Love and Wine', never abusive like other alcoholics, firm in his friendships and invariably gentle, a sort of man-woman. His art too was androgynous, for he was supremely the painter of Arcadia, with its unregulated pleasure and unthreatening sexuality. Because he was an Arcadian painter, it was right that he should eschew the Christian heaven and inhabit 'Groves of Everlasting Dawn'.

It was the death not only of a likable man Behn mourned but of a fellow-artist who could give her and her friends 'Immortalitie'. His works improved on their human subjects and had a less physical and more refined effect on the viewers than the originals had:

> The Face and Eies, more Darts receiv'd from him,
>   Then all the Charms she [Nature] can create.
> The Difference is, his Beauties do beget
> In the inamour'd Soul a Vertuous Heat:
>   While Natures Grosser Pieces move,
>   In the course road of Common Love.

Despite its refinement, however, Greenhill's brush is thoroughly eroticised. Painting and poetry can create a body which exists in three dimensions and responds softly to the touch. The result is baroque metaphysics, with *putti* floating over cloud-like breasts:

> So bold, yet soft, his touches were;
> So round each [part,] so sweet and fair.
> That as his Pencil mov'd men thought it prest,
> The Lively imitating rising Breast,
> Which yield like Clouds, where little Angels rest.[29]

In the end, the vision fades and, though his pictures have preserved others in their prime, they have not preserved the painter.

Behn probably wrote her elegy for Greenhill in company, even, again, collaboratively. Like 'The Disappointment', it was first published as the Earl of Rochester's.

The combination of poetic development and libertine excitement resulted in one of Behn's most successful pastoral poems, 'The Golden Age'. Like 'The Disappointment', it was based on a French original, but was also a greatly expanded—198 lines of pindarics—adaptation of the famous Act I chorus of the pastoral play, *Aminta*, written in the previous century by the Italian poet Torquato Tasso. In the poem, Behn brought together many of the themes of this period of her life, while providing her own happy resolution to the problem of 'Disappointment'.

The myth of the Golden Age to which Behn so constantly refers goes back as far as Hesiod in about 700 BC, but her apprehension seems closest to Ovid's in Book I of his *Metamorphoses*. It refers to the period before the Olympian gods seized power, a time when gods and men lived together amicably under the benign rule of Saturn or Cronos and under the influence of the goddess Justice or Astrea, Behn's own pseudonym. Subsequently, it was imagined as a time of civilization, but without its discontents, an era of fecund plenty without effort, when war, work, property, shame and sexual constraints were unknown. In the pastoral age, agriculture had not been invented, or, as Behn put it, 'The stubborn Plough had then, / Made no rude Rapes upon the Virgin Earth; / Who yeilded of her own accord her plentious Birth; / Without the Aids of men.' In the Renaissance, the Golden Age was reimagined with great intensity, especially by Tasso. His poem was made into an English version, which, however, played down the sexual freedom at the heart of Tasso's lines.[30]

Dryden was worried that the Golden Age subverted the Christian myth of Eden, and he sometimes equated it with the Hobbesian state of nature.[31] Other consistent monarchists saw that it undercut the Royalist notion that kings owned power from God and that people were born subjects.[32] But Behn shared with Tasso, Rochester, Wycherley and Otway a sense of yearning for past innocence, and her time of pleasure was not subverted by Christian considerations. Nor was it undercut by the use she made of it for a common or uncommon seduction—in the most obvious reading 'The Golden Age' is an invitation to bed by an ungendered speaker.

Behn feared that sex had become trammelled with economy, that love was a kind of trade, and that intercourse was physical and mercenary. Desire depended on constructed subterfuges, on clothed nakedness and illicit pleasure, while passion was created by the politics of honour, rights, property and authority. In her imagined Golden Age, here a pre-pastoral time which reached the pastoral world of seduction only at the end, no one hoarded riches for themselves and sex was pleasure not power. Since the male institutions of power, from kingship, religion and property to honour and shame, were absent, 'Nymphs' could be 'free, no nice, no coy disdain, / Deny'd their Joyes, or gave their Lover pain'. 'Joyes' were not transitory but 'everlasting, ever new'. No virginity, no impotence, no satiety. Since there was no shame, there was no need for constricting clothes and all the cumbersome pretence of Restoration fashion which dictated stiff oppressive undergarments and a free-flowing exterior. Woman was not bound in corsets or in repressive sexual codes.

It was a fantasy world where all were aristocrats; no domestic or agricultural labour was required. As there was no plough to pierce the virgin earth, no sword, so, it is implied, there was no erect penis either. Sexual joys were not dependent on potency. There was no heterosexuality only sexuality and the snake which poor Cloris found so limp had here no 'spightful Venom' at all, 'But to the touch were Soft, and to the sight were Gay'. Ease and sex could both arrive without 'the Aids of men'. Had Cloris and Lysander strayed into the Golden Age realm, they would not have suffered 'Disappointment'.

Much of the power of the utopia in 'The Golden Age' comes from the invocation of its opposite, the leaden world of money, war, trade, merchandise and sexuality as commodity. In this world, the false concept of honour has induced shame and made men and women both commodify sex. So the woman herself ties up her hair:

> The Envious Net, and stinted order hold,
> The lovely Curls of Jet and shining Gold,
> No more neglected on the Shoulders hurl'd:
> Now drest to Tempt, not gratify the World,
> Thou Miser Honour hord'st the sacred store,
> And starv'st thy self to keep thy Votaries poor.

> Honour! that put'st our words that should be free
>   Into a set Formality
> Thou base Debaucher of the generous heart,
> That teachest all our Looks and Actions Art....[33]

The poem ends invoking the lines which Tasso also had invoked, from the Roman poet Catullus: 'Suns can sink and rise again: for us, when once the brief light has ended, there is a night of perpetual sleep.' Or as Behn puts it, 'The Sun and Spring receive but our short Light, / Once sett, a sleep brings an Eternal Night.'

'The Golden Age' is a felicitous poem, although, wanting to find fault where he could, Pope quoted some lines out of context in his *Art of Sinking in Poetry*; stopping Behn in mid-sentence, he made her exemplify the florid style. Irritated into even more egregious misreading and misquoting was a contemporary lampoonist who would come to be the scourge of the liberated Mrs Behn, a man with a background not far from her own, the former servant Robert Gould. Immune to the wit of a lethargic Cupid using his bow only when he felt men were ignoring sex, Gould made Behn summon ten thousand 'wanton Cupids' scattering 'lecherous Darts'; Behn had presented only 'A Thousand Cupids' fanning their wings, occasionally sending a dart to an 'uninspir'd' shepherd. Meanwhile Behn's amorous swains and shepherdesses became men servicing lusting virgins. The 'Golden Age', as rewritten by Gould, argued a want of 'Chastity' in its author and outdid the filth of Rome and Greece.[34]

The 'Golden Age' theme colours another poem of Behn's probably from this time, in which she portrayed herself as a sort of mythical Astrea, the guardian of the easeful aristocratic realm. The King had reappointed the estimable Duke of Ormonde as Lord Lieutenant of Ireland, and Ormonde had set off in August 1677 with a retinue of two earls, two viscounts 'and several other noblemen and gentlemen'.[35] To one of these gentlemen, just possibly his younger son, the untried and earlier troublesome Earl of Arran, Behn may have addressed her 'Farewell to Celadon'.

'Celadon' was one of Behn's most commonly used pastoral names, the initial association with Scot having long since been broken. Although it was often given to 'swains' with whom she, as Astrea, could be associated, it might refer to anyone. The only hint of identity in the poem is that the man is young, rich, noble and loyal.[36]

An autonomous and tranquil aristocrat, Celadon had been in a Golden Age by being at home on his estate, where ease, amorousness and pleasure attended his days. Now he was being urged into a debased world in which aristocrats could no longer leave business to the underprivileged and factious; they must become the bulwark of a needy monarchy. Conventionally in pastoral poems, a kind of masculine effort disrupts a feminine peace. Here the King crashes through the poem as the Almighty, Jove and Caesar, responsible for Celadon's 'fall' from 'easie quietude'. Behn implied no disloyalty, but she was rarely admiring of the *acts* of Charles II. She no doubt remembered her own experiences when, in the poem, she described the royal service as 'hurry, noise, and news'. None the less, however much a nobleman might wish to leave politics to the underprivileged, 'To him to whom forgetful Heaven, / Has no one other vertue given, / But dropt down the unfortunate, / To Toyl, be Dull, and to be Great', he must be about royal business. The only consolation is that, in his few hours away from 'Toiles', Celadon may establish a wistful pastoral world in Ireland and have again his Damon and 'some dear Shee' to tumble on the 'Mossey Beds'.

Because men tended to write prologues and epilogues and to be recorded more than women, Behn seems largely to move in a masculine literary world during these years. As she gained fame, however, she attracted younger women poets and would-be playwrights. One was the plain, clever, witty (and later scandalous) Elizabeth Taylor, daughter of Sir Thomas Taylor from Maidstone in Kent, whom Behn probably met through the widespread Colepeper family. Although reputedly the lover of Thomas Colepeper of Preston Hall, namesake of Behn's foster-brother, this spirited and extravagant lady went on in 1685 to marry the trimming judge, Francis Wythens, possibly in imitation of Behn's later fortune-hunting girls.[37] She seems to have had the same literary Royalist taste in poets as Behn, being a great admirer of Cowley, and she wrote very creditable songs, which had fairly wide manuscript circulation. Later Behn published her work, including her pleas (made ironic by later circumstances) to 'Virgin Pow'rs' to defend her from improper love.[38] In lampoons Betty Taylor had a hectic sex life and loved the bottle.[39]

Another friend of this time was 'Ephelia', who may have been Behn's link to Rochester's enemy, the Earl of Mulgrave. Her 'infant Muse' now 'i'th'Bud', Ephelia was far more successful than Katherine Philips and even Aphra Behn at secrecy (she still manages to hide her identity). Like Behn, she seems to have become a Londoner. Possibly she was a failed actress and possibly freckled or red-headed, since the name was close to the Greek term for freckles. One or two references to 'Easiness' suggest she lost her 'honour' young. The portrait accompanying her poems displayed a woman with abundant ringlets, large eyes and almost naked breasts; on her falling gown is the miniature of a man, presumably the object of her passion. The reader is left to decide whether the semi-nakedness expresses grief or the foolishness of the man who could run from such substantial charms.[40]

Ephelia may have been briefly intimate with the Earl of Mulgrave, often called Bajazet after the proud Turkish sultan. An anonymous poem of complaint circulating at this time, 'Ephelia to Bajazet', was quickly burlesqued in a work written as if by the vain Mulgrave: 'in my deare self, I center ev'ry thing....If heretofore you found grace in my Eyes, /

Be thankfull for it, and let that suffice.' Possibly 'Ephelia' did write the first poem or possibly the whole exchange of submissive woman and dominating man was a Rochesterian game, with Etherege writing the Ephelia verses as Rochester wrote Bajazet.[41]

Behn and Ephelia, mocked by Robert Gould as a 'ragged jilt', were brought together in satire, for both were impudent and wrote for bread.[42] Indeed they may even have collaborated on some verses in the paper-war about the nature of women started by the misogynistic Gould and spiritedly continued by 'Sylvia' of *Sylvias Revenge*. Possibly his knowledge of both women prompted Rochester to assume the mask of the witty and bleak female poet, Artemiza, who warns herself:

> Dear Artemiza, poetry's a snare:
> Bedlam has many Mansions: have a Care.
> Your Muse diverts you, makes the Reader sad;
> You Fancy you'r inspir'd, he thinkes, you mad…
> …Whore is scarce a more reproachfull name,
> Then Poetesse.[43]

If the poem is written with Behn anywhere in mind, however—and it has something of the gossipy voice of her verse epistles—it is not fierce. Poetry appears a snare and delusion for everyone, not only for women, and general satires 'against the Poets' warn all of them that Bedlam will be their end, a warning later exemplified by the horrid fate of Nat Lee, who, falling into insanity, was confined in chains in the dark. Certainly Behn was not publicly upset about the poem, knowing that, in any case, a man could scorn the type yet hold her in high esteem. In epilogues and prologues Behn herself often echoed the male viewpoint, that women's art should be in pleasing men rather than in writing, but this did not make her lay down her pen.

The comic misogynous urbanity of Rochester was not shared by all his readers. Robert Gould took up the whore-poetess conjunction to very different effect, damning both Behn and Ephelia:

> …*Hackney Writers*, when their Verse did fail
> To get 'em Brandy, Bread and Cheese, and Ale,
> Their Wants by Prostitution were supply'd;
> Shew but a *Tester*, you might up and ride:
> For *Punk* and *Poetess* agree so Pat,
> You cannot well be *This*, and not be *That*.[44]

But Gould, wreaking on women much of his own social frustration, saw any trespassing on male preserve as an affront: 'Songs Obscene fit not a Woman's Pen.' Satire is a male province. Behn did not agree.

CHAPTER 16

❦

The Rover and *Thomaso*

'I will gaze – to let you see my Strength'

With her work circulating in manuscript, Aphra Behn was by now fairly well known as a poet, and even limited association with the Rochester circle must have increased her fame. She was pleased to find Edward Phillips (Milton's nephew) mentioning her in his compilation of poets, *Theatrum Poetarum* (1675), although he reserved his highest praise for the dead Katherine Philips as 'the most applauded....Poetess of our Nation'. Ironically she was perhaps more gratified to be included in a widely read satire on playwrights called the 'Session of the Poets', which might have been by Elkanah Settle since it mocked Dryden, Shadwell and Otway, his foes of the moment—as well (very mildly) as himself. Certainly Otway, ridiculed for his lice, mange and pride, assumed it so and attacked Settle back. It could just as well have been by Rochester, however, or a combination of wits.[1]

Like the Countess of Winchilsea's 'Circuit of Apollo', it was in the 'session' mode in which the god had to award a prize to the leading playwright. Each stepped forward. The Laureate, Dryden, was eliminated because it was rumoured he might be ordained and go to Oxford, Etherege because he was idle though witty, Wycherley because he was not a professional 'Trader in Witt' but a 'Gentleman-Writer', Shadwell because he was bibulous and vain, Nat Lee because he was clever only when drunk, Settle because he was out of fashion and so on. After Ravenscroft came his friend Aphra Behn:

> The Poetesse Afra, next shew'd her black Ace;
> The Lawrell, by a double right was her owne,
> For the Plays she had writ, and the Conquests she had won.
> Apollo acknowledg'd, 'twas hard to deny her,
> But to deal franckly, and Ingeniously by her,
> He told her, were Conquests, and Charmes her pretence,
> She ought to have pleaded a Douzen yeares since.

213

She was about thirty-five at the time, and the poem was generous considering the usual mockery of a sexually aware woman of her age. She shared her black arse (both dark colouring and licentiousness since darkness and sexual ardour were conventionally tied) with the King, who is reported by Burnet to have quipped to an opponent, 'At doomsday we shall see whose a— is blackest.'[2]

In the end, the actor-manager-adapter Tom Betterton points out that 'since Poets, without the kind Players, may hang' and since he had not rushed vulgarly into print, the prize should be his; so it is agreed. The unprovocative point is made that play-writing is communal, and poetic pretension absurd in a commercial, collaborative world.[3]

As at the beginning of her career, so now in the late 1670s, Aphra Behn was mapping out several plays. She hoped that, staggered through the months, they would provide a reasonable income. Possibly to compensate for Hoyle's financial defection, she may now have made some arrangement with Betterton for a yearly payment. Many playwrights shunted between the two playhouses; Behn seems to have been loyal to the Duke's.

Abdelazer had taught her the quick benefits of adaptation or revision and her next play, *The Town-Fopp*, was made from George Wilkins's Jacobean drama, *Miseries of Inforst Marriage*, last printed in 1637. It concerns a hero, Bellmour, prevailed on for the sake of his inheritance to jilt his beloved, Celinda, and marry Diana. He grows dissipated from shame but, after much agonising, all is righted in one of those marriage annulments Behn so often fantasised. (In the source play the hero has to adjust to a *real* marriage and an unwanted wife, as well as two sons he has hitherto been calling bastards.) The only casualty in Behn's play is Bellmour's sister who, dreading poverty, marries the unsavoury Sir Timothy Tawdry, a foppish rake without the rake's saving wit. The poor girl probably reflected Behn's own occasional feelings in the depth of her affair with Hoyle when she exclaimed: 'Wou'd I were in *Flanders* at my Monastery again.'

So much worldliness, drinking and dissipation were portrayed in Sir Timothy that there was no room in the play for any sympathetic raffish character like Alonzo in *The Dutch Lover* or for a comic portrait of the fop, as in Etherege's *The Man of Mode*, produced earlier in 1676.[4] The actions of Bellmour are hard to make either funny or heroic, since he simply distresses the simple Celinda, as well as Diana who, when her sexual overtures are sternly repulsed, reasonably echoes Alcippus of *The*

Forc'd Marriage in asking, 'Why, since you could not love me, did you marry me?' In his dissipation in the brothel, Bellmour has some comedy, but his self-hate is more tragicomic than comic, and the potentially satirical scene is not allowed to comment, as it might have done, on the erotic politics of sexual relations.[5] Below the level of the hero, there is a Restoration easiness across sexes that sits ill with the stern attitudes of the original play.[6] Abandoned by Bellmour, Diana falls for Celinda dressed as a boy; the latter is horrified by the display of explicit female desire, but, on learning her mistake, Diana simply exclaims, 'Bless me!— did I then love a Woman?' She does not seem unduly upset.

All in all, *The Town-Fopp* was a less successful and careful job than *Abdelazer*, with some long undramatic speeches left in and a muddled morality. Yet it has interest in being Behn's first *London* comedy, catching her sense of metropolitan life and culture. A nurse says to Sir Timothy, 'I live without Surgeons, wear my own Hair, am not in Debt to my Taylor… who wakes thee every Morning with his Clamour and long Bills, at thy Chamber-door.' Whores scrap over clients and debate the status of kept women and prostitutes, growing philosophical over the changing times: since surface is everything, the stale woman with a fine petticoat, right points and clean garnitures is more valued than the pretty novice.

The Town-Fopp was staged in the autumn season of 1676 probably in September. No cast list is given, but Betty Currer may have played the aptly named mistress of Sir Timothy, Betty Flauntit.[7] The pert, vivacious Currer from Ireland was one of the new actresses at the Duke's, her whorish reputation offstage being eminently exploitable in the *double entendres* of prologues and epilogues.[8] Over the years she would inspire Behn to some sprightly comic writing, especially once Elizabeth Barry had veered towards pathos. A cheeky epilogue was supplied for the play by Mr E. R., probably Ravenscroft, who had appreciated the saucy poem Behn sent him in his sweating-tub and was sorry for his delinquency. The play was successful enough to be revived in November when Nell Gwyn went to see it and it was printed in 1677 by Magnes and Bentley.[9]

After *The Town-Fopp* came several anonymously published adaptations, probably commissioned by Betterton. One or two might have been collaborations between himself and Behn. This is made more likely from the speed with which they were published, since Betterton was never in a hurry to get his plays in print, as the 'Session of the Poets' indicated, though the 'Stage has been dishonoured with 'em many a time'.[10] The first was another City play, *The Debauchee*, put on in about February 1677 and printed by a man hitherto unassociated with Behn, the legal publisher John Amery. It was a slightly shortened revision or rather translation into more modern, elegant and abstract English of Richard Brome's comedy, *A Mad Couple Well Matched* of 1639.[11] To bring it up to date, the authors provided a new London geography, translating old taverns and tourist spots into contemporary ones. The changes quickened the old play's pace, but destroyed some of its crude vernacular quality.

Compared to Behn's secure plays and adaptations, *The Debauchee* gives little wit to women, allows an uncharacteristic dignity to a City knight, penetrates far into the trading classes and allows some decidedly democratic sentiments. Like Sir Timothy Tawdry of *The Town-Fopp*, its rake hero, Careless, is a bit too unpleasant, too unthoughtful and unwitty to make the comic saving at the end entirely palatable. Yet, some of the less pleasant components of Behn's later rakes may derive from him: for example, Careless considers becoming a gigolo, a role Behn later allows one of her 'heroes'.

The prologue to *The Debauchee* was by a 'Person of Quality' and it painted an ebullient portrait of the spark as spectator, a type Behn must have had to deal with throughout her career:

> …you come bawling in with broken *French*,
> Roaring out Oaths aloud, from Bench to Bench,
> And bellowing Bawdy to the Orange-wench;
> Quarrel with Masques, and to be brisk, and free,
> You sell 'em Bargains for a Repartee,
> And then cry, Damn 'em Whores, who ere they be. [12]

The epilogue was again signed Mr E. R., probably Ravenscroft, although some have found a claimant in the Earl of Rochester.[13]

In the summer, the 'bawling' upper-class youths were supposed to have gone to the country, leaving the playhouses to provide 'Vacation Chear' to the 'honest Tradesman'. This was the theme of the prologue to the next anonymous revision, which might again be by Behn or partly so: Thomas Middleton's *No Wit, No Help, Like a Woman's*, first performed before the Interregnum and now called, in its revised state, *The Counterfeit Bridegroom*.[14] It was not meant for 'sparks', said the author, since Middleton satirised neither marriage nor City wives; besides it had a decidedly secondary cast, with few major actors included, as was common in the unfashionable summer months. To please the projected audience, this play, like *The Debauchee*, gained a bawdy drunk scene; it also displayed a woman 'in her Nightgown'.

Together with *The Dutch Lover* and *The Town-Fopp*, Behn's anonymous plays and parts of plays formed an important group in her life: as her transition from tragicomedy to her strongest dramatic mode, farcical social comedy. In all of them, the components were difficult to unite, and heated heroics were too thoroughly discomposed by the urbane flytings of witty couples or by the sheer nastiness of the action presented. Perhaps the generic instability echoed an instability in Behn's own life. She wanted to be witty, light-hearted and urbane, yet her own experience, as well as habit, pulled against the style. She never entirely rid herself of the vision of the tragicomedy of life, but she never again immersed herself so entirely in it either.

The transition was complete in the last of her anonymous plays, an adaptation-cum-imitation rather than a revision-cum-adaptation like the others, in which at last she moved close to Ravenscroft's formula of light intrigues round a 'gay couple'. It was based on Thomas Killigrew's Interregnum play, *Thomaso*, and called *The Rover*.[15] To Behn's delight it proved immensely popular. For the first time in her work it put the 'gay couple', including the sympathetic Restoration rake, firmly in the centre. It could do so since the Duke's now had a notable comedienne in Elizabeth Barry, whom Behn could coach in precisely the gestures she wanted for her heroines.[16] The popularity had a downside, however, since it obliged her to admit authorship and end her anonymous run.

The Spanish Don Juan figure had been a prankster and seducer, but, as he travelled through Italy and France, he became serious, took on philosophical libertine views and avoided repentance and reform. In the Restoration, he was infused with the popular version of Hobbes's philosophy and associated with libertine court wits, although he also acquired a commercial sense of the world in which everything had a market value, the price desire would pay.

Court and theatre were symbiotic and it was an endearing aspect of the former that it liked to see itself portrayed, sometimes even mockingly. While in the 1660s Charles II's defeat at Worcester, his exile and Restoration underpinned the tragicomic theme of the true king restored, his amorous progress in the 1670s gave substance to the rakish Cavalier, and the character appeared frequently on the stage. In 1675, for example, Wycherley put on *The Country Wife* with a hero so intent on sexual gratification he was prepared to claim impotence to follow his desires.

The following year came a more admiring portrait in Etherege's *Man of Mode*, in which the patrician and arrogant Dorimant, many years later alleged to be based on Rochester, was a devil with something of 'the Angel yet undefac'd in him'; master of men, women and language, he was the most perfect theatrical libertine.[17]

Necessarily the character was mildly political. Shortly after the Restoration, Charles II ordered Killigrew not to portray on the stage any 'representations of scenes in the cities of London and Westminster'.[18] So theatrical politics had to be coded. When the increasingly vocal opposition wanted to mock the court, it could attack the rake figure and everyone would know the target, as they did when Shadwell put on *The Libertine* at Dorset Garden in 1675, making of the rake an ugly seducer. It would be equally understood if one staged a sympathetic rake. Hoyle's treatment of Behn, coupled with her desire to follow fashion, ensured that she too would create such a character, but with a difference.

The name of Thomaso had been jogged in Behn's mind by a production of a curious play called *The Siege of Constantinople*, acted both at court and at Dorset Garden in November 1674. It was by her playwright-friend, Henry Nevil Payne, whose staunch Royalism may have been influencing her to think more specifically of state politics herself. The play was a kind of political allegory featuring the King and his ministers and revealing the treachery of some subjects during the last Dutch War. In the idealised picture of Thomaso, it portrayed the upright James, Duke of York.

Beyond making a living in espionage with its professional loyalty, Aphra Behn had not been singular in her Royalism. Her early plays clearly expressed it, but also implied criticism of privilege and arbitrary rule. Now in the late 1670s, as King and Parliament jockeyed for power in echo of the 1640s, some clearer public commitment was wanted. She did not toe the complete Royalist line expressed in Filmer's *Patriarcha*, which grounded kingly power in the 'natural' rule of a father in his household; instead, she was closer to Hobbes who, putting order over chaos, simply argued for a strong government. This would be based on hereditary kings because of precedent not 'nature'; power should be vested in them whatever their individual characters, for, like Margaret Cavendish, Behn believed a foolish head better than a factious heart in a state. By taking sides, Behn would alienate part of the theatre audience but, since the court was still the largest patron, there was much to recommend expressing its views. The safest thing was to be nostalgic and set the rake-Cavalier before the Restoration, a period as complex as the present, but now mythologised into simplicity. It was long since 1660 and the glamour of Interregnum activities had grown with Restoration disillusion. For Cavaliers, it had been an irresponsible time when money was none the less not the measure of a man.[19]

Perhaps, remembering the past, Killigrew suggested turning his cumbersome, old-fashioned but engaging *Thomaso* into an actable play. Or perhaps Behn approached him. He was a far more important figure in society than she, but neither he nor she could have avoided noticing her superior play-writing skill.[20] By now Behn had a string of satisfactory performances behind her, revealing her ability to make taut and theatrical what was once lax. Yet, given her anxiety over plagiarism, it was strange she believed she might borrow so recent a play with impunity. Perhaps, since she knew she improved what she changed, she thought that what she improved she owned. She may, too, have remembered an earlier involvement in the play as amanuensis, in the Low Countries, before the Restoration.

As she carved it out of the ten-act, two-part play of *Thomaso*, *The Rover* was moved from Madrid to the rebellious Spanish colony of Naples during carnival, in part perhaps because her recent failure, *The Dutch Lover*, was set in Madrid. Behn made no effort to capture the strangeness of location that Killigrew found in southern cities—heat, evaporated rivers, and biting lice.[21] The play opens in the manner Behn would make her own, with two young girls talking, Florinda in love with the English Cavalier, Belvile, but promised elsewhere and the assertive Hellena, designed a nun. Their spiritedness suggests that their brother, Don Pedro, will have a hard time controlling them. He is not helped by the carnival, into which the young women escape, one eager to test her lover and the other to find one. Soon they are enmeshed with the soldier Belvile and his friend, Willmore, who has newly arrived from sea in a randy state—echoes of the riotous sailors young Prince James had commanded in pre-Restoration Rotterdam. Hellena is quickly hooked; Willmore is attracted but fascinated also by Angellica Bianca, the famous courtesan, who has advertised herself for sale through a portrait. By pulling this down and treating her as a commodity in which shares might be bought—like a ship—Willmore kindles Angellica's interest and, as they reveal the sexual charge between them, her maid fears her lucrative mistress will become a lover and jealous dupe—as she does. A third Englishman, the bumpkin Essex man, Blunt—one of those to whom, in Rochester's words, nature 'does dispense, / A large Estate, to cover Want of Sense!'—is less lucky in his choice of woman: the whore Lucetta arranges for him to be duped, robbed and dumped back on the street almost naked.[22] In the end, most of the characters are coupled, although Angellica remains bitter and alone—the man who would follow her is pulled back on to the stage as she leaves. After some sparring about matrimony, Willmore agrees, despite his dislike of the state, to take Hellena and her large dowry.

So what did Behn lift from *Thomaso*? The answer is, most of the play, although the breaking up and reassigning of speeches makes *The Rover* something new.[23] For example, she gives to Hellena some of the speeches of Killigrew's more modest heroine, Serulina—parts of these have gone also to Florinda—but she adds words originally spoken by men. Behn had been impressed with Killigrew's scene in which Thomaso's friend, describing what it would be like for Serulina to marry her old rich suitor, portrays the physical horrors of the ageing male. When the words about carcases, impotence and belches are spoken by young Hellena and delivered at the beginning of the play, the effect is startling, and the character of Hellena distinguished sharply from Serulina's. But something is lost too. Although Behn takes this dismembering of a man's body from *Thomaso*, she omits that of the old woman: '*One whose Teeth, Eyes and hair rests all night in a Box*, and her Chamber lies strew'd with her loose members, *High shooes, false Back, and Breasts.*' Hellena would have been less comic repeating this.

Angellica Bianca, a character in both *Thomaso* and *The Rover*, is a more substantial figure in Killigrew, the discussion of whom opens the play. She is flanked by several other whores, who also consider the state and profession of prostitution; in *The Rover* the whores are reduced and the virgins increased, so that a happy denouement in multiple marriages can be accommodated. Killigrew's Angellica has a more thoughtful grasp on the female situation than Behn's, but she is also more of a conscious exhibitionist, believing that her action will live on the stage and be a theme of discourse. In fact, her bravoes (servant-bullies) declare that she would have got more 'in a Booth with the Elephant' than with her picture. In the end, neither in *Thomaso* nor in *The Rover* does Angellica entirely fit into a comic mode: Behn could not make an amusing version of Hippolyta, the woman who internalised her shame in *The Dutch Lover*, but at least she did not demand the submission Killigrew required of his courtesan.[24]

Thomaso has more success as a rake than Behn's Willmore. He is a divided man, whose reformation at the end is appropriate, as it could not be for the jauntier Rover. He controls the events which, in Behn's play, are largely controlled by the plotting Hellena. So, when

Thomaso disguises himself, he does it consciously. Willmore, however, is constantly 'disguised' by being drunk and fuddled; he disrupts rather than forms plots.

The two come together, however, in refusing to revere women, assuming they are after sex like men. So Willmore's comic effort at raping Florinda, paralleled in the *fool* but not the hero of *Thomaso*, becomes a comic expression of both their views: that forceful men are really fulfilling female desires. It may sound—and is—misogynous, and to a modern audience is menacing, but it needs to be seen in cultural context.

First, Puritans and Dissenters tended to condemn rape and wife-beating, so that male violence had a whiff of the Cavalier about it. Second, in heroic plays of the 1660s and early 1670s, rape had become the ultimate property crime; Behn's tendency to trivialise it was an escape from this degrading circumstance. And third, when the tragic presentation of rape by male playwrights in the theatre was almost always voyeuristic, pandering to the sadism of the male audience, Behn's resolute refusal to allow rape dramatic seriousness can appear decently reactionary.[25] (Notably, however, when a woman like Florinda does face rape, the scenes are discontinued because the woman is of 'Quality'; Behn would, it appears, have had little sympathy with any complaining rape victim of the lower ranks. It is also significant that, although her romantic heroines suffer violence, her spirited witty ones face no such challenge, as if, with sense, a woman ought to be able to avoid the threat. Perhaps in this distinction Behn, who must have known the controlling fear of male violence even when held in abeyance, was commenting on a perceived male fantasy: of a spirited, witty and sexy woman who is not intimidated when confronted with inescapably superior male force.)

Inevitably Behn omitted much: farcical scenes and some bawdiness, for example. Later audiences, worrying over the impropriety of *The Rover*, should have taken comfort that Behn did not include descriptions of two sisters as 'ovens' which burn cakes or make them come out as dough, or of the hot one as a dog leaping on and dirtying men. She also largely avoided the profound questions which had clogged the comedy: why chastity is wanted in a wife when experience is valued in a horse, hawk or hound; how women can be simply divided into whores and virgins, when both categories include the respectable and the lewd (Behn to some extent lets Hellena question the double standard, but she is, after all, chaste, so the questioning has less power than it does in the whores); what happens to a rover in inevitable old age. *Thomaso* sees 'a gray Wanderer' out of doors in the 'Winter' of his life, an old beggar not a rake, a tragedy to himself. Behn was right: this was not the stuff of her sort of comedy.

Behn's Rover is the heir of Alonzo in *The Dutch Lover*, macho and sexually attractive to desperate southern women. His insouciance is alluring and he has the best lines in the play. He avoids the deep misogyny of Wycherley's Horner and, in the list of actors, he is described as 'A Loyal and Witty Gentleman, only addicted to rail against Women'. He is not emasculated by his easy acceptance of limited female power, as many Restoration heroes are: Mark Antony in Dryden's *All for Love* is, for example, 'unbent, unsinew'd, made a Womans Toy'. Men are more robust and more ridiculous in Behn. But Willmore is also a drunk, and his repetition of the fool's episode in his attempted drunken rape brings him suspiciously close to the villainous Sir Timothy Tawdry of *The Town-Fopp*, who prided himself on his self-indulgence in wine and women. For those who later saw Rochester in the portrayal of Willmore, his constant drunkenness and roistering interventions must have been the clearest sign. Yet the Rover was given none of Rochester's social power. Where the icily controlled and stylish Dorimant of *The Man of Mode* lived after the Restoration and could have position as well as charm, Willmore, a man with stinking linen, has to make do with a society of exile. His power is only in personality and sex.

Some of the ambiguity in *The Rover* may have been gained by time. Behn and her contemporaries never ceased to point out that language was part of the seducing game, but our more romantic age finds it hard to separate apparently sensitive language from truth; so we find Willmore's words true because well expressed, although his moral remarks are part of his amorous stratagems. He upbraids Angellica for being a whore, while he himself will wear the clothes she has given him. Is his upbraiding 'true'? Or is it part of the seduction through seriousness? Because of his charm, the rake gets more than he ought in a just world: is it that the charming and entertaining not only usually *do*, but also *should*, win? Or is Willmore simply a male 'whore'?

So too with Angellica, with whom it is hard not to empathise because of her 'sincerity' (and blank verse). Willmore declares lovers' vows made to be broken by a sensible man. They are a fictional pact. But Angellica, trying to reconcile libertine and romantic love, now believes in fictional social words. Willmore puts her straight, accusing her of being spoilt for ordinary life by flattery, that is heightened words. The scene in which she learns the limits of the romantic language she thought she had taken from Willmore echoes that other moment of realisation between unequals: Caliban with Prospero in *The Tempest*. Caliban has learnt his master's language and has derived no benefit from it except an ability to curse. Both Angellica and Caliban are, in the last resort, gullible fools.

The audience is intended to enjoy the high spiritedness of the witty heroine, Hellena, who is necessarily a little saucy and sexy, a little anarchic and transgressive, answering Willmore's condescending address of 'Child' with 'Captain', so mocking his masculine pretension to authority. She is the heir of a whole line of spirited Restoration girls who combat men's desire to confine them 'just in [their] rambling Age' and she too sets out to employ her assets 'to best advantage'.[26] In her, the treacherous mercantile imagery which Behn mocked in poems seems liberal and sensible, supporting disobedience to what is unjust and allowing free trade for women. It is the tyrants and those who would interrupt commonsensical commerce who bear the blame.

Hellena assumes a multiplicity of roles: gypsy fortune-teller, nun, lady, and boy, so escaping the enclosure of a daughter and concern for portions and jointures. At the same time she avoids Angellica's mistake in raising desire through an image and deflating it with her simpler person, since she keeps it raised through a series of shifting selves. Had it not been carnival time, she could not have taken such licence, as her exasperated brother is aware. In masquerade, Hellena can flirt and make sexual overtures to a man she does not know, since the disguise allows the rare pleasure of seeing rather than simply being seen. Hellena has some distinction in ending the play in cross-dress and avoiding a scene of absorption back into society, but, like other witty heroines, she remains a virgin who seeks marriage, one whose virginity and financial worth secure the husband.[27] To turn from idealised love and marriage was to enter the libertine world with its misogyny and lonely pregnancies: at this threshold Hellena draws back. Without romantic love or wifehood, woman is not elevated to a free agent but, in a world controlled by men, degraded into a 'cunt', as numerous lampoons informed her.

So Hellena answers Willmore's demand for love without marriage by declaring she would then get 'A cradle full of noise and mischief'. An ideal society of sexually equal men and women existed only in the Golden Age. The new sexuality had to be negotiated, not enjoyed by unmarried women, it seemed. There may have been moments when the unmarried—perhaps now unmarriageable—Aphra Behn did not find her attraction to the sexually withdrawing Hoyle so very fatal.

The Rover explores vision, both male and female. Most of the watchers within the play, especially the secret, disguised or masked ones, are women, although Willmore knows the power of eyes when he says, 'I will gaze—to let you see my Strength.' In moments of danger for women, however, such as the near rapes, both men and women spectators are forced to see through male eyes. Willmore insists that he has a right to possess what he has looked at so long—indeed he manages to go from the portrait of Angellica to the real person without even paying. In a way, he suggests the enormous power of the watching (though paying) audience in the theatre who really do control. As it says in the prologue, 'Poets are Kings of Wit, and you appear, / A Parliament, by Play-Bill, summon'd here.'

In the case of *The Rover* the watching was benign, and on 24 March 1677 the play was excitedly received. It was slightly behind the playwright's moment and right in the popular mode. There was little problem of political analogy: lovers' vows did not affect political vows, and Willmore, without faith to women, keeps faith with his prince. Elizabeth Barry triumphantly played Hellena, a character probably tailored to her skills. Some thought her more apt for Angellica, since she was already appearing in lampoons as a mercenary whore charging 'fifty shillings a week', but, for others, it might have seemed a high theatrical moment: the first *starring* of the most celebrated Restoration actress in a play by the foremost female playwright.[28] William Smith acted Willmore to Betterton's Belvile and was much acclaimed. For once he had outshone Betterton, and he came to see the part as his own special one. Don Pedro was played by the Catholic actor Matthew Medburne, and the comic Cave Underhill, skilled at lumpen parts, was right for the fool, Blunt. The cadaverous new comedian Thomas Jevon, Shadwell's brother-in-law, made his Behn début in a minor role; she would lovingly exploit his mimicking talents later on. The song in the play was set by Simon Pack, a well-known composer of light music. The dividends of the month of March, in which *The Rover* may have been the only new play at the Duke's, rose to £37 16s 8d.[29]

Possibly Behn supplied her own prologue; if so it was an example of her mystifying ventriloquism. It had a defensive tone, blaming claques and, with extraordinary cheek, attacking other playwrights for stealing good lines. It does not *assert* the writer is a young, rather ill-natured and unseasoned man, but it implies it, although, at thirty-six, the female Aphra Behn was the composer of at least six staged plays, possibly more, and was eager to please. For those who knew the author, it was a duplicitous piece of writing, but fair enough in the theatre. It paled beside the duplicity of the postscript accompanying the printed work.[30]

The inevitable had happened: there came 'a Report about the Town (made by some either very Malitious or very Ignorant) that 'twas *Thomaso* alter'd; which made the Book-sellers fear some trouble from the Proprietor of that Admirable Play'. At which stage Behn could have apologised or stated her source in Killigrew, who had, after all, himself borrowed the self-marketing of the whore from Brome's *The Novella*.[31] That she did not indicates her infection of secrecy—neither openness nor repentance was her way, in literature or in life.

Instead, she brazened it out with a postscript attacking others for what she herself had tried to do. She might 'have stoln some hints' from *Thomaso* but this would be 'a proof, that I valu'd it more than to pretend to alter it, had I had the *Dexterity* of some Poets, who are not more Expert in stealing than in the Art of Concealing'. Moving from the subjunctive, she then declared, 'I, vainly proud of my Judgment, hang out the Sign of *Angellica* (the only stoln Object) to give Notice where a great part of the Wit dwelt.'

Who knows what she meant? Was she comparing herself to Angellica Bianca, whose initials she shared, or was she drawing attention to Killigrew's play, since this is the only name of a main character that remains the same across the two works?[32] Was the wit hers or Killigrew's? If the former, why would she choose the one incident Killigrew had clearly taken from another source? Was there a sly allusion to her earlier involvement in the play, of which some of the wit might just have been hers? She gave the reader no time to ponder, for she dashed onwards, 'I will only say the Plot and Bus'ness (not to boast on't) is my own: as for the Words and Characters, I leave the Reader to judge and compare 'em with *Thomaso*, to whom I recommend the great Entertainment of reading it.' She must have assumed not many would plough through Killigrew's ten acts. She finished by making her truest point, that, if the play had flopped, no one would have bothered to attack her: 'Therefore I will only say in *English* what the famous *Virgil* does in *Latin; I make Verses, and others have the Fame.*' It was an impudent quotation.

Realising the success of the play, the publisher Amery issued a new title page advertising it as a 'Comedy', but keeping it anonymous— although the authorship was becoming widely known. Soon Behn felt she might as well get what credit she could. So, when he reissued it again, Amery added 'Written by Mrs. A. Behn' to the title page and inserted into the postscript the words 'especially of our Sex': the passage now read, 'I shou'd have had no need of imploring Justice from the Criticks, who are naturally so kind to any that pretend to usurp their Dominion, especially of our Sex, they wou'd doubtless have given me the whole Honour on't.' Her sex could not bring down any more opprobrium on her head than was there already and it might let her counter criticism by complaining of discrimination.[33]

Langbaine, 'the great detector of plagiarism', usually excused Behn because she wrote for bread and improved her originals.[34] The outright lie about *Thomaso* rankled, however, and he wrote of this and the sequel, 'These are the only Comedies, for the Theft of which, I condemn this ingenious Authoress....I cannot acquit her of prevarication; since *Angelica* is not *the only stol'n Object*, as she calls it: she having borrow'd largely throughout,' to such an extent that she 'could not justly call these Plays her own'.

Whatever Behn's duplicity with the play, *The Rover* gained an important admirer: James, Duke of York, the King's brother. He enjoyed it and told the playwright so. For Behn he presented the possibility of patronage and income, although the Duke was always freer with his praise than with his purse, and his encouragement of Otway, for example, led to nothing substantial. He also stood for the glamour of power and privilege, and perhaps, after years in thrall to John Hoyle, a simple and transparent manly heroism. It can have done the Duke no harm in her eyes that he disliked Lord Arlington.[35] The praise transfixed Behn in a posture of public admiration which she retained far longer than most of James's supporters. It also made her realise that she had a winning theatrical formula and she used it to the hilt over the next years.

CHAPTER 17

❦

Sir Patient Fancy and City Whigs

'I have almost run out of all my stock of Hypocrisy'

Aphra Behn was fascinated with jargon, signs, cant and idiosyncratic chatter. She was writing for public entertainment and her method was to study what a particular audience wanted and then give it to them. This included a good deal of mimicry both of what they despised and feared and, more insidiously, of what they valued. By the beginning of 1678, her taste and that of the courtly element of her audience seem to have coincided. Restoration comedy was at its most sophisticatedly cynical and even Otway, so mawkishly moral at times, was putting on a play ridiculing conventional morality.

Yet, even as it flowered, the mood of cynicism and indulged hedonism began to wane. In 1676, Savile had written to Rochester in the country that London was 'full as foolish, and full as wise, full as formall, and full as impertinent as you left it, there is noe one contradiction you left in it but you will find again at your returne, noething changing in it but some few mortall lives'.[1] But by now Rochester, the chief rake, was ill and beginning to feel the cold winds of mortality. There were even rumours that he was showing interest in theology. Savile himself was a regular in the sweatshops taking a 'masse of Mercury' for his venereal disease. The statesman, libertine and part author of *The Rehearsal*, the Duke of Buckingham, whom Behn never much liked, was physically failing: his teeth were false and he smelled bad to the cleanly Nell Gwyn.

The court frightened pious Protestants and ordinary citizens as the site not only of licentiousness but also of Catholicism and arbitrary rule. Indeed, Algernon Sidney went so far as to link royal debauchery with absolutism when he suggested that Charles II was depraving his people with his fetid example and so preventing their resistance to his policies. The French connection exaggerated the fear, for Louis XIV of France was regarded as the garish exponent of both Catholicism and absolutism. His English cousins, the militantly Catholic James and his equivocal brother King Charles, might well be his allies, the enemy within. Charles tried to placate Protestant opinion by marrying James's unwilling daughter Mary, a girl of fifteen, to his Protestant nephew William of Orange, son of his eldest sister Mary. William was nearly twice Mary's age and five inches shorter, and the gloom of the wedding was lightened by the King's indulgence in the kind of buffoonery that made Willmore endearing and absurd.[2] Behn wrote no poem on the event—she was not yet a political panegyrist, nor did she care for Dutchmen.

By now, someone even closer to the King was exercising the thoughts of the nation. Fear of a court conspiracy to impose absolutism and Catholicism, or even of a military coup by James, provoked whispers, then loud talk, of changing the principle of succession and excluding Catholics from the throne. The name of the Protestant James, Duke of Monmouth, the King's eldest illegitimate son, was canvassed as a ruler, and the astute Earl of Shaftesbury, an old Cromwellian turned Royalist, turned opposition, saw in both uncle and nephew a destabilising promise. He set about harnessing fear of despotism to the cause of Exclusion and Monmouth's candidacy.

Like Dryden and other loyal supporters of the Duke of York, Behn had long been intrigued by Monmouth, both as a handsome, skittish Cavalier and as the dark shadow of legitimate Stuart power, the embodiment of Charles II's sexual prowess which was both admirable in a monarch and disastrous for a realm. Unlike his father, whose youth had been spent in exile, acting below his true rank, Monmouth, his mother dying early, had grown up the spoilt darling of the court, caressed by his father and grandmother and accepted openly as the eldest son of the King. He was also publicly brought up in the Protestant religion, which made him distinct from the regular male royal family, with its dye or at least patina of Catholicism. As a Protestant and a King's son, he had been married off in his early teens to the heiress Countess of Buccleuch, whose surname, Scott, he took as his own.

Monmouth had his father's popular touch and he was charming to everyone. He was dangerous to the state as the only one of the King's illegitimate children who could have claimed the throne and, with his charm and Protestantism, be supported by a good number of citizens: he was the eldest as far as anyone knew and he had been born before Charles married his Queen, Catherine of Braganza. So, had the King declared himself married to Monmouth's mother Lucy Walters, there would have been nothing to disprove the match. Unfortunately, as well as being charming, Monmouth was rather stupid, as Behn and the thinking part of the nation could see, though he compensated a little for this by sharing his father's lack of principle. Monmouth himself probably came to believe in the rumours that the King had indeed married his mother, and that there was a box of documents which would prove it. Charles, however, strenuously denied it and opposed any claim by his beloved son. Kingship, including his own possession of it, relied precisely on legitimacy and absolute succession.

In the polarising of King and Parliament, Charles and his brother James against the Earls of Shaftesbury and Monmouth, the abusive labels Whig and Tory were first heard to denote a wide spectrum of ideologies or beliefs—in time they would be used for political parties. 'Tory', deriving from the Irish word 'toraidhe' applied to the dispossessed Irish who attacked English settlers, suggested support for the royal brothers in their desire to strengthen the prerogative against Parliament and, more extremely, belief in the King as God's representative on earth. A Tory would, on the whole, maintain the Duke of York's right of succession. The 'Whigs', whose name derived from the expression 'Whiggamore raid' applied to a band of Scottish Covenanters in the 1640s, were staunchly Protestant; they favoured some form of constitutional monarchy and inevitably became associated with 'Exclusionists' who opposed the accession of James or at least wished to hedge him in with Parliamentary constraints. Tories feared the Whigs were using the London 'mobile' or Wapping rabble to gain their ends; the Whigs feared the Tories were using French subsidies and Jesuit plotting.

The polarising included Aphra Behn. Her contempt for the mob, obvious from the moment she put pen to paper, was influenced by her attitude to the theatre audience, an uncontrollable mass swayed by the loudest critic and unable to distinguish between good and bad, true and false. In its roused state, it had immense power and had always to be cajoled. As she wished to control her audience, so Behn wished the King to control his people. Her tentative doubts over arbitrary authority, expressed in her earliest plays, disappeared under the increasing fear of democracy, mob-rule, or anarchy. Her enthusiasm for Shakespeare bolstered her views, for he too had dreaded 'the blunt monster with uncounted heads, / The still-discordant wav'ring multitude'.[3]

Whigs were often Dissenters—old Puritans, as she always saw them— often City merchants and traders. Behn's political principles were those of a 'pseudo-aristocrat', not one born into the upper classes, but one who had internalised their views and images and who aimed to support their privilege and pretensions and to enjoy and serve their culture. She had had few conventional morals early in life—perhaps her own sexual habits had influenced her, perhaps her experience of Puritan hypocrisy in Canterbury. Certainly by now, having mixed with the demi-monde and the theatrical community and enjoyed the fringes of louche aristocratic society, Behn had an investment in the institutions that underpinned them: the King and his court. These were the ratifiers of the connection between free living or expression and witty art.

Aphra Behn did not relish a return to the old times and was horrified by any growth in City or democratic power—she never wished to see constraining sexual morality linked with politics again. Dreading the connection of introspection and coercion in the opponents of the court, she noted that those who thought much about forms of drama wished to impose rules on others and those who thought most about themselves expected others most to appreciate them and be like them, wishing to legislate their morality. Behn did not equate intelligence with this introspection, as later ages would do; she considered that a resolute triviality was as intellectually reasonable a response to an analysis of the human predicament as concentration on the 'depths' of something presumed to be the 'self'.

Other, less psychological circumstances were also driving Behn into greater public commitment to one side. State politics were infecting drama and Nat Lee advised poets to give up disinterestedness or starve: 'Turn then, who e'er thou art that canst write well, / Thy Ink to Gaul, and in Lampoons excell.'[4] Playwrights had to take sides: Elkanah Settle became a Whig pamphleteer and rabble-rouser with his spectacular pope-burning processions; Shadwell grew thick with Shaftesbury. The defenders of James were slower to group. In the end they were theatrically wiser, however, since on the whole the theatre audience was Tory.

After wavering, Dryden settled down in the Tory camp, as did Otway and a new intense young Irish and strongly Protestant dramatist, Nahum Tate, with whom Behn rather unaccountably became friendly. She herself was one of the few not to waver publicly (although public commitment, useful for business, did not preclude advantageous private involvement with influential men of other views). She was a Tory. She supported the rule of hereditary males and accepted that men of lower rank and all women except queens should have nothing directly to do with government. As she wrote in a late story: 'I cannot alter Custom, nor shall ever be allow'd to make new Laws, or rectify the old ones....'[5] Royal government should provide stability and, except in the basic tie of subject and monarch, leave freedom to its subjects in all other relationships.

Some playwrights responded to the times with serious discussion in tragedy, but Behn knew its two-edged nature when it enacted the breakdown of social order. Intending to appear a Tory, Nat Lee, for example, managed to put on one play exposing Romish cruelties at precisely the wrong moment and another in which the hero argued the need for curbs on 'raging Kings'.[6] In any case Behn was not ready to write propagandist drama, or perhaps she had not yet been paid to do so. To continue the libertine message—but with more sophisticated ambivalence—to follow the trend in Wycherley and Otway for harsh, sexually amoral plays, and to swipe at Puritan 'cits' were political acts enough. Despite the attacks on *The Rover*, it had undeniably been a success and Betterton was eager for Behn to repeat it—although, since she had no intention of coming clean, she should disguise her borrowing a little more. What better than to use the same formula: an elastic source, sexual intrigue, some political implication, and comedy unsullied by tragedy?

At this pregnant moment, a 'Gentleman' translated Molière's last play, *Le Malade imaginaire*, which had been staged in Paris in 1673 and printed two years later. The gentleman might have been one of several of her educated acquaintances: Ravenscroft, who had plundered Molière for two farces, the Catholic Matthew Medburne, who had acted in Behn's plays and already translated Molière's, *Tartuffe;* most likely he was James Wright, another Middle Temple lawyer like Ravenscroft. A translator and theatre historian, Wright translated the Molière play and probably shared his manuscript with Behn—he did not publish it.

Behn had been slow in coming to the French dramatist, whom there's no evidence she read in the original, but the farcical skit, *Le Malade imaginaire*, mixing music, speech and dance, tweaked her fancy. She would make something more plotted and less choreographed.[7] She would also make something more indecent than anything she had staged before. The play, *Sir Patient Fancy*, would have the energy of *The Rover*, but provide no perfect romantic couple as foil to the compromises and contingencies of the central pair.

Sir Patient Fancy is less earthy, more bawdy and more substantial than *Le Malade imaginaire*, with touches from Ben Jonson who, from the moment Behn found her most successful form in sex comedy, was increasingly present in her plays.[8] Molière allowed little sexual intrigue, whereas a general erotic feeling pervades *Sir Patient Fancy*: mothers and daughters vie for lovers and not everyone is fussy over his or her copulating partner. The old rich Puritan, Sir Patient Fancy, who replaced Molière's hypochondriac, dotes on his pretty young wife and displays the amorousness for which cits were constantly mocked, calling her monkey face and indulging in baby talk. He even does 'the office of my Women', that is, he 'dresses and undresses me,' the implication being that he cannot fulfil his more manly duties.

The spectre of impotence appears again in the vulgar lover, Lodwick, who, coming to meet his intended bride, Isabella, Sir Patient's daughter— chastely, for who, he asks nastily, 'would first sully the Linen they meant to put on?'—is appalled into seeming impotence by her desire. His anxiety evaporates when he learns that the desire emanates not from Isabella, but from her delicious step-mother, who takes him for her beloved Wittmore. He is ushered in to Lady Fancy's bed where he performs to satisfaction in the darkness. Behn had opened *The Amorous Prince* with suggestion of sexual activity, but it had been love in Arcadia between two young people: she had not before tried anything like the beginning of a scene of Act III, where, after his session with Lady Fancy, Lodwick is presented 'as just risen in Disorder from the Bed, buttoning himself, and setting himself in order'.

The amorality is compounded when, although discovered, nothing very terrible follows, since both are discreet and hypocritical. In parallel fashion, Wittmore, observing Isabella whom he is pretending to court as cover for his affair with her step-mother Lady Fancy, notes that she is very pretty and inviting: at that point he is restrained from pursuing her only by 'my Vows to the fair Mother'. It is a kind of moral libertinism more disturbing than Willmore's spontaneous version. The one piece of principle to which Behn subscribed, the iniquity of compelled marriage, seems repeated in *Sir Patient Fancy* in echo of *The Forc'd Marriage* and *The Town-Fopp*; yet, even this is vitiated when it is clear that want of money rather than a father's pressure drove the young Lady Fancy to marry the old rich man. Behn's marital separations at the ends of her plays are all optimistic in the context of actual seventeenth-century practice, but this one, where the woman is separated and left independently rich, is conspicuously so.

Lady Fancy is a complex creation, part heroine, part anti-heroine. Her justification for her adultery and hypocrisy in an earlier pledge to Wittmore is balanced by testimony from her maid: 'Now am I return'd to my old trade again, fetch and carry my Ladyies Lovers, I was afraid when she had been married these night-works wou'd have ended.' Lady Fancy realises how much femininity is a game and sex just a pleasure, so she spends little time repining for having slept with the wrong man: 'I was so possesst with the thoughts of that dear false one, I had no

232

sense free to perceive the cheat.'[9] At the end, the place she reaches is beyond marriage. Even the young blades cannot match her callous self-assertion and she avoids the apologetic tone that creeps into Wittmore's speech. *Sir Patient Fancy* becomes the first work in which Behn attempted to include women in the libertine space. From now on they would often inhabit it but the wisest would know it was a fantasy space.

On first sight, it seems strange that Behn should have qualified Lady Fancy with Lady Knowell, the conventionally amorous older woman who wants both a husband and fame as a learned lady. She is the widow of another puritanical City alderman like Sir Patient, in whose view she has degenerated into a 'fop'. Based partly on characters in Molière's mocking *Les Femmes savantes*, Lady Knowell is allowed, if not a lover, at least a dignified retreat: she had always urged her fortune rather than her charms, but at the end she is discovered to have been testing the young man rather than lusting for him, a motif found in earlier drama too.[10] Yet, at thirty-seven, Behn must have been a little sensitive to male mockery of ageing amorousness and have had some sympathy for Lady Knowell's desires.

The absurd erudition the widow reveals is not specific to women as in Molière, but more commonly found in university-bred men: Behn's usual butt. Lady Knowell is made to follow snobbish men in repudiating translation of the classics, which Behn herself thoroughly endorsed.[11] Yet, when Lucretia, her frustrated daughter, remarks of her mother, 'Methinks to be read in the Arts, as they call 'em, is the peculiar Province of the other Sex,' Isabella more cautiously replies, 'Indeed the Men would have us think so, and boast their Learning and Languages; but if they can find any of our Sex fuller of Words, and to so little purpose as some of their Gownmen, I'll be content to change my Petticoats for Pantaloons, and go to a Grammar-school.'

The main fool of the play is the usual rustic bumpkin, this time a '*Devonshire* Knight' called Sir Credulous. His three years at the University, never a happy circumstance for a limited man in a Behn play, have taught him one particular code which he can no more forget than he can his dead mare Gillian. He fancies himself as a 'Country Wit', not knowing this to be a contradiction in Restoration drama.[12] His concern for animals, whether seen as friends or assets, is as absurd as the family values country people and cits both display. In courtly circles, a relative represents potential cash, and Sir Credulous's sentimental feeling for a purse of broad gold given by a grandmother marks him out a fool. Yet, even he knows the marriage laws: ingeniously forced to part with his coins to the woman he intends to marry, he comforts himself: 'when I have married her, they are my own again.'

Politics inheres in Sir Patient Fancy, presented as a Whig Dissenter. His name probably reminded the audience of Sir Patience Ward, a substantial London merchant, strong Protestant, and sheriff of the City.[13] His fame as the lord mayor who inscribed on the Monument to the Great Fire his opinion that the Catholics had started the conflagration lay in the future, but his views were already known; in Behn's play Sir Patient accuses 'French papishes' of having a 'design to fire the City'.[14] As an anti-Catholic who equates convents with the theatre and the court as corrupters of youth, Sir Patient looks back longingly to 'the good days of the late Lord Protector' and praises 'a good Commonwealths-man' who sent his sons to Geneva for a 'virtuous Education' in Calvinist principles.[15] By the end of the play Sir Patient learns that one might as well be cynical: he intends to 'turn Spark…keep some City Mistress, go to Court, and hate all Conventicles'. Too much moral concern for others corrodes a family and a state. The cynical have the advantage of being tolerant and unshockable into extremes of behaviour when human nature fails to live up to unreasonable ideals.

As with Killigrew, so with Molière, Behn adds female scheming and she even provides a child go-between, Fanny, who mimics amorous intriguing language. The play opens with the kind of knowing young women of the town who have happily replaced the ingénues of her first works, talking the sort of liberated talk that makes the subsequent restrictions and arranged matches of brothers and aged fathers ridiculous: 'the Insolence and Expence of their Mistresses has almost tir'd out all but the Old and Doting part of Mankind,' one remarks for example. Isabella expresses the play-acting that the pretence of female innocence and actual subordination forces on rational women:

> Custom is unkind to our Sex, not to allow us free choice, but we above all Creatures must be forced to endure the formal recommen-dations of a Parent; and the more insupportable Addresses of an Odious Foppe, whilst the Obedient Daughter stands—thus—with her Hands pinn'd before her, a set look, few words, and a mein that cries—come marry me: out upon't.[16]

In fact, the acting teaches women also to direct; so, when Wittmore is discovered by her husband, Lady Fancy quickly tells him, 'keep your distance, your Hat under your Arm, so, be very Ceremonious, whil'st I settle a demure Countenance.' Lady Fancy becomes an impresario, forcing Wittmore into something of Willmore's foolish role. She makes narrative of all contingencies, a lover in the wrong place, a loud watch, a chair tipping over, to the point where she is forced to exclaim, 'I have almost run out of all my stock of Hypocrisie.' Wittmore admits, 'I'me a Damn'd dull fellow at Invention' and Lodwick is advised, 'You were best consult your Mother and Sister, women are best at intrigues of this kind.'[17] In a tight place, men can only reach for their swords, women are ready with fictions.[18]

Sir Patient Fancy is a veritable comedy of discourses. As conversation, it is as clever as *The Rover*, while Behn's contrapuntal technique, used first in the whispering scenes in *The Amorous Prince*, is perfected as Wittmore and Lady Fancy talk *doubles entendres* aimed at each other and at the eavesdropping Sir Patient Fancy. Groups converse animatedly at cross purposes. Sir Patient is much tickled by his name which, following a habit picked up from *The Debauchee*, Behn makes him use as a tag— 'Patience is a Virtue.' He speaks the biblical language of Dissent, which is both hypocritical and too extreme since Lady Fancy remarks that such cant covers sexual desire: the brethren 'do so sneer upon me, pat my Breasts, and cry fie, fie upon this fashion of tempting Nakedness'. In Dissenting language, London becomes a place of Iniquity, where 'the Young men are debaucht, thy Virgins defloured, and thy Matrons all turn'd Bawds!', a place full of 'immodest Revellings, and Profane Masqueradings'. Sir Patient addresses people as if at a public meeting and covers ordinary failing with rotundity.[19]

In cynicism, *Sir Patient Fancy* surpasses Behn's earlier plays. The swapping of bodies in beds implies that any body will do and there is no reason to suppose that the couples that end the play will be static.[20] The conclusion of the Fancys is sourer than the ending of Molière's play or of the Molière adaptations by Otway and Ravenscroft, and Lady Fancy's exultation with Wittmore by the bed of her assumed dead spouse is as cruel as anything Behn had written: 'That which the Slave so many years was toiling for, I in one moment barter for a Kiss…I now having no more to doe, but to bury the stinking Corps of my quondam Cuckold, dismiss his Daughters, and give thee quiet possession of all.'[21]

Sir Patient Fancy was produced on 17 January 1678, equipped with a prologue, spoken by Betterton and written by a friend. Perhaps this was Ravenscroft again or Otway or, given the ironic reference to Pope Joan—'Defend us from a Poet *Joan* again!'—conceivably Henry Nevil Payne, who grasped any opportunity to attack anti-popery. The mythical

Pope Joan had become a notorious and lewd figure in anti-papist propaganda, used to frighten good Protestants with the excess and gender
chaos of Catholicism.[22] She formed a neat analogue to the Poet Behn,
who had dared to invade the male realm of dramatic poetry.

The female poet's threatening assertiveness was exemplified in the
epilogue which Behn herself wrote and appropriately gave to the actress
Ann Quin, who had played the aspiring Lady Knowell.[23] Quin quoted
a male spectator, heir to the 'fop' Behn lambasted in her Epistle to the
Reader of *The Dutch Lover*:

> I Here, and there, o'reheard a Coxcomb Cry
> Ah, Rott it—'tis a Womans Comedy,
> One, who because she lately chanc't to please us,
> With her Damn'd stuff, will never cease to teaze us....

After this reminder of *The Rover*'s success, the epilogue swerved into a
seemingly serious plea for a more splendid present for women based on
their cultural past:

> What has poor Woman done, that she must be,
> Debar'd from Sense and Sacred Poetrie?
> Why in this Age has Heaven allow'd you more,
> And Women less of Wit than heretofore?
> We once were fam'd in Story, and cou'd write
> Equall to men; cou'd Govern, nay cou'd Fight.
> We still have passive Valour, and can show
> Wou'd Custom give us leave the Active too,
> Since we no Provocation want from you.[24]

The passage may refer to the Elizabethan age of aristocratic female
culture or, more likely, to something fantastic, the age of romance and
Amazons as presented in La Calprenède and de Scudéry, when women
did daring deeds. Behn's positive female models were nearly always
mythical or royal.[25]

So ringingly feminist in isolation, the verse slides into the present,
declaring itself one of Behn's mediated addresses. It is not just the author
speaking as an aspiring lady, but the actress and professional playwright
doing their number and pleasing men. Mrs Quin is there to seduce the
audience. Players submit to spectators, as women to men. Whatever
they did in romance and the past, women do not now fight fiercely and

so do not 'scorn and cudgell ye when you are Rude'. The epilogue collapses into the conventional cajoling of spectators. Behn's clever women negotiate a man's world rather than seeking to change it. Since they are raised to please and play-writing is pleasing, 'pray tell me then / Why Women should not write as well as Men.' The sexual attraction of men and women always subverts any feminist agenda.

The cast of *Sir Patient Fancy* was impressive. Betterton took Wittmore and the new comic actor, Anthony Leigh, played Sir Patient Fancy, coupled, as he increasingly was, with the reliably funny James Nokes as the effete and gullible fop, Sir Credulous Easy. Growing notorious for tough unconventional women, Betty Currer played Lady Fancy.[26] The flirtatious Emily Price was Lucretia and Thomas Farmer, one of the King's violinists and a prolific composer of music for songs by Ravenscroft, Otway, Lee and Dryden, provided his usual stolid fare. Behn expected success but braced herself for remarks on her 'hints' from Molière, on her politics, on her form, and on women writers.

Not everyone had comments of course, for several had not really come to watch the stage at all. The Earl of Arran, who saw 'the French play' on 19 January, was more concerned to record whom he met, while the King's chief mistress, Louise de Kérouaille, in deep distress at the triumph of a new rival from France—the dashing and spirited Hortense, Duchess of Mazarine—'got up, had herself dressed, and dragged herself to her Sedan chair, to be carried to the French play, where she heard the king was to be with Madame Mazarin'.[27] She could not have noticed much. Others did not let *Sir Patient Fancy* and its polemical epilogue pass unnoticed, however. Shadwell countered with *The True Widow*, mocking Behn's style of farcical comedy; possibly even Dryden glanced at her when, in *Oedipus*, he insisted on tying lack of traditional dramatic regulation to political chaos: 'when you laye Tradition wholly by, / And on the private Spirit alone relye, / You turn Fanaticks in your Poetry.' Behn refused this link.

She had to contend with more specific and immediate criticism as well. This was worse than she had anticipated, suggesting she had slightly misjudged the times: she was loudly accused not only of plagiarism, as expected, but also of bawdiness. The country was full of scorn for the royal mistresses and contempt for petticoat rule. A woman playwright, openly peddling bawdry in the theatre àt such a moment, became just another symptom of a world turning upside down again. The only course for Behn was to rush into print with the text, so that a more informed judgement could be made. She could also exploit the notoriety by providing a vindicatory preface, as she had done with *The Dutch Lover*. The disorganised 'To the Reader' was attached to a carelessly printed text by her new publishers, Jacob and Richard Tonson (with whom Magnes and Bentley had been associated, so it was a reasonable progression). Perhaps they were unimpressed with her status and yet, although Jacob had a dazzling future career, it was now only in its early stages: if anyone were doing a favour with the collaboration, it was probably Aphra Behn.

As in her preface to *The Dutch Lover*, Behn followed Restoration fashion in creating fictional characters for critics, an amalgamation of foppish dress and vacant attitude. It was a device adopted by Dryden and Ravenscroft as well, but it was more comic employed by a woman creating men. She began on bawdry. Could the critics who grumbled at it know anything about sex? Behn asked. Perhaps they were too old or too prudish to judge on the matter or perhaps they had not listened to the play: 'if such as these durst profane their Chast ears with hearing it over again, or taking it into their serious Consideration in their Cabinets; they would find nothing that the most innocent Virgins can have cause to blush at.' Then she turned to the old charge of plagiarism. Against those who 'cryed it was made out of at least four *French* Plays', she claimed she 'had but a very bare hint from one, the *Malad Imagenere*... but how much of the *French* is in this, I leave to those who do indeed understand it and have seen it at the Court'. She hoped these consisted of like-minded Royalists who agreed with the play's political tenor and could overlook other aspects.

Both defences were dubious. Behn had purloined the plot from Molière and some of the language from the translator—although the borrowing was nothing like as large as that from Killigrew's *Thomaso*. As for bawdry, it was certainly possible for an innocent but perceptive virgin to blush at the antics of Lodwick in his soon-to-be step-mother's bed.

Then, having defended, Behn attacked. Both criticisms of bawdry and plagiarism were due to her sex:

> The play had no other Misfortune but that of coming out for a Womans: had it been owned by a Man, though the most Dull Unthinking Rascally Scribler in Town, it had been a most admirable Play.[28]

Often Behn saw her denigrators as men, but she was also aware that criticism came from women or was instigated by them. She admired racy, witty, ambiguous ladies like the King's new mistress, the Duchess of Mazarine, who gambled, went cross-dressed, enjoyed wit of all sorts, and would tie herself to no man, not even the King. Conversely, she sniffed at those who displayed conventional marks of femininity, moistening handkerchiefs with tears she could never believe were not artificial. She was so aggrieved that only men were allowed to express sexual and amorous feelings candidly that she turned on her own sex in frustration. As a result Behn came close to the satiric male view of women: 'if they durst, all women would be Whores.'[29]

Behn had often spoken of this with Otway, whose conception of woman was far more sentimental than her own. Even he took Behn's point, however, that women who complained about so-called bawdy plays were prudes and hypocrites. When he had to defend his cynical *Souldier's Fortune*, Otway wrote: 'I have heard a Lady (that has more Modesty than any of those she Criticks, and I am sure more wit) say, She wonder'd at the impudence of any of her Sex, that would pretend to understand the thing call'd Bawdy.' This sounds like Aphra Behn over a tankard.[30]

Although much in her address is robust, Behn also showed a more vulnerable, petulant side. She was a jobbing poet, obliged to write 'for Bread and not ashamed to owne it', so she courted public favour. This was fine, but she went on to add, 'though it is a way too cheap for men of wit to pursue who write for Glory, and a way which even I despise as much below me'. This snobbish attitude, foreshadowed in the Epistle to *The Dutch Lover*, was hardly an advertisement for her play.

Caught in enmeshing statuses of sex and class, Aphra Behn was, then, both defensive and scornful of her own work. She defended it as equal or superior to the regulated stuff penned by university-educated men, whose learning was irrelevant or inappropriate for the theatre. At the same time, she subordinated it to work written for 'Glory'. Here she invoked not so much gender as class, that touchy distinction between amateur and professional. It was constantly made among writers but, even as she loudly reasserted it, she began to suspect it might be both false and pernicious. She wrote for 'bread' and yet her irritation and defensiveness suggested some ambition for 'Glory'.

There is, too, something personal in her insistence on professionalism. Whatever she, Aphra Behn, felt obliged by the public and the times to write, there was in her view nothing bawdy in her private life. She was now not even a kept woman. That was one implication of the statement that she wrote for 'bread' without shame.

CHAPTER 18

❦

The Popish Plot and *The Feign'd Curtizans*

'Common Sense, was *Popishly affected'*

The theatre had responded uneasily to England's anxious politics. Now it was outclassed, for no playwright from Dryden and Behn to Settle and Shadwell thought up anything quite as extraordinary as the Popish Plot, the drama performed on the national stage in 1678.

Its context was the perennial English fear of Catholicism harking back to the reign of Bloody Mary in the mid-sixteenth century and engraved on the popular mind through Foxe's *Book of Martyrs*, which described in macabre detail the fiery fate of Protestants under Catholic rule.[1] Although in England Protestantism was flourishing—Catholics made up only between 4 and 5 per cent of the population—in Continental Europe it was in retreat in major states such as France and the Spanish colonies. Also, the few Catholics there were in the country tended to be in high ranks because only the wealthy could afford priests and withstand the intermittent financial persecution. Now popery had penetrated the highest circle of all through the militant Catholic convert, James, Duke of York, heir to the throne, flanked by two of the most expensive (and French) of Charles's mistresses, the duchesses of Portsmouth and Mazarine. In this threatening national and international context, English Protestantism inspirited itself with outpourings of sentiment on the Accession Day of Elizabeth I, now a Protestant icon. At the climax of a procession of cardinals scattering indulgences for the murder of Protestants and of Jesuits plotting villainy, an effigy of the Pope was pitchforked into a bonfire at Temple Bar.

For Protestants, Catholicism was not just a sect but a virulent political force. In *An Account of the Growth of Popery and Arbitrary Government*, the poet Marvell saw it as part of a conspiracy 'to change the lawful government of England into an absolute tyranny, and convert the established Protestant religion into downright Popery'. He was appalled by what attracted Aphra Behn: 'colourful Vestments, consecrations, exorcisms, whisperings, sprinklings, censings and phantasical rites'. Behn was highly dubious about the common embodiment of this fear in the Jesuits, whose reputed cunning she regarded as overrated. (They were thought to be especially amoral since they possessed a philosophical justification for regicide.) When she wanted to mock her times, she presented rumours of 'two *French* Jesuits plotting to fire *Amsterdam*, and a thousand things equally Ridiculous'.[2]

In her doubts about huge conspiracies, Behn was in a small minority and the chief creators of the Plot could build on popular prejudices, that Catholics had been responsible for the Civil War, Charles I's execution, and the Great Fire of London. It was a small step to assume that they were now proposing to assassinate Charles II and then massacre the Protestants, with the help of the Pope, the Jesuits and Louis XIV. The lack of originality in the scenario made it familiar and convincing.[3]

The Plot was adumbrated in the hot month of August by Israel Tonge, a fanatical parson and ex-Puritan, whose London church had been burnt in the Fire. Some felt his intellects had been singed in the conflagration, which he attributed to the Jesuits. Tonge informed a sceptical King, who handed the matter to his ministers. In September, Titus Oates, the source of the information, made a statement on oath before Sir Edmund Bury Godfrey (the magistrate who had been unimpressed with Mary Carleton's spiritedness in 1663). The Popish Plot which would convulse the nation and drive several great and little men to the scaffold had begun.

Behn mocked the pig-like Oates whenever possible—although she did not, like other denigrators, allude to the homosexual practices for which he had been dismissed as a sea chaplain. He had a complicated past: ordained in the Church of England, converted to Catholicism, Oates had travelled to Valladolid where he failed to study for the priesthood, and to the seminary of St Omer, from which he was expelled. This limited but first-hand knowledge was invaluable when he made the implausible claim that he had carried treasonable material between the Jesuits in St Omer and England. Forged letters were produced and Oates even made their ineptitude incriminating: Jesuits wrote in disguised hands, he declared.

The decisive event came on the evening of 17 October 1678: Sir Edmund Bury Godfrey was found dead in a ditch. According to the insatiably nosy Gilbert Burnet, the body was bruised and the neck broken, and, it was thought, Godfrey might have been strangled before being moved and pierced with his own sword. The contemporary recorder, Narcissus Luttrell, noted that his stick and gloves were carefully placed against a hedge, and his money and watch left in his pocket; so there could be no suspicion of the murder as part of a common theft.

Had Godfrey died of natural causes? Had he killed himself? Had he been killed by Roman Catholics as a known persecutor? Or had he been killed by dissident Protestants to lay suspicion on the Catholics and stir up trouble?[4] Court Catholics saw Godfrey as a depressive who had committed suicide, the strangling coming after to give the appearance of murder (which his family would wish since a suicide's goods were confiscated by the state). The overwhelming belief of the populace was that he had been done to death by Roman Catholics.

Once a respected, austere, and melancholy man, Godfrey now grew mythical.[5] His death had occurred by Primrose Hill, in earlier times apparently called Green Bury Hill: Green, Berry and Hill were the names of the three hapless men who were condemned for his murder. Months later, the sky went dark for half an hour in morning service, as Godfrey's ghost walked the earth, appearing significantly in Queen Catherine's Catholic chapel.

If Aphra Behn expressed her opinion at the time, it was privately or anonymously, but, a few years later, when several sensible people doubted aspects of both murder and Plot and when the court Catholics were in the ascendant, she declared them clearly: the whole lying edifice had been constructed of false ambition, corrupt judiciary, Church and Parliament playing on 'the restless People', she wrote. Godfrey was a 'Melancholy *Self-Murtherer*', whose death was used for mischievous political ends.

After Godfrey's death, Titus Oates could spread his net wide. The Duke of York's part in the plot had so far been minimised, but he had a weak flank in his former secretary, Edward Coleman, a fanatical Catholic convert with grandiose ideas. Coleman had been sending letters to Louis XIV's personal confessor, ludicrously urging on both the French king and the Pope to intervene in English affairs. His papers proved a gold mine, condemning him and tarnishing James. The Duke was discovered apologising to the Pope for the marriage of his daughter Mary to the 'heretic' William of Orange.

Oates also lighted on the Queen's physician, Sir George Wakeman, who was supposed to help with the poisoning of the King, as well as Charles's mistress, the Duchess of Mazarine. He implicated an assortment of Catholic noblemen, including the ageing Viscount Stafford, Behn's acquaintance from the journey to Antwerp. With the country raised to fever pitch, Charles II did not withstand the pressure, and five

Catholic lords, including Viscount Stafford, were taken to the Tower at the end of October for allegedly plotting to kill the King.

The winter of 1678–9 was given over to hysteria. Chalices and other Catholic *bric-à-brac* turned up everywhere and a warren of underground rooms and passages was allegedly discovered under London. Guards were posted on buildings, every noise was investigated, and the King was urged to tighten security about Whitehall, changing locks and preventing free access. Committees and tribunals met and dissolved. As Burnet later put it, 'believing was then so much in season, that improbabilities or inconsistencies were little considered'. Rochester wrote, 'things are now reduc'd to that extremity on all sides that a man dares nott turne his back for feare of being hang'd.'[6] It was beyond the control of the King, Parliament or the governing classes.

Catholic servants were seen as a fifth column and several were imprisoned on suspicion that they would kill their masters or burn their houses. The Queen and the Catholic royal mistresses, the Duchesses of Mazarine, Cleveland and Portsmouth, discreetly dismissed some of their Catholic retainers—although, as a Protestant, the Duke of Monmouth managed to keep his Catholic barber for the best part of another year. Much hatred was directed at these ladies, especially at the Duchess of Portsmouth, a direct emissary of Louis XIV and seen as a national disease and contaminator of the King. It was happy for Nell Gwyn that her wit reputedly came to her aid when, in Oxford, she was stopped by a hostile mob which took her for her French rival. She is supposed to have quelled the militant crowd by shouting, 'Pray, good people, be civil; I am the *Protestant* whore.' But in fact no whore of the King could have felt entirely secure.

Booksellers and printers had much to gain from the furore and presses were in constant production of pamphlets, broadsides, and summaries of trials and confessions. But cashing in on the Plot was not entirely safe. The evidence on which people were being arrested was after all mainly textual, a matter of letters and notes, and it was easy to fall from zeal into sedition.

The crisis led to an outpouring of political comment by such theorists as John Locke and Algernon Sidney, which set the terms of political debate for centuries to come. Yet there was an old-fashioned ring to pamphlets of the time. The monarchy was reeling but Tories could think of nothing beyond restating the old theory of divine monarchy, formulated before the Civil War had shown how easy it was to kill a king. Meanwhile, the Whigs fell back on theories of Roman republicanism which had done duty several times before. Beyond this restated difference, both sides were shocked by the power of the mob or 'Mobile', and both were increasingly aware of the influence of public opinion.

As patriot and national hero, Titus Oates had been installed in Whitehall; he now affected gorgeous episcopal dress—silk gown, lawn sleeves, rosettes and rose scarf. He was romancing with impunity and had even reached the childless and Catholic Queen, something of a sitting target. The King, who had failed to carry out Catholic policy with enough alacrity, was to be poisoned using the Portuguese ambassador or, if this failed, the 'Queen would procure the Doing of it' with her doctor, Wakeman. Even Godfrey's murder was now placed in the Queen's apartments at Somerset House, although the informants had difficulty pointing out the rooms when questioned.

Behn liked this no more than the King. She admired Catherine as royal and dignified and, when she addressed her formally six years later, she called the accusations '*Perjuries*...black and foul'. Happily the Queen displayed '*Steady Graces*' becoming analogous to 'our Blest *Saviour*' when taunted and pierced with thorns:

> ...Heaven (to make the *Heroin* understood,
> And Hell it self permitted loose abroad,)
> Gave you the *Patience* of a *Suffering God*.

Behn was as quick to make kings and queens into Christ and God as the opposition was to turn them into devils and Babylonian whores.

> Your pretious *Life* alone, the Fiends disdain'd,
> To Murder home, your Vertue they prophan'd;
> By Plots so rude, so Hellish a Pretence,
> As ev'n wou'd call in question *Providence*.

Charles put the matter less exaggeratedly: the Queen was 'a weak woman, and had some disagreeable humours, but was not capable of a wicked thing: and considering his faultiness towards her in other things he thought it a horrid thing to abandone her'. He was firm in his support, even if his declaration fell short of Behn's rapture: 'This the *Great Lord* of all Your Vows beheld, / And with disdain Hells baffl'd rage repell'd.'[7]

At the end of the year Behn's friend and fellow playwright, Henry Nevil Payne, was seized; he sensibly proclaimed his Protestantism. Medburne, the Catholic actor and translator of Molière, had less opportunity and he died in prison.[8]

It was at this inconvenient moment, at the end of the year, that Parliament became aware of the secret Treaty of Dover of 1670, entered into by their King with his cousin, the King of France. The revelation had come about partly through scandal.

In the summer of 1678 Savile wrote of 'terrible doeings att Paris betwixt my Lady Cleaveland and her daughter Sussex....whilst ye Mother was in England the daughter was debauched by our Embassdr Mr Montaigue'.[9] Anne, Countess of Sussex, had already shocked her mother by becoming intimate with the King's bisexual mistress, the Duchess of Mazarine.[10] Since Mr Montague had been the lover of Barbara, Duchess of Cleveland herself, the mother was not best pleased to find her daughter her rival. She wrote a stream of horrified and indignant letters to Charles as the girl's father and Montague's employer, accusing the ambassador of openly criticising the King and plotting against his ministers. Montague hurried to England to clear himself, but was sacked by his irate employer. He bided his time, schemed with Shaftesbury, and then revealed the correspondence between Charles and Louis XIV in which he himself had taken part. This showed the government offering peace with France and the reconversion of England in return for a subsidy which would render Charles independent of Parliament. The revelations reinforced the damage of Coleman's letters. Popery and arbitrary government became fused in the popular mind.

By now, the first executions were occurring; a Catholic banker who was said to have been prepared to kill the King was followed in early December by James's ex-secretary, Coleman, condemned by his own injudicious writing. He was hanged, drawn and quartered at Tyburn on 3 December, expecting to the last a reprieve from those he had served. He was a warning to all agents and spies and confirmed the power of the letter to save or destroy.

The uproar in the nation hit playwrights in their pockets. The theatre faced stiff competition from courthouses and public tribunals, and, along with the other dramatists, Behn moaned that this 'cursed plotting Age' had 'ruin'd all our Plots upon the stage'.[11] At the same time the Plot spurred *political* play-writing, which gained authority by analogy and could be commissioned by both sides. However, Behn as a woman had to be careful. So often rebellion was seen in gender terms, with armed revolt being masculine and insidious subversion feminine; it would be easy for a woman to be regarded as a covert plotter. If such as Queen Catherine could be suspected, a female playwright who had already invoked an image of the whorish woman would be fair game.[12]

Although she remained cautious now, when times became propitious

Behn retrospectively praised the one man who stood firm and had to go into temporary exile for his firmness: Roger L'Estrange, the royal propagandist and censor. He had the distinction among apparent Protestants of being openly against Titus Oates from the beginning, trying to rescue 'the *World* from stupid Ignorance'. Behn agreed with his version of the Plot as a matter of perjury rising from national decay:

> Grave *Judges, Church-men*, and whole *Senates* now,
> Ev'n *Laws* and *Gospel*, were corrupted too.
> By *these* misled, the restless People Range
> Into a Thousand *Errors*, New and Strange;
> To every *God*, to every *Idol-Change*.
>
> Unknown *Religions* first their *Poyson* hurl'd,
> And with *New Lights* Debauch'd the giddy World;
> Not the *Rebellious, Stubborn Hebrew Race*;
> More falsely forbidden *Worships* did embrace.
> Hence Universal *Feuds* and *Mischiefs rose*,
> And *Friends* to *Friends, Parents* to *Sons*, were Foes.
> The Inspired *Rabble*, now wou'd *Monarchs* Rule,
> And *Government* was turn'd to Ridicule;
> ...*Perj'ries, Treasons, Murthers*, did ensue,
> And total *Dissolution* seem'd in View.[13]

In such unstable times, code was the mode: playwrights could allude to political events, rather than stating what could not easily be repudiated if things took an unexpected turn. A useful device was the pointed revision of Shakespeare who was beyond prosecution. Otway turned *Romeo and Juliet* into *Caius Marius*, Edward Ravenscroft adapted the bloody *Titus Andronicus* into an horrific picture of civil strife, while Dryden used *Troilus and Cressida* to present a vision of political corruption.[14] Another device was the Roman play, like Nat Lee's *Lucius Junius Brutus*, which showed the turmoil that accompanied the ending of a monarchy. These serious Tory plays warned against confusion in the state, but the fear of anarchy they overtly displayed did not quite eradicate the other fear of tyranny, the obsession of the Whigs.

Behn was not in the habit of using drama to air great political questions, and she had no patron or commission to write direct propaganda. Also it was more politic to suggest the falseness of appearance and the equivocation of signs than to declare the Popish Plot fraudulent. In *Sir*

Patient Fancy she had already shown she agreed with Dryden in opposing the virulent power of extreme Puritan speech, which she saw as creating public fear. Unlike him, she concluded that farce more than tragedy was an appropriate response. In the crisis she assumed the public might want something jolly in tone. It was a gamble, however, and she put on her new play, *The Feign'd Curtizans*, in the early spring of 1679 with some trepidation.[15]

Behn chose to circumvent the charges of plagiarism levelled at *Sir Patient Fancy* and *The Rover* by providing an original play. Inevitably, though, there were loud echoes, both of herself and of earlier play-wrights. While she never admitted she had overstepped the limits of propriety, Behn also made sure her new work did not offend morality quite as thoroughly as *Sir Patient Fancy*, and there are more convention-ally misogynous lines.

The Feign'd Curtizans was set in Italy, in Catholic Rome, where, as in *The Rover* and *The Dutch Lover*, vengeful southern patriarchs made the alterna-tive to marriage not spinsterhood but the convent or the brothel. The setting might have been intended to compliment Mary of Modena, the young second wife of the Duke of York, who had married an English man as Behn's two heroines do in the play. (In 1673, when she was four-teen, Mary had been forced to relinquish her desire for a convent to marry the almost forty-year-old widower Duke of York—to the dismay of the Protestant citizenry. She was beautiful, her dark fragile looks contrasting with the heavier features of James, his recently dead first wife Anne Hyde, and their daughters Mary and Anne. Her strange presence was caught in the lampoons that greeted her arrival, including one ascribed to the Earl of Rochester which became extraordinarily popular called Signor Dildo. Since this instrument was hardly a novelty in England, it is unclear why it should have become entrenched in the entourage of the teenaged bride. If the setting were a compliment—there is evidence Behn joined Elizabeth Barry in admiring the young Duchess—then it was mistimed since, in the month of the play's production, the Duke and Duchess of York were forced into expedient exile. In any event, Rome had more obvious significance, especially when the play concerned amorous plots which turned out to be trivial and when the Roman girls who pretended to be whores were revealed as chaste. The whore, 'La Silvianetta', like the Great Whore of Roman Catholicism, existed only in the imagination.

Behn did not need to underline the point, but she did so in her prologue all the same. Like *The Rover*, which she said could not be popular since it was set during a 'popish carnival', she argued that her new play must be damned because set in Rome (and because wit was considered 'Jesuitical'), rather hoping that the play would have the same success as its predecessor. In fact not much is made in the play of Rome as the centre of Catholicism, and the church functions, as it usually does in her works, as a place of assignation and amour. As one lady puts it, she goes to St Peter's with no 'other Devotion, but that which warms my Heart for my young English Cavalier'.

The Feign'd Curtizans follows *The Rover* in concerning Behn's usual group of intermeshed young people trying to form themselves into suitable couples. Various virtuous virgins have escaped to Rome, where, confusedly, two of them take the whore's name of La Silvianetta. They meet the usual band of desirable and desiring Englishmen: Belvile and Willmore are transformed into Sir Harry Fillamour and Galliard, Florinda and Hellena into Marcella and Cornelia. Galliard declares the libertine creed of the momentary state: he will not love till hair and eyes change colour, for he hates 'the lazy stay'. Desire, he announces, 'knows no time but the present' and he has Willmore's robust, misogynous attitude to rape when he exclaims that, in Roman times, 'noble Rapes, not whining Courtship, did the Lover's business'. In fact, however, he is far less devil-may-care, much less drunken than Willmore. Hedonism, so criticised by moralists, could now only be lightly expressed. Yet, this hedonism becomes the only defence against factionalism and intolerance. When Fillamour rails against the times that caress the coward, reward the villain and give beauty to fools, Galliard declares it all 'Mere accident'—there is no need to read providence into history and so breed anger and fear. Galliard's hedonism is not preferred to the more romantic passion of Fillamour, any more than Willmore was preferred to Belvile in *The Rover*, but he gets the best lines and the wittiest lady.

Cornelia expresses a libertine contempt for the reputation and status her sister holds dear. Although disguised as a courtesan, Marcella remains alarmed at the word and Cornelia reasonably responds, 'can you be frighted with the vizor, which you your self put on[?]' Indeed, the disguise has revealed to Cornelia how much there is of life she did not know. The knowledge is not what a virtuous woman should have, for now she concludes that, if Marcella's lover fails to rescue them,

we have no more to do than to advance in this same glorious Profession, of which now we only seem to be:—in which to give it its due, there are a thousand satisfactions to be found, more than in a dull virtuous life.[16]

She has a point in the context of Restoration London, where the rewards of warming the King's bed, or even that of a man less elevated, were certainly substantial and most working women in the theatre were 'kept' at one time or another. Although Marcella urges: 'However we may rally, certainly there's nothing so hard to woman, as to expose her self to villainous Man,' Cornelia knows that virginity must be sold in some way.[17] Either the girls market themselves or they return home, where Marcella must be disposed of to an ogre and Cornelia, like Hellena, pent up in a convent to secure more capital to her family. Remembering the dissatisfied nuns she had seen in Flanders, Behn gives Cornelia the usual grumble against enforced incarceration: she would 'whistle through a Grate like a Bird in a Cage'. Whilst Cornelia acts wildly in the short crucial interval between childhood and marriage, however, she does not go as far towards libertinism as the married Lady Fancy. In the end, she remains like Hellena a libertine only in sentiment, though when the comedy and masquerade are over she tries to salvage something by declaring she will be a most mistress-like wife.

Men desire but, as usual, do not need to plot very deeply, exclaiming as men all round Behn were doing over politics: 'the Game's too deep for me.' The woman, however, cannot afford to stop planning and analysing: not for her the man's indulgence in fury, violence and misogynous abuse. Instead, she must always look to her performance. Men can be themselves, women must act and disguise, play parts from start to finish.

Marcella overtops Florinda of *The Rover* in her verbal skills and her disguises. She needs to, for her lover is more attracted to a courtesan than Belvile had been and is even less able to see virgin and whore as one. When he claims to Marcella, acting as whore, that he has seen her face on a virtuous woman in a dream, she replies

> You only dreamt that she was virtuous too;
> Virtue it self's a Dream of so light force,
> The very fluttering of Love's Wings destroys it;
> Ambition, or the meaner hope of Interest, wakes it to nothing;
> In Men a feeble Beauty shakes the dull slumber off.

Indeed she ventriloquises so thoroughly she begins to sound like Angellica before her fall into love and Hellena in her gallanter moments: when urged to constancy Marcella as whore cries

> ...'twere to cheat a thousand,
> Who between this and my dull Age of Constancy
> Expect the distribution of my Beauty...
> Was all this Beauty given for one poor petty Conquest?

She feigns so thoroughly she almost affects herself and, fearing she is going the way of Cornelia, she suddenly breaks off her 'dissembling'.[18]

The direct political commentary in the love plot is sparse. The unwanted suitor is deformed, which gives point to Marcella's loathing and reminds the audience of the popular caricature of Shaftesbury as monstrous and deformed. But, on the whole, the politics is reserved for the comic subplot. This concerns two other English arrivals, Sir Signal Buffoon, successor to Blunt, and Sir Credulous, the young country squire, heir to £8,000 a year in Behn's own county of Kent. His wealth is presumably from sequestrated Cavalier property and his knighthood bought to aggrandise the family, where Fillamour's marks the baronet. The young fool is on the grand tour with his chaplain and tutor who is to preserve him from popery; the main effect of his travels so far is his habit of converting English names and words into a garbled mixture of Romance languages. He even insists on calling his man Giovanni, instead of plain Jack Pepper from Kent—perhaps a sly poke at Behn's foster-brother, the Kentish Colepeper. The chaplain is the farcical Tickletext—a delicious name Behn had already introduced into *The Town-Fopp* for Lord Plotwell's silent chaplain—one in a long line of lusty and hypocritical Puritans who 'tickled' texts.[19] Although 'in the Autumn' of his age, 'when Nature began to be impertinent', Tickletext still believes that a young lady could dote on him: this lack of realistic self-estimate marks out Behn's fools, young or old, men or women.

As with Sir Patient Fancy, Behn can, with her pair of squire and tutor, mock the nationalism of Protestant Dissent which breeds fear, as opposed to the easy internationalism of Catholicism. Tickletext and Sir Signal respond to foreign culture with ignorant credulity and slavish imitation or with a chauvinism that allows unfavourable comparison of the massive St Peter's in Rome to an English country church. When Tickletext reduces Roman art to superstition, idolatry and popery, it allows Fillamour to declare the absurdity of seeing 'harmless Pictures' as idolatrous, a point against which the Accession Day crowds would vociferously bray. In Fillamour, Behn expresses a Utopian belief that the true old gentry are tolerant, even if the Puritan variety appear bigoted. In fact, anti-Catholicism was found equally in every rank.[20]

The elevation of law into 'The Law' and the replacement of morality with the sophistry of legal argument Behn saw as characteristic of Dissenters, Whigs and City merchants. Tickletext is persuaded that 'Fornication [is] licensed' in Rome and he reasons, 'when its licens'd, 'tis lawful; and when 'tis lawful, it can be no Sin'. Trying to extricate himself in the brothel, he cries to the supposed courtesan: 'by what authority dost thou seduce with the allurements of thine eyes, and the conjurements of thy Tongue, the wastings of thy hands, and the tinklings of thy feet, the young men in the Villages?' Since he is now in the city of Rome, not in the villages, it seems he has made this morally muddled speech before in Kent. Cornelia responds: 'give him clean straw and darknesse, / And chain him fast for fear of further mischief.'[21]

Tickletext is a clear Oates-ish figure, a travelling chaplain given to quoting scripture in self-gratifying or erotic contexts. He is fascinated with Romish finery and absurd foreign fashions, in echo of Oates's episcopal magnificence, and is eager to affect the luxury he condemns. Both reinterpret texts and actions at will, making up new narratives to fit events as they are exposed. Sir Signal catches his tutor Tickletext in pursuit of a whore and uses his language against him: 'for you I say to be taken at this unrighteous time of the Night, in a flaunting Cavaliero Dress...going the high way to Satan to a Curtizan! and to a Romish Curtizan!' Tickletext momentarily admits to being 'Paid in my own Coyn', but then adjusts his story: he is about the conversion of a papist whore. When this new story threatens to make Tickletext seem mad, Sir Signal shows he has learnt the lesson of adaptation: he quickly explains that his tutor is having a fit, 'a whimsie—a maggot that bites always at naming of Popery'.

Behn's stage directions for her play suggest considerable theatrical planning, and *The Feign'd Curtizans* was staged with all the resources of the Duke's Company. Nokes played Sir Signal Buffoon and Underhill Tickletext. The romantic leads were taken by Smith as Fillamour and Betterton as Galliard. Elizabeth Barry, who, during her retirement for pregnancy, claimed she was going to 'quit the *World*', was back on the boards playing Cornelia. Betty Currer, who also spoke the prologue in the character of a real courtesan, was Marcella, while Mary Lee, who had played the leading role of the Queen in *Abdelazer*, played the third roving woman, Laura Lucretia. It was an impressive cast and the prompter Downes declared the play well acted.

Yet it did not take. Its trivialisation of the Catholic threat had been risky and Behn had not caught the public mood. Written prophetically before the first night or elegiacally after it by herself or a friend, the prologue grumbled that wit had fallen out of fashion and that Betty Currer's charms, like the play's, were going to waste:

> *Suspicions, New Elections, Jealousies,*
> *Fresh Informations, New discoveries,*
> *Do so employ the busie fearful Town,*
> *Our honest calling here is useless grown:*
> *Each Fool turns Politician now, and wears*
> *A formal face, and talks of State-affairs;*
> *Makes Acts, Decrees, and a new Modell draws*
> *For regulation both of Church and Laws;*
> *Tires out his empty Noddle to invent*
> *What rule and method's best in government:*
> *But Wit, as if 'twere Jesuiticall,*
> *Is an abomination to ye all.*
> *To what a wretched pass will poor Plays come…*[22]

The alternative drama of the Plot, with its conception of the 'Whore of Babylon', had seduced the public, and the playhouse had become a cast-off mistress. The beautiful Mrs Currer *'neglected at eighteen'* in her tattered clothes, stood for the 'neglected' theatre in these *'hellish times'.*[23]

Behn must have been disappointed with the reaction, for she knew hers to be a skilfully constructed play. She retained enough faith in it to try at last for patronage for the printed version. She fancied a woman but, for a person like herself, associated with theatre bawdiness, whose private life had not been impeccable, one of some ambiguity was needed—like an established royal mistress. Behn seems to have been much attracted to Hortense, Duchess of Mazarine, but it was not the moment to dedicate a play to a Catholic whore, accused as a potential poisoner of the King.[24] As for the powerful Louise de Kérouaille, Duchess of Portsmouth, Behn tended to share the nation's distaste for this French agent—called 'Fubbs' by the King and 'Squintabella' by her rival Nell Gwyn. This was perhaps unfortunate, since Portsmouth was a devotee of the theatre and was said to have given Otway twenty guineas for *Venice Preserv'd.*

It was probably Otway who suggested Nell Gwyn, although it seems that Behn had been thinking vaguely of her since the inception of the play. She was the obvious choice, although she had herself received very few dedications.[25] She had left the stage just when Aphra Behn was making her début, but she continued to visit the theatre. She now had two children by Charles II, 'two noble branches'. Although she was regarded as the commonest of the King's major mistresses—and she herself made much of being a whore to irritate the snobbish Portsmouth—and although Burnet dismissed her as 'the indiscreetest and wildest creature that ever was at court', Behn did not make the mistake of putting herself on the same social level as Nell Gwyn. She addressed the wealthy mistress as a great lady because she shared the King's bed in similar manner to a wife and because she was at court where Behn was not.[26]

So the dedication was conventionally eulogistic. Indeed, like her earlier used form, the pindaric, it was positively formulaic: 'the Poet begins with the commendation of [the dedicatee's] Country....From thence he falls into praise of...his Person, which he draws from his great endowments of Mind and Body, and most especially from his Hospitality, and the worthy use of his riches.' In this example, the successful playwright, Aphra Behn, begged to have sanctuary under the illiterate Nell Gwyn's gracious influence, where her tender laurels could thrive. Nell was the sort of vivacious, talkative woman who worked the system and Behn always admired this: the 'Sex' in general could only benefit from her success, for she refuted the common misogyny that 'will allow a woman no wit'. Nell Gwyn's physical and mental attributes were outrageously flattered and, in the next century, Dr Samuel Johnson found the dedication offensive in its 'meanness and servility of hyperbolic adulation'.[27] In fact, it was no better and no worse than most others of the time and certainly did not outdo Dryden's fulsome address to the rising political star, the Earl of Sunderland, before his *Troilus and Cressida*. Perhaps it offended because it was a transaction between two women.

Although it was Nell Gwyn's Protestantism which made her a suitable dedicatee at this moment, Behn made nothing of it. Indeed there was not much room for God where Nell herself had become the deity. Behn also made nothing of any political power Nell might be supposed to have had. The attacks on the royal courts of Charles I and Charles II most often centred on their allowing improper female power and it would be playing into opposition hands to suggest any female influence at all on the King. It was one thing to have a sexy king, quite another to have an effeminate one—as men influenced by women were inevitably termed.

It is possible that Nell Gwyn appreciated *The Feign'd Curtizans* if she watched it or had the manuscript copy read to her. Behn had tried to lighten the tone of the times as Nell Gwyn herself tried to do. Possibly the royal mistress was influential in having the play performed at court in the following year. At any rate she must have acceded to Behn's request to dedicate the play to her and it was customary to give some money to the dedicator. The usual rate was £7 to £10 depending on the importance of the work, the dedicatee and the author. Aphra Behn and Nell Gwyn were both important in their ways, though novices in the patronal tie.

Yet it is possible too that Behn miscalculated in print as in performance. Although she was not ironic in her words and made absolutely no connection between her feigned courtesan and the real one, conceivably Nell Gwyn was not best pleased to be associated with Catholic pseudo-whores.

Had Nell been able to read, she would have had definite cause of vexation, since the publisher Tonson had delivered one of the most carelessly printed works Behn ever produced, equalled only by her first and last plays. It muddled characters and names, made people exit who had never entered and printed much as a bizarre sort of prose-poetry. Strange that Behn should have allowed her first dedicated work to emerge in so ragged a form. But, perhaps by the time it was being printed, she had already despaired of its popularity with either the public or its dedicatee.

CHAPTER 19

Deaths of the Earl of Rochester and Viscount Stafford

'Here's no Sedition hatcht, no other Plots'

Not all dramatists confined plotting to the theatre and Behn herself may, at this time, have become involved in the unsavoury activities of informing, seditious copying and ghost-writing for people of various persuasions. Publicly, however, she was staunch, as an admirer declared:

> Long may she scourge this mad rebellious Age,
> And stem the torrent of Fanatick rage,
> That once had almost overwhelmed the Stage....
> ...while that spurious race imploy'd their parts
> In studying strategems and subtile arts,
> To alienate their Prince's Subjects hearts,
> Her Loyal Muse still tun'd her loudest strings,
> To sing the praises of the best of Kings.[1]

If Aphra Behn *were* recruited for any secret activity, the link may have been one of two men generally dismissed as rogues but whom she went out of her way to praise: the playwright and propagandist Henry Nevil Payne who, it was said, actually made money from informing, and the arch villain and double dealer, Thomas Dangerfield.

In the fraught days of the Popish Plot, Payne busied himself with pamphlets and lampoons, possibly at the distant request of the Duke of York or someone else at court who feared the effect of the national anti-Catholic mood.[2] Perhaps it was his loyalty and the consistency of his Catholic sympathy without any clear Catholic belief that allowed Behn to call him a faithful *'English* Subject', admirer of 'Truth', 'man of Wit', 'Eminence' and piercing 'Judgment'.

Payne had already been in trouble. Saddened by the execution of his Catholic friend, Edward Coleman, he had written an elegy making the dead man a martyr and himself a supplicant for his intercession. He thus had difficulty portraying himself as a 'good Protestant' when he was taken before the Privy Council in January with the offending manuscript in his pocket. Though he pleaded that his work had not been intended for publication, he was labelled 'homo pernitiosus & seditiosus & machinosus' and confined in the King's Bench prison for 'high misdemeanour on act of the said verses'.[3] There he was recruited as a propagandist or 'Pen-man' by the Catholic lords still imprisoned in the Tower, and employed to write both plays and pamphlets supporting the Catholic cause. The go-between was the Catholic convert, the 'Popish midwife', Mrs Elizabeth Cellier, a witty lewd woman in Burnet's words, who had ministered to a large number of eminent Catholic women, including Mary of Modena, Duchess of York.[4] Certainly one satirist made the link with Payne when he gave Cellier the words: 'as for the Muses, they are my Handmaids. Don't I direct the Pen of the great Nevil here present? I taught him to Pray in Verse to the Saint and Martyr Coleman.'[5]

Another suitable agent found by Cellier starving in Newgate prison was Thomas Dangerfield, who claimed to be a Roman Catholic. She relieved his needs, moved him first to the King's Bench, where he met up with Nevil Payne, then extricated him and redeemed his coat from the pawnshop. Presumably she did not know what she later knew: that his 'name [was] Recorded in 28 places, having been Transported, Burnt in the Hand, five times Adjudged to the Pillory, seven times Fin'd, twice Outlaw'd for Fellony, and broke the Goal in several places eight times'.[6] Nor did she realise that the keeper of Newgate thought him such a dangerous person when in prison that he 'never durst talk with him alone'. Cellier's view was rather different: her Dangerfield was a man of courage whose 'Condition and Capacity' she had thoroughly sifted.

When Payne came out of prison, he tended to slacken in his output and hang around the theatre; so Dangerfield took over as private scribe and pamphleteer.[7] Cellier promoted him and soon he was impressing James and was even introduced to the King. His experience as a forger made him doubly useful, for the Catholics had a plan—or were persuaded by Dangerfield to have a plan—which they hoped would take the heat off them and divert attention from the Popish Plot. A Presbyterian, ultra Protestant plot would be invented, together with an underground army which would have Monmouth as general, his followers Ford, Lord Grey, and Thomas Armstrong as lieutenant-generals, and Viscount Stafford as paymaster-general. The forged proof would be placed by Dangerfield in the lodgings of a Colonel Mansell and then 'discovered' by Dangerfield.[8] In the event, the device (or Dangerfield) was so clumsy that it was quickly suspected and Dangerfield was taken to prison. The trusting Cellier sent him instructions on how to handle interrogation.

By now Dangerfield either doubted her, scented more reward from the other side, or had been double-dealing all along. He turned King's evidence, going out of his way to implicate Henry Nevil Payne and Mrs Cellier, whose house he caused to be searched. Incriminating evidence was found at the bottom of a meal tub—hence the name of the affair, the Meal-Tub Plot. Cellier and her associate Lady Powis, wife of one of the imprisoned lords, were taken: the former to Newgate and the latter to the Tower, as befitted their ranks. Payne was also apprehended.

Behn later blamed Payne's misfortunes on 'National Distractions'. Otherwise so excellent a subject would not have been persecuted. In her view, he was always 'the same Man still, unmov'd in all Turns, easie innocent; no Persecution being able to abate your constant good Humour, or wonted Gallantry'.[9] She might have found it harder to say the same for Dangerfield, whom James's later chaplain, Father Warner, thought an *agent provocateur* throughout. But, although she admired heroism, Behn did not like a man worse for saving his skin.

'The Dumb Virgin', a short story written or inspired by Behn, may bear on her attitudes at this time. In it, a long-lost Venetian son turned Englishman enters an Oedipal plot, ignorantly seducing his dumb sister and killing his father. The narrator, associated with Behn, claims to have seen this man at a masquerade, 'as fine an *English* Gentleman, as I ever saw step in the Ball'. She 'made bold to ask him some peculiar questions, about affairs at Court, to most of which he gave answers, that shew'd his education liberal, and himself no stranger to quality; he call'd himself *Dangerfield*'.[10] At the end of the story the dying Dangerfield, whose crimes have been inadvertent, addresses the narrator:

> '*Madam*, said he, *I was your Countryman, and woud to Heaven I were so still; if you hear my story mentioned, on your return to* England, *pray give these strange turns of my fate not the name of crimes, but favour them with the epithet of misfortunes…*'.

The narrator hopes she has 'done him the justice…to make him be pity'd for his misfortunes, not hated for his crimes'. Conceivably, Behn was one of the few people in London to find some integrity in this notoriously false but obviously charming man, despite violently untoward appearances—as she did in Henry Nevil Payne. History decides who are rogues, but the contemporary truth is inevitably more complex.[11]

As for Cellier, whom Behn seems not to have known, though she must have provided a warning against overt politics for women, she was acquitted through a legal loophole that prevented Dangerfield's testifying against her. She unwisely followed her acquittal with an exulting pamphlet that blamed Protestantism for the execution of Charles I and branded her recent accusers 'Hangmans Hounds'. As Father Warner remarked of the staunch lady, she lacked 'keenness of judgment and calm of mind—pardonable defects in the weaker sex'.[12] As a result, she was condemned for libel and sentenced to stand on the pillory. So virulent was feeling against the new Whore of Babylon that she was allowed to put up a wooden shield to defend herself against the pelting of 'Bones, Stones, Turnips, and Rotten-Eggs'.[13] Behn knew that the misogyny unleashed by Cellier and the Plots could envelop any woman when a satire, attacking the 'Rhiming Fops that Plague the Town', depicted her 'with Bawdry in a vaile / But swearing Bloodily, as in a Jayle'.[14]

Needing to continue making a living, Aphra Behn had to negotiate the stormy time and avoid the pillory herself: she required a play that would be less flippant than *The Feign'd Curtizans*, but still relatively innocuous. Perhaps her first published dedication reminded her of her first composed drama, to which she had once sketched out her first written dedication, the still unstaged *Young King*. She looked at it again and saw it had possibilities.

Indeed it even had some political relevance. Its story of a man born to be king but barred from his proper place by superstition could relate to the Duke of York, now in strategic exile in Catholic Flanders. Were he to become king, the play appears to warn, his periods of exile would have done him and his country no good. L'Estrange had anticipated the point at the Restoration when he remarked how difficult it was for a returned exile 'to distinguish betwixt Truths and Appearances; especially for a Prince so long unwonted, and so much a Stranger to his People'. In his exile in Behn's play, prince Orsames learns 'a deal of Awe and Reverence to the Gods' and that 'his natural Reason's Sin', but little else.[15] Had the play been entirely written at this period rather than being, as Behn insists, a revision of an early one, it could be construed as criticism of the King himself, who had, many thought, weakly acceded to the exile of the rightful heir to the throne.[16]

Although she was confident that much of the old play could stand, it also required modernising. Behn must have smiled at some of her former notions, such as the absolute gendering of the sexes, an essential sexual character that education might try to but could not pervert.[17] She would always be sceptical about the power of education to supersede the teaching of experience, but she was no longer sure of the absolute difference in male and female sexuality. She also wondered at her romantic placing of country over city, although she had expressed a pastoral preference to Emily Price. The bluff soldier who had seen cities only in ruins had a heroism in *The Young King* lacking when he was transformed into the rustic buffoon of her later comedies.

It cannot be accurately known what Behn added; perhaps the fool as fop, since he is a feature of the 1670s rather than the 1660s, but probably the rather smutty sexual awakening of Orsames, unlike anything in her earliest plays or in her source, La Calprenède. This draws on the rewritten and much applauded 1667 version by Dryden and Davenant of Shakespeare's *The Tempest*, in which the authors parallel Miranda with a *man* who has never before seen a woman. Orsames sees his first woman variously as a goddess, a female, and a sex object. Initially breasts are the rise and fall of familiar waves but quickly they betoken 'other Wonders yet unseen, / Which these gay things [her clothes] maliciously do hide'. The new sexual feelings are uncontrolled by social decorum and Orsames tries to jump on each woman he sees, insisting she undress at once and instruct him what to do. He even responds sexually to his own mother, declaring when she exlaims, 'But I am your Mother': 'No matter; thou'rt a Woman, art thou not? And being so, the Mother cannot awe me.' Innocence does not baulk at incest.

More certainly, Behn added the horror of the rabble, the Wapping boys increasingly associated with Monmouth and Shaftesbury, the 'Monster-people' of Otway's *Caius Marius*. They would be most elegantly stilettoed in Dryden's *Absalom and Achitophel* as 'God's pampered people, whom, debauched with ease, / No king could govern, nor no God would please'.[18] In *The Young King* the good Royalist soldier asks the 'Rabble of Citizens' why they want a king when they had not done so before, to which comes the reply, 'That's all one, Colonel, we will have a King: for look ye, Colonel, we have thought of a King, and therefore we will have one: hah Neighbours! a substantial Reason.' The citizens express the popular English resentment at the country's loss of international place since Cromwell; they want a King because ''tis first a new thing to have a King,—a thing—a thing—we have not been acquainted with in our Age; besides, we have lost the Victory, and we are very angry with some body, and must vent it somewhere.' When pushed further the citizenry admit it prefers civil strife to war against an enemy nation. As Orsames is restored, he is warned

> though the World be yours, it is not safe
> Depending on a fickle multitude,
> Whom Interest and not Reason renders just.[19]

Charles II did not need to learn this lesson in the early 1660s when Behn was writing the first draft of the play, but by 1679 his son Monmouth did.[20]

In her attitude to the mob or rabble, Behn was as knee-jerk as her opponents to the papists. For all the contemporary fear there was very little serious violence in London, and the huge crowds that assembled for the November Protestant festivals of Guy Fawkes and Queen Elizabeth's Accession Day never attacked Whitehall or assaulted Catholics indiscriminately. It was part of Tory propaganda to see Whigs as amazing manipulators of a threatening homogeneous mass, when in fact they had little organisational power and the crowd had many different agendas.

For her new prologue, Behn alluded to an up-to-date comic event of 23 June 1679. After a curious episode in the militia in Flanders, possibly nursing a heart broken by Elizabeth Barry, Thomas Otway attended the theatre where he encountered a blustering young man buying oranges from Orange Betty. This was John Churchill, future Duke of Marlborough and hero of Blenheim, but at present gigolo to the King's ex-mistress, Barbara, Duchess of Cleveland. Either the price or the fruit offended and Orange Betty's shriek was heard after the crack of a cane. Inspired by his stint in the militia, Otway challenged Churchill. Reports are unclear whether or not a real duel followed, but most likely the pair battled it out with canes; by most accounts Otway came off best. It was the height of his martial career, the depth of Churchill's.

Behn was much amused by her friend's performance which gave her another opportunity of treating male pretension, predicament, and violence mock-heroically:

> *Cudgel the Weapon was, the Pit the Field;*
> *Fierce was the Heroe, and too brave to yield.*
> *But stoutest hearts must bow; and being well can'd,*
> *He crys, Hold, hold, you have the Victory gain'd.*
> *All laughing call—*
> *Turn out the Rascal the eternal Blockhead.*[21]

At the end of the play, Elizabeth Barry, who probably played Cleomena, stepped forward to speak the epilogue, 'at his Royal Highness's second Exile into *Flanders*' as the printed text expressed it. In creaking couplets, it conjured up an unambitious theatrical Golden Age vision, obverse of the factious London world, a vision in which Monmouth is contained and James is not '*forcd by Arbitrary Votes to fly / To foreign Shores for his Security*'. Of the '*Lord of May*' alone it can be said:

> *No emulation breaks his soft Repose;*
> *Nor do his Wreaths or Virtues gain his Foes:*
> *No politick mischiefs can disturb his Reign,*
> *And malice wou'd be busie here in vain.*
> *Fathers and Sons just Love and Duty pay;*
> *This knows to be indulgent, that t'obey.*
> *Here's no Sedition hatcht, no other Plots,*
> *But to intrap the Wolf that steals our Flocks....*[22]

Behn always had trouble yoking monarchy with pastoral indolence. In 'The Golden Age' she had fantasised a pastoral world without kings and, in 'Farewell to Celadon', she let the King destroy pastoral bliss. Here she forces pastoral and monarchy together in a paradox of power in repose.

With the theatre so problematic, Behn now looked around for other ways than play-writing of making a living, ones that did not carry with them the risk of prosecution for libel or sedition. Perhaps in another genre she might even acquire some of the literary status about which she was so ambivalent. Many of her plays had been pleasing and quite good, some were mediocre, all followed rather than led fashion. They used the conventions with skill, but the genre of bawdy intrigue comedy was not the highest. Poetry had more cachet. Behn's poems had been circulating among a coterie of readers for some time and, with a little help, she might attempt to publish in the prestigious mode of poetic translation from the classics. Perhaps she mentioned her desire to Tonson, who, like other booksellers, served as publisher, distributor, agent and even patron. Tonson may have mentioned the matter to Dryden.

Although as a professional Tory Behn publicly admired Dryden, she had had little personal contact with him. He had been writing mainly for the rival theatre and was more of a court figure than she. Now times were even worse for the King's than for the Duke's Company and it actually had to close for part of one year; Dryden was therefore looking around for other outlets for his writing and perhaps other alliances. In the summer of 1679 he left town to spend some months in Northamptonshire, but, before he went, he organised a volume of translations for Tonson from Ovid's *Heroides*, a collection of monologues spoken by famously abandoned or grieving women. It was to be published early in the new year. Despite her ignorance of Latin, he asked Behn to join the project.[23]

Behn probably hoped for Greek Sappho, her great predecessor. By the seventeenth century Sappho had an ambiguous reputation, perceived by some as a promiscuous lover of women and a suicide, by others as a great lyric poet and feminine victim of heterosexual passion. Her image had recently been popularised in a soft-focus, rather sentimental version by French writers and this made it possible for respectable men to call respectable female poets by her name—Katherine Philips had been 'the English Sappho' for example.[24] Behn might have done justice to this multi-faceted figure if she had had a chance; in fact she was assigned Oenone lamenting her faithless lover Paris, lured away by Helen of Troy.

It is unlikely that Behn had help from Dryden himself since, in the early months of 1680, he was recuperating from a vicious attack in Rose Alley made by bullies hired perhaps by the Duchess of Portsmouth or by the Earl of Rochester, both of whom had been mocked in a work ascribed to him. One of her university-educated theatrical or legal friends, Nahum Tate or Otway, both in the volume, might have given Behn a prose translation or, since she was remarkably fluent with poetry, might have translated orally while she turned the words into couplets. Or James Wright, who most likely helped with the Molière translation behind *Sir Patient Fancy*, might have come to her aid: he was known to translate from Latin as well as French.

Her 'translation' differed from work by men who knew Latin.[25] In his preface Dryden wrote of Behn, 'I was desir'd to say that the Authour who is of the *Fair Sex*, understood not *Latine*. But if she does not, I am afraid she has given us occasion to be asham'd who do.' It was a compliment to someone he obviously did not know well and it fitted with his conception of feminine modesty, but Behn so routinely lamented her lack of classical learning that he was probably telling the truth. Where the others in the volume used literal translation or paraphrase, hers was, Dryden said, 'in Mr *Cowleys* way of Imitation only'. She liked the parallel. Cowley had called his free and cultural translations of Pindar 'libertine', allowing the writer to supply the 'lost Excellencies' of the original language with those of a later. The author became a 'pattern' and the translator could write as the author would have done had he lived in the translator's times.[26]

Dryden was serious about his volume and provided a substantial introduction. It began with a summary of Ovid's life which included the kind of tart remarks on imperial morals that might have been risky in a man less highly regarded. In his hands the Roman Ovid began to sound like a Restoration gentleman, even appreciating English rank. Probably Behn felt a twinge of jealousy as she noted the kind of authority a man could command even when saying routine things.

Mindful of the erotic charge in Ovid's 'tenderly passionate' work, Dryden went on to insist: 'of the general Character of Women which is Modesty, he has taken a most becoming care; for his amorous Expressions go no further than virtue may allow, and therefore may be read, as he intended them, by Matrons without a blush.' Ovid was also commended for giving 'lower' characters such as Oenone 'Images after a Country Life'. Whether Ovid, whose steamy life he had just delicately negotiated, was truly writing for unblushing matrons was as doubtful to Behn as the natural association of women with modesty. As for the lowering of the tone when lower-ranked characters spoke, this was something she did not follow when she wrote her section—or rather she did not regard her Oeone as 'lower'. Instead she saw her as a theatrical amalgamation of several lamenting ladies: dropping the passive accept-ance of a prophecy of Paris's infidelity which marked Ovid's Oenone, Behn gave her character the dishevelled hair and wild gestures of the more active Ariadne and Sappho.

Some of Ovid's sentiments were translated into Behn's own mode. For example, she made Oenone mock her successful rival Helen:

> ...Rape hides the Adult'rous Deed.
> And is it thus Great Ladies keep intire
> That Vertue they so boast, and you admire?
> Is this a Trick of Courts, can Ravishment
> Serve for poor Evasion of Consent?

Female sexuality or desire should always be frankly acknowledged—at least when one is young.

It was not a political volume, but Behn could not entirely omit politics and she socialised what in Ovid was essentially a private affair.[27] So Paris merges into Monmouth and the prize for which he abandoned Oenone was less Helen of Troy than royal power, that 'fatal Pomp, that cou'd so soon divide / What Love, and all our Vows so firmly ty'd!' Like Monmouth, Paris was seduced by old grave men who whispered to him 'Renown, and Glory' and promised to change his shepherd's crook for a sceptre.

In a later edition Dryden added another version of 'Oenone', by John Cooper. It seems to have been no slight to Behn, however, since her version was retained and since Cooper was her old 'Brother' of the pen described so warmly in 'Our Cabal'. Indeed Cooper later wrote that, had Behn been able to give her words to Oenone at the time, the nymph 'soon her perjur'd Lover had regain'd / In spight of all the fair Seducers tears'; meanwhile Ovid would not have tried to write at all, but fallen in love with Aphra Behn instead.[28]

Behn hoped that Dryden's pointed reference to her ignorance of Latin would save her from adverse comment, but it did not. True she was omitted from Matthew Stevenson's *The Wits Paraphrased*, which poked most fun at Sir Car Scrope's rendering of 'Sappho to Phaon'. However, Behn appeared quite clearly in a later satire by Matthew Prior, which not only called her 'blind translatress' and 'Female Wit' but pointed to her 'Lewdness' and 'the ruin of her Face'. Probably she was not much concerned, for the young Prior was a colleague of Shadwell's and a Whig.[29]

She was more irritated by what followed. Tonson had persuaded a young Tory, Alexander Radcliffe, to counter the mockery of *Wits Paraphrased* with another mockery, *Ovid Travestie* (1681). The picture Radcliffe drew of Sappho as a woman entertainer, a ballad maker and writer sweating in her garret, her rent unpaid, may have drawn a little from Aphra Behn, and it may also have brought her to his mind. For he went on to produce a medley called *The Ramble: An Anti-Heroick Poem*, in which in a section called 'News from Hell' he allowed a truly annoying claim to be advanced. The 'censuring Age' damned

> a Woman, 'cause 'tis said,
> The Plays she vends she never made.
> But that a *Greys Inn* Lawyer does 'em,
> Who unto her was Friend in Bosom.

Behn might not mind being mocked for her affair with Jack Hoyle, but she objected strongly to doubts about her authorship, especially from a man who probably knew Hoyle. Radcliffe too was a Gray's Inn lawyer.

* * *

Still reluctant to create an original play or to put her name on a printed text, Behn followed *The Young King* with *The Revenge*, an anonymous, partly revised, partly adapted version of Marston's Jacobean play, *The Dutch Courtezan*, a dark City tragicomedy of a whore's intended vengeance on her seducer and betrayer.[30] The play was probably staged early in 1680 and may have 'dishonoured' the stage 'many a time' after that.[31] Given some of the additions uncharacteristic of Behn, it could have been a collaboration of Behn and Betterton.[32]

Most of the material is in the original play, with a few contemporary comments added. As in *The Feign'd Curtizans*, popular anti-popery is ridiculed: a robbed tradesman immediately cries that the thief is a 'Jesuit in disguise, sent from beyond Sea to ruine honest Citizens', while his female accomplice must be 'some Priest in Petticoats'. Later, hearing tall tales of 'Giants in Scarlet, with Triple Crowns on their heads', he fears 'the Nation will be over-run with Poperie indeed'.

The Revenge would have to be classed as revision with cuts and interpolations if there had not been some fundamental changes, mainly to adapt parts to the Duke's Company actors: the thin and wiry Jevon played someone whom Marston had called thick and stub-bearded, while, most significantly, Elizabeth Barry, famous for the pathos she had just magnificently displayed in Otway's *The Orphan*, was playing the seduced Corina. Consequently Corina was transformed from a comic Dutch whore speaking broken English into a pathetic fallen woman with every justification for revenge on her seducer.[33] In the flurry of marriages with which this play, but not Marston's, ends, Corina's achievement of the absurd Sir John must be part of a happy conclusion. Certainly it is better than the torture and 'severest prison' that Marston's Dutch whore faces.[34] However motivated by theatrical needs (and at odds with Marston's moral about lust for a whore being quite distinct from love of a wife), the changes make *The Revenge* a fascinating slice of literary history. A Jacobean work has bypassed the Restoration mode that Behn had made her own and approached eighteenth-century sentimental drama, in which wrong-doing is explained and humble whores humiliated and forgiven.

The Revenge was performed in the first part of 1680 and seems to have proved quite popular, with Williams as the hero and the scandalous Charlotte Butler playing the virtuous heroine.[35] Emily Price played the cunning foil. The play was published anonymously without prologue or epilogue to give any inkling of the author, and, like *The Debauchee* and *The Counterfeit Bridegroom*, was never acknowledged. The ascription, surer than that of the other two anonymous plays, rests with the collector and recorder Narcissus Luttrell, who was so convinced it was Behn's that he bound it in a volume with other 'Comedies' of 'Ann Behn'.

For some time now Aphra Behn's health had been poor. If the Elisabeth Johnson in the burial register of St Bride's for 10 April 1679 is Behn's mother, dying aged sixty-five, then Behn would recently have lost her nearest relative. Such a close death may have prompted thoughts of her own. She was now suffering from aches and pains in her limbs and back which depressed her spirit. So it may have been at this juncture that she tried to follow the austere regime of her acquaintance and fellow traveller to the Caribbean, Thomas Tryon. Believing that all physical ills of man were due to self-indulgence, Tryon attributed the Fall to the killing and eating of animals, and he condemned meat, tobacco and alcohol.[36] Later, when his *Way to Healthy Long Life, and Happiness* came out, Behn wrote a commendation assimilating his doctrine of health to her vision of the Golden Age, 'When the whole race was Vigorous and Strong…When Christal Streams, and every plenteous Wood / Afforded harmless drink, and wholsom food'. Since the passing of these idyllic days, humanity had become enfeebled by ingesting poison and ruining the body, then trying to restore it with bad medicines: 'Till sinking Nature cloy'd with full supplys / O'er-charg'd grows fainter, Languishes and dies'. Tryon was for Behn a 'saving Angel', however mocked by others: 'Let Fools and Mad-men thy great work condemn, / I've tri'd thy Method, and adore thy Theme.' It would be interesting to know for how long she avoided alcohol.

In July 1680, further grief was added to poor health when Behn heard the news that the Earl of Rochester had died at the age of thirty-three. He had left London in April already very ill. Opinions differ on his ailments, but they included kidney stones and neurosyphilis. His affair with Elizabeth Barry had been decidedly ended, although he had still written bitter letters to her from time to time, and he had been reconciled with his long-suffering wife and pious mother in the country. Soon there were rumours of a conversion to Anglican piety, and the indefatigable cleric Gilbert Burnet was summoned to the deathbed to dispute theology. As a loud critic of courtly corruption Burnet was keen to make as much mileage as possible out of the event and he quickly published his account of the dying rake Rochester, the conversion, and his own part in it: 'All the town is full of his great penitence,' Burnet could soon crow.[37]

Behn lamented the death, but pointedly ignored the conversion. When the King had heard of it, he had doubted and dispatched an emissary to Oxfordshire to find out the truth; he was told that Rochester had gone mad, a condition that fitted the occasional course of syphilis. Perhaps Behn subscribed to this view or at least assumed that a man racked with pain and anticipating a gruesome death could not well weigh the evidence of Anglicanism.

Yet Burnet's full account must have had some truth in it which she wished not to see: she preferred the atheistical author to the penitent. Nat Lee, who had been mocked by Rochester and had moved over to his enemy Mulgrave, took a similarly robust line in *The Princess of Cleves*, where Rochester became the 'Spirit of Wit' who 'had such an Art of guilding his Failures, that it was hard not to love his Faults'. But Lee went further in seeing the conversion as trickery: 'He well Repents that will not Sin, yet can, / But Death-bed Sorrow rarely shews the Man.'[38] Mulgrave agreed; he had always been jealous of Rochester's publicity coups, and now saw him bringing one off even in death.

Given Rochester's huge poetic talent and learning, Behn decided to mourn the Earl in a formal pastoral elegy. She was used to writing poems of praise and it is difficult to cull out opinion from the conventional phrases, but she evidently saw in Rochester one of the greatest poets of his age. Her refusal to accept the Burnet version of the end— her Rochester 'ne're shall rise from Deaths eternal Night'—suggests just how much she had been affected by the philosophy implied in his poetry, as well as by the pastoral vision that avoided any notion of an afterlife.

Behn did not see Rochester as he had seen himself in the conversations with Burnet, as wasting his life and talents, but as splendid, eternally young and noble. She was always moved by physical beauty which she called 'godlike'; tall, lean and self-assured, Rochester had been simply inimitable. Later Robert Wolseley, his friend, wrote 'Sure there has not lived in many ages (if ever) so extraordinary, and, I think I may add, so useful a person as most Englishmen know my Lord to have been... for as he was both the delight and the wonder of men, the love and the dotage of women, so he was a continual curb to impertinence and the public censor of folly.' In Behn's words,

> He was but lent this duller World t'improve
> In all the charms of Poetry, and Love;
> Both were his gift, which freely he bestow'd,
> And like a God, dealt to the wond'ring Crowd.
> Scorning the little Vanity of Fame,
> Spight of himself attain'd a Glorious name.

It was the testimony of a professional woman to a glittering amateur man. For Rochester, social and political power had been so easy to grasp. Born aristocratic and male, there was little for which he needed to strive. He could afford satire with a 'Sting', indulge his 'dear instructing Rage', dabble in loyal and opposition politics, and, having flesh so easily to hand, grow disgusted with it in poems of transcendental longing. Behn's elegy made nothing of the ambiguities of the libertine caught in *The Rover* which the drunken, violent as well as charming and witty Rochester embodied. It was not the moment for complexity.[39] She expressed only appreciation and perhaps some satisfaction that she, a commoner, was writing an elegy to an earl.

Some remained disdainful of the outpouring. In his *Essay upon Poetry*, the Earl of Mulgrave criticised women elegists in particular, and may have had Behn in mind when he said 'harmonious numbers' were not enough: thought and genre should be in absolute unison. 'Trifles' approved in the moment would not stand the test of time. If he were referring to Behn, he was wrong, for her elegy was reprinted in the eighteenth-century collected edition of Rochester's works.[40]

Others commended her poem, including those who were shocked by her more risqué verse. Among these was Rochester's half-niece, the unhappily married Anne Wharton.[41] She herself was a poet, encouraged by the elderly Cavalier, Edmund Waller, to think 'some worth' in her 'dull Rhymes'. Having read the elegy, she was clearly not offended by Behn's attitude to the conversion. Although she herself was moved by Rochester's exemplary death, in her own elegy she too went against the notion of a vicious man made suddenly good by religion when she saw Rochester's *earlier* influence tending to wisdom and civilisation.

Anne Wharton used verse to address the older, more distinguished Aphra Behn, who forced 'an Homage from each Generous Heart'. As Behn's social superior, she felt she might hazard a criticism also. Behn should, she advised, 'Scorn meaner Themes, declining low desire, / And bid your Muse maintain a Vestal Fire'. That way Behn would have Sappho's 'Wit, without her Shame'.[42]

However qualified the 'Condescension'—and she was attuned to its niceties—Behn was pleased to receive it and she replied in another poem, entitled 'To Mrs. W. On her Excellent Verses (Writ in Praise of some I had made on the Earl of Rochester) Written in a Fit of Sickness'. In this she negotiated the social (and poetic) distance by praising Anne Wharton through the undeniably great Rochester, whose 'Mighty Soul' was revived in his niece. Waller had anticipated the conceit when he claimed that Rochester continued to live in Anne Wharton. Happily Wharton adored her uncle, and was not offended by the manoeuvre. The title of the poem suggests that Rochester's death had contributed to Behn's ill health.

Within it Behn referred to 'the Silent Hours' of grief, the 'Weary Nights, and Melancholy Days; / When no Kind Power my Pain Reliev'd', which gave an hallucinatory quality to her vision of the coalesced Rochester–Wharton. The conjunction of sickness, pain and grief had led to depression, that psychosomatic state which, despite her gaiety and vitality, often haunted Behn:

> Sad as the Grave I sat by Glimmering Light,
> Such as attends Departing Souls by Night.
> Pensive as absent Lovers left alone...
> So dull I was....

She was not, however, too 'dull' to take up the criticism made by Anne Wharton. As an 'image' of Rochester, Wharton had a right to correct Behn, who had been taught by him, but Rochester was unlikely to have condemned desire or urged a 'Vestal Fire'. The 'loose Neglect' Behn admitted to having corrected under Rochester's influence was a matter of style, not content.

Anne Wharton relished the correspondence with so famous a literary woman as Behn, but Gilbert Burnet was now in a commanding position with the family, and, when she sent him a copy of Behn's verse response, he did not approve. Deeply conservative on women, he castigated anyone who did not follow the modest feminine path, and he rebuked the young Wharton for writing in praise of such a person:

> Some of Mrs Behn's songs are very tender; but she is so abominably vile a woman, and rallies not only all Religion but all vertue in so odious and obscene a manner, that I am...heartily sorry she had writ any thing in your commendation....The praises of such as she is are...great reproaches.

A few days later he returned to the attack:

> I am very much pleased with your verses to Mrs Behn; but there are some errours in women, that are never to be forgiven to that degree, as to allow those of a severe vertue to hold any correspondence with

them. And so many grosse obscenities as fell from her come under that qualification, if I can judge aright.[43]

The same advice came from another pious friend, William Attwood. Wharton should flee so contaminated a person as Behn, with her 'loose Desires' and hedonistic teaching, and emulate the chaste Katherine Philips instead:

> When counterfeit *Astraea*'s lustful Rage
> Joyns to Debauch the too Effem'nate Age;
> Draws an Embroider'd Curtain over Sin,
> And jilts with Promises of Bliss within:
> 'Tis time for you with all your Wealth of Thought,
> Forth from your lov'd Retirement to be brought....
> You best can tell the Charms of vertuous Joy;
> Despising *Venus* with her Wanton Boy.[44]

In fact poor Anne Wharton, ill perhaps with venereal disease contracted as a child, did not have much time to associate with either Venus or Behn. Over the next years she lived mainly in the country in Buckinghamshire, and died at the early age of twenty-six. Behn printed her own reply to Wharton in her first collection of poetry in 1684, and, in her *Miscellany*, published after Wharton's death, anonymously reprinted Wharton's poem called 'Despair'.[45] Oddly, she did not reprint the poem Wharton had written to *her*; perhaps the family or Burnet obstructed the publication.[46]

The year 1680, so depressing politically and personally, ended with another blow. After months in the Tower, Behn's old acquaintance Lord Stafford, now nearly seventy, was finally tried before the Lords for his part in the largely fictitious Popish Plot. The political climate was less hysterical than it had been a few months before, but the recent Accession Day had none the less featured effigies of L'Estrange and Mrs Cellier along with the usual popish bugbears. Behn had not known Stafford well, but her travelling companion from Antwerp, Sir Bernard Gascoigne, had spoken highly of him. His wife and several children were devoted to him, although his kin were not; as Evelyn tartly remarked: 'Lord Stafford was not a man beloved, especially by his own family.'[47]

The events of the early part of the trial Behn probably had directly from Sir Bernard Gascoigne. He was in court watching in disbelief as

Lord Stafford was gradually caught in the noose. With only his daughter's notes to help him in his defence against a charge of treason, Stafford had to combat deafness, a heavy cold, and natural irascibility. Sir Bernard was not there for the later part, however; he had been spotted, and a cry had gone up to eject the Catholic.

Stafford was found guilty, though Evelyn declared of Titus Oates's perjured evidence: 'Such a man's Testimonie should not be taken against the life of a Dog.'[48] His relatives had been divided on the verdict, the Earl of Arundel voting against death, the Earl of Sunderland for it.[49] The sentence was conventionally gruesome: 'you must be drawn upon a Hurdle to the Place of Execution; When you come there, you must be Hang'd up by the Neck, but not till you are dead; for you must be cut down alive; your Privy Members must be cut off, and your Bowels ript up before your face, and thrown into the Fire; then your Head must be severed from your Body, and your Body divided into four Quarters; and these must be at the disposal of the King.' The City authorities wanted to carry out this barbaric ritual, but accepted Charles's intervention, and Stafford was allowed to die as befitted a nobleman, by the axe only. Even Burnet had to admit 'Lord Stafford behaved himself during the whole time, and at the receiving of his sentence, with much more constancy than was expected of him.'[50]

He was executed on 29 December on a special scaffold erected on Tower Hill. So popular was the spectacle that people rented out space at even distant windows for a guinea a head.[51] Stafford read out a prepared statement showing that he had used the time since his sentence in proper Catholic contrition, despite being badgered by Burnet to change his faith to Anglicanism. One of the anxieties was that the convicted would not confess at the last, or might even declare their innocence on the scaffold. Although in a Catholic's case this was explained by absolution and lack of a proper Protestant sense of guilt, it still worried many that Stafford claimed ignorance of any Catholic plot: 'I have always held that Christianity and the truth is never to be brought in with blood.' In the words of the diarist Roger Morrice, he 'very peremptorily with the greatest asseveration, and in the most plain words, denyd the guilt he was charged with, and avowd his inocency even to his very thoughts…'.[52]

Although Burnet considered that Stafford died 'without any shew of fear or disorder', he also asserted that the Viscount 'vanished soon out of men's thoughts'. This was Whig optimism. Shortly afterwards,

Stafford's ghost, like Sir Edmund Bury Godfrey's, was apparently haunting informers. Reports of such activity indicated that he lingered on in popular memory as the sufferer of an unjust death.

Sickened at this latest display of lunatic anti-popery, Behn was at least pleased that Stafford, the only aristocratic Catholic martyr of the Plot, died a 'glorious death'. 'Here Noble *Stafford* fell, on *Death's* great *Stage*, / A *Victim* to the Lawless Peoples Rage,' she wrote. Echoing the redemptive Christ himself, Stafford

> Calm as a *Dove*, receiv'd a shameful Death,
> To undeceive the *World*, resign'd his *Breath*;
> And like a *God*, dy'd to redeem *Our Faith*.

As for his killers,

> At *Golgotha* they glut the'r Insatiate *Eyes*
> With *Scenes of Blood*, and *Humane Sacrifice*,
> *Men Consecrate* to *Heavn*, were *piece-meal* hew'd
> For Sport and Pastime, to the brutal Crowd.
> The *World* ran *Mad*, and each distemper'd *Brain*,
> Did *strange* and *different Frenzies* entertain;
> Here *Politick Mischiefs*, there *Ambition* sway'd;
> The Credulous *Rest*, were *Fool* and *Coward-Mad*.
> The Wiser *few*, who did th'*Infection* shun,
> Were those most liable to be *undone*:
> *Honour*, as *Breach* of *Priviledge*, was detected;
> And *Common Sense*, was *Popishly affected*.[53]

In case the parallel was not crystal clear, Behn provided a note that, for Jerusalem's Golgotha, the reader should understand Tyburn, the site of English executions just outside London.[54]

If it sounds as though Behn had become Catholic here, the date and circumstance of the composition of these lines should be noted. They occur in the poem to the propagandist Roger L'Estrange, printed long after the Popish Plot, during a Catholic monarchy and after Stafford's treason had been quashed; in their language they pay tribute to L'Estrange's always extreme vision. In contrast, in the poem Behn wrote earlier to Stafford's son, printed in 1685 probably before the accession of the Catholic King James, Stafford was a saint and a 'necessary Victim to the frantick Croud', but not a redeemer. In further contrast, in the winter of 1680 Behn was among 'the Wiser *few*...liable to be *undone*', who published no thoughts on Stafford at all.

As usual, then, Behn expressed what it was expedient to express, but the timing and theatricality of her final response to Stafford do not invalidate its genuineness, if only as part of a complex attitude to complex times. Payne and Cellier could warn her of the fate of the outspoken and more single-minded.

CHAPTER 20

❦

The Second Part of The Rover and The Roundheads

'Our Sister's vain mistaken Eyes are open'

As a woman of the theatre, an admirer of the court and a despiser of the mob, Aphra Behn was a publicly committed Tory, a supporter of kingly power and prerogative. The aftermath of the Popish and Meal-Tub plots was not, however, a moment to express violent anti-Whig feelings. Shadwell, the most skilled Whig dramatist, was on the attack, hitting out at arbitrary government and the decline of individualist Protestant values, and even Dryden offered a play to 'the people' in which he allowed some anti-Catholic satire. Charles II's fortunes were at a low ebb, and his chief mistress, the French Duchess of Portsmouth, was wooing Whigs. The insecurity caused some to waver and write ambiguously, ready to interpret or reinterpret depending on the fortunes of Monmouth or the Duke of York. Behn chose to pull back: if it were wise to muffle Tory opinions, other themes might come to the fore, stifled when politics had to predominate. At the same time, the political upheavals were edging her towards a more serious conception of theatre, to a position closer to that of the earlier denigrated Ben Jonson. She never wrote comedies of humours in his manner, or approved dramatic rules, but his satirical use of farce was attracting her.

The Duke of York had praised *The Rover*, subsequently seen twice at court. He suggested a sequel. Behn was receptive since she had been recalling her play while she grieved over Rochester, its partial inspiration. Perhaps there was another work to be mined from *Thomaso*, one that would imitate the elements of the first *Rover* but subtly change them. She decided to try. Hoping for a repeat success, Betterton encouraged her.

The Second Part of The Rover has similar characters to the first, although the only absolute links are Willmore and Blunt. Hellena has died a month after marrying, because she insisted on following Willmore to sea. He has not mourned her, but regrets the dissipation of her dowry. Indeed, he almost hints that he wished to be rid of her since he mentions that *she* insisted on coming to sea with him; the Hellena who only fantasized gender equality would have been unsurprised. Willmore is now in Spain, like his predecessor Thomaso. Intrigues follow, and again he is forced to choose between virgin (Ariadne) and whore (La Nuche). This time he chooses the latter. Willmore and La Nuche reject riches and security for an apparently equal love.

In the early 1670s Behn had followed the trend in denigrating arranged unions and supporting marriages of love. By the time she wrote *The Rover*, she was questioning aspects of the institution of marriage itself, as well as its relationship to prostitution. By 1681, she had moved beyond *Thomaso* into a more radical consideration of the different social expectations of men and women which necessarily undercut the whole concept of marriage. So the dissonances harmonised at the end of the first *Rover* were intensified in the second. Behn, who may once have wanted marriage to Hoyle, now accepted that no marriage was equal to courtship. In this she was in tune with the profound scepticism about human institutions that had come to permeate the theatre. At the same time, nothing in the play suggests that equality is possible between men and women, and there is thus a sour sweetness to the ending.

Ariadne is given the same mixture of virginal care and libertine philosophy as her predecessor Hellena: 'I love a man that scorns to impose dull truth and constancy on a Mistriss,' she exclaims. She fails to capture the Rover, however, and instead ends in matrimony according to her family's wishes. Is she a victim of a repressive society, or an example of a woman's gaining what she subconsciously wants, much like Laura Lucretia in *The Feign'd Curtizans*?[1] Despite her greater success, La Nuche does not differ substantially from Angellica Bianca of *The Rover*. She gets her man because she does not require the 'formal foppery of marriage'; Angellica did not demand it either. But La Nuche comes closer to Hellena in accepting that the Rover will not be faithful. Where Angellica had wanted to kill him because of his roving, Hellena had accepted it in theory—though combatting it in practice. La Nuche does the same. As in the earlier play, Behn did not follow Killigrew in musing on the implications of the roving libertine life for men and women as they aged.

La Nuche is not more controlled than Angellica but, where Angellica erred in placing romantic desire over self-interest, La Nuche displays a perversity deeper than Angellica's or Ariadne's, a psychological need to damage herself which may be related to her outsider status. When, through her arrogance and greed, she alienates both lovers, she realises that her power is simply dependent on men and that women alone are truly impotent. Such a complex female figure increasingly fascinated

Behn in the 1680s and the predicament may have responded to something in her own life—or in that of Elizabeth Barry who, this time, played the whore not the virgin.[2]

The Second Part of The Rover is both more farcical and sterner than the first *Rover*. The callousness of libertinism is more apparent, and the fools, Blunt and Featherfool, more clearly extend and shadow the activity of the central rake. Sex and other appetites are to be gratified, and the rest is simply an edifice constructed on them. Since women are interchangeable and the chase everything, then the fools should be free to pursue two monster women for their money: although Willmore baulks at this, it in no way violates his codes. Yet the effect is, as so often in the uneasy works of Behn's middle period, less subversion than demonstration; here is the effect of libertinism, she seems to say, but it is still better than alternative hypocritical creeds.

Willmore himself has changed between 1677 and 1681. He is less comic and drunken, harsher and more philosophically libertine. Right at the beginning of the play his callous attitude to the charming Hellena of *The Rover* makes him a darker character than his previous incarnation, a darkness that modifies the impression of the earlier Willmore for those who were watching both plays. In many ways, he embodies Behn's fear in 'Love Arm'd' that the libertine could not be tamed, whatever the 'happy ending' of *The Rover*. Perhaps he was a compliment to Rochester, for this second Willmore has something of the aristocratic, wayward charm of the Earl, something of the cynicism and protean character as well as the cruelty. Indeed the connection is made explicit in the mountebank section, a tribute to three men who were now important in her literary life: Thomas Killigrew the begetter, the Earl of Rochester and, through the echo of *Volpone*, the dramatist Ben Jonson.[3]

The Cavaliers had prided themselves on their disguises. The stories of Charles and Wilmot, Rochester's father, after the Battle of Worcester turned on their ability to represent other types of people, while always hinting at hidden nobility. Rochester was his father's son, and grew notorious for his masks: he had been a porter, a beggar, a merchant, a landlord of an inn, and even a woman. But the summit of his impersonation had been his transformation into Dr Alexander Bendo.[4]

In Burnet's prissy words, Rochester had been 'under an unlucky Accident, which obliged him to keep out of the way'—probably this referred to the ugly episode at Epsom when the drunken Earl, along with the playwright Etherege, attacked a constable; in the affray, one of their companions was killed.[5] Rochester promptly disappeared.

Simultaneously, handbills were distributed on the streets of London, proclaiming the arrival of the great Italian doctor, Alexander Bendo. Soon the town rang with his 'extraordinary performances' and people flocked to Tower Street, where they saw a splendid bearded figure in a gown of green, lined with exotic furs, a jewelled medal hanging from his neck. Bendo could be observed concocting potions out of various ingredients, from ashes and soot to lime, chalk and clay, using scales and accompanying his actions with a patter of strange tongues. He could fasten loose teeth and redden aged gums, it was averred. He could also tell the future from an examination of warts and moles. Since these were often in immodest places about a woman, he claimed that he would not look at hidden female markings himself but leave this to his wife, before whom women need not be diffident. Rochester of course acted both Bendo and his wife. When the King suddenly forgave his erring friend, Bendo had to disappear. A rumour went round that he and his assistants had been spirits all along and had returned to the underworld. The medicines they had sold were thrown away in fear.[6]

Willmore of *The Rover* did not disguise himself but, in *The Second Part of the Rover*, Behn conflates her Willmore with Killigrew's mountebank (himself calling on Volpone's antics in Jonson's play) in honour of Rochester's exploit, which, Saint-Évremond declared, was 'in every Body's Mouth'. The disguise fits within a work that is much concerned with transformation: a man even becomes a clock. But if Burnet, who had popularised the Bendo exploit by mentioning it in his record of the deathbed conversion, saw Behn's play, he must have been irritated at this glorification of the pre-conversion trickster. He would also have disapproved the nihilistic ending, in line with Behn's elegy to Rochester. In mockery of Burnet, Willmore declares: 'Love still, like Death, does to one Center tend.'

Even more attracted to farce as a response to the human predicament than she had been in 1677, Behn now felt able to accommodate some of Killigrew's grotesque elements, which she had earlier disdained. These included the subplot of the monstrous Jewish heiresses, one a dwarf, the other a giant, huge enough for two men.[7] She treats them with unexpected sympathy, giving them personalities in a way Killigrew had not, and she even omits the anti-Semitic (but social) remark, that 'the Jews their parents couzen'd the poor of a Nation to give it to these Monsters' so they themselves could be fairly robbed. Indeed the suitors are more monstrous than the women they court: Featherfool is forced to hide a pearl by eating it and is threatened with dissection, a nice touch since it was usually monstrous women who were objects of dissection.[8]

The main comment on the *contemporary* moment is the ambience of spying. People watch other people in all Behn's plays, especially *The Rover*, for it is one of the stocks-in-trade of the theatre. In this play, however, it reaches new heights, as Ariadne watches Willmore watching La Nuche watching an old whore, Petronella, deceive Featherfool. The times were equally wary.

If she was politically reticent in the play, Behn was partisan in her epilogue, in which she attacked the violently anti-Catholic Whig propagandist Elkanah Settle for his part in the Accession Day pageants and for his virulent *Female Prelate...the Life and Death of Pope Joan*. Hoping to ingratiate herself with the beleaguered court, she nailed her colours firmly to the royal mast and mocked any notion that she would ever dedicate a play to the 'Almighty Rabble'.[9] Instead, she presented it to the man who had asked for it, the man who, in most people's eyes, was the ultimate cause of the political strife: James, Duke of York, himself. The parallels between James and Willmore were inescapable. Again in exile from political troubles, James was like an old Cavalier before the Restoration; he was associated with the sea like Willmore and his absent 'prince'; and like Willmore he was something of a rake, although not on the scale of his kingly brother. He had aggravated his position during the Popish Plot by seducing his wife's Maid of Honour, the plain, witty Katherine Sedley, who bore him a daughter.

The Duke's reaction is unknown if he ever saw the play, but it seems that the first *Rover* pleased him more, since he ordered this rather than the second to be acted twice at court when he was king. In this he was in line with posterity, which did not take to the second work despite its initial success, its music and spectacle of platforms, dancers, horse and horseplay.

As the Popish Plot petered out, the theatre had still to compete with political spectacle. The wealthy Whig nobleman Ford, Lord Grey, was stage-managing a royal Monmouth show in the provinces to build up Monmouth as a credible successor to his father and alternative to his uncle, the Duke of York. In Parliament, there had been an accelerating drive for the exclusion of James. The King did not relish this, seeing it almost on a par with the execution of his father and as a distinct threat to himself. Behn agreed, writing of the '*Ingratitud*' of a body that, instead of voting 'against His *Right* and *Fame*' should have been raising '*Eternal Altars*' to James. But this was not the prevailing mood and, fearing violence from the City, the King chose Oxford as the site of his next Parliament, a place that had been the headquarters of Charles I in times of strife.

There in March he staged the event which Dryden termed 'the publick *Theater*'. Secure in his subsidy from the French king, which he had recently managed to increase, he had no pressing need of Parliament to grant him money, and no intention of compromising over the issue of the succession.

Charles had arrived with his women, the Queen, Nell Gwyn and the Duchess of Portsmouth, on the 14th; Shaftesbury, some Whigs and a group of armed men came on the 19th, with Monmouth, Lord Grey and thirty followers arriving on the 22nd. With all the cast in place, the King was asked to legitimise his bastard son Monmouth. He gave the reply 'that his Majesty was none of those that grew more timorous with age, but rather he grew the more resolute the nearer he was to his grave...'. His life 'after Fifty' was not of such value to be preserved 'with the forfeiture of my Honor, Conscience, and the Laws of the Land'. When he had called Parliament, he had given signs that a long sitting was expected. But now he passed to the Lords, retired, swiftly dressed up in his formal regal robes stashed away in a sedan chair, returned and dissolved it. Such a performance Nell Gwyn as former actress must have applauded. So must Behn, for an attitude of cynical tolerance interrupted with a swerve into heroics was the sort of manoeuvre she gave to her rakish heroes in more domestic settings.[10]

Back in London after the Oxford show, Charles and his court went on the vindictive offensive, intent on removing troublesome Whigs and Dissenters from office. Titus Oates was demoted, and his allowance stopped. Shaftesbury was arrested for treason and sent again to the Tower—though, to the fury of the Tories, a Whig jury acquitted him with an 'ignoramus' verdict at his subsequent trial in November 1681. Grey and Monmouth decided to visit Tunbridge Wells to 'divert' themselves.[11] The King was cock of his kingdom again.

Since the initiative lay with Charles II, abuse of the Whigs returned to fashion, and, since censorship had inadvertently lapsed, a pamphlet war erupted. The Royalist propagandist Roger L'Estrange, 'Towser the buldog', back from exile in Edinburgh, seized Whig pamphlets when possible and refuted them in a deluge of replies. It was now sensible to be on the establishment side. If an author pursued 'a Story...having in his eye the Affairs of his own Country' and intended to write 'against the establish'd Settlement of the State', he should, thought a critic in *A Comparison between the Two Stages*, be dealt with as a libeller. In any case, the theatre had always been associated with the court for, as the prologue to the first play presented to Charles after the Restoration declared, 'They that would have no king, would have no *Play*.' Tory playwrights and poets were urged on by the King and L'Estrange. Not since the early Restoration had the theatre been so coopted for a political agenda.

To be of assistance to the 'establish'd Settlement', Dryden produced his propagandist masterpiece, *Absalom and Achitophel*, a mock-heroic poem ridiculing Monmouth and Shaftesbury through the figures of biblical characters, and giving a humorous gloss to the peccadilloes of Charles as King David—the nation much enjoyed sharing the King's sex life. Prudently he omitted some of the awkward parts of the story, such as Absalom's sexual ousting of his father in copulating with the royal concubines, as well as the tragic biblical outcome in which Absalom was killed for his rebellion.

Behn's poetic contribution was many notches below Dryden's, but she did her bit, for she, like Ephelia, feared the threat of Monmouth supported by Shaftesbury and Grey. She was as tolerant of the King's illegitimate sons as anyone and honoured them as noblemen: in *The Dutch Lover* she had made of Quintana's villainous bastard a hidden aristocrat, but, as a base-born admirer of aristocracy and monarchy, she valued legitimate royal birth even more highly: only kings coupling with queens produced kings. Any other view threw open the whole Hobbesian world of power and, in this state, anyone might struggle for supremacy and ruin the peace of the rest.

Surnamed Scott through his marriage, Monmouth could be associated with Scotland and verses in an approximation of a Lallans or Scots dialect 'To a Fine Scotch Tune' would be immediately recognisable as political comment. For example, Behn's 'Silvio's Complaint' figured a 'Noble Youth', apt to dance, pipe and charm, now lamenting ''Twere better I's was nere Born, / Ere wisht to be a King.' He curses 'Old *Thirsis*' for leading him astray and warns: 'Ye Noble Youths beware / Shun Ambitious powerful Tales.' In another ballad, 'To a New *Scotch* Tune', Young Jemmy, a graceful charming 'Lad, / Of Royal Birth and Breeding', is 'ruin'd' by ambition. The reduction of Monmouth to the naïve shepherd, 'Poor *Jemmy*', was a technique many used to cut the threatening figure down to size. Behn's song was published anonymously in at least two broadside versions.[12]

With much 'dunning', Behn was probably paid for her loyal propaganda work in ballads and perhaps lampoons, which, since she refers to 'His Sacred Majesty' being frequently in debt to her, had clearly been commissioned. Yet the theatre remained her most lucrative source. She was ready now to use her pen for specifically political purposes, although not prepared to abandon her chosen genre of farcical comedy and follow Lee and Otway into 'serious' drama. 'In this Age 'tis not a Poets Merit, but his Party that must do his business; so that if his Play consists of a Witch, a Devil, or a Broomstick, so he have but a Priest at one end of the Play, and a Faction at 'tother end of the Pit, it shall be fam'd for an excellent piece.'[13]

To take financial advantage of the difficult times and to say something to the nation, Behn speedily wrote four plays, two adapting and two using old plays. All were performed within months of each other from 1681 to 1682: *The False Count, The Roundheads, Like Father, Like Son* and *The City-Heiress*. The first and third of these were not primarily political and they flopped, the second and fourth were and they succeeded. It was not the moment to avoid being partisan: the Tories would be offended and neutrality did not attract Whigs.

In the epilogue to *The False Count*, written by 'a Person of Quality', Behn is made to insist she had taken 'five Days' to produce the work. Possibly this was tongue-in-cheek, mocking boastful male colleagues like Ravenscroft and Shadwell who prided themselves on speed; possibly it was true. The production was, the epilogue claimed, a 'slight Farce' suitable for a Whiggish citizen audience which cared nothing for wit or clever bawdry.

The pretence that the piece was written for the Whigs was in keeping with the claim in the prologue, which comically played on Behn's known Tory partisanship, so strenuously asserted in the dedication to *The Second Part of The Rover*: she, Aphra Behn, hitherto 'a most wicked Tory', had, it averred, been converted to Whiggism, for 'Our Sister's vain mistaken Eyes are open.' She had learnt to value her 'Interest' and had written a 'Recantation Play'. The pretence allowed the prologue backhandedly to deliver a ferocious attack on Whig acts and attitudes, as well as to provide the court with a testimonial to Behn as Royalist propagandist:

> *'Twas long she did maintain the Royal Cause,*
> *Argu'd, disputed, rail'd, with great applause;*
> *Writ Madrigals and Dogerel on the times,*
> *And charg'd you all with your Fore-fathers crimes;*
> *Nay confidently swore no plot was true,*
> *But that so slyly carri'd on by you.*[14]

Despite the ironic nature of the description of Behn's Whig conversion, curiously the play *does* allow expression of the Whiggish opinions she usually avoids: the sense that lordly breeding can be faked, that an honest merchant, not perfumed like a lord but wearing 'cleanly Linen', is not contemptible, that a man's 'Appetite increases with his Greatness', that the City habit of making gentry of their children—hoisting the 'Daughter's Topsail…above her breeding'—is stupider than the Dutch one of raising them for their parents' calling, that 'good Clothes, Money, and an Equipage,—and a little Instruction' do make a 'Gallant', and that, with enough money, a repellent chimney-sweep can be passed off in foreign parts 'for what you please to make him'. The more basic reality, however, remains as snobbish as ever: a shoemaker will never really be a gentleman, nor his daughter a lady. And property is not, as Whigs supposed, the basis of civic identity and worth.

Although essentially a City play (albeit set in Cadiz), *The False Count* was based in part on Molière's skit, *Les Précieuses ridicules*, which mocked a couple of romance-addicted cousins who expected to be courted at the length of multiple volumes. Instead, they were humiliated by their rejected suitors' device of disguising lackeys as nobles to woo them with the flowery speech and flattery romance demanded.[15] Well aware of her own romance-reading past—indeed one of Molière's girls chooses her own poetic pseudonym of Aminta—Aphra Behn found such young women less ridiculous and was not keen to present their defeat by a sensible father.[16] So she changed the butt to parvenues, the former English cobbler, Francisco, and his stuck-up daughter, Isabella, and made the father more odious by putting him in her old plot of elderly merchant husband and young witty wife. The fault of the unsympathetic characters is not, as in Molière, a yearning for a more romantic and empowered life, however comically presented, but a mistaken belief that money can buy others, in the father's case a young wife, in the daughter's a man of 'quality'. The only connection between Molière's young women and Behn's upstart one is an exaggerated sense of self-worth.

Ill-bred father and daughter are thoroughly disagreeable. Francisco is not bound by civilities that temper the violence of hierarchy, whether of sex or class, and he veers between infantilising his wife in the manner of Sir Patient Fancy and calling her his slave and merchandise: '[Y]our true bred Courtier', perhaps just as misogynous underneath, is 'more ceremonious in his Civilities to Ladies than Men'. Francisco fears plots where they are not and fails to see them where they are, in neat comment on London, where the absurd Popish Plot covered the growth of the real, potentially anarchic plot of excluding the legitimate James from the throne. Francisco is fooled through ignorance—he supposes Turkey close to Cadiz—while Isabella is brought down through the kind of ludicrous ambition for which Titus Oates was famous: at the height of his power Oates thought himself worthy of a title. In the marriage of Isabella and the chimney-sweep as nobleman, Behn may also have called on the stories of Mary Carleton and her foiled desires.

Like *The Second Part of The Rover*, there is complexity in *The False Count* beyond politics: the cynicism of money and the instability of rank and gender. Guilliom, the chimney-sweeper, is assumed to be available for any lordly sport, but, once transformed, he is threateningly disruptive and he cannot easily be returned. As he observes, ''tis a harder task to leap from a Lord to a Rogue, than 'tis from a Rogue to a Lord.' His rudeness becomes lordly freedom, and his exuberant speech has only to drop the references to brooms and chimneys to form the exaggerated code of nobility. He abuses his 'servants' coarsely—but Rochester was famous for wittily abusing his.

So many of Behn's plays had ended with Utopian dissolutions of unwanted marriages: this seems to be on course when, towards the end, Francisco unexpectedly interrupts the progress by insisting that consummation of his marriage *has* occurred despite many hints of his impotence. So the marriage must simply be ignored for the happy ending, in which Francisco gives his wife to her lover like any other commodity. Earlier on, the sense of woman simply as a sexual body had bred exaggerated fear in Francisco, who sees lesbian monstrosity where there is only female intrigue: 'I have known as much danger hid under a Petticoat, as a pair of Breeches. I have heard of two Women that married each other—oh abominable, as if there were so prodigious a scarcity of Christian Mans Flesh.' The monstrosity of the woman given in whoredom (according to one scheme of values) does not strike him.[17]

The False Count is a knowing, although not a witty or bawdy work, which manages well its stage business of darkness and doors. It plays with issues, and its own form: a servant hopes for a 'comical end' when her mistress veers towards tragedy, a lover fits himself for his part in 'this Farce' and then worries that the 'plot' may miscarry, so that they make 'a Tragedy of our Comedy'. Despite its advantages and her proven actors, however, Nokes as Francisco, Antony Leigh as Guilliom and Betty Currer as Isabella, with Elizabeth Barry coming on to do the epilogue, *The False Count* did not please when staged before the King in the autumn of 1681. Behn published it with no dedicatee.

Clearly, to succeed 'in an Age when Faction rages, and differing Parties disagree in all things', Behn would have to be cruder and more explicit.

Audiences were so rowdy that plays were nearly drowned out; in the pit Whigs sat 'with a pious design to Hisse and Rail', while 'the Loyal hands ever out-do their venom'd Hisse'.[18]

Behn's next play had much in common with *The False Count* in the way it relished middle-class female pretension to aristocratic ceremony.[19] It had some political complexity, raising though not settling the serious problem of loyalty to the wrong side. What is owed to a Parliamentary husband? What is the nature of a contract or an oath to a defeated man or regime? What is honesty when the heart and tongue have different codes? Yet in general *The Roundheads*, set in London just before the Restoration, greatly simplifies matters made problematic in the earlier play, reducing rank complexity and abandoning allusion for direct polit-ical attack.[20] The use of an Interregnum subject enforced the Tory point, that Whig agitation in the 1680s repeated republican unrest in the 1640s and 1650s and that Dissenting Whigs were just old Civil War Presbyterians: 'every poor Ape, Who for Changes does gape' is really trying to bring back the '*Good-Old-Cause*'.[21] Behn's play was as up-to-the-minute as it could be in its old-fashioned combination of sixties Royalist comedy and eighties abuse.

Although, as usual, she did not admit her source, the work was an adaptation of Tatham's propagandist play *The Rump*, concerning the last days of the republic when the army and the 'Rump' Parliament—whose name had already generated a vast quantity of farting backsides and buggery jokes—struggled over the legacy of Oliver Cromwell. Tatham's crude play had been put on privately between the fall of the Rump and the arrival of Charles II, and it thinly disguised the names of the principals, General Lambert as Bertlam for example. As so often in English plays, the Scots were ridiculed, and this aspect allowed Behn to bring in the contemporary 'Scott', Monmouth, as well as the Whigs.

The time of the play, 1659 and early 1660, was probably a significant period in Behn's own young life, and she may have remembered talk of the figures she now presented. Cromwell had just died, and his son Richard had become Protector. The army chiefs failed to rally behind him, and the canting Fleetwood, Oliver Cromwell's son-in-law, along with the oafish Desborough, his brother-in-law, and various uncouth upstarts (in Royalist terms) recalled the remnants of the Long Parliament. This body, nicknamed the Rump, assumed power. (Perhaps residual feeling for William Scot made Behn omit his father from her play, despite his involvement in the Rump's revival; his place was taken by Thurloe, Cromwell's chief of intelligence, described as 'Trapanning the Kings liege people', of whom Behn may have had some secret and sour memory.[22]) Quarrelling inevitably broke out, especially with the powerful General Lambert, as Behn always assumed it would when there was no legitimate leader.[23] At this point General Monck, with his army in Scotland, came forward to take control, and invite in the King. The Roundheads were reduced to their original roles of pedlars, cobblers and scroungers of kitchen slops. In Behn's play, much is made of Roundhead low birth and uncouthness, complemented by absurd passion for the people—the list of characters actually includes 'A Rable Of the sanctified Mobil[e]'. Although the London crowd had participated in the Restoration, Behn was so appalled at the Whig mob of the Popish Plot years, whipped up through wild processions and pope-burnings, that she could not imagine its being other than recalcitrant and dangerous.

Tatham had written lengthy 'shrew' scenes in which the ladies Lambert and Cromwell quarrel over who is grander—although, in reality, Cromwell's wife had been mocked for her *homely* demeanour. Behn used part of these scenes, but omitted the frequent humiliation of the Protector's widow, making her instead a dispossessed, dooming Queen Margaret figure out of Shakespeare's history plays. As usual, Behn was disinclined to mock anything connected with the dead Cromwell except his ostentatious state funeral. His follower in the play, the Oliverian commander, is really a Cavalier in his heart, suggesting that even a pseudo king like Cromwell is better than the anarchy of Parliaments. As a sign of this general respect, Behn presented neither Protector nor seventeenth-century King on the stage: proper government appeared only in the symbol of the crown itself.[24]

What Behn added to Tatham was love interest, this time between Roundhead women and Cavalier men who, despite opposing the materialism of the Roundheads, end with their ladies and the money. She also provided an Oatesish Puritan hypocrite—here called Ananias Gogle, heir of Tickletext in *The Feign'd Curtizans*, who had himself been called 'my amorous Ananias' in echo of Jonson's famous Puritan in *The Alchemist*. Both probably used the image of the 'enthusiastical buffoon preacher', Hugh Peters, famous for his ranting sermons and lasciviousness; Behn went out of her way to introduce his name into *The Roundheads* despite his playing no part in the events of 1659–60.[25] As usual Puritans, pretending to control sexuality, control only appearance, and Gogle remarks, 'the Sin lyeth in the Scandal.' But he is not solely comic, for his canting, levelling language influences the people: 'You are a Knave of Credit, a very Saint with the rascally Rabble, with whom your

Seditious Cant more prevails, your pretious hum and ha, and gifted Nonsense, than all the Rhetorick of the learn'd or honest.'

Behn uses the misogynous fear of petticoat rule to make her point that no one but the legitimate king should govern. The sense that, if rank goes, proper sex inequality must follow, lies behind Tatham's female council scene, which Behn borrows for her cause, although she adroitly moves it into the final act of her play, and allows it to be penetrated by two Cavaliers in drag. Since her main butt is not women, she does not include Tatham's exchanges about cosmetics and perfumes which allow women to be 'sented a street off'; instead, she emphasises the ridiculous Puritan notion of democracy, with its appeal to law and rights, and gives the exchange—'in a Free State, why shou'd not we be free?' answered, 'Why not? we stand for the Liberty and Property of our Sex'—to a man pretending to be a woman and a Cavalier lady pretending to be a Puritan. As in Tatham and countless other writers of the time, women in *The Roundheads* are solely sexual beings: political posturing precedes bed. In this misogynous presentation, Behn does not necessarily temper her more basic feminist feelings, for nowhere else does she refer to women's substantial role in the Civil War.[26] Sceptical of political 'progress', she always saw women's only hope of influence not in any doctrine of universal freedom and rights but in their subtlety, their performative abilities, and their sexual manoeuvring.

The historical Frances Lambert had been famed for her arrogance and beauty. In Behn she becomes a pushy wife who openly henpecks her husband, like so many middle-class women in Tory plays. She even demands that he make her queen, rather as Isabella in *The False Count* demanded to be noble. Both upstart women act preposterously, in keeping with their ambition: as Lady Lambert remarks, 'I thought I'd been so Elevated above the common Crowd, it had been visible to all Eyes who I was.' Lady Lambert, always only the 'little Actress', is brought down not by presumption but by something Behn respected more (while always aware of its dangers for women): sexual feeling. Lady Lambert has this for a man who, on first meeting, sees not a potential queen but 'a thing just like a Woman'.

As in *The Rover*, the woman's gifts to the man do not render him a despised gigolo or give her the status of a keeper, but simply diminish her. Under Loveless's tutelage, Lady Lambert drops social for sexual desire and becomes eager simply for the 'Common Civilities due to my Sex alone' at which Cavaliers had always excelled. When, at the end of the play, a soldier pursues Lady Lambert, believing with some justice that she did more damage than her lord, he is mocked by Loveless for hunting a woman. The Restoration is close, the time when women—outside of the court and theatre—will be put back on to their pedestal of subordination and respect and the intellectual gender freedom of the Puritans will become lewd. In the satires, the Rump Parliament was often portrayed as a monstrous wife, where the Free Parliament, which opposed it and, under Monck's guidance, brought in the King, was the virtuous wife. Uncharacteristically, Behn had to rely on this imaging when she made her Puritan women, insubordinate and rebellious to improper Roundhead husbands, look forward to a future of obedient wifeliness to (slightly insalubrious) Cavaliers.[27]

In Behn's formulation, Cavalier against Roundhead becomes the common plot of youth outwitting age, and taking its women. Politics falls into chaos and sexual struggle; government is reduced to bedroom farce, as in the brilliantly orchestrated scene where the Committee of Safety begins to rule, gets drunk, dances wildly, ending in Lady Lambert's bedroom. There they sing of the 'lean Carrion', Shaftesbury, and of themselves as those who, being

> ...Rogues that are Resolute, bare-facd and Great,
> Boldly head the rude Rabble in open Sedition,
> Bearing all down before us in Church and in State.
> Your Impudence is the best State trick.
> And he that by Law means to rule,
> Let his History with ours be related,
> Tho' we prove the Knaves, 'tis he is the Fool.[28]

In the bedroom Loveless is concealed in a couch on which Lord Lambert inevitably sits. When Lambert feels movement, he shouts 'a Popish Plot'.

The Roundheads was crude, farcical, and intermittently misogynous—the City was like a woman raped and left with legs open to the wide world, an unpleasant image from Tatham which Behn in propagandising mood did not suppress. The play was also effective, and it had its purpose in giving its author a new sense of self: as a playwright with a clearly political agenda. This was expressed in her dedication.

Where she had once scorned Jonson's idea of 'Edifying Plays', Behn now saw them teaching political correctness.[29] The Roundheads was not simply light-hearted amusement, but a 'small Mirror of the late wretched Times'. So poets, including herself, were transformed from entertainers earning their shillings into 'Prophets as of old they were'. Such an idea reinforced a line in the epilogue of *The Second Part of The Rover*, in which Charles became the King of Poets and his peers the poets secured 'beneath his Laurels Shade'. Betrayal by poets was as drastic for the state as the betrayal by peers.

As Tory propaganda, *The Roundheads* overtopped *The Second Part of The Rover* and *The False Count*, indulging in no comic undercutting of Cavaliers. Royalism became synonymous with virtue, and libertinism was translated into love, lust being left to the canting Puritans. The play proved deservedly popular, enlivening for the Tories a cold winter, the first of three such. It helped to dampen the effect of Shadwell's Whig play, *Lancashire-Witches*, acted at Dorset Garden earlier in the year, and probably inspired Crowne to add his farcical *City Politiques* to the Tory attack. Behn was exultant, keen to exaggerate her political effect and make imaginary Whigs say of her play '*what, to name us...she deserves to be swing'd*'. The propaganda of which her play was a part evidently helped reinforce court power and celebrating Royalism became the order of the day. Some pieces with Parliamentary sympathies were even forced into private theatres.[30]

When published, *The Roundheads* was made the more insulting to Monmouth by being dedicated to his half-brother, the equally illegitimate and Protestant but loyal Duke of Grafton. The son of Barbara, Duchess of Cleveland, and the husband of Lord Arlington's daughter, Isabella, Grafton had just been made Colonel of the First Foot Guards—Behn liked to catch people on the way up. The dedication was the usual fulsome flattery and appeal to a young man 'whom Heaven and Nature has form'd the most adorable Person in the whole Creation'. She admired pretty young men and, following convention, tended to use beauty to stand in for any good quality. None the less, this was one of her most over-the-top performances—especially since many regarded Grafton as uncouth and ill bred—and it was as well that Samuel Johnson, who so lamented her less outrageous Nell Gwyn address, did not see it. '[T]he Poet's Flattery seldom reaches the Patron's Vanity', however, 'and what's too strong sea-son'd for the rest of the World, is too weak for their Palates'.

After her success with *The Roundheads*, Behn may have thought she had earned the right to relax her political stridency. If so, she was wrong and her next adaptation, *Like Father, Like Son*, was not even published after its failure on the stage. Its prologue, however, survived and provided another reason for the failure: that, ironically, it had to compete with the Duke of York. James had returned from exile to join the King at the Newmarket races and his well-wishers had rushed to greet him, thus deserting pits and boxes:

> So we who having Plotted long to please,
> With new Parts, new Cloathes, new Face, new Dress;
> To draw in all the yielding Hearts o'th' Town,
> His Highness comes and all our Hopes are gone.[31]

Inevitably Behn turned back to overt propaganda and, in late April, came the last of her run of political plays: *The City-Heiress*.[32] A better work than *The Roundheads*, it was innovative on two counts. It began Behn's serious analysis of the danger and perversity of female desire, foreshadowed in *Sir Patient Fancy* and *The Second Part of The Rover*, while the hero's quotation from 'The Disappointment'—'he saw how at her Length she lay, / He saw her rising Bosom bare; / Her loose thin *Robes*, through which appear / A Shape design'd for Love and Play'—initiated her habit of intermeshing works to form a single coded fictional world. This teased the reader/ watcher into guessing the author's 'life'—or perhaps wondering what a life was apart from narratives and images.

Borrowing bits from the pre-Interregnum playwrights, Philip Massinger and Thomas Middleton, *The City-Heiress* primarily followed the latter's *A Mad World, My Masters*, but is not an adaptation like *The Roundheads*. In keeping with the times, it translated the unpleasant original characters of the early seventeenth century into the political and comic types of the 1680s. Middleton's old uncle figure became the alderman Sir Timothy Treatall, for example. Hypocritical, greedy, Whig and Dissenting, Sir Timothy was probably a composite figure of several Whigs such as the now Lord Mayor, Sir Patience Ward, and the notoriously whoring alderman and virulent anti-papist, Sir Thomas Player. Since, however, the play followed hard on the heels of the political sensation of the theatrical season, Otway's *Venice Preserv'd*, people may well have been looking for mockery of Lord Shaftesbury. (Although it is not universally agreed that Shaftesbury was represented in Otway's character Antonio, many believed that the playwright had turned the ageing, ailing and clever Earl into a fetishistic masochist, intent on flagellation from his mistress Nicky Nacky.) Behn did not disappoint expectation and, like many others, she alluded to Shaftesbury by referring to the invented Tory episode of his seeking the elective crown of Poland: in her play Sir Timothy is fired by the ludicrous offer but then returned to his status of London alderman. His money will be restored only if he promises to support the royal brothers and stop meddling with Exclusion.[33]

Despite its title, the centre of *The City-Heiress* is held by the poxed hero Wilding, choosing as usual between two women, and by the rich widow, Lady Galliard, who here plays the courtesan's role. In keeping with the greater conservatism of a primarily political play, this time the rake-hero *marries* a virgin, but the chemistry between Wilding and the adult Lady Galliard is so great and her passion so well communicated that it is hard for the play to follow *The Rover* rather than *The Second Part of The Rover* and donate the desired man to the proper and clever heroine.

Lady Galliard is passionate and free—she was played by Elizabeth Barry, who had just played La Nuche—and, like Angellica of *The Rover*, she feels love stronger than prudence and interest. Unlike Lady Fancy, she is not a libertine but remains the conventional woman reared to modesty, yet overwhelmed by sexual desire. She succumbs knowing, as many naïve girls do not, that neglect will follow. Sexual freedom in the context of the double standard is inevitably imprisoning, and Lady Galliard ends diminished by her affair with Wilding.

Another Rover with some of the harshness of the second Willmore and the rhetorical power of the first, Wilding, played by Betterton, subjects Lady Galliard to the seductive language Behn both admired and, as a woman in society, feared to hear. Beauty should still be the reward of love, he argues,

> Not the vile Merchandize of Fortune,
> Or the cheap Drug of a Church-Ceremony.
> She's onely infamous, who to her Bed
> For interest, takes some nauseous Clown she hates:
> And though a Joynture or a Vow in publick
> Be her price, that makes her but the dearer whore...
> All the desires of mutual Love are vertuous.
> Can Heaven or Man be angry that you please
> Your self and me, when it does wrong to none?[34]

It was the sort of plea Rochester made in his heyday before he encountered Burnet. It was often the prelude to sex, then male disgust at female sex, then rejection.

Both Lady Galliard and Wilding tiptoe round marriage. He proclaims that he 'had the honest Reputation of lying with the Magistrates Wives' but now he is reduced to 'a Husband-Lover!...Thus the City She-wits are let loose upon me, and all for you, sweet Widow'. Meanwhile she exclaims against marrying a man with 'half a dozen hungry Vices, like so many bawling Brats at your back, perpetually craving, and more chargeable to keep than twice the number of Children...'.[35] Both know the truth, however, that he does not need marriage and that for her only marriage can do. Lady Galliard can truly say, 'I understand not these new Morals.' There is no libertine space for women who have already internalised the conventional morality and tragic progress: 'when you are weary of me, first your Friend, / Then his, then all the World'. Loving so intensely that she sees Wilding as 'all / That Man can praise, or Woman can desire', Lady Galliard pays for fulfilled desire the 'high Price' of her virtue. She knows the consequence:

>...A Whore? Oh, let me think of that!
>A man's Convenience, his leisure hours, his Bed of Ease,
>To loll and tumble on at idle times;
>The Slave, the Hackney of his lawful Lust!
>A loath'd Extinguisher of filthy flames,
>Made use of, and thrown by...

In the end, when she gives in through pure sexual desire, Wilding crows:

>All Heaven is mine, I have it in my arms;
>Nor can ill Fortune reach me any more.
>Fate, I defie thee, and dull World, adieu.
>In Loves kind Fever let me ever ly,
>Drunk with Desire, and raving mad with Joy.[36]

Despite his diseased status, he gains in stature while she is left with remorse and jealousy. It is a powerful picture of gender difference in sex and the warfare between men and women outside Arcadia. The woman may be intellectually attracted to the male libertine creed but she cannot, without the cover of marriage and the conquest of her moral upbringing, follow it and survive in society. Lady Galliard is forced to screen her fall with marriage to her would-be rapist, looking, like poor Ariadne of *The Second Part of The Rover*, fondly back at the man she loves.

Otway's complex sexual concerns seem to have entered *The City-Heiress* and there is even a leering and voyeuristic uncle pushing a nephew into vicarious rape.[37] Fittingly, then, Otway offered Behn a prologue for Elizabeth Barry to speak. He and Nat Lee seem now to have replaced

Ravenscroft in closeness; each needed the others in these impecunious times, and Otway would have been paid for his words. A 'Person of Quality' provided a suggestive epilogue, clearly written for the scandalous Charlotte Butler, who comically played the virgin in the play—Butler is made to refer to her whorish reputation which, she claims, will make her role hard for the audience to swallow. The play therefore began and ended in 'petticoats'. The cast-off mistress who finally gets the Whig knight, Sir Timothy, was played by Betty Currer, so famed for her saucy mistress roles, and Sir Timothy and his friend were acted by the comic duo of Nokes and Leigh. Music was provided by Giovanni Draghi and Langbaine declared the whole performance well received. The printed version was brought out by Daniel Brown who had also published Behn's other most political play, *The Roundheads*, making more careful jobs of both than Tonson had done with her earlier plays.[38]

For her dedicatee for this success Behn chose carefully, another Protestant who would become very important to her: Henry Howard, Earl of Arundel, the future seventh Duke of Norfolk and son of the great patron of the Royal Society. His strategic conversion during the Popish Plot had just been rewarded and he had become Lord Lieutenant of Berkshire and Surrey. Behn appreciated him as the only Howard peer to vote for his great-uncle Stafford—'May Heaven and Earth bless you for your pious and resolute bravery of Mind, and heroick Honesty, when you cry'd, *Not Guilty*'—but others regarded him as 'a very vicious man', a trimmer and a time-server. Probably Arundel was generous to Aphra Behn since she later referred to him as her patron.

The dedication welcomed the revival of royal spirits. The Stuarts were popular again after 'troublesome times, this Age of Lying, Preaching, and Swearing'. The bubble of the Popish Plot had burst: 'The Clouds already begin to disappear, and the face of things to change, thanks to Heaven, his Majesties infinite Wisdom, and the Over-Zeal of the (falsely called) *True Protestant Party.*' But heaven and royal wisdom were only part of the cause Behn knew. The Tory propaganda which she had helped create tarred the grumblings of the 1680s with the rebellion of the 1640s, making Exclusionists of whatever hue into rabid republicans. Behn wanted 'seditious Fools and Knaves... [to] become the business and sport of Comedy, and at last the scorn of that Rabble that fondly and blindly worship 'em'. Certainly she had helped in the former task and she could feel proud of her part. It did not matter to her that others saw this Royalist campaign as a vicious attempt to silence dissent and freedom of expression.

CHAPTER 21

❦

Free-thinking in Politics and Religion

'Beyond poor Feeble Faith's dull Oracles'

Behn had reluctantly followed the times in using plays as overt propaganda and was glad of some success in the mode. With satisfaction she reflected on the popular *Roundheads* and *The City-Heiress*: of the latter she wrote, 'It has the luck to be well received in the Town; which (not for my Vanity) pleases me, but that thereby I find Honesty in fashion again, when Loyalty is approved and Whigism becomes a Jest where'er 'tis met with.'[1] Perhaps she even celebrated the moment by commissioning a portrait of herself by Lely's successor as court painter, John Riley. A shy, diffident man, no lover of conviviality and taverns like her dead artist friend Greenhill, Riley is unlikely to have encountered Behn socially. But, unpopular with court ladies, he did paint women of her rank, including, on one occasion, a governess in the royal household. He had writers such as Edmund Waller among his sitters and to these he gave an inward, brooding quality quite distinct from Lely's more extrovert images. The portrait of Behn, surviving now only in engravings, is serious, even sombre, but compatible with the one ascribed to Lely five or so years earlier.[2]

With Behn's success the Whig Shadwell was thoroughly vexed. Gleeful over the failure of her unpublished play, *Like Father, Like Son*, he was incensed at the good reception of *The Roundheads* and *The City-Heiress*, and, in *The Tory Poets, A Satire*, he fulminated against both works as shams. He made Otway into Behn's pimp because he had supplied her with a prologue:

> Poetess Aphra, though she's damn'd today,
> Tomorrow will put up another play;
> And Otway must be pimp to set her off
> Lest the enraged bully scowl, and scoff,
> And hiss, and laugh, and give not such applause
> To *Th'City Heiress* as *The Good Old Cause*.[3]

Other less Whiggish poets were displeased with Behn's efforts as well. Believing that wicked writers would 'pluck down a Judgment on the Times', Robert Gould was furious at the spectacle of the impudent Mrs Behn portraying rewarded rakes and cursing virgins.[4] He had been uneasy as each of her plays was performed, but he positively seethed when, in *The City-Heiress*, he saw intercourse implied in the rumpled clothes of Wilding and the laments of the widow, Lady Galliard. With visceral horror he watched Behn moving into the political and literary centre as a 'Female Laureat' and lashed out at her:

> What tho' thou brings't (to please a vicious Age)
> A far more vicious widdow on the Stage,
> Just Reeking from a Stallions Rank Embrace,
> With Ruffled Garments, and disordered Face,
> T'acquaint the Audience with her Slimy Case?[5]

It says something for Behn's personal discretion that Gould, who probably did not know her personally, seems to have had little specific to charge concerning her sexual life, when he dismissed Dryden's wife as a whore, Dryden as a lecher, and Otway as a drunk. The worst he could say of Behn was that she had become '*Sapho*, famous for Her Gout and Guilt'.[6]

Wycherley also took this moment to comment ribaldly, if affectionately, on Behn, as one theatrical trooper to another. She could take his remarks with a pinch of salt, since he himself was being savagely lampooned as the latest gigolo of the King's ex-mistress, Barbara, Duchess of Cleveland.[7] His poem was called 'To the *Sappho* of the *Age*, suppos'd to Ly-In of a *Love-Distemper*, or a *Play*' and it responded to the sexiness of *The City-Heiress* in particular.

Wycherley created a prostituting past for Behn, in which she had flaunted her 'Parts' to the town, where now she flaunted plays, and had borne children, where now she bore works: 'Barren Wits, envy your Head's Off-springs more, / Than Barren Women, did your Tail's before.' This was the first and last anyone heard of Behn's child-bearing. Wycherley also placed her with Ravenscroft in the sweating-tub for 'Clap':

> Now Men enjoy your Parts for Half a Crown,
> Which, for a Hundred Pound, they scarce had done...

more Men, now you please the more...
Who, to be Clap'd, or Clap you, round you sit,
And tho' they Sweat for it, will croud your Pit;
Since lately you Lay-In, (but as they say,)
Because, you had been Clap'd another Way;
But, if 'tis true, that you have need to Sweat,
Get, (if you can) at your New Play, a Seat.[8]

As Shadwell could not avoid the correspondence of pimp and prologue, so Wycherley could not resist the analogies of writing and child-bearing, poetry and prostitution, claps and the clap, made resonant by a *female* playwright. It was hard for any woman to avoid the connection of writing and sex, almost impossible for someone like Behn, exhibiting on the public stage and apparently once kept by a man. Wycherley's *main* point, however, was the steaminess of Behn's recent popular offerings, the watching of which would serve quite as well as sweating-tubs. It was a sort of compliment.

However naughty her plays, Behn's new political stature meant that she was now asked to supply committed prologues and epilogues herself. Her first known commission was for *Romulus and Hersilia*, an anonymous Roman tragedy. The £10 or so she gained was useful, but she may also have felt attracted to the play's Amazonian subject, reminiscent of Edward Howard's *New Utopia* and her own *Young King*, though its heroine Tarpeia is more consistently heroic than her back-sliding Cleomena. In propagandising mood, Behn played with the Roman setting of *Romulus* as she had in *The Feign'd Curtizans*: 'ours is a Virgin *Rome*, long, long before / Pious *Geneva* Rhetorick call'd her Whore'. In the extreme language characteristic of the belligerent Roger L'Estrange, she ridiculed the Protestant Whigs as stinking rats and weasels gnawing the royal lion's beard, then, when he roared, skulking away. Incensed like all the Tories at Shaftesbury's acquittal through the 'ignoramus' verdict of the packed Whig jury in November 1681, she asked in a series of raucous rhetorical questions:

What have ye got ye *Conscientious Knaves*,
With all your *Fancy'd Power*, and *Bully Braves?*
With all your *Standing to't*; your *Zealous Furies*;
Your *Lawless Tongues*, and *Arbitrary Juries?*
Your *Burlesque Oaths*, when one *Green-Ribbon-Brother*
In Conscience will be *Perjur'd* for another?

> Your *Plots*, *Cabals*; Your *Treats*, *Association*,
> Ye shame, Ye very Nusance of the Nation,
> What have ye got but one poor Word? Such Tools
> Were *Knaves* before; to which you've added *Fools*.

The epilogue spoken by Lady Slingsby, as the tragedienne Mary Lee had now become, was equally pointed. Tarpeia, the character she played, had been innocent once; she had grown treacherous through love:

> *Love*! like *Ambition*, makes us Rebels too:
> And of all Treasons, mine was most accurst;
> Rebelling 'gainst a *King* and *Father* first.
> A Sin, which Heav'n nor Man can e're forgive;
> Nor could I *Act* it with the face to live.

Not even death can expiate 'a Treason gainst the *King* and *State*'.[9] The reference to Monmouth was clear.

But, in fact, the King *could* forgive; consequently these uncompromising words were unappreciated. Although Charles's 'pleasure is to be dissatisfied and angry with the Duke of Monmouth, yet he is not willing that others should abuse him…'. The *True Protestant Mercury* of 16 August 1682 described what followed:

> *Thursday* last being Acted a Play called The *Tragedy of Romulus* at the Dukes Theature [sic] and the *Epilogue* spoken by the Lady *Slingsbey* and written by Mrs *Behr* [sic] which reflected on the D. of *Monmouth* the Lord *Chamberlain* has ordered them both into custody to answer that affront fo the same.[10]

How Behn got off is unknown. Possibly she echoed Mrs Cellier, who pleaded her sex when accused of libel: 'If I was a foolish vain Woman, and did seem to speak some vain words…which I did not understand the Consequences of, I hope a word vainly spoke by me, shall not be brought against me to convict me of a Crime.'[11] Although an enemy gloated that 'Sappho with her wondrous empty shew / [Of] Torie faith, yet shan't unpunished go,' quite possibly Behn was never taken into custody.[12] The Lord Chamberlain was, after all, her old associate, Lord Arlington, whose daughter she had just fulsomely flattered in her dedication to the Duke of Grafton, and she herself was an accepted Tory propagandist. No more was heard of the matter.

Behn's forthright condemnation of Monmouth probably had the advantage of bringing her to the attention of his enemies, such as Rochester's old sparring partner and Dryden's patron, the trimming Earl of Mulgrave. Recently Mulgrave had published anonymously his *Essay on Poetry*, a powerful literary analysis of verse in his age which, in contrast to any remarks Behn made about poetry, looked forward to the eighteenth-century aesthetic and expressive views rather than to the more political and social ones of his own time. It also attacked some prized contemporaries, including the dead Earl of Rochester, but Behn knew that her idol was strong enough to withstand any assault. On Monmouth's disgrace, Mulgrave had received many of his preferments—while Monmouth had apparently taken over Mulgrave's former mistress, Lady Henrietta Wentworth. Now, in November 1682, Mulgrave followed Monmouth into disgrace, as Luttrell records:

> The earl of Mulgrave is fallen into his majesties displeasure (by pretending courtship, as is said, to the lady Ann, daughter to his royall highnesse), and is forbid comeing to Whitehall and St. James, and hath all his places taken from him.[13]

James's daughter, the young Princess Anne, was third-in-line to the throne, so Mulgrave's offence was heinous.

At this awkward juncture, Mulgrave seems to have turned to the professional poet, Aphra Behn, to provide him with a poem as a peace offering to the princess and to the court. This was not an uncommon act, even for a poet as skilled as Mulgrave, and Dryden himself was occasionally supplied with appropriate verses by jobbing poets.[14] For Behn, it was a useful commission from a man whose style she declared she admired, and for him she wrote verses as if composed by the Roman poet Ovid to the granddaughter of the Emperor Augustus, his beloved Julia. Ovid had been banished from Rome for Julia's sake, as Mulgrave was from the English court for Princess Anne's.

Male ambition, political or sexual, was a disturbing, truly Promethean force, and Behn did not entirely deflate it by giving her 'Ovid' the stereotypical language of female complaint, of the sort she had used for Oenone. The famous Mulgrave pride remained: languishments and tears were 'Artillery which I ne'r sent in vain', but there was also a genuine sense of pain, not only for baulked love, but for ruined self-esteem: physical suffering was preferable to psychological, wounds to the scorn of the court.[15]

Whatever the subtlety of the picture, many readers saw only crude compromise and unholy alliance between the vain Earl and the lewd poet.[16] It again incensed Robert Gould, jealously watching Behn's sideways movement towards the court and the great. Truly the shameless pair deserved each other, he sneered: 'sure Heav'n never Joyn'd a happier Pair: / He kind, as Lovely! you, as good as Fair!'[17]

The libertinism that marked so many of Behn's recent plays had been influenced by the classically educated men she had come to know and admire, especially Jack Hoyle and the Earl of Rochester. Like many other intelligent women, she had bewailed her exclusion from the classics. Now, however, more and more works were being 'English'd...this Age being pretty kind to us females in such assistance'.[18] But, although several people, including Rochester and Dryden, had attempted part of the great philosophical poem, *De Rerum Natura*, by the Roman Lucretius, no one had yet made the whole accessible to those unlearned in Latin.[19] So it was with excitement that Behn received a copy of a complete translation, along with a request to write a poetic commendation for the second edition. She gladly agreed.

The work was by a young man from Wadham College, Oxford, Thomas Creech. Since one of the commendations warned him against the theatre, Behn may have encountered him there, but it is more likely that Tonson both commissioned the commendation and later introduced her to Creech. In her poem, she shows no personal acquaintance with the author whom she addresses as the 'unknown Daphnis'.[20]

Creech knew he was dealing with dangerous matter, even after two thousand years, for Lucretius had taught the classical doctrine, that all things and all living beings were combinations of atoms. 'The rise of Things, how curious *Nature* joyns / The various Seed, and in one Mass combines / The jarring Principles.'[21] All being corporeal, piety was exploded and death could be faced, as it was in Lucretius, without comfort or discomfort. Divinity, if any divinity there were,

> live[s] in Peace,
> In undisturb'd and everlasting ease,
> Not care for Us, from fears and dangers free,
> Sufficient to His own felicity.
> Nought here below, nought in our power He needs,
> Nere smiles at good, nere frowns at wicked deeds.

Institutional religion became 'Tyranny' and 'holy Cheats'.

This was shocking in a Christian country and all the translators were anxious not to be associated with the author they were busily publicising. Dryden declared that his time with Lucretius confirmed his Christianity and Behn's foster-brother, Thomas Colepeper, studied Lucretian atomism only to pronounce it frivolous. Like these, Creech, a lugubrious and apprehensive young man, felt obliged to apologise for his work, and his friend Nahum Tate helped him by praising his purging of Lucretius' poison. Scenting Tory embarrassment, however, Matthew Prior roundly mocked the young man for hypocrisy: 'The Wits confirm'd his Labours with renown, / And swore the early Atheist for their own.'[22]

Behn saw *De Rerum Natura* very differently from Dryden and Creech: as a powerful and triumphant assertion of rationalism and materialism using the atom theory. Released by Lucretian philosophy, Reason in her baroque vision has a libidinal, liberating quality playing like Cupid over all including faith:

> It Peirces, Conquers, and Compells
> Beyond poor Feeble Faith's dull Oracles,
> Faith the despairing Souls content,
> Faith the Last Shift of Routed Argument.[23]

She knew the religious implications of what she was saying and that this deification of reason sounded remarkably Hobbist. The Anglican position was that reason could lead *up* to the mysteries of faith, but never equal or supersede them: the famous opening lines of Dryden's *Religio Laici*, published some months later, makes the orthodox point: 'pale grows Reason at *Religions* sight.' That Behn was approaching what the seventeenth century termed 'atheism' and was growing known for her free-thinking is apparent from a later comic verse epistle by a Tory curate, also an acquaintance of Creech's, who flattered her by admitting that, under her influence, he might 'e'n believe the World was made by Chance, / The Product of unthinking Atoms dance'.[24]

Behn may not so thoroughly have understood the possible *political* implications of Lucretius. Dryden opposed him partly because he associated his message with rebellion: the circumscribing of power in God led to the circumscribing of it in the King. Behn so disliked clerical power, however, that she took every opportunity of mocking priests and their law, a position more common among radical thinkers and republicans like Hoyle than among Royalists, who tended to understand the need of an established church to support an established king. Behn seems to have felt she could be daring in religion without impinging on politics, so that destabilising the Christian God did not necessarily desta-bilise Charles II. Hobbes, who saw religion as the arm of the state, could have put her right.[25]

Behn came closer to Dryden in her admiration of Lucretius on sex. Indeed, Dryden called *De Rerum Natura* 'the truest and most Philosophical account both of the Disease and Remedy, which I ever found in any Author' and, in his own translation, he added some of Lucretius' explicit description of sexual intercourse omitted by Creech.[26] Given the common cultural assumption of active, vital male form and passive, cold female matter, Behn must have smiled to encounter the feminine Venus as the primary energy within the universe. Although he was man-centred, when it came to individual human beings Lucretius did acknowledge female desire.

In Lucretius' analysis, sexual union, always wanted, was always momentary, therefore always disappointing and embittering. The sexual urge was irrational and anarchic, and the '*secret* wound' was the insa-tiability of desire. Even orgasm did not entirely satisfy, as 'the *loose airy* pleasure slips away.' Behn had revealed a frank attitude to sexual matters when she wrote 'The Disappointment'; in Lucretius, she met a mate-rialist and explicit description of what underlay disappointment and desire.

She was excited and wrote of her enthusiasm in her commendatory poem for Creech. First, however, she thanked the young man for his work. Comically using the Lucretian atomic theory, she portrayed herself as composed of slow-moving particles, so that her mind was all concerned with love and 'Womanish Tenderness'. She could not rise to Creech's 'Strong Manly Verse'. None the less, she wished to declare her debt to Creech—greater than any man's, for he had rescued her from the 'ignorance of the female sex':

> Thou by this *Translation* dost advance
> Our Knowledge from the State of Ignorance;
> And Equallst Us to Man.

In the epistle to *The Dutch Lover*, Behn seemed to mock male classical learning, but, in fact, her butt had been the pedantic and affected char-acters learning could create. Here she suggested the value of classical knowledge for sensible, inquiring people of either sex. Women's exclusion had been based on custom, not nature.

Behn made her feminist point lightly, for the assurance of her poetry and her stance of public compliment now rendered any presumed inferiority conventional: nobody, it was implied, was very much superior to her, man or woman. Indeed, as Robert Gould feared, poetry was already conferring a kind of status independent of gender. Where, in Lucretius, savage man had been tamed by love, fire and clothing, in Behn's work poetry (and by implication the poet) performed this function. Whatever she might comically and conventionally say about her poetic inferiority to Creech, she was proving at the very moment of writing her own poetic status.

As in her verses to the little known Anne Wharton, here again Behn tended to slide off from praise of the unfamiliar into consideration of the analogous but truly great and known. She extolled Wadham College, the 'Sacred Nursery', for begetting not only Creech, but also 'the soft, the Lovely, Gay and Great' Rochester, as well as a man she seems increasingly to have known in this period, Thomas Sprat, 'Loyal Champion of the Church and Crown' and biographer of Cowley, one of Behn's first poetic loves. Through Sprat Behn managed a swipe at Gilbert Burnet, whose criticism of her she may have known and who was famously at odds with Sprat. Both men had preached political sermons on the same day, Sprat appealing to the King, Burnet successfully wooing the Commons; Behn referred to the event when she portrayed Sprat as 'above the thanks of the mad senate-house'.

She finished her poem and sent it off to Creech in January 1683. He received it with dismay. The reference to 'poor Faith's dull Oracles' was too much; obviously Behn understood nothing of his delicate position as a fellow of a university where orthodoxy was nominally required or of his hopes of taking holy orders and receiving a secure college living. He did not have much opportunity to register his unease, for it is about this time that Behn seems to have left the country.

Late in 1683 Behn claimed that she had been 'at *Paris* last Spring' and the claim is supported by the fact that, from this time onwards, she became assured in her knowledge of French culture and language, as well as more contemptuous of French people.[27] When she had written *Sir Patient Fancy* in 1678, she had implied that she knew little French, but, from 1684, she translated French at top speed, using authors hardly known in England.

She knowledgeably discussed the differences between the two languages, commented on the hazards of translation, and wrote authoritatively of the importance of drama to a state, a topic much debated in Paris in the 1680s. Either she was lying earlier, or she had, about this time, a sojourn in France or Flanders that gave her new competence.

Perhaps she went on another spying mission or took part in some undercover activity. If so, her employer might have been the present Secretary of State, Robert Spencer, second Earl of Sunderland.[28] Sunderland was a protegé of Arlington and nephew of Shaftesbury. As she might have remembered, he had also been an inmate of the Sidney nursery in the Interregnum, when his mother, Dorothy Sidney, had lodged at Penshurst. Since those early days, Sunderland had become a slippery politician; some thought him Machiavellian and cunning, others simply opportunistic and selfish. A satire of 1680 makes him a 'Cringing Cheat', a 'Silver Eel' who has 'wrigl'd thro' the Mud to Fortunes Wheel / Slipt into place improperly by Fate'.[29] With misgivings Rochester had watched his rise through court intrigue, especially with the King's French mistress, Louise, Duchess of Portsmouth, seeing him as one who 'wold bribe us without Pence, / Deceive us without Common Sense / And without Pow'r enslave'.[30] Evelyn, who greatly admired Sunderland's wife, disapproved the Earl's extreme 'Court ambition'.[31] Behn cannot have approved his voting for Stafford's death, but she could not afford political grudges. The Earl was close to the stage, an acquaintance and patron of Dryden, Otway, and Betterton, and, if she met him, her Kentish connections would have made a link, though he was well above her sphere socially.

Sunderland had been Secretary of State from the late 1670s and would be so with one gap until 1688. The gap came from his flirtation with the Exclusionists—according to Evelyn he thought that they would *win*, not that they were right—but he retrieved Charles II's favour in 1683. From then on he intended publicly to cleave to royalty, but keep all options open, whether embodied in Monmouth, the Prince of Orange or Louis XIV. It is just conceivable that Behn was required to find out something of these options in France or generally bring back 'Intelligence'.[32] Behn may also have had her own agenda for her travels. Gould mentioned gout and Wycherley pox, and she herself had described indifferent health in the early 1680s. Paris was a centre of medical knowledge and several noblemen went there to find cures for their venereal complaints. Behn, too, may have journeyed in hope of some relief from her ailments.

In Paris, Behn might have touched the fringes of grand and respectable society, less handicapped than in England by the notoriety of her bawdy plays. So she could encounter the *'précieuses'*, intellectual women who held salons in which relations between the sexes were regulated by intricate codes. One of the hostesses was Mlle de Scudéry, the famous writer of French romance; Behn had probably read her when young, although her references are mainly to de Scudéry's fellow romancist, La Calprenède; she had more recently met her in Molière's mockery in *Les Précieuses ridicules* and *Les Femmes savantes*, used for her own *False Count* and *Sir Patient Fancy*. The heyday of the female salons had been the early seventeenth century, when aristocratic women had presided and politics been much discussed. Now salon conversation was mainly literary, philosophical, and gallant, and many of the *salonistes* were not of the highest rank. Hence they had become fair game for Molière.

Three charming and sociable men who mingled with the *précieuses*, Tallemant, Fontenelle and de Bonnecorse, may have encountered Aphra Behn during a stay in Paris. The first, the Abbé Paul Tallemant, a gallant, courtly cleric, had, when still in his teens in 1663, published *Voyage de L'Isle d'Amour*, which charted the psychological course of love through allegory. The Abbé was famously good company, the soul of parties and known for his quick wit; so Behn must have been surprised to find so little displayed in the *Voyage*. The second, the witty, popular and sceptical Bernard de Fontenelle, nephew of the tragedian Corneille, was a young man in his twenties, already a journalist and playwright. Behn and he held rather different political views, since Fontenelle opposed absolutism—although the distinction was mainly due to the difference between France and England, for they thoroughly agreed in their elitism and scorn for the mob.[33] Like Tallemant, Fontenelle had a grounding in religious controversy but, where Tallemant studied doctrine to defend Catholicism, Fontenelle studied to destabilise it and was robustly anticlerical. Third, Balthazar Bonnecorse from Marseilles, had, nearly twenty years earlier while consul in Cairo, written an allegorical love work in prose and poetry called *La Montre* (The Watch), which de Scudéry's brother persuaded him to publish. It had done well and de Bonnecorse had enjoyed a modest fame. Later, however, it grew notorious through an attack from the famous critic and poet, Nicolas Boileau who, despite a later admission that he had not read it, labelled it trivial and wordy.[34] The attack stung the author, but it gave *La Montre* renewed currency. All three men and their works would be useful to Behn in the future.

Among English expatriates in Paris Behn may have met was an intellectual boy of seventeen called George Granville. He was the son of
Bernard Granville, who had been Groom of the Chamber to the young
Duke of Gloucester in the Interregnum and who, as a distant connection of the Sidneys and a close one of the Albemarles, might just have
been known to her at that time. Having achieved his MA in Cambridge,
where he had excelled at Latin verse, young George was enjoying France
and running up debts. He was given to romantic enthusiasms for older
women, having, at the age of eleven, dedicated his life to the winsome
Mary of Modena, and he was fascinated by the theatre. The theatrical
Aphra Behn was probably his next enthusiasm. For her he would become,
with Creech, the first of the young men who enlivened the 1680s, as
middle-aged men like Killigrew, Marten, Scot, Gascoigne and Ogniate
had stimulated the 1660s when she herself was young.[35]

Back in England, Behn was lodging in St Bride's in the house of a Mr
Coggin, round the corner from Tonson's shop in New Street, where
both Shadwell and Sprat also lived. She appears as 'Mrs. Bene' in a list
of lodgers drawn up after a precept of 28 June 1683, probably a government attempt to make a census of the shifting lodgings population of
London. Although the document has no date, if it follows other listings
it can probably be assigned to the end of June or July.[36] That she was
still not a head of household, like her fellow dramatists, Dryden, Shadwell
and Tate, may have irked her, but she was never sufficiently well paid
or frugal enough to set up in independent style.

When she contacted Tonson, Behn was not best pleased to discover
that Creech had been so anxious about her commendation for his *Lucretius*
that he had actually changed the most offensive lines. They now praised
rather than denigrated faith, having been transformed into 'Faith the
Religious Souls Content / Faith the secure Retreat of Routed Argument'.
She thought it presumptuous, but there was nothing to be done now—
though she registered her feelings with Tonson: 'As for Mr. Creech, I
would not have you afflict him with a thing can not now be help'd, so
never let him know my resentment.' She did not want to offend the
reputedly touchy Creech.

Behn realised she had come back to a new professional and personal
scene. Her friend Ephelia was probably dead, since several miscellaneous
and raffish poems by Behn, Rochester and others had been added to
her original verses to form a new edition of her works, often a sign of
an author's absence. Killigrew too was gone, having lost control of his

company long before his death. Professionally it was the change in the theatre that most touched her, however. Killigrew's old King's Company had been declining through the troubled period of the Popish Plot, and its demise was hastened through violent actors' quarrels. Soon there was nothing for it but to amalgamate with the more successful Duke's. For the rest of Behn's life there would be only the United Company playing at two locations, Drury Lane mainly for drama, Dorset Garden for spectacle. Happily, most of the Duke's Company actors survived the merger.

When competition between the two Companies was at its height, between twelve and twenty-five new plays had been staged each season. Now the United Company, needing to economise and having at its disposal *all* the old plays, expected to put on only three or four. Although Behn was an established playwright and could anticipate a number of revivals, inevitably the theatre could no longer be her major source of income. 'The Poets lay dormant,' one later recalled.[37] It was well that, over the years, Behn had been dabbling in prose and poetry. Neither of these promised the easy money she was used to as a quick and efficient adapter of plays, but, for the moment, she had no choice but to use what skills she had.

The change coincided with another major shift in Behn's thinking and mode. She had defeated tragicomedy with farcical comedy and social comment with political assertion. But, in the defeat, she had, to some extent, lost the opportunity of investigating the effects of social coercion on the thinking individual and of deeply probing female passion and sexuality. Now, as she moved out to include other discursive genres in her repertoire, she came to look more at woman in society and to face for them less theatrical solutions. Consequently, she darkened her once half-admiring presentation of the rake figure. What would such a man be like in ordinary social life? she asked.[38]

There were other questions too. What of the incipient 'female rake' she had created? How would the witty flirtatious woman comport herself outside comedy and inside or outside marriage? Although a female rake was not really possible within society, could she exist on the periphery? If so, would she have to pretend *all* the time? Would she have constantly to use the codes of the very femininity her sexual being denied? Was it possible for a woman to attract a man without playing the feminine game, a game deeply influenced by the absolute distinction of men and women which the spirited woman, aspiring to act and speak like a man, had been bridging? Was sexual pleasure for the woman at its height only when the game was not understood? Thereafter, was it the game, the masquerade, that became the primary pleasure, avoiding as it did the inconvenient outcome of pregnancy?

Behn would start to answer these questions in prose.

CHAPTER 22

Love-Letters between a Nobleman and his Sister

'I have my tools about me'

While Aphra Behn was on the Continent she may have used her sleuthing powers to gain a meeting with a friend or servant who knew first-hand of the scandalous doings in the family of Monmouth's most noble follower, Ford, Lord Grey. With her penchant for gossip, she would have probed and thus obtained the second chapter of a story begun in England in late September 1682.

At that time, along with a large proportion of the reading public, Behn had noticed an advertisement in the *London Gazette* for a runaway, Lady Henrietta Berkeley, 'a young lady of a fair complexion, fair haired, full-breasted and indifferent tall'. A reward of £200 was offered for her return. Like the item in the *Gazette* on the failed beheading of Tarquini nearly twenty years before, it was the very thing to spark Behn's literary interest: sex and rank worked into scandal.[1]

The event was made piquant by the relationship of the people involved. Lady Henrietta had eloped with her brother-in-law Ford, Lord Grey. Although ostensibly the Duke of Monmouth's ardent supporter, Grey was said to have resented his wife Mary's reputed affair with the Duke though lampoons portrayed him as pimp more than cuckold. The affair of Grey and Lady Henrietta had been public long before the elopement: as one gossip had written in June, Lord Grey 'as the report goes, saith that he married the eldest sister and expected a maidenhead, but not finding it, hee resolved to have one in the family, if any be left'.[2] Both young Berkeley women were libidinous 'By nature or by education', loving 'the act of generation'.[3]

With Lady Henrietta still missing, Lord Grey was caught and arrested for conspiring 'to commit whoredom, fornication, and adultery'. He was placed in the Tower. The scandal was by now 'the talk of the Town', while letters between aristocratic ladies bruited the news through the provinces. One wrote excitedly, ''Tis serrting he has delewded her and entised her from her father, but wheare she is not yet knowen...he must soon produce her, or his Lordship must remaine a prisner.'[4] In fact, Henrietta was at a milliner's house near Charing Cross and she emerged, pregnant, for the trial.[5]

This began in November 1682, with the crown represented by the future 'hanging judge', the infamous George Jeffreys. Lord Grey was accused of contriving by 'impure ways...the final ruin and destruction of the lady Henrietta Berkeley, then a virgin unmarried, within the age of 18 years'.

The court scene was dramatic. Grey had an impudent, confident look through most of the proceedings, while Henrietta's mother dissolved in tears of shame and grief; Lord Berkeley was so choleric he could hardly contain himself. Accorded little opening, Lady Henrietta demanded, 'Will you not give me leave to speak for myself?' The answer was a firm 'No'. When ordered to return to her father, she had her moment, however, for she announced, 'I will not go' and dramatically proclaimed, 'My Lord, I am married.' The husband was a William Turner. Satirists were surprised: they had thought she meant to marry someone called Forrester and then live a respectable life of vice.

There was no more to be done: Grey was released and, after a 'great scuffle about the lady, and swords drawn on both sides', Lord Berkeley went home without his daughter. Henrietta and Turner were taken to the King's Bench prison but, when they proved their marriage, there was no detaining them either. After much debate as to which Turner Henrietta had married, it was concluded he was in fact Grey's gentleman and that the marriage was clearly for the convenience of his lord. What sort of man he was is unclear, but a lampoon called him 'grizly'.[6]

The trial had been sensationally summarised in the newspapers; then it was published in full. The diarist, Roger Morrice, was hooked, but admitted that both parties would have been wiser hushing the whole matter up.

Over the next months, Grey was entangled in matters even more serious than incestuous sex—for so an affair between in-laws was regarded, man and wife having become one flesh. He had long been associated with Shaftesbury, joining him in denouncing James and taking part in the Accession Day pageants, and he had latterly been linked with Monmouth. Along with other disgruntled men including Shaftesbury and Colepeper's cousin, Algernon Sidney, he busied himself collecting weapons and plotting an armed rising in the City. The story is succinctly told by the diarist Evelyn on 28 June 1683:

After the Popish plot there was now a new, and (as they called it) a Protestant plot discover'd, that certaine lords and others should designe the assassination of the King and the Duke as they were to come from Newmarket, with a general rising of the nation, and especially of the citty of London, disaffected to the present government; upon which were committed to the Tower the Lord Russell, eldest son of the Earle of Bedford, the Earle of Essex, Mr. Algernone Sydney, sone to the old Earle of Leicester, Mr Trenchard, Hampden, Lord Howard of Escrick, and others. A proclamation was issued against my Lord Grey, the Duke of Monmouth, Sir Thomas Armstrong, and one Ferguson, who had escaped beyond sea...[7]

The assassination attempt, which Grey and Monmouth probably condoned but did not organise, was foiled because a fire in Newmarket on 22 March 1683 meant that the King and his entourage returned from the races a week earlier than intended. They rode unscathed past Rye House where the shooting was supposed to have occurred.

The fall-out was bloody, since examination of the assassination uncovered details of earlier rebellious projects. The Earl of Essex slit his throat in the Tower, while the heroic William, Lord Russell, was painfully executed, though thought innocent by many. Thomas Armstrong was captured in Holland and executed at Tyburn without trial, while Algernon Sidney was condemned and killed mainly for his republican writings, neither completed nor published. Sunderland made no more move to save his cousin Algernon than he had his kinsman Stafford. Although her politics were by now so divergent from Algernon's, Behn must have been affected by this Sidney death and seen its relevance to a writer: anyone might fall foul of a change of regime and she too could lose much by being known for the wrong sort of writing.

Monmouth fled to his mistress Henrietta Wentworth at her house in Bedfordshire, famous for its secret closets and trapdoors. Everyone knew where he had gone, for the affair, scandalously encouraged by her mother, was of long standing. In November he came out of hiding, confessed to his implication in plots, was taken back into favour, had second thoughts when the Duke of York insisted the confession be published in the *Gazette*, retracted it, and fled. Shaftesbury, ailing by now, left for Holland where he shortly died.

Arrested on 25 June 1683, Lord Grey denied his part in the assassination plot. Knowing his involvement in almost all other conspiracies, however, he prudently resolved not to join Essex and Russell in the

Tower. So he organised an alternative and alerted Lady Henrietta. Conveniently for his plans, his guard fell asleep at the crucial moment and he nimbly escaped.[8] He then crossed the Thames pursued by a soldier who, when his boat caught them up, was persuaded off, and Lord Grey landed at the Pickled Herring on the south side. From there he went to his home in Uppark, where he hid in the woods with a man called Ezekiel Everest, a former customs officer (later he would turn agent, betray Grey to the English authorities, and apologise for his help in the escape, the 'only Crime I am guilty of against his Majestie'). Grey and Everest, with Lady Henrietta, Turner and one or two servants, then travelled to Chichester, where the *Hare Pink* captained by a wooden-legged Dissenting man was ready to take them out of England. They had, however, mistaken the tides and had to travel up and down the shore for six hours in one account, hide in the wood in another, before the crossing could be made.

The current head of intelligence, Sir Leoline Jenkins, who received all this immense detail from his agents, must have gnashed his teeth at the fecklessness of the authorities who failed to arrest the fugitives during all this time. No doubt the escape route was oiled by Lord Grey's considerable wealth.

Such a story of rebellion and sex demanded treatment and someone in the government—perhaps the politically ambiguous Sunderland—wanting to discredit Monmouth through his henchman Grey, persuaded an astute and speedy author, most probably Aphra Behn, to write it.[9] The theatrical Whigs were in retreat and Behn had herself admitted, in the dedication to *The Roundheads*, that the Tories had won the stage battle. In the dedication of *The Duke of Guise*, however, Dryden and Lee declared the 'glorious Work' of Tory revenge 'yet unfinished'. Propaganda was always needed and the theatre was not the whole country. The campaign had to move from drama into fiction.[10]

The letter form had been used for propaganda in the Interregnum, persuading in 'a more gentle, and familiar way' than satire.[11] In this genre, which caught the reader alone, Behn, already known for her anti-Monmouth sentiments, could provide something more subtle and oblique than her direct attacks. She could make the Duke a corrupting presence, not a rather foolish actor, and connect him with a politics that moved from laughable farce to disturbing erotics.

Behn had kept up her fiction-reading, but, over the cynical 1670s, her love of La Calprenède had diminished. She had not taken to his

English imitators and now preferred the Spanish rogue narratives, such as Alemán's *Guzman* and *Lazarillo*, to which she referred in her plays. Her interest in romantic fiction was rekindled, however, when she read a new translation by her admired Roger L'Estrange of *Lettres portuguaises*, rendered as *Five Love-Letters from a Nun to a Cavalier*.

In the manner of La Calprenède's romances, this work purported to be historical, real letters from a nun in Portugal who had been abandoned by her lover, a French officer. But it was different from La Calprenède, more psychologically interesting and faster-paced. Like Ovid's epistles, with which Behn had so recently been working, *Lettres portuguaises* gave voice to the loving, abandoned woman, but it also allowed her to be fascinated by her own extreme emotions. Since Behn was always on the lookout for ways of making a better living, she undoubtedly noted its popularity.[12]

Other works would also have influenced her form. In 1679, her three plays, *The Forc'd Marriage, Abdelazer* and *The Town-Fopp*, were advertised by her old publishers, J. Magnes and R. Bentley, in a volume purporting to be the *Apology: or, the Genuine Memoirs of Madam Maria Manchini...eldest Sister of the Duchess of Mazarin....* This was actually by a French fiction writer in exile in Holland, Gabriel de Brémond, though based on the Mancini sisters' experiences. Brémond was eager to gain patronage in England, and it is just conceivable that his usual publishers, whom he shared with Behn, Richard Bentley and James Magnes, asked her to translate the anonymously published work. She was an admirer of the King's mistress, the witty, well-read, vain and cross-dressing Hortense Mancini, Duchess of Mazarine, and Hortense was the sister of Maria and joint heroine of the narrative.[13]

Behn possibly caught up with the other work by Brémond during her stay in France, if she had not already read Bentley's Englished version from 1676. This was *Hattigé*, a short novel commenting on the amorous doings of Mazarine's predecessor, Barbara, Duchess of Cleveland, the first important mistress of Charles II.[14] La Calprenède had woven fiction into what he regarded as history; but Brémond was, like the unfortunate Lady Mary Wroth in James I's reign, making a story of contemporary scandals which everyone knew.

For Behn, *Hattigé* was inspiring, with its hothouse atmosphere of odorous love amongst jasmine and tuberoses, its hints of naughty doings, and its theme of expanding desire. Yet *Hattigé* veiled sexual activities. Behn was planning something longer and more erotic. A large part of her life had already been spent describing love in pastoral Edens or in modern brothels. She had, however, rarely treated sexual obsession, except perhaps in the 'Love-Letters to a Gentleman', which had concentrated on psychological enthralment, and in the depiction of the Queen in *Abdelazer*. Both writings were now far in the past. The infatuated Angellica in *The Rover* was not the central character in her play, nor was Lady Galliard of *The City-Heiress*, who caught something of the predicament of an older woman in love. Neither fell outside her society for the sake of sex.

Aphra Behn had certainly been in love—the public assumed a long affair with Hoyle, which she herself invoked when she wished to pass as an expert on amorous affairs. With Hoyle, however, sexual love may rarely have been satisfying, may even have been unconsummated. Later, it was transformed into something between obsession and friendship. No other lover had been publicly talked about for Behn. Now, after a time of relative propriety, hard work and some ill-health, she appears to have become rejuvenated possibly from her travels, with renewed sexual and literary energy, prepared to declare that life was not worth living or literature written without some sexual impetus.

Loving and writing coalesced in a poem called 'To *Damon*' in which Behn wrote to ask if 'Damon' could identify a writer of some anonymous verses. Desire, she noted, crept up on a person 'In lone recesses'. Its pimp was the letter. The received verses had been

> fill'd with praises of my face and Eyes,
> My verse, and all those usual flatteries
> To me as common as the Air;
> Nor cou'd my vanity procure my care.

All conventional stuff, but mind worked on words to render them a philtre darting 'pain / Thro every pleas'd and trembling vein'. Then the body blushed and trembled. The whole experience had been mediated by writing; the reader brushed the verses with her imagination and formed an erotic 'Image' that enthralled her body.

An awakening to sex is caught, too, in another poem of this period called 'On Desire'. Desire is a poetic spot of time, properly existing in the fantastic Golden Age, in Arcadia; in the *real* world it is transgressive and wounding, a subtle disease. It was an apt image, since Behn knew well that any sexual passion would at this stage be at odds with her 'fame' and would, if known, make her ridiculous:

Oh! mischievous usurper of my Peace;
Oh! soft Intruder on my solitude,
   Charming disturber of my ease,
   That hast my nobler fate persu'd,
And all the Glorys of my life subdu'd.

Most irritating was the untimeliness of the emotion. Had Behn had such a passion at more suitable years, she might have combined love with interest or honour. She was probably exaggerating when she wrote that 'princes at my feet did lye,' but she could certainly have coupled herself with or been kept by a man of some status, had she had her feelings more opportunely. In an early poem, 'Damon, being asked a reason for Loveing', a young woman rebuffs a well-heeled lover by taunting him with his taciturnity. Given Behn's later pride in her fluency and Hoyle's complaints over her garrulity, this might well convey a memory. In the past, men's words, their beauty, their gifts and offers had failed to awake 'the unform'd somthing—to desire'.

Yes, yes, tormenter, I have found thee now;
And found to whom thou dost thy being owe,
'Tis thou the blushes dost impart,
For thee this languishment I wear,
'Tis thou that tremblest in my heart
When the dear Shepherd do's appear,
I faint, I dye with pleasing pain,
My words intruding sighing break
When e're I touch the charming swain
When e're I gaze, when e're I speak.
Thy conscious fire is mingl'd with my love,
   As in the sanctify'd abodes
   Misguided worshippers approve
   The mixing Idol with their Gods.
   In vain, alas! in vain I strive
With errors, which my soul do please and vex,
   For superstition will survive,
   Purer Religion to perplex.[15]

Her only comfort is her usual arrogant assumption, that what she feels others also feel, and that chaste and apparently asexual women are fraudulently hiding similar sexual feelings.

The novel which I believe Aphra Behn began at this time seems to have been written in the white heat of resurgent erotic feeling, which may well have been confined to the head and pen. Hoyle had told Behn she was too passionate and unrestrained and, by portraying a series of intense women who lost in the sex game through being uncontrolled, she had implicitly agreed. She was now over forty, the age of the absurd mothers and widows of Restoration comedy like Lady Wishfort and her own Lady Knowell, who were advised by the ends of their plays to leave sex to their daughters. Perhaps writing was a way of neutralising what had so embarrassingly come upon her in middle age. But the book was also a celebrating of an aristocratic promiscuous concept of love that took no notice of what was abandoned for it. By now, Behn was certain that there should be no Whiggish hoarding of the self for fear of religion or ridicule. One must take risks since

> who can be happy without Love? for me, I never numbred those dull days amongst those of my life, in which I had not my Soul fill'd with that soft passion; to Love! why 'tis the only secret in nature that restores Life, to all the felicities and charms of living; and to me there seems no thing so strange, as to see people walk about, laugh, do the acts of Life, and impertinently trouble the world without knowing any thing of that soft, that noble passion, or without so much as having an intreague, or an amusement... with any dear she, no real Love or Cocettre.[16]

Behn admitted her own situation, that she still had the torments of love while living without its fulfilment. Such objectless erotic feeling, although inconvenient, was still preferable to sexless calm and indifference:

> (A Medium, I confess, I hate,)
> For when the mind so cool is grown
> As neither Love nor Hate to own,
> The Life but dully lingers on.[17]

Behn's mind was not 'cool', then, when she sat down to fictionalise the scandal of Lord Grey and Lady Henrietta, and she had her own agenda beyond the political one. In the past, she had been attacked for the sexual charge in her plays, but prose could deliver it a hundred times more effectively. Thus, an intended piece of propaganda became a great erotic novel: *Love-Letters between a Nobleman and his Sister*.

* * *

Perversely, having denied or ignored her sources in so many of her plays, Behn here invented one: a French text to which she would keep 'close'. The novel was set in a France which she might know—indeed, as part of the pretence that the story was French not English, she made the probably true claim that she had been in France earlier in the year. In the fiction, the civil wars of the French Fronde were supposedly raging, but no English reader could fail to see the allusion to Monmouth in Cesario, to his lover Lady Grey in Mirtilla, to her husband Lord Grey in Philander, to *his* lover and *her* sister Lady Henrietta Berkeley in Silvia, and to Henrietta's husband-of-convenience Turner in Brilljard.[18]

Politics comes to the fore early in the book and Silvia is Tory to Philander's Whig. Silvia assumes that Philander aims at individual glory in his plotting and that she can use the good character of the King to persuade him out of it:

> What has the King, our good, our gracious monarch, done to Philander? How disoblig'd him? Or indeed, what injury to mankind? Who has he oppress'd? Where play'd the tyrant or the ravisher? What one cruel or angry thing has he committed in all the time of his fortunate and peacable reign over us? Whose ox or whose ass has he unjustly taken? What orphan wrong'd, or widow's tears neglected? But all his life has been one continued miracle; all good, all gracious, calm and merciful: and this good, this godlike King, is mark'd out for slaughter, design'd a sacrifice to the private revenge of a few ambitious knaves and rebels, whose pretence is the public good, and doomed to be basely murdered.[19]

As a description of Charles II this is laughable;[20] yet it allows the erotic and the royal to merge in the King's body: 'I never approach his sacred person,' writes Silvia breathlessly, 'but my heart beats, my blood runs cold about me, and my eyes overflow with tears of joy, while an awful confusion seizes me all over.' The images of Charles and James in Behn's royal panegyrics will stress the erotic quality of power, in keeping with the renewed Stuart mythography, in which the body of the king holds the authority he wields. Such images express the divine-right doctrine, but without stating what had by now become a rather discredited, even absurd, notion.[21]

Philander is represented as a libertine. Yet, instead of making her earlier link of Royalism and exciting libertinism, Behn here allowed another common cultural connection: of libertinism, selfishness and rebellion. Philander embodies her considered belief that those who opposed tyranny and authority did so not out of desire for universal liberty, but from desire of power for themselves. Philander *poses* as a Whig, but he is in fact an unprincipled and power-hungry individualist, resenting the sexual affront of Monmouth while taking no heroic action, and disliking the rule of anyone, whether legitimate king or 'bastard'.[22] He exists in a Hobbesian natural realm beyond Royalist authority and Whiggish Parliamentary contracts.

Most people are stupid and are led by whoever has the will, Philander believes. One of these is Cesario himself, whom Philander can use for his own ends: 'he is so dull as to imagine that for his sake, who never did us service or good, (unless cuckolding us be good) we should venture life and fame to pull down a true monarch, to set up his bastard over us.' Philander continues with Cesario / Monmouth, he confesses to Silvia, because, in the vacuum that would follow a coup, there is no reason why he himself should not be the new power as well as another:

> when Three Kingdoms shall ly unpossest, and be expos'd, as it were, amongst the raffling Crowd, who knows but the chance may be mine, as well as any others, who has but the same hazard, and throw for't; if the strongest Sword must do't, (as they must do't) why not mine still?[23]

The only genuine ruler is appetite in a commonwealth world where anyone with strength and cunning can control. Shorn of divine significance, the King is indeed but a man. In this case why should not any individual be king, if he has enough self-assertiveness, strength and desire?

Despite some sexualised politics, however, the domestic and erotic intrigues are Behn's main subject in her book. She makes little of the known political plots and less of the dramatic trial of Lord Grey, although she uses some of the telling details. For example, Lady Henrietta was said 'to have gone away with only a night gown and slippers'—a lampoon added that it was a multi-coloured, striped night gown or loose morning dress, and the petticoat was symbolically red and white. Behn exaggerated the informality in her fiction: Silvia 'thus undrest, walk'd towards the Garden', then dashed outside to the waiting chariot. The lack of clothes means that she must stay suggestively in bed until Philander arrives.

Although there are a few letters from others, the bulk of the book unfolds the sexual passion and develops the writing skills of the central pair. Philander, the elder, almost coaches Silvia in rhetoric. This is appropriate since it is the 'irresistible *Idea* of Silvia that attracts him, the woman mediated through his imagination, which she herself can help to create. The body itself may fade, his mental image will not. Platonics supersedes erotics at times and Philander becomes the imaginist of sex. He desires to 'encounter what I already so much adored in *Idea*, which still I formed just as my fancy wished'.

In Behn's poem 'On Desire', the erotic blurs sight, so that the ideal not the real can be contemplated. Such a state is romance or disease, and it is this that Silvia suffers at the outset: 'a strange disorder in my blood, that pants and burns at every Vein...'.[24] She is then coached in writing and soon she sees that desire is not enough. She must go about to raise desire or recapture it in the object if she is to keep her man. She also learns that her own desire and simulation of desire are interchangeable in their effect of arousing desire in another. The great temptation of erotic epistolary fiction is narcissism. The eighteenth-century novel, often written by men pretending to be women, was addicted to mirror scenes, in which heroines stare fixedly in their glasses and then form their bodies into images of desire for their lovers and their readers, and almost for themselves. In *Love-Letters*, the erotic description of the beloved by the lover consciously panders to this narcissism at first. Both Philander and Silvia respond lustily to pictures drawn of each other and of themselves and, as they grow more sophisticated, the pictures become more aware, more hyperbolic. But, as hyperbole increases, so individuality decreases, and the reader sees, in the end, the 'hot brute' drudging on. There is a price for the woman's development: 'we are only safe by the mean Arts of base Dissimulation, an ill as shameful as that to which we fall.' Narcissism turns into an assessment of the self for another, a commodification of the body.

Such representing is connected with what Lucretius had perceived at the heart of sexual politics: desire for mastery. Behn had read that the desire to dominate and destroy was the dark side of love, and she had experienced it herself. The irrational, destructive and almost brutal idea of sexuality emerged in the presentation of the love act as close to violence, 'vain violence' of sex in Dryden's phrase:

> often with a furious Kiss
> They wound the balmy Lip; this they endure
> Because the Joy's not perfect, 'tis not pure:
> But still some STING remains, some fierce Desire
> To hurt whatever 'twas that rais'd the FIRE....

The male desire to rape emerges even from the early letters: 'violent' love attracts Philander and he fantasises rushing on Silvia with no 'respect or Awe', wanting 'excess of pleasure'. He threatens to express his masculinity 'and force my self with all the violence of raging Love…and Ravish my delight'.[25] When the private fantasy becomes public, Philander sees vast masculine scenarios of erotic power: he will enter Silvia's house and put it 'all in a flame' to prevent her marriage to another man. He visualises stabbing the bridegroom at the altar and torturing the bride. Even when Philander enters the feminised pastoral world, the Arcadia into which he claims love has pulled him, he manages to bring violence with him: for Philander, the rural wind becomes the male lover of coy boughs, which are treated 'with a transported violence'. At one point he expresses the hedonistic Arcadian vision so dear to Behn with its infantile sexual passivity: he wants 'to take [Silvia] without controul to shades and Palaces, to live for ever with her, to gaze for ever on her, to eat, to loll, to rise, to play, to sleep, to act o'er all the pleasures and the joys of life with her'.[26] The vision is so passive, however, that he cannot accommodate it and he soon thinks of death.

Sexual experience also moves the now educated Silvia to a kind of violence by destroying her feminine inhibitions. It brings her closer to a man in the thermal categories of the time, which saw males as naturally hotter than females. Once suppressed in the name of femininity, burning anger flows free, and what only discomposed Silvia when she was a maid 'now puts me into a violence of rage unbecoming my sex'. In other writers, desire exaggerated, then thwarted, becomes feminine hysteria; it is a measure of Behn's innovation with the character of Silvia that she makes her neither an hysteric nor a melancholic, but something closer to a violent man. Yet she never equates men and women—their social conditions are simply too different. However robust, Silvia must always fear abandonment, as did Ovid's women, the Portuguese Nun, the writer of 'Love-Letters to a Gentleman'—and 'Mrs Affora' herself when suspecting herself deserted in Antwerp.

Long after the politics had subsided, sexual explicitness kept *Love-Letters* popular with the public. Within the conventions of the time, it is indeed an arousing book. Here is Philander approaching Silvia:

I beheld thee extended on a Bed of Roses, in Garments which, if possible, by their wanton loose negligence and gaiety augmented thy natural Charms: I trembling fell on my Knees by your Bed-side, and gaz'd a while unable to speak for transports of joy and love…I ventur'd to press your lips with mine…[and]…by degrees ravisht a thousand Blisses…her short and double breathings heav'd her Breast, her swelling snowy breast, her hands that grasp'd me trembling as they clos'd, while she permitted mine unknown, unheeded to traverse all her Beauties, till quite forgetting all I'd faintly promised, and wholly abandoning my soul to joy, I rusht upon her, who all fainting lay beneath…[27]

Despite all this impassioned, erotic prose, however, Behn's mocking obsession with male sexual failure still makes comic the first effort at consummation between Silvia and Philander. The passage above continues: 'my useless weight, for on a sudden all my power was fled.' Not all his beloved's charms, clasps and sighs can call the 'fugitive vigor back'. When this is coupled with Silvia's statement, that Philander's 'complection render'd him less capable of the soft play of Love, than any other Lover', it appears that he, perhaps like John Hoyle, is not good at foreplay.

Here erotics and politics come together again. Behn had already realised that the comic quality of the rake, so brilliantly exposed in *The Rover*, could be harnessed for propagandist purposes. The powerful Philander with his impotence, his ravings, his extreme language and his inept planning, is often absurd. The absurdity is neatly caught in the aftermath of the failed consummation. Philander has to escape from Silvia's room in female clothes, symbol of his late disappointing performance. In these he is apprehended by her amorous father, who falls on the disguised man, now forced to counterfeit a female voice and demeanour. As a 'failed' lover, a kind of woman, Philander must submit to the father who can boast, 'I have my Tools about me' and places a bag of money in one of his hands and a penis in the other.

Humour not only serves politics, it could also fulfil a personal purpose. In her love for Hoyle, Behn seems to have gone deep into herself and come close to obsession. Without entirely losing her emotional dependence on Hoyle, she had then moved from this self-destructive phase, concentrating on the surface, taking on more and more masks, gaining friends and using her humour to deflate any rising panic. Although she might burn and sigh erotically, she was not, she hoped, a candidate for romantic martyrdom a second time—as *Love-Letters* suggested. She intended to be armed with a lethal combination of erotics and humour to offset her obsessive nature.

Licensed on 20 October 1683, *Love-Letters* was published in 1684 by Randal Taylor. He was known as a 'trade' publisher, one who could serve as a front for several booksellers and, in his lowly position, be a kind of bulwark against prosecution, while not directly financing publication himself.[28] Often trade publishers were binders and could claim complete ignorance of the work if it got into trouble—usefully so for it was even more dangerous to write prose propaganda than poetry:

> Though truth in prose may be a crime,
> 'Twas never known in any time
> That one was hanged for writing rhyme.[29]

The work probably did well, for there was a great vogue for secret texts and for erotic fiction. It was as well for the remnants of Behn's reputation that she brought it out anonymously. There were naughty books around, even pornographic ones—*L'éscholle des Filles*, for example, to which Samuel Pepys ashamedly masturbated and which Horner of *The Country Wife* denied possessing—but they were not openly written by women.

Since it was anonymous, scandalous and possibly dangerous, Aphra Behn did not dedicate her book to the great, but instead addressed an obscure man called Thomas Condon, apparently a young captain and firm supporter of the Duke of York, her longtime hero.[30] From his description, it seems that, though no patronage could be expected from him, he had materially influenced the work by his physical charms, and he must have been in the secret of the authorship. Indeed it is possible that he actually inspired Behn's erotic feelings. Darkly she alludes to a scandal of an amour in which Condon had done something 'base, silly and unmanly'. Since she claims she 'too well knew the story', she may have been involved.

Except in his politics, Condon is, Behn insisted, close to the luscious Philander, a man like Hoyle attractive to both sexes:

> that I may believe *Silvia* truly happy, give me leave to fansie him such a person as your self, and then I cannot fail of fansying him too, speaking at the feet of *Silvia*, pleading his right of love with the same softness in his eyes and voice, as you can do when you design to conquer.

The personal notion led Behn to rhapsody: 'you are young as new desire, as beautiful as light, as amorous as a God, and wanton as a *Cupid*, that smiles, and shoots, and plays, and mischiefs all his fond hours away.' She prays that Condon, like Philander, will not love unlawfully—possibly it was a veiled allusion not only to Grey's incest but also to homosexual love (an 'unmanly' act?) which may have caused her pain with Hoyle. But mainly Behn warns Condon not to hoard his body and mind as a 'lazy Lover'; he should go into circulation—like her book.

CHAPTER 23

The Great Frost and *Voyage to the Isle of Love*

'A body has no creditt at the Playhouse as we used to have'

Between the advertising of *Love-Letters* and its printing, London suffered another of its great winters. Despite considerable cold, in the previous year the Duke of York had complained that his 'ice-house' had not been filled, but the winter of 1683 and 1684 answered his wishes.[1] The severe frost lasted from 15 December until 5 February. The Thames froze solid and Luttrell reported 'above fifty coaches' sliding on the ice while whole oxen were roasted for the gathered crowds. 'Most sorts of trades' sprang up, including puppet shows and three or four printing houses. (This was probably necessary for them since the frost closed some presses for as long as ten weeks.) People bought ballads and 'tooke a fansy to have their names Printed & the day & yeare set down, when printed on the Thames'.[2] According to lampoons, men and women even copulated in the booths on the ice.[3] It was a release after the scared years of the Popish Plot, a passing interlude of early Restoration spirit.

In her newly receptive state, Aphra Behn ignored the matter of her bowdlerised commendation and celebrated Twelfth Night with young Thomas Creech, who had come down from Oxford for Christmas. Despite the Protestant lack of sympathy for the tale of the three kings, the feast of the epiphany, the last of the midwinter festivals which lightened the long, hard and very dark winter, was observed in much the same way as Christmas came to be later. Many superstitions attached to it: for example, that the thorn tree at Glastonbury which grew from Joseph of Aramathea's staff bloomed at midnight. Like almost every event in England, Twelfth Night was celebrated with bonfires and a wassail bowl, but the centre of the feast was a rich cake baked round a bean and sometimes a pea. The man who received the bean was chosen king of the feast, the woman with the pea became queen.

The cake was a yeast-raised rich offering of almonds and sugar, based on a pastry of butter, wheat and eggs.[4] 'To make a great Cake', a cook was instructed to 'Take two gallons of fine flower and a halfe,' add it to five pounds of currants, half an ounce each of mace and nutmeg, a pound and a half of butter, cream, rose-water, sack, three-quarters of a pound of sugar and a pint of ale seasonings. It was all extremely expensive and Pepys records his 'excellent Cake' made by the maid Jane costing him 'near 20s'. Jane was fortunate in this excellency, for anything yeast-based could go seriously wrong—as it seems to have done for Behn, who supplied the cake for this occasion. Perhaps she tried to make it herself—in any case, she called the result 'lamentable'.

As a gregarious person, she enjoyed the evening, which she found particularly memorable because she had met 'A Man whom I shall ne're forget'. He was a 'True Tory' and, in her usual hyperbole, 'A God in Wit, tho Man in look'—in plain words, not overly handsome but very funny and perhaps sexy. In Behn's open frame of mind he had had an enormous effect on her and, when she later wrote to Creech asking him to pass on her 'vast esteem', she complimented both men by declaring the guest worthy of Creech. This sounds like a first sighting of Tom Brown, a youth of nineteen who, like Behn, admired Creech's *Lucretius*.[5]

Thomas Brown, son of a Shropshire farmer, became a good classical scholar and went to Oxford in 1678. There his avid enjoyment of sociability merited expulsion by Dr Fell, which he avoided by turning a Latin epigram into the memorable rhyme, 'I do not love thee, Dr Fell'. Intending to make a living by wit on the edges of the theatre, he had come to London but, failing at first, he had had to resort to teaching in a school. Trying to rid his ashes of the 'Load of Dirt' thrown on them, his posthumous biographer wrote, 'Fortune obliged him to prefer Money (which he only wanted) to Reputation.'[6]

After some years he returned to London, at a time when 'Politicks and Polemicks had almost driven Mirth and Good Humour out of the Nation.' '[H]is wit soon procur'd him a numerous Acquaintance' who liked his jaunty conversation, easy-going manner, malicious wit and satirical sallies. Brown was greatly in demand by those with time to pass agreeably and he spent much of his in the tavern. The company he amused was willing to pay for his wine, but not his clothes and lodgings and, since he was 'of an Humour not to chuse his Acquaintance by his Interest', he continued to lack money for necessities, however much he preferred it to reputation. But, in one instance, there is a hint that he did have some 'Interest' in his acquaintance. After Behn's death, when he had taken to faking correspondence for a living, Brown included his old friend in an exchange called *Letters from the Dead to the Living*, in which he imagined Aphra Behn and the '*Celebrated Virgin*' actress, Anne Bracegirdle, trading insults.[7] Although an unkind response to old friendship, the letter purportedly by Behn fits well with her tendency in the early 1680s to see chastity as hypocrisy or lack of opportunity, and to admire women who negotiated sexual conventions with 'cunning' and 'Managements': 'Experience has taught me to judge of my own Sex to perfection, and I know the difference there is between being really virtuous and only accounted so.' The pseudo-Behn moves in a company of promiscuous women friends who delight in cross-dressing, 'Shifts and Evasions'.

Anne Bracegirdle's supposed answer is more damning. The middle-aged Behn is portrayed with a young male entourage:

> You were the young Poets *Venus*; to you they paid their Devotion as a Goddess, and their first Adventure, when they adjourn'd from the University to the Town, was to solicit your Favours; and this advantage you enjoy'd above the rest of your Sex, that if a young Student was but once infected with a Rhiming Itch, you by a butter'd Bun could make him an establish'd Poet at any time.

Behn never had the power to make anyone an 'establish'd Poet', even if she had, as the bun image implies, been sexually serviced by him, but she could be of some help. In her next anthology of poems, *Miscellany*, she published five works of Tom Brown's, including two that might bear on their relationship.

In 'The Parting', 'Damon' quits 'his dear *Amyntas*' for 'cruel bus'ness'. This sounds like an excuse to a lady for leaving early. (Behn herself supports the impression in a later prologue in which she imagines 'old and tough' widows abandoned by young and '*drunken Sot[s], that had kind hours, / And taking their own Freedoms, left you yours*'.[8]) In 'On a Token sent me by a Lady', the lady sends money to the poet and freely 'told my friend—let that be drunk for me'. He is properly grateful: 'Each Jovial Glass, your fair Idea gave.' Behn was generous to needy poets: she was reported to have helped the now ill and indigent Otway, and later reminiscences bear out the impression of care, sometimes appreciated, sometimes not, as well as her poetic nurturing.[9]

Brown makes his Behn into the poets' whore, a woman who sleeps with Dryden or a Whitefriars ballad-monger if he will praise her. She preys on young men poets both for sex and for rhymes: 'well might you be esteem'd a Female Wit, since the least Return your Versifying Admirers could make you for your Favours, was, first to lend you their Assistance, and then oblige you with their Applause.' Yet, with all this, her amorous intrigues and her tireless efforts to please a fickle audience, her reputation never rose above 'the Character of a bawdy Poetess'.[10]

The picture of the lusty Behn, coinciding with Wycherley's, is part of the conventional mockery of a public woman. Behn herself helped paint the portrait with her demand that women be allowed to express their sexual feelings as freely as men and her insistence that chastity and prudery were simply masks over universal female desire. The picture may have had a grain of truth in it. Behn may simply and scandalously have enjoyed the company of young men; she may have had an amorous flirtation or two; she may have been strictly chaste, hence the heated quality of her compensatory prose; or she may even have had sexual intimacy—possibly of the *coitus interruptus* sort that her continued scenarios of 'disappointment' suggest. If so, and if Tom Brown was one of her partners, he may have felt justified in using her in turn.

Behn herself drew many robust pictures of older women desiring sex and knowing its price. One was in the 'cast-mistress' of the old African king in *Oroonoko*, who is courted by Oroonoko's friend Aboan for ulterior purposes: she had not

> forgot how pleasant it was to be in Love: And though she had some Decays in her Face, she had none in her Sence and wit; she was there agreeable still, even to *Aboan*'s Youth; so that he took pleasure in entertaining her with Discourses of Love. He knew also, that to make His Court to these She-Favourites, was the way to be great; these being the Persons that do all Affairs and Business at Court.[11]

Most likely Behn was somewhere between Brown's picture and that drawn by the editor of the 1702 edition of her plays, who wrote: 'Those who had the happiness to be personally acquainted with her were so charmed with her wit, freedom of temper and agreeable conversation that they in a manner ador'd her.' She was appreciated by the 'more sensible part of mankind' and loved by 'men of all ranks'.

It is just possible that Brown not only created the insatiable, lustful Behn, but also, in his insistence that she stole from men like himself, alluded convolutedly to his *own* habit of ascribing to her what *he* had in fact written. If this is the case, he was helped by another young man she might have met at this time, Charles Gildon from a noted recusant family, who would subsequently mar his position by depleting his inheritance and marrying unwisely. Both young men (Gildon was twenty-four years her junior) exploited Behn as thoroughly after her death as Brown implies she exploited men before. They were aided in this by Samuel Briscoe, an eccentric bookseller who needed money as pressingly as Brown and Gildon, and who went bankrupt in the late 1690s. In the publisher John Dunton's words, 'by contracting a friendship with Tom Brown, [Briscoe] will grow rich as fast as his author can write or hear from the Dead, so that honest Sam does, as it were, thrive by his misfortunes…'. One of the 'Dead' must surely have been Aphra Behn, whom Briscoe began publishing in 1696 when the successful dramatisation of *Oroonoko* gave her name sudden currency. Briscoe himself was unwise enough to remark on '[t]he General Doubts that Posthumous Works create of their being genuine'.[12]

If this scenario is true, then some of the poems Briscoe published and ascribed to Behn in the eighteenth century, many of which fitted into the lubricious picture he and Brown were creating to sell her works, may be as dubious as that picture. For example, one poem published by Briscoe with the spurious 'Remains' of Tom Brown and dated to this time, was a curious attack on the notorious Moll Howard, now leading a loose and decadent life at Tunbridge Wells.[13] The occasion was supposedly a rumour that she was to marry the Earl of Kildare, much satirised as a loathsome ninny. Quite why Behn should attack the one-time mistress of the Duke of Norfolk, her powerful patron, is unclear; if she did, she was either two-faced or multi-faceted, depending on one's intellectual standpoint.

At this frosty time when she was entertained by Creech and may have met Brown, Behn purportedly took part in a short-story writing competition in which she elected to imitate the French comic fictionist, Scarron, by writing a tale of a 'mighty *Cake*' reminiscent of her 'lamentable' Twelfth Night one which Brown had probably seen: 'Memoirs of The Court of the King of Bantam'. (Bantam was common cultural currency for the strange and grotesque. *Sir Patient Fancy* had already referred to it when Sir Credulous was persuaded to serenade his lady with the 'King *of Bantam*'s own Musick'. In 1682, however, Bantam became sensational when its 'monkey-like' ambassadors visited London, with their 'fat slaves, who had no covering save drawers', in the diarist John Evelyn's shocked words.)

'The Court of the King of Bantam' tells of the outwitting of a stupid rich man, Mr Wou'd be King, who is duped by a younger brother, Friendly, the name of Behn's hero in *The Revenge*, who manages thereby to provide a dowry for his daughter and a keeper for his pregnant mistress.[14] The story is saturated with theatre, referring to popular plays of the time, from Beaumont and Fletcher's much revived *King and No King* to Nat Lee's tragedy *The Rival Queens*, and to the 'Airs in the last new Plays', of which several were Behn's. The gull, Mr Wou'd be King, acts in the insolent way at the playhouse so often described by Behn and her fellows: failing to listen to the play, he gets up part way through and condemns it as 'Damn'd Bawdy'. The work he fails to see is Ravenscroft's *The London Cuckolds*—in his Bracegirdle letter, Brown accused Behn of having been a mistress of Ravenscroft.

The story could certainly be Behn's, and there are persuasive touches of her in the homosexual desire that drink brings out in Mr Wou'd be King. Yet it is also possible that, many years later, remembering their first meeting on Twelfth Night and the plays and excitement of his early season in London, Tom Brown wrote the story under her name, consciously putting in those 'persuasive touches'.

He was chronically short of money at this time, and was himself translating Scarron into English for Briscoe. In 1696, Gildon helped Briscoe bring out a one-volume edition of *The Histories and Novels Of the Late Ingenious Mrs. Behn*, consisting of the known and published short stories along with 'Love-Letters'. Another edition would need a new angle to sell. How better to provide this than for Gildon or Brown to write short stories as if by Behn and, if Brown were the author, to compose one in the manner of the man he was translating, Scarron? When the story, also published by Briscoe, came out in 1698 Gildon was worried about the difference between Behn's baroque prose fiction style and that of the new work: 'The Stile of the Court of the King of *Bantam*, being so very different from Mrs. *Behns* usual way of Writing, it may perhaps call its being genuine in Question.' The answer he gives is that it was done for a wager to see if she could write in Scarron's style.[15]

Two other Scarron-like stories that might have come from Behn's hand at this time—or Brown's or Gildon's later—are 'The Adventure of the Black Lady'—which, in *All the Histories and Novels* of 1698, Gildon declared clearly confessed its 'admirable Author'; and 'The Unfortunate Happy Lady', first published in 1700 by Briscoe. Like 'The King of Bantam', both stories cited specific locations in London, especially Whitefriars where Behn had lived.

In the manner of 'The Court of the King of Bantam', 'The Black Lady' dates itself by reference to a theatrical performance: of John

Wilson's *The Cheats*.[16] It too has self-conscious touches of Behn. Having lost trunk and friends in alien London, the dark-haired heroine responds by sending out for 'a Pint of Sack'. But other curious elements are less typical. Proving pregnant, the heroine keeps to her room to hide her 'great Belly'. One of the Scarron stories that Brown translated was 'The Useless Precaution', in which the man's beloved kept to her room because she was in the last stages of pregnancy.[17] In her condition, the 'Black Lady' is forced by her officious friends to choose life on the parish or marriage to a man she has come to loathe; the Overseers of the Poor who search for her are called rapacious 'wolves' who prey on the poor. Is this Behn getting at her father—a onetime Overseer of the Poor? Or Brown, knowing more than most, getting at Behn?

The other short story is linked to Behn's drama through the name Wilding, used in her latest play, *The City-Heiress*. He becomes the villain of 'The Unfortunate Happy Lady', though, quite unlike any recent rake in Behn, he is both witless and forced to reform through his sister's indulgent generosity. The story is also linked to *The Dutch Lover* through the initial situation of the heroine, Philadelphia, established in a brothel which she takes for a respectable house. Like one of Behn's spirited theatrical heroines, Philadelphia tries comic plotting, but only after she has, unlike Behn's girls, revealed her romantic essence in tears and doleful tales. Later, she romantically falls ill for six weeks on hearing that her lover has been lost at sea. She extricates herself from the brothel not through pert talking or clever trickery but by impressing the hero with her virtue. The ending gives the woman the social power she never quite achieves in any Behn work.[18]

In *The Rover*, Angellica, disliking Willmore's stinking buff, had dressed her man but he had gone off with his new clothes to flirt elsewhere. Encountering her lover in clothes 'as rotten as if he had been bury'd in 'em', Philadelphia provides linen, hat, shoes, stockings and sword from a 'Sale-shop', but, when he shows proper gratitude, he is measured by 'the best taylor in *Covent-Garden*' and given 'three of the most modish rich suits made that might become a private Gentleman of a thousand pounds a year'. It sounds like a fantasy of the impecunious Tom Brown's.

There are other problems, too. The tone of the story is broken when the narrator says that the widow Philadelphia is besieged by as many suitors 'as our dear King *Charles*, whom God grant long to Reign, was lately by the Presbyterians, Independants, Anabaptists, and all those canting Whiggish Brethren'. The list sounds as though it is there to remind any frequenter of the playhouse of the old propagandist playwright, Aphra Behn. But other aspects would not: for example the ending where Philadelphia simply gives a girl to Wilding, as if arranged marriages become satisfactory when organised by matriarchs rather than patriarchs. Then there is the praise of the chapel-going Councillor Fairlaw and his family, more suitable to Tom Brown, a committed Protestant, than to Behn. Fairlaw believes a humble posture only due to God 'and the King sometimes' and, as his name suggests, he uses the law, usually maligned by Behn, to right Philadelphia as much as he can. When he, an old man, married her, the marriage is justified by the prudence and sorrow of Philadelphia, who is proposed to Fairlaw by his dying first wife as 'an excellent Nurse to him', a woman who will 'prolong his life by some years'. Young Behn heroines tend to marry old men simply for money, while old men marry for sex, not nursing.[19]

Behn was a great ventriloquist. So were Gildon and Brown, who wrote, 'Those who rob the *Modern Writers* study to hide their Thefts.'[20] Answering a charge of literary fraud, Tom Brown's imaginary 'Scriblers' exclaim, 'our empty Pockets have Occasion to be Replenish'd.... We dare do any thing for Hunger .... What a God's Name would you have us do? The Bailiffs are perpetually inquiring for us, the Booksellers Teizing us, our Landlords Persecuting us for Drink, Washing and Lodging; and must we do nothing to deliver us from the Plagues we lye unde.'[21] If this is true of Tom Brown, it is hard to see why Behn with her chronic shortage of money failed to publish her entertaining stories in her lifetime—or indeed why Briscoe and Gildon did not do so in 1696 when, also needing money, they entitled their volume of Aphra Behn's fiction *The Histories and Novels...In One Volume*.[22] (The volume of novels, written by Behn or her ghost, proved initially popular. In 1731 William Twiss was sentenced to transportation for stealing books including 'one call'd Mrs Behn's Novels' while Walter Scott's grand aunt remembered reading the work with great pleasure when she was a girl. Living on into the more squeamish nineteenth century, the old woman looked again briefly at the first story, then advised that the volume be burnt.)

The bookseller Tonson's shop at the Judge's Head in Chancery Lane on the corner of Fleet Street formed a congenial meeting place, and wine flowed there, no doubt paid for immediately or ultimately by the authors. On one occasion during the Great Frost, Aphra Behn had, by her own admission, become 'in Wine'. Although she claimed she drank to keep out the intense cold, she felt herself much enhanced, as she wrote later in her comic verse letter to Thomas Creech. She was not self-conscious about a middle-aged person tipsy—indeed it was something of a poetic image, putting her in the literary company of the Ancients such as Horace, and noblemen such as Rochester, who had all fixed the tie of wine and wit:

> ...when 'twixt every sparkling Cup,
> I so much brisker Wit took up;
> Wit, able to inspire a thinking;
> And make one solemn even in Drinking;
> Wit that would charm and stock a Poet...
> I say 'twas most impossible,
> That after that one should be dull.[23]

During this pleasant inebriated time she promised to show Creech her latest work. She would leave it at Tonson's for him.

Enlivened by shifting intimacies and sherry wine, still the frost went on, as did the activity on the Thames, especially near the Temple stairs. The result of the cold interacting with the fires on the river was a thick fog. 'London, by reason of the excessive coldnesse of the aire hindring the ascent of the smoke, was so filld with the fuliginous steame of the Sea-Coale, that hardly could one see crosse the streete...& every moment was full of disastrous accidents.'[24] Usually much traffic went by water but, with the Thames frozen, it had to go by road and this added to the congestion of private coaches, tradesmen's wagons, and sedan chairs. No wonder there were so many accidents.

One happened to Aphra Behn, just as the snow was turning into hazardous slush. She had been to Whitehall to try to squeeze money from the King for her propaganda, noting in passing that Charles was 'oft in Debt... / For Tory Farce or Doggerell'.[25] She then intended to go to Tonson's to leave her work, a 'scrap of Nonsense' for Creech to read. She also hoped to meet him there. She had wanted to introduce Jack Hoyle to him since he was, she said, a great admirer of Lucretius, probably meaning both of the philosopher and of Creech's translation. But, on her way from Whitehall through Charing Cross to Chancery Lane, as the carriage, perhaps her own coach but more likely a hired hackney, passed the Pope's Head Tavern and the Temple, it was overturned. Behn was tumbled out on to the ice. She made an unedifying spectacle, soaked to the skin in dirty slush. Since keeping warm simply entailed putting on more and more of the same garments, she was swathed in petticoats, now all sopping. She looked, she moaned, like a discomfited Whig after the discovery of the Rye House Plot, or like one of her male characters in sexual embarrassment after 'too much fire':

> Even so look'd I, when Bliss depriving,
> Was caus'd by over-hasty driving,
> Who saw me cou'd not chuse but think,
> I look'd like Brawn in sowsing drink.

Although the result was an injury to her hand—'Scribling Fist was out of joynt, / And ev'ry Limb made great complaint'—Behn was most upset to be missing her meeting. She neither delivered her material nor saw Creech at Tonson's before he left for Oxford.

What Behn had wanted to show him was probably her first translation from the French: Tallemant's *Voyage to the Island of Love*, with which she had taken great pains. When she did get the poem to him, Creech found it very sexy indeed—he said as much in a long commendatory work. Behn was an arousing agent, who led both the chaste and the warm into sexual fantasy: 'Each languishes for thy *Amintas* Charms, / Sighs for thy fancied Raptures in her Armes…In the same Trance with the young pair we lie, / And in their amorous Ecstasies we die.' Later, the poet Anne Finch, Countess of Winchilsea, asserted, 'the art of the Muse is to stirr up soft thoughts, / Yett to make all hearts beat, without blushes, or faults.'[26] This was an enterprise the older poet could not easily have imagined; yet there is some evidence that Creech's poem calling her 'Loves great *Sultana*' who allows the reader to 'suck the sweet destruction in' pleased Behn as little as her original poem on his *Lucretius* had pleased him. Strange really, since she had said as much of '*soft*' Cowley, who melted her hero with his erotic poems.[27]

The Island of Love was less translated from, than inspired by, Tallemant. Behn's pastoral poetry had suggested she was fascinated with cartographies of love, the *Carte du Tendre*.[28] So she was, in choosing Tallemant, taking the advice of the Earl of Roscommon, whose *Essay on Translated Verse* was probably circulating in manuscript at this time. He argued that translators should pick originals partly from sympathy with the author: 'seek a *Poet* who *your* way do's bend, / And chuse an *Author* as you chuse a *Friend.*' Thoughts and styles should agree so well that the translator is 'No Longer his *Interpreter,* but *He!*'

Yet however congenial he was, Tallemant was also clearly judged inadequate by Behn, for her own work is far longer than his. Considering that she later lamented the embellishments of French writers who took '*twenty Lines, to express what an* English *Man would say, with more Ease and Sense in five*', it is ironic that Behn made a 2196-line poem of Tallemant's slim prose and poetry.[29] In fact French of the time was growing more abstract and taut, and English translators, with none of the restraints of reverence that the classics sometimes imposed, tended to add their own concrete examples and specific details—as Behn herself did. Although rococo in style, Behn's poem was far more erotic than Tallemant's. *The Island of Love* was published at much the same time as *Love-Letters* and, for those accepting her authorship of both, gave a steamy impression of Aphra Behn. Whether this mirrored a sudden promiscuous reality, a middle-aged sexual spree, or a rich imaginative life fed by a mixture of amorousness and sexual restraint was probably as little known to most readers then as now.

Tallemant's *Voyage to the Island of Love* tells of a miserable lover, Tircis, who writes to his friend of his allegorical voyage. Behn turns Tircis into Lysander who encounters the fair Aminta, the name she had used for herself in her poems to Boys and Hoyle: Lysander loves and eventually beds Aminta and then loses her through death. Like 'The Golden Age', the work is mostly a long seduction poem of the *carpe diem* variety. Aminta is urged to forget reputation and esteem,

> *Mistaken Virgin, that which pleases me*
> *I cannot by another tast and see;*
> *And what's the complementing of the World to thee?*[30]

The sex act becomes a strenuous journey in which the lover is accosted by Honour, Respect and Jealousy, until he finds Opportunity. Copulation occurs in the Bower of Bliss, the name used by Edmund Spenser for a dangerous threatening realm in his Renaissance allegory, *The Faerie Queen*. Behn softens the Bower into a Golden Age place of mutual ecstasy, not quite as indolent as the state in her earlier poem, but more of a realm of gentle pastoral orgy, as lovers' whispering '*Is all is heard: Silence and shade the rest*'. It seems a more decent version of Rochester's London, where nightly beneath the trees of St James's Park 'Are Buggeries, Rapes, and Incests made'.[31]

In *The Island of Love*, Behn took on a male persona, speaking through the male lover and looking through male eyes. But there are touches that reveal her poetic female narrator, such as—again—the description of a failed love-making even in the Bower of Bliss, as the man suddenly lies 'all dead' between the arms of the 'disappointed Maid'. This time, however, the lady does not run off, and soon 'vast Seas came rowling on, / Spring-tides of Joy, that the rich neighboring shoar / O're-flow'd and ravisht all great Natures store.' (Needless to say there was nothing of this in Tallemant.) Behn is also there in the sense of love as flirtation, foreplay, and anticipation: the '*Little Arts to please*' are expanded from Tallemant's fifteen lines to forty-five, and include music, song, dance, gaiety and prodigality.

The realm of love has the ease of the Golden Age, expressing again something of Behn's ideal of sexual quietude, her association of arousal and indolence. It lacks the ferocity of Lucretian sex and the busy nature of ordinary life. In this pleasant realm, the melancholic, the politician and the philosopher forget what embitters their days. Evidently fatigued by her own period of subservience to state politics, Behn sees the Island also as a place of poetry not propaganda: '*Eternal Musick, Gladness, Smiles and Sport, / Make all the bus'ness of this Little Court.*'

The Island of Love is delicately saturated with sex; the poem is far more suggestive than Tallemant's, with even nature having sexual resonance, and the prude and the slut exposed as equally sexually obsessed. With his checked but constant desire for consummation, Lysander has wet dreams in which he tastes '*the last Mystery* of Love' before waking or, after heavy petting, ends 'fainting on the sacred floor'. Surrounded with Honour and Respect, Aminta is yet overcome by lust at the end, and she yields with the breathless punctuation of Cloris in 'The Disappointment': '*I am—disarm'd—of all resistance now.*' When Behn gets to Love itself as a creative agent, it is not the Christian but the Lucretian concept she expresses:

> Whilst yet 'twas *Chaos*, e're the World was made,
> And nothing was compos'd without his Aid.
> Agreeing *Attoms* by his pow'r were hurl'd,
> And *Love and Harmony* compos'd the World.

For the woman, however, it may be discomposing as well: by the end of the work, Aminta, sexually fulfilled, is dead in the Bower, decomposing into a 'stiffening Face'.

Although the poem stays mainly in the allegorical realm, the coaches and liveries of Restoration London peep through, the jilts, politicians and whores, the cabals and mobs. When the lover is distracted, he becomes like 'a new Religion, / As full of Error, and false Notion too'. As in 'The Golden Age', religion is the enemy of nature and love, Lucretian 'Holy Cheats' that spread 'infection' to the healthy.

Shadowing the progress of the lover is a progress of a politician. The Princess Hope does not keep promises to lovers nor, it is implied, to ambitious men:

> Her Promises like those of Princes are,
>   Made in Necessity and War,
>   Cancell'd without remorse, at ease,
> In the voluptuous time of Peace.

In the presumptuous lover who disdains *'common Mistresses'* may be something of the presumptuous politician Mulgrave, who had aimed as high as the Princess Anne, and may have used Behn to help make his peace; but above all he is the Duke of Monmouth, *'The Peoples Darling'*, always pushed on by a 'Politick throng, / The Rabble Shouting as he passed along'. Behn has, however, learnt not to be quite as harsh as she had been in the epilogue to *Romulus*: Monmouth is not now a criminal but a fool.[32]

The length of Behn's poem suggests both inclination and commercial need. It was a dire financial time for playwrights. Nat Lee had gone mad under the strain and was, following current treatment, being whipped, starved and exhibited into sanity in Bedlam. Wycherley mocked the paradox: 'You, but because you starved, fell mad before, / Now starving does your wits to you restore.' Failing to prise £20 out of his publisher, Wycherley too was locked up in debtors' prison.[33] Dryden was begging an advance on his government salary, and Otway, 'tho he's very fat, he's like to starve.' When she visited the latter, reputedly to 'lend' him £5, Behn was probably reminded of the horror to which poverty could lead.

In *The Luckey Chance* a couple of years on, she gave a graphic picture of her hero, an old soldier like Otway, at the lodgings of a 'poor woman', disturbed by the Billingsgate voice of the stinking landlady and by a blacksmith's hammer. His room is the size of a tub:

He may lie along in't, there's just room for an old Joyn'd Stool besides the Bed, which one cannot call a Cabin, about the largeness of a

Pantry Bin, or a Usurer's Trunk, there had been Dornex Curtains to't in the Days of *Yore*; but they were now annihilated, and nothing left to save his Eyes from the Light, but my Land-ladies Blew Apron, ty'd by the strings before the Window, in which stood a broken six-penny Looking-Glass…which could but just stand upright, and then the Comb-Case fill'd it.[34]

(As ever in the Restoration one should not be too affected by seemingly realistic touches, since the passage is also based on a description of a garret in Dryden's first comedy *The Wild Gallant*, which also compares the space to the size of a usurer's iron chest and notes that a 'penny Looking-glass cannot stand upright in the Window'. Dryden adds the even more unpalatable detail of a chamber-pot which, if spilled, would completely inundate the room.)

Behn's hero was attended in his garret by one unpaid footman who has become a familiar companion rather than a servant. Money is owed everywhere, to the landlady, to taverns, alehouses, chandlers, and laun-dresses, while the hero—for whom the amorous landlady has pawned her best petticoat, her new Norwich Mantua, and her apostle spoons— has only a cloak to skulk out in at night and 'a pair of piss-burn'd shammy Breeches'.

Although only thirty-three like Rochester at his death, Otway was now beyond skulking out.[35] He had reputedly written four acts of an affecting tragedy, superior in Behn's view to anything he had written before. She told him to show it to Betterton, but Otway wanted to finish before taking this step. Behn then 'acquainted Mr. Betterton with this interview, who immediately made all possible enquiry after him, till about a month afterwards he was informed of his death on Tower Hill'.[36]

To avoid such a plight herself, Behn packaged *The Island of Love* with some of her old poems and, unadventurously, entitled the whole *Poems upon Several Occasions*.[37] She then tried to persuade Tonson to increase her fee:

As for the verses of mine, I shou'd really have thought 'em worth thirty pound; and I hope you will find it worth twenty-five; not that I shou'd dispute at any other time for 5 pound wher I am so obleeged; but you can not think what a preety thing the Island will be, and what a deal of labor I shall have yet with it… pray speake to your Brother to advance the price to one five pound more, 'twill at this time be more then given me, and I vow I wou'd not loose my time

334

in such low gettings, but only since I am about it I am resolv'd to go throw with it tho I shou'd give it. I pray go about it as soone as you please, for I shall finish as fast as you can go on. Methinks the Voyage should com last, as being the largest volume.... I wish I had more time, I wou'd ad something to the verses that I have a mind to, but, good deare Mr. Tonson, let it be 5 pound more, for I may safly swere I have lost the getting of 50 pounds by it, tho that's nothing to you, or to my satisfaction and humour; but I have been without getting so long that I am just on the poynt of breaking, especially since a body has no creditt at the Playhouse as we used to have, fifty or 60 deepe, or more; I want extreamly or I wo'd not urge this.

The instability here—the pride in her past earning power and indifference to money, together with the pleading in an attenuated present—echoes Behn's begging Antwerp letters of nearly twenty years before.

Although he had advanced £11 to Otway, and Brown referred to him as often keeping 'the Infant-Poet warm', Tonson was not a generous man and he must have considered he had not offered a poor fee for the volume in the first place. It did not approach the £50 Dryden got for a translation, a figure the poet was trying to negotiate up to fifty guineas— and never in her life did Behn come near the 250 guineas Dryden received in 1699 for his *Fables*—but it was not contemptible for a poet of her standing.[38] Perhaps nothing came of the appeal and both felt aggrieved. Although Behn used Tonson as surety for a small loan in the following year, she did not publish with him again.

Henry Higden, a translator and friend of Dryden's, knew that poetry needed to arrive in a panoply of recommendations, sometimes written by the author in self-praise. Behn too knew how to present a volume and her *Poems* appeared embroidered with hyperbole of the sort she supplied for others. The commendations functioned like modern blurbs rather than reviews, written to puff and advertise the book. They would have been glanced through by prospective purchasers, who would have encountered a coterie of mutually admiring men and women; they conversed with each other in a charmed circle which both excluded and invited readers. The entry fee for the reader was the purchase price.

In Behn's volume, there was of course Creech, as well as John Adams, a fellow scholar of King's College and commender of Creech's *Lucretius*, and John Cooper (possibly appearing twice as J. Cooper and J.C.), her 'Brother of the Pen' who had written the alternative 'Oenone' for Dryden. The general sentiment was that, had Behn lived of old, she would have been worshipped as a divinity and, more pertinently, that, despite her long 'translation' of *The Island of Love* and the accusations of plagiarism, she had no need of 'foreign aid', having 'wondrous store' in her own 'tunefull breast'.[39] 'To the excellent Astrea', declaring humility that the writer cannot equal Behn in wit and poetry, is signed J.W., possible initials of the theatre historian, James Wright.

One poem, '*To the Lovely Witty* Astrea', conventionally praising her 'beauteous' face and mind, had seemingly been supplied by Dryden and Behn was sensible of the 'honor'. Unfortunately, Tonson had either been precipitate in promising to deliver the Laureate or Dryden had forgotten his obligation. Most likely, he demurred when he read the book with its erotic poems. He was no longer as sure of Behn as he had been in 1680 when he received her 'Oenone' for his volume. Elegising the young poet Anne Killigrew, formerly Queen Mary of Modena's Maid of Honour, he paused to lament that the muse had been made 'prostitute and profligate... / Debased to each obscene and impious use'—although happily Anne Killigrew's poetry was 'Unmixed with foreign filth, and undefiled'.[40] Dryden did not mention Behn in this passage, but neither did he include her in his short list of famous women poets, Katherine Philips and Sappho.[41] In Behn's volume, the poem that *appeared* to be by Dryden was actually by Tonson himself. Later he owned to writing it, for he had a healthy contempt for authorship. On occasion, he could be as free with poets' names as the forging Tom Brown and Sam Briscoe.[42]

If the choice of puffers was, in the main, personal, the choice of dedicatee was political. *Poems upon Several Occasions with the Island of Love*, Behn's only original volume of verse, was dedicated to James Cecil, son of another of Colepeper's Sidney cousins, the eighteen-year-old youth who had just become fourth Earl of Salisbury. Behn intended to arrive early, being 'ambitious to be first in the Croud of Your Admirers, that shall have the honour to celibrate your name'. Perhaps because of the indecorousness of a middle-aged woman's addressing a youth, some coupling of her name with young men, or the inclusion of the erotic *Island of Love*, lampooners immediately raised eyebrows at the dedication, as Gould had over her poem for Mulgrave:

> *Astrea* with her soft gay Sighing Swains
> And rural virgins on the flowery Plains
> The lavish *Peers* profuseness may reprove
> Who gave her Guineas for the Isle of Love.[43]

Yet the address probably represents no more than an astute approach to a man just arrived at his honours, who shared Behn's devotion to the Duke of York—Salisbury was a Tory despite his father's Whig allegiance—and who had 'Guineas' to give.

As Silvia had argued in *Love-Letters*, and Behn never wearied of emphasising, the aristocracy had its purpose in the monarchy's defence: 'You that are great, are born the Bulwarks of sacred Majesty.' Now a new theme was grafted on to the political one: stability also needed the *artist*. Aristocracy must support the throne above and sustain the poet below. So the patron of the poet is the patron of England. Culture and politics should go together. The theme coincided with Behn's greater need for patronage owing to her loss of theatre revenue, but it was also a political insight which she would develop over the next years.

Behn's *working* conception of this poet remained contradictory, however. She claimed that her 'little Piece' was begotten in 'lazy Minutes'. The claim refers either to the general poetry in the volume and may be true, or to *The Island of Love*, in which case it belies the 'deal of labour' admitted in the letter to Tonson. In both cases, it associates its author with the 'gentlemen' poets—despite the fact that 'hard Fate has oblig'd me to bring [poetry] forth into the censuring World.' Behn was consistent in tying an elite art to an elite political system, but she had not yet worked out the position of the *professional* poet in the scheme.

The next dedication of poetry, to a collection of her own and others' work, entitled *Miscellany* and published early in the following year, 1685, enlarged on the political theme of the Salisbury dedication. Consequently, it became the clearest statement of Behn's political views in the mid-1680s. The dedicatee, the eligible and much-pursued bachelor Sir William Clifton, was a rich Nottinghamshire gentleman and landowner of the old breed, a Royalist whose worth 'bore the Royal stamp'.[44] In the stiff hierarchy Behn wished England to be, the Stuarts were at the apex, with the Sir Williams below, their 'Quality and Fortune' in turn elevating them 'above the common Crowd'. Although Behn never accepted the basis of the hierarchy in the domination of man over woman, she yet saw the analogy of the King to the nation with the gentleman to his neighbourhood.

Acting as a kind of monarch and representative of the great Monarch, the landlord civilised his community with 'Noble Hospitality': Clifton treated 'the under-world' around him and made people honest and loyal where else-where for want of such great Patrons and Presidents [precedents], Faction and Sedition have over-run those Villages where Ignorance abounded, and got footing almost every where, whose Inhabitants are a sort of Bruits, that ought no more to be left to themselves than Fire, and are as Mischievous and as Destructive. While every great Landlord is a kind of Monarch that awes and civillizes 'em into Duty and Allegiance; and whom because they know, they Worship with a Reverence equal to what they would pay the King, whose Representative they take him at least to be if not of God himself... he's their Oracle, their very Gospel, and whom they'll sooner credit; never was new Religion, Misunderstanding, and Rebellion known in Countries [counties] till Gentlemen of ancient Families reformed their way of living to the new Mode, pulled down their great Halls, retrenched their Servants, and confined themselves to scanty Lodgings in the City....[45]

Behn did not question why these admirable men were rushing to London or why she herself did not try to become a poet in a country hall. In fact she did not question much at all, for she was largely expressing Royalist ideology.

After the disasters of the Popish Plot and the Exclusion Crisis, through sheer indolence and the luck of a better economy the King had temporarily stabilised his vacillating and duplicitous domestic policies in an alliance of crown and gentry. This gave an appearance of peace to the next few years—for some that is, since there were many Dissenting victims about which Behn cared not a fig. On a larger timescale, however, the old patriarchal concept of squirearchy supporting monarchy was at odds with the monarchy's efforts to centralise royal power—with which Behn also agreed, since it stressed the King as absolute ruler.[46] Indeed, even as she addressed Clifton, he was helping Secretary of State Sunderland to pack Parliament with Tory Anglicans on the King's behalf. Seeing politics in terms of personalities, Behn never thought out how squires could be analogous to an absolute monarch who would need precisely to break their powers to be absolute. The vision she had was not unlike James's: of a fatherly monarch sustained by devoted nobility and squirearchy, both helping to control a foolish Parliament, city and rabble. It may have been the consonance of their confused opinions that helped make Behn one of the Duke of York's most devoted followers; conversely, it may have been her desire to be considered James's devoted follower that made her express such opinions.

If Behn's leaning towards the Duke of York's views was evident, her attitude to Charles II as a man (though not as a king) was more ambivalent, as this dedication suggests. Sir William valued the court, but did not shine there: he was content, Behn wrote, not always to behold 'the Illustrious Pattern of all Glorious Vertue in your King', whose bounty he did not need—and presumably was not getting. Behn's slight ambivalence to the King was augmented by her choice for her volume of her friend Nahum Tate's long, violent poem, 'Old England'.[47] This was in the advice-to-a-painter mode that Marvell had made famous after the disastrous Second Dutch War in 1667. Swerving from lambasting the encroaching City and 'fanatics', it rendered the times a confusion of cast-off mistresses, catamites, wine and effeminate fops, and it ended with warnings to Charles to stir himself to secure his brother's succession.

Miscellany included ten recent works of Behn's, among which were two curious ones, a paraphrase on the Lord's Prayer and an epitaph for the last of seven dead children. Both were in common genres—Waller and Anne Wharton had made paraphrases of the Lord's Prayer for example— the curiosity is that Behn should have written them. The Epitaph was, however, probably commissioned and, in transforming the dead child into a cupid-like angel babbling heavenly music, it showed more conceit than feeling. As for the paraphrase, it quickly shifted from God to the King, to whom honour, glory and praise were as appropriate on earth as to the deity in heaven. It also sheered off from amazement at the 'Wondrous condescension of a God' to more mundane thoughts of its author's own predicament: 'With all our flatter'd Wit' she and her friends could not earn their 'daily Bread' and 'Trespasses' were so seductive they could hardly be resisted:

> ...how sweet were made
> The pleasures, our resistless hearts invade!
> Of all my Crimes, the breach of all thy Laws
> Love, soft bewitching Love! has been the cause;
> Of all the Paths that Vanity has trod,
> That sure will soonest be forgiven of God.

Charles II had much the same attitude and had been taken to task by Burnet for it. When, after her death, Tom Brown mocked the Catholic converts, he included a dig at Behn's poem, her 'strange fit of Piety' interrupted by '*Cupid*' a 'private Act of Toleration for a little Harmless Love'.[48]

By now Tom Brown seems to have replaced Creech in Behn's affections, for, apart from the ambiguously named 'Out of *Horace*, omitted in Mr. Creech', Creech's name is missing from the volume with its many translations. Perhaps relations had changed since the jolly Twelfth Night, perhaps Behn had been really upset by Creech's public emphasis on her sexiness. Or she may have offended a moody man. It was easy to do. In response, her pastoral to John Howard, son of the executed Viscount Stafford, made the insulting claim that Howard outshone 'Daphnis' (Creech's sobriquet) at translating.[49]

With the eclipse of Creech, Behn seems to have moved colleges, from Wadham in Oxford to King's in Cambridge. There Henry Crisp and John Adams, both acquaintances of Creech, were fellows. Crisp was a young relative of Thomas Colepeper's, his father having been the executor of Colepeper's father's will. Behn must have liked the young man and patronised him for friendship and old times' sake, since his many rhymes in *Miscellany* are dire.

Hoyle too was probably still on the scene since lampooners found no one else with whom consistently to link Behn. She had always been fascinated, enthralled or amused by self-regarding masculinity, the shifty glamour of some men, their egoistic vitality, their subtle indulgences of themselves that allowed them to talk when they would, be silent when they wished and silence women at will. Such men always found Behn too overwhelming and garrulous, and, instead of countering her, took refuge in taciturnity and disdain. A man might ignore such emotional behaviour in another man, but a woman, raised to please, could not simply withdraw and needed instead to probe until she had upset herself and allowed him the indulgent comfort of rage.

The type, clear in the early Hoyle, recurs in Alexis, who may have been another poetic image of Hoyle, but is more likely to be a replacement, a second version of the same type. Alexis's poetic theme is that it is best not to consummate love since it always leads to disappointment—eternal dissatisfaction, tied not so much to the nature of things as to an assumption of superior sensitivity in the man, was a traditional male theme. As a woman, Behn inevitably redefined the concept, so that what men tried to write as universal metaphysical dissatisfaction became simply a male sexual peculiarity. Alexis fears consummation as the end of love with women because men have the sexual habit of scorning women after sex: ''tis a fatal lesson he has learn'd, / After fruition ne're to be concern'd.' So women, however beautiful and intelligent, are downgraded:

> In vain the mind with brighter Glories Grace,
> While all our joys are stinted to the space
>   Of one betraying enterview
> With one surrender to the eager will
> We're short-liv'd nothing....

Men, not women, always love the absent and find fault with the cruel and the kind, as Silvio in *The Dutch Lover* amply showed when he blamed his beloved for not taking pity on him and threatened her with death when she apparently did. Here Behn restates the female double bind that had concerned her throughout her writing years:

> Since Man with that inconstancy was born,
> To love the absent, and the present scorn.
>   Why do we deck, why do we dress
>   For such a short-liv'd happiness?
>   Why do we put Attraction on,
> Since either way 'tis we must be undon?
>
> They fly if Honour take our part,
> Our Virtue drives 'em o're the field.
>   We lose 'em by too much desert,
>   And Oh! they fly us if we yeild.
> Ye God! is there no charm in all the fair
> To fix this wild, this faithless, wanderer.[50]

Dissatisfaction was predicated on male disdain for women; as for women, they were too busy trying to please to have time for such inward-looking thoughts.

Behn knew she opened herself to abuse by her familiarity with young and old; Alexis obliged, for he could be priggish as well as silly. If he is indeed Hoyle, then Hoyle was still attacking her garrulity as well; if not, then, Behn was still talkative and attracted to men exasperated by this trait. Both piqued and amused on this occasion, she decided to answer the 'kind opinion', that 'unflattering Glass, / In which my mind found how deform'd it was'. She had been having a pleasant, animated talk with a man, knowing well that a sexual charge enlivened her wit. Sounding like the morose Hoyle of the letters, Alexis had watched the flirtatious discourse sourly and then expressed his disdain. Behn's response to his carping was a witty fantasy of female humility. Although she had been impertinent and vivacious all her life, she would now try to become as 'perfect' as Alexis saw himself. She would eschew vain men who prided themselves on their 'prate' and admire only the taciturn: 'For ever may I listning sit, / Tho but each hour a word be born.' It was a neat turn of reproach.[51]

Perhaps, like so many of Behn's characters, Alexis was a composite. If so, a component might have been the dedicatee of *Love-Letters*, Thomas Condon, who according to Behn chose rather to 'be singular, and sullenly retire, than heard with that noisie Crowd'. Setting 'just value' on himself, he shunned 'the publick haunts, Cabals and conversations of the Town'. Another component might be George Granville, Behn's probable acquaintance in France. He was out of London during most of these years, so is less likely than Condon or Hoyle to have been present at a social gathering with Behn, but he might have held Alexis' views of female inadequacy and he did not marry until 1711.

If Granville *did* contribute to 'Alexis', however, he could also be supportive and kind, as when he wrote this tribute to his friend:

> Some for your Wit, some for your Eyes declare;
> Debates arise, which captivates us most,
> And none can tell the Charm by which he's lost.
> The Bow and Quiver does DIANA bear;
> VENUS the Dove; PALLAS the Shield and Spear:
> Poets such Emblems to their Gods assign,
> Hearts bleeding by the Dart, and Pen be thine.[52]

It was conventional stuff, but Aphra Behn, smarting from Alexis' criticism, was glad she could inspire it.

CHAPTER 24

❦

Death of Charles II and Coronation of James II

'there is an unspeakable pow'r and pleasure in obliging'

A phra Behn entertained a number of ideas which were especially unconventional for a woman. She believed that sexual passion should result in enjoyment in the flesh and not be allowed to develop into a mind-binding construction such as love or romance. Romantic love was the enemy of necessary self-promotion and she saw it as a mistaken result of culture. Sexual desire was implicated in women's social and psychological oppression, and, while it could be eulogised as the fuel of life at one moment, at another it was an inevitably masochistic and addictive drug. Nowhere was sexual desire free from other desires, for ease, for significance, for mastery and for degradation. On her own pulse she knew that one did not always act in accordance with one's insights and that there was a perversity at the heart of things. She might mock those who believed in romance, but she too had been inspired by desire for the unattainable, perhaps more than once. Over the next months, Behn investigated her ideas of romance and perversity and, in the process, inevitably scrutinised herself as a sexual being.

First, however, she had a debt to pay. Fletcher's late Renaissance play *Valentinian* had been adapted by the Earl of Rochester before his death. Rochester had retained much of the wording of the old work but radically changed the effect. Both new and old plays aired the perennial problem of what to do with a bad ruler but, where Fletcher had solved it by assassination, then revenge, Rochester had left the future ambiguous and democratically allowed common soldiers to commit the resolving murder. The rape of Lucina by the Emperor sets matters in motion in both works, but, far more than Fletcher, Rochester luxuriated in the act, making the passive, sensuous body of the victim centre stage in voyeuristic Restoration fashion. Behn may not have cared for this exposure of vulnerable female flesh which, after her earliest works, she tended to avoid. While sharing its absorption in royal sexuality she may also have

343

disapproved the play's obvious attack on Charles II in the person of the libidinous Emperor. Yet, she probably had enough admiration for the play, and for Rochester to feel complimented if she were, as seems possible, invited to prepare (or help to prepare) *Valentinian* for the stage, as well as providing a prologue.

Since she had listened to his strictures on the 'vile' Mrs Behn, Anne Wharton's enthusiasm for Burnet may have cooled. He had too ardently praised the hated Mulgrave's *Essay Upon Poetry*, which censured her uncle Rochester, the 'late Convert', for his 'Bawdry barefac'd' and his 'nause-aous Songs'.[1] So, when she planned to organise a performance and printing of her uncle's work, Wharton may have felt free to approach Behn for professional help. She occasionally came from the country to stay at her husband's lodgings in London, but, since she was near death and suffering from headaches, sore throats and sore eyes, complicated by the effects of mercury treatment, she probably did not actually meet Aphra Behn. It was just as well since Wharton was notorious for her social pride, the 'desperate greatness' of her spirit.[2]

Rochester's manuscript of 1679 had a cast list suitable for the King's Theatre of the time, but there is no record of an actual performance. When it was staged sumptuously on 11 February 1684 by the United Company, the female lead – the raped Lucina – was taken by Elizabeth Barry, and a prologue written by Behn was spoken by Sarah Cooke. In the acting career of both Barry and Cooke, the Earl had been instru-mental. So the play became a tribute to Rochester from four women on whom he had had great influence: the poets Aphra Behn and Anne Wharton, and the actors Elizabeth Barry and Sarah Cooke.[3]

In the revised play, a few of Rochester's scenes are shifted to make more contrasts in tone, but the potentially offensive subject of homo-sexual paedophilia remains. The Emperor wantons with the 'sweet-fac'd Eunuch' in whose 'moist Kisses' he bathes his 'Love-scorch'd Soul'. When interrupted by his would-be murderer, he is prompted to one of the few moments of tenderness Rochester added to Fletcher's text: 'spare the gentle Boy! / And I'le forgive thee all.'[4] Later, when her own work was attacked yet again for being bawdy, Aphra Behn listed *Valentinian* as one of the best plays she knew, noting that its bawdiness was ignored by women because it had been written by a man. Possibly her own part in its presentation made this ironic.

Speaking Behn's prologue for the first day, Sarah Cooke argued that *Valentinian* was like an assured beauty; so railers had better talk among themselves rather than criticise:

Fam'd and substantial Authors give this Treat,
And 'twill be solemn, Noble all and Great.
Wit, sacred Wit, is all the bus'ness here,
Great *Fletcher*, and the Greater *Rochester*.
Now name the hardy Man one fault dares find,
In the vast Work of two such Heroes joyn'd.

Behn's prologue was printed first in the edition of the following year,
which Anne Wharton may have organised. It preceded one for the
second day, intended for Barry and written by another of Rochester's
protégés, the young satirist John Grubham Howe.[5] This sneered at
'Ladies of mature Age', bidding them go home and quench their embers
with their pages, rather than sit patched and painted in the boxes. The
edition also had a preface, written specifically to counter Mulgrave's
attack on Rochester. It had probably been commissioned by Anne
Wharton from a friend she shared with her uncle, the bulky Robert
Wolseley. Wolseley had been all eagerness for the task, fancying himself
the Earl's literary heir, and he had contributed a long, learned and
initially unsigned piece having nothing to do with the play, but much
with the vindication of Rochester.[6] In it, the Earl was seen as Anne
Wharton also saw him, not as a libertine but as a 'continual Curb to
Impertinence, and the publick Censor of Folly'.

Subsequently, Wolseley, Howe, and others concerned with *Valentinian*
were attacked in a lampoon called 'Letter to Julian' (Julian was a notorious distributor of libels, mainly of a Whiggish tenor).[7] Only Behn was
omitted, as she had been from *Wits Paraphrased*, the attack by Matthew
Stevenson on Dryden's Ovid volume, to which she had contributed
'Oenone'. This also had come from the workshop of Julian, to whom
it was dedicated. Perhaps Behn had friends in low places, or perhaps
her own copying past (and present) allied her with some of the lampoon-
writers who, in response, withheld their mockery.

Happily, satirists were unaware of Behn's authorship either of *Love-
Letters* or of a companion play. *The Younger Brother*, published and
performed after her death, cannot be firmly dated, but reference to
the exhibition of a rhinoceros in 1684 suggests composition about this
time, as does its central subject of female sexual adventuring. In *The
Younger Brother*, Mirtilla is an unfaithful woman who is unmasked but
left unrepentant at the play's end. She has followed her desires, unper-
turbed where they led, and has thus spent much of the play enamoured

of a youth who is in reality her lover's sister. When enlightened, she is not greatly disturbed.

Being married and possessing the social and sexual security no unmarried woman could have, Mirtilla appropriately speaks lines that echo Willmore's in *The Rover*, although she is a better rhetorician and narrator than he and far more adroit in intrigue: 'Till now I never found the right Use of long Trains and Farthingals,' she exclaims when hiding a lover in her skirts. Taxed with falseness to her oaths, she responds, 'shou'd Heav'n concern its self with Lover's Perjuries, 'twou'd find no leisure to preserve the Universe.' Marriage is a 'Fond Ceremony', a trick devised by age to 'Traffic 'twixt a Portion, and a Jointure'—though, like the heroines of *Sir Patient Fancy*, *The Fair Jilt* and *Love-Letters*, Mirtilla has not been married off by a tyrannical parent but has bestowed herself. She pursues pleasure and power, but, as a woman, she must use her sexual desirability to fulfil her desire for power: so she claims her conquest of a prince gives her as much pride as a man would have 'if thou hadst won his Sword…Look round the World, and thou shalt see…Ambition still supplies the Place of Love. The worn-out Lady, that can serve your Interest, you swear has Beauties…. All Things in Nature Cheat, or else are Cheated…You never knew a Woman thrive so well by real Love, as by Dissimulation'.[8]

The recipient of this speech of Mirtilla's is George Marteen, given the name and character of the man Behn so much admired in Surinam two decades before. So the play is a comic allusion to her own obscure past, both physically (in Surinam) and politically (she had openly admired republicans and Parliamentarians in the 1660s—possibly as men rather than politicians, and possibly in part due to her complex, never quite resolved, relationship with William Scot). George Marten had succumbed to the plague just after Behn left Surinam, but his famous republican brother Henry had, despite his regicide past, only recently died, thus perhaps jogging her memory of the family. In her play the brothers Marteen (the lengthened name indicates which Marten Behn meant, since Henry was very particular about the spelling with an 'e') were spendthrift and self-indulgent, to the disgust of their puritanical father Sir Rowland (based on the parsimonious Sir Henry Marten). In contrast to his more robustly dissolute brother, the hero George lives a schizo-phrenic life, passing for a sparkish leisured gentleman on purloined money, while forced to appear an apprentice to his father. Seeing the commercial possibilities of so handsome a piece of flesh as his son, old Marteen decides to 'sell the young Rogue by Inch of Candle'—auction him as long as a candle burns.[9] Mirtilla had at least marketed herself.[10]

It is unclear why Behn did not stage *The Younger Brother* at its moment of writing, but, having failed to do so, she could not easily insert it into another season. It had good moments, but the exposition of the plot at the beginning is undramatic, more like some of the short stories than a play, and there are creaking parts. After Behn's death, her young friend, Charles Gildon, possessed the manuscript. He made no immediate effort to put the play on. In April 1695, theatrical competition resumed and new works were wanted. The Middle Temple lawyer and soldier turned dramatist, Thomas Southerne, drew especial attention to Behn by scoring great success with his plays based on her stories, particularly *Oroonoko*, staged in late 1695. So Gildon rushed Behn's play into performance early in the next year. It flopped, although he claimed he had made it suitable for the times by cutting 'that old bustle about *Whigg* and *Tory* and adding a '*Rake-hell*'. (Gildon was not treating Behn with especial irreverence, since he went on to 'improve' Shakespeare's *Measure for Measure* in 1699.) *The Younger Brother* was probably not bettered by the changes, which, in any case, did not address the problem that, by the late 1690s, elderly fooled cuckolds and successful jilts had fallen from fashion on the stage. Of course it is possible that, like some of the late short stories, this post-humous play was *all* forgery, inspired by the single remark in Behn's *Oroonoko* that she had displayed George Marten on the stage. If so, it is curious that Gildon would have misjudged popular taste with so morally lax a work. The scene in which Mirtilla 'Opens Olivia's Bosom, shews her Breasts' to prove her a woman is close to a similar raffish scene in Wycherley's *Plain-Dealer* (a probable source of much of the play), and is more in tune with the 1670s and early 1680s than with the late 1690s.[11]

With its easier anonymity and its option for private reading rather than public performance, the novel was a better medium than drama for Aphra Behn to investigate what Mirtilla embodied and which did not much concern male writers: female rakishness and desire. So now she may well have taken up her pen to continue *Love-Letters*, interrupted to prepare the poetry volumes for the press and compose another play.

Sequels were always a problem, for they had difficulty equalling the original. Behn solved this by writing in a different mode. She moved her lovers out of the erotic pastoral world of Part I which they shared with Lysander and Aminta of *The Island of Love*, past mutual love, and into the stage world of sexy intrigue and duplicity, encapsulated in *The Younger Brother*. Part I had followed the *Lettres portuguaises* in allowing letters to stand alone; in Part II, however, they were accompanied by a decidedly unreliable narrator. Consequently what had once appeared sincere because it expressed a single passionate point of view was now undercut, whilst characters read for ulterior as well as surface meanings. Moving from Part I to Part II of *Love-Letters*, then, the reader learns of Behn's un-Puritan opinion, that language did not refer to a true inner life at all, but was always instrumental, social, and rhetorical, and that it could be distorted at will.

Much of Part I of *Love-Letters* is paralleled in Part II, often farcically, for example in the sexual experiences of Philander and his servant Brilljard, husband of convenience to Silvia. A useful nullity in Part I, Brilljard has now woken up to his manhood and desires the wife he has married for the convenience of his lord. When he believes himself about to bed Silvia at last, to rise to the challenge and avoid his master's initial 'disappointment', he takes an aphrodisiac. Unluckily other bodily needs come to the fore and 'intollerable gripes and pains' have him dashing in and out of bed in most unamorous manner.[12]

Before Silvia had left her father's house, her abandoned sister had told her what to expect from a future with Philander who had betrayed one woman and would another, leading his victim for ever beyond the pale of polite society. Her arguments echoed those made to Lady Henrietta Berkeley by Bishop, later Archbishop, Tillotson, urged by the family to bring the erring daughter back to virtue. Yet, however the historical Lady Henrietta responded, Behn's Silvia did not follow the common trajectory: she was abandoned certainly, but she did not recant or die. Instead she adapted to betrayal.

This came quickly. Shortly after their arrival on the Continent, Philander is separated from the pregnant Silvia. Love depends on the body and, in its absence, he cools—although, unlike the Henrietta of lampoons who was 'ugly grown', Behn's Silvia continued resplendently beautiful.[13] The betrayal devastates Silvia and, initially, she responds like the Portuguese nun, imagining her own death or at least reclusiveness. Then, however, she veers from the path. She will survive *in* the world, and for this she needs money. Her maid points out the only way forward: '*love and int'rest always do best together, as two most excellent ingredients in that rare Art of preserving beauty!*'[14] Silvia sees that she must market herself: young and greedy, 'she considers her condition in a strange Country, her Splendor declining…'. She must not only use her body but become a decoder and analyst of the language of the body the better to manip-ulate other bodies and understand her own. In his satire on the libertine Tory translators, the hostile Matthew Prior had told Behn to 'Describe the cunning of a jilting Whore, / From the ill Arts her self has us'd before'. Concerned with her public reputation, Behn cannot have relished this advice, but she *was* fascinated by the stratagems of women in the sexual market-place. Silvia was an excellent medium for such a study, as for a reply to a version of Behn's long-standing question: is a female rake, especially an unmarried one, possible?[15]

In Part I of *Love-Letters*, the ingenue heroine had faced the sophisticate Philander; now in Part II, the worldly Silvia and Philander face other ingenuous characters, a brother and sister Octavio and Calista who have not been steeped in Restoration court culture. Octavio is a sincere man, believing love to be absolute, true and uncontingent; he takes the passions of the heart as his authority and is self-deluded. Fascinated with Philander, he never sees his love for Silvia as part of a homoerotic tie, and, enthralled by Silvia, he does not consider her disgrace and cruelty aspects of her allure.[16] For Octavio and others like him, the knowing Silvia is a sort of fire-ship, the contemporary term for a woman carrying venereal disease. *Her* disease is the provocation of romantic love or desire in others, which leads them inevitably to poverty and degradation.

Once her 'condition' and value are no longer fixed, the theatrical Silvia consciously plays parts, fending off her lover Octavio in imitation of the selfish tyranny of virginity. She does not actually *fake* virginity, like the whores in Cleland's *Fanny Hill*, but she reveals its artificial nature by acting out its supposed results. Under this tyranny, Octavio becomes a 'slave' and the hauteur which she derives from a just sense of her market value Octavio insists on converting into the self-esteem of the virginal heroine of romance. Indeed Silvia seems now thoroughly aware of the male desire that women appear a touch infantile and capricious. Freud sees this as narcissism, fascinating to men because it allows them to seek the fantasy of a lost childhood paradise in women. Absolutely no child, Silvia plays at being a child, for what else is the enigmatic female supposed to be?[17]

That Silvia utterly fascinated her author is clear from the treatment in the final part of *Love-Letters*, completed by Behn a year or so after Part II.[18] Offered marriage, wealth and security by Octavio, Silvia abandons them all for the momentary gratification of feeling renewed power over Philander. Meanwhile, with far less to lose, Philander has been intrigued at the sight of his leader Cesario besotted anew by his ageing love, Hermione (she is over thirty), and wonders if he too can resurrect passion; Philander's obvious test is Silvia. The result is that the pair fall into each other's arms. Then, inevitably, 'Love decay'd, and ill Humour increased: They grew uneasy on both sides, and not a Day passed wherein they did not break into open and violent Quarrels, upbraiding each other with those Faults, which both wished that either would again commit, that they might be fairly rid of one another.'[19]

To free herself from Philander Silvia requires more money and, here, she is helped by the much duped Octavio, who, reduced by her treatment to entering a monastery—albeit with great baroque *éclat*[20]—bestows a pension on her in the mistaken belief that she is penitent. Her other aid is her once despised husband, Brilljard, who becomes her lover and confidant, helping her to use Octavio's money for greater allure. Soon she has entrapped a rich young nobleman Alonzo by playing in quick succession a young boy, a loose woman, and a romantic object. (A role she resolutely refuses to play is that of mother. It is difficult to remember that, during her progress, Silvia has borne a child.[21])

In portraying Silvia in all three parts of *Love-Letters*, Behn reveals how she herself was enthralled by aristocratic freedom, that certainty of caste that allows even a woman to act outrageously, to follow an un-bourgeois route of excess or intemperance.[22] Having married beneath her, Silvia might have declined from a free aristocrat into an ordinary wife, but she refuses to accept the status, just as she refuses to marry Octavio despite obvious inducements. The aristocratic Philander's continued attraction is that he cannot be a husband.

As La Nuche of *The Second Part of The Rover* showed, Behn was as curious about perversity as about excess. Although the narrator comments that Silvia baulks 'at nothing that might carry on an Interest, which she resolved should be the business of her future life', this is simply not the truth. Jilting Octavio, she flees with Philander, disliking him even as she goes, hating him as she sees her jewels sold to pay for his needs. The woman who was passionate in Part I, rational and controlling in Part II, becomes sexually self-destructive in Part III.

Silvia's analogue in perversity is the 'Countess' of the closing pages of Part III, heiress of a widow whom Behn may have helped portray in *The Debauchee*, one who could only love when abused.[23] The Countess frankly gives her terms for seduction as 500 pistoles. Going to her as a potential customer and lover, Alonzo suddenly finds her maid more appealing, and he exchanges 50 pistoles for the unexpected virginity. The Countess happens on this betrayal, and in the moment of voyeurism and degradation of desiring a man after her maid, she is fired by Alonzo for the first time. But he, like Philander, is not fond of a willing woman, and is unimpressed when she waives her fee: 'she caress'd me with all imaginable fondness; was ready to Eat my Lips, instead of kissing them, and [was] much more forward than I wish'd.'[24]

For Silvia, the only relationship left at the end of the novel is with Brilljard, the ambiguous servant-husband-master, the man who can pimp to her transvestite punk:

> She continues her Mans Habit, and he supplyed the place of *Valet*, dress'd her and undress'd her, shifted her Linen every day; nor did he take all these Freedoms, without advancing a little farther upon occasion and opportunity, which was the hire she gave him to serve her more Lucky Amours; the Fine she paid to live free, and at ease. She tells him her adventure, which tho it were Daggers to his Heart, was however the only way to keep her his own; for he knew her Spirit was too violent to be restrained by any means.[25]

For many years Behn had investigated the phenomenon of the *male* rake. She admired Rochester who had mythologised himself as promiscuous, drunken, violent, misogynous and frivolous, and she had been aware in him of the heady mixture of apparent rebellion and actual power: the man who treated women in a libertine way was the same man who was at the apex of the patriarchal system and demanded a chaste wife and legitimate heir. In her plays, Behn had gone some way to providing a rakish *woman*, especially in the women married to old men but desiring young lovers: Lady Fancy in *Sir Patient Fancy* and Mirtilla in *The Younger Brother* were obvious examples. Outside marriage but within society, however, such a woman was always a prize for the rakish man, who inevitably mitigated her rakishness. The male rake momentarily pretended that men and women were equal, but the commonsensical woman knew they were not.

A woman could not really conquer sexually, for the Restoration accepted that the sexual act ended a woman's power over a libertine. In the end, although she felt no love for him at all, Philander was the only man Silvia 'feared': Philander feared no one. She could, then, sexually dominate only a non-libertine man, but this man would be too womanish in his emotions to keep her desire raised. Ringing the changes in gender and class, the pseudo-tie of Silvia and Brilljard, pimp and punk, was the one relationship that either could bear without boredom or perverse pain. It ended Behn's fullest answer to her question of whether there could be a female rake. Set within culture and society, this swordless being had only sex and her monstrosity to gain the power she desired. Transgressing the social bonds and the norms, she became a parasite, beyond the pale, while the male rake remained deep within it, for 'Custom has favoured [men] with an Allowance to commit any Vice.' As Silvia proved, it was the nearest such a woman could come to autonomy.

In this repeated analysis there was probably some self-reference. Despite being lampooned for lewdness, Behn saw herself controlling emotions to which she would like to have given rein and compromising to live within her society, however lax. Like Silvia, she too was spendthrift, hating to 'hoard' herself or her money. In her heroine, Behn perhaps fantasised what might have been had she been born in another rank, had less verbal skill and less dependent emotion. In the portrait of the perverse relationship of Silvia and Philander, there may, also, be some distant comment on Behn's own lifelong connection with Hoyle, the bisexual man for whom she could never have been enough. Perhaps she no longer had any pressing sexual passion for him and other men were no doubt occupying her mind. Yet Hoyle may still have influenced her emotional life and the relationship may have kept her ultimately from being respectable. Certainly there are analogies between *Love-Letters* and the letters from the 1670s. Silvia puts up with just such contrary behaviour from Philander as Behn seemed to have done from Hoyle: each is driven to 'the very brink of Despair' before the man casually makes a peace, for which each is pathetically grateful. Meanwhile, Philander accents his power by drawing up 'Articles of Agreement, as should wholly subdue [Silvia] to him...', controlling her public expression. If the letters can be credited, the lawyer Hoyle, too, had worried about Behn's public face and insisted on articles of obedience.

Inevitably Hoyle was much in Behn's mind at the time, for it was early in the year of the publication of Part III of *Love-Letters* that he was finally arrested for repeated buggery in his Temple chambers with the young Benjamin Bourne—he who had as a boy probably run messages between Hoyle and Behn. With Bourne, now about seventeen and apprenticed to a poulterer, Hoyle admitted to 'sev'all indecent acts' but, probably bribed by Hoyle, the youth later retracted his main charges, and an *ignoramus* verdict was brought in. Satirists, however, found Hoyle guilty and he entered the Earl of Dorset's satiric catalogue of 'Our Most Eminent Ninnies' together with his 'he-mistress'. Bulstrode Whitelocke was more forthright: Hoyle was 'an Atheist, a Sodomite professed, a corrupter of youth, & a Blasphemer of Christ'.

* * *

By now Behn may have been borrowing money which she could not easily repay. A part of her debt could be honoured in a dedication and it may have been for this reason—as well as the guarding of her anonymity—that she addressed Part II of *Love-Letters* to the relatively obscure Lemuel Kingdon, paymaster-general of the forces in Ireland.[26] She seemed to be alluding to her prodigality with borrowed money when she claimed: 'I never was of a nature to hord any good to my particular use... there is an unspeakable pow'r and pleasure in obliging....' She had known Kingdon for some time, since she had sent a copy of the first Part to him in Ireland, although he was back in London before the publication of the second. Kingdon was neither simply a purse nor yet an amorous object like Condon, but more of a friend: 'I think you born to put the ill natur'd world in to good Humour,' she wrote.

Generous friends could only do so much and the theatre, however attenuated, must have remained in Behn's mind her best *potential* provider. So she set about writing the kind of farce that should appeal to the court. The King liked Italian *commedia dell'arte*, now assimilated into French culture, with its stock characters of Harlequin and Scaramouch, its hobby horses and pantomimic tricks. Indeed it had become so associated with the court that Otway has a snobbish character urge in a play, 'But dear Mr. *Malagene*, won't you let us see you act a little something of Harlequin? I'le swear you do it so naturally, it makes me think I am at the *Louvre* or *Whitehall* all the time.'[27] It was a taste that appalled Dryden, who crustily complained that 'Th'*Italian* Merry-Andrews...quite Debauch'd the Stage with lewd Grimace.'[28] He particularly disapproved of Ravenscroft, who had become the major exponent and apologist: 'Great Wits refrain this writing, 'cause 'tis low, / They oftner write to please themselves than you.'[29]

Behn was increasingly attracted to the stylised comedy of the *commedia*, and under its influence she had learnt to give her comics more freedom. Where in *The Dutch Lover* she had berated the comic actor for unscheduled fooling, five years later she had introduced *commedia* characters into *The Second Part of The Rover*, giving them the encouragingly freeing direction, 'Harlequin meets him in the dark, and plays tricks with him.'

The *commedia* improvisations were rarely transcribed. In 1684, however, the French scenario for a production, *Arlequin Empereur dans la Lune* by Fatouville, *was* printed. Behn decided to adapt it for the English stage and call it *The Emperor of the Moon*. With his scepticism and interest in amateur science, the King would relish mockery of the more bizarre beliefs of some 'scientists', of alchemy and rosicrucianism, for example. The work was intended to be light, frothy and funny, a mixture of comic verbal play and absurd transformations. Behn was optimistic of success.

At about the same time, she also began a sequel to her popular *Island of Love*. Here she was in some difficulty, for, unlike Tallemant, she had killed off her heroine and dismissed the hero. The solution was to elevate the cynical recipient of Lysander's earlier romantic verse-letter, Lycidus, into the main character. As for a heroine to contrast with the faithful Aminta, it was easy to find a name: Silvia. As Behn had moved from the romance of Part I of *Love-Letters* to the intrigues of Part II, from the light *Rover* to the darker *Second Part*, so she began to follow *The Island of Love* with a sequel that replaced passion with amours.

Then, both play and translation were interrupted by startling news.

The King (and with him the court) had grown wearily voluptuous. As he pondered the 'unexpressable luxury, & prophanesse' of a royal Sunday, the disapproving Evelyn caught the elegiac decadence:

the King sitting & toying with his Concubines Portsmouth, Cleaveland, & Mazarine: &c: A French boy singing love songs, in that glorious Gallery, whilst about 20 of the greate Courtiers & other dissolute persons were at Basset round a large table, a bank of at least 2000 in Gold before them, upon which two Gent: that were with me made reflexions with astonishment, it being a sceane of uttmost vanity; and surely as they thought would never have an End: Six days after was all in the dust.[30]

On 2 February, the King woke with convulsions. Prayers were offered throughout the kingdom for his recovery, while his doctors prevented it by purgings, bleedings, head shavings, and a general military attitude to doctoring. Even Dryden commented on the 'malice' and 'pious rigor' of the royal physicians. For someone so often compared with a goat, it was perhaps fitting that one remedy should entail the King's swallowing of a stone taken from the stomach of a rare goat.

Despite a rallying, Charles died on 6 February. Possibly he expired with piety like his famous subject, Rochester, since he was urged into the Catholic last rites by James and the Duchess of Portsmouth. He certainly died with courtesy, apologising to his long-suffering Queen, recommending his mistresses to James's care, and blessing his bastards—apart from the absent Monmouth. The moment so dreaded by the nation had come: the succession of a Catholic king.

Behn's political stature had risen over the last months and she felt nearer to the court than she had ever been. Her plays were put on there and she had made a public stand of commitment to the Tory Royalist cause and personally to James, Duke of York. In the view of some people, excluding the satirist Robert Gould, the bawdy she-playwright had been subsumed into the professional propagandist. The King's death seemed a moment of breakthrough. For the first time Behn would publicly join the ranks of the poets who hymned the court in the hope, usually vain, of receiving some largesse or favour. However thickly surrounded by other poetasters and minor versifying courtiers, she relished the significance. Her growing sense of the importance of poets as bulwarks of an elite of monarch and aristocracy accompanied her increasing sense of herself not just as an entertainer but also as a writer with political and philosophical opinions to express. The role of pane-gyrist allowed a female agency that was not sexual and seductive alone, as she had implied in the past. The mockery of satirists like Gould had simply added to her sense that she could, in some way, indeed be the 'Female Laureat'.

Behn's first big public performance was her elegy for Charles II. One of a large group that included Dryden's long *Threnodia Augustalis*, her poem might have been commissioned by a nobleman such as the Duke of Norfolk or by James himself. Unlike Dryden's, it was probably not paid for in advance.[31]

Court poets were used to making each detail grist to their mill. If the sun shone on a royal show, the heavens were blessing it; if it were cloudy and raining or even stormy, this also became a sign from the gods. The usage was at its most baroque in Behn's ode on Charles II, in which the events between his falling ill and his dying, much discussed in a nation that was quick to suspect poison and foul play, became biblical. When, reeling from his appalling treatments, the King managed to rally for a few days, this rallying became the equivalent of Christ's crucifixion and resurrection.

Behn's ode on Charles II's death was not the best of her state poems, but it had the most urgent political purpose. Its ending was concerned less with Charles than with the succession of James, so that the work became an enactment of the orderly and desired transfer of legitimate political power from one brother to another. Both Dryden and Behn were eager to tie the brothers together to counter the rumours of poison and to outweigh the more emotive and dangerous bond of father and son, Charles and the illegitimate Monmouth. Both poets made Charles and James into something resembling lovers, a kind of David and Jonathan pair of 'Dear Partner[s]' who must become pseudo father and son in succession. Inevitably, the marriage tie of King and his barren Queen was downplayed.

Although many, including the chief minister Sunderland, had fanta-sised a world without James, suddenly it was full of him. Yet, though he assumed the throne with surprising ease, many were less convinced of James's abilities than Behn. A hostile report drawn up for Shaftesbury indicated the danger: 'He is every way a perfect Stuart, and hath the advantage of his brother only that he hath ambition and thoughts of something he hath not, which gives him industry and address even beyond his natural parts....His religion suits well with his temper; heady, violent and bloody, who easily believes the rashest and worst counsels to be the most sincere and hearty.'[32] The huge difference in character between the royal brothers was commonly expressed, as it was in Behn's poem, through Moses and Joshua, the lawgiver and the soldier. James as Joshua worried many who feared a period of war, as well as a regime of inflexibility and vigour. Behn, however, whose public commitment to James was absolute, hymned these qualities in her hero; where Dryden identified himself with Charles, she had already moved towards his successor. No doubt, like Sunderland on a grander scale, she believed she too might benefit from declared loyalty to unfettered royal power; none the less, it is strange that such an adaptable, flexible woman should have supported so famously unadaptable a man.

Having made her political point in the elegy on Charles, Behn sat down to write a second public ode, this time to the widowed queen, Catherine of Braganza, for whom she was as free with Christian images as she had been for her royal spouse. She began by apologising for ignoring the Queen and continued with startling honesty about her motive: 'Griefs have self-interest too.' In other words, Behn had first to write poems for those most likely to pay: her sponsor in the elegy had presumably asked for concentration on the new king.

The final and longest of Behn's public political odes celebrated the coronation, which took place on 23 April: *Pindarick Poem On the Happy Coronation Of His most Sacred Majesty James II*, nearly eight hundred lines of baroque extravaganza in praise of her '*Godlike Patron*' James and his wife, Mary of Modena. For it, Behn invoked her Muse and the powers of the spheres:

Come ye soft Angels all, and lend your aid,
　Ye little Gods that tun'd the Spheres,
　That wanton'd, sung, and smil'd and play'd,
When the *first World* was by your *Numbers* made
And Danc'd to *order* by your *Sacred Ayrs*!
Such *Heavenly Notes* as *Souls* Divine can *warm*,
　Such wond'rous *touches* as wou'd move
　And teach the *Blest* to *Sing* and *Love*!
And even the *Anger* of a *GOD* wou'd *Charm*!

Like the other poems in the series, Behn's seized on every possible favourable detail, while ignoring what more hostile writers would stress: that the crown nearly fell off James's head and that one of the poles of his canopy broke, both ominous to the less committed. There is no admission of selectiveness, however: the Stuart grandeur inspired only truth-telling. It was Behn's old dream of Golden Age transparency, when people 'tell us what you mean, by what ye say'.

The form she chose was suitable for her subject: James liked degree, precedence and controlled spectacle, and the coronation was carefully planned. So was the poem, which versified the published order of the ceremonial and provided a roll call of processing aristocrats. These were men and women who, Behn hints, might want her eulogistic services in the future, as well as deserving them here: 'Each would a noble Song require.'

The peers at the coronation would mostly betray James and their oath three years later when they defected to his Protestant son-in-law, William of Orange, but, for the moment, all was loyalty. If there were some irony in the depiction of the Duchess of Norfolk, 'the *Generous, Gay* and *Great*, / To whom each *Muse* officiously resorts'—considering what satirists were writing about this famously adulterous lady—there was none in the portrait of her equally lampooned husband, 'NORFOLK! the greatest *Subject*', a man beloved at home and adored abroad. He was 'True to *his King, his Honour*, and *his Word*'. Also, he was Behn's '*Patron* Lord', the equivalent of the Roman Maecenas, celebrated sponsor of Virgil and Horace under the Emperor Augustus. Presumably the Duke— or Earl of Arundel as he then was—had paid handsomely for the *City-Heiress* dedication.

Generally unpopular because of her religion, Mary of Modena much appealed to Behn. She was a striking slender woman with dark hair and eyes. Indeed so riveting was the spectacle of female loveliness, of '*Snowy*

Neck', '*Ebon Hair*' and 'fair rising *Breasts*', that Behn occasionally forgot that her subject was primarily James.[33] She treated Mary to baroque Catholic imagery which stressed not only her natural beauty, but also her iconic robed majesty. Behn enjoyed theatrical effect and could accept the transformation wrought by robes and crown: she had seen the actresses with their smudged faces and mottled skins in the tiring-room translated into alluring beauties on the stage below the flickering candles.

The King and Queen lived on a plane above ordinary mortals and their sexual activities were beyond their subjects'—indeed, when it came to Mary's much-awaited pregnancy, Behn would even suggest that they took longer to produce children. In the *Coronation Ode*, Mary was such a sexual force that she provoked joy 'too fierce for *any* sense' but the King's. Considering the danger from the late King's illegitimate son, there was some point to Behn's insistence that Stuart monarchs would be best employed coupling with their divine wives.

In its use of the coronation only as an outward show for the benefit of the people, Behn's *Ode* was politically correct in the Stuart mode. Power and government moved from one king to another at the moment of Charles's death, as her elegy had indicated, and the coronation in the Abbey was there 'not to *make*, but to *confirm* the *King*'. The Stuarts insisted on the absolutes of their power, the divinity of kingship. Even the cynical Charles II accepted the ceremony of touching for the King's Evil or scrofula, suggesting that he too wished to be seen, in Behn's words, as 'True *Representer* of the Pow'rs Divine!'

At the climax of the crowning, her verse struggled for the condition of music to express 'All Raptur'd *Joy*! all perfect *Extasie*', the vision of 'the third *Heav'n*... / Where *Glory* sits Enthron'd above the *Stars*'. The magnificent picture gives way to her political hope, echoing Nahum Tate in his poem in her recent *Miscellany*, that the new King will rule the people as a rider controls his horse:

> You mount the unruly *World* with easie *force*...
> The wanton *Beast Restive* with ease has lain,
> And 'gainst the *Rider* lifts the sawcy *heel*;
> But now a skilful *hand* assumes the *Rein*.

She never had much time for democracy. The people usually became brutes in her political analogies.[34]

The genre in which Behn was writing, the Pindaric ode, had the advantage of allowing the poet to concentrate on him or herself, as well as the person addressed. So the poet might allude to the need for money, providing it was couched in suitable terms. One of the attractions of James over Charles was his suffering. Both brothers had been in exile, but James had been shunted off to the Low Countries and Scotland *since* the Restoration, during the Popish Plot upheavals. He could thus provide a fine analogy for the poet, whose life had also been chequered and who had experienced toil, care and '*Vicisitudes* of Night'. James should be generous from sympathy. In view of her powers, Behn felt justified in making a claim on this generosity:

> Oh Blest are they that may at *distance* gaze,
>   And *Inspirations* from Your *looks* may take,
> But how much more their happier Stars they Praise,
>   Who *wait*, and *listen* when you *speak!*
> Mine for no *scanted bliss* so *much* I blame,
> (Though they the *humblest* Portion destin'd me)
>   As when they *stint* my *noblest Aim*,
>   And by a silent dull obscurity
>   Set me at *distance*, much too far
> The *Deity* to view, or Divine *Oracle* to hear!

In other words, Behn would like now to be at court, as well as to be rewarded.

It seems a strange place to put in a claim for pay and position, but Dryden, who had received a great deal more than Behn had, used his elegy to point out that Charles had given very little to poets, expecting them to sing away and eat nothing. For Behn's point, it was useful that Mary of Modena's family had been patrons of the Italian epic poet, Tasso, and could be pictured as the embodiment of magnificent feudal patronage.[35]

Behn's coronation poem must have pleased, since it was published in various forms and reprinted by the royal publisher in Scotland. One 'Lady' reader was especially impressed and responded by composing a Pindaric to Behn herself as 'sole Empress of the Land of wit', both masculine and feminine in cleverness and tenderness. This staunch 'Lady', sometimes identified with Behn's successor as Tory poet and playwright, Delarivier Manley, thought that Aphra Behn should now be rewarded by the new King for her 'unlabour'd Song' with something substantial like a house. It would be called Arcadia in honour of the realm in which Behn had spent much of her imaginative life:

May the just Monarch, which you praise,
   Daine to acknowledge this.
   Not with a short applause of crackling Bays
   But a return that may revive thy days;
   And thy well-meaning grateful loyal Muse
   Cherisht by that blest theam its zeale did chuse.
Maist thou be blest with such a sweet retreat,
That with contempt thou maist behold the great;
Such as the mighty *Cowlys* well-known seat.
Whose lofty Elms I wou'd have all thy own...
The new *Arcadia* shou'd the Grove b.e nam'd
And for the guift our grateful Monarch fam'd.[36]

It was a conventional plea. The poet Cowley had famously been unable to purchase a small house when he wanted to retire from the world until his patrons secured a lease for him. Behn, it is implied, is a female Cowley and should be treated as such. Alas, no house and grounds materialised, however. Her huge effort seems to have yielded her little in goods, money or status.

None the less, the new reign generally improved conditions for Tories and Behn could not yet have despaired. Titus Oates was convicted of the perjury he had long been practising and was whipped through the streets. The disapproving Burnet swiftly left the country and became a naturalised citizen of Holland, where he grew into a trusted confidant of both William and Mary. Dryden was confirmed as Laureate and the Whig Shadwell was blacklisted by the theatre. The Licensing Act was renewed and Roger L'Estrange, now knighted, returned to control the press. The attainder of treason was removed from Stafford. And *The Rover* was put on at court.

CHAPTER 25

Farewell to the Theatre:
The Luckey Chance and *The Emperor of the Moon*

'We cannot help our Inclinations, Sir'

The serene first months of James II's reign were interrupted by the event so long feared and predicted: the illegitimate and Protestant Duke of Monmouth made a bid to oust his uncle James and seize the throne.

Colonel Bampfield, who had loomed large in the dispatches of Scot and Behn from Antwerp in the 1660s, had been silent for many years. Now, having lost his position in the army, he resumed activity with more time on his hands than ever. Consequently, he was even more eccentric, garrulous and lugubrious. He had, however, something to tell, especially about the escaped rebels involved in the Rye House Plot, the most notorious of whom were Monmouth and Lord Grey.[1] Sunderland suggested the government send someone over to Amsterdam to meet Bampfield and pump him. If Behn were approached because of her past, she had the good sense to decline the mission.

Monmouth was already raising loans in Holland for the enterprise: 'A great part of the goods made over as a security...were my lady Henrietta Wentworth's, or her mother's...', confessed the wealthy Grey later.[2] He and Monmouth chartered ships and purchased arms, while Turner (Lady Henrietta Berkeley's 'husband') helped recruit about eighty men. James had pleaded with William of Orange to send Monmouth packing from Holland; yet it was from Holland that the Monmouth invasion was launched.

The rebels decided to land in Lyme Regis in the west of England, where Monmouth had once been popular. Because of bad weather the trip took a lengthy eighteen days and James's quicker agents had anticipated him with the news in Whitehall. On landing, Monmouth at once issued a declaration, mainly composed by Robert Ferguson, one of his more extreme followers: cautiously it claimed the throne, but incautiously attacked James for a multitude of fantastic crimes, including starting the

361

Fire of London and poisoning Charles II.[3] By now, the 80 followers had swelled to 6,000; they were equipped with some, but insufficient, Dutch arms and they remained a small and undisciplined army with which to face the trained militia of the King. Although one of his generals was the competent John Churchill, later Duke of Marlborough and victor of Blenheim, James modified his advantage by putting the inept Christopher Monck, Duke of Albermarle, in charge of the Devon militia. Monmouth's cavalry was commanded by Grey.

The two sides met in an unglamorous way at Bridgeport. Grey fumbled and an officer asked Monmouth to replace Grey in future cavalry engagements. Monmouth refused. Then, on the night of 5 July, the rebels attacked the royal forces in the fog at Sedgemoor. Grey again mishandled the cavalry and his men fled the field, leaving the Duke and his infantry unprotected. After the rout that followed, Monmouth was advised by one of his few remaining supporters to take a boat for Wales from the nearby coast; from there he might escape to Holland. Grey persuaded him to go east—towards the Royalist soldiers.

On 8 July, the exhausted Monmouth was found asleep in a ditch, his pocket containing a manuscript book of spells and charms for combatting death in battle and opening prison doors. He was captured and taken to London. There he wrote childish and ill-ordered letters to James and his Queen, begging for mercy and blaming everyone but himself:

> my misfortune was such, as to meet with some Horrid People that made me beleve things of your majesty, and gave me so many false arguements that I was fully led away to belive, that it was a Shame, and a Sin before *God*, not to doe it.

Now he had learnt 'an Abhorrence for those, that put me upon it; and for the Action it self'.[4]

Monmouth was questioned by the King and Sunderland, tried and sentenced to death. On the scaffold he was as infatuated with his mistress, Henrietta Wentworth, as he had been in the previous years when they had 'imagined themselves man and wife....The poor duke alleged a pretence, very airy and absurd, that he was married so very young that he did not know what he was doing, and that my poor Lady Henrietta he regarded as his wife before God, and she was a visionary on her side.' Facing death, he was more concerned with returning a talismanic toothpick case to his beloved than with his political place in history. So he wasted his critical, political moment on the scaffold.[5]

When Behn came to fictionalise the execution in the last and third part of *Love-Letters*, she gave Monmouth little sympathy. She made much of the toothpick case presented to him by Henrietta, so portraying him as the stereotypical would-be ruler destroyed by effeminating and uxorious love.[6] She did not give the detail of the bungled death, in which the executioner failed to sever Monmouth's head after five blows with his axe and was forced to cut off the rest of the neck with a long knife (unlike Tarquin of *The Fair Jilt* he was not saved by popular tumult). It was rumoured that James had ordered a blunt axe for his nephew.[7]

For Hermione (Henrietta Wentworth) and her ageing charms Behn did, however, display some final sympathy: she depicted her taking to her bed on the news of Monmouth's end, vowing to starve herself to death—'and she was as good as her word'. Outside fiction, Rochester's friend Henry Savile diminished the event: 'My Lady Henrietta Wentworth is dead, having sacrificed her life to her beauty by painting so beyond measure that the mercury got into her veins and killed her.'[8] The demise of both was no doubt satisfactory to Sunderland, who had recently flirted with Monmouth and did not wish it known.

Behn was clear where she stood. James was the '*Representative of Heaven*', the '*Saving Angel, who preserv'st the Land*', a man '*Soft and Forgiving, as a God*'.[9] Not everyone agreed with her. Judge Jeffreys, who had presided over the trial of Lord Grey for the abduction of Lady Henrietta Berkeley, was the main instrument of the new King's sledge-hammering justice, and the judgements he meted out to the Monmouth rebels were grue-some. The offender was hanged, drawn—i.e. organs pulled out before dead—and then quartered, the limbs pickled and sealed in tar and dispatched about the country. The process was extremely expensive, at about 27s a victim. It was also long, so much so that often only two or three were dispatched in a day, and the punishing of a hundred or so seemed to last an age. Hence the exaggeration of the numbers killed. None the less, most regarded Jeffreys as bloodthirsty and not many praised him. One of those who did was Aphra Behn.

Jeffreys was fascinated with the theatre, and he and his wife often entertained the young up-and-coming actor, William Mountfort. Indeed lampoons suggested some intimacies, especially between Mountfort and Jeffreys' wife. On one occasion, the tipsy Jeffreys had Mountfort mimic the quirks of his fellow judges and comically ridicule the law, to the grave disapproval of the more serious in the company.[10] Not overly grave about the law herself, Behn may have been present at some of these unseemly revels, for Mountfort and his new wife, Susannah, began to appear in her plays about this time. Jeffreys was also a friend and associate of the subservient, trimming, and hedonistic Judge Wythens, now the husband of her poetic friend, the former Elizabeth Taylor.[11]

For Behn, Jeffreys, a handsome and witty man if his portraitist and she are to be believed, remained primarily a zealous Royalist who had, in her words, 'so absolutely attach'd' himself 'to the interest' of the King that he had no purpose in life except to serve him, despite the fact that he had been persecuted in the 'Rabble-ruling times' of Charles II. But, except for herself and Elkanah Settle, now as violent a Tory as formerly he had been a Whig, the poets did not rally to him. Loyalty, it seems, did not bring popularity. In the next reign, when the Monmouth Rebellion was mythologised as part of England's fight for freedom, he would be demonised as a cruel monster, the 'Western hangman'.

Nor did loyalty bring money for poets. After the Monmouth Rebellion, Behn had used her dedication to Lemuel Kingdon of the second part of *Love-Letters* to compliment him on his unobtrusive Royalism. Then she went on:

> I am so good a subject that I wish all his Majesties work done by such hands, heads and heart, so effectual and so faithful, and then we shall fear no more Rebellions, but every man shall bask securely under his own Vine, that has one.—For my part I have only escap'd fleaing by the Rebels to starve more securely in my own native Province of *Poetry*....

Her situation was exacerbated by the fact that Tonson seems to have dried up as a source of loans and Behn had to borrow money elsewhere—although using him as surety. In August 1685, at about the time she was moaning about her poverty to Kingdon, she wrote an IOU to Zachary Baggs, later treasurer (and probably at this time sub-treasurer) of the United Company:

> Whereas I am indebted to Mr Baggs the sum of six pound for the payment of which Mr Tonson has obliged himself. Now I do hereby empower Mr Zachary Baggs, in case the said debt is not fully discharged before Michaelmas next to stop what money he shall hereafter have in his hands of mine, upon the playing my first play till this aforesaid debt of six pound be discharged. Witness my hand this 1st August 85.[12]

She was still managing to spend her earnings before she received them.

To alleviate her immediate poverty further, Behn may surreptitiously have turned to an earlier standby, copying for money within a scriptorium of men and women. In the Bodleian Library, Oxford, is a manuscript verse miscellany of lampoons entitled 'Astrea's Booke for Songs & Satyr's', most of which was written between 1685 and 1688. It was copied by several people, one of whom, joining the manuscript late in 1685, on page 101, may be Aphra Behn. The handwriting resembles the clear script of Behn's letter to Zachary Baggs, while, on the cover, is scrawled the subtitle 'Bhen's and Bacon'. 'Beans and bacon' was a common phrase, which Behn had met in Tatham's *The Rump*, where the crude Parliamentarian, Desborough, is made to exclaim, 'my *colon* begins to cry out *beans* and *bacon*. Possibly the bawdy and coarse satires copied into the manuscript were intended as antidotes for the nation.[13] (If so, a restorative might have been the 'sack possett', for which a recipe was also provided.)

Writing and copying lampoons to exhibit 'the Faults of the Great and the Fair' was a thriving business throughout the 1670s and 1680s.[14] The main operator was Robert Julian, often called 'Secretary to the Muses', who had famously lost his ears through his career in libel. He supplied material to poets such as Robert Gould (and possibly Behn herself), commissioned to write for a coterie clientèle. He also used scribes to copy works for distribution to individuals, coffee houses, taverns and brothels; Ravenscroft describes Julian as employing 'too Clarks'.[15] On the cover of 'Astrea's Booke' the name of John Somerton is doodled along with 'Bhen', which makes it more likely that the manuscript was a commercial venture rather than a private collection. In 1684, Julian had been convicted of publishing libels on the King and others; he was put in the pillory and bound over for good behaviour for life. Successors immediately replaced him: Captain Warcup, possibly the father of Behn's friend Emily Price, was dubbed 'second scandal Carrier of the Town' to the first, named John Somerton or Summerton.[16] A fictitious letter to Julian from Brown's *Letters from the Dead* also mentions 'your Successor *Summerton*', noting, as contemporary lampoons did, Somerton's subsequent 'madness', during which the libelling business collapsed.

In the mid-1680s, Somerton was in his heyday as distributor and writer of lampoons and newsletters, and it is quite likely that he supplied Behn and other copyists of the manuscript with scurrilous works. Towards the end of the volume there is a list of names and addresses, in which

New Street, Behn's own place of lodging, figures more than once. There is also the name of the printer, R. Holt, whom she was using during these years, while on the cover but not in Behn's hand, is the address in Paris of the Duke of Norfolk, Behn's patron 'Maecenas'.[17] He might well have been one intended recipient of the manuscript through his Parisian address; the Duke himself was in England during these years. If Norfolk *did* read the manuscript, he cannot have relished it: it presented him as 'a famous cuckold' and masochist, sneaking into bed with his infamous relative, Moll Howard. Meanwhile, his wife, celebrated by Behn in her *Coronation Ode*, appeared 'less sparing of her arse than eyes'; she was famed for her 'Dissolute lewdness, falseness, and ill nature'.[18] Perhaps, however, like insolent prologues, the lampoons were enjoyed by their victims: Tom Brown has Julian declare that noblemen wanted his libels 'tho' their own folly and their Wives were the Subject'.[19]

In public, Behn loudly disapproved the Whiggish political stance of the verses copied into 'Astrea's Booke', which lambasted James II, Roger L'Estrange, Hortense, Duchess of Mazarine, Dryden and Sunderland, all of whom she revered or served. So the possibility exists that, in involving herself in such an enterprise—she was working on the side opposed to the one she overtly espoused—was in short as politically two-faced and cautious as a good many others. It is not known by whom Somerton was employed, but Julian certainly worked in part for the Earl of Dorset, who was called his 'great Maecenas'. (Like Rochester and Mulgrave, Dorset both wrote for and patronised Julian.) In James's unsatisfactory reign the disaffected nobility, including Dorset, were working hard to provide a context for the usurpation of the throne by William and Mary, using every resource possible of disinformation, spying and libel. The last is illustrated in 'Astrea's Booke', which has a high proportion of verses appearing uniquely or for the first time. If this manuscript is part of Dorset's propaganda-factory, as it might have been, Behn was working for the Whigs and her activity would fit with her composing of a graceful 'Pastoral Pindarick' for Dorset's marriage in 1685, the only time she addressed the nobleman directly.[20] Indeed, her remark that she had only 'song' to give Dorset since she was not 'blest with Flocks or Herd' could be a comic allusion to her activity and her necessity.

There is, however, much against the notion that Behn was working purposely for the Whigs. In her *Coronation Ode*, she praised Dorset among all the noble peers apparently supporting James, but implied a rebuke when she declared 'His looks made good to day, all he e're spoke or

Write.' Presumably she knew of Dorset's recent undercover activities. She herself was associated with the Tories throughout her life both by fellow Tories and by opposing Whigs. If she were prepared to work clandestinely for the latter at this point, it seems curious that she did not search out Whig patrons more than she did or make something of her past activity once it was clear in 1688 that William had come to stay. Most likely, Behn was, in 'Astrea's Booke', copying for money for anyone who was prepared to pay, attracted to the work as a satiric writer who needed to know town gossip. This interpretation is supported by the fact that, to the side of several of the poems, are comments written in her presumed hand that express anger at the contents. For example, next to lines that charge L'Estrange with abandoning the royal cause for Cromwell in the Interregnum, 'when to Noll's our Charleses fate gave Place / I coud abjure th'unlucky Royal Race,' the hand wrote 'A damnd Ly', an exclamation repeated when it came to the line in which L'Estrange is made to admit, 'I servd him [Cromwell] as a faithfyll spy.' These would be unhelpful marginalia for a Whiggish employer. If the hand was Behn's, she was doing hackwork to keep body and soul together in a time of penury and her heart, it seems, was not much in alliance with her copying fingers.

The play Behn mortgaged to Zachary Baggs when she borrowed £6 was probably *The Luckey Chance*, the final in her series both of intrigue comedies starting with *The Rover* and of City plays beginning with *The Town-Fopp* and *Sir Patient Fancy*.[21] More than these last two, it breathed the localised physical London she knew—Whitefriars with the George Tavern and the liberty of Alsatia, where debtors could hide from arrest; Lincoln's Inn Fields, its theatre temporarily closed now, home to tramps and thieves; the Monument with its inscription (commissioned by Sir Patience Ward, a butt of *Sir Patient Fancy*) blaming the Fire of London firmly on the Catholics; and the swirling Thames at high tide under London Bridge. There was a sense of scribbling and speaking London too, with allusions to Snow-hill in Holborn where lampoons and ballads were printed, to Sir Roger L'Estrange's newspaper, *The London Gazette*, and to bawdy cockney slang, with its mingling of sex and money: 'hot cockles' for vagina, 'Sir-reverence' for a turd, men 'broke' in money and women.

Behn had probably written most of *The Luckey Chance* earlier, since it attacks the enemies of the Popish Plot and Exclusion Crisis years, rather than those of James II's reign. It was probably performed in the late

Spring of 1686 in Drury Lane by the United Company and proved the last mainly original drama Behn would stage.[22] Happily, it was one of her best. She knew she was fortunate to have it put on, that it was indeed a 'Lucky Chance' for her. As she pointed out in her prologue, the amalgamated company was relying mainly on old plays to which it now had complete access, and living playwrights were experiencing 'Dearth and Famine' or at least 'small' credit. Behn, however, had authority in the theatre and she was not only produced but enabled to hire the best musicians for her work: John Bowman, an actor and singer who had joined the Duke's Company as a boy in 1673, sang a fine song, probably by Robert Wolseley, her old collaborator on *Valentinian*; music came from the court musician, John Blow.[23]

The Luckey Chance echoes and varies *Sir Patient Fancy*, rather as *The Second Part of The Rover* does the first, but it may also have called on the scandal of Behn's poet friend, Elizabeth Wythens, née Taylor, who, it was said, had married Judge Wythens while still loving Sir Thomas Colepeper. After the marriage in Westminster Abbey, Elizabeth left her husband and moved in with her lover, who sued Wythens for financial support of the children she brought with her. After the judge's death in 1704, Elizabeth married Colepeper. Some such arrangement and implied progression seems anticipated in *The Luckey Chance*.

The play takes up the Restoration theme, famously realised in Wycherley's Pinchwife in *The Country Wife*, and already treated by Behn in *Sir Patient Fancy* and *The False Count*, of an older man demanding exclusive possession of a young wife whom he owns only through money. Sir Feeble declares his marriage will be lawful 'when I've had Livery and Seisin of her Body', the legal terminology rendering her person his paid-for commodity. Characterised by the conventions of Tory plays, the old City knights are frequently impotent—a fact stressed, as in *Sir Patient Fancy*, by the old man's habit of undressing his baby wife. They are uxorious with their awful infantile talk of 'little white Foots', and 'little round Bubbies', superstitious and avaricious. As usual, the comic chaos is the fault of such old men who have overstepped the limits of their power, not of the young bloods who want to rob them of it.

Ravenscroft had realised the changing morality in the theatre and declared of his last play, 'No double sense shall now your thoughts beguile, / Make Lady Blush, nor Ogling Gallant Smile.'[24] Judged beside *Sir Patient Fancy*, *The Luckey Chance* seems a conscious effort on Behn's part to avoid the usual 'sottish Censures' by pleasing the public with more conventional morality. So she created a slightly more respectable, more constricted world than formerly, one in which the chaste heroines have greater virtue than Lady Fancy and even than Hellena or Ariadne of the two *Rovers*. Each keeps her virginity (or chastity) until she disposes of it to the correct man, but the earlier heroines did not prate about it: here Leticia declares her guide religion, while Julia, Lady Fulbank, insists she will not wear her beauties 'in a dishonest Bosom'. In *The Rover* and *The False Count* no pity was spared for old men who lost their women, but Leticia is surprisingly tender about Sir Feeble, who has tried to possess her—'it grieves me to consider how the poor old Man is frighted'—while Lady Fulbank rejects her husband only when she learns he has gambled her away.

The young men, too, are less daring, less libertine. Still separated from the City, they are no longer of the court and more of the town, and they have none of the Cavalier glamour of Willmour and Belvile. Gayman, whose other name is rightly Wasteall, is driven to real experienced poverty by his amour and, in his schizophrenic life of town wit and pauper, must have called on Behn's knowledge of the shifty Tom Brown, as well as poor Otway. Nor is the contrast between them and the City elderly as great as before, and the impression is close to that of *The Younger Brother*, where the hero, whose 'Parts [were] not form'd for dirty Business', yet appears before his father 'Drest like a Prentice', his fine clothes and equipage kept outside the City. Bellmour fears to appear openly until he can legally do so and Bredwel, afraid to 'steal a City-Heiress', is happy to have the woman without her money. But there is much harshness too. Willmore had clothed himself with money from sex, but Gayman sets up as a straightforward male prostitute and his sordidness is unglossed: '*She pays and I'll endeavour to be civil.*' He goes where he believes some ugly old woman has seen his face, shape and youth and 'thinks it's worth her Hire' and he is prepared to 'moil on in the damn'd dirty Road', drudging through the night to look gay by day.[25] It is an interesting gender reversal. Gayman is no better than Angellica Bianca and, fittingly, he does not, at least within the play, get the woman he wants in marriage.

The contrasts that have underpinned Behn's earlier plays are no longer absolute. The old knight treats his wife as a commodity and a moveable good, but, in gambling for her and offering Sir Cautious £300 for a night's use of Lady Fulbank—whatever his motive—so does her lover. Although the play finds the elderly frantically trying to hold on to their wits, their gold and their women, the generosity with which they finally offer to release the young women brings characters together in a way quite foreign to the bitter rakish ending of *Sir Patient Fancy*: 'I find *Sir Feeble* we were a Couple of old Fools indeed, to think at our age to cozen two lusty young Fellows of their Mistresses,' says Sir Cautious.

Love for young or old coalesces in being imaginary. The old fantasise pleasures they cannot take, but so do the young. Gayman ruins himself to make a rich self-image with which to court Lady Fulbank, who in fact does not want his money, having already married for it herself and being prepared to use it for his benefit. Each has had a faulty image of the other, just as Sir Feeble and his child wife, Leticia, have. To possess Lady Fulbank, Gayman is prepared to court his stinking landlady and act as a male whore. When he actually achieves what he desires, a night with his beloved, he does not know her and calls her 'a Canvas Bag of wooden Ladles'.[26]

Later, when Gayman has won sex with her, Lady Fulbank believes herself to be sleeping with her husband 'in cold imagination' and begins by 'shyly' turning away, 'faintly resign'd'—until 'excess of Love betray'd the Cheat'. Gayman's happy involvement in the second transaction, organised by the husband rather than the wife, indicates that he is more comfortable bargaining with a man for a woman than in allowing the woman the autonomy and power Lady Fulbank takes. There are echoes of *The False Count*, where an old husband is persuaded to donate his wife to another, but that play was a less ambiguous depiction, with more willingness assumed in the lady.

Early in the play, Julia Fulbank had offered herself to Gayman when her husband died, mockingly seeing herself as a property leased to the one, but temporarily occupied by the other—much as the Cavalier lady had done in *The Roundheads*. Yet, when her husband offers her the same bargain after Gayman has taken the imagery to its conclusion and bought her, Julia recoils. Having slept with two men against her will, she now stands on her 'Freedom and my Humour'. In the language she herself chooses, Gayman has made her a 'Prostitute' and 'Adulteress', and she seems as likely to cleave—although not in bed—to the old Sir Cautious, who has learnt sense, as she is to her lover.

Yet, it is not all independence and spirit, for in the end what freedom could Lady Fulbank have without falling outside society like Silvia? Her wit makes her seem to dominate both Gayman and Sir Cautious, who do not match her verbally, but each has more control of her than she of them. Her last speeches claim that the assignation she had arranged with Gayman was terminated as pre-arranged without consummation;

yet, when Gayman tells of the scene, he does not stress that no sex occurred, as it would be to his advantage to do. The audience cannot know whether or not the encounter was innocent. The future, too, remains unclear. Lady Fulbank taunts Gayman for describing her as a 'Canvas Bag of wooden Ladles', but the taunt has a teasing rather than an angry ring. As usual with Behn, the stance of women towards men is not simple and unambiguous. Physical attraction cuts across political feminism.

In several works of this time, reality and fiction intermingle: Lady Fulbank's situation is as far as possible from the independent and ageing Behn's and yet Behn seems to have given her something of her own public image. The mark of self-revelation is often an allusion to talkativeness and dominating wit. Lady Fulbank is accused of loving 'to pass for the Wit of the Company, by talking all and loud'. Behn often accused other women of playing the modest feminine game, especially in the theatre: Lady Fulbank assures her husband she cannot 'simper, look demure...Cry fie, and out upon the naughty Women, / Because they please themselves—and so wou'd I'. She boasts, 'I value not the Censures of the Croud' and declares,

> We cannot help our Inclinations, Sir,
> No more than Time, or Light from coming on—
> But I can keep my Virtue....

Behn, too, often declared her contempt for the 'Croud'.[27]

This time the 'Croud' or 'the Generality of the Town' did not 'censure' Behn's play. The actors had done her proud, with Nokes, Leigh and Jevon playing the comic citizens, and Elizabeth Barry doing the female lead; the coming comedienne, Susannah Percival (soon to be Mountfort), made her Behn début as the second heroine, Diana. Over fifty now, Betterton still felt himself equal to the amorous part of the hero. Probably the milk punch—to which John Bowman claimed he was introduced by Behn—flowed when she collected her third night's earnings, minus, one may assume, Zachary Baggs's £6.[28]

Yet there were the carpers. After the first performance, following custom, the witty part of the male audience repaired to an upstairs room of Will's coffee house, 'the merriest place in the world' to discuss the play.[29] As a woman, Behn was excluded—a fact that was doubly irritating to her on this night, for she heard that a Wit of the Town, a Friend of mine at *Wills* Coffee House...cry'd [the Play] down as much as in him lay, who before had read it and assured me he never saw a prettier Comedy. So complaisant one pestilent Wit will be to another, and in the full Cry make his Noise too.[30]

Something similar had seemingly happened with the now-dead Otway over *Abdelazer*, so she was used to men's treachery through their desire to run with the witty herd. Yet, it was annoying when such comment threatened the reception of a money-making play. Since Dryden usually presided on the first-floor room at Will's, this may be a reference to him, but a 'Wit of the Town' does not sound like the Laureate.[31]

Behn learnt that her work was criticised for being bawdy. It was the old story, but she was hurt since she had tried to make her material more moral. She had given the play to some noble ladies to read before she put it on, and neither they nor Sir Roger L'Estrange, who licensed it, nor Killigrew's son Charles, now Master of the Revels, had found it indecent. Other ladies of quality saw it more than once and commended it. The elevated list of supporters helped to bolster her self-image, of a woman whose 'Conversation [was] not at all addicted to...Indecencys'.

As in the past, Behn tried to persuade someone to tell her exactly what was amiss with the work, but all she could discover was that people were upset that Anthony Leigh opened his nightgown when he came from the bride chamber. If he did so, she sniffed, it was a 'Jest of his own making'. (Unfortunately the text belies her, for she had indeed written Sir Feeble, Leigh's character, as a flasher, but his age and predicament make the scene comic. She may of course have added the direction *after* she discovered the source of the criticism, thus simultaneously grumbling at and taking advantage of the notoriety.)

Behn always found men stripped or in undress funny, but it was often the place where she fell foul of modest opinion. It was as if no one quite wanted to comment on her other related fixation: impotence. Blunt's scene in his drawers later contributed to the removal of *The Rover* from the eighteenth-century stage. There was no reason why a woman should not write of such topics as male undress any more than men, but the fact remained that they had not done so in the past and would not do so again for a very long time. Behn's insistence that she be allowed to play gender games and speak as one of the lads always landed her in trouble, which in turn made her furious. Expressed and public irascibility she also associated with men or unconventional women—as Silvia of *Love-Letters* attested.

Since she could not hold forth at Will's herself, Behn stopped the printing of *The Luckey Chance* to dash out a preface. She was irritated at attacks on her play, convinced they were due entirely to her sex. Although she was not quite, as with the failed *Dutch Lover*, in the situation Mulgrave mocked in his *Essay upon Poetry*, where playwrights 'rail at th'Age they cannot please', she did reiterate her old point from the 1670s, that she was merely following the conventions of the sort of comedy she wrote. While she might expand, transgress a little perhaps, she could not differ substantially from other playwrights:

> I make a Challenge to any Person of common Sense and Reason... any unprejudic'd Person that knows not the Author, to read any of my Comedys and compare 'em with others of this Age, and if they find one Word that can offend the chastest Ear, I will submit to all their peevish Cavills.

Why on earth would she stand out by being exceptionally bawdy? she reasonably asked. 'I must want common Sense, and all Degrees of good Manners' to go about *purposely* to offend an audience. She had, after all, repeatedly declared her prime aim to please.

Having been so long in the theatre, Behn knew her subject: 'Had I a Day or two's time...I would sum up all your Beloved Plays, and all the Things in them that are past with such Silence by; because written by Men: such Masculine Strokes in me, must not be allow'd.' And she ran through a tradition of stage bawdy that included the great Dryden, Ravenscroft, Crowne and Etherege, as well as the approved early writers, Beaumont and Fletcher. Then followed the most moving of her statements:

> All I ask, is the Priviledge for my Masculine Part the Poet in me, (if any such you will allow me) to tread in those successful Paths my Predecessors have so long thriv'd in, to take those Measures that both the Ancient and Modern Writers have set me, and by which they have pleas'd the World so well. If I must not, because of my Sex, have this Freedom, but that you will usurp all to your selves; I lay down my Quill, and you shall hear no more of me, no not so much as to make Comparisons, because I will be kinder to my Brothers of the Pen, than they have been to a defenceless Woman; for I am not content to write for a Third day only. I value Fame as much as if I had been born a *Hero*; and if you rob me of that, I can retire from the ungrateful World, and scorn its fickle Favours.[32]

It was good ringing stuff, emotional and unstable, similar to the final letters from Antwerp many years ago, when Behn had played on her sex and asserted her autonomy, been at once defenceless, defensive and authoritative. Now she wanted 'Fame' in the masculine term of glory, not the feminine one of goodness, chastity and modesty; yet she also wanted to play at being a 'defenceless Woman'. She both accepted the gender divide of the time that made wit and poetry mainly masculine in the context of what a man was and could do, and mocked it when she declared that she, a woman, wanted to be a man, a hero, and display her 'Masculine Part'. Only with this hermaphroditic manoeuvre would she be treated fairly.[33]

Undoubtedly Behn was right. She *was* criticised more heavily because she was a woman writing. What she never acknowledged, however, was that times were thoroughly changing for everyone. There was a backlash against the frank, sexy Restoration woman and—against the male rake and libertine as well: both were moving towards their new eighteenth-century place as temptress and villain.[34] Morality was more and more wanted in art, if not necessarily in life. Behn had provided some, but not enough for those still scandalised by the tone of Charles II's reign. Bawdry attracted of course, but was falling foul of the critics more seriously than before. Admitting that 'few Poets...are left,' she must have noticed that her theatre generation was passing. Yet, it was easier to blame the common fate on her sex.

The preface to *The Luckey Chance* repeated Behn's defences of *The Dutch Lover* and *Sir Patient Fancy*, but it differs from them in one respect: she no longer insisted that comedy was trivial and that she wrote it only for money. This was the central point of her dedication of the play to Laurence Hyde. In the past, she had argued that comedy was inconsequential and contemporary, so there was no reason a woman could not write it. Since it did not aim to teach, no claims need be made. Now, after her experience with the Popish Plot, Behn had arrived at the old opinion of Sir William Davenant in the Interregnum and become aware of the power of drama, which joined poetry as a form of statecraft. Plays were 'secret Instructions to the People, in things that 'tis impossible to insinuate into them any other Way'. The times were much in need of instruction, now that the Tory triumphalism of Charles II's last years had ceased and James's Catholic policies were upsetting the nation.

Brutal and unstable though it was, Behn had a very real fear of the end of the period of Restoration. The society in which she had moved and which allowed the sort of verbal cross-dressing now shocking the public had always been fragile. It had consisted in a small coterie of people sure of gender and rank and thus able playfully to destabilise both; for a few years it had been close to a source of power in the court and associated with aristocracy. If its critics in the nation at large did not see it as the best location for an intellectual woman to flourish in, Behn herself found it a nurturing and bracing space; it allowed her to play parts and speak speech quite forbidden outside.

She had probably addressed Laurence Hyde before this dedication, since she declares, 'You have an Art to please when you deny; and something in your Look and Voice has an Air so greatly good, it recompences even for Disappointment.' As 'great Persons' in classical times and the French Cardinal Richelieu in modern had patronised drama, so should English politicians like Hyde. Perhaps he might have done so but, for once, Behn's timing was wrong. She had described Hyde, second son of the dead Chancellor Clarendon, now created Earl of Rochester and President of the Privy Council, as 'above that Envy which reigns in Courts', his loyalty imposing 'Silence upon Malice it self'. Hyde was *not*, however, above malice and envy, and he was suffering from his royal brother-in-law's efforts to convert him to Catholicism. Lacking the deviousness of the Earl of Sunderland, he was unable to string James along with hints and promises. Disliked and undermined, he was dropped by the King and soon left court. Sincere Protestants were becoming thin on the ground.

Behn continued to need money—probably there had been other debts besides that to Zachary Baggs. Her health, always precarious but seemingly improved through 1684 and 1685, took a turn for the worse towards the end of 1686. No doubt she consulted expensive physicians, including Dr Bellon, who, according to 'Astrea's Booke', lived 'next doore to the Gold Bottle in Salisbury Streete neare Salysbury house in the Strand'. He probably charged a good deal since he was a noted doctor and wrote on medical matters.[35]

Behn's symptoms recorded in her stray remarks and in lampoons make it uncertain what was wrong. Her limbs were aching and sometimes she had trouble walking and writing. She may have had a form of arthritis or sciatica or she may have suffered from what the satirist Robert Gould accused her of, gout, the symptoms of which were pain in legs or arms or hands, the sort that Behn lamented. It was not immediately fatal, but could cause death as it travelled to the heart. If this were the problem, she could have started it as long ago as Surinam, where gout was reportedly endemic.[36] Or she may, like so many men and women of the time, have had some long-standing venereal complaint, which revealed itself in the slow distorting of the limbs and in pain very like arthritis. Both Wycherley, who knew and respected her, and Gould, who probably did neither, declared that she was 'clap'd'. Some years later the woman of letters, Lady Mary Wortley Montagu, was reminded by a nobleman that several 'remarkable poetesses & scribblers' had 'given very unfortunate favours to their Friends', in other words, infected them with venereal disease. In the list is 'Mrs Been', a lady 'famous indeed in [her] generation'. This is the stuff of misogynous satire, but there may be some truth in it. The disease was remarkably common.

Whatever the matter was, it was unpleasant and worsening, and lampooners made much of it:

> Doth that lewd *Harlot* that Poetick Quean,
> Fam'd through whitefryars, you know who I mean
> Mend for reproof, others set up in spight
> To flux, take glisters, Vomits, purge & write,
> Long with a Sciatica she's beside lame[37]
> Her limbs distortur'd Nerves shrunk up with pain
> And therefore I'll all sharp reflections shun
> Poverty, Poetry, Pox are plagues enough for one.[38]

It is characteristic that Behn's next play, the one she concluded during this horrible predicament, should light-heartedly ridicule some of the fantastic medicines of the day.

The Emperor of the Moon had been interrupted by Charles II's death and Behn knew she was finishing and presenting it two years after its moment of inception, in a worse theatrical climate. She would not, however, publicly blame theatrical decay on King James. Rather, it was due to the ignorant and envious public and to factional politics, which she once hoped had died with the Popish Plot: 'the only diversion of the town now, is high dispute, and public controversies in taverns, coffee-houses, &c.' Behn had to rival this noise more than ever, for her aim was to please the people not, as formerly, a king.

More narrative than her source play, *Arlequin, The Emperor of the Moon* was necessarily more coherent than its original, as Behn boasted, the French being 'content with almost any Incoherences'. (Earlier in her life she had regarded chauvinism as a Whig infection, but her short stay in France seems to have improved her language and increased her distaste for the people. Behn was now in tune with the anti-French mood in the country.) She was not about to interrupt a lifetime's habit and admit her debt, especially to a French work, and she allowed *Arlequin* to have provided only 'a very barren and thin hint of the Plot'.[39]

The story of *The Emperor of the Moon* is one of gullibility. This had been the mark of Behn's old City knights, although the scene here is supposedly Naples—incidentally connecting it with her other popular Neapolitan play, *The Rover*. Doctor Baliardo believes in a lunar world equivalent to the earth and holds to the comic rosicrucian doctrine, that only spirits should copulate with mortals. So convinced is he that he denies his daughter, Elaria, and his niece, Bellemante, their merely terrestrial lovers. Soon there are 'stratagems a-brewing', aided by Scaramouch and Harlequin.

The Emperor of the Moon caught the public mood in its mockery of belief in science and medicine, its contempt, so usual for Behn, of pedantic male scholarship, as well as its scorn of alchemy and astrology, increased now she and the nation knew of Monmouth's gullibility.[40] Medicine and love are comically entwined as wounds of the heart become physical and metaphysical; science and superstition merge. Telescopes and microscopes, the discoveries of Kepler and Galileo, founders of the new astronomy, are useless in the hands of fools who, with or without them, can see what they expect, in this case fantastic lunar voyages and other worlds remarkably similar to the Earth.[41] As Scaramouch comments, echoing Behn on many a foolish university student, 'this reading of books is a pernicious thing.'[42] Books like telescopes can only be of value to the already sensible; otherwise they magnify stupidity.

The Emperor of the Moon is a play about theatre, transformation, and pageantry. Harlequin concludes couplets, making them appear on Bellemante's tablet as if by magic. Scaramouch is an apothecary with a portable shop—another tribute to Rochester as Bendo here—a woman with a child, and a piece of tapestry. Disguises abound: Harlequin becomes ambassador from the moon and declares he can do whatever he wishes, even tickle himself to a laughing death.[43] Baliardo's house becomes a theatre within the theatre; dancers emerge from tapestries, revealing the theatricality of all life—indeed, when Elaria questions whether her father is mad, Bellemante shows that the theatrical circumstances of life might drive anyone so. The emphasis is on spectacle, on taking theatrical show to its limits.

In the final spectacular scene, Behn demanded ten blacked actors, two descending chariots, the embodied signs of the zodiac landing on the stage to a symphony of music, and the moon changing phases and coming on as a machine which opens to disgorge the lunar emperor to the sound of flutes. It is an operatic display, in which almost the whole cast—including Underhill as Dr Baliardo, Leigh and Jevon as Scaramouch and Harlequin, and the Mountforts and Rochester's protégée Sarah Cooke as the romantic leads—is assembled; spectacle follows spectacle, and a real marriage occurs within a fake scene. Finally, Baliardo, chastened by his exploded belief in the spectacle's reality, elegiacally echoes Shakespeare's last hero Prospero and commands: 'Burn all my Books.'[44] It is a triumphant finale to a play—and, as it turned out, to Behn's theatrical career of seventeen years.

The prologue prepared for the farcical pantomime of the play by taking stock of theatrical history—and inevitably Behn's own, since her work spanned a good deal of the Restoration. First, it argues, there was heroic drama, heroes and gods thundering across the stage. Soon, the audience was cloyed with 'Magnificence', weary of a bustle about love and honour. Then came 'humbler Comedy', which flourished until spectators grew uncomfortable at pictures of themselves and hid behind the excuse that women should not be seeing such stuff. But it was all 'feigned niceness'. Farce followed and people grumbled again. Nothing was left to try but something from a sixpenny raree show, like the famous speaking head which supposedly repeated what people said if they talked into its mouth.[45]

At this point, the prologue, spoken by the skeletal comic actor Jevon (for whom Behn had written her Harlequin, described in the play as a worn-out herring), was interrupted by this mechanical head. It rose on a twisted post from under the stage, accompanied by a booming voice. The joke was that, in Behn's version, the head had a Scottish or northern accent quite unlike Jevon's and was given to singing Scots songs; what with this and Jevon's not speaking loudly enough, the theatrical 'Cheat' was betrayed. When this too passed, there would be only puppets left to entertain, appropriately since they echoed the woodenness of people who could not value art.[46]

However insulting the prologue, *The Emperor of the Moon* captured the spirit of the times when it was put on in March 1687, the only new theatrical work of the month. Despite Gould's envious strictures, it avoided any bawdry and ambiguous morality and was sheer farce, the nearest England had seen to pantomime.[47] For Behn, it was also the nearest she had come to the Jonsonian play with its stylised

characters and tight construction. Sure of her own powers and achievement, she could afford to allow comparison of her work with that of
the man with whom she had been so often berated and yet with whom,
because of her name, she had been coupled. Some of her alchemical
vocabulary came from Ben Jonson's *Alchemist*, and the fantastical physical humour approached his, as when Scaramouch joked about the fire
and metal god Vulcan turning the smith's faeces to iron: when consti-
pated, he could be cured with a magnet.[48] With its advantages and
innovations, *The Emperor of the Moon* became second in popularity only
to *The Rover*, exceeding *The Luckey Chance*.[49] Indeed it became so well
known that, in 1711, the *Spectator* could refer familiarly to it when a
player asserted he had acted 'several Parts of Houshold-stuff with great
Applause', among them 'one of the Men in the Hangings in the *Emperor
of the Moon*' (26 March 1711).

Intended formerly for King Charles himself, the dedication of the play
now went unsolicited to another Charles, whom Behn seems to have
known slightly, the young Marquis of Worcester, cousin of her patron,
the Duke of Norfolk. She passed swiftly over the necessary eulogy of his
'Mighty Mind' and 'uncommon Wit', spending more time on his 'Glorious
Father', the ex-Cromwellian and now staunchly Tory Duke of Beaufort,
who had played an active part in quelling the Monmouth Rebellion.
Perhaps she hoped for future patronage from this greater nobleman.
Although writing farce, the genre Dryden and other educated men thought
vulgar, Behn wanted to raise *herself* above the vulgar. So she insisted that
her version was not 'meant for the Numbers, who comprehend nothing
beyond Show and Buffoonry', but for such connoisseurs as the Marquis.
Her paradoxical, snobbish contempt for people, combined with her clear
desire for large audiences, fed on her conviction that no *readers* would
include themselves in the ignorant crowd.[50]

Invoking for Worcester her old vision of strong monarchy supported
by nobles supporting artists, Behn now made a symbiotic relation of
nobility and creative talent that somehow avoided the horror of the
plebeian market economy, encouraged the arts, and strengthened the
state. Such a Utopian patronage system had resulted in the English
Renaissance of Shakespeare, Fletcher, and Jonson and the flourishing
of many theatres where there was now only one. Given her Whig and
Protestant significance, Elizabeth I was not mentioned, but her shadow
was there, rebuking James II and his poor theatrical record.

Accepting the pedagogic and civic value of plays, that art and the
artist were part of the body politic, Behn now became mentor, not

simply client, to the aristocracy as she had been before, reiterating the point made in the Clifton and Hyde dedications, that a flourishing nation needed a flourishing theatre. '[S]ome leading Spirits, so Generous, so Publick, and so Indefatigable' must support it. Otherwise, people would find diversion in the dangerous activities of political and religious dispute, as they had in the Popish Plot and were showing every sign of doing again. Not only the young Marquis but James II should take note.

CHAPTER 26

Seneca Unmasqued and *La Montre*

'talking all, purely to prevent a dumb Entertainment'

James II wished to re-establish Roman Catholicism through freedom of worship not coercion, believing that tolerance would inevitably lead to Catholic supremacy. Since she appreciated religious tolerance whatever its cause, Behn supported his efforts, as did Henry Nevil Payne, and the pair probably wrote government propaganda. Behn could not, however, avoid noticing that it was the aim of re-establishing Catholicism rather than religious tolerance that struck the bulk of the populace; most equated the former firmly with arbitrary government.

In the country at large, to be a Catholic was even now not especially advantageous but, around the King, it was increasingly so. In Evelyn's sour words, 'Romanists [were] swarming at court with greater confidence than ever had been seen in England since the Reformation' and, to some, it appeared that a Catholic conversion was the only route to court and royal patronage. Despite success with *The Emperor of the Moon*, Behn still could not find the contemporary theatre a secure source of income and, along with other political poets who wished to prosper, she must have felt the kind of pressure the dying Rochester had suffered from Burnet. Dryden succumbed and was converted to Catholicism. He had been moving in the direction for some months, but the timing made his enemies rejoice.

Behn probably shared the nation's cynicism and, feeling her own relative obscurity, she may, in a moment of pique against a man she envied as well as admired, have written a vicious and popular attack on the conversion. It was called by various names from 'Satyr on Doctor Dryden' to 'On Dryden Renegade' and it mocked the Poet Laureate for his opportunism. On more than one manuscript, Aphra Behn's name has been added to the poem and this is sufficient to make her a serious candidate for authorship. The lampoon's mockery of Catholic doctrine would be unusual for her, but not quite foreign: in *The Island of Love*, she had recently written, 'No pamper'd *Levits* are in Pension here; / ...No Oyl, fine Flower, or Wines of mighty price, / The subtle Holy Cheats to Gormandize'—not the words of someone who valued priests or transubstantiation, a major Catholic belief. In *The Fair Jilt*, the story she now created from the sensational events in Antwerp in the 1660s, Behn exploited English obsession with popery as extravagant ritual and secret vice by setting her heroine in a beguinage so lax it comes close to the lewd picture of nuns as cloistered whores so beloved of contemporary pornographers.

Yet, there is much against Behn's writing the verses on Dryden too. First is that she herself was hinting publicly at a leaning towards the faith.[1] It is unlikely that she ever became an open Catholic—or she would have been mocked along with other converts. She might have been a 'Church-Papist', someone who was a Catholic in some circles, but attended Anglican services to be on the safe side; more likely, given her repeated scepticism, she used her cultural sympathy for Catholicism to suggest a beneficial belief. Second, although Behn's relationship with the Laureate had been chequered and she may privately have assumed something of Rochester's later dislike, Dryden had been conspicuously kind in taking her into his Ovid project and praising her verse. She was always complimentary of him in her published poetry and, only a few years earlier, she had written to Tonson of Dryden 'in whose esteeme I wou'd chuse to be rather than any bodys in the world'; in a recent dedication she called him 'the charming and Incomparable Mr *Dryden*'. True, he did omit her from his tradition of modest female poets (all dead it should be noted), and, after her death, he referred to the licence which gave 'some scandall to the modesty of her sex'. Yet he also accepted that times had changed and that Behn had never been more lewd than himself: 'I am the last man who ought, in justice to arraign her, who have been myself too much a libertine.'[2]

A further three considerations are, first, that the verses are rather out of Behn's own line—her accepted satire tends to be more baroque, more suggestive, less crude, less explicit and less funny than this poem; second, that, at about the time Dryden's conversion was provoking satire among the wits, she copied 'Dryden Renegade' into 'Astrea's Booke' under the heading, 'Another on Mr Bays', an oddly unpossessive action if she had in fact authored it. Finally, Behn was a firm and sometimes paid supporter of the monarch whose chief poetic servant Dryden was and whose religion he now shared.

If Behn did not write the satire, someone wished to make it appear that she did, perhaps to deflect attention from another, perhaps to make tension between two of the foremost 'Tory Poets'. As with the posthumous short stories, a candidate may again be the violently anti-Catholic Tom Brown, who made great literary hay out of Dryden's conversion. He acknowledged verses beginning 'Traytor to God, and Rebel to thy Pen, / Priest-ridden Poet'; he also wrote a lampoon called *The Laureat* (1687) in which Dryden is 'Condemn'd to Live in thy Apostate Rhimes' and is abused as a 'Scandal to all Religions, New and Old', a 'lewd... Profligate'.[3] Brown badgered Dryden throughout his life and even after it: 'His Death, alas! affected ev'ry Body, / And fetcht deep Sighs and Tears from ev'ry Noddy,' he mocked.[4] It does not seem beyond possibility that he was the author of the earlier mockery as well.

As for Behn, Dryden's friends cannot have assumed any ill-will in her, or suspected her authorship. In his elegy, Alexander Oldys imagined her as one of the poets greeting Dryden on his arrival in heaven—incidentally providing the only image of Behn in a Christian afterlife.

In reality Dryden, Behn, and the other playwrights were all in the same boat, all searching for any means to make an adequate living, whether this meant trying to ingratiate themselves with the court, writing lampoons, or copying for whoever would pay. From the ascribed publications of the time, it seems above all to have meant making 'Servile translation[s]'. Over these years they poured from Behn's pen.

Although it was considered a lesser art than original composition, translation had some status through association with the classics. So, in this necessary strategy, as in her switch to state panegyrics, Behn increased her literary if not her financial status. Indeed, her very casualness in translating for publication suggests a new and comfortable confidence.

She had given the subject much thought, some of which she expressed in a commendatory poem to Henry Higden, Dryden's friend, yet another witty lawyer from the Middle Temple with poetic ambition. He had translated a satire of the Roman Juvenal for Tonson, putting it into modern dress on the reasonable assumption that Juvenal's brutal Rome much resembled Restoration London. His 'Brat', as he called his work, was not popular, and either Tonson dropped Higden, or Higden dropped Tonson. When he translated a further Juvenal satire, Higden turned to Randal Taylor, the trade publisher who had brought out part of Behn's *Love-Letters* and whom he probably had to subsidise. To gain a better reception for this second volume, he commissioned some renowned praise-writers: Dryden, Behn and Elkanah Settle.

Higden had been thoroughly vexed by the Whig playwright Thomas Shadwell, who had borrowed his manuscript of the Juvenal translation, quickly printed his own version, and then mocked those who paraphrased the ancients, or in his image 'patched silk with homely wool'. Shadwell's insistence that only a few elite moderns like himself could understand the classical writers was directed, Behn surmised, at herself as well as Higden, since Shadwell cared for her no more than Higden. She was, therefore, doubly pleased to be asked to write for the new volume, which quite flouted Shadwell's opinion on classical translation. In his commendatory poem, Dryden saw Higden tempering Juvenal, making us 'laugh our Spleen away'. Behn, however, saw him as actually allowing greater expression to spleen; to Higden's list of *bêtes noires*—fops, rich upstart citizens, the waddling 'Body Politick', gigolos and the decaying old—she could therefore add her own personal ones: clergymen and canting female spectators.

Behn knew Higden's previous volume had failed and she was ready with comfort. Some had agreed with Shadwell in being uneasy at a modern-dress production of Juvenal and Higden had been blamed for choosing to render Latin hexameters as English tetrameters, where heroic couplets might have seemed more proper. (Dryden later chose this form when he himself wrote an English rendition of Juvenal.) So, Behn repeated what she had said to Edward Howard back in 1671 when his play had flopped: failure was the fault not of the ambitious and innovative author, but of unsophisticated and conventional readers.

> Perhaps there may be found some *Carping Wit*,
>   May blame the Measures of thy *Lines*,
> And cry,—Not so the *Roman* Poet writ;
> Who drest his *Satyr* in more lofty Rhimes.
> But thou for thy Instructor *Nature* chose,
> That *first* best Principle of *Poetry*,
> And to thy Subject didst thy *Verse* dispose,
> While in Harmonious Union both agree.
> Had the *Great Bard* thy *Properer Numbers* view'd,
> He wou'd have lay'd his stiff Heroicks by,
> And this more *Gay*, more *Airy* Path pursu'd,
> That so much better leads to *Ralliery.*
> *Wit* is no more than *Nature* well exprest;
>   And He fatigues and toyles in vain
>   With *Rigid Labours*, breaks his Brain,
> That has *Familiar Thought* in lofty Numbers drest.[5]

Now that she considered poets with aristocrats as the guardians of the ordered state, Behn was eager to defend those who were attacked for serious work. Sensible poets must stick together as surely as peers. As for translators, the best principle was to follow nature, to write what came naturally to the time and place in which they lived.

Behn herself could not work on the classics without help and for her own next translation she turned from the crude satirical Juvenal to the smooth, sceptical and epigrammatic Frenchman, the Duke of La Rochefoucauld. He was a daring choice for a woman author, since he was famous for finding vice in the apparently most robust virtue, a habit more suited to an aristocratic man than to a common woman.[6] Inevitably La Rochefoucauld associated Behn again with the Hobbes–Lucretius group of freethinkers and sceptics, and with the pre-conversion Rochester. Despite all the pressures to Catholic piety, it seems that she had not much changed her religious views.

Yet Behn's attraction to the *Maximes* suggests some subtle movement within her overall sceptical position. Lucretius had allowed a vision of pastoral serenity, but now Behn saw something more savage in human nature, while her faith in reason, so ringingly expressed in her poem to Thomas Creech, had shifted towards Rochester's doubt—albeit without Rochester's Christian tinge. La Rochefoucauld too was thoroughly scep-tical of reason's ability to control the needs and desires of the body. He revealed his opinion in mockery of the Stoical Roman philosopher, Seneca, who believed that virtuous action could be brought about by right reason. In contrast to Seneca, La Rochefoucauld saw virtue linked to far less savoury impulses. This mockery Behn made central to her cynical translation, which, consequently, she called *Seneca Unmasqued*.

La Rochefoucauld was merciless in analysing the self-interest involved in human conduct, even in behaviour of the most idealistic type. He showed that 'there are very few Virtues very pure in the World, and that in the greatest part of our Actions, there is a mixture of Error, and Truth, of Perfection, and Imperfection, of Vice and of Virtue'. He found the heart of 'villanous Man corrupted by Pride and Self-Love'. Behn had long thought as much herself.

The cynical remarks on royal statecraft—clemency often being a mixture of laziness, fear and vanity, for example—had pertinence to the Stuarts, but she avoided noticing it. She also left without comment maxims about the supreme importance of chance or luck in life and of temperament in happiness. About three-quarters of the way through, however, she awoke and reordered maxims to create a section entitled

'Of Love'. Here people became foolish through overwhelming, often contrary passions in which self-interest always functioned: 'Even the most uninterested Love is no other than a Commerce where our Self-love proposes a Gain.' Closer to hatred than friendship, love was indefinable, softening the mind and pushing the body towards enjoyment 'after a great deal of mysterious trouble and expectation'.[7]

Seneca Unmasqued was far less polished than Behn's earlier French 'translation', *The Island of Love*. She had spent a great deal of costly time on the latter, and she could not afford as much again: writing was physically laborious and she probably did not wish the expense of an amanuensis. So *Seneca Unmasqued* was often careless and incorrect, as when Behn rendered 'On est quelquefois aussi différent de soi-même que des autres' as the muddled, 'We are oftentimes farther from knowing our selves than we are from that of others.' Whatever its difference in quality, however, the work was mischievously tied to *The Island of Love* through the two characters, Lysander and Aminta, who intruded into several maxims on love. Behn even personalised the pair to herself and a lover when she translated the French 'on' as 'I'.

Three maxims in particular suggest self-reference: 'If you believe you love *Amynta*, for the love of *Amynta*, you are deceived,' 'You ought to indure and bear with that fault in *Amynta*, which she has Wit and Candor to own,' and 'I am more happy in being deceived by *Lysander* than in being undeceived.' They lead intentionally and codedly to the dedication of the work by 'Astrea' or Behn, so often called 'Aminta' in poems, to a man named 'Lysander'. He is the double of the person who entered *The Luckey Chance* to accuse the heroine of talkativeness and who, as Alexis, had blamed Aphra Behn for the same fault.

As ever, she guarded more than she revealed, for much of the jokesy, seemingly intimate address to Lysander in her dedication was actually an unacknowledged translation of a French foreword to a 1665 edition of La Rochefoucauld. This tried to place the *Maximes* in a Christian context in which self-love was also condemned, and was probably added to counter church criticism of its pervasive cynicism. Behn omitted the Christian placing, but kept the familiar tone. Thus, with the help of the French mediator, she was 'at this time' able to put herself on to a level with the aristocratic La Rochefoucauld, the 'Duke'—and the English earls, Rochester and Mulgrave: 'speaking for him, and my self...I can speak of nothing under *Monsieur* the Duke and I'. She could then assume the prestige of the amateur aristocrat: if the work does not please, she quipped, ''twill spoil neither of our Reputations: since we both of us pretend to some other Pieces, that have indured the Test, and passed for Good and Currant Wit.' In this insouciant mode Behn could separate herself from 'the Dramatick poor Devils that depend on the uncertain Humours of the Stage and Town' and from the 'trading Poet[s]'; instead she could become a courtly 'Man of Quality and Wit'.[8] The manoeuvre by which she feigned being what she so palpably was not resembles her ploy at the beginning of *The False Count* when, in a violently Tory prologue, she declared herself a convert Whig.

Yet this time Behn *wanted* to be part of what she counterfeited. Consequently, she could not easily keep up the pretence. When she mocked Seneca for despising worldly blessings while enjoying wealth, love and pleasure, she made him into an early Roman version of the hypocritical Puritan and alluded to her own real predicament: 'I should have loved to have been a Philosopher at this rate, and could be contented amidst such abundance, to have recommended and extoll'd Moderation and Poverty to the World.'

'Lysander' emerges vibrantly from the dedication. He sounds a little like the old Hoyle in his censorious self-satisfaction, and a lot like the recent Alexis. There is more about business and virtue than Hoyle provoked, less about political difference, which, since Behn had been so thoroughly and publicly politicised by the Popish Plot years, would now have been a chasm.[9] Hoyle was apparently taciturn with her, but otherwise a facetious wit, as well as a bully and a brawler, whereas this Lysander is a grave young man. While Behn is teasingly fond of Lysander–Alexis, she does not appear romantically obsessed with him as she had been, fitfully, with Hoyle. Although he appears with the 'Complexion' of a lover, Lysander with Alexis seems to be holding back for some reason. By now Behn knew the best and worst of Hoyle—as did the public—and would not have had to speculate from 'Complexion':

there is not one Sentence but is applicable to some body or other, so you will find many that will touch your self: and many more that I doubt not but you will lay at my door, especially any Satyr on our Sex: but since there is wherewithal to quit Scores, do your worst. I know too well you have abundance of Gravity, to the loss and destruction of many an honest hour, which might have been past more gayly if you had pleased to have laid by that (sometimes necessary) humour; and that face of dull business, enough to mortifie all thoughts of Mirth about one. I know you have a great deal of that which my Reflections tell you passes for Vertue, nay even your self it deludes

387

with that Opinion, as well as the World: you should be a Lover too, if one will believe you or your Complexion; and to my knowledge you have goodness enough to pardon all the faults you will find here, at least you dissemble it well, and that will do as well. These Motives, joyned to the desire I have to let you see you are more in my head than you imagine, oblige me to chuse you from out the number of my few Friends, to address this part of my handy-work to.

Again Behn refers to the man's taciturnity and his criticism of her loquaciousness, as she had in the supposed letters to Hoyle and in the more recent Alexis poems:

I am so us'd to be impertinent in *Lysanders* Company that 'twill appear no more strange than what he is entertained with every time I have the happiness of seeing him: where his grave silence, and scarcity of speaking (afflicting enough to me) gives me an occasion to run into the other Extreme of talking all, purely to prevent a dumb Entertainment, for which I have many times met with wise Reproofs, as 'tis very likely I may now, and which will as little work upon the temper of a Woman of my humour, as Mercy to a hardened *Whig*.[10]

This was no dedication to the great for money. That Behn decided to throw away a begging opportunity argues either a sense of the carelessness of her work or an overpowering personal need to say something in public to this fascinating and infuriating man. Presumably her 'few Friends' recognised the portrait.

An equal mixture of the carelessness and skill displayed in *Seneca Unmasqued* went into the rendition of *Aesop's Fables* soon afterwards. Behn's recent poetic publications, especially the *Poems upon Several Occasions* with *The Island of Love*, had given her a reputation for competence, and, when the (predominantly) Whig Francis Barlow, the painter and engraver, wanted to reissue his 1666 volume of Aesop engravings, a work dear to his heart, he turned to her despite their political differences. The original work, some sheets of which might have perished in the Great Fire which destroyed so many publications, had had verses by Thomas Philipott stretching from six to sixteen lines. The irregularity made the engraved pages untidy, the longer poems often being squashed to fit the space allowed. The work might be better served with her tiny, concise and uniform verses of four lines for the fable and two for the moral.[11]

Behn's main source for her verses was Philipott, his words and rhymes sometimes being identical to hers. As no doubt with some of the collaborative theatrical updating, Behn was here refashioning an English style of twenty years earlier, smoothing, generalising, omitting out-of-date linguistic crudeness and, in this case, infiltrating her own views. In the process she lost some of the earlier vigour. All being elegant, it was difficult to inject a shock into mock heroics, and the fable in which a rhetorical wolf leisurely questions a drowning vernacular fox loses its comedy. (Indeed the colloquial Philipott is generally better at animal 'speech' than Behn.) Sometimes, too, Behn was just more slapdash than Philipott and in Fable XL, 'The Porcupines and Adders', she made a moral in which his contrast of force and fraud was collapsed into a similarity of force and war. But sometimes her elegance worked:

> *An hungry Viper neare a Black Smiths forge,*
> *Snatcht at a file his eager maw to gorge,*
> *But the tough steele his feebler teeth repells,*
> *Its dinted force his jaws with anguish fills.*

As with parts of *Seneca Unmasqued*, Behn set the fables in the present English culture of debauchees, fops, sparks, aged lovers, and gilded equipages. The toad exploding with venom became the would-be wit. Ageing herself, she was preoccupied with horrific age, the old man pressing himself on the young girl, the old 'worn out Beauty' trying to pass 'for eighteen'.

Religion, important to Philipott, was largely abandoned and Barlow asked Behn to replace it with politics. Fables were famously used for political purposes and the addition would be a selling point. Clearly *selling* was the purpose for the flexible Barlow, since, on the analogy of cardgames and games of state, he had already produced series of playing-cards with cartoons that adapted to changing times: his one on the Popish Plot from a Whiggish point of view was, when the Titus Oates stories collapsed, redone to reveal Whig corruption instead.

Behn of course had no difficulty with the commission. Monmouth had been dead for two years, although his cause of a Protestant alternative was alive. He became a youth misled and his mistaken ambition was set in a context of opposition corruption, plots and sham trials. As ever, Behn avoided sympathy for the underdog, whether the victim of royal anger or the poor. Everyone, illegitimate son or poor man, would be better if he stayed in place. As for democracy, it should be roundly resisted: no inch should be given to the rabble, lest they take all. Where Philipott, who had just survived the Civil War, reflected on the damage of civil strife, Behn pushed the Stuart Royalist message of strong central government—so much so that she sometimes ignored the fable and tacked on a quite different, clashing moral. In Fable XXII, Philipott's appropriate conclusion was that the poor often did not get their rightful share, squeezed as they were by the rich and powerful. Perhaps revealing herself the daughter of an Overseer of the Poor in her attitudes, Behn omitted the compassion and made this into 'Proud Senatts thus by easy Monarchs thrive / Incroaching on their whole prerogative.'[12]

Despite all this philosophical and political work, Behn knew her reputation in translating was for amorous writing. She was fluent and skilful there, where she could be awkward and tired in other modes. So, despite her feeling that she had been insufficiently rewarded for *The Island of Love*, it was her fluency that made her take up the French allegory *La Montre* by de Bonnecorse, as well as the second part of de Tallemant's *Voyages*, which she had begun to translate before Charles II's death. Both were long and there were times over the next months when Behn must have rued the day she had set up as an authority on love. Earlier on in her poetic career, she had expressed earthy sentiments in pastoral mode. These translation-imitations were more simply elegant, more *précieuse*, more French. She made no great claim for them, as she was doing by now for her plays and original poetry, perhaps knowing they were in a style that would not survive her time.

Published in 1686, *La Montre* was not a 'servile' translation. Closer to Behn's habits in *The Island of Love* than in *Seneca Unmasqued*, it formed one in a line of interlocking pastoral works, different from the tone and tenor of her contemporary plays. As in *Seneca Unmasqued*, Behn again revealed her increasing need to surround herself with a fictive world in which characters travelled from one book to another, while an image of herself flitted in and out. Its hero was actually a friend of the character, Lysidas, from *The Voyage to the Island of Love* and the talkative author made a guest appearance, as she had in the dedication to Lysander in *Seneca Unmasqued*.

Balthazar de Bonnecorse's original work of 1664 was a fantastic account of the lover Damon's day, organised by his demanding mistress Iris and regulated through a watch, the centre of which is a Cupid indicating hours and duties.[13] In 1671 de Bonnecorse had allowed the man to make a gallant reply. Behn combined both works in a mixture of prose and poetry, freely translated into the English language and, occasionally, culture—Damon walks in St James's Park and the Mall— although, in the main, it still breathes of Parisian salons more than London taverns. Damon's wonderfully leisurely day begins with his lying in bed for an hour and dressing for another, as he languidly tells his valet to spare the perfume and let him be negligent in dress because his love is absent. At the end of the instructions and the day, Damon responds by providing an allegorical heart-shaped watch case, decorated with cyphers encoding love, and a looking-glass which hourly tells Iris of her charms. This allows Damon to write the kind of amorous cata- logue of complexion, hair, eyes, mouth, neck, and hands more sensually enjoyed by Philander in *Love-Letters*. The picture of the lovers, only occasionally veering towards the erotic, is far more static and playful than anything in *The Island of Love*.

Now and again Behn grew inspired to write originally. For example, she expanded the short section on visits of friends into a discussion of how a woman might be fooled by seductive men. Armed with La Rochefoucauld's maxims about self-love, she wrote: 'I have seen a Man dress, and trick, and adjust his Looks and Meen, to make a Visit to a Woman he lov'd not, nor ever cou'd love…and only for the Vanity of making a Conquest upon a Heart, even unworthy of the little Pains he has taken about it.' Undoubtedly she herself had suffered from such company, especially in her time of relative fame. Again, Behn suggested her continued susceptibility when she deplored the man who 'lies in his Looks, he deceives with his Meen and fashion, and cheats with every Motion, and every Grace he puts on: He cozens when he sings or dances, he dissembles when he sighs; and every thing he does, that wilfuly gains upon her, is Malice propense'. Yet the lady in the scene admits vanity is universal and that she herself sometimes finds 'a secret Joy in being Ador'd, though I even hate my Worshipper'. Nothing is simple where sexuality is invoked.

Then Behn herself, Behn as *Aminta*, Behn as author-lover, Behn as talker and mocker of silent men, made her unscheduled appearance. It was as if, knowing her own notoriety, she could not resist putting in a coded signature. So the 'angry Aminta' lambasted a self-assured flatterer and, when Damon is urged not to have an 'unnecessary, and uncom- plaisant Sullenness', Behn inserted her own poem to Alexis, in which she is accused of 'Loving a Talker'.[14]

Her customary themes peeped through as well, lovers as gamesters throwing dice or the erotic charm in gossip, news and scandal:

> *When I hear a Swain enquire*
> *What Gay* Melinda *does to live,*
> *I conclude, there is some Fire*
> *In a Heart Inquisitive:*
> *Or 'tis, at least, the Bill, that's set,*
> *To shew*, The Heart is to be Let.[15]

In another place, Behn swerved off to praise Windsor Castle—and the new waterworks made by her old inventor friend, Samuel Morland.[16] (Poor Sir Samuel needed some support these days since, having abandoned marrying impecunious young women—like Carola Harsnett—who invariably died, he had decided in 1687 to improve his own sorry financial position by wedding an heiress—only to find himself as thoroughly duped as the Carletons by their supposed 'German Princess'.) Although Behn had obviously received no house and garden for her sycophancy in her Pindarics, it sounds as if she had at least been invited inside a royal palace: in the passage she stressed she was looking at the 'In-side of this magnificent Structure' as well as the outside. She had not been there before and the splendour of Charles II's refurbishment astonished her. Always moved by opulent art, she was enthralled by the carvings of Grinling Gibbons and the wall paintings of Antonio Verrio; she thought it all a fitting setting for 'the most Fair, and most Charming of Queens, and the most Heroick, Good, and Just of Kings…such Earthly Gods'.[17] Evidently Behn was preparing for another panegyric assault on the court.

La Montre was a huge work which, following habit and convention, she called 'this little unlaboured Piece' when she dedicated it to the young lawyer, Peter Weston. He was chosen because he was *not* one of the young men she had formerly honoured, but instead a beautiful, witty, *modest* and *religious* youth, a rare combination. Anxious about the public reputation for erotic writing she had gained from *The Island of Love*, Behn used the opportunity to insist that she too honoured 'chaste' love and that she had here presented a couple who did not end in bed. Far from the Rovers of the 1670s, Weston was praised for his 'Abhorrence to Lewdness'. To such a man she was 'A. Behn' not Astrea. It is hoped that his 'Happy' parents, to whom he was such a credit, paid her for the dedication and that he appreciated it when he became an eminent barrister.

La Montre marked the entry of a new publisher in Behn's life, William Canning and his printer Holt, mentioned in 'Astrea's Booke'. With Canning she would be closely identified during her final years—indeed she became his major author. For this first venture with him Behn provided commendatory poems from her friends, Nahum Tate, George Jenkins, and Richard Ferrar. Predictably they praised her for improving on de Bonnecorse—Jenkins actually claimed she made a writer out of the Frenchman who had little merit before she softened the coarseness of his 'Rubbish': 'We owe to thee, our best Refiner, more / Than him, who first dig'd up the rugged Ore.'[18] Outside the circle of well-wishers, however, the mocking Matthew Prior thought the pretty frothy work too long:

> The Poetess Sung: at length swore She'd prove
> That She and Jack Hoyle taught the whole Age to Love
> And on with't She ran, nor had ended 'till now
> But Phoebus reprov'd her, and gave her to know
> That her Tongue went too fast, and her Love watch too slow.[19]

Avoiding the eroticism of *The Island of Love*, *Lycidus*, to which Behn returned after a gap of two or three years, also differed from the chaste *La Montre*. Using both Tallemant's first and second *Voyages*, Behn produced a new work, closer to the French original than *The Island of Love* had been; it was more worldly and sophisticated than either *The Island of Love* or *La Montre*.

Lycidus, the new hero, becomes a hedonist and extrovert, rendered so by experience: 'I was ly'd and flattered into Wit, jilted and cozen'd into Prudence, and, by ten thousand Vows and perjured Oaths, reduced to Sense again; and can laugh at all my past Follies now.'[20] Henceforth, he is resolved to pursue love 'in such a manner as it shall never cost me a sigh'. In *Lycidus* coquetry and flirtation replace the romance and languor of *The Island of Love*, and characters assume not pastoral but theatrical names like Bellamante and Belinda. The god of love is no longer the power of the earlier poem, certainly not the tyrant of 'Love Arm'd' from *Abdelazer*, instead he rules 'with Reason and with Wit'. He ridicules 'Whining Passion', suitable only for 'Boys and formal Asses', and accepts love as masquerade—Lycidus is just as successful with his false sighs as with his sincere:

> I never vow'd nor sigh'd in vain
>   But both, tho false, were well receiv'd.
> The Fair are pleas'd to give us pain,
>   And what they wish is soon believ'd.
> And tho I talk'd of Wounds and Smart,
>   Loves Pleasures only toucht my Heart.

The hints of a Restoration world of wits, coxcombs and fops have increased—although politicians are scarcer—and people fear lampoons as well as rejection. Always fascinated by social and intellectual codes, Behn relished the description of the realm of Intelligence, suitable only for a few, where communication occurs with signs, cyphers and half-words—an Arcadian version of Antwerp. The true lover becomes the fooled spy who has insufficient intelligence, but, for the fake one, the pleasures are evident: he can with the aid of codes take 'all freedoms, without controul'. The danger is solipsism, a descent into a private code, for 'there are as many Languages as persons', as well as a tiring promiscuity—when once the self is separated from words, there is no end to the roles it can play.

Cynically Lycidus succeeds in bedding two women. The effect is more comic than erotic as the verse falls into doggerel rhythm. The end finds the hero caught by one beloved *in flagrante* with the other. He has overplayed matters and he has little option but to turn from women to glory. He will pursue a public career, as his female lovers of course cannot.

Behn's many additions to Tallemant tend towards complexity, to understanding the mechanism of feeling, the selfish love of a lover on the rebound, the confusion in the mind which registers conflicting emotions, the duplicities of regret. Without allowing herself to enter her poem directly as in *La Montre*, Behn as author yet gives a sense of an older literary and amorous person looking elegiacally back over experience; to the description of the new lover of the beloved she adds youth, where the French had only beauty, and she interrupts the work to lament her own 'easiness', resolving 'to be no longer a *Mark-out-fool* for the Rhiming Wits...to aim their Dogrel at'.[21] Embittered life must be mitigated by amorous play, a play that has little to do with 'truth'. In *Seneca Unmasqued* and a poem beginning 'Cease, cease, *Aminta* to complain', written at about the same time, Behn declared a preference for pleasing duplicity:

> I lov'd my Life too eagerly away
> To have disturb'd thee with too long a stay.
> Ah! cou'd you not my dying Heart have fed
> With some small Cordial Food, till I was dead?

In this poem the speaker determined to accept her misery when abandoned by a 'Youth' for someone else, realising sadly that she had simply loved 'too late'. Resignedly she awaited the moment when her 'hopeless love' would die of its own accord.[22] Lycidus too accepts the death of love but, being a young man not an ageing woman, he does it more noisily and egoistically. In the end, however, for all their half sincere, half insincere posing, young man and older woman come together in being 'in a Humor not to dye', whatever died within and without them.[23]

The ending of *Lycidus* sounds like Behn's own farewell to her Rochesterian world and her genre of escapist and enriching pastoral poetry:

> I lookt back on all those happy shades, who had been conscious of my softest pleasures, and a thousand times I sighing bid 'em farewel, the Rivers, Springs and Fountains had my wishes that they might still be true and favor Lovers, as they had a thousand times done me. These dear remembrance[s], you may believe stay'd some time with me, yet I wou'd not for an Empire have return'd to 'em again, nor have liv'd that life over a new I had so long and with so much pleasure persu'd.[24]

As Behn's pastoral poetic career began, according to her memoirist, with a prophetic vision of a Cupid floating on the Thames between England and Holland, so it closed here with an elegy to her created Arcadia.

Although the poems affixed to *Lycidus* also have an elegiac quality, there is one notable exception. In these final years, Behn's verse came to be dominated by women—or perhaps it's more accurate to say that she was simply impressed with beauty and youth wherever they were found, in man, woman, boy or in those delicious beings who refused to submit to gender simplicity. Her half-utopian, half-earthy feelings were most perfectly captured (and hidden) in a poem which could indeed be by a man to a woman, a woman to a man, a woman to a woman or one of either sex to a transvestite or, as the last line suggests, an hermaphrodite—in short any kind of being as long as s/he is young. It is the sort of poem Mirtilla of *The Younger Brother* might have written.

'To the fair Clarinda, who made Love to me, imagin'd more than Woman' opens:

> Fair lovely Maid, or if that Title be
> Too weak, too Feminine for Nobler thee,
> Permit a Name that more Approaches Truth:

And let me call thee, Lovely Charming Youth…
Against thy Charms we struggle but in vain
With thy deluding Form thou giv'st us pain,
While the bright Nymph betrays us to the Swain.

With her pastoral sexual imagery, Behn can as ever touch on risqué matters, even though the setting here is explicitly not Arcadia but England where a concept of 'Crime' exists and sex is fixed:

In pity to our Sex sure thou wer't sent,
That we might Love, and yet be innocent:
For sure no Crime with thee we can commit;
Or if we shou'd—thy Form excuses it.
For who, that gathers fairest Flowers believes
A Snake lies hid beneath the Fragrant Leaves.

Thou beauteous Wonder of a different kind,
Soft *Cloris* with the dear *Alexis* join'd;
When e'r the Manly part of thee, wou'd plead
Thou tempts us with the Image of the Maid,
While we the noblest Passions do extend
The Love to *Hermes*, *Aphrodite* the Friend.[25]

At one minute seeming a 'beauteous Woman', at another Clarinda hides the 'Snake', so often the penis in Behn's erotic poetry. She is Cloris and Alexis, manly and maidenly, Amazon—Clorinda was an Amazonian character from Tasso—and girl, a physical version of the intellectual and sexual Behn, praised by her admirers as both masculine and feminine. The final line declaring that love is given to Hermes, the male, friendship to Aphrodite, the female, keeps her or him a divided hermaphrodite.

'Hermaphrodite' was a tricky term: sometimes it was associated with alchemy to denote a kind of perfection from the creative union of opposites; elsewhere it was used for a freak, as when Behn herself was mocked as 'an Hermaphrodite' with 'neither Witt enough for a Man, nor Modesty enough for a Woman'. It could also denote an effete man or a bisexual woman: a relative of Colepeper's wife, Anne Frecheville, Lady of the Bedchamber to the Princess Anne, was described in one satire as having 'another sex to spare' and in another as 'Hermaphrodite' Frecheville with her dildo.[26] Clarinda is the epitome of all the seductive and ambiguous boy-girls Behn had for so long been creating, the Hellenas, Silvias and Olivias. Indeed so, for, above all, Clarinda is of the theatre— especially the Renaissance theatre from which Behn took so much inspiration.

The other poems of *Lycidus* express a more everyday reality. Some time in an autumn, probably of 1687, Behn went to Tunbridge Wells again for her health, taking with her two women friends, Gloriana and Eliza, whose mundane identities are unknown. Perhaps one might be the generous Madam Welldon of the posthumous dedication to *The Widdow Ranter*, a dedication which Behn was said to have desired; perhaps Eliza was Betty Taylor, her old poetic friend with a tendency to tipple. The visit was recorded in several poems by herself and her friends. Apolitical and gently gallant, they tended to avoid the passion caught in 'On Desire', which was published with them, as well as the shaded final tone of *Lycidus*.

Behn's group of friends is a muted older version of the one described in 'Our Cabal' many years before. Much of the society revealed in the poems is mild, quaint even, slightly absurd and intimate, and the hothouse sexual atmosphere caught in the earlier collections has diminished. One man sends a poem to Behn in thanks for a bottle of orange flower water; another dispatches a basket of fruit. Writing in verse from London to Tunbridge, a man complains that he cannot compose with Aphra Behn gone from the city and another moans of lethargy in her absence. Half London seemed to have disappeared to Kent and 'general dulness has possest the Town.' For one friend, the effort of rhyming has been too much and he will in future—that is if he cannot get down to Tunbridge himself—lapse into prose. Meanwhile, he salutes the three female friends, his 'mistresses', Gloriana, Eliza and Astrea. For all her years and ailments, Astrea is still the 'Charming Nymph', the 'Goddess of the Spring', 'alwaies Airy, Witty, Gay'.

With her reputation as analyst of love, Aphra Behn seems to have become an adviser or 'agony aunt' for the young. One woman wrote that, having been disappointed in a man she was prepared to receive, despite his owning no 'Sheep nor land'—a man to whom Behn may have introduced her—she was now planning to dedicate herself to Behn instead. Possibly her dedication included the writing of the 'Memoirs' some years after her friend's death, with its paradoxical concern both to rescue Behn as a modest woman and to display her as she is here, the 'gay and free' doyenne of love.

As *Lycidus* and its attached poems function as a kind of farewell to

Arcadia, so a Pindaric Behn wrote to the second Duke of Albemarle 'on his Voyage to His Government of Jamaica' concludes her line of political poems urging men from ease into business. The first one, written many years before, had been to 'Celadon', forced to leave for Ireland. By now, both the times and the characters have changed. The late 1680s had few Arcadian realms left and Christopher Monck, Duke of Albemarle, Granville's cousin and son of the great Interregnum general George Monck, was not the witty Celadon of the 1670s, but simply a wealthy man, to many a 'Scandal to that high name from whence he sprung'. Behn omitted the fact that he was a gambler who had run up vast debts to the Duchess of Mazarine, and a drunk called 'brawny *Kit*' in lampoons.[27]

During the Monmouth Rebellion, Albemarle had been given a chance to redeem himself, but James's victory at Sedgemoor owed nothing to his confused deployment of the Devon contingent, and he seemed to have little future at court.[28] But then he had the luck to become involved in an apparently hare-brained scheme: to set up a committee of Gentleman Adventurers to pay for an expedition to salvage a Spanish treasure ship, wrecked in the Caribbean. This had been in 1685 and, to popular amazement, in mid-June 1687 the expedition returned with vast quantities of treasure. Fabulously, he became £90,000 richer. Three months later, Albemarle was *en route* for Jamaica as governor. Between the revelation of money and his embarkation, Behn fired off her poem: he had become a possible patron. Recording the change in the times, herself and her subject, the effect of the verses was very different from those addressed to Celadon voyaging to Ireland. Celadon was going with reluctance, in no doubt that the leisured pastoral world he was quitting was more valuable than Irish politics to which he was called. Albemarle, however, is now urged to forsake an ease which seems more brutish than charming.

Behn's elegiac phase of poetry and translation was rounded off by a poetic death. Edmund Waller, the Cavalier poet who had made Penshurst into Arcadia for her and whose work she had admired when still a girl, the poet whose elegance, coupled with that of Abraham Cowley, had heralded the new age of smooth pastoral verse, died in October 1687 at eighty-one. It seemed the end of a literary era. A volume of elegies was planned and among the seven invited to write were Behn, her young friend Granville, and the Duchess of Mazarine's noble French admirer, Saint-Évremond. She and Saint-Évremond were the only writers of distinction in the volume.

Like so much in these years of ill-health, her poem was self-revelatory, even self-pitying, albeit in the conventional mode of Pindarics:

> How, to thy Sacred Memory, shall I bring
> (Worthy thy Fame) a grateful Offering?
> I, who by Toils of Sickness, am become
> Almost as near as thou art to a Tomb?
> While every soft, and every tender Strain
> Is ruffl'd, and ill-natur'd grown with Pain.

She should write a work of fancy, wit and judgement to such a poet but, in her present sickly state, her verses 'like Transitory *Flowers*, [will] decay'. Harping on her theme, that poet-prophets who, in the past, 'got so great Renown' were now ignored to the detriment of the state, she alludes to her other great evil: lack of money. Observing the decline of poetry, the richer Waller had yet been shielded from the effect, since '*Fortune* Elevated thee above / Its *scanty Gratitude*.' So he could do what Behn could not: scorn 'th'unthinking *Crowd*'.

Between allusions to her ill-health and her poverty, Behn described what Waller had meant to her in her youth. He had expanded her soul, taking her out of herself. Using her favourite biblical character of Moses, she made Waller into a poetic Charles II: Waller had led poets out of the dark morass of impenetrable style into the glories of clarity and elegance. Now, however, the darkness, poetic and political, was coming again: Waller in his '*Circulary Course*, didst see / The very *Life* and *Death* of Poetry'.

When she had written her poem, Behn sent it off to Abigail Waller, the poet's daughter-in-law, with a covering note apologising for any weakness in the verse,

> I can only say I am very ill and have been dying this twelve month, that they want those graces and that spirit which possibly I might have dress'd 'em in had my health and dulling vapours permitted me, however madam they are left to your finer judgement to determine whether they are worthy the honour of the press among those that celibrate Mr Waller's great fame, or of being doomed to the fire.

Happily her poem was not so 'doomed'. But, though it was the best in the volume, it might not entirely have pleased Mrs Waller. For, as Behn had ignored Rochester's conversion, so now she omitted mention of Waller's devotional verse. Close to death in her own apprehension, she was not preparing for it with Christian piety.

CHAPTER 27

❧

Part III of *Love-Letters* and Court Poetry

'very well understood by all good Men'

A phra Behn's sense that an era was coming to an end had much to do with her ill-health and perception of mortality. Where others yearned to retreat into childhood Christianity, she held to her scepticism: dissolution implied increase of pain followed by numbness and nothing. On a political level, her attitude also came from public events or, rather, a development in her understanding of them. This was codedly chronicled in the last, third, part of *Love-Letters*. What brought it about?

At the end of the second part, the intention of the work seemed to be in line with Behn's darkening picture of the once-celebrated rake: that the libertine Philander would observe political misery and suffer personal failure. So the story would become a Restoration parable about the self-destructive nature of political and libertine desire. In fact, the third part of *Love-Letters* swerved from this trajectory into something more cynical and anarchic: instead of taking Grey to destruction as the fictional fable seemed to require, it followed history and moderately rehabilitated him.[1]

The public image of Grey was clear. Long seen as the pimp for Monmouth, he was now, after Sedgemoor, both pimp and coward: '*Gray* turn's Tails, with his Horne made away: / God Curse me quoth *Gray*, if longer I stay....' None the less, he had pleaded for his life with more success than his leader Monmouth, cleverly weaving together confession and extenuation, admitting he had sinned against God in rebelling against his sovereign and confessing his role in the various plots and rebellions of the past years. Sensibly, he deflected blame on to the dead Earl of Shaftesbury and supported his confession with betrayal of his fellow rebels, at whose trials he testified. His great wealth also played its part: his price was apparently £40,000. Lampooners took note of the treachery: '...let there in his guilty Face appear, / The Rebells Malice, and the Cowards fear, / That future Ages in thy peice may see

401

/ Not his wife falser to his Bed, than to all Parties he.'[2] This view had been lightly anticipated by Behn in her first two parts of *Love-Letters*. In Part III, however, it collapsed and Philander was allowed neither simple treachery nor simple cowardice.

Behn began her *volte face* by reversing the relations of Monmouth and Grey. Cesario's mistress pimped for Philander rather than Philander pimping for his leader, as Grey was alleged to have done. Then Behn depicted Philander not as a selfish opportunist, but as a divided man within the rebel camp, in the thick of the invasion though, sadly, no longer believing in the cause. His actions at the ensuing Battle of Sedgemoor were then glossed:

> Some Authors in the Relation of this Battle affirm, That *Philander* quitted his Post as soon as the Charge was given, and sheer'd off from that Wing he commanded...he disliked the Cause, disapproved of all their Pretensions, and look'd upon the whole Affair and Proceedings to be most unjust and ungenerous: And all the fault his greatest Enemies could charge him with, was, That he did not deal so gratefuly with a Prince that loved him and trusted him; and that he ought frankly to have told him, he would not serve him in this Design; and that it had been more Gallant to have quited him that way, than this; but there are so many Reasons to be given for this more Politick and safe Deceit, than are needful in this place....[3]

Whatever readers might think of Grey after this treatment of Philander, they would surely judge the narrator of Part III of *Love-Letters* unprincipled. Behn was running out of invention and this passage was the nearest she came to expressing embarrassment publicly and to displaying her own complicity in unscrupulous politics.

As befitted a playwright of many voices, Behn could express a predominant view while holding various other ones balanced in her mind. The ability was surely embodied in the men with whom she had been friendly over the years, William Scot, George Marten, Jack Hoyle, Thomas Killigrew, Thomas Dangerfield and Henry Nevil Payne. All were ambiguous, unclear, flexible, two- or three-faced, possibly treacherous and violent men. It was as if Behn's own complex protean personality, as well as her outsider status in the aristocratic society she hymned, demanded such friends. As a professional writer and a hanger-on of the upper orders, she had to project a single image; yet, while publicly expressing political clarity as part of this image, she might also have communicated other murkier aspects of herself by consorting with those whose views and personalities were decidedly unclear or subversive, sometimes even opposite to her publicly professed ones. Behn was a rational Tory Royalist on the hustings and in the theatre, but, in more secretive moments, alone with her pen, she was also something that defied single labels. In the case of *Love-Letters*, however, her ambiguities were probably exploited (anonymously) by her commissioner into something close to conscious perfidy. In Part III more than the other parts, it was becoming clearer that this commissioner was the slipperiest man with whom she had had dealings, the Earl of Sunderland.

In 1683 and 1684, Monmouth had been a threat which needed controlling by Sunderland, so the discrediting of Grey could have been a means. By now, the oppositional politics that the dead Monmouth and the living Grey stood for was less *immediately* threatening, but, paradoxically, more powerful and potentially more invasive. After the treatments of Parts I and II and the known public scandals, Lord Grey would have to remain a dubious and ambiguous figure in Behn's work, but, to make the new political point, he would also need to be rehabilitated from downright villainy as much as possible. This interpretation may seem far-fetched, but intelligence activities included the disinformation and control of information through lampoons and fictions, just as much as spying.

An extraordinary feature of the later sections of *Love-Letters* is that, allowing for transformations and amalgamations of people and happenings, the events Behn chronicles for Philander follow so closely those of history. The actions of the first part had been common currency in London where the transcripts of Grey's trial for seduction were sold in the streets. The second part had been like a theatrical intrigue comedy and the plot had almost written itself with little help from history. But, with elongations, shortenings and re-arrangings of place and time, what she wrote in Part III followed in the actual rebel footsteps of Grey and Henrietta as they trundled around the Low Countries and Germany.

A month after arriving on the Continent with Henrietta Berkeley, the real Lord Grey, who according to lampoons had grown 'desperately poor', had sought employment with the Duke of Brandenburg in his territory of Cleve. Behn, however, held back Philander's move there until towards the end of Part II to elaborate on the relationships of both Silvia and Philander with Octavio within a context of absences and arrivals.[4] For the later Continental movements of Grey and Henrietta there were no pamphlets to hand and no reports in the *Gazette*.

During the Popish Plot, news had been disseminated as never before in unlicensed news sheets, but these had been largely suppressed in the Tory backlash after the Exclusion Crisis. To gain any reliable information, one had to be on the mailing list of the manuscript newsletters compiled by the clerks in Scotland Yard for the Secretaries of State; these had a monopoly of licensed news from spies, intercepted letters, and weekly reports from domestic and foreign correspondents. Behn was not one of the agents and ambassadors having access to these newsletters, although she might have seen them. Even this source, however, would not give her quite the detailed knowledge she evidently had. How did she come to know what she knew?

She may of course have had informants who travelled to the Continent at this time. The narrator speaks of talking to a page who is in love with Silvia, for example. Or she might have been used again for more espionage. If so, there is a delicious possibility that Behn took her Parts I and II of *Love-Letters* with her to the Low Countries and that Lady Henrietta read the book which made her notorious and came to know the author between Parts II and III. It is unlikely, however. Bampfield was back in place as an agent, garrulous as ever, and he mentioned no middle-aged 'shee spy'. Mainly, Behn's poor health argues against travel, as does the regularity of her productions in London.

A further, more likely possibility is that Behn read or heard of Grey's unpublished confession, to which Sunderland of course had access.[5] In addition, she may have seen secret-service documents which minutely recorded the activities of Grey and his entourage as they travelled round Holland, Flanders and Brandenburg.[6] Were Sunderland her commissioner, he could authorise Behn to inspect the original writings.[7] If she *did* read Grey's long-winded confession, she would have found no trace of Lady Henrietta, for her lover glossed over her seduction and elopement as a period of his own illness, and his escape from England became a solitary matter. Grey presented himself as a lonely and impecunious exile on the Continent, like Killigrew's Thomaso. He downplayed his part in the Monmouth preparation, concentrating on his simple desire to find somewhere he 'might live cheap' as he faced a prospect of 'being always a vagabond, and that a poor one too'.[8] Did Behn perhaps feel here the first stirrings of sympathy for a man who was undoubtedly a rogue but one not so far removed from her Willmore except in politics, driven to expedients not far from her own?[9]

Behn could not have been *much* surprised by anything she read. As far back as 1684, she had already been creating an unstable, fickle and deceitfully self-indulgent figure to stand in for the austere Lord Grey. There were not many who would at that time have portrayed Grey as *already* unfaithful to Monmouth, as she had. But she could have *known* nothing. Now, as she considered the facts, she may have started to wonder at history and quiz its prime movers. How could Monmouth have been so speedily snuffed out? She had understood his appeal, his handsomeness, his affability, and the charm that not even she could give his uncle. Why had he presented in the end so little challenge to James? Many would have benefited from a tame Protestant prince with legitimate issue. Who wanted Monmouth to make trouble but not succeed?

The Earl of Sunderland had been the assiduous follower of William of Orange before the Exclusion Crisis and he had always preferred him as a candidate for the throne over Monmouth (although he had made some overtures to Monmouth when life at court became especially tough). Indeed, in 1680, William of Orange admitted 'he had more obligations to my Lord Sunderland, and more marks of his friendship, than he had from all the ministers these ten years'.[10] Falling foul of Charles II through his mistimed support of Exclusion, Sunderland had apparently abandoned William's interest and regained the trust first of Charles and then even of James. Perhaps, however, he had not abandoned his first allegiance after all. Could it be that Sunderland and William were playing a deep game, hoping to destroy Monmouth first and then James?

Behn did not know but, rifling through secret papers, she may have begun to suspect. First they wanted Grey harmed as an instrument to destroy Monmouth; now, Monmouth gone, he might be useful to help destroy James and was to be rehabilitated. Could Sunderland really be looking beyond the King? Could he be the puppeteer of Grey, the puppeteer of Monmouth?[11] Were there really no good noblemen but only cynical manipulators facing one or two foolishly honourable men who would inevitably lose in the political games? In which case, the heroic James II, with not an ounce of guile and cynicism in him, would inevitably fail. Behn had long believed that aristocrats were the bulwark of the monarchy. What if they should prove as treacherous or as flexible as commoners like herself had to be?

Sunderland, who was present at the interview of Monmouth and James, lifted no finger to save Monmouth, who yet proclaimed that he could save himself if he were to say the word. This word was presumed by some to be 'conversion'. James himself later came to believe it was 'Sunderland', however. That Monmouth remained silent on politics suggests he expected reprieve even on the scaffold—had he been treacherously promised something to keep quiet?[12] The treachery could spread backwards, too, over the last years. Could Sunderland, who had had little to do with the crushing of the Rye House Plot, have intervened to let Lord Grey slip nimbly away to involve himself fatally with Monmouth? The story of escape through a sleeping guard had always been difficult to swallow.

Behn's book ends with Cesario-Monmouth mounting the scaffold, still prating about his Hermione, a political anti-climax analogous to the failed sexual climax of his follower Philander in Part I of *Love-Letters:* both are bungled critical moments, political or sexual.[13] Pardoned by the King, Philander is back in the centre of the court. The exemplary moral tale promised at the end of Part II has not been delivered. In its place is a comic and cynical realisation of the corruption of personal and political life, both in aristocrats and in those who serve them.

Behn did not believe in huge Machiavellian plots such as Titus Oates had invented. Her description of the peripatetic English opposition in Europe under Monmouth, reminiscent of the useless Cavalier activity of the Interregnum, reveals her usual opinion, that politicians muddle through in a mixture of selfishness and opportunism, rather than strategy and plot. If she momentarily suspected the devilish plotting that the historian in James's exiled court came to see, and so communicated it, codedly, in her work, she *mainly* apprehended in Sunderland flexibility, opportunism and avarice on a high level. The Earl flowed where power was or was likely to be, and he found in the rich Lord Grey both expedient treachery and rich pickings. So Behn's novel ended:

> *Philander* lay sometime in the *Bastille*, visited by all the Persons of great Quality about the Court; he behaved himself very Gallantly all the way he came, after his being taken, and to the last Minute of his Imprisonment; and was at last pardoned, kiss'd the King's Hand, and came to Court in as much Splendour as ever, being very well understood by all good Men.

Known to 'all good Men' for what he is, Philander saves his skin, while Cesario, like Monmouth (and Stafford before), goes his simple way to death.[14] Behn was suggesting what anyone of commonsense knows, that Grey's type of man always flourishes, but she was giving some warning as well. She had begun *Love-Letters* in 1684, with the fear that Philander's amorous plotting would destabilise family and kingdom; she finished it in 1687 with Philander at the centre of the realm, one ruled not by the cynical Charles but by the guileless James. In this interpretation, the last act would be both absurd and tragic, beyond the scope and sardonic tenor of the book. As in her plays, so in prose, farce was Behn's predominant genre, not tragedy.

When Sunderland read Part III of *Love-Letters*, he perhaps saw a use for it beyond state politics. Like King Charles, he had an ungrateful son, Robert Spencer. As early as 1681 when the lad was only fifteen, Evelyn thought he would 'prove an extravagant man; for though a youth of extraordinary parts, & that had all the Education imaginable to render him a worthy man; yet his early inclinations [are] to vice'.[15] As Behn knew from lampoons, he was called 'Lewd rakehelly Spencer'.[16] Sunderland blamed his wife for spoiling the boy but his own excessive gambling made him no great parental model. In one action, however, Robert upstaged his father. James II's policy of appointing or promoting Catholics to high office was in full swing and Sunderland was embarked on one of the longest conversion processes in history, each year taking one step away from Canterbury and one small one nearer to Rome. Then in April 1687 Robert was gravely wounded by the congregation of a church in Bury St Edmunds after he had drunkenly assaulted a clergyman, and his family learnt the astounding news that he had, on his expected deathbed, become a Catholic. It was a piece of statecraft worthy of his father and it was all James needed: when recovered, young Robert was employed on state business, sent to deliver condolences on the death of Queen Mary of Modena's mother. He sank to the occasion and was so drunk when presented to Louis XIV in Paris that he could not speak a word.[17]

Sunderland continued his advice and threats to his son, but neither worked. In Behn's Part III of *Love-Letters* he may have seen another opportunity for admonition, qualified by a woman's tact. The book was not coming out under her name and she agreed to dedicate it to Robert Spencer, probably with a fee from Sunderland; so she gave the profligate and violent young man her usual fulsome treatment, along with some advice. In response to his drunken brawling, Behn suggested Spencer take more care of himself, while she sugared over his appalling record of crimes as 'youthful sallies' which he must try to curtail. Probably her advice had little effect, but, happily for Sunderland, he was relieved of his trying son the following year, through an overdose of brandy.

In public politics, Behn continued to hymn the increasingly doomed King and Queen. She also continued writing coded fables of absurdity and treachery that followed on from *Love-Letters*. The illiterate and foolish Monmouth, the ultimate dupe of the novel brought closer to his uncle in his sincerity and gullibility, would be replaced by similarly doomed but more heroic men and women, by Oroonoko, Bacon, and Isabella, set far from England but also deep in its heart.

Like Part III of *Love-Letters*, the short story *The History of the Nun* drew on Behn's memories of Flanders and touched on real events such as the French invasion at the end of the Dutch war and on the Turkish siege of Crete. Unlike *Love-Letters*, it *claimed* to be true.[18] The story unsettles judgement with its divided message, being easy to read but difficult to assimilate and, as in Part III of *Love-Letters*, the effect is partly due to the use of an unstable, even duplicitous narrator, and to the multiple purposes of the tale.

The plot of *The History of the Nun* is of a broken vow to the cloister, followed by inadvertent bigamy. The heroine Isabella, once a whole-hearted nun, elopes with a man whom she marries. Then, believing her first husband dead in war, she marries a second, only to be confronted with the first. She kills him and persuades the second husband to dispose of the body, but, in a moment of panic at the shame of it all, she sews the corpse of the first husband to the coat of the second; so he drowns when he pitches the dead bundle into the river and Isabella becomes a double murderess. She is caught and nothing remains but to make a good show on the scaffold, which, unlike Monmouth, she does. Isabella eroticises the space in such a way that the final effect, like that of *Love-Letters*, is sardonic rather than tragic.

The overwhelming message that emerges from *The History of the Nun* is Behn's conviction that inclinations change: Isabella's suffering follows from feelings pent up by a culture that refuses to acknowledge the Lucretian truth, that change is the only constant in human nature. From being prevented from following ordinary and natural desires and changing her mind as her body matures, Isabella is led into real crime. In this way, the story is in dialogue with both *Love-Letters* and *The Fair Jilt*, written at about the same time. The heroines of the last two respond to their culture by becoming knowing, manipulative women; desperately wanting to live by the pious fixed standards she has internalised, the good Isabella ends doing more damage than either of her wicked sisters, Silvia and Miranda. The stated message of the story is, however, quite different and is stridently political. More strenuous with a point of view than in *Love-Letters*, the narrator insists on seeing the tale of profound sexual emotion as a caution against the heinous act of disloyalty or vow-breaking. The Church here stands in for the King, whose subjects would follow Isabella at their peril.

The messages of *The History of the Nun* both suit and do not suit Behn's dedicatee, the Queen's cousin and Charles II's old mistress. Routinely called the 'Queen of Lust', Hortense Mancini, Duchess of Mazarine, had famously broken her marital vows and entered and exited a good many convents.[19] So she was a curious recipient for a cautionary tale against vow-breaking, although more suitable for a psychological one of unnecessary damage, especially considering the distinction between her present, pleasant life and that of the tragically fated Isabella. For the tale as political warning, she was, perhaps, more appropriate and in the dedication she became the sort of loyal figure that Behn could drench in hyperbole.

Yet Mazarine seems to be more than simply a court lady and loyal Royalist, and the dedication is suffused with a greater homoerotic yearning than Behn usually allowed herself. As with the Nell Gwyn epistle, she stressed that she and Mazarine shared a sex. Nell Gwyn was the cynosure, the woman who proved misogyny wrong, but she had died soon after Charles II and Mazarine was now simply the brightest and best. She had cost Behn some 'Inquietude', but the author wanted, all the same, to tell her 'how infinitely one of Your own Sex ador'd You'. Behn insisted that her love surpassed that of men: nowhere had the Duchess 'subdu'd a more intire Slave'.

During James II's rule, Mazarine was living comfortably out in Chelsea, a lampoonist noting that her old age and grey hair were not quenching her amorous or gaming desires. Together with her admirer, the French noble Saint-Évremond, she supported the remnants of the Cavalier court culture the Stuarts represented for Behn, her male and female outfits and independence gaining her the name of an Amazon. Mazarine enjoyed the musical entertainments put on by Saint-Évremond using James Paisible, Rochester's delicious musician, for whom Behn herself had written words in the 1670s. Many attended soirées, including Behn's young friend George Granville. For years Behn had desperately wanted to be of the royal court. Perhaps, now that her hopes of this were fading, she set her sights on this more louche, ambiguous and achievable one in Chelsea. If she came closer, however, she was never close enough and there is no evidence that she was ever of Mazarine's company; the intense dedication was speculatively written. The social yearning expressed in the Nell Gwyn dedication appears again, then, but where in the earlier address it was ambitious—the future was still before her—here, after a decade of sustained pleading to be let in, it was elegiac: 'Fortune has not set me in such a Station, as might justifie my Pretence to the honour and satisfaction of being ever near Your Grace.' It was a poignant admission of failure. The witty entertainer does not join the society she amuses.

Behn's next (and most literal) French translation, *Agnes de Castro*, was a *précieux* and macabre tale of close female friendship standing against male sexual obsession. It was based on a mythical story from Portugal and, given the wide circulation of *Lettres portuguaises* which had promoted Portugal as the land of passion, it was not surprising that Behn had competitors in her hurried work.[20] Considering the strictures against vow-breaking in *The History of the Nun* and the theme of male and female ties in *Agnes de Castro*, the latter might have been a more appropriate story to have dedicated to the errant and bisexual Duchess of Mazarine. For her dedicatee Behn chose, however, not a privileged court figure but another outsider like herself, Sir Roger Puleston, who, before the Restoration, had taken part with Colepeper, Willoughby and Strangford in Sir George Booth's Royalist rising. In Behn's political frame, he was successor to her earlier dedicatee, Sir William Clifton, loyally affecting the country around him and shedding gentlemanly beneficence. Puleston had delivered a lifetime's support to the Stuarts, but, as he had been little concerned with recent politics and lived far from London, he was not part of the caballing and lewd town like Mazarine and Sunderland. Behn did seem to know him a little, however, since she referred to his easy conversation and affable temper, while the praise of his generosity sounds as if she had benefited from it.

As so frequently in these late dedications, Behn's main interest was herself. She had not been taken up by the court, had not been significantly patronised by any of the great:

> It would be a happy World for us Traders in Parnassus, if, like those in the Moon...we cou'd Barter, pay Debts, and obligations with Poems and Dedications: But this is a World not Generous enough for such noble Traffick. Like *Homer*, we may sing our Verses from Door to Door, but shall find few List'ners that understand their Value, and can recieve 'em as they ought.... In our Age the Noble *Roman* Poets wou'd have Starv'd....

Yet she noted darkly that 'The Building of the Halcyon points us not out more certainly to Calmest Seas, than the Flourishing of the Muses does to a Happy State.' Sir William Davenant had made much the same observation in a republic and it was sad that under a monarchy she had to reiterate it.

The Mazarine and Puleston dedications reveal that matters had not gone as swimmingly for Behn as the *Coronation Ode* of 1685 had hoped. Less flippant and intelligent than his brother, James II showed no sign of being impressed anew with her theatrical wit, and he had not become her special patron. Indeed he had hardly patronised any significant author. Obsessed with his Catholic mission, the King had offended not only his former allies at court and in the nation—the gentry and the Anglicans—but also the needy artists. Most court writers fell silent or departed. It was some comfort for Behn to be able to write collective disappointment as the decline of literature and the downfall of the state. None the less, if as playwright and fictionist she was not in royal demand, as poetic propagandist she could still be useful in the trying months to come.

CHAPTER 28

❧

A Discovery of New Worlds and Poems for James II

'And POETS shall by Patron *PRINCES live'*

Aphra Behn's ill-health was by now expensive and constraining and, with royal patronage sluggish, she turned to further translations from the French as the quickest literary task. It was a common manoeuvre; as an anonymous satire unkindly expressed it, after despairing of 'eating at a full third day', playwrights left 'stage-practice, chang'd their old vocations, / Attoning for bad plays, with worse translations'.[1] Despite Behn's wonderful facility with verse, prose was easier than poetry and she resolved to continue in the mode, but, after so much amorous hyperbole with *Lycidus* and *La Montre*, she must have fancied something more weighty.

Behn may have turned to Fontenelle's *A Discovery of New Worlds* after some prodding from her young friend Charles Gildon who, raised for the Catholic priesthood, had grown increasingly irreligious. At the same time, the work was probably commissioned by the publisher William Canning, who seems to have been largely living off Behn during these years.[2] She had to work fast, for the playwrights and literary hacks were scraping round for projects—she had acknowledged the competition in her hurried publication of *Agnes de Castro*.[3] Now she heard that, yet again, a rival translation was 'doing by another hand'. To get her book out first, she had no time to 'supervise and correct the Sheets before they were wrought off; so that several Errata have escaped'.[4] Bluntly she announced that she could '*either…give you the* French *Book into* English, *or…give you the subject quite changed and made my own*'; since she had '*neither health nor leisure for the last*' she would '*offer you the first such as it is*'.

This candour concluded a long and possibly derivative preface to *A Discovery of New Worlds* entitled 'Essay on Translated Prose', indicating that, as usual, Behn had been thinking about her practice. In the past, her ignorance of Latin had prevented her from commenting much on translation theory, but her competence in French was emboldening. She was aware of the Earl of Roscommon's work on poetry, pleased to see him taking issue with Shadwell's demand for literal translation. Roscommon had respect for the translator's skill: 'Composing is the Nobler Part / But good Translation is no easie Art'; a translator must be 'Discreet, and Bold'.[5] Behn was also aware of Dryden, although she chose to omit mention of him here. In fact, however, neither from Roscommon nor from Dryden could she have received much comment on prose. She was one of the few English writers to take up this subject.

The 'Essay' treated the idiosyncrasies of particular languages and made the common patriotic point that French sounds well but English means more.[6] Commenting on linguistic change, the necessary acceptance of immigrant words, Behn claimed she would use the term 'Tourbillion' instead of 'Whirl-wind' because the English equivalent was not exact. People were cautious about employing a French word, tending instead to paraphrase it, but slowly the foreign word became current. She was helping the process. She had recently read Higden's 'Preface to the Reader' before his Juvenal satire, noting his point that some cultural adaptation was necessary in translation. Yet she decided that Paris was not London and that she would keep the French allusions rather than anglicising them. Her work in the last years had given her a thorough competence in French and she could risk declaring, 'I have endeavoured to give you the true meaning of the Author, and have kept as near his Words as was possible.'[7]

Any modesty suggested by the ending of the 'Essay', which remarked on her ill-health and lack of time, was much belied by what preceded it: in the 'Essay', Behn corrected scientific errors and commented on the original author with learned reference to the philosopher Descartes, whom she thus implied she had read.[8] It was audacious for a non-aristocratic woman to take issue with learned men and make authoritative comments on areas usually reserved to them (although Fontenelle himself was regarded by original scientists as something of a lightweight). But, if she had not the physical stamina to write an original work of science, as she confessed, Behn wished it well known that she had the mental equipment. In this, she went rather further than her predecessor, the scientific Margaret Cavendish, who frequently stressed her incompetence in learning.[9] Even more audaciously, she also stuck out her literary neck by hinting that much of what she was writing was parody.

In *The Emperor of the Moon*, Behn ridiculed the gullible who expected a moon world complete with earthly hierarchies. Fontenelle she considered weakened his work on the existence of other planetary systems by imagining men in the Milky Way. Yet, she approved his popularising of the new thought. In her commendatory poem about *Lucretius*, she had praised Creech for making philosophy easy and inviting, suitable for any capacity: 'No hard Notion' interrupted understanding. Fontenelle was doing something similar in his *New Worlds*, with the science of Copernicus and especially Descartes, who had written in the 1630s and 1640s but was little known in England outside academic circles. She and Fontenelle were taking 'the middle way' to the public.

Fontenelle's main point was that the stars were equivalent to other worlds, and the Earth was thus reduced to a subordinate place in the cosmos. The problem was of course religion, as both Fontenelle and Behn knew. With Creech, she had happily embraced the freethinking position against his fear, but she had since then learnt circumspection or, rather, equivocation. Although Fontenelle was careful to blur the line between fact and fantasy, remaining respectful of the 'delicate Niceties of Religion', Behn piously took him to task for omitting any mention of God. This apparent and exaggerated piety was, however, exploded by her use of the Bible to undercut itself.

Oscillating between serious point and parody of the scholastic method of dispute, Behn gave a dazzling display of biblical chapter and verse that must have bemused the serious readership of her old dramatic prefaces mocking preachers and pedants. The upshot was that the Church's opposition to the Copernican system as incompatible with the Bible became absurd. She concluded: '*Thus I hope I have performed my Undertaking, in making it appear, that the holy Scriptures, in things that are not material to the Salvation of Mankind, do altogether condescend to the vulgar Capacity; and that these two Texts of* Psal.19. *and* Josh. 10. *are as much for* Copernicus *as against him.*' To come to this point, Behn had put forward many decidedly comic arguments. For example, the Hebrews in the Bible have the moon and sun stilled for their benefit; so she asked, '*Now when by this Miracle they had the Light of the Sun, of what Advantage could the Moon be to them?*' The various miraculous interruptions God makes are so radical that it would take '*nothing less than two or three new Miracles, all as great as the first*' to '*set the World in Order again*'. In the meantime, His activities become '*Inconveniences*' for everyone else. It was pretty much tongue-in-cheek, rather like her paraphrase of the Lord's Prayer. Just in case she might have been too offensive, however, Behn concluded, '*I hope my Readers will be so just as to think, I intend no Reflection on Religion by this Essay; which being no Matter of Faith, is free for every one to believe, or not believe, as they please.*'[10] The double tone, so useful in this period, was one at which

Behn was now skilled. She needed it, for she had before her the example of Charles Blount, one of Rochester's later coterie of freethinkers, who had recently had his sceptical book suppressed.

With all her equivocation and parody, Behn knew she had a serious point. She was not really concerned with science—Descartes' notion of liquid whirlwinds which moved each planet and star around in a series of interacting vortices was not critiqued as it might have been by reference to Isaac Newton, who had just disputed it with his more satisfactory idea of gravity (nor was it absolutely clear why she could not use the English word vortex, already employed in English for Descartes' concept). Rather, her concern was with a history of thought as a human construction, the sense that religion was an ideology that could be destabilised by *new* systems of thought. Here again Behn was following Lucretius and Hobbes in mocking archaic and stupid pedantry, especially when applied to religion.

Within the same year, Behn came before the public with an even more controversial work, Fontenelle's *History of Oracles, and the Cheats of the Pagan Priest*, itself based on a Dutch treatise by A. Vandale, *De Oraculis Ethicarum*, a covert attack on Catholicism. It was a comparative history of pagan religions, in which myths were brought together and compared. The plot was the slow disengagement of reason from superstition. Behn's translation came out anonymously, with no publisher's name on the title page.[11] Perhaps Canning had become anxious.

Behn's choice of work to translate placed her again firmly with Hobbes who, in the twelfth chapter of *Leviathan*, had scandalously discussed the pagan cheats in the same breath as Christian expedients.[12] So too in Fontenelle, the oracles of the pagans were undercut, just as the miracles within the 'Essay' had been. The mockery stopped short of Christian miracles, but the implications were present. Priests of all sects seemed master frauds, duping a credulous and stupid people. However, the Dutch philosopher Spinoza had been much criticised for openly denying miracles; Behn was careful not to become quite so clear.

The issue of pagan and earlier religions was sensitive in England. The Anglican position was straightforward: old oracles were from daemons and miraculously ceased with the advent of Christ. Milton put the matter properly when Jesus tells Satan in *Paradise Regained*, 'No more shalt thou by oracling abuse / The Gentiles; henceforth oracles are ceased/... for they shall find thee mute.'[13] Fontenelle argued that the pagan oracles were priestly fraud from the start and so could not stop in this way. Indeed, they continued *after* the triumph of Christianity, which suggested that paganism had declined for political and social rather than divine reasons. The oracles, he declared, were simply silenced through Christian imperial action and there was no sudden transition from paganism to Christianity.

In making this claim, Fontenelle inevitably mocked the early Church Fathers who were responsible for much of the dogma and who, to make God more powerful, had accepted the notion of supernatural oracles defeated by Him. As he expressed it, 'to gain a little upon the pagans, there was a necessity of yielding to them what they maintained with so much obstinacy.' Christians allowed 'something supernatural in the Oracles...and so Daemons were to be brought upon the stage'.[14]

Inevitably this sort of historical investigation of origins threatened modern Christianity as well. Thus, with seemingly limited aims, a study of paganism became a critique of the state religion. Its opponents were quite aware of the subversive implications, and faithful Anglicans and Catholics would answer the case for many years after Behn's death.[15]

That Behn chose or agreed to translate this work as she had chosen or agreed to praise Lucretius must suggest something of her attitude to religion in general. This seems to have been fairly constant over the years for, as early as the epistle to *The Dutch Lover* in 1673, she had noted the confusion of early science, religion and poetry. With all her political enthusiasm for James II and appreciation of the tolerance at which, from one view, he was aiming, she can have had virtually no sympathy for his sense that a particular sect, Roman Catholicism, had a monopoly on truth. She might by now have accepted with Hobbes that a single religion tended to the coherence of the state, but, with Protestantism so entrenched as it was in England, Catholicism was surely inappropriate.

The parlous condition of the government, reeling under James's zeal was displayed in the new dominance of the Scots at court, to which Behn's dedicatees of these months testified. Scots were not usually of much account in the English government, but the King's ability to antagonise almost all his natural English followers meant that he had had to turn to the nation that had often supported him and with whom, as a Stuart, he had an ancient connection. So, except for Sunderland and George Jeffreys (to whom Behn, in a complex political/religious move, dedicated her *History of Oracles*), the usual bevy of English aristocrats and politicians was replaced at court by untried Scots. In the past, Behn had shared the English distrust of the 'schismatics'; she now followed her King in acquiring an 'Esteem' for Scotland.[16]

A Discovery of New Worlds was dedicated to one of the new men, the Earl of Drumlangrig. He was a Privy Councillor in Scotland and allied to Sunderland, who used him to help topple his enemy, Laurence Hyde, Earl of Rochester, the earlier dedicatee of Behn's *Luckey Chance*. *Lycidus*, which came out about the same time, was addressed to a far more important man, the unlikeable, handsome and vain Earl of Melfort, the Scot who was fast becoming Sunderland's most formidable rival. As a converted rather than a converting Catholic like Sunderland, Melfort was powerful in his association with the Jesuits, with extreme Catholics, and with the Queen. So he was not as easily ousted as the Protestant Rochester had been. Nor was he easy to flatter, and Behn was even forced to use his receipt of the newly revived (and much mocked) Order of the Thistle to congratulate him.[17]

In the circumlocutions in which all needed now to express themselves, Behn praised Melfort for not looking beyond James: he was not one who weighed 'Advantages by Probabilities only, and fancying the future to out-poyse the present, cast there their Anchor of Hope'. In other words, he had not opened negotiations with James's son-in-law, the Protestant William of Orange over the water. For his benefit, again she trotted out her belief that 'the Royal Interest' is 'so greatly…the Property of Nobility' that nobles should support the monarch over life and fortune, especially one 'so truly just, so wise and great' as James II.

At this point, a new factor agitated politics. In her brief life, Queen Mary of Modena had suffered eight pregnancies, all resulting in miscarriages or short-lived infants. So, news of her being with child again did not immediately alarm those whose political hopes rested on James's death. By early 1688, however, it was known that the pregnancy was going well, and Behn's friend, the literary cleric Thomas Sprat, helped draw up plans for a day of thanksgiving and prayers for the birth of a boy.

Though there was little enthusiasm in the nation—"tis strange to see, how the Queen's great Belly is everywhere ridiculed'—James's enemies and critics grew anxious.[18] The birth of a boy would continue Catholic sway and, in the event of the King's death, result in the regency of the ultra-Catholic and increasingly haughty Mary of Modena. The anxious naturally became devious. Ciphered messages flew between London and The Hague where William was always in waiting. Indeed his propaganda machine was already in action and his pamphlets were being widely distributed throughout England. He needed only to accelerate the activity. The few loyal poets that were left to James were ordered to work.

It was a difficult moment for propaganda. If a poet wrote glowingly of the event and a girl were born, William would have been needlessly offended, since his wife Mary, James's eldest daughter, would remain the heir; but, if it were a boy and the poet had been silent, this would upset James. If one were going for the former option, one might as well line up with the extreme Catholics, who saw the pregnancy as a miraculous sign of England's impending conversion and assume the miracle would include correctly sexing the child.

Behn's *Congratulatory Poem to her most Sacred Majesty, on the Universal Hopes of all Loyal Persons for a Prince of Wales* was one of the few robustly to express the extreme Catholic position—which is why it was published both in London by the very pro-James Canning and in Edinburgh by the King's own printer.[19] It claimed that the 'Mighty blessing is *at last* arriv'd' and 'the Wond'rous work achiev'd'. While it is God who has taken his time in the matter, Behn also gave the comic impression of a lengthy earthly conception: 'monarchs are not fashion'd at a Heat'. Her conceit was again the godlike monarch, 'For *Gods* and *Kings* ally'd most nearly are', a god now begetting a saviour son. Like his predecessor, the child will 'call the wand'ring, scattered Nations home' and princes will come to worship him as they did Christ. It was no more over-the-top than the *Coronation Ode* but, since the child had not even been born, there was some audacity in hailing him 'Royal boy'. As for Mary, to whom the poem was addressed, she was only the 'Sacred vessel', exhorted to guard her pregnancy with care.[20]

In fact this faith in the birth of a boy, which loyal poets were urged to express, helped increase Protestant suspicion of a *fake* pregnancy. Probably Behn's poem was one of several works that fed into the much credited story, that the whole matter was a fraud and that a baby boy was, at the crucial moment, to be smuggled into the royal bed in a warming-pan.

In her poem, the hostility to William was overt: the new child would overthrow all the designs of the Dutchman. Yet, there was some uneasiness amidst the celebration. Behn used the image of fortune's wheel being arrested by the birth, as if the downfall of James were inevitable without it, and again she noted the silence of the Muses. This was due to their fright by Mars. Decoded, the image meant that the martial William was causing writers to defect. Against such political realities she could only assert a personal vision:

> A young APOLLO, rising from the Gloom,
> Dress'd in his Father's brightest *Rays*, shall come...
> And bless the Earth with New-*created* LIGHT.

As for James, the child would quell 'sawcy Murmurs' and make him '*Absolute*'. Behn ended ringingly, 'You *will*, you *shall*, and *must* for ever Reign.' In such strenuous linguistic effort she herself seemed mimicking the divine word.

As ever, however, her own concern was patronage. James had not stimulated it: his son would.

> He the faint *Muses* shall a-new inspire,
> And from his *Beams*, kindle their useful Fire:
> His Rights Hand *Crowns*, his Left shall *Lawrels* give;
> And POETS shall by *Patron* PRINCES live...

This forlorn faith in generous royal patronage had been Aphra Behn's hope throughout the 1680s; it was ironic that it should come to rest with the child who would grow up to be the Old Pretender—with no patronage in England at all.

On 10 June, the happy event occurred and a Prince of Wales was born. Apart from those who, like the Duchess of Mazarine, had felt the baby kicking in the womb, a whole army of people witnessed the birth, including Charles's Queen Catherine and Lady Sunderland, though, significantly, not James's daughter Princess Anne, who chose to be absent. Bonfires were ordered in celebration on 17 June and again on the 29th, when it seemed the child would live. Sunderland decided at last to become a Catholic.

Behn was ready with another poem, this time for James rather than his wife. *A Congratulatory Poem to the King's Most Sacred Majesty, On the Happy Birth* was published by the loyal William Canning, who also packaged the two birth verses together as *Two Congratulatory Poems*. Obviously such work was aimed at the King not the country, which dreaded the implications of the event and was seething with warming-pan rumours. Behn linked the new poem to the *Universal Hopes* by addressing again the 'happy *KING*' and insisting on the child's divinity, as well as its future ability to unite all into '*One SOUL*'—if not into '*One FAITH*'. But the new work added little to the earlier one and showed signs of strain; clearly Behn was finding it difficult to cap or equal her previous performance. Yet, however constrained and tedious the *Congratulatory Poem*, she did use it to make a few useful personal and political points.

First, that she, Aphra Behn, had been hymning James for many years now and had not been afraid to foretell this '*Glorious*' moment. She would like the King to take more note than he had. Second, that William would be mightily put out: 'Methinks I hear the *Belgick* LION Roar, / And Lash his *Angry Tail*', frustrated at the birth of a prince 'Whose BROWS his *Boasted Laurels* shall Adorn'. Here William was reduced to a farcical villain howling like the devilish opposition in the *Coronation Ode*. Third, the child was truly James's, for his eyes proved him a Stuart, of 'the *Forgiving* KIND'. In this, apart from scotching warming-pan nonsense, there may have been some implied advice to James on recent disastrous events. Having raged at the Archbishop of Canterbury and six Anglican bishops for refusing to read out his Declaration of Indulgence to Catholics, the King had sent them to the Tower. It would certainly have been better for the country if James had forgiven them before matters reached this dangerous pass. When, just after the birth, on 30 June, the Anglican bishops were acquitted by the courts, it was to 'mighty rejoyceing, in ringing of bells, discharging of gunns, lighting of candles, and bonefires in several places'.[21] James had sunk further in popularity.

Behn was quite aware that she had written a tired poem. Diplomatically, she blamed this on her joy, which had been too great for '*Thought* or *Wit*'; so she had produced only '*Scanty VERSE*', too narrow to contain all she wished to say.[22] In reality, she might have been irritated at delayed or inadequate payment; in addition she was possibly by now hampered by political fears.

Like many affable, talkative people, Behn had a competitive streak, which had grown stronger in her later years. In the preface to *The Luckey Chance*, she had insisted that she was equal to any man as a playwright and, even in the dedication to the translated *Agnes de Castro*, she had felt obliged to stress the excelling power of her portrait. So, when John Baber appeared to denigrate her as a court poet, she was prepared to fight hard.

Baber was the son of a Presbyterian royal physician, one of those who had helped Charles II out of life. He was the frequent butt of lampoons, some copied into 'Astrea's Booke'; one called him 'sly Mr Baber' who is 'a plaguy sharp writer of satire'. Behn knew the practice of self-mockery—'*in Lampoons…your selves revile*' because '*None else will think it worth their while'*—and she must have suspected Baber as the author of this gentle satire.[23] Although lampoons suggested he was a writer of ballads and even a provider of the scurrilous Julian, Baber had had only two acknowledged works published, one on the coronation and the other on the birth of the Prince of Wales. They were suitably careful and courtly, making the high principled and stubborn James into a model of justice and peace. Often Baber and Behn echoed each other: in his coronation ode, Baber alluded to the awkward fact that the sublime couple had failed to produce an heir as quickly as was desired and he too suggested that heaven took its time to make a king.

Baber thought Aphra Behn had started a fight by claiming in her *Universal Hopes* that very few poets were writing loyal poems, thus drawing attention to her own achievement and his silence. His small output suggests he was slow to compose and lacked his rival's facility. So, when he did finally publish his poem on the royal birth, he addressed Behn's readership directly. In her assumption of a boy she had, he complained, been premature, almost hubristic, raising the possibility of 'Abortive Joyes': '*Some could not Bridle their Officious Rhime, / But must bestow an Heir before the Time.*' Given the demands of court propaganda, Behn must have found this below the belt.

More troubling because nearer her own insecurities was the clear dig that Aphra Behn was a professional writer, part of the '*Writing* Tribe'. Beside these dull mercenary hacks, he, John Baber, a court poet, did not need the absurd hyperbole they churned out. Where Behn offered her skill as poet in return for money, he offered the unmercenary loyalty of a gentleman. In addition he blamed the '*Writing* Tribe' for failing to create a proper representation of James II. With such charges Baber had laid himself open and had only himself to blame for the hatchet job Behn undertook.

The similarity of Behn and Baber, even to the mediocrity of their poems on the birth of the Prince of Wales, meant that, in mocking him, she inevitably mocked herself. So she was forced to deflate the image of the godlike royals which she too had been busily creating. Her poem on Baber thus became a rare glimpse of the political Behn in undress.[24] Had she been less concerned with herself, she might have paused to consider whether a beleaguered monarch was best served by a squabble between two of his few supporters.

To counter the accusation of premature rejoicing, she used gossip she had unearthed: that Baber had in fact finished *his* poem before the birth, had offered it to a publisher, and then, in cowardly fashion, held back until he was sure of the child's sex. Beside this cowardice she emerged both daring and loyal. Her main attack was, however, stylistic. Baber's grasp of metre was faulty and he had to pad out his lines with '*Dids*, and *Does*, and a quaint *Simely*' to make them scan. Behn easily reduced the opening—'Nine Months a Loyal Zeal has Fir'd my Breast; / Which for Nine Muses could not be at Rest'—to nonsense, the lucky jingle of nine and nine being fatuous: 'The first thy *Loyalties* short date Rehearses; / The next, how Damnably thou Pump'st for Verses.'

Behn had even more fun with Baber's accusation of hyperbole, the very stuff of the panegyrist. It is comic to watch the great mistress of exaggeration literalising Baber's conceits and making his routine claims ridiculous. For instance, she demolished his image of the trading City without a soul, its '*Maces* and *Furrs*' like '*Roses* after *June*' once royal favour was lost: this was quite incomprehensible, Behn snorted, roses blooming after June would be prized, and maces and furs were nothing like them.

As for Baber's notion of himself as a gentleman-courtier, she easily countered it. Usually Behn extolled and craved the courtly life but here, to deflate Baber, she reduced it to what she must always have known it was, an endless waiting on the King, wearily attending 'His Couchees, and his Levies'. The life suited Baber, who saw everything in terms of outward show, belittling a disgraced peer as a dirty garter ribbon and a cashiered colonel as a man without a laced coat. All poets wanted something for their dreary attendance, she pointed out, and, if not money, it was an honour or a title.

Gleefully Behn developed Baber's unwise boast of not being a professional. Indeed he was not. And he might have escaped censure 'had not [his] Unlucky *Rhiming Spirit*, / Writ *Satyr* now, instead of *Panygerick*'. Amateur writers of panegyrics could be indulged because they did no harm and might be rewarded for loyalty, if not for art. Baber should have jingled out a welcome to the new prince, as he had for the coronation. Satire such as the attack on herself was, however, the province of the *real* professional writer and Baber had been foolish to encroach: 'Why so sharp Squire *Bavius* on your Friends?' (Bavius was a poet from the time of Augustus; he was synonymous with bad verse and malice towards the more gifted.) Behn in her turn had to be 'sharp', for Baber had attacked her in her real business.[25]

The most perplexing of Baber's accusations concerned the representation of the King, for Behn could see that she and Baber did not differ much politically, although he went a little further than she did in seeing

James as a reformer, as well as conserver. To ridicule Baber, Behn had actually to ridicule what she usually supported and to defend what she commonly mocked. For instance, she had to defend the usually maligned City: 'She's still in Favour; and deserves to be, / Inspight of all thy ill-timed Poetry.' Also, Baber had praised James's disastrous persecution of judges and Anglican bishops: to attack him she even risked sounding Whiggish by accusing Baber of the foolish belief that

> ...because the *Judges* Chaines is gone,
> The gaudy Triffle lost, the Man's undone:
> Dull Fool, that ne're to Merit gave its due,
> But thinks all Vertue to consist of Show:
> As if the Man, once Worth his Prince's Grace,
> Must with his short-liv'd Frown become an Ass.
> A Prince's Favour, then by the same Rule,
> Shou'd make him Lov'd, or Wise that is a Fool.

If the collector Narcissus Luttrell had not written 'By Mrs. Behn' on the copy of *To Bavius*, which he immediately acquired, one might be forgiven for doubting the authorship of this anonymously published poem. Clearly it was not for the eyes of the King.[26]

Whatever she thought in private and wrote anonymously, Behn's main professional business was to praise the loyal actors and eulogists, both now in need of bolstering. She began with her old friend, the playwright and Stuart propagandist, Henry Nevil Payne, who had the advantage of having prospered under James II and thus been enabled to show his 'Bounty' to her. To him Behn dedicated her Antwerp story, *The Fair Jilt*; in the dedication references to the hero, 'prince' Tarquin, gave way to those of a greater Prince, the object of both their veneration:

> I present you with a Prince unfortunate, but still the more noble Object for your Goodness and Pity; who never valu'd a brave Man the less for being unhappy. And whither shou'd the Afflicted flee for Refuge, but to the Generous? Amongst all the Race, he cannot find a better Man, or more certain Friend.

James seems to have recognised this and urged Payne to write retaliatory pamphlets.

In 'Astrea's Booke', Behn had refuted in the margin an attack on the

much denigrated Roger L'Estrange, who had dominated Royalist propaganda through all her working life.[27] Now he was required by James
to counter the versions of recent history put out by Burnet over in
Holland.[28] As part of his Tory organ, the *Observator*, L'Estrange had
produced a *Brief History of the Times*, aiming to capture the past for the
Stuarts—or, in Behn's words, rescue 'the *World from stupid Ignorance*'. More
specifically, it was intended to settle the matter of Edmund Bury Godfrey's
death in the Popish Plot days, a fine example of the triumph of Whig
propaganda—as the warming-pan story was also fast becoming. As with
Payne, she was needed to commend L'Estrange's effort. Her response
in *Poem to Sir Roger L'Estrange* was to add to his '*Truth*' with her own vision
of recent history as a series of fictions: paradise lost, truth betrayed by
perjury, and virtue banished by fraud and flattery. The result was a
present of corrupt laws, false religion and a misled 'restless People'.

L'Estrange had used his *History* not only as propaganda but also as
self-vindication. He had been a man driven from comfort and ease by
zeal in the cause. So Behn alluded to his chequered years, his exile
during the Popish Plot, his effigy burnt on Accession Day, his return
and rededication to the royal crusade. For him, she used the religious
vocabulary usually reserved for royalty, and L'Estrange was translated
from a propagandist into a prophet: what he preached was truth, not
opinion. Publicly silent when L'Estrange had been driven into exile in
Scotland, she now found it easier to look back at a past made deceptively
clear than to cope with a turgid present.

Another enterprise in which Behn became involved at this time was
a literary work made propaganda by the moment. At least it was intended
as such when advertised in April 1688 (although, unhappily, it seems
not to have arrived in public until July 1689, politically a very different
time). This was Nahum Tate's English edition of Cowley's huge Latin
work, *Of Plants*, dating from the Interregnum and early Restoration.
Aphra Behn was asked to 'translate' Book VI called 'Of Trees'.

She seemed unaware of an earlier translation of 1680 and, since she
could not easily read Latin, she must have had help in her writing from
a classically educated friend, probably Nahum Tate himself. One or two
errors suggest that Behn was working from ear, that she was hearing an
oral version and rendering it there and then into couplets. However she
did it, the result was smooth and fine. Like Dryden with Ovid's *Heroides*,
Tate went out of his way to praise the only female translator in the
volume and the only person without Latin. Behn's book, he claimed,
'o'ertops the others'.

Like Behn's admired Edmund Waller, Cowley had lived through the trying times of the Civil War and Interregnum. According to his biographer Thomas Sprat, he had travelled 'where-ever...the King's Troubles requir'd his Attendance'. The circumstances of his return to England were, however, obscurer. Sprat claimed that he came as a Royalist spy and 'was advis'd to dissemble the main Intention of his coming over, under the Disguise of applying himself to some settled Profession. And that of Physick was thought most proper...he proceeded to the Consideration of Simples...retir'd into a fruitful Part of *Kent* where every Field and Wood might shew him the real Figures of those Plants of which he read...'. In case this might seem accommodation with the enemy, Sprat continued,

> instead of employing his Skill for Practice and Profit, he presently digested it into that Form which we behold.... The two last [books] speak of Trees, in the way of *Virgil's Georgics*. Of these the sixth Book is wholly Dedicated to the Honour of his country. For making the *British* Oak to preside in the Assembly of the Forest Trees, upon that Occasion he enlarges on the History of our late Troubles, the King's Affliction and Return, and the Beginning of the *Dutch War*, and managed all in a Style, that (to say all in a Word) is equal to the Greatness and Vigour of the *English* Nation.

It was this important, deeply political sixth book that Behn was asked to put into English couplets. It stretched to 1,726 lines.

The work was closer than her other Latin 'translations' of Ovid and Horace to the original. Perhaps she did not want to deviate too far from Cowley, whom she reverenced as one of the great poets, or, perhaps, noting Cowley's attacks on the Dutch and his triumphalist Stuart rhetoric, she was keeping an option open of hiding in the future behind the words of a poet now dead.

Behn was used to many of the devices of the work, as well as to the main allegory of talking trees.[29] Years before she had written of a voyeuristic juniper. The oak, as symbol of English stability, had gained great significance from Charles II's often-told story of his seclusion in its branches after the Battle of Worcester. In keeping with this incident, the Stuarts saw themselves as planters not destroyers of trees, guardians of woods and of the nation. In Cowley's poem, Charles actually became a woodland deity. In contrast, Evelyn associated the Parliamentarians with the destruction of forests in the building of ships for war and trade, both activities supported now by the modern Whigs.[30] William of Orange was suspected by some of wanting to rule England so as to embroil it in a French war; so he too would need to cut down trees for wood. He could not, then, be construed as the guardian of the English oak like the Stuarts.

Book VI ends with a rousing description of the Battle of Lowestoft or Solebay, which had taken place on 3 June 1665, just before Behn set out on her spying mission to Antwerp. In this battle, the English under James, then Duke of York, had defeated the Dutch, and a Dutch ship named the *Orange* had been the last to threaten the English before catching fire from cannon shot. The poem was tailor-made for the present moment.

For Behn, Cowley's verse became something beyond a vehicle for politics (and for the modern reader a tedious exercise in the skimming of footnotes) when she reached line 586. She was discussing the laurel, used by kings to adorn their conquering brows, when she suddenly deviated from her text:

> And after Monarchs, Poets claim a share
> As the next worthy thy priz'd wreaths to wear.
> Among that number, do not me disdain,
> Me, the most humble of that glorious Train.

At this point she wrote in the margin: 'The Translatress in her own Person speaks.' Then she went on:

> I by a double right thy Bounties claim,
> Both from my Sex, and in Apollo's Name:
> Let me with *Sappho* and *Orinda* be
> Oh ever sacred Nymph, adorn'd by thee;
> And give my Verses Immortality.[31]

Behn's enormous esteem for royalty made the claim for the artist an important one, echoing the language used for James himself in the dedication of *The Second Part of The Rover*: he 'made double Conquest' by his sword and virtue and took the laurels. But it also confirmed the impression given by her state poems and many of her dedications that, although she revered kings and their semi-divine and prophetic roles, she more and more valued the artist as both their subordinate and their creator. It was perhaps an inevitable progression as kings tottered on their thrones.

Behn's admirers often compared her to major male writers and she herself, blaming the wrong-headedness of those who would not accord her the fame she deserved, insisted that she wrote like any man. Yet, when she came to make this direct plea for significance, it is in a woman's tradition that she saw herself: that of the equivocal Sappho and the irreproachable Katherine Philips.[32]

There was little influence of either of these women on her work, but both, like Behn herself, were concerned with their reputations. The 'Matchless Orinda' was tireless in covert self-promotion before her early death and Sappho, most famous of female poets, was the first writer to claim explicitly that song confers immortality on the singer. In linking herself with Orinda, Behn may have been conscious again of Dryden's separation of her from her apparent rival, but she was probably also recalling Cowley's own elegy for Katherine Philips, in which he claimed that, if there were a 'Woman *Laureat*', it would be Orinda. Although the notion had been most clearly expressed for her by the antagonistic Robert Gould in his lampoon 'The Female Laureat', Behn, too, might have claim to such a post. It was perhaps some comfort to the ailing, over-worked woman who, in these last months, had had to push her pen so relentlessly for a tottering governmenr.

CHAPTER 29

The Widdow Ranter and *Oroonoko*

'frightful Spectacles of a mangl'd King'

By 1688, everyone in London political circles felt trouble imminent. It was impossible not to sense the movement of illicit messages back and fore between England and Holland, and the King's loyal subjects were simultaneously strident in his support and anxious for themselves. Behn responded with her usual propaganda and panegyric, but now, even more than before, she shadowed them with part tragic, part cynical reflections on the regime and the man she was hymning. Her covert fears were expressed in a pair of related works, the play *The Widdow Ranter* and the short story *Oroonoko*, both set in the New World of her youth, when she had briefly called herself an 'American'.

Perhaps her recent use of the name George Marten in *The Younger Brother* had opened up memories, but Behn may also have been coming to suspect that the old label suited her. Although she had socialised with some of the great in London and with many of the wits, she had always been an outsider, someone from away, someone who had had to sing for her supper. She had desperately wanted to be of the court of Charles II, then of James II, then even of a counter-court with Mazarine in Chelsea, as her dedication of *The History of the Nun* suggested. All her efforts had been abortive. Through them, however, she had always assumed that royalty, courtiers, and the aristocracy were the ultimate insiders. Now, with the state shuddering, she saw that there was really no inside in England, no safe place and she felt in London a similar sense of duplicity and instability to that experienced years ago in Surinam. Everywhere was 'America'.

It was not a moment to stage her only unperformed play, *The Younger Brother*, which exhibited infidelity largely unpunished and used the last name of a famous republican for its hero. Yet, she did not wish to start another before the old was produced. The court was, however, on a drive to recapture public opinion and it was at last commissioning playwrights.[1] Probably Behn was approached, perhaps with the offer of a prologue and epilogue from the Poet Laureate, Dryden. If so, she could not refuse.

The time for crude theatrical propaganda of the sort that had marked the Popish Plot years was over. People were no longer clear about issues. So Behn responded not by straightforward mockery of democracy and praise of monarchy as in *The Roundheads*, but by showing what chaos would come if a legitimate authority were absent and if all felt it their right to govern and choose governors, as in America. People would only stay in their correct social places when the central authority was noble, legitimate and absolutely fixed, as both kings Charles and James had thought. The events described in a pamphlet, *Strange News from Virginia; Being a full and true Account of the Life and Death of Nathaniel Bacon Esquire*, published in 1677, provided the germ of an American story that could become a lesson to England: 'This Country wants nothing but to be Peopl'd with a well-born Race to make it one of the best Collonies in the World...'.[2]

The Widdow Ranter or, the History of Bacon in Virginia was the first play to be set in British colonial America, but no one could fail to see that the Virginia of the 1670s spoke to the England of 1688. Reverting to Behn's old genre of tragicomedy, now suited to the troubled times of change, *The Widdow Ranter* included a tragic vision of basically good men led astray and a comic one of vulgar men empowered during the absence of a strong governor. In early Restoration tragedy, men such as Behn's hero Bacon would have been placed exotically in Renaissance Spain or pre-Columbian America, but, here, he was in a mismanaged colony; he was thus forced from being a glowingly simple hero, destroyed by social forces in the manner of Dryden's early heroes, into becoming a commentary on a complex reality that sullied and diminished as well as destroyed him. In this context, masculine heroism came under closer scrutiny than ever before in Behn's works.

The Nathaniel Bacon of history was an English settler of good family from East Anglia who, having been imprudent, was equipped by his father to travel to Virginia to recoup his fortune. Temporarily leaving his wife in England, he arrived in America, bought land in Henrico County and, as a man of substance, became a councillor. The trouble he suffered on his plantation from marauders, as well as his own insubordinate spirit, soon led him into conflict with the Governor, whom he felt to be too lenient on the Indians (Native Americans). Failing to galvanise the administration, he attacked these natives himself and his spirited actions attracted other frustrated and plundered planters. Soon he was at the head of a troop in rebellion against the colonial government.

Much of Bacon's language invoked the old Commonwealth: he spoke of 'Libertyes' and 'the cause of the oppressed'. So his uprising could appear the first American revolt or, nearer to home, an echo of the Monmouth Rebellion. At the same time, however, he took a high patrician tone, castigating the administrators of Virginia as men of 'vile birth' and no education who had let the arts and sciences stagnate. Such men were 'spounges' which had 'suckt up the Publique Treasure'. This elitist emphasis was the basis of Behn's portrait of Bacon as her usual noble hero, a man of birth and breeding in contrast to other vulgarian Virginians.

The historical Bacon and the Governor both declared themselves doing the King's will, but, when Whitehall heard of the rebellion, it swiftly sided with established authority. The King issued a proclamation 'for the Suppressing a Rebellion lately raised within the Plantation of Virginia'. In the midst of the unrest, Bacon simply died: 'Hee lay sick… of the Bloody Flux, and…accompanyed with a Lousey Disease; so that the swarmes of Vermyn that bred in his Body he could not destroy but by throwing his shirt into the Fire as often as he shifted himself. Hee dyed much dissatisfied in minde…'.[3] Some murmured that he was made worse by excessive brandy-drinking. Clearly straight history would not do for drama.

For her play, Behn disposed of the Governor, so allowing the heroic Bacon to oppose only ill-born Virginians and be the nearest thing to royal authority in the colony.[4] Her work could then end happily, anticipating the true Governor's arrival. Bacon would be vanquished, but so would the base-born councillors whose absurd authority derived from the debased law; the excuse for Bacon would be gone.[5] Behn also omitted mention of the reprisals that marked the quelling of the historical Bacon rebellion. Charles II had accused the Governor of hanging 'more men in that naked Country, than he had done for the Murther of his Father'. In Behn's play, there was such chaos that no one managed to be hanged at all and the play concluded with multiple marriages.

Eliminating Mrs Bacon, Behn made Bacon romantically in love with an 'Indian Queen'—an heroic emotion mocked as affected by cynical onlookers. (The figure, a stock one of heroic romance, might just have been based on the widowed Cockacoeske, Queen of the Pamunkeys, who allegedly had a son by an English colonel and felt the dual allegiance to Native Americans and settlers given in romantic terms to Behn's young queen. Cockacoeske, a far older and more substantial personage, fled *from* Bacon, however, and was more concerned with supplies, troop movements, and the control of her own goods than with romance.)[6] Behn's 'Indian Queen', a delicate Europeanised conception—she is as 'timorous as a dove' with 'no Amazonian fire' about her—could wear the full set of feathers Aphra Behn had brought from Surinam; presumably the prop now belonged to the United Company, which must have wanted opportunities to use it. The Restoration theatre liked mixing western ways with cultural exotica.[7]

In Behn's play, Bacon is no longer allowed to die lousily in bed like his historical counterpart. Instead, he commits Roman suicide on the battlefield, for, like the rebellious Allin of Surinam, who had tried to kill the Proprietor Lord Willoughby in the 1660s and whom Behn probably remembered when writing the play, Bacon himself is inspired by heroic Roman example. He is

> a Man indeed above the Common Rank, by Nature Generous; Brave, Resolv'd, and Daring; who studying the Lives of the Romans and great Men, that have raised themselves to the most Elevated fortunes, fancies it easy for Ambitious men, to aim at any Pitch of Glory, I've heard him often say, Why cannot I Conquer the Universe as well as *Alexander?* or like another *Romulus* form a new *Rome*, and make my self Ador'd?[8]

Such ambition now belongs in the theatre. Little can be achieved in a world where the admiring man who speaks these words intends to oppose the heroic Bacon, solely because of an 'Interest' he has in the new governor.

In his obsession with love in death at the expense of more political realities, Bacon resembles Monmouth. Dying by his own hand rather than by another's, however, he feels able to utter the proper political words that James must badly have wanted from his nephew on the scaffold: 'never let Ambition—Love—or Interest make you forget as I have done—your Duty—and Allegiance.'[9] With his staunchness, heroism, and political naïveté Bacon is both Monmouth and the martial King James of Behn's *Coronation Ode*. Characters within the play remark on his theatricality, his heroic sense of himself on a stage. He wants to reduce war to chivalrous duels—even though his Indian opponent is merely a 'mad hot-brained youth'—and rhetorical confrontations, even though his antagonists use words only for deceit.

Bacon is, the onlookers suspect and some of his followers fear, in the

wrong play at the wrong moment. The glamorous and glorious conception of personal power he holds resembles that of heroic drama, not late
tragicomedy. He has the consciousness of the mythologised 1640s, when
cavaliering was swashbuckling, or of the 1660s, when the myths were
fashioned, the early jubilant years of the Restoration with their fantastic
hopes of a Golden Age and incorruptible power. Bacon believes in a
kind of transcendental politics, true for all times and places, a belief
based on heroic myths and deeply embedded in masculine classical
literature like Plutarch's *Lives*, which he takes to be true. He also has faith
in the integrity of language: the oath and word of honour. Renaissance
tragedy, especially of Shakespeare, persistently expressed a belief that
oratorical virtuosity could dominate the rudest rabble. The Restoration
had abandoned the notion, but it remains dear to Bacon's heart.

Bacon is made more anachronistic by the other, unheroic characters
in the play. In the 1670s, Behn's rakes had been wandering Cavaliers;
now they are more like economic migrants, seeking solvency rather than
empire—much as George Marten and his Interregnum cronies had
always done in the New World. But they do not even do this with gusto.
Like *The Luckey Chance*, *The Widdow Ranter* presents men willing to sell
their bodies for money but not to work at 'business'. The newly arrived
gambler, Hazard, will try for a rich marriage but, if he fails he, like
Gayman, will take up a kind of prostitution: 'A Younger Brother may
pick out a Pritty Livelihood,' says his friend. Having just arrived in the
new country, he remarks to the hospitable but low-born councillors, 'I
was not bred to Merchandizing Sir, nor do intend to follow the Drudgery
of Trading...I was not born to work Sir.' He is actually prepared to
fight to defend the honour of his idleness.

The comedy of the play is mainly provided by the Virginian councillors, colonial versions of Behn's City aldermen. Royalist mythology had
always fastened on the low origins of anti-monarchists, as *The Roundheads*
testified, both in the 1640s and the 1680s. Here Behn directs her social
disdain to anyone who aspires to inappropriate place and fails to recognise that the gently born, even if card-sharpers and fortune-hunters, are
natural rulers. The social chaos of Virginia has allowed a bankrupt
farrier to become a preacher through forging his ordination papers and
a tell-tale pickpocket to become a Justice of the Peace. The response of
these dignitaries to any rehearsing of the scandalous truth is not the
duel of a gentleman but the law of common people: they will dishon-
ourably sue, not honourably fight. In Virginia, the law is absurd in
abstract and disgraceful as administered by vulgar men. It is corrupting

when confused with ethics. Without a legitimate king, England would be as bad, for it, too, would have to rely on the Law. One of the ill-bred councillors asks, '[I]s it fit that every impudent fellow that pretends to a little Honour, Loyalty & Courage, should serve his king and Country against the Law? no, no, Brother, these things are not to be suffer'd in a Civill Government by Law Establisht.' Law becomes the opposite of loyalty, as democracy of honour.

In the hilarious drinking scene of the Committee of Safety in *The Roundheads*, written during the Popish Plot furore, Behn had reduced non-monarchical government to a farce of vulgar self-interest. In still more tense times, she repeated the device here, as the Virginians set up court aided by a bowl of punch with 'a great ladle or two in it'. Their first item before they move on to the domestic bickerings is to vote themselves a new larger punch bowl. Such is democracy, Behn seems to say, such the people's ability, such the quagmire on which the apparently secure edifice of the government of a realm is built. As one onlooker remarks, 'The Country's well, were but the People so.' Despite all the political perceptiveness which her creation of Bacon implied, Behn could still not look beyond a single figure, the royally sanctioned Governor, for any political resolution. Only this man will properly separate Native Americans and English, base- from well-born, and show who is master.[10]

Chaotic Virginia is also home to the tobacco-smoking, buffalo-eating widow Ranter, who shares the title of the play with Bacon and, with her exploits in martial cross-dressing, burlesques him. She has the spirit, almost crudeness, that Behn's pure young heroines can no longer afford. The Ranters had been a radical sect in the Interregnum, but, by the late Restoration, they were largely forgotten and the term was used for a roistering man or a whorish woman: Ranter is a roistering woman.[11] As such, she lives high, giving gargantuan banquets to anyone of a jolly disposition, smoking and drinking in the morning, downing pints of punch through the day, riding like a man in the evening, and roundly abusing her servants like a lord. She has gained her money through inheriting from Colonel Ranter, who had bought her as an indentured servant off a ship from England, then married her, and conveniently died. She is aware that her attraction must be largely in her purse; without it, 'I might sit still and sigh, and cry out, a Miracle! a Miracle! at sight of a Man within my doors.'[12]

Ranter sees herself as a good 'Commodity' for a young fellow with his fortune to make. But in fact she wants Dareing, one of Bacon's followers, an older man who is not especially attracted to her wealth, having more complex desires. Dareing is persuaded to take her rather than the younger woman he loves, only if she stays in the male dress she has donned to pursue him and proves herself in fighting: 'I never lik'd thee half so well in Petticoats.' Yet, the depiction is not subversive—it cannot be for, as Behn knew, if pushed to any limit, the theatrical woman in breeches simply became a rogue and a freak. She would do this in *Sir Anthony Love*, a startling play of the 1690s by Behn's new play-writing friend, Thomas Southerne, who doubtless thought of Ranter when he created his heroine. She too stays in men's clothes but goes further than any of Behn's cross-dressed women in refusing the romantic role, choosing to give her lover to a more feminine girl.

In the portrait of the frank, free and cheery widow, Ranter, praised as 'good-natur'd and Generous' and never 'melancholy', there may be a compliment to Madam Welldon, the dedicatee chosen by the editor in accordance with Behn's wishes, a lady 'Eminent for Hospitality'.[13] It is hard, too, not to see in the widow an image of Aphra Behn herself. Ranter tried to make life 'as Comical' as possible and was irritated at belief in the stars as fate; she liked punch, and Behn was remembered for her milk punch. So with love: Ranter wanted it but asked, 'why should I sigh and whine, and make my self an Ass, and him conceited....'[14] With Behn, Ranter dominated company and promoted good cheer, but both felt stricken when not attended to and appreciated. The exaggerated picture of a libidinous Ranter which Dareing made to tease the widow reflects the exaggerated satire which credited Behn with vast sexual feats: 'half a dozen [such women] wou'd ruine the Land,' said Dareing of Ranter, 'debauch all the men, and scandalize all the women.'[15] Fittingly, when the play was performed posthumously, the role of Ranter was taken by the actress for whom Behn had so often written and on whose naughty reputation (as on her own) she had capitalised, Betty Currer.[16] If the widow *were* a portrait, however, it would reflect only one aspect of Behn's complicated personality. It could not, for example, include her intellectual and imaginative powers or the melancholy of ill-health. It would have taken account of her humour, though, for Behn would have transposed her snobbish literary self into an illiterate and rich former servant.[17]

Oroonoko was probably written between the announcement of Queen Mary's pregnancy and the birth, since it was printed by William Canning just after the *Happy Birth* poem, in which it was advertised for sale. Behn had long contemplated the story and had told it often in company, with a tone her writing never caught. The rehearsing meant that the writing was quick, an afterthought: on her own admission she wrote it out in '*a few Hours*' and '*never rested my Pen a Moment for Thought*'. Charles Gildon added the detail that the room was filled with company. Behn had always had the knack of composing wherever she was; it had fuelled her scorn for those who made a palaver of writing.

Oroonoko was both Behn's own story, based on memories of Surinam, and a sardonic-tragic extension of the last part of *Love-Letters*, with its sense of corruption triumphant deep within a state. This time, the state was a definitely doomed one, since her readers knew of the later fate of Surinam, to which Behn referred in the work: its conquest by the Dutch. England itself could now fall to the Dutch. So, in this famous tale, memories of Surinam were overladen with contemporary anxieties, and the people of America—Trefry, Marten and Behn herself as narrator—stood for the increasingly powerless English loyalists of 1688, while the crude Banister and the rogue Deputy Governor Byam did duty for Burnet and William of Orange.[18]

Together, *Oroonoko* and *The Widdow Ranter* clarify the little sympathy Behn felt for ordinary victims of slavery and hierarchy. Like Charles I, James II, and Bacon, Oroonoko is a martyr to unworthy popular rule. For Behn the evils of democracy which killed her heroes were so great that they diminished other possible evils. England's colonies became places for the worst elements in society, a dumping ground for its misfits. It could, therefore, only be redeemed by aristocratic control. Had the noble Governor, the King's vice-regent, been present in Surinam or Virginia the tragedies would not have occurred. Neither Native Americans nor slaves would have rebelled. This point was stressed to Behn's dedi-catee, Lord Maitland: if he had been able to protect Oroonoko, the latter 'had not made so Inglorious an end'.

With Cesario and Octavio of *Love-Letters*, Behn had begun to inves-tigate absurd and tragic male heroism. In Oroonoko as in Bacon, she contemplated the admirable person deceived by himself and by worldly men, now quite unsuited to the modern age. Each has something of the swashbuckling quality of her early Cavalier rakes, but the type is no longer at ease in the world. More clearly than *The Widdow Ranter*, however, *Oroonoko* warned, celebrated and despaired of the man Behn had so long publicly supported. In the story the hero, noble, sincere, heroic, and a little absurd, is no match for the cunning and brutal forces around him. While panegyric praised the royal family as if no dangers were nigh, then, Behn's most famous short story functioned as a coded warning to King James of what might happen if he were not on his guard. *Oroonoko*, a richly evocative tale, is not straight allegory of course, and the fictional character of the slave prince is not simply a substitute for James, but the story *is* surely being informed by the impending political tragedy of an historical man. If James and his followers failed immediately to see the analogy, Behn made it clearer in the dedication: '*Men of eminent Parts are as Exemplary as even Monarchs themselves...'Tis by Comparison we can Judge and Chuse!*'

There were many parallels between the black slave and the 'black' Stuart. First, James and Oroonoko, both called Caesar, speak the heroic language of Restoration drama, which Bacon had also used. It was a language suited mainly to the theatre and to a court where the King aspired to absolute distinction from his subjects—the sort of court which the Restoration fantasised in tales of Turkish sultans and African kings. Second, Oroonoko and James both mistimed magnanimity. *The Happy Birth* had taken up the theme which ran through many of the political works of the Stuart period, including Behn's, of royal mercy or forgiveness. Certainly James should have forgiven the bishops before matters got out of hand and he had to arrest and try them. Forgiveness could also be inappropriate, however, and Charles I had reputedly fallen because of his indulgent forgiveness of his enemies. In *Astrea Redux*, just after the Restoration, Dryden praised the 'mildness' that Charles II had inherited from his father, but, by *Absalom and Achitophel* in the Popish Plot years, he was urging the King not to be foolishly and naïvely merciful. In her *Coronation Ode*, Behn had wanted James to grasp the reins of the unruly horse of the people. Now in *Oroonoko* she shows the political folly—as well as personal grandeur—of forgiveness. With Oroonoko she is warning James of the possible defection and treachery of those he had forgiven, men such as Lord Grey, to whom he had shown extraordinary clemency, and perhaps the Earl of Sunderland himself. Moreover, forgiveness betrayed could make a man run to the other extreme. Too forgiving when he had it in his power to harm, Oroonoko turned to threatening horrific vengeance on the colonists when powerless to inflict it.

Third, Oroonoko is defeated by the cruelty of his opponents and by his own naïveté and dread; so too James II was inspired by fear, that the fate of Charles I would be visited on his son. Charles I had been killed and James II had killed his nephew Monmouth. There was no precedent for royal deposition or defeat without death. That a death of James would be caused by a daughter and son-in-law in a Lear-like tragedy made it the more dreadful. In *Oroonoko* Behn pandered to the King's fears by presenting the 'frightful spectacle of a mangled king'. How could she or James know that political violence was giving way to violent verbal politics? Few could have anticipated the mundane, sordid petering out of King James II and his reign.

Like Oroonoko and James, Imoinda and Mary of Modena have curious parallels—indeed Imoinda is almost an anagram of Modena. Both women are romantically loving. As so often with feminine attributes and notions, Behn explains this in terms of culture, in this case, a foreign tradition in which the husband is a god. English husbands are no longer so regarded by fickle English wives, but King James is constantly termed a god in Behn's poetry and the foreign Mary's devotion to him was much noted. The veneration of their husbands, rare in Behn's society and her fictional works, marked out both women as heroic and different. Bacon managed to kill his beloved by accident, while Oroonoko killed Imoinda intentionally. If James fell, no one knew what would happen to the much hated foreign Queen Mary, whose pregnancy, like Imoinda's, was precipitating the tragedy. Many must have assumed she could not survive.

On one level, Behn's emotions were thoroughly engaged with Imoinda and Oroonoko, but she allowed some estranging details into the story. Like the Queen, Imoinda is an exotic beauty. Her tribal scars distinguish her even from Oroonoko, for, where he has only a few carvings, she is covered in birds and flowers. Unlike actual African tribal marks from the Gold Coast, Imoinda's presumed home, hers are in the aesthetic forms appreciated by Europeans, so that she seems 'jappaned'. It was some years since Behn had been in Surinam and her notion of slavery probably had more to do with the East where slaves, often Christians, could be regarded as treasured objects rather than workhorses.[19] Yet the seemingly throwaway detail of the *comprehensive* patterning is so peculiar that some distancing of the character is inevitable. It is exaggerated by the news that, after her murder by Oroonoko, the decorated object is transformed into a corpse whose 'Stink... almost struck them dead'. So too with the hybrid figure of Oroonoko, real and romantic, heir of the great classical slave Aesop, whom Behn has so recently been contemplating; he is made alien in his gruesome death. At one point he appeared to be heading towards the noble tragic fate of Charles I, but this progress is subverted when he is chopped to death, smoking a pipe while his 'Members', ear, nose and arms are hacked off and thrown on the fire. Only 'at the cutting of this other Arm, his Head Sunk, and his Pipe drop'd.' Oroonoko, who had recoiled from the self-mutilation of the strange Native Americans, is mutilated into strangeness himself

Such repeated estrangement might have had a semi-political, semi-personal purpose. As the Baber poem suggested and her writing of *The Widdow Ranter* and *Oroonoko* confirmed, Behn held multiple views and, as she lauded the loyal, she also understood inevitable disloyalty. So, as narrator of the story, she often included herself in the 'we' of the whites and even shared their fear of Oroonoko's possible cruelty when baited. Her absence at crucial moments was ascribed to her physical female weakness, but it might also signify a kind of reluctant disloyalty. In Surinam, Behn had inevitably been part of the often brutal and deceitful European society; so in London, whatever her emotional ties, she remained a member of the non-courtly, non-royal people who must go on living with their kind. As well as admonishing James and his Queen, then, the story may have worked as a covert investigation of her own position in relation to her hero and heroine. She was lamenting a misguided monarch while leaving herself some small room to redefine both him and herself, should events overtake her. Both in *Oroonoko* and in *The Widdow Ranter* genres wobble as romance collides with violent reality and heroics jostle farce.

Behn concludes her story of *Oroonoko* by boasting of her verbal power. Partly this is to compensate for her inability to protect her hero and heroine in the tale and to provide some form of fame or immortality, now their unborn child is dead. For William Scot, whom she felt she had let down in Antwerp, she had had merely her letters to give in the end. For Dangerfield and Nevil Payne, she had simply tried to set the record straight. In short, for all of these men she had had only a pen with which to do them 'Justice'. Behn, too, wanted 'Justice' for herself, and, in *Oroonoko*, she again expressed the desire for poetic fame inserted into the Cowley translation. She hoped that 'the Reputation of my Pen is considerable enough to make [Oroonoko's] Glorious Name to survive to all ages.' If it did, hers would survive with it. After comparing painting and writing in her dedication to Lord Maitland, Behn exulted that 'the Pictures of the Pen shall out-last those of the Pencil, and even Worlds themselves.' The exaggeration revealed how far she had come since she had seen herself as the author of a middling sort of play.

Lord Maitland was one of James's Scots and, with him, Behn could continue to pay '*the Obligations I have to some of the Great Men of your Nation*' and emphasise her new enthusiasm for Scotland which, despite the '*Barrenness of [the] Soil*', produced so many admirable men. Although the nephew of the Protestant Duke of Lauderdale who had ruled Scotland autocratically in the 1670s and son-in-law of the virulently Protestant Earl of Argyll, recently executed as part of the wider Monmouth Rebellion, Maitland, like Dryden and Melfort, was a recent Catholic convert. So Behn could gain extra merit with the court through a dedication of *Oroonoko* to a Catholic. Maitland was therefore praised not only for his learning and loyalty—he is of course an aristocratic bulwark of monarchy—but also for his religion: *''tis only Men of so elevated Parts, and fine Knowledge; such noble Principles of Loyalty and Religion this Nation sighs for. Where is it amongst all our Nobility we shall find so great a Champion of the Catholick Church?'* Then, after publication of *Oroonoko* in June or July, that is, just after the controversial birth of the Prince of Wales and the warming-pan rumours, Behn or possibly Canning thought better of so public an endorsement of Catholic loyalty. The last sentence was excised from other copies of the work.

In June 1688, the same month as the 'Happy Birth', Henry Sidney, younger cousin of Colepeper and uncle and close friend of Sunderland, obtained the signature of several nobleman on a letter in cipher which he sent to William of Orange. The letter invited William to invade his father-in-law's kingdom. James continued writing his own letters to his nephew William in his usual simple and kindly way.

By late September, even James, surrounded as he was by the rival sycophancies of the Earls of Sunderland and Melfort, felt things amiss and began to reel back his Catholic policies and appointments. Some Protestants were restored to office and the army; the hated Sunderland was dismissed. It was all too late. The situation had grown critical: London was in an uproar with rumours of Catholic atrocities and there were frequent mob attacks.

On 5 November, William of Orange answered the nation's call by landing in Torbay. He brought with him printing presses to print pamphlets which were distributed all over England through the penny post and through booksellers who were given them to sell for their own benefit.[20] Burnet, who had come over with William, was much involved in the campaign and it was probably his influence that made the pamphlets insist on the fraudulent birth of the Prince of Wales.[21] James's propaganda machine was outclassed. Some rushed to defend the King, others like Behn's young friend, George Granville, yearned to do so. Most stayed away.

At this point James had one of the most unlucky and vicious

nosebleeds in history. In fact, it was more of a haemorrhage, accompanied by insomnia, vertigo and headaches. The loss of blood led to hallucinations of his murdered father which eroded his courage, as did the defection of his former followers, including his daughter Princess Anne and many of the nobles Behn had praised in dedications and in her *Coronation Ode*. The court disintegrated around him. In early December the Queen and baby Prince left for France. James tried to follow, was caught, and then allowed to slip away. It was tragedy turned into farce. The Stuart monarchy which had been Behn's political life was ended.

James's escape was a relief to William, but a stunning humiliation for the King's supporters. Behn's feeling for James had been genuine and deep, if probably never unalloyed. His past encouragement of her plays had made a personal bond, while her public praises of him had helped rivet her to him. She understood expedience—she well knew of it in poets and in herself—but she must have felt deeply saddened and disappointed. The divinity of royalty she had so baroquely hymned never had much to do with the actual royal men and women, but she admired gracious public behaviour. This flight was not a gracious act.

By fleeing like his father, rather than standing firm as he himself had done in 1685 in the face of Monmouth, James opened the way for usurpation. Had he remained in London, he would most likely have rallied support. More people than Aphra Behn still had memories of the Civil War and feared the anarchy that might follow any disturbance of the strict hereditary principle. The English were wary of foreigners and William was a Dutchman. James could have capitalised on the animosity this stern, astute and unprepossessing man quickly aroused. But the very traits Behn had so often lauded in the King kept him, like Oroonoko, rigid until he broke and, although courageous in past battles, he lost his nerve with his health and his confidence. He could not stay to compromise, for compromise was what a divine king should not do. It was a shock to discover that, despite his belief in sacred monarchy and its binding oaths, men found it easy to betray him. Behn's analysis of heroic men, Oroonoko and Bacon, written before James's flight, was proving fatally true—even down to the physical collapse.

Sunderland, dressed as a woman, fled to Holland. He had of course kept options open and, like Philander of *Love-Letters*, could be counted on soon to return 'in as much Splendour as ever'. It was no surprise to Behn to find that Lord Grey had not heeded a call to support the man who had so unexpectedly pardoned him. Later he was seen among the followers of William of Orange who, in time, gave him an earldom. Melfort and Maitland escaped to the Continent, but Jeffreys, fleeing disguised as a sailor, was assaulted by a mob and put in the Tower, where he died a few months later. The Duke of Norfolk, Behn's Maecenas, prudently went abroad, then joined William once James left his kingdom; so he took part in yet another coronation and Behn lived to savour the irony of her earlier words: 'so long as the Royal Cause has such Patrons as your Lordship, such vigorous and noble Supporters, his Majesty will be great, secure and quiet.' Drumlangrig had anticipated him: he had become the first Scot to abandon the King and accept the new ruler.

Further down the scale, men moved with the times. The Aesop illustrator, Francis Barlow, attuned as ever to the popular will, quickly produced a new pack of playing cards, detailing the 'Crimes' of James II and the arrival of William as saviour. Jacob Tonson, the publisher, made a hefty profit out of a reissue of *Paradise Lost*, which had been pretty coolly received in 1667. Nat Lee, the playwright, said to have been always a Whig at heart despite his frequent bouts of Toryism and the aid James II had given him in Bedlam, moved swiftly over to the new rulers. But not everyone could so easily turn: Roger L'Estrange was imprisoned and Henry Nevil Payne fled to Scotland. Loyal support for James, which Behn had so often lauded, became illegal Jacobitism.

CHAPTER 30

❖

End of Stuart Dynasty and Death of Aphra Behn

'I like the Excluded Prophet stand'

William and his supporter Gilbert Burnet had expected an enthusiastic welcome from the English nobles, as well as from the
common people who had supposedly suffered under Stuart rule. Neither
group acted as it should. The people had been jubilant only as long as
they were ignorant of the Dutch William, while the nobles hung back.
Parliament too was recalcitrant.

By January 1689 there was acrimonious debating over what to do
with the throne. Some thought it should be left to James, but with
administration vested in the Prince of Orange as regent; some believed
it should be declared vacant through James's flight. In which case, it
should go to his daughter and Protestant heir, Mary, with her powerful
husband as prince consort. Two other monarchical options were mooted:
that the hereditary principle should be waived and the Prince of Orange
become king or that William and Mary, both with a Stuart parent,
should rule jointly.[1] William declared roundly that he would not hold
'anything by apron strings' and refused to 'have any share in the government unless it was put in his person, and that for the term of life'.[2]

In poor health and always irritated by political wrangling, of which
he had experienced a good deal in the United Provinces, William was
intensely irritated by the public discussion. He was well aware that the
country was at his disposal and that he could declare himself king without
much opposition or help from anyone. He found it demeaning that the
realm he had just liberated or conquered should be considering in so
public a manner what to do with him. Never affable at the best of times,
he let his temper sour and, at the end of January, Evelyn noted that he
'shew'd little countenance to the noblemen and others, whoe expected a
more gracious and chereful reception when they made their court'.[3]

During these difficult weeks of negotiations, Burnet, who had worked
so tirelessly for the Orange cause, worried at the resentment William

442

was inspiring, even in those who had been foremost in inviting him. He needed some quick propaganda besides his own to focus opinion on the benefits the new ruler was conveying on the English. In this spirit he probably approached Aphra Behn. He did not care for her morals, but he had preached morality to Charles II and had no fear of taint. As for her political opinions, although Burnet knew she had been a skilled apologist of the old regime, he had some reason to hope they might be changed, or, more accurately, they might be bought. He heard she was ill and would therefore be in need of support and money.[4] He may also have believed her the author of the vicious satire on Dryden's conversion, as well as knowing of some activities that later ages did not.

Burnet might have been encouraged by Behn's most recent publication, a light story of amorous intrigue set in France called *The Lucky Mistake*, dedicated, after James's flight, to her young poetic friend, George Granville.[5] When he read this dedication, he would perceive no hint of Jacobitism, despite the fact that Behn, a supporter of James, was writing to another supporter at what she called 'this Critical Juncture'. Indeed, her reference to the nation's need to have its 'Laws and Liberties' defended was, in the present context, at least ambiguous.

During the crisis, Granville had retired in disgust to his mother's house in Yorkshire, from where he expressed his poetic contempt for the world and its degeneracy. Fittingly, then, Behn praised him for his pastoral passivity. This quality had first been celebrated in her character, Celadon, before he bestirred himself to go to Ireland on political business, but it had been denigrated in the poem to Christopher, Duke of Albemarle, written in more fraught times. The renewed celebration of non-involvement which this praise implied appeared to include herself. Both she and Granville would rather not be drudging 'Slaves of State', it seems.

And yet Burnet must have known that, whatever the wealthy Granville might do, Behn would be freed from politics only by death. If not turning Jacobite, she could only follow the advice in the manuscript satire on Dryden: 'when the act is done and finish't cleane / what shold the poet doe but shift the scene.' Burnet, who had famously converted the libertine Earl of Rochester to Anglicanism, could surely make of this needy woman a Williamite.

Behn was no doubt amused at the approach. She knew what Burnet had thought of her—indeed he thought most witty women lewd—but she must also have seen that he admired her poetic skill.[6] The request indicated it. She would refuse of course, for it was only months since she had mocked the 'Belgick lion', but she would do so publicly and in code. If she could not give Burnet the clarity he requested, she would give the equivocation she imagined he half expected. A man such as Burnet could read into, as well as read.

On its surface the work she wrote, *A Pindaric Poem to the Reverend Doctor Burnet*, was heroic, suitable for an old supporter of James II, for whom she was overtly risking her professional future. In it she denied the use of her pen to the man who was *de facto* ruler of the country, the Prince of Orange and Nassau. Yet, both in literary and in state politics, the denial was equivocal, suitable for an author who would need to go on writing whoever ruled in England.

The *Pindaric Poem to Burnet* painted an affecting portrait of Behn as isolated poet, a portrait which the Pindaric form and Burnet's invitation allowed her to make:

> The Brieze that wafts the Crowding Nations o're
>   Leaves me unpity'd far behind
>   On the Forsaken Barren Shore,
> To Sigh with Echo, and the Murmuring Wind...
> ...while the Chosen Seed possess the Promis'd Land,
>   I like the Excluded Prophet stand,
>   The Fruitful Happy Soul can only see,
>   But am forbid by Fates Decree
> To share the Triumph of the joyful Victory....

'Ruin'd in the Universal Turn', she was reduced to cataloguing her 'Indigence and Lost Repose' as her 'Meager Furies'. She did not quite convey humility but she did catch the melancholy of a Muse without its lover, of a court poet without a king.

In fact, her Muse was working fast, but what she had written was a remarkable Pindaric to *Burnet* instead of William. The replacement was not impudent, for it gave Burnet the role of *agent* of the Glorious Revolution. He it was who had helped make William the conqueror. It was a parodic version of the point to which Behn had long been tending, that the pen is mightier than the sword and that the state needs its writers. In her new configuration, James as usual remained the simple soldier, a sort of Trojan Hector. William became Odysseus, sly maker of the Trojan horse, who captured Troy by deceit before arms. Because, despite his army, William was not delivered primarily as a soldier, as he had been in Behn's poem on Mary of Modena's pregnancy, he could be seen the more as a creation of Burnet, who moulded him into the embodiment of power.

Although Baber had earlier been rude about her royal portrait, in this poem as elsewhere Behn insisted that she followed L'Estrange in dealing with the 'Truth' when it came to the King. So James II had simply been delivered by history. Dealing in propaganda not truth, however, Burnet had to create a fictional image of the new ruler, William. It had all worked out well for him, and Burnet had made the fickle public accept the new order created in the time of 'post-truth'. In other words, he had seduced the country with his pen—and, it is implied, made a nation of whores. (Significantly, Behn did not allude to the piece of Burnet's propaganda which had been most effective: she had acknowledged that the Stuart monarchy had been shaken by the fiction of the Popish Plot, but now she omitted mention of his insistence on the fraudulent birth of the Prince of Wales.)

Burnet's would-be seduction of the nation was enacted in miniature with Behn herself. Her coy Muse became a humble but honest English maiden, enticed by the notoriously tempting cleric. She probably recalled Dryden's lines in *The Hind and the Panther* of Burnet as a 'portly prince, and goodly to the sight...Broad back'd, and Brawny built for Loves delight, / A Prophet form'd, to make a female Proselyte'.[7] As the seducee, Behn was the inferior, a woman of the past, while Burnet was a man of the future. She was detached from power, while he was at the centre of the new regime; she was principled and poor, while he was flexible, unprincipled and rewarded; she was a writer only of feminine pastoral, while he was a master of all styles, now heroic, now honey-tongued, seducing with 'Language soft as Love'.

Despite these contrasts, all serving her claim to feminine humility, Behn also used code and allusion to undercut her surface point, that, being of the old order she must perish with it. She declared she laid no claim to heroic poetry, especially heroic panegyric—she 'never durst, like Cowly, tune her Strings, / To sing of Heroes and of Kings'. Yet the claim was palpably absurd: Behn was even then addressing Burnet in Cowley's heroic pindaric form and both were aware that she had just written reams of court poetry to two kings. At the same time, they both knew this to be a hoary poetic manoeuvre, used by the Latin poet Horace and by Cowley himself, a man who had had to shift and turn to cope with changes in power. He, too, had declared himself the 'Excluded Prophet' and then moved on and in.[8]

With this claim went some literary-political awareness. From the present dearth of heroic poetry Behn must have seen not just that poets were holding back, but that the genre was going out of fashion. Heroic pindaric poetry had been part of the panoply of sacred kingship in which the Stuarts had wrapped themselves and which, many thought now, had helped them separate themselves from political reality. Men like Shadwell had always found it distasteful. Now, it palpably did not suit the far from divine, more down-to-earth, and actively heroic William. If, then, Behn was, like Cowley before her, a forsaken prophet, it was in a context where there was no further occasion for 'prophets'. Even in the old order, Behn had never been a much rewarded one. She had constantly hymned the tie of Stuarts and patronage, been sycophantic in her praise, and yet here she was declaring her poverty. Something must be allowed to be amiss. There might be other routes.[9]

Beyond political implication and allusion was Behn's desire for literary fame, admitted both in the Cowley translation and in *Oroonoko*. Now in this *Pindaric Poem* she revealed how she saw it slipping from her as she understood a truth of the new context, a truth beyond her earlier realisation that a state needed writers. This was that the state also governed *literary* fame. Fame, or, in modern terms, entry into the canon, was predicated on acceptance by an elite that controlled culture. The elite consisted of those with political authority. So, in the new world of Burnet and William, the writer of approved propaganda alone was an artist.

The ambiguous politics of *A Pindaric Poem to Burnet* fitted the moment. The refusal to praise William was clear, but little else. James who, by February, was preparing with French help to retake his kingdom was not revered as the present king, but entirely as a former master who had fallen, while William, not king indeed, was yet conceded to be the future. Had the work been written after the coronation, the insistence on calling the Prince by his Dutch title of Nassau would have startled a cautious reader. In the early months of 1689, however, it was not significant and Burnet must have felt he need not despair of Behn's support in the long run. Even in *her* poem James was a failed king.

She was in large company. Her old acquaintance Thomas Sprat, now Dean of Westminster, was trying again to set the needs of new allegiance within a framework that would not entirely sully it. Like Behn, Sprat implied it was his fidelity to the old regime that made him worthy of trust by the new.

Events were moving quickly in the early weeks of 1689. Coming to the only possible conclusion, Parliament announced that James II had abdicated and that the throne was vacant. On 6 February, the crown was offered to William and Mary jointly, with the administration vested entirely in William's hands—as he insisted. As soon as the news was conveyed to Holland, Mary set out for London. She arrived in Greenwich in mid-February, to be welcomed by William and her sister Anne. There was the kind of general rejoicing with bells and bonfires that the rather ungracious Dutchman William could never inspire in England, and court poets and artists took heart at her presence.

Before landing, she had worried about the demeanour she should adopt in her native country, where her father had just been vanquished by her husband, and many were mindful of *King Lear* and its viperous daughters.[10] In France, Madame de Sévigné imagined Mary stepping over James's body and sneered that she had been 'the procuress of her husband in his bid to take possession of the Kingdom of England'.[11] Aware of such attitudes, Mary accepted her husband's instructions that she show no public sorrow for her father's fate when she entered Whitehall. She acted too well and many onlookers, including Evelyn, were shocked at the gaiety with which she took possession of the old King's house.

Probably Burnet read correctly the political meaning of Behn's *Pindaric Poem*. He realised that her fascination for power was undimmed, but noted her implied cynicism. So he may now have suggested she take on the more welcome task of applauding James's daughter. Praise solely of Mary was a common strategy for James's old supporters who wanted to remain in London and receive some patronage. Behn obliged without equivocation. *Her Congratulatory Poem to her Sacred Majesty Queen Mary, upon her Arrival in England* was hurriedly written: Narcissus Luttrell bought a copy for 2*d* only two weeks after Mary landed.

In this new poem, Behn could be more open about affection for 'an Unhappy dear Lov'd *Monarch*' than she had been in the *Pindaric Poem*, following her old habit of praising a lesser person by subsuming him or her into the greater. In earlier poems, Rochester had overpowered Anne Wharton and Thomas Creech, just as young Howard had been overwhelmed by his martyred father, Lord Stafford. Here Mary could more subtly disappear in James, within the conceit that she was his double, another Stuart deity revealing 'all the Lines of your great Father's face'. Given this doubled identity, Mary did not need the authority provided by a writer, as William had needed Burnet's. Her authority was from God as James's had been, as well as from her father. One monarch had been metamorphosed into the other.

Behn was comfortable celebrating a powerful woman—her politics of absolutism, not based on paternal rule of father in his household, had never insisted power be masculine, only legitimate and hereditary. Indeed, she had always had more ease in associating herself with female than with male royalty, Catherine than Charles II, Mary of Modena than James II. She enjoyed the interaction of the female body with the state: Catherine the martyr, Mary of Modena as lover of James and the nation, and now Mary, a regnant queen who would rule through 'Beauties'. Behn's Muse was often female. Mary, the Stuart queen, slid easily into this role, inspiring her 'Genius with new Life and Flame'. Always sensitive to female attractions, Behn had conveyed the charms of Mary of Modena, as well as of Nell Gwyn and the Duchess of Mazarine. The new Queen too was beautiful, demanding flamboyant imagery. The unfortunate levity of her arrival in Whitehall was glossed as lack of 'Formal Nicety', part of her sweet affability. None the less, no reader could fail to note that the portrait was more muted than that of Mary's step-mother.

Like the *Pindaric Poem to Burnet* and all Behn's panegyrics, these verses to Mary were as much about herself as her ostensible subject and about the poet's role in politically tempestuous times. She began in self-contemplation, taking up the image of the *Pindaric Poem*, of herself as 'Excluded Prophet', resolving to publish no more 'fruitless Songs' for '*Brittains* Faithless Shore'. Facing a republic, Cowley and the Interregnum Cavalier poets had grievingly accepted a private pastoral life, taking their Muses with them. But Behn's Muse wanted public nourishment and did not care to retire. If Behn had invoked the image of rural retreat, it had usually been as prelude to rescue. Although, then, the poem began by placing the poet in a dark covert by the Thames, under willows through whose thick shade no light could penetrate, the retreat sounds as much like seclusion in St Bride's as in the country. After all, it was mid-February, not a time noted for the thick shade of willow leaves.

Whether the pastoral world she invoked was inside or outside, it began by being empty: not a nymph or faun in sight. Presumably William had frightened them away since they had been very present in 1685. Soon they returned, however, their arrival echoing that in the *Coronation Ode* for James. Relieved of her unwelcome isolation, Behn could join in the general rapture, moving from the winter of James to the spring of his daughter:

> *Maria* with the Sun has equal Force,
> No Opposition stops her Glorious Course,
> Her pointed Beams thro' all a passage find,
> And fix their Rays Triumphant in the Mind.

Soon the poet was properly overwhelmed by the glamour of true royalty: 'What Human Fortitude can be / Sufficient to Resist a Deity?' Behn was incorrigible where it came to the Stuarts.

In her poem, the political wrangling of the 'several Factions, several Int'rests' which had so irritated William was quelled not by his force but by his wife's presence: 'Great Caesar's Off-spring blest our Isle, / The differing Multitudes to Reconcile.' Past loyalty was served by the absence of any mention of the real ruler of the country, Mary's mastering husband, soon to be crowned William III. So the old King James, 'Great Lord, of all my Vows', was asked for his permission for Behn to pay tribute to the daughter who was 'a Part of You'—though notably she did not wait for the exiled King's reply. Whatever James was planning in France, there was no opening for his return in his old supporter's poetry.

What else could she have done? Much ailing by now, Aphra Behn had still to look to her possible future. She could not flee with James and the remnants of his court to Paris. James's exile included a palace and largesse from his cousin, King Louis XIV. A poor poet's flight abroad or to the country might simply be self-destructive, more like the magnificent, pointless resistance of the slave Oroonoko. Behn was a sick woman, probably now with no close family. She could hardly get around London, let alone make a journey outside. The rural seclusion in which she had symbolically placed herself at the outset of her poem to Mary was not an option without private means. She was a professional, political poet and her work was to hymn power in as principled a way as she could while earning a living. The heroic poet Cowley himself knew that court poetry could not be written in exile or to the loser: 'it is so uncustomary, as to become almost *ridiculous*, to make lawrels for the *Conquered*.' Though in war the pen could accompany the sword, 'when the event of battel, and the unaccountable *Will* of *God* has determined the controversie... we must lay down our *Pens* as well as our *Arms*, and we must march out of our *Cause* it self...'.[12] So, inevitably, *A Congratulatory Poem* aimed at making peace with the new source of power. It cannot have been exactly what 'great NASSAU' wanted but, as Behn wrote at the end of her *Pindaric Poem* to Burnet, he had other pens to 'immortalise his Name'. Maybe the satirist who called her 'machiavellian Behn' thought she went too far, but the country would be a den of Machiavellians if such political trimming deserved the label.

Perhaps, though, she had gone further than her Stuart loyalist publisher, William Canning, wished to follow. He had published the poems on the birth of a Prince of Wales and was then a co-publisher with Richard Bentley of the Mary work, but the *Pindaric Poem to Burnet* was brought out by Bentley alone, a man who may well have been involved in anti-Stuart propaganda before James's flight.[13] Certainly Behn went beyond Henry Nevil Payne, who could not be coopted for William and Mary, or Dryden, who did not supply a poem for the new rulers—though Shadwell, his old enemy, added insult to injury by faking one for him.[14] Shadwell of course provided work on his own behalf as well. His efforts met with approval, and in March he was rewarded with the laureateship, replacing his old antagonist, John Dryden.

On 11 April, William and Mary were jointly crowned in Westminster Abbey, guarded by Dutch soldiers. For the first time in English history monarchs swore to govern according to 'the statutes in Parliament' and, after the ceremony, there was no touching for the King's Evil. This was not a divine monarchy. Burnet, upholder of the gender proprieties and fitting symbol of the new regime that would promote moral values in society and theatre, preached the coronation sermon. The crown was carried by the illegitimate son of Charles II, the Duke of Grafton, dedicatee of Behn's most politically committed Stuart play, *The Roundheads*. Her old friend Thomas Sprat, who had a few months earlier organised prayers of thanksgiving for Mary of Modena's pregnancy, assisted at the service as current Dean of Westminster, showing that he could negotiate this Revolution as he had negotiated the Restoration nearly thirty years before.

If Aphra Behn picked up her pen to hymn the moment, she had to let it fall again. For on 16 April, five days after the coronation, she died.

It was commonplace to blame death on doctors and pharmacists, and the 'Memoirs' was no exception: 'her Death' was 'occasioned by an unskilful Physician'. Probably there was some truth in it. Behn's old enemy Gould described druggists

> (Who, *Leach-like*, cleave to the poor *Patient* close,
> And suck their *Purses* full 'ere they break loose;)
> With their damn'd, long, unconscionable *Bills*,
> Bring in as many Pounds as they deliver *Pills*.
> Thus *Fools*, with *Villains* wilfully complying,
> Are made to pay for dying.[15]

This is certainly possible for Behn. Many died of their 'cures', especially when these included hefty doses of mercury and new hot dung.

Also chronic pain persuades its sufferers to search, even irrationally, for relief and, despite her pleas of poverty, Behn was probably not as poor in her final year as she had been earlier; she had something to lay out on physicians and quacks. Her commendation of the mystical herbalist, Thomas Tryon, and her attraction to Cowley's *Of Plants*, which lengthily described the curative properties of plants, prove her interest in health and medicines, and she probably had some belief in doctors, although she did note that a person best knows his or her own body. She routinely ridiculed quacks, along with lawyers and clerics, but she omitted from *Sir Patient Fancy* Molière's opinion, that 'Most men die of their cures, and not their diseases'. She might have been better served had she followed the new ruler rather than the old: where Charles II had been famously helped to death by excess medical advice, the always sickly William considered himself alive only because he avoided doctors.[16]

As well as sickness and cures, Behn had thought much about the moment of death, the act of dying itself. Lord Stafford's end on the scaffold in 1680 had been an example to the nation in the art of dying well. In her translation of La Rochefoucauld, she noted that heroism in death was not confined to the well-born: Vratz the highwayman and murderer had put on as great a show as any peer. In the last years, her fiction too had been engrossed with death, especially the spectacular version: of the accepting Isabella of *The History of the Nun*, of the stoical Oroonoko, of the foolish Tarquin of *The Fair Jilt*, of the misguided Cesario of *Love-Letters*, and of the Oedipal Dangerfield of 'The Dumb Virgin'.

Although each character was heroic in some way, however, each also had some grotesqueness that prevented a completely heroic depiction and made the whole inharmonious. If disharmony was part of staged death, it was even more so of private inadvertent dying. In public, Behn knew that people could rise to heights caused less by heroism of spirit than by fear of disapproval. In private, it was different. In her translation of La Rochefoucauld, she distanced herself from Stoicism. The Roman philosopher Seneca had believed in the mind's control of the body, but Behn had no such illusion and probably did not expect great things of her dying self. She accepted the pain of death and the fear of the pain. Everyone dreaded death she thought, and most clung to life, even when it seemed intolerable: 'Tho wrackt with various paines yet life does please / Much more than death, which all our pressures ease.'

Although Behn loved the panoply of religion, she had shown little faith in other-worldly comfort, and she was not important or suggestible enough for Gilbert Burnet to give her the time he boasted of lavishing on the dying Earl of Rochester. So she looked forward to a dissolution of the body and a return to those amorphous atoms which Lucretius had seen as the essence of life and death. In her elegy for Rochester and in her translation of La Rochefoucauld, she expressed the Lucretian view of 'Death's eternal Night', of *'nox perpetua'* not the *'lux perpetua'* of the Christian mass. In her last performed plays, one heroine declared, 'I cou'd not have pray'd heartily if I had been dying,' while a hero, unfazed by black magic, asserted, 'I am for things possible and Natural.' Behn did not feel the need of compromising an intellectually libertine life with the repentance that had allegedly terminated the Earl of Rochester's.

By dying in the week of William and Mary's coronation, Behn avoided outliving her age: she would not see stately Dorset Garden, scene of all her theatrical triumphs, left to 'rats and Mice, and perhaps an old superannuated jack-pudding to look after', in time pulled down or 'converted to more pious use' to atone for its 'levity' and 'transgressions'.[17] Instead she had come in and out of literature within the Restoration and she would be firmly linked with its culture and theatre. It was the kind of unison of experience and history that usually occurs only in fiction, when the era and the central consciousness fade in tandem. This was as it should be, for Behn's life, with all its trials and physical pain, had been theatrical and fictional in the highest degree.

The small groups of witty and vicious, paradoxically potent and impotent men and women whom Behn admired and served contributed little to the political and social future beyond provoking reactionary moralities. Together, they and Behn became a hiccup in the erratic but irresistible development of English culture towards democracy, individualism, capitalism, consumerism, pursuit of happiness, human rights, the sanctity of life, spiritual craving, and family values. Yet, before the demonisation of this brutal and glittering age, Aphra Behn experienced to the full its libertarian and libertine possibilities; in it she had been allowed to experiment with styles of living and writing in the way few women could do or would wish to do for centuries to come. For Behn and for her friends, the theatre had been life and the metaphor for life. It would be a long time before any woman would again feel able to accept so thoroughly the theatricality of her demeanour or to remain so masked that nothing about her could be declared 'authentic'. It would also be a long time before a woman would be free to ignore or criticise marriage and motherhood. Or indeed to find death grotesque and funny. Or to display state power and domination as openly erotic. Or to hate commerce and the feckless poor. Or to delight in and mock sex. Or openly to pursue pleasure and ease.

According with her wish to settle with Orinda and Sappho, Aphra Behn *did* have immediate influence on women and women writers. As Virginia Woolf remarked, she had given them the 'right to speak their minds' and, for a short time, their bodies. A few years after her death, the writer of the prologue to her last performed play, *The Younger Brother*, revealed that Behn had made writing women as natural as watching women: 'The Ladies too are always welcome here, / Let 'em in Writing or in Box appear.' Yet, by becoming a byword for lewdness, Aphra Behn also had a negative influence on female authors, helping to construct the prevailing feminine style that would restrict their content and manner for several centuries. She had not planned that Blunt's missing breeches in *The Rover* should shock a later audience and, as she said, she would have been insane if she had purposely gone about to offend popular taste, even of the future; yet perhaps to be vilified as an unfeminine *woman* would not much have distressed her. Although she wished to be remembered with female poets, in the last resort her desire was not to appear simply as a *woman*-writer at all—indeed a *woman*-anything. Her reiterated point was that she wrote as anyone did, and was as good as (almost) any man. Sex and gender were fluid, fun and funny, to be used, celebrated, mocked, and bent for one's purposes, but they did not denote essential qualities. They were the subject of art not its determinants.

Aphra Behn was buried in Westminster Abbey, probably allowed there by Thomas Sprat. With felicitous error, the burial register recorded the death not of the secretive Mrs Behn, but of the public 'Astrea', patron and poet of Arcadia. She was placed in an outside position, in the East cloisters 'near the door that goes into the church' in the words of her foster-brother, Thomas Colepeper. A few years later the slippery Tom Brown joined her there, as did the actor-manager Tom Betterton, arguably the most influential man in her life. A black marble slab was placed on her grave. Unusually for a woman it mentioned no family at all, no father, mother, sibling, husband or child, nor any place and date of birth.[18]

Perhaps John Hoyle, a follower of Lucretius and doubter of the afterlife, wrote the lines inscribed below her name on the slab:

Here lies a Proof that Wit can never be
Defence enough against Mortality.

But it is as likely that she made this little rhyming preparation for her own death, including reputation in the decay of the body.[19] Like Keats, yearning for literary fame while declaring that his name was written on water, she too might, in mingled disillusion and hope, have denied what she most wanted. Or, since everything about Behn is equivocal, the lines may not have been referring to literary fame at all, but may simply have expressed the truth that even the wittiest of people must die.[20] In later centuries, the austere, elegant gravestone was recut and is now quite legible.[21] It terminates the wheelchair ramp down which schoolchildren leap to land heavily on the tomb. Not a spot for quiet contemplation, but perhaps a fitting memorial for a woman who lived in tumult and bustle.

NOTES

✤

Introduction

1. John Dryden, 'Life of Lucian', *Works of John Dryden*, Prose 1691–1698, vol. XX (Berkeley, 1989).
2. W. H. Hudson, *Idle Hours in a Library* (San Francisco, 1897).
3. George Savile, Marquis of Halifax, *The Lady's New Years Gift* (London, 1688), p. 96.
4. Julia Kavanagh, *English Women of Letters* (London, 1863), p. 22.
5. John Doran, *Their Majesties' Servants. Annals of the English Stage* (London, 1888), vol. I, p. 239.
6. It is not strictly true that Behn was the first professional woman writer since, as Elaine Hobby has noted, there were women such as Hannah Woolley, writer of cookery and advice books, and Sarah Jinner, writer of almanacs, and no doubt others earning a living by the pen before Behn, *Virtue of Necessity: English Women's Writing 1649–88* (London, 1988). Behn was, however, the first to earn her primary living over a long period of time through writing in male and elite forms. Several women before Behn had written plays, most of these women being of noble birth and connected with coteries of writing women. In the fourteenth century Katherine Sutton, an abbess, rewrote the Easter liturgical dramas, while, in the sixteenth, Mary Herbert (née Sidney), Countess of Pembroke, wrote a pastoral in honour of Queen Elizabeth I, herself a translator of parts of plays. Elizabeth Cary, Viscountess Falkland, wrote the first full-length original play by a woman, *Mariam, the Fair Queen of Jewry*. In the reign of Charles I, Queen Henrietta Maria wrote and performed plays along with her ladies-in-waiting, and, in the Interregnum, the daughters of William Cavendish, Duke of Newcastle, and his second wife, Margaret, wrote closet plays. Just before Behn, during the Restoration, Frances Boothby and Katherine Philips exhibited their one or two plays on the public stage, and Margaret Cavendish, Duchess of Newcastle, published her closet dramas. None the less, it has been estimated that, in the seventeenth century as a whole, women's writing made up 0.5 per cent of all works published.
7. *A Room of One's Own* (Harmondsworth, 1992), pp. 82–5. For a discussion of Woolf's attitude to Behn, see Virginia Crompton's dissertation "'Forced to write for bread

and not ashamed to owne it": Aphra Behn, Court Poetry and Professional Writing in the 1680s' (Norwich, 1994).

8. Maureen Duffy, *The Passionate Shepherdess: Aphra Behn 1640–1688* (London, 1977) and Angeline Goreau, *Reconstructing Aphra: A Social Biography of Aphra Behn* (New York 1980). I am indebted to both these, especially to Duffy's ground-breaking investigation of Behn's early life.

9. 'The Laugh of the Medusa', *New French Feminisms*, ed. Elaine Marks and Isabelle de Courtivron (New York, 1981), p. 245.

Chapter 1

1. *The Letters from Dorothy Osborne to Sir William Temple* (London, 1942), p. 207.

2. *Bishop Burnet's History of his Own Time* (Oxford, 1833), 6 vols.

3. *The Life and Times of Anthony à Wood, antiquary of Oxford 1632–1695 described by Himself* collected by Andrew Clark, 5 vols. (Oxford, 1891–1900).

4. *The Diary of John Evelyn*, ed. E. S. de Beer (Oxford, 1955), III, 246. Hereafter called Evelyn.

5. *The Diary of Samuel Pepys*, ed. Robert Latham and William Matthews. 10 vols. (London, 1983), vol. 11, 17 August 1661. Hereafter called Pepys.

6. Quoted in Julia Cartwright, *Sacharissa* (London, 1901), p. 107.

7. Behn would have been interested in the female commentators on the royal accession, the little known Rachel Jevon and the soon to be famous Katherine Philips or 'Orinda' as she was named, who composed 'On the faire weather at the Coronacon' in which, like Dryden, she made the sudden advent of the sun on a rainy day into the heavens shining on the crowning. For a short account of Philips, see Patrick Thomas's introduction to volume 1 of the *Collected Works of Katherine Philips, The Matchless Orinda* (Stump Cross, 1990).

8. 'The History of the Life and Memoirs of Mrs. Behn', published in 1698 in *All the Histories and Novels Written by the Late Ingenious Mrs. Behn, Entire in One Volume*, the third edition of the prose works. It was printed in London for Samuel Briscoe. Henceforth it is referred to as 'Memoirs'.

9. *Selected Poems of Anne Finch Countess of Winchilsea*, ed. Katharine M. Rogers (New York, 1979), p. 72.

10. The manuscript collection, including the 'Circuit of Apollo' on which the note occurs, is in the Folger Shakespeare Library, Washington. Despite some irritation at the apparent mystification of Behn's background, there is evidence that Winchilsea admired some aspects of the earlier writer and was influenced by her. Unlike Katherine Philips, Finch sometimes wrote erotic pastoral in the manner of Aphra Behn.

11. See Thomas Colepeper's eighteen-volume manuscript 'Adversaria' (British Library

Harley MSS 7587–7605). Behn appears in two places, as 'Mrs Aphara Bhen' and 'BEENE the famos female Poet'. Hereafter BL.

12. Some of Colepeper's projects were feasible, such as the iron grate, some less so, such as the device to allow divers to stay underwater without air pipes. See *Calendar of State Papers*, Domestic, 1687–89, pp. 57 and 201. Hereafter *CSP*.

13. The case for Eaffry Johnson has been persuasively made by Maureen Duffy in *The Passionate Shepherdess*.

14. Bishops Transcripts, copy in the Centre for Kentish Studies, County Hall, Kent, Maidstone. Unhappily there is a gap in the Smeeth records of christenings from 1639 to 1662.

15. One might speculate that George was deaf since Aphra showed an uncommon interest in sign language, introducing it into her comedies. It also occurs in a late story ascribed to her called *The Dumb Virgin*, where the heroine uses 'the significative way of discourse by the Fingers' (*The Works of Aphra Behn*, ed. Janet Todd, 7 vols., London, 1992–6, vol. 4, p. 344; hereafter called *Works*). John Lacy's *The Dumb Lady: Or, The Farriar Made Physician* (1672) tells of a young lady who pretends to have been struck dumb on her wedding day and there is some association of dumbness and repression, but no one else wrote serious fiction investigating the subject. For the general interest in sign language see Kenelm Digby and George Sibscota's *The Deaf and Dumb Man's Discourse* including *the Method they use, to manifest the sentiments of their Mind* (1670).

16. In the De L'Isle Papers in the Centre for Kentish Studies, the Colepeper children are mentioned as nearly starving in London. See Chapter 2, n. 2.

17. Elizabeth Denham was born on 28 February 1613, and George baptised in Smeeth on 22 August 1620.

18. On his marriage licence Elizabeth and George Denham's father was termed a 'gentleman of Mersham'.

19. There seems to have been no break between the families since, in later life, Elizabeth's mother lived close to her daughter's family. When she remarried, she was described as 'of St. Margaret's', a nearby church. She may even have been sharing the Johnsons' house. In which case Aphra grew up close to her mother's slightly more elevated trading family.

20. See the Canterbury Burghmote Minute Book 22 December 1648. Jane Jones was the first to alert scholars to these records in her article, 'New Light on the Background and Early Life of Aphra Behn', published in *Notes and Queries* and reprinted in *Aphra Behn Studies*, ed. Janet Todd (Cambridge, 1996), pp. 310–20.

21. March 1649, Minute Books.

22. 24 July 1649; court records Canterbury Cathedral Library A/C 4.

23. The catalogue at Canterbury Cathedral Library records the Overseers' Account Book for St. Margaret's for the relevant period but the volume seems to be missing.

24. There were many suggestions on how to decrease the parochial burden and silence the 'loud noise for *Liberty and Property*, tho the invading that of *others* is only aimed at'. See *A Plain and Easie Method: Shewing How the Office of Overseer of the Poor may be managed* (1686).

25. Dedication to *The Roundheads* (1682), *Works*, vol. 6, p. 362.

26. See P. Crawford, 'The Sucking Child: Adult Attitudes to Child Care in the First Year of Life in Seventeenth-Century England', *Continuity and Change*, I, 1986.

27. Cited in Antonia Fraser, *King Charles II* (London, 1993), pp. 73 and 79.

28. The original Johnson mother may have been followed by a step-mother and the woman to whom Behn refers in her Antwerp letters may be a step-mother.

29. The sexual point cannot be stressed, however, since many in the Restoration were fascinated by the entanglement of sexuality, power and family, especially Behn's friend Thomas Otway.

30. See Pedro in *The Feign'd Curtizans* and Trickwell in *The Revenge*, *Works*, vol. 6.

31. In 1647, there was a riot in Canterbury over banned Christmas celebrations. The mayor, who tried to make all shops open, was thrown into the ditch. Riots broke out, which were then given a Royalist tinge. They were easily quelled. An instigator in these riots was Roger L'Estrange, the later Royalist propagandist whom Behn much admired.

32. Her mockery was common. The end of the Rump was greeted with a volley of lampoons and broadsides on this sort of line:

> Now the *Rump* is confounded,
> There's an end of the *Roundhead*,
> Who hath been such a bane to our *Nation*.
> He hath now plaid his part,
> And gone out, like a *fart*,
> Together with his *reformation*....
> *Kings* and *Queens* may appear
> Once again in our *Sphere*,
> Now the *Knaves* are turned out of door.

'The Second Part of Saint George for England', Brindley pamphlets, Huntington Library, California.

33. In a survey of 23 Stuart women's diaries, three-quarters were heavily devotional, see S. H. Mendelson, 'Stuart Women's Diaries and Occasional Memoirs', *Women in English Society 1500–1800*, ed. M. Prior (London, 1985).

34. See Peter Lake, who contrasts 'the formally patriarchal content of puritan ideology and the subtle ways in which the personal godliness of individual women could be invoked to subvert that patriarchalism', 'Feminine Piety and Personal Potency:

the Emancipation of Mrs Jane Ratcliffe', *The Seventeenth Century*, vol. 11, 1987, pp. 150–3.

35. Despite her attraction to Catholicism, it is unlikely that Aphra was raised a Catholic or that she had much to do with Catholics in Kent. Bartholomew would have to have been at least nominally Protestant to hold his post and the Denhams do not appear a Catholic family. There were very few open Catholics in the county and the faith tended to be confined to higher social ranks who could afford to maintain priests trained in foreign seminaries. The laws against Catholics were draconian though frequently unenforced. It is possible that Aphra, like the famous 'Popish midwife' Elizabeth Cellier, was raised a Protestant but was attracted to Rome by the excesses of anti-papist Protestants.

36. *The Emperor of the Moon* (1687), Act I, Sc. I, *Works*, vol. 7, p. 164.

37. The image of an infinitely bounteous nature, located sometimes in a pastoral world and sometimes simply elsewhere, might of course have been the obverse of a harsh reality. Kent was a county of great contrasts in wealth, and, as prices rose through the troubled 1640s, the Johnson family cannot have remained untouched. Those in middling circumstances would be anxious about falling lower down the scale, and rising prices must have posed both a financial and a social threat.

38. Again Behn shows her un-Puritan tendency, for girls were informed in such tracts as Thomas Salter's *The Mirror of Modesty* that they should read only pious books about 'virtuous virgins and worthy women' and avoid songs and sonnets. The tract also demanded that girls not lie or talk much. This could not have suited Behn either.

39. Osborne, *Letters*, pp. 56 and 70.

40. Roger North, *The Lives of the Norths*, ed. Augustus Jessopp (London, 1890), vol. 1, p. 46.

41. Hannah Woolley, *Gentlewoman's Companion* (London, 1675), p. 13.

42. In *England's Pen-Man: Crocker's New Copy-Book* by Edward Crocker (1671), there are examples of various hands, Secretary, Roman, Italian and Court.

43. Some of the copying Aphra Behn may have done would have been legal, as well as literary. For a description of circulating manuscripts, see Harold Love, *Scribal Publication in Seventeenth-Century England* (Oxford, 1993).

44. An example is Mr Bevan's school at Ashford. The curriculum consisted mainly of ornamental attainments, needlework, reading, writing and, increasingly, French. See L. A. Pollock, 'Teach her to Live under Obedience: The Making of Women in the Upper Ranks of Early Modern England', *Continuity and Change*, 4, 1989.

45. Bathsua Makin, *An Essay to Revive the Antient Education of Women* (London, 1673), p. 26. Sir Ralph Verney desired French for his goddaughter but was horrified by any notion she might learn Latin, *Memoirs of the Verney Family during the Seventeenth Century*, ed. F. P. and M. M. Verney (London, 1925), p. 501.

46. Many new schools were being founded from which girls were sometimes explicitly excluded, as at Harrow, or in which they were confined to the lowest levels. See K. U. Henderson and B. F. McManus eds, *Half Humankind: Contexts and Texts of the Controversy about Women in England 1540–1640* (Urbana, 1985).

47. Cavendish, *Philosophical and Physical Opinions* (1655).

48. *A Serious Proposal to the Ladies* (1694).

49. *Works*, vol. 1, no. 11.

50. For an account of the pamphlets concerning Mary Carleton, see *The Counteifeit Ladies*, eds Janet Todd and Elizabeth Spearing (London, 1994).

Chapter 2

1. Thomas was son of Sir Thomas, the fifth of the twelve sons of Sir Anthony Colepeper of Bedgebury.

2. The De L'Isle Papers C 82/14 1 Feb 1637, Kent Community Archives, Maidstone. The union started badly. In 1637 the Countess of Leicester wrote to the Earl, 'This night your newe brother in law is come to visitt me wich is a verie extravagant sivilitie, for I never saw the mans fase in my life, and have not hard on word from your sister since her marieg wich makes me wonder the more at this caviliers complement. What shee finds in him I do not know but if he be not a verie ase I am deseaved' (C82/14). Soon they learnt that 'the poore man is very sadd for his two children [Thomas and Roberta] that att this instant lye dying here in London.' Happily this did not happen and, through Sidney patronage, Colepeper was given a brigade to command after the previous incumbent was discharged as a Catholic. In fact, Sir Thomas Colepeper was not as lowly as the Sidneys liked to think since he had been one of the lieutenants of Dover Castle under Charles I, a position that would be taken by Algernon Sidney during the Interregnum, and he had flourished sufficiently to buy the estate of Hackington near Canterbury, which remained in his son's possession.

3. On the death of his parents, Strangford and his wealth had passed into the wardship of the Crown, and Charles I had sold the administration of it to Sir Thomas Fotherley for the sum of £2,000. Fotherley, who was described by the Countess of Leicester as 'non of the honestest', proved as unsatisfactory as his now dead mother and the boy appealed to his uncle, the Earl of Leicester, to be his guardian instead. On Fotherley's death in 1649, Leicester became Strangford's guardian. See *CSP*, Dom., 1640–1, 434, for a dispute of a petitioner with Fotherley. Strangford is called 'his Majesty's ward'.

4. Strangford would charge that the Earl had been receiving some thousand pounds a year from his estates. He, however, had 'neaver received any of my Rents my Selfe'.

5. Eager to link herself with her famous uncle, Sir Philip Sidney, and to the *Countess*

of Pembroke's Arcadia, Wroth called her work of 1621 *The Countess of Montgomerie's Urania*, Urania being a character in the Arcadia and the Countess being the sister-in-law of the Countess of Pembroke.

6. *The Poems of Lady Mary Wroth*, ed. Josephine A. Roberts (Baton Rouge, Louisiana, 1983).

7. In an unpublished paper, Sharon Valiant speculates that Behn was physically connected with Wroth. Wroth had an illegitimate daughter who married Lovel. There was a Lovel tutoring in the Sidney household and Valiant considers that Behn might have been his daughter and therefore the granddaughter of Lady Mary Wroth. I have not followed this speculation since I imagine Behn would have boasted of such a tie to the aristocracy. As well as writing *Urania*, Wroth also composed a pastoral play called 'Love's Victorie' rather on the lines of *A Midsummer Night's Dream*. The manuscript came into the possession of Sir Edward Dering, a Kentish gentleman known to Colepeper's mother and a supporter of Katherine Philips. There is no proof that Behn knew the Dering family, but she used a variant of the name in one of her last plays, *The Widdow Ranter*. By that time one member of the family, Charles Dering, had become known as a rake and a duellist and the comic fight with a woman which she gives her character might just refer to this man's obstreperousness in the theatre.

8. In *Reconstructing Aphra*, p. 12, Goreau claims that Colepeper lived with his guardian, the Earl of Winchilsea's steward, on their estate just outside Wye, p. 12. On p. 309 she also claims that Lady Elizabeth Finch was 'the daughter of Sir John Fotherley, who had been Thomas Culpepper's original guardian and was steward of the Earl of Winchilsea'. I have not been able to duplicate this information. Jane Jones has pointed out that on p. 284 of his thesis 'The Community of Kent and the Great Rebellion 1640–1660' Alan Everitt mentions a John Fotherby and a Sidney Fotherby, Winchilsea's 'agent'. This man may have been confused with the Fotherley who was Lord Strangford's guardian.

9. *The Roundheads* (1682), *Works*, vol. 6. The prince's tutor was Lovel, a man already involved in Royalist activities when at Penshurst. He travelled with his charge to the Continent.

10. 'Memoirs' and William Oldys, 'Choice Notes', *Notes and Queries*, 2nd series, 11 (London, 1861), pp. 201–2.

11. In the same letter L'Isle exposed more personal irritation against the energetic and favoured Algernon. He found it 'very extrordenary that the younger sonne should so dominere in your house that....it is not only his chamber but the greate roomes of the house, and purhaps the whole he commands'. In time Philip, though inevitably succeeding to the title, would be largely disinherited by his father. De L'Isle papers, C83/51, Kent Community Archives.

12. In later life L'Isle was inclined to solitude, but a letter suggests it was not always

so: a friend writes that he wishes he could send L'Isle 'a little Spanish mistress' to spoil his walks. Quoted in Julia Cartwright, *Sacharissa*, p. 129.

13. *Works*, vol. 4, p. 170.

14. *Works*, vol. 4, pp. 170–1.

15. L'Isle may be too grand a figure and someone with learning further down the social scale may have functioned as Aphra's mentor. Given Behn's tendency in her late stories to suggest her codes by using the initial to indicate the real person on which a character was based (as in *The Fair Jilt*) the man hinted at might have begun with V. In which case candidates could come from the Verney family or from the Vernattys. Philibert Vernatty was a crooked treasurer and merchant connected with Tangiers where he 'lived like a prince'; he greatly irritated Pepys (see BL Sloane MS 3509). Nicholas or Nathaniel Vernatty was mentioned as a friend of Behn's Kentish friend, Jeffrey Boys, and appears to be referred to in her poem 'Our Cabal'. The notion of Behn's contact with a literary family comes largely from the background of the other writing women comparable to her, Katherine Philips and Margaret Cavendish. Cavendish was part of a largely literary group which included her writing daughters-in-law, women of her own age, Jane and Elizabeth Cavendish.

16. When taken back into the fold, Strangford declared he had over £4,000 in debts but, when Algernon came to sort matters out, he found the indebtedness more like £6,000. For a full discussion of Algernon Sidney's relationship with Strangford's inheritance, see Jonathan Scott, *Algernon Sidney and the English Republic, 1623–1677* and *Algernon Sidney and the Restoration Crisis, 1677–1683* (Cambridge, 1988 and 1981).

17. *CSP*, Dom., 1655.

18. When the Strangfords returned for a short time to Kent in 1657 they were offered a small house nearby which 'displeased them'.

19. *CSP*, Dom., 1656, p. 4.

20. The meeting near Gray's Inn was in early July 1659 and the uprising was intended for 1 August; 'one called Lady Willoughby a Catholic' heard of the plot and laid her knowledge before the chief of intelligence Thomas Scot, giving him particulars not only of the meeting of Royalists but also the intended day of rising. This was ironic since Thomas Scot's son William just might have been implicated in the plot. Scot, 'Confessions of transactions in the service of Parliament, 1660', BM, Stowe MS. 189. fol. 73b.

21. See Edward, Earl of Clarendon, *The History of the Rebellion and Civil Wars in England*, ed. W. Dunn Macray (Oxford, 1958), vol. VI, Book XVI, section 37.

22. At the Restoration, Thomas Colepeper was sure he deserved a reward and in June 1666, he was claiming in a petition that he had lost £10,000 by his loyalty. It is not clear what was done for him but he was soon corresponding with the King's minister, Lord Arlington, about subversive activities in Kent. As balance for Sidney arrogance in the Interregnum, it would be pleasant to think that he was the 'young'

Colepeper who in 1663 had the pleasure of offering the now impecunious and exiled Algernon Sidney a foreign command.

23. The difficulty of tracing women can be exemplified by a 'Margaret Smith' in *A Collection of the State Papers of John Thurloe*. She provided intelligence from Bruges to Thurloe in July 1657 concerning the King's troops and vessel-building for an invasion of England. The name may be a code for a man since there seems some evidence that he or she was at sea, but its use would suggest that a woman spy was not unthinkable. Later s/he writes again as from Blanck Marshall, while signing Margaret Smith, Antwerp, 28 June 1658. In July Blanck Marshall is writing from Bruges in desperate need of money; s/he has assumed the name Jo. Harrison. On 12 August Jo. Harrison or Blanck Marshall writes several times from Bruges, on one occasion almost entirely in code. In November the name is again Margaret Smith. In the index to the Thurloe papers, this agent is listed as Elizabeth Smith, spy on the king. For Aphra, the problem is exacerbated by her surname: among the spies, Johnson was one of those easy common names turned to in haste—even the King used it on occasion. But it is possible that one of the many male Johnsons mentioned in the secret service papers of Thurloe and Hyde in the early 1650s was her father, e.g. December 1657, William Lockhart, ambassador in France, wrote to Thurloe 'on behalfe of one Johnson, a prisoner in the custody of one of your messengers, who was taken about twelve months since at Rye, upon suspition of his being an intelligencer'. A John Johnson, possibly a Scot, was an agent in Rotterdam; he sent a letter in April 1658 suggesting that Monck's army had gone over to the King and renounced Parliament.

24. Although, happily for them, both Willoughby and Killigrew were loud Royalists at the Restoration, neither was impeccable politically and there is evidence that each either changed or played on both sides. Such acquaintances, therefore, suggest political activity but not clear-cut political principles. The early Aphra was not necessarily a confirmed and single-minded monarchist.

25. Occasionally there would be a lull in the opposing documents collected by Thurloe in London and Hyde across the Channel. When this happened, as it did on 29 May 1654, Hyde exclaimed, 'We are at a dead calm for all manner of intelligence,' *CSP*, III 244. But such exclamations were rare.

26. See *The Memoirs of Anne, Lady Halkett and Ann, Lady Fanshawe*, ed. John Loftis (Oxford, 1979).

27. The English Augustinian nuns settled in Louvain at St. Monica's, another convent Behn may have known. For an insight into the nuns' life see *The Tixall Letters; or, the Correspondence of the Aston family, and their friends, during the 17th century*, ed. A. Clifford (Edinburgh, 1815). Other laxer groups called the '*Gallopping Nuns... Chanonesses, Begines, Quest's, Swart-Sisters*, and *Jesuitesses*' are mentioned in Behn's short story, *The Fair Jilt*.

28. The archives in Ghent have some details of finance and personnel of the English convent, but little else. See Sint-Baafs Reeks B no. 2773, Rijkarchief Gent, and Reeks XXI and XXXV, Stadsarchief Gent.

29. Thomas Killigrew, *Thomaso, Or The Wanderer: A Comedy, Comedies and Tragedies* (London, 1664).

30. *CSP*, III, p. 607. It rather sounds as though Mary Knatchbull kept up some of her political activities, for an account of her a few years later refers to her moving when the 'new stormes in England began' as though she would be sure to be involved. See vol. XVII, *Publications of the Catholic Record Society*.

31. In the Ghent archives, Mary Knatchbull describes the poor financial state of the convent during the Interregnum when it was in debt of almost two years' income. On 1 April 1661 it was claimed that the convent 'subsists by the portions of such as proffess a moungst us', Reeks B, 2773, Rijksarchief Gent. Other possibilities are that Behn went to a convent briefly as a child; Elizabeth, Pepys's wife, born the same year as Behn of a Kentish mother, was according to her brother briefly in an Ursuline convent at the age of twelve. Or that she was in a lowly position in one: in *Love-Letters*, *Works*, vol. 2, p. 217, the maid Antonet says that at the age of six she went to a convent as the playmate of a noble girl and that the pair stayed there for seven years. To girls without money, there were also subordinate serving positions available, but Aphra Behn seems not to have been the type for this sort of role. A final possibility is that Behn considered entering a convent later as an adult, perhaps in Antwerp in the mid-1660s. Many older women did so, including one of Winefrid Themelby's relatives. But again Behn would have needed funds.

32. *The History of the Nun*, *Works*, vol. 3, p. 214. In another story Behn describes a Protestant young girl believing she 'had happily got into the company of Angels' and having 'heard talk of Nunneries, and having never been out of her own Country [county] till within four or five days, she had certainly concluded she had been in one of those Religious-houses now, had she but heard a Bell ring, and seen 'em kneel to Prayers, and make use of their Beads, as she had been told those happy people do', vol. 3, p. 370.

33. *Works*, vol. 2, p. 382.

Chapter 3

1. A continuation of their work might have been necessary for many agents who expected reward at the Restoration since it soon became clear that royal largesse could not extend to all who had served the King in exile. A few days into the reign found Pepys worrying where to find the month's pay promised by the King to the ship's crew that ferried him to England.

2. James A. Williamson, *English in Guiana 1604–68* (Oxford, 1923).

3. See William Byam, 'The Description of Guyana', BL Sloane MS 3662.

4. With the help of Byam, Willoughby had shifted from his initial support of Parliament and had tried to hold Barbados for the royal cause. He failed and, after his defeat, was restricted to his estates in Surinam. But he was eager to return to England. So, after a short time, he left Surinam to Byam. In England Willoughby was imprisoned and released only on condition that he return to Surinam. He was by now too deep into plotting and he did not set out until well after the Restoration. Having backed the winning side, Willoughby was confirmed in a large portion of the proprietorship, now shared with Clarendon's son, Laurence Hyde, under whom Byam continued as Deputy or Governor.

5. Adriaan van Berbel, *Travels in South America, between the Berbice and Essequito Rivers and in Suriname (1670–1689)*, trans. Walter E. Roth (Georgetown, Guyana, 1925).

6. This absence of sheep did not prevent Aphra from 'seeing' them in the colony when she came to write *Oroonoko*. Although it was only after James Lind's work in the mid 18th century on the effect of citrus fruit on scurvy that the connection of Vitamin C and the disease was widely known, the discovery had often been made and forgotten in the past. An authoritative recommendation of the juice of lemons is to be found in James Lancaster's account of his voyage to the Indian Ocean in 1601, see Purchas His Pilgrimes, vol. 2, 393.

7. Thomas Tryon, *Friendly Advice to the Gentlemen-Planters of the East and West Indies* (1684).

8. *Plantation Justice* (1701).

9. *Colonising Expeditions to the West Indies and Guiana*, ed. V. T. Harlow, Hakluyt Society, 2nd ser., 56 (London, 1925), pp. 174–7.

10. Henry Adis, *A Letter Sent from Syrranam, to His Excellency, the Lord Willoughby of Parham, General of the Western Islands, and of the Continent of Guianah, &c. Then residing at the Barbados*...dated 10 December 1663, printed in London in 1664. Adis was perhaps not an entirely reliable witness: he wrote such pamphlets as *A Fannaticks Alarm* (1661) in which he called himself 'a Baptized Believer, undergoing the Name of a Free-willer; and...called a *Fannatick or a mad man*'.

11. *Othello* was the most popular Shakespearean tragedy of the Restoration, allowed on the stage in its original form. With its domestic drama, it was considered especially appealing to women. When the playwright Southerne later made his Imoinda white, he drew on the image of *Othello* with its exotic, erotic tie of black man and white woman. That coupling with a black man was regarded as a trait of a prostitute in the Restoration can be seen from the lampoons on Charles II's mistress, the Duchess of Mazarine, and his daughter, the Countess of Sussex. A satirist described a 'loathsome filthy Black. / Which you & *Sussex* in your arms did take' ('Rochester's Farewell', BL Harley MS 7317).

12. The most famous proponent of the theory that Behn took all her description from

books is Ernest Bernbaum in 'Mrs. Behn's "Oroonoko"', *George Lyman Kittredge Papers* (Boston, 1913), pp. 419–33.

13. George Warren, *An Impartial Description of Surinam upon The Continent of Guiana in America. With a History of several strange Beasts, Birds, Fishes, Serpents, Insects, and Customs of that Colony etc.* (London, 1667). For further information on Behn in Surinam, see J. A. Ramsaran, '"*Oroonoko*": A Study of the Factual Elements', *Notes and Queries* (1960), p. 144, and Bernard Dhuicq, 'Further Evidence on Aphra Behn's Stay in Surinam', *Notes and Queries* (December 1979), pp. 524–6.

14. Banister was much involved with the English settlers and their new Dutch masters after the second loss of Surinam following the Treaty of Breda. See *CSP*, Col., 1668.

15. It is of course possible that the father was a stepfather and so the name would not be known. But again, given Aphra's prominence, it is likely that such a connection would have emerged and there is no one in the records I have studied who clearly fits the role.

16. *Works*, vol. 7, pp. 298 and 302.

17. Richard Head, *The English Rogue described, in the Life of Meriton Latroon, a Witty Extravagant* (London, 1666).

18. There had been at least one colonial woman, Anne Bradstreet, who had published literary work, but this evidently did not make the New World a glamorous location. Despite the fact that Bradstreet referred to the Sidneys in her *Tenth Muse Lately Sprung up in America* (1650), Aphra Behn made no mention of her in any of her published writings, accepting only Katherine Philips as her modern literary forerunner.

19. Robert Sanford, *Surinam Justice. In the Case Of several persons proscribed by certain Usurpers of Power in that Colony* (London, 1662). Sanford spent his 'whole puerility and adolescence' in the West Indies.

20. Lady Forster, in Henry Nevile's *Newes from the New-Exchange, Or, The Commonwealth of ladies, Drawn to the Life, in their severall Characters and Concernments* (London, 1650).

21. BL Add. MSS 47133.

22. PRO, April 20/30, 1683.

23. Robert Sanford, *Surinam Justice*, p. 9.

24. When Joanna also arrived, she too petitioned Cromwell, admitting that William Scot had 'lost his office through his own fault'. Cromwell must have had some regard for Thomas Scot for he granted a life pension of £20 a year to Joanna.

25. Thomas Scot, 'Confessions of Transactions'. See too *The Speeches and Prayers of Major General Harrison, Mr. J. Carew, Mr Justice Cooke, Mr. H. Peters, Mr. T. Scott… Together with Severall Occasionall Speeches and Passages in their Imprisonment till they came to the Place of Execution* (London, 1660).

26. Perhaps had Thomas Scot apologised rather than justified himself, he might have

shared the fate of the regicide, Colonel Hutchinson, whose devoted wife wrote an abject letter for him to sign, thus gaining his life but adding personal shame to political misery.

27. Thomas Scot's widow and William's stepmother did manage to secure part of the property later.

28. See Edmund Ludlow, *A Voyage from The Watch Tower*, ed. A. B. Worden, Camden 4th series, vol. 21 (London, Royal Historical Society, 1978).

29. *CSP*, Ireland, 1660–1.

30. *CSP*, Col., 1661–8, pp. 166–7.

31. There were several of Thomas Colepeper's Kentish relatives in Surinam, including Crisps. Behn later knew Henry Crisp well.

Chapter 4

1. *The Dutch Lover* (1673) and *Works*, vol. 1, no. 104.

2. *A Voyage to the Island of Love*, *Works*, vol. 1, no. 51, ll. 86–116.

3. See also Dryden's *The Satyrs of Aulus Persius Flaccus*, the Fifth Satyr, for another description of the miseries of sea travel.

4. See 'The Dumb Virgin' and 'The Unfortunate Happy Lady' where the hero is shipwrecked on the coast of North Africa and enslaved there for six years by 'people less merciful, than Seas, Winds, or hungry wild Beasts in pursuit of their Prey', *Works*, vol. 3, p. 80. A pretended version of this fate is used in *The False Count*. For a Kentish account of an Englishman enslaved by Africans at Calabar in 1668, see Watts's *True Relation*. He thought the life of a slave of the Africans worse than that of a galley slave of the Moors and Turks.

5. Perhaps Aphra's father, if he *had* accompanied her, was served so.

6. *The History of the Bucaniers of America; From their First Original down to this Time* (London, 1699). This work has purported accounts by Exquemelin, Basil Ringrose, and the Sieur de Montauban. See also Basil Ringrose, *The dangerouys Voyage and hold attempts of Captain B. Sharp and others upon the coasts of the South Seas. From the original Journal of the Voyage, written by B. Ringrose* (London, 1684). Although it was only after James Lind's work in the mid 18th century on the effect of citrus fruit on scurvy that the connection of Vitamin C and the disease was widely known, the discovery had often been made and forgotten in the past. An authoritative recommendation of the juice of lemons is to be found in James Lancaster's account of his voyage to the Indian Ocean in 1601, see *Purchas His Pilgrimes*, vol. 2, p. 393.

7. Huntington MS HM 171919.

8. See Carl and Roberta Bridenbaugh, *No Peace Beyond the Line: The English in the Caribbean 1624–1690* (New York, 1972).

9. There are no full and extant English maps of Surinam published in the early 1660s

but there is a manuscript one in two versions. One was probably copied by a Dutch person, given his script and use of Muller for Millard and Davenpoort for Davenport; possibly it was made from an English map in Holland after the ceding of the colony (or before to help with the conquest). The second is an unsigned MS in Brown Library drawn in ink and colours with additions in ink in a seventeenth-century hand. There is also an engraving after 1667 as *A New Draught of Surranam upon the coast of Guianna*. All three maps represent Surinam under the English but they have different names on the plantations and are not necessarily copies of each other. The first of these maps came into the possession of William Blathwayt, who may have obtained it when he was a clerk in the embassy of Charles II in The Hague from 1668 to 1672. As a clerk he needed to know something of Surinam since he was relaying information about the treatment of the English settlers. See Gertrude Ann Jacobsen, *William Blathwayt: A late seventeenth-century English administrator* (New Haven, 1932).

10. In *Oroonoko* Behn calls this Parham House, the name also used for the government house in the capital.

11. BL Add. MS 70010.

12. Yearworth recounts to Harley a rumour 'that your Honour have sould that plantation too my Lord Willoughby'. BL Add MS70010.

13. Thomas Tryon, *Friendly Advice*.

14. Adis, *A Letter Sent from Syrranam*. The letter is followed by a reply from Lord Willoughby, dated Barbados 23 January 1664. The title of lieutenant-general was a military one, and the confirmation of Byam suggests either that the post might have gone to another or that Willoughby had only recently been confirmed by the King in the power to create such titles.

15. Antoine Biet, *Voyage de la France equinoxiale en l'isle de Cayenne* (1654).

16. *CSP*, Col., 1664.

17. BL Portland MSS. It is not known precisely what his offence was.

18. Sanford, *Surinam Justice*, p. 3.

19. Behn may have been prepared for her liking by having read an engaging little book of letters entitled *Coll. Henry Marten's Familiar Letters to his Lady of Delight* published in 1662 when Marten was in the Tower. When later in her play, *The Roundheads*, Behn mocked the Parliamentarians from just before the Restoration, she mentioned but did not portray Henry Marten, although he had been the butt of satirists for his politics and his womanising.

20. Sir Josiah Child, *A New Discourse of Trade* (London, 1694). The government insisted that the indentures should be made 'freely without delusion, persuasion or any other Sinisterly means' and demanded that servants be bound before one or more JPs, a record being kept at the Court of Quarter Sessions. The indentured person granted to his or her master for a number of years, usually seven, total service; in

return the master agreed to pay the passage and provide food, clothing and lodging during the period of the indenture. At the end many servants found themselves in a dreadful state without land or resources. In a generous case, he or she might receive, as one man did, a breeding sow, 35 acres of land at 2*d* per acre per annum and corn sufficient to sow two acres of land. Before they were freed, however, many indentured servants died, for their lives were of less value to their masters than those of their slaves. In all the colonies of the Spanish, Dutch, English and French, indentured servants were beaten to death: one employer was said to have killed over a hundred. See the case history of the pirate Esquemelin in *The History of the Bucaniers of America*, Ringrose, 1699.

21. *Works*, vol. 7, p. 299.

22. *CSP*, Col., 1667, p. 528. In Thomas Southerne's dramatisation of *Oroonoko*, two young women who have gone to Surinam to find husbands, having become 'shop-worn' in London, pretend to be related in this way. Aphra may have had something of a marital aim herself.

23. Enys's report is summarised in *CSP*, Col., 1661–8, p. 577.

24. I am not suggesting that Behn bases all of her *Oroonoko* on Allin but his being white is no impediment to her taking some details from the story. In 'An exact narrative of the state of Guyana', Ashmolean MS, Byam recounts some 'insolencies of our Negroes', with a few rebelliously escaping to the woods, which may also have some bearing on Behn's tale.

25. *An Exact Relation of The Most Execrable Attempts of John Allin, Committed on the Person of His Excellency Francis Lord Willoughby of Parham, Captain General of the Continent of Guiana, and of all the Caribby-Islands and our Lord Proprietor* (London, 1665).

Chapter 5

1. Sir Walter Ralegh landed in the mouth of the Orinoco in 1616. See his *Discoverie of the large, rich and beautiful Empyre of Guiana, with a Relation of the great and Golden Citie of Manoa (which the Spanyards call El Dorado)...Performed in the yeare 1595* (London, 1596) and *Sir Walter Ralegh's apology for his last voyage to Guiana*.

2. *Works*, vol. 2, p. 95. cf. Warren's *Impartial History*, 'There is a constant Spring and Fall, some leaves Dropping, and others succeeding in their Places: But the Trees are never quite divested of their Summer Livery; Some, have always Blossoms, and several degrees of Fruit at once.'

3. For a discussion of colonial vision see Mary Louise Pratt, *Imperial Eyes: Travel Writing and Transculturation* (London, 1992).

4. Over a hundred years later the eel was still the prize exhibit of the region, as can be seen from Alexander von Humboldt's famous accounts of South America.

5. Warren, p. 13. Among other animals, armadillos were a craze with European

collectors and no antiquary could be without a stuffed one. They tended to be seen as miniature rhinoceros and be depicted in allegories of America.

6. 'The Description of Guyana', BL Sloane MS 1956, 3662.

7. Aphra Behn probably read Montaigne between visiting Surinam and publishing *Oroonoko* in 1688 since her likely acquaintance, Charles Cotton, was translating the essays in the 1680s.

8. June 16, 1663, *CSP*, Col., 1661–8, p. 425.

9. During the 1660s there were slave raids on the Surinam settlers but other colonies such as Jamaica and Barbados fared worse. Some of the uprisings passed unnoticed in London, but others made the news in the years between Behn's return and her publishing of *Oroonoko* in the late 1680s. In 1675 there were reports of a 'Conspiracy of the Negroes' who had intended to establish an Ashanti-style monarchy under an 'Ancient Gold Coast Negro'. But the plan was discovered through a female domestic slave who overheard a would-be rebel trying to recruit. One hundred and ten were arrested and six burnt alive, *CSP*, Col., 3 Oct. 1675, p. 294.

10. Feathers loomed large in early portraits of Native Americans, a Portuguese painting of the epiphany in about 1505 providing a headdress of Brazilian feathers for one of the Magi. By then, some examples of featherwork had reached Europe and several artists such as Dürer included the radial crown of feathers in their drawings. There was a misconception that Native Americans also wore skirts of feathers—Behn obviously did not see one and did not record it.

11. Agent Enys's report made a similar point: 'The greatest infelicity of this colony is that his Majesty is not rightly informed of the goodness thereof.'

12. In about the 1640s Albert Eckhout, a professional artist, went with Johan Maurits to Brazil to draw figures, animals and plants. His picture of an African king, possibly of the Congo (he seems not to have visited Africa), is the kind of exotic but Europeanised vision Behn has of Oroonoko. The picture features a curtain, column, balustrade, and European crown.

13. Warren, p. 19. Harley's agent Yearworth describes the arrival of a slave ship captained by Sir John Wood, which Aphra may have witnessed. It had 130 blacks on board, having lost 54 on the voyage (BL Add MS 70010). Before her visit to America Behn may have seen a few black Africans probably as footmen and pages to the rich and aristocratic, but she had certainly never seen them in a group as she would have done in Surinam.

14. Hilary Beckles, *White Servitude and Black Slavery in Barbados, 1627–1715* (Knoxville, Tennessee, 1989), p. 117.

15. See the Dutch manuscript map in The Hague Rijkarchief of the 'Goud-Kust'.

16. Anthony à Wood, *Life and Times*, vol. 11, p. 425.

17. Montaigne, 'On the Cannibals', *The Complete Essays*, trans. M. A. Screech (Harmondsworth, 1993).

18. 'The Essay on Translated Prose', *Works*, vol. 4, p. 76.

19. Richard Blome, *A Description Of the Island of Jamaica; With the other Isles and Territories in America, to which the English are Related* (London, 1678), p. 37.

20. For example, when the hero awakens to see the heroine, La Calprenède's character says, 'Great Goddess...pardon to a stranger the errour he may have committed against your Divinity; had I known this sacred place, I would not have prophan'd it by my presence', while Aphra's exclaims, 'Great Goddess, pardon an unlucky Stranger, / The errours he commits 'gainst your Divinity, / Who, had he known the Grove had Sacred been, / He wou'd not have prophan'd it by his presence.'

21. Isabella, Strangford's wife, was dead and he had little hold left on the Sidneys.

22. Behn may have taken the name from a famous tragicomedy of Beaumont and Fletcher, *Philaster: Or, Love Lies a Bleeding* (1609). Katherine Philips used the name in her works for the Welsh Royalist, John Jeffreys of Abercynrig.

23. The cross-gendered education of Fletcher's characters was more adhesive. The girl found it hard to 'suffer like a woman' and the boy belligerently to assault whoever gets in his path.

24. Portland Collection, University of Nottingham Department of Manuscripts, Pw2 Hy221.

25. Alternatively, the reference might just have been to Ferdinando's brother, Henry, of whom their father noted that his 'unguided temper' had carried him to Barbados. See Raymond Gorges, *The Story of a Family through Eleven Centuries, being a History of the family of Gorges* (Boston, 1944).

26. So bad was the situation in Barbados that in September 1663 a Corporation of Barbados Adventurers was looking for new land to settle. It had turned its attention to Surinam.

27. By the time Harley received the information of the departure of both Astrea and Gorges, he himself was *en route* for England, having been banished by Willoughby.

28. After the departure of the tenants and Harley's return to England, Byam checked that everything was in 'good order' at St John's Hill. He ordered silk grass to be planted, put '5 negros' to work there and proposed a new manager, a William Gwilt, to look after things. See letters of Byam to Harley's attorney, 24 July 1664 and to Harley in November 1665, as well as Gwilt to his father on 24 July 1664. BL Add MS 70010.

Chapter 6

1. There are other claimants but none so far very compelling. Beane is a common London name, see, for example, Richard and Ephater Beane in registers of St Katherine's by the Tower. *The Calendar of Treasury Books, 1660–1667* lists two possible Beanes but no Behns. The first is a Humfrey Beane, merchant and farmer of excise

in various southern counties, especially Essex; he was also involved in collecting excise from alcohol in London. This Beane survived the plague and does not die or disappear when Mr Behn drops from Aphra's life. He goes on being a farmer of excise for the southern and eastern counties, petitioning and being petitioned against and he is still flourishing in the 1670s, when he seems to have become an alderman. (Incidentally his subcommissioner of excise in Kent and East Anglia was in 1671 a Charles Johnson.) The second Beane is a slightly more likely but less visible candidate, Isaack Beane, described as a merchant, who on 9 November 1660 was petitioning with a Benjamin Hassall for release of goods seized by Edward Watkins, the head searcher in London. Presumably he had had incoming goods seized, wrongfully he believes, which makes him involved with shipping. After this mention he disappears from Treasury papers. The Port Books throw up some candidates but I have found none with an overwhelming case.

2. *The Luckey Chance*, *Works*, vol. 7, p. 227. The old man (*senex*) was also a stock figure in comedy, including *commedia dell'arte*.

3. Johannes Nenne Postma, *The Dutch in the Atlantic Slave Trade 1660–1815* (Cambridge, 1990), p. 145.

4. In addition, the English government wanted to prevent the importation of arms for a possible 'fanatic' or republican rebellion in England helped by the republican Dutch; again it was in the interests of those ships carrying such arms to be as secretive as possible and to keep in their holds as many colours as they could in the hope that one would please the ships they met or the ports at which they had to call.

5. See *CSP*, Col., August 14, 1655, entries 219, 219, i–vi. I am grateful to Keith Davey for disentangling the various *King David*s.

6. *CSP*, Dom., pp. 253 and 276.

7. This Norwegian ship was allowed by King Charles to participate in certain trading activities around the shores of England—it was carrying deal both before and after the date on which Aphra probably travelled from Surinam to England—though it was never considered more than a foreign ship; indeed it was open to the kind of theft that British inhabitants saw as their right in regard to 'foreign bottoms'. See Art. 30 of Dutch complaints in *A Catalogue of the Damages for which the English Demand Reparation from the United-Netherlands. As Also A List of the Damages, Action, and Pretenses for which Those of the United-Netherlands demand Reparation and Satisfaction from the English* (1664), which listed the grievances of the East India Company against the Dutch and the grievances of the Dutch East India and West India Companies against the English: '*Lawrence Kettles*, Merchant *of Amsterdam*, saith, That in *May* 1659 his Ship named the *King David*, (*Oche Alberts... Master*) laden with *Salt* at *St Uvall*, and bound for *Dronton* in *Norway*, was taken and carried to *Dunkirk*, by Captain *Louis de Hay*.' There it is said in reply 'that the Captain was neither an *English*

Subject, nor had any *English Commission*, and therefore the *English* cannot be responsible for his action'. This Scandinavian ship sailing a northern route was licensed by Charles II to trade as a Norwegian ship in July 1661 despite being Dutch-built (*CSP*, Dom., 1661/2, pp. 34 and 47). In 1665 Thomas Middleton wrote to Pepys of the goods on board the prize ship the *King David* and had leave from the commissioners of prizes to land them if a warrant could be procured. In 1666 there is a report of the Lords Lauderdale, Arlington, Ashby and Berkeley about a dispute between a merchant, John Hammond, and the Earl of Morton, that the *King David* of Druntheim, Norway, was freighted in August 1664 by Hammond to go to Norway and return laden with deal, but had in fact been driven by harsh weather into the Orkneys. In April 1665, the lading was condemned in the Admiralty, as war had been declared with the Dutch in February 1665. Since the goods had been loaded before the declaration of war between England and the Dutch Republic, however, the authorities advised release of the cargo on payment of reasonable charges. They would give no opinion of the ship itself, however, since it was principally Scandinavian. Despite this clear statement, in July Hammond was complaining that the Earl of Morton had none the less disposed of some of the goods from the ship and suffered others to perish. It seems fairly unlikely that a ship would go to the West Indies to trade illegally after it had been permitted to trade legally as a Norwegian ship in 1661. The reason that a biographer would try to take it to Surinam is the mention of Oche Alberts or Oge Albert, Dutch master and owner of one-sixteenth of the ship. In the letters purportedly from Antwerp, Behn writes of an 'Albert'. Throughout this study I have referred to the United Provinces as 'Holland', although Holland was in fact only one of the Dutch provinces.

8. The name spelled Behn was uncommon in England but present in northern Germany. This Johan Behn is the only one so far found who was born at a suitable time. There are many Beans and Bens in England, variations other people used for Aphra, and a will is recorded for an 'Afra Beane' of Kent in 1651. Aphra was particular with the spelling of her last name.

9. Incidentally a fair number of English, Dutch and New World sea captains were called Johnson. A captain received about 50 Dutch gilders a month—the first mate would get around 36. The Holland Johnsons or Johnstons were often military and naval men and many were in shipping. For example, in August 1655, the *St James*, with Peter Johnson of Amsterdam as master, was taken by the English as it sailed home. The owner was William Belin de la Garde, merchant of Amsterdam who owned many ships including also the *Golden Fortune* with a Francis Johnson; among other Dutch ship owners there was the Widow of Heertgen Johnson, while the heirs of a Daniel Johnson, merchants of Amsterdam, lost a ship to the English in January 1657. Leonard Johnson traded illegally in negroes and sugar in Jamaica.

There were also English Johnsons in shipping, such as John Johnson, the master of a ship called the *Dove* of London belonging to a group of English merchants; this was seized off the Shetland Islands by the Dutch some time before 1663. Such Johnsons may have been distantly related to the Kent family; if so they give Aphra Behn an appropriate maritime and international context.

10. Pepys, *Diary*, 3 Oct. 1665, vol. VI, pp. 257–8. This was said of an eminent merchant who died in the plague, but would also be true for small operators, especially those who had not left a will, as Mr Behn probably did not.

11. The name of the hero has some similarity to Yoruba names such as Okonkwo or Oro, but the slaves Behn portrayed were from near 'Coromantine'. Curiously the word Coromantine may have prompted her to the choice of name because of its closeness to another nearby South American river, the Coromanine.

12. The 'Memoirs' account of the royal meeting, if true, tends to confirm Behn's function in the colony: an audience with the King or even his substitute is an unlikely event for the daughter of a barber, unless she had been to the New World for a purpose.

13. In its early years the Royal Society acquired 'rarities' of various kinds. The first dated gift in the extant catalogue was made on 18 May 1661. A 'Repository' for the gifts was founded and they were sent or presented at meetings to Mr Hooke, the Curator of Experiments from 1662. In 1679 a Catalogue of the Repository was printed which included several natural and cultural objects from America, e.g. 'A West-Indian bow, arrows and quiver' and 'An Indian Peruque, made not of hair but feather, a mantle also of feathers', *Musaeum*, p. 367.

14. See *The Lismore Papers*, 2nd Series, ed. A. B. Grosart (Private Circulation, 1888), vols IV and V; F. W. Stoye, 'The Whereabouts of Thomas Killigrew 1639–41', *Review of English Studies*, vol. 25, 1949, pp. 245–8.

15. It was an odd genre to choose for autobiography, but in this he resembled Margaret Cavendish, Duchess of Newcastle, who also wrote autobiographical and philosophical plays.

16. See epilogue to *The Parson's Wedding*; Alfred Harbage, *Thomas Killigrew Cavalier Dramatist 1612–83* (Philadelphia, 1930), p. 45; and 'A Ballad, call'd a Session of Poets', Dyce MS, Victoria and Albert Museum.

17. See Germaine Greer, *Slip-Shod Sybils: Recognition, Rejection and the Woman Poet* (London, 1995), pp. 197–213.

18. For a discussion of Killigrew's politics, see J. P. Vander Motten, 'Unpublished Letters of Charles II', *Restoration*, Spring 1994, vol. 18, 1, pp. 17–26, and 'Thomas Killigrew: A Biographical Note,' *Revue belge de philologie et d'histoire*, LIII, 1975, 3, pp. 769–75. See *Thurloe State Papers*, vol. VII, a letter to Thurloe, October 18, 1658: 'As for Charles Stuart his having been in Holland; surely you had my memoriall complaining thereof, which was even at the very time while he was in Holland;

and at the very time I had an accompt from one Killigrew of his bed-chamber of every place where he was, and the time, with his stay and company of which also I gave you an accompt in mine by the last post.' Although both Thomas and his son Henry could have been referred to here, it is rather more likely to have been Thomas. The letter puts Killigrew into an ambiguous light but Vander Motten warns against jumping to premature conclusions.

19. Killigrew was a friend of Willoughby's and Harley's and had two sons in the West Indies.

20. See Duffy, *The Passionate Shepherdess*, p. 66.

21. MS V a 20, Folger Shakespeare Library.

22. If Mr Behn died of the plague he was not recorded. The bills of mortality listed numbers rather than names as the pestilence increased.

23. There is a Johan Behn born in Hamburg in 1635, who went to Gluckstadt and then to Copenhagen where he died in 1709. If this is the *King David* Behn, and Aphra's husband, he would have been a widower for twenty years and Aphra never a widow. In view of *The Abraham's Sacrifice* reference, this seems unlikely. See Chapter 10.

24. *Works*, vol. 1, no. 67.

25. A similar libel on the Dutch was printed by Behn in her *Miscellany* of 1685. It was by 'Mr. Nevell', which probably indicated her friend Henry Nevil Payne.

26. See Pepys, *Diary*, 2 Feb. 1664.

27. *An Exact Survey of the Affaires Of the United Netherlands* (London, 1665), pp. 81–2.

28. Pepys, *Diary*, 10 July 1666.

29. *Works*, vol. 1, no. 64.

Chapter 7

1. The description comes mainly from the letters quoted in the 'Memoirs'.

2. *CSP*, Dom., 1664–5, pp. 426–7. The allusion is almost certainly to Scot.

3. The letters to De Witt are in The Hague archives. Bampfield writes in French.

4. Oudart had a long Royalist past, having been amanuensis to Charles I. After his period as an agent in Holland, he would return to England to become Latin secretary to Charles II. Corney was proud of having won over a secretary of the directors of the East India Company, although the man wanted a handsome salary for any information, 3000 florins a year and a thousand in advance. Whitehall of course wanted his information before payment.

5. The taking of Corney and Oudart formed part of a series of intelligence acts and followed the arrest in London of a secretary to the Dutch ambassador. See H. H. Rowen, *John de Witt* (1986), p. 617.

6. *CSP*, Dom., 1666, pp. 318, 343, 358.

7. In the Act of Parliament 1665, such men as Scot and Bampfield would be deemed guilty of treason if they did not surrender by an appointed date.

8. It was not easy to engage someone new on the spot for, since the outbreak of war, there had been no direct packet-boat service from Holland to England and all letters had to go through Flanders.

9. Arlington was just concluding the rivalries of the Interregnum by helping to oust the old chancellor, Edward Hyde, Earl of Clarendon. Clarendon had taken a moral stand with the King while Arlington, in Burnet's words, had the 'art of observing the King's temper, and managing it beyond all the men of that time'. At the height of the Anglo-Dutch conflict he would follow Killigrew in improving his estate by marrying a Dutch heiress who brought him the huge dowry of 100,000 gilders. Killigrew's part in the ousting of Clarendon was even less honourable. Clarendon had been as dismayed as anyone to hear of the pregnancy of his own daughter Anne by the Duke of York and her insistence on marriage. Queen Henrietta Maria was loud in opposition to her son's match—which to his credit the King insisted must go forward—and Killigrew, her long-time friend, helped out by claiming he had bedded Anne, so that the child she was carrying was not necessarily James's.

10. Colepeper did not succeed, but he did become one of the King's gunfounders, responsible for the movement of ordnance round Kent. *CSP*, Dom., 1662–3, p. 3.

11. It was not a mission that a very respectable lady would have undertaken. The secret relationship with a man, if discovered, would have blasted the reputation of anyone. Even in the more turbulent times of the Interregnum, Ann Murry had found her name compromised by her visits to the dashing Colonel Bampfield.

12. See *The Right Honourable the Earl of Arlington's Letters to Sir W. Temple, Bar. from July 1665...to Sept 1670, 2* vols, ed. Thomas Bebington (London, 1701), vol. 1, p. 83.

13. Inevitably all groups declared their prime motive to be the service of the King. In the posthumous 'Memoirs' of Aphra Behn, her employer is given, with some romance, directly as the King; he employed her because of her reputation for wit, secrecy and her 'Management of Publick Affairs'.

14. Thomas Cheney, son of another Thomas Cheney, is the only suitably aged Cheney from Kent in the very incomplete Morman archives. He was christened on 5 February 1636. A George Cheney, son of George and Elizabeth Cheney, was born in Bishopsgate and christened in April 1648 but there seems no reason to connect him with Behn.

15. Charles Cheney's captain was Nicholas Stewart of Sir John Norton's regiment in the division of Alton, co. Southants. See *Treasury Books*.

16. Since there is a Piers mentioned in the Countess of Leicester's letter to her husband about Sir Thomas Colepeper, it is also possible that he was from Kent. See the De L'Isle Papers C 82/14 1 Feb 1637 in the Centre for Kent Studies.

17. Finally Behn was to pump Scot about the dissident English and Scots in Holland.

She was especially to gain information about Edmund Ludlow, the old Commonwealth leader whom the English feared. Neither Aphra Behn nor her masters realised that Ludlow had been transformed into the arch-enemy by earlier misinformation from Scot himself, trying as Scot always was to impress the authorities by his knowledge of important men.

Chapter 8

1. Desmarches was doing another errand for Williamson with a young lad called Robert Yard. The boy was to go to Holland to continue his study of languages and Sir Antony was happy to escort him; indeed he declared to Williamson a little later that he was caring for the lad as if he had been his own son.

2. *CSP* Dom., 1665–6. The letters from Behn and others which chart her progress are held in the Public Record Office, London, SO 29. Parts are quoted in *CSP* and a transcript of the Behn letters is provided in W. J. Cameron's *New Light on Aphra Behn* (Auckland, 1961). Corney's correspondence is in PRO SP 77/35.

3. One daughter, who was originally in the convent in Louvain, was persuaded to leave by Stafford, who thought the location unsafe in time of war. In 1667 she went instead to the convent of the Augustinian Canonesses in Antwerp. Possibly Behn met her there.

4. Ogniate moved about a good deal and might just have been on the boat with Behn and Desmarches. A correspondent of his, writing on 17 July 1666, directed a letter to either England or Flanders.

5. Antwerp had been the home of the learned Anna Maria Van Schurman, who had argued the fitness of women for intellectual endeavour. But Behn seems not to have known of her. She did not refer to Van Schurman or, in later years, add her name to the list of female writers into whose company she wished to insert herself.

6. The records are in the Antwerp city archives: Pk 2259 Ket.4; 2295 Off. A 17; 2320 Off.B17; Rk 2259 Ket.4; 2295 Off A17; 2320 Off. B17. There was more than one tavern called the Rosa Noble in Antwerp, but the one in St Katelijuevest O. seems to be the only flourishing establishment at the time Behn was in the city. It was, alternatively, called the Roode Lelie.

7. Beyond desire for vengeance, Corney had legitimate business in Antwerp. With England ranged against both Holland and France, Arlington was trying to negotiate other alliances, usually scotched by the French through their network of agents and large sums of money. Only Munster remained neutral and Corney, established in Brabant, was to help negotiate between the English government and the Bishop for a full twelve months.

8. Sara Heller Mendelson makes the suggestion that Behn was sent by Killigrew precisely because she would not be known as an agent and jeopardise Scot's

position with the dissidents. Scot's palpable fear every time he was in Behn's company suggests, however, that he expected others to know who she was. See *The Mental World of Stuart Women* (Brighton, 1987), p. 122.

9. Perhaps Scot did not like the sight of a brother associated with Albemarle. His father had mistakenly regarded Albemarle, then George Monck, as his 'greate friend' and the mistake had cost him his life.

10. Scot also confided to Behn what she probably did not know, that he had dealt with Arlington the year before. Now he gave information on a man in Ludgate prison in London pretending to be an informer, when he was really a 'Rogue' and agent of the Dutch; the man was signing up agents in English ports to gain information on merchant shipping. Unfortunately Arlington knew this already.

11. BM Luttrell Collection, III 95. See also *A True and Perfect Narrative of The great and Signal Success of a Part Of His Majesties Fleet Under His Highness Prince Rupert, and His grace the Duke of Albemarle, Burning One hundred and Sixty Dutch Ships within the Ulie: As also the Town of Brandaris upon the Island of Schelling, by some Commanded Men under the Conduct of Sir Robert Holmes, the Eighth and Ninth of this instant August* (London, 1666).

12. The troop movements and the disgrace of Admiral Tromp were not presented as information from Scot, although Scot did later provide some details of Tromp's fall and replacement. Perhaps in her desire to please or pad out her points, Behn was showing how dispensable Scot was.

13. Another associate of the treacherous Bampfield was a John Wright or Write, who had been a merchant in London employed by the Dutch to spy for them within England. It seems unlikely, but it remains a possibility, that this was Behn's brother-in-law or a relative of his. Her sister Frances had, according to Colepeper, married a man possibly called Write who had been with Mr Behn on the *King David*, a ship with Dutch connections. Arlington probably knew of Wright, but the proposed treachery of Temple could well have been new to him.

14. Algernon Sidney's work was not printed until 1698, long after sections of it had formed part of the prosecution in his trial for treason.

15. *Works*, vol. 7, p. 226.

16. Arlington, *Letters*, vol. 1, p. 96.

17. Behn did not appeal to Sir Mark Ogniate possibly because he was back in England in December. At that time he was issued a pass to export six geldings to Flanders.

18. It must have sounded pretty absurd in London but in fact Antwerp was notoriously expensive. A Richard Brathwait was writing from the Low Countries to a Daniel Fleming asking urgently for £100 to discharge a bond. He pointed out that 'tymes make money very difficult to Come by' (Folger Shakespeare Library MS V.b.226).

19. In presenting Scot, Corney had the problem of wanting to portray a sottish rogue *and* a dangerous traitor.

20. Possibly Halsall had been fooled by Write who, Corney asserted, was in league not

only with Bampfield, as Scot had declared, but also with Scot himself. Despite his protestations to Behn, Scot was still Bampfield's lackey, Corney averred.

21. Someone else was having a go at Corney as well, and Whitehall was wary of using him in further undertakings. See Arlington, *Letters*, vol. 1, pp. 100–1.

Chapter 9

1. 'Sir Thomas' may also have been another man within the intelligence network, Maureen Duffy makes a case for Sir Thomas Gower. Or he could be a relative of Colonel Colepeper's such as Sir Thomas Colepeper of Hollingborne. Or he could be Sir Thomas Godfrey of Hackington, the nearest Sir Thomas to Behn's childhood home, one of the various Sir Thomases mentioned in the De L'Isle papers, or even Sir Thomas Taylor, father of Elizabeth Taylor with whom Behn was later acquainted. None is quite right. For example, Gower seems too highly placed to be upset that Aphra Behn did not use him as a messenger and too influential to see a close friend's daughter threatened so ferociously by debt as she was, while Sir Thomas Colepeper of Hollingbourne was a pedantic man who seems an unlikely associate for a female spy and her mother.

2. This proposed use of him is the last that is heard of Behn's brother. Possibly he died, for Behn implies that she was free of male relatives in the 1670s. Possibly he is the Samuel Johnson in the Treasury papers who turns up in August 1680 as a soldier in Barbados, petitioning for arrears of pay. Samuel had been in Sir Tobias Bridge's company and had been promised preferment in Flanders.

3. Nipho had spent some £750 in two years, including a payment of £240 to one spy for expenses—it was such a large sum that he was now trying to get an increased allowance from Arlington. He cannot have had much spare money for Behn.

4. Scot also brought up Algernon Sidney from time to time, here in connection with the Quaker agent, Furley. Both men were resolved 'to shape som designe for Ingland'.

5. See the 'Memoirs'. Another who gave the same news was the agent Peter Du Moulin, a Huguenot used by Arlington to supply naval and political reports on Dutch public opinion. He wrote from Amsterdam at the end of May 1667 about the Dutch fleet's preparations for assault in revenge for the incident on the Vlie.

6. Like the one for 20 September, this letter survives only in a clerk's summary in Whitehall. It retains the pieces of information which could be speedily given, and reduces the lengthy justifications and pleadings to which Scot was addicted to the simple 'if hee had money hee could doe much more.'

7. It is unlikely that Behn went to Holland at this juncture but there is a reference in a letter of 27 November 1666 by Thomas Corney to 'the lady's safe arrival in Holland'. By this time Corney was not habitually referring to Behn in this way.

In the same letter he asserted that most of the treason was emanating from agents in Flanders, especially the merchants there. Antwerp was no doubt the centre. This and other letters suggest that, by November, the English agents in the Low Countries were spending more time abusing each other than spying on the Dutch.

8. The lack of reports (as opposed to letters begging money) in the series of letters in the Public Record Office between September and December suggests that a good number of Behn's letters went astray, then or later.

9. In this long quotation, I have written out abbreviations such as 'yt' for 'that' and 'Ldp for 'Lordship' to make the reading smoother.

10. PRO S.P. 29/182. Reprinted in Cameron, pp. 84–6.

11. The letters, forming part of the 'Memoirs', may have been partly forged but they may also have been based on real letters Behn wrote to a friend or relative in England.

12. In the 'letter', a 'Woman of some Remains of Beauty' called Catalina tells Behn that she herself is actually married to Albert, who had deserted her on their wedding night. By the end of the story both Behn and Albert seem to have forgotten Catalina.

13. Unlike Behn, Bruin with its variants Bruyne and Bruyn, is a Dutch name.

14. 'Memoirs', pp. 21–2. In the end, even if the suitor were prepared to become a keeping man, Behn still felt reluctant to ignore his age, bulk, and deception of his friend Albert, whom he knew to be in love with her himself.

15. *Works*, vol. 3, p. 35

16. Behn tended to use the initial of a real person when creating a disguise. This was espionage practice, too, as in the case of Aphra-Astrea. Cf. *Thurloe State Papers*, VII, 47: 'Hee told the major, that the false names alwayes began with the first letter of their owne name, and that hee had a list of three hundred counterfeit names.'

17. Tarquini was frequently in litigation, on one occasion over a farm owned by Susanna Oosterlincx, presumably a relative of his wife's. When, later, money was obtained, it seems not to have been shared with his wife's sister, Anna Louisa, as it ought. So, in 1662, the two sisters were in court, Anna Louisa arguing that she had a right to half the income from the farm but had been refused it. Tarquini was ordered to pay the money but did not. Further litigation followed.

18. In Behn's story much is made of Tarquin's claim, shared by his Italian military family, that he was descended from the Tarquin kings of Rome. The claim is quietly dropped at the end of the tale when Tarquin returns to a merchant family. Behn's emphasis on this descent may be a compliment to the royal James II, much in her mind at the time. For the detailed background to the story through Dutch language sources, see J. P. Vander Motten and René Vermeir, "'Reality, and Matter of Fact": Text and Context in Aphra Behn's *The Fair Jilt*', *Review of English Studies*, New Series, vol. 66. no. 274, 2015, 280–99.

19. Stadsarchief, Antwerp, 2367, 7553; Proc supp 4006.

20. See the manuscripts in the Stadsarchief, Antwerp: Processen suppl. 7127 and 2368; Inventaris PR 198.

21. '[S]he ceas'd not to purstue him [the monk, Henrick] with her Letters, varying their Style; sometimes all wanton, loose and raving; sometimes feigning a Virgin-Modesty...by a Cunning peculiar to a Maid possess'd with such a sort of Passion.' The writing does duty for sexuality which Miranda, as a young beguine, cannot display quite as easily as the uninstitutionalised Silvia in *Love-Letters*; so it becomes 'wanton' and 'loose'. *Works*, vol. 3, pp. 20–1.

22. Written on 22 March 1667 to De Witt. See *Brieven aan Johan de Witt*, letter 6, ed. Robert Fruin and N. Jepikse, vol. 2 (Amsterdam, 1922), p. 298. The fuller originals are in the archives in The Hague: 1.01.03; 1.01.04; 3.01.17; 3.20.66.01.

23. There was an Edward Butler in Flanders, Latin secretary to the Duke of Ormonde, *CSP*, Dom., 1661–2, p. 47 and 1665–6, p. 349. See also H. A. Hargreaves, 'A Case for Mister Behn', *Notes and Queries*, June 1962, pp. 203–5; *New Light on Aphra Behn*, pp. 292–3.

24. *CSP*, Dom., 1663–4, p. 607.

25. It was probably more than coincidence that Behn travelled to and from the Continent with noted Roman Catholics and that both Sir Antony Desmarches and Sir Bernard Gascoigne were friends of Arlington and Ogniate. See Evelyn, 22 July, when Evelyn meets Ogniate and Gascoigne with Arlington near his house at Euston.

26. See Alistair B. Fraser and William H. Mach, 'Mirages', *Scientific American*, January 1976, pp. 102–11, and Walter Tape, 'Topology of Mirages', *Scientific American*, June 1985, pp. 120–9. I owe this reference to Mary Anne O'Donnell.

27. The incident is recorded in the 'Memoirs' and borne out by *CSP*.

Chapter 10

1. MS jest book (Va 302) in the Folger Shakespeare Library, Washington.

2. See *CSP*, Col., Nov. 6, 1668, and HMC 14th report, app. 2, vol. 3.

3. Behn felt some comfort when she later heard that the English had recaptured Surinam. Shortly afterwards, it was ceded by the English to the Dutch at the Peace of Breda when the English received New Amsterdam, renamed New York, in its place. Most of the Surinam settlers were forced to leave, but a few chose to stay and agree to be loyal to the state of Zealand.

4. See Arlington, *Letters*, vol. 1, pp. 159–74.

5. *London Gazette*, 16 June, no. 165.

6. Clarendon, *Life*, 1759, p. 421.

7. Pepys, *Diary*, June 12. There seems to have been only one hero: the Scot, Captain Archibald Douglas, who died deserted on his burning ship. Marvell described him

in 'The Loyal Scot' and set his example against that of the corrupt court. The poem's erotic praise of valour—Douglas's head falls 'on the flameing plancks... / As one whoe huggs himselfe in a warme bed'—may have influenced Behn in her verses describing valour, especially the Duke of York's.

8. See Peter Fraser, *The Intelligence of the Secretaries of State and Their Monopoly of Licensed News 1660–1688* (Cambridge, 1956), p. 73.

9. Oudart was, however, reimbursed for his fines and, on 23 February 1666, Sir George Downing was advanced £300 for him. It was generous but the same paragraph records the advance of £700 to Sir George to bring his wife and effects back from Holland.

10. Behn gave no hint of Butler's character, but there is a Butler in the Earl of Rochester's correspondence described as 'a gentleman of the cloak and gallow shoe' (a Puritan who wore other shoes in bad weather to avoid taking a coach). Yet he is also described as having 'debaucht' a young maid employed as a dresser at Henry Hazards' girls' boarding school in Kensington. He sounds the sort of puritanical hypocrite Behn never ceased to lampoon in her works. See *Letters of John Wilmot, Earl of Rochester*, ed. Jeremy Treglown (Oxford, 1980), p. 71.

11. Arlington usually had only £2500 a year for intelligence. During the period of war the amount must have been a good deal higher, however.

12. Albert is telling Astrea of the projected assault on the Medway, another proof that the letter was written after the events: 'you may depend on it, my charming *Astrea*... we have that good Correspondence with some Ministers about the King, that... we look on it as a thing of neither Danger nor Difficulty,' 'Memoirs', p. 7.

13. Behn's petitions to the crown during this time are printed in 'Aphara Behn', *Notes and Queries*, 2nd ser. 8 (1859), pp. 265–6.

14. Arlington, *Letters*, vol. 1, pp. 379 and 384.

15. Dedication to *The City-Heiress*, *Works*, vol. 6.

16. See *CSP*, Venetian, 1667–8, pp. 30, 186; and 1669–70, p. 74; Howard became ambassador to Morocco around this time.

17. This and the other posthumous stories have been published in the complete works of Behn because they have some claim to be by her, although, in several cases, the claim is highly dubious. With its outright linking of narrator with the historical Aphra Behn, 'The Dumb Virgin' seems closest to the authenticated stories, *The Fair Jilt* and *Oroonoko*. For comments on the authenticity of the others, see Chapter 23.

18. For more detail on this, see Jane Spencer's edition of *The Feign'd Curtizans* in *The Rover and Other Plays* (Oxford, 1995).

19. See Phyllis S. Lachs, *The Diplomatic Corps under Charles II and James II* (New Brunswick, 1965).

20. Ann Leuellin, for example, was the 'Administratris of one Robert Leuellin', a merchant, who with Humphrey Beane and other English merchants had a ship

called the *Sarah* seized in August 1656 off the coast of Guinea by two Dutch ships; see *A Catalogue of the Damages* (1664), p. 7.

21. Arlington, *Letters*, vol. 1, p. 397.

22. The government clearly pursued the case above and below board. The agent of Arlington, secret negotiator and expert in marine affairs, Sir Peter Pett, called the King's advocate in Ireland, was issued a royal warrant on 13 May 1670 for £100, the money being royal bounty for services done in connection with the *Abrahams Sacrifice*. On 30 July, another money warrant of £100 (dated 2 Aug.) was issued to Pett in the same connection. Blathwayt was in touch with Pett but probably did not know exactly what he was doing. See Arlington, *Letters*, vol. 1, p. 397.

23. Incidentally Blathwayt may also have been interested in speaking to Behn about Surinam since he was involved in negotiating with the Dutch over the English settlers.. He was a great collector of maps and the owner of the most detailed one of Surinam.

24. The letter is in the Huntington Library, Pasadena. See James Fitzmaurice, 'Aphra Behn and the *Abraham's Sacrifice* Case', *Huntington Library Quarterly*, 1993, vol. 56, no. 3, pp. 319–27.

25. Behn probably avoided offering her services as an agent within the country, since such people were very unpopular when discovered, and she was as little likely to be paid as she had been abroad.

26. *Reflections on the Weekly Bills of Mortality* (London, 1665).

27. John Graunt ascribed the low birth rate to the habit of men's keeping their wives away in the country, *Natural and Political Observations on the Bills of Mortality* (London, 1662), p. 62.

28. See *Rules of Civility* (London, 1673).

29. James Wright, *Humours and Conversations of the Town* (1693), p. 87.

30. Rochester, *Letters*, p. 76; *The Character of A Town-Miss* (1675), p. 4. The town miss was also a prostitute, but some of her manoeuvres of delicacy and dressing were necessary to any woman without family who wished to flourish.

31. Below the level of Ladies of the Bedchamber and the young Maids of Honour, taken usually from the Royalist gentry who needed rewarding for their services to the King in exile, the court could still allow some functions for women who were close to it but not quite of it. One did, however, need money for these as well.

32. 'To my Lady Morland at Tunbridge', vol. 1, no. 25, and 'To Mrs Harsenet. On the Report of a Beauty, Which she went to see at Church' (*The Muses Mercury*, July 1707). It seems likely that the *Muses Mercury* version came from an early manuscript and that, when she came to print the poem in her first volume of poetry in 1684, Behn changed the name of the recipient to use her better-known married name. By 1684 Carola had been dead for a decade.

33. Anthony Hamilton, *Memoirs of the Court of Charles the Second by Count Grammont* (Bickers, 1906).

34. Rochester, 'Tunbridge Wells', *The Poems of John Wilmot Earl of Rochester*, ed. Keith Walker (Oxford, 1984), pp. 69–74.

35. The instruments were destroyed in the Fire. The government placed frequent advertisements in the newspapers declaring that the postal service was confidential and that the letters entrusted to its care were delivered to the recipients untampered with.

36. *An Alphabetical Account of the Nobility and Gentry, Which are (or lately were) related unto the several Counties of England and Wales* (London, 1673).

37. G. J. Gray, 'The Diary of Jeffrey Boys of Gray's Inn, 1671', *Notes and Queries*, 159, no. 26, December 1930, p. 455.

38. 'On the first discovery' (no. 79 in *Works*, vol. 1) seems more personally resonant than many other love poems and it did not appear in the 1684 volume. It is possible it was written much later but, since it was printed in *The Muses Mercury* from another source, it may have been in manuscript circulation long before publication in *Lycidus* in 1688. Perhaps it had been lodged with Boys. Another poem that appeared in the 1684 volume and in *The Muses Mercury* in a different version may also date from this time and concern Jeffrey Boys (although it may refer to a later—or fictional—lover) is 'The Dream' (vol. 1, no. 30), in which 'Fond *Astrea*' saw Cupid weeping because Amyntas had stolen his bow and tied up his wings. To this she exclaimed, ''twas then thy Darts / Wherewith he wounded me;… / He stole his Pow'r from thee.' She would set Cupid free if he would wound Amyntas in return and it was agreed. She untied him and he flew off, crying 'Farewel fond easie Maid.' She awoke and found herself enthralled to Amyntas through Cupid's power.

39. See Harry R. Hoppe, 'English Actors at Ghent in the Seventeenth Century', *Review of English Studies*, vol. 25, 1949, pp. 305–21.

40. James Howell, *Epistolae Ho-Elianae*, ed. Joseph Jacobs (London, 1892), vol. 1, pp. 317–18.

41. See, for example, Robert Lovelace, who was possibly tilting at Cavendish in 'On Sanazar's being honoured with six hundred Duckets', *Poems*, ed. C. H. Wilkinson (Oxford, 1930), p. 200. Dorothy Osborne pronounced Cavendish 'a litle distracted'. Katherine Philips's poems appeared in 1664.

42. Evelyn, *Diary*, III, pp. 465–6.

43. The accusation was, however, perennial. In the 1580s Barnaby Rich found London gentry given to effeminate fashions with dire consequences for their manhood. See L. Woodbridge, *Women and the English Renaissance: Literature and the Nature of Womankind, 1540–1620* (Urbana, 1986).

44. Rochester, *Letters*, p. 67.

45. See also Thomas Shadwell, *A True Widow* (1678), Wycherley, *The Country Wife* (1675), and Samuel Vincent, *The Young Gallants' Academy* (1674).

46. *The Gentlewoman's Companion* (London, 1675), pp. 35–6.

47. Francis Kirkman, *The Unlucky Citizen* (London, 1673), pp. 260–1.

48. The effect of putting on a vizard or mask was a kind of anonymity, as Pepys again noted in February 1667 when he watched or failed to watch *The Maids Tragedy*, having his eyes firmly fixed on the lady beside Sir Charles Sedley. She kept her mask on all through the play and yet managed to impress Pepys as 'a virtuous woman and of quality', while wittily taunting Sir Charles with her knowledge of him. As for Pepys, he never heard 'a more pleasant rencontre' though he thereby 'lost the pleasure of the play wholly'.

49. Above these was the gallery where servants, apprentices and poorer citizens could sit for a shilling.

50. At home Behn could *read* plays, for it had become customary to print a text shortly after the performance. Whether Behn continued with other sorts of reading is doubtful. So she may have missed Milton's publication of *Paradise Lost*, as well as Margaret Cavendish, Duchess of Newcastle's biography of her husband, the Duke. The collected poems of Katherine Philips she probably did see.

Chapter 11

1. See *Tixall Letters*, vol. II, pp. 59–61.

2. Margaret Cavendish, dramatised introduction to her 1662 collection of *Plays*.

3. Miss Cottington was referring to Boothby, who drew attention to 'this uncommon action in my sex'. If Philips's works are labelled adaptations, Boothby is the first woman to write an *original* play for the English public stage. *Marcelia* was performed by the King's Company and licensed for publication in October 1669. Since the date of Cottington's letter is not absolutely certain, it could just about refer to the Duke of Newcastle's play called *The Humorous Lovers* at the Duke's playhouse which Pepys thought by his wife. He regarded it as 'the most silly thing that ever came upon a stage'. See Mendelson, p. 129. However, *The Humorous Lovers* is most likely to be by William, to whom it was attributed in the 1677 edition.

4. Edward Howard was satirised with his brother, Robert, in Thomas Shadwell's *The Sullen Lovers* (1668).

5. In *A Continuation or Second Part of the Letters from the Living* by Thomas Brown, Captain Ayloff and Mr Henry Barker (London, 1793) there is the unreliable suggestion that Ravenscroft was Behn's lover and her helper.

6. See the prologue to the revised version of Jonson's *Every Man in His Humour* (1616), where Jonson takes issue with Shakespeare's Wars of the Roses plays.

7. In her life-long engagement with Ben Jonson, Behn came close to Margaret

Cavendish, who was equally critical and fascinated (Jonson was closely associated with her husband's family). Cavendish also praised Shakespeare for his 'natural' art. See *Sociable Letters* (1664), no. CCXI: 'one would think [Shakespeare] had been Transformed into every one of those Persons he hath Described…he was a Natural Orator, as well as a Natural Poet.'

8. 'To the Reader of *The Jealous Lovers*' (1632), which Behn adapted as *Like Father, Like Son* in 1682.

9. This and the previous derogatory remarks come from 'A Satyr on the Players', BL Harley MS 7317. Nokes played transvestite parts such as the nurse in *Romeo and Juliet* and in Otway's *Caius Marius*.

10. Dryden wrote lines in his partly authored play, *Sir Martin Mar-all, or The Feign'd Innocence* (1667), 'purposely for the Mouth of Mr Nokes'.

11. See *The Tory-Poets: A Satyr* (London, 1682).

12. Colley Cibber, *An Apology for the Life of Mr. Colley Cibber, Comedian*, ed. Robert W. Lowe, 2 vols (1889; New York, 1966), vol. I, pp. 154–5.

13. If Behn had indeed helped Killigrew with *Thomaso* before the Restoration, she might have been introduced to Betterton as a potential adapter and collaborator, or simply as a clear transcriber. In 1669–70, Betterton was making *The Amorous Widow: or, The Wanton Wife, A Comedy* out of Molière's *George Dandin* and Thomas Corneille's *Le Baron d'Albikrac*. In *A Biographical Dictionary of Actors, Actresses, Musicians, Dancers, Managers, and Other Stage Personel in London, 1660–1800* (Carbondale, Ill., 1973), vol. II, Philip H. Highfill, Kalman A. Burnim, and Edward A. Langhans speculate that Behn may have helped Betterton with the adaptation and it would, in view of her future, be an apt title with which to make her début. Ascription is difficult with Betterton because his adaptations were not published until many years later but there seems no reason to associate *The Amorous Widow* with Behn. It is a lively, sophisticated early sex comedy, set specifically in London, mocking age and aged desire and promoting fashion and youth; it is quite different from and more modern than the style of Behn's early tragicomedies. In addition, the dialogue is rather more long-winded than Behn's, even in her early plays, and more aphoristic.

14. *The Genuine Works in Verse and Prose, Of the Right Honourable George Granville* (London, 1732), p. 122.

15. Interestingly, there is similar instability in Frances Boothby's *Marcelia* (London, 1670), which accepts Stuart theory in making an absolute separation of subjects and princes: 'The King is by that awful name secure; / Subjects are bound what they do to endure.' Then, however, it presents the King as courting an engaged woman in possible reference to one of the many amours of the actual Stuart King, Charles II.

16. *Works*, vol. 5, p. 76.

17. Others have the same knowledge—Philander instructs his sister on how to use her

feminine charms on their father by hanging on his cheek and mingling talk with kisses—but they do not quite deconstruct femininity with this knowledge.

18. *Works*, vol. 5, p. 25.

19. Charles Gildon's *Life of Mr. Thomas Betterton* (London, 1710).

20. Preface to *Don Sebastian, King of Portugal* (London, 1690). Cuts were restored in the printed text.

21. After Behn's death women playwrights were certainly involved in rehearsals. The dramatists Catherine Trotter and Mary Pix were mocked in *The Female Wits* (1697) for their roles in staging a play.

22. *The Female Tatler*, 1709–10, no. 41, ed. Fidelis Morgan (London, 1992), p. 94.

23. The Otway incident need not necessarily have happened at the first performance.

24. 'Session of the Poets' (1676).

25. On the whole, in these years theatre-managers were trusted to be careful over content, since Charles II had put authority into their hands.

26. In the 1670s house charges were about £25 a night. See Judith Milhous, 'The Duke's Company's Profits, 1675–1677', *Theatre Notebook*, 32, 1978, pp. 76–88.

27. *The Laws of Poetry* (London, 1721), pp. 37–8. See Roswell Gray Ham, *Otway and Lee: Biography from a Baroque Age* (New Haven, 1931), p. 61.

28. The secrecy of Behn's professional life is enforced by the fact that on 31 May 1670, the avid theatregoer, Samuel Pepys, fearing for the safety of his eyes, stopped writing his *Diary*. Behn had still four months to go until her début. It is interesting to speculate what he would have written. He would probably have appreciated Behn's sense of theatre and her endeavour to make her plays various, although he might not have accepted her general tenor: he had more of an admiration for Ben Jonson than she had, and he thought her much admired *Othello* 'a mean thing' when he read it on a boat, though he had earlier 'esteemed [it] a mighty good play'. But, in the end, it is impossible to guess Pepys's reaction: the difference between his being 'mightily pleased' and 'mightily dissatisfied' depended on his mood, ladies in the audience, and his sense of other people's opinion, as well as on the playwright's dramatic skill and the production.

Chapter 12

1. See the dedication to *The Spanish Friar* (1680).

2. The Printing Act of 1662 ensured that copyright resided in the Stationers' Company rather than the author, but the author was now free to sell the initial work, unlike in the years before the Interregnum.

3. Osborne, *Letters*, pp. 82 and 218.

4. Elkanah Settle complained of the difficulty of getting a play text published in his dedicatory epistle to *The Empress of Morocco* (1673).

5. Though political affiliation is certainly not absolute among publishers, Magnes appears to be largely in the Royalist camp, but, since he died in 1679, he did not have to take sides when party factions became intensified. He also published French works usually in translation, including Brémond's *Hattigé*, which Behn seems later to have read.

6. Behn expressed this fear in the dedication to *The Young King*, *Works*, vol. 6.

7. The second edition made some much needed emendations, for example Falatio is happily renamed Falatius and Erminia marries the 'General' Alcippus rather than the 'Genetall'.

8. The play was matched only by her posthumous play, *The Widdow Ranter*, and almost by *The Feign'd Curtizans*; see endnotes to these plays in vols 6 and 7 of *Works*.

9. For further information about Behn's dramatic sources, see the head notes to the plays in *Works*, vols 5–7. It is curious that, in her 1662 *Plays*, Margaret Cavendish, boasting of the originality of her works, declared she avoided precisely the sources of Behn's early plays, French romance and Spanish prose: 'I ne'r took Plot…from Romance, nor from Don Quixot, / As others have, for to assist their Wit, / But I upon my own Foundation writ.'

10. *Works*, vol. 5, p. 109.

11. See the 1724 edition, *Plays Written by the Late Ingenious Mrs. Behn*.

12. Thomas Dring acted as bookseller for several famous literary authors, such as Wycherley, Dryden, Milton and Mlle de Scudéry. This meant that he financed the publication and was responsible for marketing as well. *The Amorous Prince* was entered in the Term Catalogue for Trinity, 10 July.

13. D. E. L. Crane, *George Villiers, Duke of Buckingham's 'The Rehearsal'* (Durham, 1976), p. 64.

14. Tragicomedy was not a form Behn could easily abandon and she returned to it at the end of her life when perhaps it best summed up her experiences.

15. Dorset was actually Lord Buckhurst at this point, but I have anticipated his later title to avoid confusion.

16. *Works*, vol. 1, no. 1.

17. 'A Pindaric By The Honourable Edward Howard, To Mrs. B. Occasioned By a Copy she made on his Play, called The New Eutopia.' It was published in Behn's *Miscellany* of 1685.

18. For another view of the authorship, see Paul Hammond in 'The Prologue and epilogue to Dryden's *Marriage A-la-Mode*', *PBSA*, 81, 1987, no. 8. James Anderson Winn has noted that Dryden himself was fairly indifferent to collecting and reprinting his shorter poems, see note to p. 379 of *'When Beauty Fires the Blood': Love and the Arts in the Age of Dryden* (Ann Arbor, 1992).

19. *Works*, vol. 1, no. 2.

20. George Etherege, *The Man of Mode* (1676).

21. *A Comparison Between the Two Stages* (1702; Princeton, 1942), p. 17.

22. [Edmund Hickeringill] *The Mushroom: or, A Satyr In Answer to a Satyre against Sedition. Called The Medal.* The satire points out '*Poets and Beauty* play *no After-Game*' (London, 1682).

Chapter 13

1. See the will, signed 1677, of John Hoyle, 8 July 1692, PRO:Prob/11/410.

2. Satirists put Barry's birthdate at just after Behn's, in 1643. See the satire on Barry, Mall Hinton and Charlotte Butler, in BL Harleian MS 6913, p. 345. In 'A Pastoral to Mr. *Stafford*' Behn refers to herself as too young for her Antwerp mission when, if born in 1640, she would have been twenty-five. *Works*, vol. 1, no. 64.

3. Hoyle's learning can be gauged from his eclectic library, which included many learned tomes, as well as such works as *Le Putanisme d'Amsterdam avec figures*. No books by Behn were found in it at his death. Hoyle was perhaps one or two years younger than Behn since he entered Emmanuel College, Cambridge, in May 1658 and Gray's Inn nearly two years later.

4. The suicide became notorious and featured in many anti-government poems, for example, 'On the Happy Memory of Alderman Hoyle that hang'd himself', where 'A wounded soul close coupled with the sense / Of sin, pays home its proper recompense.'

5. Attitudes towards homosexuality and bisexuality seem fairly relaxed in Behn's circles, despite the capital statutes against sodomy. R. Trumbach has argued that this was the last generation in which the typical representative was a sodomite 'with his whore on one arm and his boy on the other' rather than the more worrying member of an effeminate and homosexual subculture which began to grow up in the late 1690s, 'Sodomitical Assaults, Gender Role, and Sexual Development in Eighteenth Century London', *The Pursuit of Sodomy*, eds K. Gerard and G. Hokma (New York, 1989), pp. 408–9.

6. The diary trails off with Boys in a fever, from which he might have died, although Blome in *Britannica* lists a Jeffrey Boys of Gray's Inn in 1683. Clearly there were other flirtations for Behn as well. In 'The Sence of a Letter sent me, made into Verse, To a New Tune', she describes receiving a letter with the kind of male threat she did not like; she turned it into verse for *The Amorous Prince*. Perhaps she constructed the lover out of male attitudes or the man may have stood out for the clarity of his threat. In the final stanza he blamed the woman for provoking and not satisfying him: if women did not act as men wished, men would 'grow to abhor, what we now do admire'. When she republished the verses thirteen years later (see *Works*, vol. 1, no. 22), Behn was more aware of absurdity than menace and she changed the last stanza to make the luckless lover slink off.

7. *Works*, vol. 1, no. 43.

8. When the Duke's Company went to Dorset Garden, the King's Company under Killigrew had the mortification of having to move into their rivals' vacated premises.

9. Behn was less pleased to hear in the hero's mouth the opinion 'Wit and Beauty seldome go together in a Woman,' while the quarrel of the two whores who discuss the precise stages of a woman's sartorial disintegration through second-hand gowns and black cloth and plain linen to 'Strip't Semar', which no wit can redeem, must have struck near the bone. It was not long since Behn had faced prison for debt.

10. Meanwhile Marcel is persuaded not to kill his fallen sister since he has sought to visit the same fate on his beloved: 'I either must my shameful Love resign, / Or my more brave and just Revenge decline.'

11. *Works*, vol. 5, p. 177.

12. *Works*, vol. 5, p. 194.

13. Some of Behn's techniques were still old-fashioned, e.g. the overuse of asides so mocked in *The Rehearsal*, but she avoided the clumsy eavesdropping of *The Amorous Prince* and relied more on gesture: Euphemia's mock swoon to reveal her beauty is carefully choreographed. Behn had developed a sense of the importance of costume and was eager to control what the characters wore.

14. Both Angel and Jevon, who joined the Company in the 1673–4 season, were known to dislike seriousness and to develop their own buffoonery, as Downes suggested.

15. Very few playwrights assumed Behn's cynicism and so they opened themselves to the kind of criticism that Jeremy Collier was already levelling at them in the early 1670s (see MS Va 312 Folger), when he countered their notion that evil and 'concupiscence' were displayed to reform the audience. Behn accepted with Collier that drama did not represent 'dull Christian marriage', and that people sought comedy 'out of jollity of heart'. Indeed she manages to sound quite like the censoring divine when she writes that 'Playes were certainly intended for the exercising of men's passions not their understandings.' Her defiant stand was of course an advertisement for her wares—the plays she wrote ought to be amusing. But it also sprang from her irritation at the pretensions of men. She always bewailed the formal education she had not received, but at times, as here, Behn's annoyance at the discrimination was tempered by her sense that men might indeed be learned without being sensible, frank or wise.

16. Shadwell had such overweening confidence that he declared of his adaptations, 'without vanity…Molière's part has not suffered in his hand' and, of his version of Shakespeare's *Timon of Athens*, that he himself had made it into a true play.

17. John Eachard, *The Grounds and Occasions of the Contempt of the Clergy and Religion Enquired into* (London, 1670), p. 12.

18. Eachard, pp. 4–5. After 1660, as grammar schools for boys began to diversify into

a new curriculum, the upper gentry insisted on sending their sons to schools which preserved the old regime with its union of harsh discipline and the classics. See M. V. Wallbank, 'Eighteenth-century Public Schools and the Education of the Governing Elite', *History of Education*, 8, 1979.

19. Behn also relished Eachard's criticism of the clergy although she did not follow him in attributing much of their scandalous backsliding to their poverty. Mendelson believes that Behn was the author of a comedy called *The Woman Turn'd Bully* written about this time and performed in 1675, which shows both learning and a mockery of learning. There is no conclusive evidence either way. On the one hand there are in the play more Latin quotations and tags than Behn usually allowed, which suggests a lawyer-author, and, on the other, Behn was known as a friend of lawyers and there is mention of 'the Nunnery at Ghent'. There is also an entry of a boisterous widow who, like the later widow Ranter, smokes publicly. Most likely the play was a collaboration.

20. Evelyn, *Diary*, ed. William Bray (London, 1852), IV, pp. 21–2.

21. Here of course Shadwell might be making the best of a bad job, since the Duke's Company still did not excel in comediennes.

22. Prologue to Ben Jonson's *The Silent Woman*.

23. Rochester, *Letters*, p. 182.

24. *Works*, vol. 1, no. 31.

Chapter 14

1. These concerts were advertised in the *London Gazette*, the first announcement appearing on 26 December 1672. After 1675 the concerts took place in Covent Garden and after 1678 near St Clement's Church in the Strand.

2. For a description of Banister's concerts, see Alan Luhring, 'The Music of John Banister' (Diss., Stanford University, 1966).

3. It is slightly more likely to have been Henry Purcell's brother since Henry's voice began to break in 1673. Although he probably sang in commercial productions after that time, Henry Purcell became mainly an instrumentalist. See Maureen Duffy, *Henry Purcell* (London, 1994).

4. *Works*, vol. 1, no. 60.

5. The letter was printed in 1718 by Tom Brown in *Familiar Letters of Love, Gallantry, And several Occasions*. If not by Behn, it seems likely that it was written to provide a titillating context for a re-publication of her poem, 'The Disappointment'. Charles Gildon and Brown were both composers of other people's letters, see *The Post Boy Robb'd of his Mail* (1692) and *Miscellaneous Letters and Essays* (1694).

6. See P. A. Hopkins, 'Aphra Behn and John Hoyle: A Contemporary Mention, and Sir Charles Sedley's Poem on his Death', *Notes and Queries*, n.s., vol. 41, no. 2, June 1994, pp. 176–85. The eight letters were printed in 1696 in *The Histories and Novels*...

in one Volume. They may be forgeries, used to fill up sheets in the volume and help sell Behn as a Tory wit and libertine. There is no firm evidence either way, but I believe them more likely to be genuine than otherwise. The letters are reprinted in *Works*, vol. 3, pp. 260–70.

7. Given the obvious jealousy expressed in the letter, it was a useless ploy to promise to see 'no Man till I saw your Face again'—especially since on this occasion Behn had seen Hoyle only a few hours before.

8. *Works*, vol. 3, p. 264.

9. *Works*, vol. 3, p. 268.

10. Without the knowledge that it was the last of the series, a reader could still feel the writer's partial recovery and foretell a change from this letter. There is a post-script asking Hoyle to come to see Behn and on a day earlier than the one he had suggested, but significantly she ends with more distance than she had before mustered when she adds 'if you can'.

11. *Works*, vol. 1, no. 18.

12. The poem echoes the epilogue of *The Amorous Prince*: 'Love in rural triumph reigns, / As much a God amongst the Swains', and takes up the conceit in the poem 'Ballad on Mr.... asking why I was so sad', where the shepherd was adorned with female trophies.

13. See B. Lewis, *British Contributions to Arabic Studies* (London, 1941).

14. The translation was published in 1649 and was reissued with a *Caveat* in 1688 expressing the popular conception of Mohammed as cunning and power hungry. For the non-blushing Moor, cf. Webster's *White Devil* (1612), where Zanche says 'I ne'er lov'd my complexion till now / Cause I may boldly say without a blush / I love you' (Act V, Scene I, ll. 209–11).

15. Dryden also minimised the activity. In the preface to *An Evening's Love*, he argued that the borrowing playwright resembled 'a curious Gunsmith, or Watchmaker: the Iron or Silver is not his own; but they are the least part of that which gives the value; The price lyes wholly in the worksmanship'.

16. Kirkman, the biographer of Mary Carleton, published *Lusts Dominion*. He attributed it to Christopher Marlowe, an attribution Langbaine accepted. The play was clearly influenced by or similar to Marlowe's works, especially *The Jew of Malta* (1589), which also depicted an exotic villain defeated though never subjugated in spirit. But, since there was an allusion to a tract concerning the death of the Spanish king, Philip II, which occurred after Marlowe's death, some of the work must have been written by another person. This later writer, possibly Thomas Dekker, was also influenced by Shakespeare's *Titus Andronicus*, where Aaron the Moor and Tamora, Queen of the Goths, are similarly outrageous. Despite the attribution to Marlowe, *Lusts Dominion* did not do well and Kirkman was still trying to sell his 1657 edition in 1661, when he gave the work a new title page. Usefully for Behn,

it does not seem that the play was performed; so she might have hoped that most of her audience would not know it.

17. For example, Behn moved the scene where the Queen persuades her old flame, the Cardinal, to abandon her son to a position where it can be interrupted by a messenger from Philip, who dashes in to urge the Cardinal to bring up his forces and save the day.

18. As usual, Behn abandoned supernatural devices. She also omitted a comic duo and old King Philip and combined peripheral characters, retaining only one comic soldier. She filled the court with courtiers and added a banqueting scene. She also clarified motivation: Osmin, Abdelazer's creature, is in her play characterised as weary of his subjection to a tyrant and he is given the role of warning Philip, in place of the two 'lowsy friars' of *Lusts Dominion*.

19. Politics is implied in lines added to the original play when Abdelazer speaks about the need to exclude Philip, now declared a bastard, despite his popularity: 'That dangerous Popular Spirit must be laid, / Or *Spain* must languish under Civil Swords.' Something is also made of the theme of political revenge. But Abdelazer's triumph, destroying almost the entire male part of the Spanish royal family, is so extreme it is difficult to see it as political comment. There are, however, one or two references to recent events in the play. In the last act when Abdelazer describes himself 'Raging as Midnight flames let loose in Citie... will ruine where it lights', the audience probably remembered the Great Fire of London a decade before. When Philip looked at Abdelazer, seeing not just black destruction but 'Plagues' to poison the world, the reference had a resonance now lost. There may even have been a reference to the Antwerp society that had so struck Behn in 1666: the Queen speaks of the spies she has round her son, as they had been round Phillander in *The Forc'd Marriage*. It is a detail not in *Lusts Dominion*.

20. See Jessica Munns, *Restoration Politics and Drama: The Plays of Thomas Otway, 1675– 1683* (Newark, Del., 1995).

21. In other plays, women are given heroic drives and find their will their appetite. In Settle's *Empress of Morocco*, for example, the heroine combines the ruthlessness of Abdelazer with the lack of family feelings of the Queen. Women are, however, considered to have an essentially feminine nature and even Settle's character has, like Lady Macbeth, to denature herself—'Nature, be gone'—as she prepares to kill her son. The man acts according to nature when he follows his appetite, the woman has to be denatured. Also, despite her villainy, the Queen follows Cloris of *The Amorous Prince* in making the feminine point, that love exists most happily in the pastoral world without honour and rank, 'In shadie Groves... / Free from the noise, and danger of the Great'. The Queen knows the political value of femininity, as she manipulates other powerful men with her 'sighs, and feigned tears'.

22. Behn may well have thought of a vehicle for Mary Lee while writing. Lee had just been

acclaimed as Mariamne in *The Empress of Morocco* and the Queen of Spain in Otway's *Don Carlos*, which again featured the winning combination of herself and Betterton.

23. Alfred Harbage, rev. by S. Schoenbaum, *Annals of English Drama, 975–1700* (London, 1964) puts the first production *of Abdelazer* in about April, with Otway's play coming after on 8 June. The next edition of 1693 took the prologue, 'Gallants, you have so long been absent hence', from *Covent Garden Drolery*.

24. See Montague Summers, ed., *The Works of Aphra Behn* (London, 1915), vol. 11, p. 431. The device of the child was also used by Otway in *Don Carlos*.

25. This is the first Behn play for which there is any financial information. See Judith Milhous, 'The Duke's Company's Profits, 1675–1677', *Theatre Notebook*, 32, 1978, pp. 76–88.

26. *Abdelazer* had two editions in Behn's lifetime, a probable revival in 1693 and a certain one in 1695, when it was staged at Drury Lane. By then it had lost its appeal and, despite a new prologue by Colley Cibber and splendid music by Henry Purcell, it did not please. Heroic tragedies had continued, but the taste for unremitting villainy without sentiment had gone.

27. The name Emily is not sure. A Mrs Price was working at the Duke's Theatre from 1676 to 1682, playing secondary parts. Thus Montague Summers speculates that this may have been the daughter of the actor-dancer Joseph Price, who died in 1673, a supposition born out by Price's familiarity with the theatre and theatre gossip. A later actress called Elizabeth Price is sometimes confused with Emily, but Elizabeth started at the United Company only in 1685 or 1686; she was famous for being seduced by Etherege and by her efforts to have herself accepted as Countess of Banbury. The possible connection of Mrs Price and Warcup is made by Galbraith M. Crump in *Poems on Affairs of State*, vol. 4 (New Haven, 1968). Captain Warcup's first name may be Edmund like the judge in the Popish Plot or, as Wilson speculates in *Court Satires*, Lenthal, p. 159.

28. 'Verses design'd by Mrs. A Behn, to be sent to a fair Lady' was published in *Miscellany Poems upon Several Occasions* (1692) with a dedication by Charles Gildon, and the other two, 'To Mrs. Price' and 'Song: 'Tis not your saying that you love…', by Samuel Briscoe in *Familiar Letters of Love, Gallantry, and Several Occasions* (1718), together with Tom Brown's spurious posthumous works. See *Works*, vol. 1, nos 93 and 97.

29. Dorchester seems likely because of the confluence of rivers. There is, however, a very tenuous link between Behn and Glympton in Oxfordshire through her involvement in the manuscript 'Astrea's Booke' which bore the Busby bookplate; the family lived at Glympton. Since Lenthal Warcup, the man tentatively labelled Emily Price's father, was from Oxford, it is conceivable that Emily Price and Behn had both been near Oxford together for a while. This is the more likely if one speculates that the Duke's Company may have been visiting Oxford. *The London Stage* records only visits of the King's Company in summer 1674, however.

30. The letter appears with the two poems in *Familiar Letters of Love, Gallantry, and Several Occasions*. Briscoe is known to have published spurious letters of Charles Sedley and the Duke of Buckingham, and the Behn work may also be so, but I have included mention of it because it may have genuine passages or be some pointer to what contemporaries believed to be her emotional life. The remarks about the attacks on the plagiarism of *Abdelazer* seem typical of Behn, who always defended her borrowings. At the same time Briscoe might have taken them from Gildon, who had revised Langbaine as *The Lives and Characters of the English Dramatic Poets* in 1698; in this there was much attention to Behn's plagiarisms.

Chapter 15

1. These letters were published without a superscription in *Familiar Letters: Written by the Right Honourable John Late Earl of Rochester... with Letters Written by the Most Ingenious Mr. Thomas Otway* (1697). The recipient was given as Barry only in 1713 after her death. Tom Brown's involvement does not inspire entire confidence in the genuineness of the letters.

2. As the strongest and most assertive actress of the period, Elizabeth Barry was constantly mocked and called a whore. Tom Brown's opinion is characteristic: 'should you ly with her all Night, She would not know you the next Morning, unless you had another five Pound at her Service.'

3. Rochester, *Letters*, p. 174. Nell Gwyn urged Savile to write to Rochester.

4. Rochester, *Letters*, p. 172.

5. Rochester, *Letters*, p. 180.

6. The birth delighted satirists: Rochester was described as fathering 'a cheddar child as his own brood, / And had he lived to Hesty's fifteen year, / He'd fucked his girl t'have been a grandfather' ('Satire on Bent[in]g' from March 1689, in *Court Satires of the Restoration* by John Harold Wilson (Columbus, Ohio, 1976), p. 115. Despite the 'cheddar' cheese remark there seems little doubt the baby was Rochester's. Rochester did not leave her anything though he did leave £40 per year for a love child called Elizabeth Clerke, while his niece Anne Wharton at her death in 1685 left the large sum of £3000 to Hesther. Whether or not Rochester followed through with his threat to take Hesther, Barry was certainly looking after the girl later and there is some evidence she became a devoted mother. She would thus have needed a good deal of money, and some of the mercenariness of which she was accused might have derived from this need.

7. Six years younger than Behn, Rochester was far more formally educated and he knew the classics intimately. It may have been with his help that Behn began to imitate and put into verse some of the translated classical texts of Horace. Rochester may also have introduced her to the form of the pastoral dialogue which she used

for 'Dialogue for an Entertainment at Court, between *Damon* and *Sylvia*' and for her adaptation of Randolph's *Amyntas* as *The Wavering Nymph*, a pastoral play which seems not to have been printed.

8. *Boscobel Tracts*, ed. J. Hughes (London, 1830), p. 151.

9. Preface by Robert Wolseley to *Valentinian* (London, 1684).

10. Rochester, *Letters*, p. 127.

11. The playwrights themselves were equally quarrelsome. Shadwell and Otway, for example, had begun as friends, then savagely fallen out. Otway also quarrelled with Elkanah Settle.

12. Rochester, *Letters*, p. 165.

13. The poem was published in Behn's collection in 1684 entitled 'Song *To Pesibles Tune*', *Works*, no. 33.

14. In the late 1670s Rochester, Blount and other rakish wits formed themselves into an atheist conventicle in mockery of Dissenting conventicles. The word 'atheist' could indicate a doubt of orthodox Christianity, rarely a denial of any immaterial being. Often it was simply used for a wicked person. If it ever did more than exist to shock good citizens, the group would have leaned towards scepticism and the line of thought that stretched from Lucretius and the ancients to Hobbes. Behn could well have been of the company.

15. *Leviathan*, ed. Richard Tuck (Cambridge, 1991).

16. Rochester, *Poems*, p. 13.

17. 'Memoirs of the Earl of Rochester', in *The Poetical Works of the Earls of Rochester, Roscommon, and Dorset*, 2 vols (London, 1757), p. iv.

18. *Works of Nathaniel Lee*, ed. Thomas B. Stroup and Arthur L. Cooke (New Brunswick, 1954), p. 564.

19. The seventeenth century had introduced the clitoris into medical textbooks, cf. the 1668 translation of *Bartholin's Anatomy*, where it is called the 'chief seat of delight in carnal copulation', and Thomas Gibson's *The Anatomy of Human Bodies Epitomised* (1682).

20. The poem comically falls into the tradition in which female voraciousness or any concern for a woman's pleasure causes failure in the man. Examples could come from many times and places, from the *Arabian Nights* or Shakespeare's *Much Ado About Nothing* or the contemporary *Learn to Lye Warm* by Arnot Bagot (London, 1672).

21. See Jessica Munns, '"But to the Touch were soft": pleasure, power, and impotence in "The Disappointment" and "The Golden Age"', *Aphra Behn Studies*, ed. Janet Todd (Cambridge, 1996), pp. 178–96.

22. The copytexts of this edition did not originate from Rochester's family. Of the 61 poems, only 34 are by Rochester.

23. In *A Review of the State of the English Nation* III, no. 131, 2 November 1706, Defoe

casually alluded to Behn as Rochester's mistress, but there is no known supporting evidence.

24. Nat Lee, *On the Death of Mrs. Behn* (London, 1689).

25. See Elizabeth Walsh and Richard Jeffries, 'The Excellent Mrs. Mary Beale' (Inner London Education Authority, 1975) and E. Walsh, 'Mary Beale, Paintress', *Connoisseur*, 131, 1953, pp. 3–8. Montague Summers describes the portraits of Behn in *The Works of Aphra Behn*, vol. 1, lxiii. The 'Beale' portrait was ascribed to Mary Beale only in 1822 when J. Fittler engraved it after a drawing by Uwins, labelling it 'Aphra Behn. From a Picture by Mary Beale in the collection of His Grace the Duke of Buckingham. Drawn by T. Uwins. Engraved by J. Fittler'. It was produced for Stowe's *Effigies Poetae* in 1824 but subsequently found its way into the 1702 edition of Behn's *Plays* published by Tonson. The original portrait was bought in 1848 by J. S. Caldwell, a literary antiquarian, in whose family it remained until Captain G. H. Heath-Caldwell sold it to Miss M. V. Wakefield-Richmond, who presented it to St Hilda's College, Oxford, in 1989.

26. The notion comes from Ned Ward's *London Spy* (1698; London, 1955), p. 119, where the narrator describes the deserted Dorset Garden open to pillage by those who would sell the pictures of the poets 'to some upholsterer for Roman Emperors'. The mention of Wright is in *Walpole Society. Vertue Notebooks*, vol. 1, p. 43. The 'Lely' portrait was later owned by Philip H. Howard of Corby Castle, who lent it to the South Kensington National Portrait Exhibition in 1866. It is now owned by Arthur Schlechter of New York, whose ancestor bought it through Colnaghi's in May 1888. There is no mention of Wright in Behn's life—unless the scrawl in Colepeper's 'Adversaria' can be read so, in which case Wright would be her brother-in-law. The speculation seems unlikely.

27. 'Lely on animated Canvas stole / The sleepy Eye that spoke the melting soul', Alexander Pope, '1st Epistle of the 2nd Book of Horace', ll. 149–50.

28. A possible candidate is the sketch made on 21 May 1873 by Sir George Scharf, first director of the National Portrait Gallery. It was taken from an oval painting of about 2 feet square, now not known (T.S.B. XIX, p. 4) and was intended for the trustees who were considering acquiring the painting from Edward Parsons. The Scharf sketch is consistent with the Lely (and later Riley) image although it gives its subject a fuller and more pursed mouth and fuller and darker hair, part hanging over her right shoulder. The hair is described as intensely rich brown, where Lely's sitter has lighter, more reddish hair; unlike in the Lely and Riley pictures, it has no ornaments. Scharf declared the painting had brown shadow and greenish tints and was 'in the style of Closterman'. Closterman was the assistant of Riley and so the portrait Scharf saw might have been a version of the Riley one, but it could also be the missing Greenhill.

29. *Works*, vol. 1, no. 15. Behn's lines were used for the epitaph on Greenhill's tomb.

30. See Henry Reynolds' translation of 1628 which omitted the phrase 'that which pleases is permitted', *Aminta Englisht*, ed. C. Davidson (Fennimore, Wisc., 1972), p. 67, n. 26.

31. Often Dryden treated the Golden Age in a quite different way. In his translation of Virgil's fourth eclogue in his *Miscellany Poems* he uses imagery of the Golden Age and peace, already employed in *Astrea Redux*. Here the Golden Age, although it erases kings and priests as well as discord, still stands for the status quo against civil strife and Whiggish liberty.

32. See, for example, Nathaniel Johnston, *The Excellency of Monarchical Government, Especially of the English Monarchy...* (London, 1686). His radical opinion that all are totally subject to the prince led to a kind of sex equality outside the Golden Age, when he asks why, if the King is not allowed to be absolute, anyone, including 'Women and Children, Madmen and Fools', should be excluded from authority.

33. *Works*, vol. 1, no. 12.

34. 'The Female Laureat', Dyce MS, National Art Library, Victoria and Albert Museum, London.

35. Thomas Carte, *An History of the Life of James, Duke of Ormond* (1736; Oxford, 1851), vol. IV, p. 526.

36. Behn had little contact with Ireland, but she may have been brought to know those who had through a fellow dramatist (and political agitator) Henry Nevil Payne. Payne had made trouble there in a previous administration or, in the words of a scurrilous account (1680), 'spawn'd abundance of Poyson, whence venemous Beasts have grown in such plenty, that St. Patrick's Miracle [casting snakes out of Ireland] is become a mere Fiction'. Behn was probably commissioned to write her poem, or she might have offered it to a witty and self-indulgent man of the sort she liked, expecting a suitable response.

37. Elizabeth Taylor's progress sounds rather like that of Lady Fancy in Behn's later play *Sir Patient Fancy*.

38. In *The New Atalantis*, ed. Ros Ballaster (London, 1991), Delarivier Manley called 'Olinda', who may be Elizabeth Taylor, 'the wittiest lady of the age... She had... the face of a wit, much sprightliness and but little beauty', p. 260 and n. 512.

39. 'A Satyr Ignis Ignibus extinguitur', Dyce MS, Victoria and Albert Museum.

40. Ephelia's beloved appears to have been a J. G. and the affair to have followed the much traced road: the man loves, the woman returns love, conceals nothing, he loses interest, she increases hers. Another object might have been the 'Philocles' of Behn's 'Cabal', the temporary beloved of Elizabeth Barry. Ephelia tried to tie him to her in one of those intense platonic relationships that Katherine Philips was so famous for depicting in her poetry: 'In a strict League, together we'l combine. / And Friendship's bright Example shine. / We will forget the Difference of Sex,' *Kissing the Rod: An Anthology of Seventeenth-century Women's Verse*, eds G. Greer, S.

Hastings, J. Medoff and M. Sanson (London, 1988), p. 283. As with Behn, however, so with Ephelia, there are problems in assuming amorous autobiography from a series of texts that play with conventional roles.

41. The main speculation comes from 'A Familiar Epistle to Julian', where 'Poor George's Muse' hoarsely 'sang Ephelia's Lamentation'. The Ephelia poems may refer to Mulgrave's affair with Mall Kirke, a Maid of Honour to Mary, Duchess of York, or to that with Carey Frazier, a Maid of Honour to Queen Catherine, and an occasional, rather implausible claimant for the identity of Ephelia. Alternatively, many hands might be at work in the poems, including Behn's. One possible allusion to Ephelia comes from a commendatory poem to Behn's *Lycidus* (1688) which describes 'Sappho' as 'weak and poor' and wearing 'At second hand… russet Laurels'. This is, however, a late reference if Ephelia did in fact die in the early 1680s and any dubious female poet tended to be called Sappho. The adaptation of Ephelia's poem 'The Twin Flame', by Monmouth attests to her fame through MS circulation. See Sajed Chowdhury, 'A Newly Discovered Manuscript Adaptation of Ephelia's "The Twin Flame",' 'Archives, circulation...', June 29, 2016. For further discussion, see *Poems by Ephelia*, facsimile, ed. Maureen E. Mulvihill (New York, 1993) and Germaine Greer's response in *TLS*, 25 June 1993, pp. 7–8 and *Women's Writing*, vol. 2, no. 3, 1995, pp. 309–11.

42. Gould, *Satyrical Epistle* (1691). If she is the author of the prologue to the single play ascribed to her, 'The Pair-Royal of Coxcombs', acted only at a dancing-school, Ephelia tried to separate herself from the professionals, declaring she composed only to amuse her friends, that women's work was too lowly to expect male attention, and that any faults should be laid to her sex. Behn was long past this sort of thing. Ephelia clearly admired Behn, whose career allowed Ephelia to claim that a woman writing a play was not common, 'though it be not rare'.

43. Rochester, *Poems*, p. 83.

44. *The Poetess A Satyr* (London, 1707) p. 3.

Chapter 16

1. Rochester's letters almost seem to deny the ascription of 'Session of the Poets' but it remains significant that they do not quite do so.

2. Burnet, *History of His Own Time*, vol. II, p. 290. The opponent was the Earl of Shaftesbury. Paula Backscheider thinks the 'black Ace' may be a reference to Oroonoko, whose story Behn may already have been telling. See *Spectacular Politics: Theatrical Power and Mass Culture in Early Modern England* (Baltimore, 1993), p. 93. Behn herself as 'Astrea' may have appeared as judge rather than judged in 'A Supplement to the Session of the Ladyes', Dyce MS, which featured such ladies as the scandalous Countess of Sussex, daughter of Charles II and Barbara, Duchess

of Cleveland. It is appropriate that, at the end, Astrea gives Adonis to 'wrinkl'd brow'd Venus'.

3. Just possibly there is another allusion to Behn in 'In defence of Satyr', sometimes attributed to Sir Car Scrope. This praises the theatre of Shakespeare, Jonson and Fletcher for satirising people and damning the age by ridiculing vice. Now the lust for money, place, fame and women is so great that the stage has no impact and there is no purpose for the moral Muse in drama. Considering Behn's expressed opinion at this time, that the stage is merely for amusement and has no moral role, there may be an oblique allusion to her in the following lines: 'The *World's* a *Wood*, in which all loose their way, / Though by a diff'rent *Path*, each goes *Astray*.'

4. The fop as a stock character appeared in the 1660s, with James Howard's *The English Monsieur* (1663) and Robert Howard's tragicomedy *The Surprisal* (1662). He had only slowly caught on. To some extent the depiction was influenced by the French dramatist, Molière.

5. This scene is based on Wilkins's degradation of his hero Scarborow, who falls a great deal further than Bellmour. In *Venice Preserv'd* (1682) Otway will, with his brothel scene, make a devastating comment on erotic politics.

6. Behn does, however, add remarks about the inadvisability of cousin marriages. Perhaps she remembered the disastrous union of Isabella Sidney and Lord Strangford.

7. In *The First English Actresses* (Cambridge, 1992) Elizabeth Howe considers this role likely since Currer had just played the similar one of Betty Frisque in Crowne's *The Country Wit*.

8. 'A Satyr on the Players' makes Currer a prostitute who is advised to return to Ireland since her going-rate in London has fallen so low.

9. *The Town-Fopp* was reprinted in 1699 and may have been played in the season of 1698–9. Probably its reprinting owed more to the sudden fame of Behn, attendant on the success of Southerne's *Oroonoko*, than to its merits. At the same time a new type of tragicomedy was coming into fashion in the late 1690s and *The Town-Fopp* might just have been more appropriate for the end of the seventeenth century than it was for the libertine 1670s.

10. A *Comparison Between the Two Stages*, p. 11.

11. The ascription to Behn rests primarily on an anonymous seventeenth-century addition to a copy of the play in the William Andrews Clark Memorial Library, Los Angeles, once owned by John Philip Kemble: 'Altered by Mrs. Behn from R. Brome's Mad Couple Well-Match'. Montague Summers did not include the play in his edition of 1915 but considered 'it is no doubt from her'. In *The Debauchee* names resemble those in Brome and the two plays are far closer than anything Behn acknowledged, which may be one reason why it remained anonymous. See Richard Brome, *Five New Playes* (London, 1653).

12. The prologue was signed E. R. which some critics have supposed to be Rochester, but Ravenscroft seems more likely.

13. According to *The London Stage*, in about May 1677 a play called *A Midnight Intrigue* was acted which might be an early version of the later Behn play, *The Feign'd Curtizans*, but there is no copy surviving. There seems, however, no compelling reason for the identification and Behn herself warned against ascribing works to her when, in the preface to *The Luckey Chance*, she claimed she had been charged 'with all the Plays that have ever been offensive; though I wish with all their Faults I had been the Author of some of those they have honour'd me with'. For a discussion of *A Midnight's Intrigue*, see Mary Ann O'Donnell, *Aphra Behn: An Annotated Bibliography*, New York, 1986, p. 46.

14. In *Some Account of the English Stage*, John Genest attributes *The Counterfeit Bridegroom* to Behn. It has also been attributed to Betterton, although Judith Milhous points out that the cast list does not include him and he was not in the habit of adapting plays in which he did not act, 'Thomas Betterton's Playwriting', *Bulletin of the New York Public Library*, vol. 77, Summer 1974, p. 375.

15. Behn probably worked from a copy Killigrew gave her. The one in Columbia University Library may well have been Behn's since her name is on each of the title pages. A few marks indicate an attentive reader.

16. See Jacques Georges de Chauffepié, *Nouveau dictionnaire historique et critique*, 4 vols (Amsterdam, 1750–6), vol. I, pp. 187–93. The recollection comes through the actor John Bowman.

17. Contemporary gossip associated the hero with the Duke of Monmouth because he was loved by two women. Edward Ravenscroft made his hero of *The Careless Lovers* regard virtue and reputation as 'Bugg-Words' for women and told the audience, 'I can no more endure a Wife, than a standing Dish of Meat.' Some people remained uneasy at the Restoration theatrical rake. When the morality of his *Evening's Love* (1668) had been queried, Dryden justified the creation of debauched but attractive heroes by the fact that he married them off at the end. He did not 'make...vicious persons happy, but only as Heaven makes sinners so; that is, by reclaiming them from vice. For so 'tis to be suppos'd they are, when they resolve to marry.'

18. PRO Sp 44/5, 'Warrent Book'.

19. There might be an allusion to the present in the loyal Cavalier mercenaries, the guileless Belvile and Willmore. Throughout the Interregnum and Restoration, English men served in regiments abroad—as Scot and Bampfield had done when Behn was in Antwerp. In 1668, Charles II tried to bring them under royal control, insisting they be kept together in regiments which would be available to the King if necessary. In the 1670s the opposition saw these forces as a Royalist army abroad outside Parliament's control. Later some troops in France were recalled, then disbanded without support, see Thomas Otway's *The Souldiers Fortune* (1680).

NOTES

20. Killigrew had written many pieces before the Restoration, but only four had ever been publicly staged.

21. Greer argues that Killigrew's claim that *Thomaso* was written in Madrid was 'almost certainly false' (*Slip-Shod Sybils*, p. 206). The description may be calling on Venice, which Killigrew certainly visited.

22. Blunt is a stock comic figure like Haunce in *The Dutch Lover*. Lucetta is the name of the character in the original *Thomaso* but Behn may have taken the name 'Blunt' from an early play of Robert Howard, *The Committee* (1662). Howard's Blunt is a Royalist who has lost his estates, where Behn's is more politically ambiguous since he seems to have remained rich.

23. In general, Behn broke up the expository speeches, keeping the substance but adding drama. For example, in the first Act where the situation of Angellica has to be conveyed, *Thomaso* has the following speech by one man:

> Know then, since the Generals death she is exposed to sale; Her price and Picture hangs upon the door, where she sits in publick view drest like *Aurora*, and breaks like the day from her window; She is now the subject of all the Love and Envy of the Town; 'tis sport to hear the Men sigh for, and the Women rail at her. And if Don *Pedro* be a Lover still, there is no need of Fayries, old Women, or Confessors, to deliver or return a Message; Now 'tis but so much a Moneth, and you are Patron; four dayes and nights in the week are yours.

In *The Rover* this becomes the interchange:

FREDERICK: 'Tis pretty to see with how much Love the Men regard her, and how much Envy the Women.
WILLMORE: What Gallants has she?
BELVILLE: None, she's expos'd to Sale, and Four days in the Week she's yours—for so much a Month.

24. At the end of *Thomaso* Part II the hero rounds on the prostitute, labelling her 'a common Whore'.

25. See, for example, Dryden's *Tyrannick Love* (1669) and *Amboyna* (1672), and Nahum Tate's version of *King Lear* (1681). It has to be remembered that all is representation and suggestion and no rape is actually enacted on the Restoration stage. Also, the physiological views of the time involved women very thoroughly in the sex act, holding, for example, that impregnation implied consent, since it could not occur without pleasure.

26. William Wycherley, *The Gentleman Dancing Master* (1672).

27. In her cross-dressing, Hellena echoes Hillaria of Ravenscroft's *The Careless Lovers*. Both go on a 'frolic' and are spurred to action through hearing themselves being scorned by their intended lovers. In breeches Hellena defeats Angellica, imparting information that makes her a more desirable match and so destroys the romance on which her rival sets such store.

28. 'On Three Late Marriages', BL Harleian MS 6913, p. 345. A good actress would get about 30 to 40 shillings though Barry seems to have managed 50 shillings. Thomas Betterton received £5.

29. Milhous, 'Duke's Company's Profits', p. 81.

30. For her two acknowledged plays of 1677, *Abdelazer* and *The Town-Fopp*, Behn had used the publishers Magnes and Bentley. But with *The Rover*, probably fearing the charges of plagiarism and wanting to keep her authorship secret, she chose again John Amery with whom she was not publicly associated and who had brought out only the anonymous *Debauchee*. Like his associate Thomas Dring, whom Behn had used for her second play *The Amorous Prince*, Amery was, among other things, a publisher of law books and probably known to her lawyer friends.

31. If she had had any hand in the updating of *The Debauchee*, Behn may recently have read *The Novella* since it followed *A Mad Couple well Match'd* in the 1653 edition of Brome.

32. In the epistle to *The Dutch Lover*, Behn declared she had not 'hung a sign' out for pedantic seriousness but for 'comedy'. In the eighteenth century, the writer and critic Richard Steele made identification more literal. Using *The Rover* as an example, he remarked that 'the Men-Authors draw themselves in their Chief Characters, and the Women-Writers may be allowed the same Liberty,' *Spectator*, 51, 28 April 1711.

33. Possibly Amery let the secret out, which might explain why, although he had done a careful job with the printing of *The Rover*, Behn did not use him again.

34. The phrase is from Samuel Johnson's life of Otway, *Lives of the English Poets*, ed. G. Birkbeck Hill (Oxford, 1905), vol. I, p. 242.

35. Unfortunately James's daughter, later Queen Mary II, did not feel the same about *The Rover*. In November 1690, the United Company had decided to celebrate William III's first birthday as king with a performance of *The Rover* accompanied by a consort of music. Colley Cibber, the actor and critic, was present. He praised Mountfort, Smith's successor as Willmore, but was hard on the author of the play:

> The agreeable was so natural to him, that even in that dissolute Character
> of The Rover he seem'd to wash off the Guilt from Vice, and gave it
> Charms and Merit. For tho' it may be a Reproach to the Poet to draw
> such Characters not only unpunish'd but rewarded, the Actor may still be
> allow'd his due Praise in his excellent Performance. And this is a

Distinction which, when this Comedy was acted at Whitehall, King William's Queen Mary was pleas'd to make in favour of Monfort, notwithstanding her Disapprobation of the Play. *An Apology* (1740).

Chapter 17

1. Rochester, *Letters*, p. 134.
2. William, a 'prince of many virtues' (Sir William Temple), was a posthumous child of enormous political importance as the inheritor of the Orange dignities. Through the following years the marriage of William and Mary would prove surprisingly close and the pair became a force to be reckoned with.
3. *Henry IV* Part II, the 'Induction', ll. 18–19.
4. Prologue to *Theodosius* (1680).
5. *Works*, vol. 3, p. 213.
6. *Caesar Borgia* (1679) and *Lucius Junius Brutus* (1680).
7. John Wilcox in *The Relation of Molière to Restoration Comedy* (New York, 1938) wrote that the play was 'a very interesting example of the manufacture of an amusing, thoroughly British farce from one of Molière's great comedies of character', p. 146. Claire Bowditch persuasively suggested Wright's translation as Behn's source in a paper given at the Aphra Behn conference, University of Huelva, 5–7 October 2016..
8. In particular, Behn must have been reading or have recently seen *Volpone*. There was a reference to it in Blunt's threat of revenge on women in *The Rover*, while in Act V of *Sir Patient Fancy*, Wittmore quotes the opening lines, 'Good morning to the day; and next my gold; / Open the shrine that I may see my saint.'
9. *Works*, vol. 6, pp. 34 and 50.
10. *Les Femmes savantes* was adapted in 1693 by Thomas Wright who was, in the early eighteenth century, reputed to own the portrait of Behn by Lely.
11. In Lady Knowell, there may be some comment on the famous bluestocking, the scientific and literary Margaret Cavendish, Duchess of Newcastle, who had recently died. Dorothy Osborne thought her quite demented; Behn never wrote directly about her.
12. Appropriately Sir Credulous is persuaded to act out a dumb ambassador in signs, while his watch becomes a 'Hieroglyphick'.
13. There was much satire on the puritanical Sir Patience Ward, including one by a lady who was arraigned for her remarks. It is just possible that this was Aphra Behn, though the stance sounds rather different.
14. In Sir Patient, the Puritan habit of assigning a cause to all accidents is pronounced: he intends to blame his impending death on a visit of Lady Knowell, 'if I die I'll swear she's my Murderer.' The 'ignorant Rabble' believe that all ills are due to the malice of foreigners.

15. Sir Patient claims his daughter 'understands more Wickedness than had she been bred in a profane Nunnery, a Court or a Play-house'.
16. *Works*, vol. 6, p. 9.
17. *Works*, vol. 6, p. 48.
18. In the dominating, unfaithful, but unadventurous and unscheming Wittmore, Behn may be putting something of John Hoyle. When Wittmore has to assume an identity, he chooses to be the son of a Parliamentarian from Yorkshire; Hoyle's father had been a Yorkshire alderman.
19. In this play wit too is a disguising of language and, in the end, the deceit of the Tory does not seem so different from that of the Whig. On the one hand Sir Patient, fearing his daughter Isabella's reputation 'ruined', immediately translates ruin into the need for a double marriage portion. On the other, Lodwick is called a man of 'honour' only after he has falsely copulated with Lady Fancy but hidden it from the world.
20. There is a description of the exchanging of bodies in beds in the comic Antwerp letters ascribed to Behn, but there the result had been a foiling of improper desires, a bringing together of husband and wife. The same effect occurred in *The Debauchee*, where husband and wife, seducer and seducee, are joined.
21. *Works*, vol. 6, pp. 75 and 76.
22. Pope Joan was also regarded as the originator of female insubordination, as the satiric *The Parliament of Women: Or, A Compleat History Of the Proceedings and Debates, Of a particular Junto, of Ladies and Gentlewomen, With a design to alter the Government of the World* (1684) makes clear. In December 1679, the anonymous *History of Pope Joan; or, a Discovery of the Debaucheries and Villanies of the Popish Faction* was acted at a school in Cannon Street and, in May of the following year, Settle put on his violent *The Female Prelate, or the History of the life and Death of Pope Joan* at the King's Theatre. It is possible that there is also a reference to a poet called 'Joan', perhaps 'Ephelia'.
23. Using a picture of Nell Gwyn speaking the epilogue to *Sir Patient Fancy*, Angeline Goreau posits Gwyn's involvement in Behn's play; see *Reconstructing Aphra*, pp. 134–5. In *The Playhouse of Pepys* (1935), Montague Summers reprints the picture and notes that it was first published in 1779. He rightly considers it an imaginary portrait. Since the same name is given for the actress of Lady Knowell as for the speaker of the epilogue, it seems most likely that this actress also spoke the epilogue.
24. *Works*, vol. 6, p. 79.
25. Cf. *Sylvia's Complaint of her Sex's Unhappiness* (London 1688): 'They fear their empire would decay; / For they know women heretofore / Gained victories, and envied laurels wore.' This text refers to the usual female icons, Amazons, Joan of Arc, Sappho and the various heroines of romance.
26. Betty Currer had also acted in *The Counterfeit Bridegroom*, which may in part be by Behn, although it was never openly acknowledged.

27. Ormonde HMC, New Series 1906, IV, 90; Henri Forneron, *Louise de Kérouaille, Duchess of Portsmouth* (London, 1887), pp. 197–8. The Duchess of Mazarine, one of the nieces of Cardinal Mazarin, had been regarded as too good to be offered as a wife for Charles II in exile. But now, as a woman running from an allegedly tyrannical husband, she was pleased to become the King's mistress and to receive a pension from him.

28. In fact men were equally attacked for bawdry, but the main attacks on Behn's friends Otway and Ravenscroft came just after *Sir Patient Fancy*, when they staged *Friendship in Fashion, The Souldiers Fortune* and *The London Cuckolds*. In the epistle dedicatory to *The Souldiers Fortune*, Otway quotes a 'Lady' exclaiming of his play "tis so filthy, so bawdy, no modest Woman ought to be seen at it.'

29. Robert Gould, *Love Giv'n O're*, in *Satires on Women*, Augustan Reprints (Los Angeles, 1976).

30. Epistle dedicatory to *The Souldiers Fortune* (1681).

Chapter 18

1. Burnet held a common view that Catholics had a prior allegiance to the Pope in Rome and could not be good subjects and citizens.

2. *Love-Letters, Works*, vol. 2, p. 264.

3. Titus Oates's own account was published on Parliament's order as *A True Narrative of the Horrid Plot and Conspiracy of the Popish Party against the Life of His Sacred Majesty, the Government and the Protestant Religion*.

4. For a modern discussion of the murder, see Stephen Knight, *The Killing of Justice Godfrey* (London, 1984).

5. See *A True Narrative and Discovery Of several very Remarkable Passages Relating to the Horrid Popish Plot* (1679).

6. Rochester, *Letters*, p. 220.

7. *Works*, vol. 1, no. 66.

8. See *Intrigues of the Popish Plot laid open* (1685) by William Smith.

9. Rochester, *Letters*, p. 200.

10. Lampoons described Mazarine's ladies, including Sussex, as 'Whores of honour'. According to one, the second daughter of Lord Willoughby brought 'Mazarin to bed'. This might mean that she acted as a midwife or possibly a lover. See *Court Satires of the Restoration*, ed. John Harold Wilson (Columbus, 1976), p. 27.

11. Prologue to *The Feign'd Curtizans, Works*, vol. 6. Dryden elaborated on the point in his dedication of *The Kind Keeper*: 'The Great Plot of the Nation, like one of Pharaoh's lean Kine, has devour'd its younger Brethren of the Stage.'

12. Behn may have written 'Tory doggerell' anonymously. Ephelia published verses on the Popish Plot in the middle of the Titus Oates furore.

13. *Works*, vol. 1, no. 82.

14. On the other side, Shadwell turned *Timon of Athens* to Whig use.

15. *The Feign'd Curtizans* was licensed for printing on 27 March.

16. *Works*, vol. 6, p. 103.

17. *Works*, vol. 6, p. 103. Cornelia and Galliard talk often in trading terms. Her body is sound goods which will 'not lie long upon my hands', while he is 'as staple a commodity as any's in the nation'. Marriage is an adventure whose participants 'are fools, and the returning cargo, that dead commodity called a Wife'.

18. The final woman of the trio of 'courtesans' is Laura Lucretia who simply has a horror of being a wife, 'That unconcern'd domestick Necessary, / Who rarely brings a Heart, or takes it soon away'. Laura not only doubles as La Silvianetta but also, for a heady moment, as a sort of young androgynous nobleman. She enjoys the resulting eroticism when she is taken by Galliard for a young 'boy': 'Pressing my willing Bosom to his Breast, / Kissing my Cheek, calling me lovely Youth'. The homosexual theme may be continued in the trickster Petro who claims he will set up with a small harlot of his own. Possibly he is contemplating pimping for a real whore or he may be considering becoming a male prostitute himself.

19. Behn enjoyed the word 'conventicle', a Dissenting meeting place, which allowed the derivative 'Conventicling' in the prologue to *The False Count*. The words and play also informed the name Tickletext.

20. See Tim Harris, *London Crowds in the Reign of Charles II: Propaganda and Politics from the Restoration until the Exclusion Crisis* (Cambridge, 1990).

21. *Works*, vol. 6, pp. 131–2.

22. *Works*, vol. 6, p. 89.

23. Since the prologue was spoken by Currer, the confession that her own principles of religion were the same as the cully's in the play, that is Protestant, should refer to her rather than the playwright, but it may do for both. The extra ambiguity comes from the fact that the 'cully', Sir Signal Buffoon, is too stupid to have any real principles at all.

24. 'The Dutchess of Mazarine understands poysoning, as well as her Sister; and a little Vial, when the King comes there, will do it,' one plotter is alleged to have said. See *The Examination of Edward Fitz-Harris, Relating to the Popish Plot* (March 1681).

25. See Thomas Duffett, *The Spanish Rogue* (1673). Nell Gwyn did appeal to women poets, however, and at about the same time 'Ephelia' wrote a panegyric praising not only Nell's beauty and honour but also her 'wealth'. Since Nell Gwyn was having money troubles at the time, albeit on a grand scale, this cannot have been a very welcome tribute.

26. For a contrary view of the dedication as parodic, see Deborah Payne, '"And Poets shall by Patron-Princes Live": Aphra Behn and Patronage', in Mary Ann Schofield

and Cecilia Macheski eds, *Curtain Calls: British and American Women Writers and the Theater 1688–1820* (Athens, Ohio, 1991), pp. 105–19.

27. Johnson's main attack is on Dryden in his 'Dryden' in *The Lives of the Most Eminent English Poets*. Elsewhere Johnson classed Behn with the despised D'Urfey as a playwright. In his 'Prologue for the Opening of Drury Lane', he wrote, 'Perhaps if skill could distant times explore, / New Behns, new D'Urfeys, yet remain in store.'

Chapter 19

1. 'Upon these and other Excellent Works of the Incomparable *Astrea*' in *Poems upon Several Occasions* (1684).

2. Payne was said to have a daughter who 'was like to turn Whore', a lady who later received the King's bounty; so his courtly ties may have been close.

3. Willard Thorp, 'Henry Nevil Payne, Dramatist and Jacobite Conspirator', *The Parrott Presentation Volume*, ed. Hardin Craig (Princeton, 1935), p. 363.

4. Burnet, *History of His Own Time*, vol. II, p. 234.

5. Cellier had been genuinely shocked by the heinous treatment of Catholics in prison—she claimed to have seen a woman in labour tortured and a man forced to drink his own urine—and she had become the main dispenser of Catholic largesse from the lords in the Tower.

6. *Malice Defeated*, p. 45, and *The Matchless Picaro; A Short Essay of the Fortune and Virtues of Seignior Don Tomaso Ganderfieldo, alias Francisco De Corombona*. Burnet called Dangerfield a 'profligate liar', *History of His Own Time*, vol. II, p. 234. See also Maurice Petherick, *Restoration Rogues* (London, 1951).

7. *Mr. Tho. Dangerfeilds [sic] Particular Narrative of the Late Popish Design* (London, 1679), p. 12.

8. See R. Mansell, *An Exact and True Narrative of the Late Popish Intrigue to Form a Plot and Then to cast the Guilt and Odium Thereof Upon the Protestants* (London, 1680).

9. *Works*, vol. 3, pp. 4–5.

10. The 'fine' man was disguised in a Turkish turban, and readers of the roguish autobiography *Don Tomazo* would have noted that Dangerfield also wore a turban. It is mentioned that the name in the story is a pseudonym; Dangerfield went by many names, including Willoughby.

11. Part of Dangerfield's reputation for roguery comes from the highly entertaining picaresque novella, *Don Tomazo*, purporting to be by Dangerfield and detailing his long involved life of counterfeiting and trickery. Given that he was still trying to establish himself as a witness and informer, for example in such accounts as *Mr. Tho. Dangerfeilds Particular Narrative*, this exposé may have been written by one of his many denigrators rather than by himself, although he was a persistent self-fashioner.

12. Father John Warner, *History of English Persecution of Catholics and the Presbyterian Plot*, ed. T. A. Birrell (London, 1953).

13. See the satiric pamphlet entitled *Mistris Celier's Lamentation For the loss of her Liberty* (1681) in which she compares her sufferings to those of Job: 'I have been gaold and pillory'd and tost and tumbl'd so as never poor woman in Travel was.'

14. Quoted in Harold Love, *Scribal Publication*, p. 258.

15. It is also implied that the people's fear of Orsames' absolutism is superstitious non-sense. James, if he became king, would prove as royally as Orsames is assumed to do. One line of *The Young King* seems to sum up the experience of kingship of the late 1670s rather than the fictional romantic kingship Behn had imagined in the early 1660s: when Orsames, having had one taste of the wonders of kingship and been then told it was a dream, asks in his real restoration what would happen if this too should prove a dream, he is answered: 'Sir, Dreams of Kings are much less pleasant.'

16. The implied criticism of Charles II would have been in tune with public opinion, since many people assumed the exile implied the King's abandonment of his brother.

17. It remains true that the girl brought up as a boy has less trouble in adapting to life as a woman than the boy brought up passively has in becoming a man.

18. *Absalom and Achitophel*, ll. 47–8, *John Dryden*, ed. Keith Walker (Oxford, 1987).

19. *Works*, vol. 7, pp. 136 and 142.

20. Other political comments suggest the 1660s. Possibly experience of Surinam urged Behn into depictions of a warm pastoral world which appears a kind of healing female space beside the bustle of the court. In *The Young King* the pastoral Urania and Lyces lament Restoration corruption where 'Oaths are like Garlands made of finest Flowers / Wither as soon as finish'd'.

21. *Works*, vol. 7, pp. 85–6.

22. *Works*, vol. 7, pp. 150–1. Unusually, Behn printed the play three years after the performance. The dedicatee, Philaster, remains obscure but I have speculated with Sharon Valiant on its being Philip, Lord L'Isle, made Earl of Leicester in 1677. Now nearing sixty, he had largely eschewed politics since the Restoration, loving 'to be at ease and not to talk of anything that related to State affairs and politics' (*Memoirs of Thomas, Earl of Ailesbury and Elgin. Written by himself*, London, 1890). L'Isle had settled into a mansion at Sheen near Richmond in Surrey, which he made the centre of a literary circle. There he entertained Wycherley and Dryden and became a friend of Rochester and Savile. He was known as a patron and, in the 1690s, Dryden dedicated *Don Sebastian* to him. Behn may have hoped for something handsome.

23. If the request had come fairly early on, Behn's excitement might have been expressed in *The Feign'd Curtizans*, where the two heroines are reading Ovid. Of course Behn

may have begun translating independently and have been approached by Dryden when he learnt of the fact.

24. *The Collected Works of Katherine Philips*, p. i. Greer notes that Anne Wharton, the poet, used the name Sappho as a term of opprobrium, *Slip-Shod Sybils*, p. 139.

25. Her other 'translations' also differed. See, for example, her version of 'Lydia, bella puella candida' compared with that of other Restoration poets. Sara Heller Mendelson makes a useful comparison of Behn with Charles Cotton, see *The Mental World of Stuart Women*, pp. 155–6.

26. Preface, *Pindarique Odes* (London, 1656). See also *Poems: Miscellanies, The Mistress, Pindarique Odes, Davideis, Verses Written on Several Occasions*, ed. A. R. Waller (Cambridge, 1905) and David Trotter, *The Poetry of Abraham Cowley* (London, 1979). Dryden also mocked literalists and he seems to denigrate Pindar for being somehow untranslatable.

27. For a discussion of Behn's translation see Elizabeth Spearing, 'The Politics of Translation', *Aphra Behn Studies*, ed. Janet Todd (Cambridge, 1996), pp. 154–77.

28. In the 1681 edition Dryden moved the 'Argument' that had prefaced Behn's translation over to Cooper's. See 'Upon these and other Excellent Works of the Incomparable *Astrea*' in *Poems on Several Occasions* (1684).

29. *Wits Paraphras'd: Or, Paraphrase upon Paraphrase. In Burlesque on the Several Late Translators of Ovid's Epistles* (1680); 'A Satyr on modern Translators' in *Poems on Affairs of State for the Year 1620 to the Year 1707* (London, 1716), vol. IV, p. 96.

30. Behn probably read *The Dutch Courtesan* long before she revised it, since its influence may be seen in several of her plays including *The Rover* and *The Feign'd Curtizans*.

31. This dating was suggested by Judith Milhous and Robert D. Hume in 'Dating Play Premières from Publication Data, 1660–1700', *Harvard Library Bulletin*, 22 (1974), p. 391. The quotation concerns *The Vintner Trick'd*, a version of *The Revenge* in *A Comparison Between the Two Stages* (1702), p. 11.

32. *The Revenge* has been given to both Behn and Betterton. In *An Account of the English Dramatick Poets* (1691) Langbaine claimed it had been ascribed to Behn, an ascription left by Gildon when he revised Langbaine. The author of *The Comparison Between the Two Stages* assigned the play to Betterton but Judith Milhous argues against his authorship in 'Thomas Betterton's Playwriting', *Bulletin of the New York Public Library*, 77, Summer 1974, pp. 375–92. *The Revenge* was not included in the editions of Behn's plays of 1702, 1716 and 1724 and Montague Summers omitted it from his edition of 1915.

33. Corina can also blame the bawd Mrs Dunwell, who was implicated in her seduction.

34. The other additions concern the 'low' characters. Instead of being merely a trickster like Cocledemoy, Trickewell is here a decayed squire, given justification for his hounding of Dashit by Dashit's earlier 'cosenin' him of 'an Estate of some two hundred a year'. Real lowlife is added in the episode right at the end of the play

with the loyal Nan, who is trying to be hanged along with her highwayman husband, so that the two can share a coffin. Its mocking comment on marriage, especially the predatory one of the Dashits, as well as its burlesque of female loyalty, may be valid but is misplaced here, since it slows down the play which should be winding down to its multiple marriages.

35. Charlotte Butler, daughter of a 'decayed knight', according to Cibber, was much mocked for her love life: 'Fam'd Butler's Wiles are now so common grown / That by each Feather'd Cully she is known… /…if She's hungry, faith I must be blunt / Sh'l for a Dish of Cutlets shew her C--t.'

36. In this, Tryon's opinion was not entirely out of the way since the humoral version of medicine did suggest that people largely caused their own problems. Tryon also favoured a strict regulated life in which there was no reading of plays and romances and in which women would go abroad veiled. Behn probably ignored these parts of the doctrine but may have tried abstinence from meat and alcohol for a while.

37. See *Some passages in the Life and Death of the Right Honourable John Earl of Rochester* (1680). Although Burnet was summoned in late June, he did not actually go to Rochester until late July and was not present at the deathbed. The conversion was reputedly brought about by the chaplain to Rochester's mother, Robert Parsons. See Christopher Hill, *Writing and Revolution in 17th Century England* (Brighton, 1985), p. 310.

38. *The Princess of Cleves* (performed 1681–2). A character who may be associated with Rochester aims to convince 'the World of the Ingenuity of my Repentance'.

39. For an elegy that started in the same pastoral mode but ended very differently, see Flatman. He described Rochester as 'the noblest of th' *Arcadian* Swains; / *Strephon* the Bold, the Witty, and the Gay', but he then ended by warning the reader to 'Live not like Strephon, but like *Strephon* die'. See *Poems and Songs*, 4th edn (1686), pp. 173–4.

40. *The Poetical Works Of the Earls of Rochester, Roscommon, and Dorset*, 2 vols (London, 1757), p. lxvi.

41. Wharton was the second daughter of Rochester's half-brother, the son of Sir Henry Lee. Rochester's mother became her legal guardian and brought her up at Rochester's home at Adderbury in Oxfordshire. See Greer, *Slip-Shod Sybils*, pp. 214–44.

42. *A Collection of Poems by Several Hands* (London, 1693). This was the second edition of a collection first published in 1672. The poem must have been sent in manuscript to Behn.

43. *Letters between J. G. [James Granger], and many of the most eminent literary men of his time*, ed. J. P. Malcolm (London, 1805).

44. 'To Mrs Wharton' in *The Idea of Christian Love… To which are added some Copies of VERSES from that Excellent Poetess Mrs. Wharton, with others to her* (London, 1688). The identification of the author as Attwood was made by Susan Hastings.

45. *Miscellany, Being A Collection of Poems By Several Hands* (London, 1685), p. 201.

46. After Wharton's death a caveat was entered in the Stationers' Register against publishing her poems and plays.

47. Evelyn, *Diary*, 7 December 1680.

48. For Evelyn's lengthy account of Stafford's trial, see *Diary*, vol. IV, pp. 225–34.

49. Having temporarily lost the King's favour through his stand over Exclusion, Sunderland was probably thinking more of himself than of any relative.

50. Burnet, *History of His Own Time*, vol. 11, p. 264.

51. See *The Protestant Domestic Intelligencer*, no. 83, 28 December 1680.

52. Morrice, 'Entring Booke', p. 287. For an account of Stafford as a candidate for beatification see S.N.D., *Sir William Howard Viscount Stafford* (London, 1929).

53. *Works*, vol. 1, no. 82.

54. In the recent Accession Day procession the image of Christ had been desecrated by a furious Protestant mob; L'Estrange described it hurled 'in *Triumph* to the *Flames*; and the Multitude Hoiting about it, and throwing Stones at it'. So too Behn portrayed 'The *Lord* of *Life*, his *Image* rudely torn, / To *Flames* was by the *Common-Hangman* born,' an action that resulted from the crude mindset of Puritans like Tickletext of *The Feign'd Curtizans*. See *Observator*, no. 189; Behn, *Works*, vol. 1, no. 81.

Chapter 20

1. Laura Lucretia in *The Feign'd Curtizans* struggles against an arranged marriage only to find herself fast within it.

2. William Smith repeated his success as Willmore—though Betterton, for once overshadowed, dropped from the cast.

3. Susan J. Owen reads Willmore more harshly. She sees the guise of mountebank as appropriate and argues that he hates the women he desires; his wit, she believes, fails to excuse all. See 'Sexual politics and party polities', *Aphra Behn Studies* (1996), pp. 15–29.

4. The stories about Rochester seem attested to in *Doctor Bendo's Bill* and *The Famous Pathologist, or The Noble Mountebank* by T. Alcock and J. Wilmot, Earl of Rochester, but the tales of counterfeiting tend to be more evident after his death than before. It would, then, be appropriate for Behn to use this aspect in a play celebrating the Rochester myth after, rather than before, his death when the first *Rover* was performed.

5. See Graham Greene, *Lord Rochester's Monkey* (London, 1974).

6. See the account of Thomas Alcock, Rochester's servant and fellow actor in the escapade, and the *Memoirs of Count Grammont*.

7. The coupling Behn imagines for the latter echoes the comic letters she purportedly

wrote from Antwerp, when she imagined herself with the gigantic Van Bruin begetting 'A Race of Giants' or something akin to 'dancing Elephants'.

8. The political satire remains general but more evident than in *The Rover*. Featherfool sums up religion in England: 'as for that, Madam, we are *English*, a Nation I thank God, that stand as little upon Religion as any Nation under the Sun, unless it be in Contradiction; and at this time have so many amongst us, a Man knows not which to turn his Hand to.' Having failed in his intrigues to become a Cavalier, Featherfool intends to return home, take the Covenant, and get rich.

9. Possibly Behn was chiding Dryden for the anti-Catholicism of *The Spanish Fryar*, despite its overall Tory message.

10. Fraser, *King Charles II*, pp. 400–7.

11. See *The Secret History of the Rye-House Plot; and of Monmouth's Rebellion. Written by Ford, Lord Grey, in 1685. Now first published from a manuscript, sign'd by himself* (London, 1754).

12. Ephelia also went into print with 'Advice to his Grace' urging Monmouth to quit his pretensions and act dutifully as a son and subject.

13. Thomas D'Urfey, dedication to *Sir Barnaby Whigg* (1682).

14. *Works*, vol. 6, p. 303.

15. Molière's girls are made snobbish and insolent; otherwise one might sympathise with their horror at finding their courtship reduced 'To the signing of the marriage contract'. There are also links between *The False Count* and Molière's *Les Fourberies de Scapin* which had already been used by Otway in *The Cheats of Scapin* and by Ravenscroft in *Scaramouch a Philosopher, Harlequin a Schoolboy* (1677). In *Les Fourberies de Scapin*, Molière in turn took his device of a young man imagined kidnapped by Turks from a galley from Cyrano de Bergerac's *Le Pédant Joué* (1654). Behn had the happy idea of making this into a fully enacted drama.

16. In Molière, the foolish Madelon has a comic but true sense of the needs of fiction which Behn must have appreciated. When her father tells her it is time to marry and that a man is provided, she replies, 'If everyone were like you a novel would soon reach its last page. A nice thing it would be if Cyrus married Mandane in the first chapter, and Aronce was married to Clelie as a matter of course!' The reference is to Mlle de Scudéry's romances. *Don Juan and Other Plays*, trans. George Graveley and Ian Maclean (Oxford, 1989), p. 7. Madelon also yearns for evenings with writers and wits, as Behn must once have done.

17. Despite his habitual impotence, his fear of castration persuades Francisco he does not deserve a 'young Wife', while Isabella learns the insatiable nature of her social ambition—she abandons her 'viscount' in the hope of being ravished by a sultan. Father and daughter are reduced at the end to a willing cuckold and a chimney-sweeper's wife.

18. Dedication to *The Roundheads*, *Works*, vol. 6, pp. 361–3.

19. Isabella of *The False Count* derives a little from Molière's Madelon of *Les Précieuses*

ridicules, who struggles to teach her maid to express herself less vulgarly. The upwardly tending Lady Lambert of *The Roundheads* will make similar efforts with her servants.

20. Other playwrights were making a similar point in tragedy where the entanglements of sex and power tended to fall into sado-masochism. See especially Otway's *Venice Preserv'd* (1682). Behn's political topicality included reference to Stephen College, the 'Protestant Joiner', recently hanged by Charles II; in *The Roundheads*, the 'Joyner' invokes the Law.

21. See *The present state of England, and The Riddle of the Roundhead. An Excellent New Ballad...* The 'game' of 1641 was declared to be beginning all over again while *Poor Robin's Dream* of the same year has people searching for 'downright *Rumpers*'.

22. One character Desbro (Colonel John Desborough), Cromwell's brother in-law, survived the Restoration. He had not been a regicide. He was mentioned in Scot's and Behn's letters during her period in Antwerp.

23. Tatham's argument sums it up:

> Fleetwood is fool'd by LAMBERT to consent
>   To th'pulling out of the RUMP PARLIAMENT;
> Which done, another GOVERNMENT they frame
>   In EMBRYO, that wants MATTER for a name,
> In brief, by force, FOOLS supplant crafty men,
>   The bauble exits, enter KNAVES again.

24. In reality, the crown jewels were less reverentially treated. They were lent to actors for example and in 1671 Colonel Blood tried to steal them from the Tower: in the struggle the great pearl and diamond fell off, the former later found by a poor sweeping woman and the latter by a barber's apprentice.

25. Burnet, *History of His Own Time*, vol. 1, p. 290. Hugh Peters was the object of much mockery in the Oxford Cavalier newspaper, *Mercurius Anglicanus*. He advocated the killing of Charles I and was executed by Charles II in October 1660. *The Tales and Jests of Mr Hugh Peters* contained traditional anecdotes said to illustrate his lasciviousness.

26. For an example of women's role, see *The Royale Virgin; Or, The Declaration of Several Maydens in and about the once Honourable City of London*. Women participated very little in any political riots of the late 1670s and 1680s, although many were accused of expressing anti-Stuart sentiments and some joined food riots. The female council or Parliament of women was a satiric genre which had been much used in the Civil War period e.g. *The Parliament of Ladies* (1647).

27. Cf. *The Life and Death of Mistress Rump* (1660) and *Mistress Rump brought to bed of a Monster* (1660). They were revisions of earlier works from 1648 e.g. *Mistris Parliament presented in her bed*.

28. *Works*, vol. 6, pp. 403–4; vol. 1, no. 48.

29. In the Interregnum and Restoration Margaret Cavendish had accepted that poets should help create a nation and support an absolute monarchy by presenting images of heroism. Behn never quite reached this position but she was coming closer to Cavendish in her realisation of the political usefulness of imaginative writing.

30. See the dedication to Shaftesbury of *Rome's Follies* (1681).

31. *Works*, vol. 1, no. 20. *Like Father, Like Son* was a revision of Thomas Randolph's *Jealous Lovers* from the 1640s. The prologue and epilogue appeared as a broadside. In the performance, the political epilogue had been spoken by Jevon and the prologue by Charlotte Butler. The latter provided yet another image for the decimation of the theatre through political conflict: it was like the poor Anglican church buffeted by sects.

32. The play is dated with reference to the Whigs' failure to hold a political feast on 21 April, a non-event mentioned in the prologue.

33. In character, Sir Timothy seems closest to the alderman Sir Thomas Player. In September 1679 he had had a great crowd of followers when he addressed the Lord Mayor on the subject of the encouragement which the papist James inevitably gave to the Popish Plot. He sparked off a pamphlet war on the subject and helped to bring about the exile of the Duke of York. See *An Account of the Proceedings at the Guild-hall of the City of London On Saturday, September 13. 1679.* Ward, as a firm supporter of the Exclusion of the Duke of York—he had been the mover of the first Exclusion Bill—was the very type Behn publicly despised. In *The City-Heiress*, Sir Timothy is further trounced vicariously when his Puritan mistress, Sensure, leaps from his bed, scattering Baxter's Protestant sermons, and mistakenly dons his robe; she is beaten by Royalists in his place.

34. *Works*, vol. 7, pp. 51–2.

35. *Works*, vol. 7, pp. 31 and 51.

36. *Works*, vol. 7, pp. 53–4.

37. A bizarre homoerotic relationship of uncle and nephew, based on Massinger's *The Guardian*, provides this context: the older man wants the younger to stand in for him, to be forthright, lusty, and pushy like his ideal of himself. The young nephew, formally courteous when sober, becomes a rakehell when drunk, and tries to do the deeds for which his leering uncle yearns. An attempted rape of Lady Galliard is part of this scenario.

38. Tonson brought out Otway's prologue and the epilogue separately as well. Brown was also the publisher of *The Young King*. For a listing of Behn's publishers, see Crompton, 'Forced to write for bread', Appendix 2.

Chapter 21

1. Even Dryden touched on Behn's success in his epilogue to Charles Saunders' play, *Tamerlane*, in 1681.

2. The Riley portrait is now lost, but c. 1721, the antiquarian George Vertue, records 'an Original picture of Mrs Aphara Behn painted by Riley the same from wch. the Print is Engrav'd by White', *Walpole Society: Vertue Note Books*, vol. 1, p. 43. The engraving by R. White exists in several copies of Behn's collected works from 1698 onwards, mainly published by Samuel Briscoe. The name sometimes appears as 'R.W.sc', hence giving rise to the misreading of 'R. Wise'. Another cruder engraving of the presumed Riley portrait is by B. Cole, with different cartouche and background from the White one. It was published in *Plays* of 1724 brought out by Mary Poulton. The same engraving was used again in *Histories, Novels* of 1735, labelled B. Cole sculpt. Montague Summers declares the presumed Riley engraving 'none other than Christina of Sweden from Sebastian Bourdon's drawing now in the Louvre' (*Works of Aphra Behn*, 1915, vol. i, p. lxiii). However, Queen Christina has a very different face, with a far more prominent nose than in any of the engravings purporting to be of Behn.

3. *Poems on Affairs of State, 1660–1714*, vol. 3, ed. Howard H. Schloss (New Haven, 1968), p. 34.

4. See *To the Society of the Beaux Esprits. A Pindarick Poem* (London, 1687), p. 5. He had made the same sort of point in 'A Satyr against the Play-House 1685': 'fair *Sappho* in her wanton fit / When she'd put *luscious Bawdry* off for *Wit*', p. 174.

5. 'The Female Laureat', Dyce Collections, V. & A. Museum, p. 607. In fact Behn had done less than Ravenscroft was doing at much the same time in his suggestive scenes of intended 'panting' in *The London Cuckolds*.

6. *The Poetess, a Satyr* (London, 1707), p. 3.

7. See 'Lampoon [March, 1676]' in *Court Satires*, p. 20.

8. William Wycherley, *Miscellany Poems* (London, 1704), pp. 191–2.

9. *Works*, vol. 1, no. 10.

10. *Newdigate Newsletter*, July 1683, and the *True Protestant Mercury* 1683, Wednesday 16 August 1682. Dryden had fallen foul of royal opinion and the response quoted here is the King's to *The Duke of Guise*. The play was forbidden. See HMC 15th Report, Appendix, pt vii, p. 108.

11. *The Tryal and Sentence of Elizabeth Cellier*, p. 16.

12. *Juvenalis Redivivus* (1683).

13. Luttrell, I, 236, November 1682. Delarivier Manley alludes to the incident in *The New Atalantis*, p. 24: 'Count Lofty, whose good sense was totally obscured by pride, cast his ambitious thoughts so high, as to pretend to the Princess, whilst yet she was a maid.'

14. Some poets even used others to correct their own verses, see 'Julian': 'In Verse to ease thy wretched Wants I write'.

15. *Works*, vol. 1, no. 64.

16. *POAS*, 1697. 'Bajazet to Gloriana' is a longer version of the poem. For the attribution, see Brice Harris, Letter in *TLS*, 9 February 1933, p. 92.

17. 'The Female Laureat'. Mendelson argues that Gould is in error here and that Behn actually attacks Mulgrave, see *The Mental World of Stuart Women*, p. 162.

18. Mary Trye, *Medicatrix, or the Woman Physician* (1675).

19. Lucy Hutchinson, the Puritan writer and biographer of her military husband, also made a partial translation.

20. The introduction is made likely by the fact that Tonson later wrote, 'mr Creech came to Town…I brought him to mr Dryden &…he was carried to mr waller the Poet. When mr Creech returned to Oxford he wrot to me to get mr Dryden & mr Waller to write some verses to put before the 2de Edition,' quoted in James A. Winn, 'Dryden's Epistle before Creech's Lucretius: A Study in Restoration Ghostwriting', *Philological Quarterly*, 71, 1992, p. 56.

21. Creech's translation *T. Lucretius… De Natura Rerum* (Oxford, 1683), p. 3.

22. 'A Satyr on modern Translators', *POAS*.

23. *Works*, vol. 1, no. 11 (variants).

24. *Poems Upon Several Occasions* (London, 1684). In *Reconstructing Aphra*, Goreau speculates that this curate, who does not relish his country situation—'Providence it seems design'd t'immure / M'aspiring soul in a poor Country Cure'—was Henry Crisp since Crisp became a vicar in Catton in Yorkshire. But the poem is dated January 1685 and Crisp was not ordained and appointed until December of that year.

25. Possibly at this time Behn may have come to know a young man Charles Blount, a deist, freethinker and former friend of Rochester in the 1670s. For him religion was simply an imposture.

26. Creech omits material towards the close of Book IV. Dryden puts this into 'luscious English' in his *Sylvae* (1685) when he describes tongues dashing into other bodies for example. For a discussion of Dryden's erotics see James Anderson Winn '*When Beauty Fires the Blood*'.

27. *Works*, vol. 2, preface. In a dedication to a late play Behn refers to Francis Hedelin, Abbot of Aubignac, a critic of the theatre and a playwright, the sort of person she is unlikely to have read had she stayed in England.

28. For a full discussion of Sunderland, see J. P. Kenyon, *Robert Spencer, Earl of Sunderland 1641–1702* (London, 1958).

29. Folger MS M.b. 12, p. 123.

30. 'The Young Statesmen: A Satire', *Poetical Works*, p. 52.

31. *Diary*, vol. IV, p. 595.

32. Also, France was fomenting rebellion in Ireland and was suspected of sending over arms and Irish soldiers in ships masquerading in English colours; Sunderland might wish to know more. The envoy to Paris at the time was Viscount Preston, who used spies to gather information to send to London. Preston could direct Behn, while Sir Bernard Gascoigne, busily spying in France over many years, could provide names of merchants and military men to contact. See Phyllis Lachs, *The*

Diplomatic Corps under Charles II and James II, p. 34. One other possibility is that Behn was a female courier taking Tory money to France for investment in foreign securities. The Whigs were eager to find out how this was done but, by 1683, it was noted that a series of court women, from the Duchess of Portsmouth and the Countess of Pembroke to a singer friend of Nell Gwyn's, had travelled to France and 'the wonder will not be great how things are managed'. See *Hastings* MS, II, 173–4; also *Court Satires*, p. 100.

33. Fontenelle wrote his main works after Behn's probable visit to France, but the speed with which she gained access to them later suggests an acquaintance.

34. Boileau, Epistre IX, *Oeuvres Complètes* (Paris, 1966), p. 134.

35. Behn may have been in France just long enough also to meet her critic, Gilbert Burnet, who, towards the end of the year, felt the need to travel with a friend for his 'health'—in fact he had upset the King by criticising his libidinous life and by reportedly helping in the composition of Lord Russell's very effective speech from the scaffold.

36. 'Returns of Lodgers and Inmates', St Bride's Parish, New Street, Corporation of London Records Office, Misc. MSS.87.4, no. 18e.

37. George Powell, preface to *The Treacherous Brother* (1690).

38. In this, Behn was in tune with the times. Although she disliked Shadwell, she may have been somewhat influenced by his attack on the rake in *The Libertine*, which was revived in May 1682. It was a ferocious depiction of the cruelty of the Don Juan type, placed within a religious context.

Chapter 22

1. In October the *Gazette* noted that another newspaper had erroneously printed the story that Lady Henrietta had written to her father telling him she was married. This, the *Gazette* declared, was false.

2. Quoted in Kenyon (1958), p. 43.

3. 'The Ladies March', *Court Satires*, p. 58.

4. See *London Mercury*, 22–5 August 1682; 29 September–3 October 1682; *Loyal Protestant and True Domestick Intelligence*, 12 September; see also *Benskins Domestic Intelligence* and *The Observator*.

5. At the trial there was much discussion about Lady Henrietta's lodgings. In one report the place had been improved by the addition of a warming-pan and candles. A maid who gave evidence claimed she was surprised Henrietta was a lady since, when she washed her shift, she found the hidden body part finer than the sleeves: ladies tended to make the sleeves finer than the body.

6. *A Letter to Ferguson* (1684). Morrice concluded that the husband was the son of Sir William Turner, the civilian, i.e. not military or in the civil law.

7. For the history of Grey's plotting, see Cecil Price, *Cold Caleb: The Scandalous Life of*

Ford Grey First Earl of Tankerville 1655–1701 (London, 1956) and K. H. D. Haley, *The First Earl of Shaftesbury* (Oxford, 1968).

8. Subsequently the guard was imprisoned in Grey's place. The fate of the participants of the Rye House Plot was described in a contemporary pamphlet, 'A True Description of the Bull-Feast', which called Lord Grey a 'Gray Gander who trod two Geese of the same Egg' and then 'fled amongst the wild Geese into the Desarts'. See also *A Letter from Amsterdam* (1684), which describes the escape of Grey.

9. One slight possibility is that one of the instigators was Christopher, second Duke of Albemarle, whom Behn later celebrated. According to Narcissus Luttrell, on 31 May 1682 he had fought an inconclusive duel with Grey.

10. If Sunderland were the commissioner, perhaps he chose Behn for the work because he knew her to be the author of a broadside called *Lady Grey's Ghost*, in which Lady Grey dreams of Lady Henrietta and her Lord as a red cow and a grey bull with horns, *Works*, vol. 2. Lady Mary's response is, 'though I love red Cows Milk naturally, I had a greater Longing to stroak the Bull', but both beasts attack her. Another dream is of herself as England seduced by Monmouth, the fool of the 'Moble, filling them with strange Notions, Whimsies and Chimeras'. Despite the anonymity of the publication, Behn might be indicating authorship by the name of the amorous Cavalier, Willmore from her own play *The Rover*, clearly identified here with Rochester. It would be a good strategy to capitalise on a popular scandal and simultaneously puff this most popular play. Behn needed revivals.

11. James Howell, *Epistolae Ho-Elianae. Familiar Letters, domestic and forren* (1655).

12. *Lettres portuguaises* seems now to have been by the Frenchman, Gabriel-Joseph de la Vergne, Vicomte de Guilleragues, but it was generally accepted in the seventeenth century as the work of a Portuguese nun, Marianna Alcoforado.

13. *Apologie, ou les véritables Mémoires de madame Marie Mancini, connétable de Colonna, écrits par elle-même* (Leyden, 1678). The narrator begins very like Behn in her short stories with generalisations about the libels against 'our Sex' and continues with her sort of derogatory remarks: ''Tis an ordinary fault of our Sex, not to endure to hear others commended.' Mancini was designed a nun, very much as Behn claims she herself was in her preface to her *History of the Nun*.

14. *Hatigé ou Les Amours de Roy de Tamaran. Nouvelle* (Cologne, 1676). In English it became *Hattigé: or the Amours of the King*. It was dedicated to the Earl of St Albans.

15. *Works*, vol. 1, no. 77.

16. *Works*, vol. 2, p. 7.

17. *Works*, vol. 1, no. 73.

18. Behn apprehended the story in theatrical terms at first: while the characters fancy themselves romantically as Antony and Cleopatra in Dryden's *All for Love*, Behn makes the Berkeley house, Durdans, a version of the many intrigue-play settings in which everyone spies on everyone else.

19. *Works*, vol. 2, p. 34.

20. The description is not far off Anne Wharton's idealised picture of Charles II in 'To Doctor Burnet upon his Retirement'. In Behn the figure of the King might be regarded as undercut by the fallibility of his substitute, Silvia's father, who roves around at night soliciting the maids for favours.

21. The relationship of Monmouth and Philander is also eroticised: Monmouth writes a kind of love letter to Philander, addressing him as 'my dear' and declaring that the morning must 'find you in my arms'.

22. The French writer, Madame D'Aulnoy, makes a rather different picture in her fictionalised *Memoirs*, written supposedly in 1675 but published in the 1690s. This created the young Lord Grey as already dominating Monmouth. But, despite being teased by Monmouth for his interest in the child Henrietta (who would have been eleven), he is no libertine and he presents himself as 'a man entirely absorbed by his family; who still plays the lover to his wife, & whose only pleasure is the society of his father-in-law, and his mother-in-law', *Memoirs of the Court of England in 1675* by Marie Catherine Baronne D'Aulnoy, trans. Mrs. William Henry Arthur (London, 1913), p. 281.

23. *Works*, vol. 2, p. 45.

24. *Works*, vol. 2, p. 67.

25. *Works*, vol. 2, p. 36.

26. *Works*, vol. 2, p. 73.

27. *Works*, vol. 2, p. 59.

28. See Michael Treadwell, 'London Trade Publishers 1675–1750', *The Library*, 6th ser., 4 (1982), 99–134, and Crompton diss., pp. 56–8. Randal Taylor's name was, however, later seen on Williamite pamphlets.

29. 'Letter to Julian', Summer 1684, printed in *Court Satires*,

30. Apparently Condon was in Ferdinando Hastings's regiment, although he was not listed among the officers.

Chapter 23

1. *CSP*, Dom., 1683, p. 40.

2. Evelyn, *Diary*, vol. IV, p. 362.

3. 'Advice to the Ladyes', Dyce MS, V. & A. Museum.

4. In a manuscript recipe book in the Folger Shakespeare Library, Va 19.

5. Leigh Hunt in 'Poetry of British Ladies', *The Companion*, no. 19, 14 May 1828, mentions rumours that Behn was in love with Creech. I have found no evidence for this.

6. The account of Brown is by James Drake in *The Works of Mr. Thomas Brown* (London, 1715), vol. III, p. 12.

7. The phrase comes from *A Comparison Between the Two Stages* (1702). Brown's *Letters* appear in his *Works*, vol. 2.

8. *Works*, vol. 7, p. 219.

9. John Wilkes, *A General View of the Stage* (London, 1762), p. 246.

10. The young Brown always had a tendency to mock older powerful women. He described the wife of the headmaster under whom he had to teach as claiming to be thirty-six when really near fifty and driven to the expedients of false hair and brandy to keep up the pretence. He also provided an unpleasant portrait of the strong-minded Elizabeth Barry. See Chapter 16, note 1.

11. *Works*, vol. 3, p. 71.

12. Briscoe was the publisher of Lee, Dryden, Wycherley and Congreve. See G. Greer, 'Honest Sam Briscoe', *A Genius for Letters: Booksellers and Bookselling from the 16th to the 20th Century* (Winchester, 1995), pp. 33–45.

13. 'A Letter to the Earl of Kildare, disswading him from marrying MOLL HOWARD', *Works*, vol. 1, no. 99.

14. Sir Philip Friendly refers to his lack of riches being due to his position as a younger brother. This was a theme of the Behn play that Brown's friend Gildon published after her death, *The Younger Brother*, supposedly based partly on George Marten.

15. Gildon's ventriloquising skills are evident. See *The Post-boy Robb'd of his Mail*, which he wrote when Behn was still alive. The various letters required different styles, some of men and some of women. Gildon went on to write stories: *The Golden Spy: or a Political Journal of the British Nights Entertainments* (London, 1709). Except for *Oroonoko*, the stories in the 1698 edition, entitled the third, have separate title pages and are separately paged, suggesting that Briscoe may originally have intended bringing them out individually. *In Familiar Letters*, Briscoe published four letters addressed to Philander and signed A. Behn twice and Silvia once. These may have been forgeries intended perhaps for a longer episode of *Love-Letters* or they may have been written by Behn when she was writing *Love-Letters* and then cut from the text.

16. *The Cheats* was published in 1684 in a new edition which might indicate a revival of the popular play, first staged in 1663.

17. *The Whole Comical Works of Monsr. Scarron*, trans. Thomas Brown and others, 2nd edn (London, 1703).

18. The closest of Behn's secure work to the 'The Unfortunate Happy Lady' is *The History of the Nun*, where the heroine hears her husband is dead and responds in great grief like Philadelphia to her lover. She is punished for her response, however, since, unlike the useful Fairlaw of 'The Unfortunate Happy Lady', the ex-nun's new husband does not die before the reappearance of the old husband/lover.

19. Tom Brown is less likely to have been the author of 'The Dumb Virgin', which was also printed posthumously, since he thoroughly despised Dangerfield and would not have used his name for a hero. See his 'A Letter from *Dangerfield* to *Fuller*, the

awkerd [sic] Plot Carpenter' in which Dangerfield is two layers down in hell with Judas Iscariot, *Letters from the Dead to the Living* (London, 1702), p. 135. It remains possible of course that Brown or Gildon completed a story that had been in part written by Behn. This may also have been the case with 'The Nun', which has much in common with Behn's earlier fictional works.

20. 'Amusements', *Works of Brown*, vol. 1, p. 4.

21. *Letters from the Dead*, p. 43.

22. The 1698 edition added three stories: 'The Court of the King of Bantam', 'The Black Lady' and 'The Nun, or the Perjured Beauty'. It also added the comic letters supposedly written in Antwerp to the 'Memoirs'. For Granville's involvement in Behn's posthumous works, see W. J. Cameron, 'George Granville and the "Remaines" of Aphra Behn', *Notes and Queries*, CCIV, March, 1959, pp. 88–92.

23. *Works*, vol. 1, no. 55.

24. Evelyn, *Diary*, vol. IV, p. 363.

25. Little of this 'Doggerell' can be discovered. Probably little has survived, although 'The Complaint of the poor Cavaliers' is an early example. Another is a dialogue called 'Tea and Coffee' from the 1680s, in which one of the voices labelled 'A. B.' is feminine. See *Works*, vol. 1, no. 54. Such dialogues as 'Tea and Coffee' were common by a single person, but possibly Behn and the man J. C. B.—perhaps John Cooper from the 'Cabal', or even her old friend Jeffrey Boys or his brother Jeremy—produced this bit of hack writing in a tavern evening. It echoes Behn in its one notion, that the sin of sham plotting might be expelled by holy water, a mockery less of Catholics than of those obsessed by Catholic habits.

26. 'The Circuit of Apollo', *Selected Poems*, p. 72.

27. F. N. W., another commender of Behn's poems, was more tactful. Comparing Behn with the chaste Orinda, he claimed that the former taught 'harmless arts of not indecent Love' with her 'Pleasant wit yet not obscene'.

28. In the comic letters Behn was alleged to have exchanged with Van Bruin in Antwerp, the elderly admirer is mocked for planning to 'set out for the *Island of Love*', thought to have been 'a *Tierra del Fuego*' for such a man.

29. 'Essay on Translated Prose', *Works*, vol. 4, p. 76.

30. *Works*, vol. 1, p. 151.

31. 'A Ramble in Saint James's Parke', *Poems*, p. 64.

32. The poetry of *The Island of Love* is often distinguished in public seventeenth-century mode:

> Doubt's the worst Torment of a generous Mind,
> Who ever searching what it cannot find,
> Is roving still from wearied thought to thought,
> And to no settled Calmness can be brought.

It is equally competent in the pastoral lyrical: the first song begins

> *This is the Coast of* Africa,
>   *Where all things sweetly move;*
> *This is the Calm* Atlantick *Sea,*
>   *And that the Isle of Love;*

> *To which all Mortals Tribute pay,*
>   *Old, Young, the Rich and Poor;*
> *Kings do their awful Laws obey,*
>   *And Shepherds do Adore.*

Works, vol. 1, p. 105. Inevitably with such poetry many of the passages turned up unidentified in contemporary miscellanies and manuscript collections.

33. *Miscellany Poems* (1704) and 'Satyr against the Poets', BL Harley 7317.

34. *Works*, vol. 7, pp. 228–9.

35. Otway's death is obscure and there are several competing stories. Anthony à Wood says he died at an inn called the Bull on Tower Hill on 14 April 1685 (*Athenae Oxoniensis*, vol. 1, p. 170). In the early eighteenth century when Otway's reputation for pathos was high, Theophilus Cibber claimed Otway choked to death on a piece of bread which he had begged (*Lives of the Poets of Great Britain and Ireland, to the Time of Dean Swift*, London, 1753, vol. 11, p. 334) and Joseph Spence has him dying of fever after chasing the murderer of a friend (*Observations, Anecdotes, and Characters*, ed. E. Malone, London, 1820, p. 100). None of the accounts much fits with Gildon's jovial 'Lover of the Bottle' whose last work was a drinking song (*Lives and Characters of English Poets*, p. 107).

36. Wilkes, *A General View*, p. 246.

37. Some of the poems had already been published in play texts as songs, others had appeared in *Covent Garden Drolery* and in other people's miscellanies. Some had been circulating widely in copied manuscripts.

38. See Henry Curwen, *History of Booksellers* (London, 1873).

39. The poems give a sense of community very much including Creech. In the long poem entitled 'Upon these and other Excellent Works of the Incomparable *Astrea*', the anonymous poet praises Behn's commendation of Creech's *Lucretius*: 'her sweeter Muse did for him more, / Than he himself or all *Apollo*'s sons before.'

40. 'To the Pious Memory of the Accomplished Young Lady Mrs Anne Killigrew', *John Dryden*, p. 312.

41. The other female poets were of course dead, as Aphra Behn was not. It is also possible that Dryden thought for a time that Behn had written the satire on him, 'On Dryden Renegade', in circulation when he was writing.

NOTES

42. *Jacob Tonson in Ten Letters by and about him*, ed. Sarah Lewis and Carol Clapp (Austen, Texas, 1948). The fact that he could risk this manoeuvre and that Behn must have approached Dryden only through Tonson suggested there was no intimacy between Behn and Dryden at this time.

43. 'Satyr against the Poets', BL Had 7317.

44. See 'A Ballad on Sr: Wm: Clifton', Dyce MS, V. & A. Museum. All the Queen's Maids of Honour prepared to captivate Clifton.

45. *Works*, vol. 1, pp. 368–70. The ideal was much expressed in the early Stuart period, see E. Heal, *Hospitality in Early Modern England* (Oxford, 1990). Its loss was deplored by more people than Behn, for example Sir John Reresby, who wrote in 1687 that hospitality had been 'much laid aside of late…which dissatisfieth the common sort of people'. He too saw it as a political problem. Others took a different view of the function of nobility and gentry, seeing them standing between the people and the imposition of arbitrary royal power. See, for example, the Whig *A Letter from a Person of Quality to his Friend in the Country* (c.1675). This Whig nostalgia was often associated with the 'Golden days of Queen *Elizabeth*' and with a nationalistic emphasis on Englishness. See Shadwell's *The Lancashire-Witches* (1681).

46. Tudor and early Stuart propaganda insisted that public service and loyalty to the monarch were the gentry's first obligation, even over loyalty to kin and lineage. See M. James, *English Politics and the Concept of Honour, Past and Present*, supplements, III, 1978.

47. The poem appeared anonymously but has been ascribed to Nahum Tate. See *Poems on Affairs of State… 1660–1714*, vol. 11 (New Haven, 1968), p. 183. Tate never owned the work which, though Royalist, was also anti-Jesuit, a position increasingly inappropriate as the Catholic reign of James progressed. If he indeed gave so lengthy a work to Behn to publish in 1682 or 1683 when she was compiling *Miscellany*, it suggests considerable friendship.

48. *The Late Converts Exposed: or the Reasons of Mr. Bay's Changing his Religion… Part the Second*. In fact Behn had given similar sentiments to Lysander in *The Island of Love*: when he tries to pray he is interrupted by earthly matters and he can think of nothing but love and Aminta, which '*Ever out Rival Heaven!*'

49. Other authors to whom Behn refers as her friends in her dedication include the dead and living: Etherege, Rochester, Dorset, Mrs Taylor, Anne Wharton, Henry Nevil Payne, Henry Crisp, and 'a Lady of Quality' who defined female wit as sexual availability and emptiness.

50. *Works*, vol. 1, no. 74.

51. In the prologue to *The Luckey Chance*, Behn describes a widow who chooses to pass her days 'With a damn'd sober, self-admiring Ass, / Who thinks good usage for the Sex unfit, / And slights ye out of Sparkishness and Wit'. It sounds like another dig at 'Alexis'.

52. 'To Mrs. Afra Behn', *The Genuine Works*, p. 59.

524

NOTES

Chapter 24

1. *Essay Upon Poetry* (London, 1682). The work was brought out again in 1685 after the preface to *Valentinian* because Mulgrave had been 'so unjustly reflected upon'. Mulgrave criticised Rochester for being too obscene to raise desire—he 'pall'd the appetite he meant to raise'.

2. The phrase comes from Goodwin Wharton, 'Autobiography', BL Add. MSS, 26,006.

3. As a young woman in the 1660s Cooke was involved in a court scandal when the lesbian Miss Hobart, one of the Maids of Honour of the Duchess of York, became attracted to her. The affair was described semi-fictionally in the *Memoirs of Count Grammont*. Behn had not written for Cooke before since the latter had been acting with the King's Company.

4. The differences can be seen in comparison between the printed text and one manuscript in the Folger (V.b. 233). For a discussion of this manuscript in relation to the BL one, see Larry Carver, 'Rochester's *Valentinian*', *Restoration and Eighteenth Century Theatre Review*, IV, 1, Summer 1989, pp. 25–38.

5. Anne Wharton may have been interested in both Behn and Barry at this time. When she died shortly afterwards she left a generous bequest to Barry's daughter Hester.

6. Wolseley's girth is mocked in one of the poems in 'Astrea's Booke' where he is also ridiculed as Rochester's echo and author of 'Prefaces which tire Men to read'. For a discussion of Wolseley, see Mary Ann O'Donnell, 'Private Jottings, Public Utterances', in *Aphra Behn Studies* (1996). Anne Wharton wrote a poem to congratulate Wolseley 'On his Preface to Valentinian', the tone suggests to Greer that the preface was a commission. Wolseley rapturously replied. See *Slip-Shod Sybils*, p. 240.

7. For Julian's implied opinions, see 'Julians Farewell to the Muses', Dyce MS, V. & A. Museum, p. 482.

8. *Works*, vol. 7, p. 382.

9. Sir Rowland's main buyer is Lady Youthly who wishes desperately to marry a young man. One might suspect Behn of a little self-irony here, but she prevents it by making her not the usual fifty or so, but eighty. In the stress on the predicament of a younger brother in both *The Younger Brother* and *The Widdow Ranter*, Behn might have been influenced by Tom Brown or one other of her new friends.

10. The other young women, though not as radical and honest as Mirtilla, are yet heirs of Hellena and the 'Feign'd Curtizans'. They adopt men's dress to avoid unwanted marriage and take stock of their money and bodies; indeed Teresia almost echoes Hellena when she declares, 'I have Youth enough to please a Lover, and Wit enough to please my self.' Olivia sees arranged marriage as prostitution without satisfaction and she adapts Whig rhetoric: 'when Parents grow arbitrary,

'tis time we look into our Rights and Priviledges.' Behn found such notions ridiculous in state politics but true enough in familial, though here they may well have been added by Gildon who admits to having reworked the play.

11. In his revision of Langbaine's *Lives and Characters of the English Dramatick Poets* (1699), Gildon boasts that, had he revised the 'jejune style' of the last three acts, *The Younger Brother* would have succeeded.

12. *Works*, vol. 2, p. 216. Some of the comic scenes of body-swapping resemble those in Behn's comic Antwerp letters. This may be because the author of the 'Memoirs' was mining *Love-Letters* or Behn might later have been mining memory. Silvia swaps her maid for herself and fools a would-be lover, as Behn supposedly does with Scot/Albert. In revenge, Albert decides to gain her through rape or subterfuge, rather like Brilljard does Silvia in *Love-Letters*. The swapping of bodies in bed was of course a conventional theatrical and fictional device.

13. See Verney pamphlets in Cambridge University Library, *A Letter to Ferguson*: 'Because she is ugly grown; and 'tis our Natures / When Beauty's gone, to think 'em nauseous Creatures.' Henrietta was said to be 'inrag'd' because another woman 'Usurps her Place and Name'.

14. *Works*, vol. 2, p. 186.

15. On Behn's presentation of Silvia there may be some influence of *The Whores Rhetoric* (1683), an English translation or adaptation of an Italian satire of 1642. While not being especially bawdy, *The Whores Rhetoric* titillated and fed the erotic misogyny of the time, as well as fitting into the sexualising of politics. The text is a dialogue between the famous bawd, Madam Creswell, and Dorothea, the daughter of an impoverished Royalist. In similar fashion to Silvia, Dorothea must work her sex because of her poverty, although she is more honest about her business than Silvia, who is shocked to hear herself described as whore. Both women learn to evaluate the parts of their body, regarding them as so much stock, and both must avoid the feminine trap of falling in love: 'The whore is not a woman' and 'she must mind her interest not her sport', pp. 144–5.

16. Philander has less difficulty, since he loves Calista most thoroughly when she is dressed as a boy 'resembling my dear *Octavio*'.

17. See 'On Narcissism' in *Metapsychology: The Theory of Psychoanalysis* (Harmondsworth, 1985) and Sarah Kofman, *The Enigma of Woman* (Ithaca, 1985).

18. After 1685 the historical Lady Henrietta Berkeley seems to have crept back to England into the bosom of her family and church. Her will names a man called Knagge, who was Grey's chaplain. Perhaps she had become an embarrassment to Grey, who wanted her made respectable. One analogue to the fictional Silvia is the pseudo-aristocratic Mary Carleton described, like Silvia, as fat, a woman who also used sex for interest. Kirkman in *The Counterfeit Lady Unveiled* describes Mary Carleton taking pride in her stratagems; he claimed Carleton was so flushed

with success at being able to pass herself off as whatever she wished that she simply cheated automatically 'any body friend or foe, rich or poor, all was fish that came to net whether *Salmons* or *Sprats*', p. 319. Other more recent scandals on which Behn might have drawn included that of the Duchess of Norfolk with a man Evelyn dismissed as 'a Dutch gamester'; one lampoon on the event is copied into 'Astrea's Booke'. Like Lord Grey and Lady Henrietta (and probably Aphra Behn herself), the Norfolks in time became direct victims of fiction in 'The Secret Letters of Amour between the duchess and mynheer', but, suitably, not through Behn. See John Martin Robinson, *The Dukes of Norfolk: A Quincentennial History* (Oxford, 1982), p. 146, and S. F. K. Causton, *Howard Papers* (London, 1862), p. 254.

19. *Works*, vol. 2, p. 365.

20. The Catholic trimmings probably came from memory of Flanders and possibly of Italy, but they could have been enhanced by observation in London and Windsor, where James had re-established Catholic ritual and pomp.

21. Defoe is often accused of male insensitivity in *Moll Flanders* in which he creates a heroine who bears and abandons a swarm of children. Behn has a similar insouciant (and Restoration) attitude to the bearing and dropping of children. A secret-service letter 'believes [Henrietta Berkeley] to be att least four months gone with child, she looked very thin, & is perfect trallop, in a plaine scarf 8c black hood'. Some months later her child was born in Cleve. A contemporary lampoon claims Henrietta was sick in pregnancy and 'scap't great danger' at the birth. *A Letter to Ferguson* (13 August 1684), Verney papers, Cambridge University Library. Little of this found its way into Behn's work.

22. To the nation the most outrageous women were King Charles's mistresses. If there is any living inspiration for the later Silvia beyond the full-breasted and irascible Lady Henrietta, it must be an amalgamation of the royal whores as delivered in satire, with Barbara, Duchess of Cleveland, prevailing. See, too, Brémond's *Hattigé* where Hattigé tires of the King and moves on to the gardener's nephew and then the gardener. She knows her needs: 'Infidelity has charms for those who know how to use it. I have a heart which wants to be its own master, and to love one person, and then another as it pleases' (p. 96). Cf. Rochester's satire 'Lais Junior'. Other satires blamed the corruption of the realm on Cleveland and used her to foretell the downfall of the Stuarts.

23. In Behn's plays, youth tends to want only youth, but, in *The Island of Love*, there was the suggestion that a pretty boy might love a woman of fifty and a blooming maid dote on an old soldier, the religious female on the libertine and the thoughtful politician on the actress: *'rarely equal Hearts in Love you'l find, / Which makes 'em still present the God of Love as Blind'*, 11. 203–36.

24. *Works*, vol. 2, p. 392.

25. *Works*, vol. 2, p. 396.

26. Part II of *Love-Letters* was printed for the author, it is not known by whom, so that it was doubly anonymous. Self-publishing was expensive. Mrs Cellier had laid out 10s a ream for printing her attack on Dangerfield which she then sold to a bookseller for 18s a dozen. Behn's book was a great deal longer. If she paid herself and waited for reimbursement from her sponsor, she was probably suffering the same fate as she had with Arlington.

27. *Friendship in Fashion, A Comedy* (1678).

28. Dryden's epilogue to Ben Jonson's *The Silent Woman*, played in Oxford.

29. Prologue to *Scaramouch A Philosopher, Harlequin A School-Boy, Bravo, Merchant, and Magician. A Comedy After the Italian manner* (1677).

30. Evelyn, *Diary*, vol. IV, pp. 413–14.

31. Along with several other poems on the King's death, Behn's work was printed for/ by Henry Playford. He seems as opportunistic as the poets themselves since he was not ordinarily a publisher of literature but of music.

32. Quoted in Kenyon (1974), p. 150. The report was drawn up before March 1679.

33. The baroque Catholic imagery for Mary of Modena had precedent in Dryden who, in 1677, had dedicated his opera, *The State of Innocence*, to her, looking on with 'the rapture which Anchorites find in Prayer, when a Beam of the Divinity shines upon them… they are speechless for the time that it continues, and prostrate and dead when it departs'.

34. The horse with rider was a common analogy for the people and their ruler, occurring, for example, in Samuel Morland's 'Brief Discourse Concerning the Nature and Reason of Intelligence'. Morland saw the English people as especially restless 'untam'd horses' who 'have thrown their unskilful riders many times within these fifty years'.

35. Mary of Modena had or would have among her ladies three women poets, Jane Barker, Anne Finch, Countess of Winchilsea, and Anne Killigrew.

36. Behn herself published the commendatory poem in her collection *Lycidus*, pp. 89–94. If Behn were known to be tangentially associated with the Sidneys, the reference to Arcadia may also be making a link with Sir Philip Sidney, whose most famous work was *The Arcadia*.

Chapter 25

1. *CSP*, Dom. 1683, pp. 97–8; PRO, SP 44/64, 45.

2. See Grey's *The Secret History of the Rye-House Plot*, p. 118, and Burnet, *History of His Own Time*, vol. III.

3. The document was primarily written by Robert Ferguson, one of the most wanted conspirators of the Rye House Plot.

4. Similar ingenuousness is revealed in Monmouth's letter to Mary of Modena: 'I would not desire your Majesty to doe it, if I weare not from the botom of my hart convinced how I have bine disceaved in to it, and how angry God Almighty is with me for it,' *An Account Of What Passed at the Execution of the Late Duke of Monmouth, On Wednesday the 15th of July, 1685,* on Tower-Hill. *Together With a Paper Signed by Himself that Morning in the Tower, in the Presence of the Lords Bishop* of Ely, *and* Bath *and* Wells, *Dr.* Tennison, *and Dr.* Hooper. *And Also The Copy of His Letter to His* Majesty *after he was taken, Dated at* Ringwood *in* Hantshire, *the 8th. of July.*

5. Monmouth seems to have been playing a role in the romantic melodrama of adultery, rather than the tragedy of history. He said, 'I have had a Scandal raised upon me about a Woman, a Lady of Vertue and Honour...I have committed no Sin with her; and that which hath passed betwixt Us, was very Honest and Innocent in the Sight of God.' He refused to follow convention and recommend his wife and children to the King; instead he approached the end with a taciturnity both heroic and childish: '*I have said, I will make no Speeches; I will make no Speeches; I come to dye.*'

6. The same effeminate image had been imposed on Charles I, regarded as unduly influenced by his queen, Henrietta Maria.

7. Apparently Monmouth felt the axe, fearing that its bluntness betokened the gruesome fate of his predecessor in opposition, Lord Russell, who 'he said had been struck three or four times'. See Burnet, *History of His Own Time*, vol. III, p. 56.

8. *The Savile Correspondence*, ed. W. D. Cooper (London, 1858), p. 286, written 24 April 1686.

9. *Works*, vol. 4, p. 347.

10. See *Memoirs of Sir John Reresby. The Complete Text and a Selection from his Letters*, ed. Andrew Browning (Glasgow, 1936).

11. Susannah Mountfort (originally Percival before her marriage in 1686, and Verbruggen after her second marriage in 1694) first appeared on the stage at the age of fourteen in 1681. Later, she became the leading comedienne of the United Company. Her father, Thomas Percival, a minor actor, had played in Behn's *Abdelazer* and *The Rover*.

12. The manuscript letter is in the Folger Shakespeare Library. Years later, in an item concerning the manuscript of Purcell's *Faerie Queen* in *The Gazette*, Zachary Baggs was mentioned as the treasurer of the Theatre Royal. Another instance of debt might be included in PRO C 4/156/48. An 'Afra Beane, widdowe', was defendant in a case concerning a debt to Sir William Rooke (a Royalist from Canterbury like Behn herself), brought by his son, the naval officer George Rooke. The document is undated and very damaged, so there is no means of knowing when the case was brought or if Beane is Behn, but it is a possibility. George Rooke declared that £10 had been given either to her or to Henry Thompson to use on her behalf; Afra Beane denied receiving any money.

13. Behn's name was frequently written as 'Bean' and she was thinking of writing a play about a man called Bacon, *The Widdow Ranter or, The History of Bacon in Virginia* (1690). On the bottom of p. 226 on the last page of a poem called 'Caesar's Ghost', the name of 'A.Behn' has been written in the hand assumed to be Behn's; it was then crossed out, possibly because she had absentmindedly and inappropriately written her name at the end of a poem she had not authored but which she had just finished copying. The identification of the handwriting as Behn's was made by Mary Ann O'Donnell, who provides a full discussion of 'Astrea's Booke' in 'A Verse Miscellany of Aphra Behn: Bodleian Library MS Firth c.16', *English Manuscript Studies 1100–1700*, ed. Peter Beal and Jeremy Griffiths, vol. 2 (Oxford, 1990) and 'Private Jottings, Public Utterances: Aphra Behn's published writings and her commonplace book', *Aphra Behn Studies*, pp. 285–309.

14. 'From Julian, late Secretary to the Muses' in Tom Brown's *Letters from the Dead to the Living*, p. 61.

15. Love, *Scribal Publication*, p. 268; prologue to *The London Cuckolds* (1682).

16. See Brice Harris, 'Robert Julian, Secretary to the Muses', *Journal of English Literary History*, 10, 1943, pp. 294–309.

17. R. Holt is listed as 'Mr Cannings printer att St. Jones Gates'. Holt printed Behn's *The Luckey Chance, The Emperor of the Moon* and *The Fair Jilt*.

18. See 'The Session of Ladies' copied out in Behn's hand, as well as 'Ladies of Honour' begun in Behn's hand but not completed; in the latter case the new hand has taken over before the libels on the Duchess of Norfolk. Other poems include Dorset's 'Faithful Catalogue of... Ninnies' and 'A New Letter to Julian'.

19. *Letters from the Dead to the Living*, p. 62.

20. It was probably a good idea to talk about the marriage in terms of shepherds rather than emphasise the bride, for Lady Mary Compton, daughter of the third Earl of Northampton and widow of the Earl of Falmouth, had rather a tarnished reputation: she was much lampooned for copulation with a footman.

21. *The Rover* was performed at court in October, so, alternatively, Behn might have been referring to this when she promised payment to Baggs. *The Stationers' Register* for 8 May 1686 has the entry '*The Disappointed Marriage, or, Ye Generous Mistris*, a comedy by Madam Beane. Lycensed Aprill the 23th by R. P.' for Edward Poole. Poole published no play of Behn's and no play of hers exists under this title. It is possible that this is an earlier name for what became *The Luckey Chance*, printed by Canning in 1687. It could also be an alternative title for *The Younger Brother*. The dating of the first performance of *The Luckey Chance* is made likely through the fact that Susannah Percival is listed as playing Diana. She married Mountfort on 2 July 1686.

22. There are, however, some sources for *The Luckey Chance*, e.g. the lady's plot of testing her lover comes from Shirley's *The Lady of Pleasure* (1637) and much of the gentlemanly low life is indebted to Dryden's first comedy, *The Wild Gallant*.

23. See Playford's *Theatre of Music* in 1687, 4th edn.

24. The prologue to *Dame Dobson, the Cunning Woman* (1683).

25. Towards the end, there may be a perversity in Gayman's action. He seems to know that his uncle has died and left him money—why has he been pretending poverty knowing it was now over?

26. Gayman is unimpressed with the amorous preparations: 'What the Devil can all this mean? If there be a Woman in the Case—sure I have not liv'd so bad a Life, to gain the dull Reputation of so modest a Coxcomb, but that a Female might down with me, without all this Ceremony.'

27. There is also an intertextual allusion when Gayman, called Philander by Lady Fulbank, is accused of making lewd verses to her under the name of Cloris, the escaping heroine of Behn's poem, 'The Disappointment'.

28. For the milk punch, see Oldys MS note to Langbaine BL (AM) 22592, f. 37. This sounds like an uncurdled version of posset for which there were many recipes, including one copied into 'Astrea's Booke'. It may have used fortified wine.

29. John Dennis, *Works* (London, 1718), vol. 11, p. 537.

30. *Works*, vol. 7, p. 217.

31. There were three groups at Will's: the Grave, the Wits and the Rabble. A 'Wit' would need to be in Dryden's section.

32. *Works*, vol. 7, p. 217.

33. The use of terms suggests a popular Cartesian conception of the self, of body and spirit or mind divided. Behn could remain a woman in body, while having a masculine or ungendered mind that wrote. It was a conception that looked back more to the humoral notions of the hot dry man and cold wet woman (in which heat was of course the source of mental and bodily strength) than forward to the gendered body-mind of the eighteenth century. For a discussion of this change in emphasis, see Thomas Laqueur, *Making Sex: Body and Gender from the Greeks to Freud* (Cambridge, Mass., 1990).

34. Also politics was leaving the theatre, and Behn's description of herself as a Royalist of 'heart and Pen' was growing irrelevant. Although not as political as earlier plays, *The Luckey Chance* touched on topical events: a controversy over the City of London's charter, continuing anti-Catholic fears, and rumours from Ireland of French invasions—neither as out-of-date as might at first seem. There was also a swipe against Holland and its bourgeois culture when Gayman impersonated the devil; the latter was addressed as *Pantamogan* in echo of the much mocked Dutch title, *Hogan Mogan, High Mightiness*.

35. See P. B. Anderson, 'Buckingham's Chemist', *TLS*, 1935, p. 612. Bellon was the author of a number of medical works. It is also possible that Bellon is the Peter Bellon who wrote a play, translated 'Agnes de Castro' and shared Behn's publishers, Magnes and Bentley.

36. People between the Amazon and the Surinam Rivers were 'strangly afflicted, with the Gout & Dropsie', BL Sloane MS 3662.

37. The original reads 'shews' not 'she's'.

38. The original reads '& plagues'. 'An Epistle to Julian', BL Harleian MS. 7317, 59.

39. All *commedia dell'arte* productions were conventional and relied on stock scenes, such as 'Scène de la fille de chambre' and 'Scène de L'Apotiquaire'. These were listed in Evariste Gheradi's *Le Théâtre Italien, ou Le Receuil de toutes les Comédies et Scènes Françoises, qui ont été jouees sur le Théâtre Italien. Par la Troupe des Comédiens du Roy de l'Hôtel de Bourgogne à Paris* (Paris, 1695). This work has selected scenes from *Arlequin Empereur*, but Volume I of the 1741 edition prints all the French scenes.

40. Although Dryden found something in astrology, to many Royalists prognostications were dangerous since they had been used for political purposes in the Interregnum and in the Popish Plot with its endless figures and analogies: Monmouth, misled by soothsayers, fitted into the Puritan–Whig pattern.

41. Behn's scepticism about what can really be seen with instruments was of long standing, if the incident with Sir Bernard Gascoigne on the boat from Dunkirk in 1667 can be credited. Then she had at first taken the allegorical apparition as a scene of painted glass.

42. Behn comically alludes to a range of fantastic 'science' works e.g. Cyrano de Bergerac's *Histoire comique ou Voyage dans la Lune* (1650), translated by Thomas Sydserff in 1659 and by A. Lovell in 1687; the classical *Lucians Dialogue of Icaromenippus*, in which Menippus describes his journey to the moon, translated by Ferrand Spence in 1684; and, especially, *The Man in the Moon* by Francis Godwin, Bishop of Llandaff, published in 1629 under the Spanish pseudonym, Domingo Gonsales. Gonsales claims he went to the moon in a machine drawn by geese.

43. This scene is based on the 'Scène du déséspoir'. See *Le theatre Italien*, 1741, vol. 1, pp. 129–30.

44. *The Tempest* V, I: 'I'll drown my book'. There is also an echo of *Don Quixote*, when the knight realises how he has been fooled.

45. See the account in the *Newdigate Newsletter*, 26 March 1687: 'A Country man haveing invented a head & soe contrived it that whatever language or tune you speak in the Mouth of it is Repeated distinctly and Audibly'.

46. The epilogue, too, sounds like the Behn of *The Second Part of The Rover* and *The Luckey Chance*. The theatre is neglected and this symptomises the rottenness of the body-politic: Rome flourished when it saw its poets as 'necessary Ministers of State', when they 'were useful in a City held, / As formidable Armies in the Field. / They but a Conquest over Men pursu'ed, / While these by gentle force the Soul subdu'd.' It is, of course, not King James's fault, but it would be good if he let some 'God-like Bounty' fall on poets for a change.

47. In his second part of *The Play-House. A Satire*, Gould mocked 'You that Write *Farce*,

and You that *Farce* Translate'. Yet he could say little against *The Emperor of the Moon* beyond repeating the charge of Behn's wanton wit and '*Luscious Bawdry*'. Contrasting rather than allying her with Jonson, Shakespeare and Fletcher, 'ye Immortal *Three*', Gould pitted Behn against the *good* moderns: Otway, now safely dead, and Wycherley and Etherege, both retired from the theatre. See *The Works of Mr. Robert Gould*, II, p. 241. Reprinted in Montague Summers, *The Restoration Theatre* (London, 1934).

48. Possibly Behn's ill-health made her think more sympathetically of Jonson, who had been bedridden for the last nine years of his life.

49. See Brian Corman, *Genre and Generic Change in English Comedy 1660–1710* (Toronto, 1993).

50. Behn now looked back nostalgically to Charles II, 'that Great patron of Noble Poetry, and the Stage, for whom the Muses must for ever mourn'. Although she may have despaired of the court for theatrical patronage, however, she was still looking to aristocratic patronage as much as to the market.

Chapter 26

1. The Catholic sympathy most conspicuously appears in the poem Behn addressed to John Howard, the son of the executed Viscount Stafford, 'Pastoral To Mr. *Stafford*, Under the Name of Silvio', *Works*, vol. 1, no. 64. She described Stafford as dying for a common faith.

2. Dryden, *Letters*, ed. Charles Ward (Durham, North Carolina, 1942), p. 127.

3. This rather uncharacteristic poem was not ascribed to Brown at the time and scholars have pointed out that he was a man to whom anything anonymous and scurrilous tended to be assigned. For the habit of ascribing satirical verse to Brown, see *POAS*, 5, 12. But the verses 'Traitor to God' *are* authenticated and, in BL MS Harl. 7319, part of 'Dryden Renegade' appears attached to them under the title 'To Mr. Bayes'. Cf. the controversy in *TLS* over the ascription of 'Mr *Higden*' to Dryden or Brown, 19 May 1995, pp. 12–13.

4. *The Late Converts Expos'd; or the Reasons of Mr. Bays Changing his Religion* (London, 1688); *A Description of Mr D—s Funeral. A Poem* (London, 1700), p. 5.

5. Cf. Pope's rather different but similarly worded sentiment in *Essay on Criticism:* 'True wit is nature to advantage dressed, / What oft was thought but ne'er so well expressed.'

6. Behn was not La Rochefoucauld's first English translator but she was the first since the authorised versions of the *Maximes* had appeared in France. John Davies translated an earlier edition. Behn seems to have used the 1675 edition, the fourth of five authorised ones. It contained 413 maxims of which she translated 391. She omitted some, repeated some, joined up some, and rearranged and added to the sequence. Possibly Behn worked on the translation

while she was in France and soon after she returned, since she supplied references from 1682 and 1683 which would still have been current in early 1684. To illustrate the gallant executions of very different men, she used the noble Lord Russell and the criminal Christopher Vratz, executed in 1682. See *The Confession And Manner of the Execution of the Three Notorious Outlandish Ruffians* (London, 1682).

7. Two final sections dealt with self-love and death, the former being always present, the latter inevitable and feared, whatever hypocrites like Seneca pretended.

8. *Works*, vol. 4, pp. 1–9.

9. Hoyle was stabbed to death by George Pitts on 27 May 1692, having provoked a quarrel. He talked 'very scurrilously against the present Government, and spake very unbecoming words against the Person of King William'. It was said that 'Hoyle, in his life-time, was a Person much addicted to quarrelling'. *Proceedings of the Old Bailey*, 29 June 1692.

10. *Works*, vol. 4, p. 2.

11. Barlow's *Aesop* was an elaborate production frequently in elegant, expensive binding. Not much care was taken by those who actually put the pages together, however, and most often texts of Philipott and Behn are intermixed. Given the fact that Behn's words are engraved over the erasure of Philipott's, a composite text is not disastrous.

12. Once she has made a political point, Behn seems unable to resist others and her overt political references tend to come in clumps. So, after this remark on Parliament, she makes the next fable into an illustration of Monmouth's 'false ambition'. The political additions were not always felicitous. Some years later, Roger L'Estrange brought out another Aesop translation and criticised recent translators for having 'Ventur'd a little too far from the Precise Scope of the Author, upon the priviledge of a Poetical License'. Part of Behn's 'Poetical License' was Barlow's commercial and her own convinced politics. Having published her verses, Behn perhaps took a leaf out of Barlow's book and either printed them, or let them be printed, as playing cards, with slightly changed copies of Barlow's engravings. The publisher might have been Randal Taylor since he also brought out political and coded playing cards.

13. Behn had actually mocked the device in *Sir Patient Fancy* when Lodwick had laid out less romantic plans for his sister according to the watch of her comic suitor: 'Beginning at Eight, from which down to Twelve you ought to imploy in dressing, till Two at Dinner, till Ten at Supper with your Lover, if your Husband be not at home, or keep his distance, which he's too well bred not to do; then from Ten to Twelve are the happy Hours the Bergere, those of intire Enjoyment,' *Works*, vol. 6, Act I, Scene I.

14. The poem first appeared in *La Montre*, beginning 'Philander, *since you'll have it*

so…' in 1686. It was republished in the poems appended to *Lycidus* in 1688, beginning '*Alexis*, since you'll have it so'. In *Miscellany* (1685) there is a poem called Song 'While, *Iris*, I at distance gaze' (vol. 1, no. 57) which, though it uses the name of the heroine of *La Montre*, describes an unhappy love that Damon, *La Montre*'s lover, does not experience except in dreams. It sounds as though the poem might have been left over from the sections for four and five o'clock in the morning of *La Montre*, omitted because the work was growing too long. Again there seems an association of Alexis and Philander, which makes more likely a possible identification of Alexis and Condon, linked through the dedication of *Love-Letters* to Condon.

15. *Works*, vol. 4, p. 303.
16. *Works*, vol. 4, p. 345. Behn urged Morland to create fountains in the Castle. He had already managed to pump water into the pond, see *London Gazette*, 12 September 1682.
17. Some impersonal praise of Cliveden, the Duke of Buckingham's house seen from Windsor makes it seem unlikely Behn was intimate with the Duke.
18. A similar claim was made in the 1660s for Katherine Philips's translation of Corneille's *Death of Pompey*: 'The copy [is] greater than th'Original' (Roger Boyle, Earl of Orrery, printed in the 1667 edition of *Poems*). The compliment to Behn is signed G. J., probably George Jenkins. If so, he is also the editor of her posthumous *The Widdow Ranter*; his admiration for Behn did not prevent his emending the play.
19. 'Session of the Poets', *The Literary Works of Matthew Prior* (Oxford, 1971), p. 63.
20. *Works*, vol. 4, p. 380.
21. *Works*, vol. 4, p. 388.
22. *Works*,vol. 1, no. 56.
23. Lysander's attitude follows the description of Tallemant, but the original is more conventional and serious than Behn's version.
24. *Works*, vol. 4, p. 421.
25. *Works*, vol. 1, no. 80. Similar gender ambiguity through the word 'youth' occurs in 'In Imitation of Horace'.
26. See 'Satire on the Ladies of Honour' (1686), BL Harl. MS 7319, p. 423, and 'Ballad to the Tune of Cheviot Chace' in *Court Satires*, p. 102.
27. To Julian', BL Harl. MS 7317. For the possibility that Albemarle might have been a commissioner of Part I of *Love-Letters*, see note 9 of Chapter 22.
28. See Estelle Ward, *Christopher, Duke of Albemarle* (London, 1915).

Chapter 27

1. Lord Grey later became a successful politician and was raised to an earldom. Lady Henrietta died on 13 August 1706; Lady Grey married again after her husband's death and died in 1719.

2. *Monmouth Routed, and Taken Prisoner, With his Pimp the Lord Gray. A Song* (London, 1685). In 'Advice to a painter' (1685) Grey is labelled a traitor to the Whigs as well as to the King; see Folger MS, p. 135.

3. *Works*, vol. 2, p. 433.

4. Octavio may in fact have been inspired by a man at Cleve, the Brandenburg ambassador M. Fucks, with whom Grey reportedly struck up a great friendship.

5. This was published in 1754 as *The Secret History of the Rye-House Plot*.

6. These documents would have come from agents and spies to the Secretaries of State, Sir Leoline Jenkins and Sunderland in Whitehall. See Peter Fraser, *The Intelligence of the Secretaries of State and their Monopoly of Licensed News 1660–1688* (Cambridge, 1956).

7. This sort of action was not uncommon. For example L'Estrange was given the papers of the Whig propagandist, Stephen Colledge, by the Chief Justice to write against him during the Exclusion Crisis.

8. *The Secret History of the Rye-House Plot*, pp. 80 and 90.

9. If she read the confession, Behn would have seen the name of Sir Patience Ward among those who had engaged to provide money for Monmouth's rebellion. Some of Behn's opinions are close to those of Grey in this document, especially in attitude to the plotter, Robert Ferguson, written off as garrulous and undependable.

10. Quoted in Kenyon, *Sunderland*, p. 78.

11. In exile James II came to believe in this elaborate treachery, see *The History of English Persecution of Catholics*, ed. T. A. Birrell (Catholic Record Society, no. 48, 1953).

12. Perhaps, too, Monmouth believed there might be family feeling, for there were those who insisted he was not the son of Charles II with Lucy Walters, but rather of Robert Sidney and thus a relative of Sunderland's.

13. After James II's removal, the death of Monmouth was rewritten more heroically. In 1690 the play *The Banish'd Duke: or, the Tragedy of Infortunatus* made of Monmouth a duped heroic figure dying less romantically than piously.

14. The phrase echoes the dedication to *Seneca Unmasqued*, where the actions of Monmouth appear ingratitude and folly 'to all good Men'.

15. *Diary*, vol. IV, p. 245

16. 'The Lovers' Session', Firth MS c. 25. p. 277.

17. The event is described in Carola Oman, *Mary of Modena* (London, 1962), p. 101.

18. The claim of factual truth may or may not be genuine since the records of Ypres, where the story is set, have not survived.

19. Mazarine is particularly viciously attacked in the satire 'On the Ladies of Honor'.

20. There seems some doubt of the sex of the author since it is variously given as S. B. de Brillac and Mlle de Brillac, but Behn assumed it was a woman and made a feminist point on female literary excellence. Although the plot mainly concerned the prince's love for Agnes, there was much on female friendship. 'The Maid' was 'so dear to the Princess' while Agnes 'lov'd *Constantia* sincerely'; indeed 'their

common Misfortune' in loving and being beloved by the same man did not change their friendship and they vied with each other in virtue not rivalry.

Chapter 28

1. 'A Satyr on the Modern Translators' (London, 1684).
2. After her death Gildon published the works of the deist, Charles Blount, as well as *The Oracles of Reason*, for which he wrote a preface declaring that reason was enough for happiness.
3. The original *Agnes de Castro*, Behn's translation, and one by Peter Bellon all appeared within the same year. Behn would have known of Bellon since he too was probably a playwright; Langbaine ascribed *The Mock Duellist* (1675) to him and he may be the Bellon mentioned in 'Astrea's Booke'. He translated several French fictional works.
4. The other translation came out in the same year. It was by J. Glanvil. The two translations are fairly close, though Behn tends to be more long-winded.
5. *Essay on Translated Verse* (London, 1685).
6. Behn concluded that English was closer to Italian, while French might be '*more agreeable with the* Welsh'.
7. Fontenelle quotes the supposed speech of the male philosopher's eager female pupil, and Behn again panders to anti-French sentiment by commenting, 'an English Woman *might adventure to translate any thing, a French Woman may be supposed to have spoken.*' She was not entirely happy with Fontenelle's condescending device. The woman listener was a hybrid, she judged, foolish at one moment, sage-like at another.
8. Behn corrected an error about the height of the earth's atmosphere. For Descartes, reason allowed a person to gain valid knowledge, to discover truth by cognitive processes. His method used an innate faculty, supposedly equal in everyone.
9. Margaret Cavendish, Duchess of Newcastle, *Sociable Letters* (London, 1664), p. 14.
10. *Works*, vol. 4, p. 85.
11. *History of Oracles* was included in the 1700 edition of *Histories, Novels, and Translations Written by the most Ingenious Mrs. Behn, the Second Volume.*
12. See *Leviathan*, pp. 75–86.
13. Milton, *Paradise Regained*, ll. 455–9.
14. *Works*, vol. 4, pp. 82–3.
15. See, for example, 'A Letter written by Dr George Hickes' in *An Answer to Fontenelle* (1709).
16. Behn had, however, toned down some of the anti-Scottish sentiment in *The Roundheads*.
17. Drumlangrig and Melfort were associated in the 1680s. Melfort and his brother, the Earl of Perth, had served under the Protestant Duke of Queensbury, governor of Edinburgh, the Earl of Drumlangrig's father. The brothers both converted to

Catholicism for James. The anti-papist riots in Edinburgh in 1686 worried James, who removed Queensbury from office and promoted the two Catholic converts. Behn probably knew little of the shifting power among James's ministers.

18. BL Stowe MS, 770.

19. George Hilton Jones, *Convergent Forces: Immediate Causes of the Revolution of 1688 in England* (Ames, Iowa, 1990).

20. While Behn was writing this hyperbole, she and her fellow scribes were probably copying into 'Astrea's Booke' scurrilous poems on the pregnancy such as 'The Miracle. How the Dutches of Modena being in Heaven prayd the Virgin Mary that the Queen might have a Son And how Our Lady sent the Angell Gabriel with her Smok upon wch the Queen Conceived', and 'Loretta & Winifred', which suggests that James was not the father of the child. Other poems in 'Astrea's Booke' include 'Tom Tyler', 'An Excellent New Song call'd The Prince of Darkness', 'The Audience' and 'The Miracle': these declare that the father was really the Papal Nuncio, Father D'Adda, a handy name for lampooners, or that the baby had been smuggled into the bedchamber in a warming pan.

21. Luttrell, vol. 1, p. 448.

22. The poets were adept at excuses. Dryden, for example, had apologised for late delivery within *Threnodia Augustalis* on Charles II's death, 'Thus long my grief has kept me dumb.' He too might have had other reasons since by 1685 payments for his Laureateship were in arrears of £1245, see James Anderson Winn, *John Dryden and His World* (New Haven, 1987), pp. 525–31.

23. Epilogue to *The Luckey Chance*, *Works*, vol. 7.

24. *To Poet Bavius* came out anonymously, quoting heavily from Baber's poem. This Behn probably did from memory or from a circulating manuscript copy, since there are many differences between Baber's printed text and Behn's quotations.

25. Behn ended by echoing an earlier satire on Baber printed in *Court Satires*, p. 43, in which he takes 'pains to make himself an ass': 'Thy Wit, thy Parts, thy Conduct, Mien and Grace, / Thy *Presence*, Cringes, and thy Court *Grimarce*, / But Swears Heaven meant thee for a perfect—As—', *Works*, vol. 1, no. 85.

26. The description of a bishop as the 'Reverend Gown, / Doom'd by his Nations Scandal' seems particularly risky.

27. See 'A Heroic Scène', p. 105, in which L'Estrange is lampooned as 'Oliver's Fiddler', accused of disloyalty and spying.

28. Burnet was being so successful as a propagandist that he constantly feared he would be kidnapped by James's agents. He went round with a bodyguard of four men.

29. The cataloguing of trees was a common device in European literature, appearing in Ovid and more recently Spenser's *Faerie Queene*, as well as in James Howell's political allegory of 1640.

30. See Evelyn's dedication of *Sylva* to Charles II in 1664.

31. The few other additions and omissions are typical of Behn: always sceptical about the institution of marriage, she chose to omit the picture of the yew as a widow mourning at the urn of her husband.

32. The author of the commendatory poem before *Poems on Several Occasions* entitled 'Upon these and other Excellent Works of the Incomparable *Astrea*' had declared even more universally, 'surely she will live, / As many Ages as are past, / As long as Learning, Sense, or wit survive, / As long as the first principles of Bodies last.' The comparison with Orinda was kept up in the commendatory poem to *La Montre* by Nahum Tate, where Behn was on a level with Katherine Philips; both were found equal to Sappho. In the commendatory poem to the later *Lycidus*, Daniel Kendrick placed Behn above Philips: 'If we *Orinda* to your works compare, / They uncouth, like her country's soyle, appear.' Anne Killigrew died in 1685, declaring 'for a monument I leave my VERSE,' *Poems by Mrs. Anne Killigrew* (1686).

Chapter 29

1. Tom D'Urfey was urged to deliver a comedy ridiculing the Dutch States General.

2. For a discussion of other pamphlets on Bacon, see my 'Spectacular deaths: history and story in Aphra Behn's *Love-Letters, Oroonoko,* and *The Widdow Ranter*', *Gender, Art and Death* (Cambridge, 1993).

3. *A True Narrative of the Rise, Progresse, and Cessation of the Late Rebellion in Virginia... by his Majestyes Commissioners* (1676). Documents relating to the rebellion are printed in the *Virginia Magazine of History and Biography*, I, i (1894) and IV.1 (1898).

4. This avoidance of portraying royal authority directly continued the trend in Behn's works. Where Dryden in *Absalom and Achitophel* had ended his poem with a too easygoing Charles II becoming suddenly assertive and centre-stage, Behn in *The Roundheads* had avoided bringing in the proper royal ruler.

5. Personal feeling may also have dictated this suppression. The large and diverse family of the Colepepers, to which Behn's foster-brother Thomas belonged, were intimately bound up with Virginia. Governor Berkeley had taken as his third wife the widow Frances Colepeper, and, when he was recalled to England shortly after the rebellion, his successor was Lord Colepeper, who arrived in the colony in 1683. Behn might have met either Berkeley or Lord Colepeper, who was soon back in England, and learnt some of the facts which she appears to know, but which do not occur in the public accounts of the uprising. Of course Sunderland's office might have been forthcoming once more. Another personal memory may have led to a possible reference to the botched trial of Algernon Sidney when Dullard says that a single witness is 'good in Law'.

6. See Martha W. McCartney, 'Cockacoeske, Queen of Pamunckey: Diplomat and Suzeraine', *Powhatans Mantle: Indians in the Colonial Southeast*, ed. Peter H. Wood,

NOTES

Gregory Waselkov, and Thomas A. Hatley (Lincoln, Nebraska, 1990), pp. 173–95. Cockacoeske was given a crown, scarlet and purple robe, striped silver and gold brocade Indian gown lined in cherry-coloured soft silk, and a bracelet of false stones in compensation after the Bacon rebellion had been quelled.

7. The same could be said of the 'Darling Indians', whom Bacon regarded as marauders. These too were Europeanised but allowed some exotic customs. Their dance '*with ridiculous Postures*' Behn may have borrowed from Richard Blome's *The Present State of his Majesties Isles and Territories in America*, published in 1687 in London, which described the 'devilish Mysteries' of Native American religion and the 'antick' or grotesque dance of 'monstrously painted' figures in horns and loose coloured hair, pp. 185–6.

8. *Works*, vol. 7, p. 299.

9. There is also an analogy between the Monmouth Rebellion and the war with the Native Americans. The young chief is buoyed up with enigmatic prophecies of the sort Behn had observed in Monmouth and exposed in her translation of *Oracles*.

10. In keeping with her softening in *The False Count* and *The Luckey Chance* towards 'good' merchants who know their limits, Behn can now allow heroine status to the widow of a merchant, Mrs. Surelove, without birth but with reasonable breeding (in the context of the colonies).

11. See *A New Dictionary of the Canting Crew* (c. 1690). In Crowne's *The English Friar*, published in the same year as Behn's play, the leader of the town sparks is generically called Young Ranter and is a brute and a brawler, while Behn herself used the terms 'rant' for boisterous behaviour in the whore in *The City-Heiress*.

12. *Works*, vol. 7, p. 307.

13. 'Knowing Mrs. Behn in her Life-time design'd to Dedicate some of her Works to you', G. J.

14. *Works*, vol. 7, p. 338.

15. Ranter also shared Behn's view of male heroism, mixing admiration and cynicism: men 'get a name in War, from command, not courage', she commented.

16. The Indian queen was played by a very different actress, Mrs Bracegirdle, making her début in a Behn play—if her possible appearance as the child Mrs Ariell at the end of *Abdelazer* is discounted.

17. Events were moving so fast in 1688 that, by the time *The Widdow Ranter* was ready, its moment was gone and it was not performed until after Behn's death late in 1689, with the satiric scene of the Virginian councillors omitted. Dryden wrote a prologue and epilogue, his first public statement since the arrival of William. Inevitably he equivocated, praising the recent triumph of William's Protestants over James's Catholics in Enniskillen in Northern Ireland, while suggesting that the former might be regarded as rebels. He insisted that Behn was not a politician or a propagandist, but simply the mistress of love: 'She who so well cou'd Love's kind Passion paint'; her play was an 'Orphan Child'.

The play flopped primarily because it was badly produced and cut: 'Had our Author been alive she would have committed [the play] to the flames rather than have suffered it to have been acted with such omissions as was made,' wrote its editor, probably George Jenkins (commender of Behn's *La Montre*), who yet published with James Knapton an expurgated and very careless version without Dryden's prologue and epilogue. Probably Tonson would not release these since he published them separately. Knapton was forced to provide the play with a substitute prologue to which he had access, one written much earlier by Dryden for Shadwell's *A True Widow*. The epilogue came from *The Covent Garden Drolery*, without even a change of pronouns to fit it for a female author. Later, the verses appeared again with changed pronouns as the prologue to a second edition of *Abdelazer*, proving the point made by Mr Bays in *The Rehearsal*, that certain lines 'may both serve for either: that is, the Prologue for the Epilogue, or the Epilogue for the Prologue... nay they may both serve too...for any other Play as well as this'. For a discussion see *Rare Prologues and Epilogues 1642–1700*, ed. Autrey Neil Wiley (London, 1940).

18. In the story, Trefry believed he could hinder the fate of Oroonoko by insisting that Byam's and the rabble's authority did not extend to Parham, the Proprietor's house. Where order has collapsed and selfish interest is ruler, however, there is no respect for this equivalent of royal prerogative.

19. Imoinda was only partly assimilated into European culture and although the pastoral name, Clemene, is donated to her, it is seldom used.

20. See Lois Schwoerer, 'Propaganda in the Revolution of 1688–89', *American Historical Review*, 82, 1977, pp. 843–74.

21. For Burnet, this was always crucial to his own position as a supporter of monarchy but a traitor to James, as he explained in his *An Enquiry Into the Measures of Submission to the Supream Authority*.

Chapter 30

1. Some time earlier in Holland, Burnet, uncured of frank speaking, had asked what William had delicately avoided asking Mary: whether in any circumstances she, as the heir, would rule alone in England. Schooled in wifely duties, Mary was horrified and absolutely refused. This conversation was unknown in England when William, the nephew of Charles and James, was invited to invade. Burnet, *History of His Own Time*, vol. 111, p. 131.

2. Marion Grew, *William Bentinck and William III* (London, 1924), pp. 150–2.

3. Evelyn, *Diary*, 29 January 1689.

4. In fact, Behn probably did fairly well financially in 1688 with three stories, the anthology *Lycidus*, and two translations. If she had £20 to £25 a volume, what

Tonson offered for *Poems on Several Occasions*, this would have brought in about £175. See Virginia Crompton's 'Forc'd to write for bread'.

5. Since *The Luckey Mistake* was published as a volume I, Behn must have intended one or two more stories to accompany it. These may have been 'The Nun' and 'The Dumb Virgin', both set on the Continent. Although two end tragically and one happily, all three stories look back to the Spanish sources of Behn's early plays and are different from the idiosyncratic hybrids of fact and fiction which she had published just before James's fall.

6. Of Elizabeth Cellier of the Meal-Tub Plot fame, Burnet had written that she 'had a great share of wit and was abandoned to lewdness'.

7. Dryden, *Works*, vol. III, ll. 454–6. When the Jacobite propagandist machine got going, Burnet would be presented as a lover of Mary II.

8. Cowley also called himself Moses who 'still alone (alas) dost gaping stand, / Upon the naked Beach, upon the Barren Sand'. See too his translation of Horace's tribute to Pindar which helps makes a line for Behn from Pindar through himself and Horace. All these poets declare modesty and exclusion. See *Poems*, ed. A. R. Waller (Cambridge, 1905), pp. 178–9.

9. Behn had used the metaphor of a coin, given value only because the King's head was upon it, in her dedication to Sir William Clifton back in 1685. Now this coin, her poetry, though of little worth in itself, was given 'value'—not converted to gold as it would be by a true king—by Burnet's invitation. The image fitted well with Behn's ambiguous opening image in the poem: she claimed she was more taken with Burnet's request than a Roman consul chosen by 'the Peoples Suffrages'. This seems a coded statement about authority: what Burnet was dealing in was not divine authority, but power held through manipulation of the people and through violence. Behn's relation to it was equivocal but she needed both to have and to be 'Currant Coyn'.

10. Comte de Pontbriant, *Histoire de la Principauté d'Orange* (Avignon, 1891), p. 247.

11. Behn may have held the common view that the crown should have been given to Mary alone. Sir Charles Sedley, for example, was unequivocally supportive of Mary but remained ambiguous in his attitude towards William.

12. Cowley, *The Essays and Other Prose Writings*, ed. Alfred B. Gough (Oxford, 1915).

13. Behn's return to Bentley might suggest her shift in political attitude. At the same time it is notoriously difficult to assign political views to publishers on the basis of their publications. Behn's works are the only specifically political works that Bentley admitted to publishing in 1689. Canning seems to have been tried for publishing a Jacobite broadside in 1690, see Henry R. Plomer, *A Dictionary of Printers and Booksellers who were at work in England, Scotland and Ireland from 1668 to 1725*, ed. Arundell Esdaile (Oxford, 1922).

14. Dryden was attacked a great deal in the autumn of 1688 and spring of 1689 by

NOTES

his literary enemies, including Tom Brown in *The Reasons of Mr. Bays Changing his Religion. Address of John Dryden, Laureat to… the Prince of Orange* was one such attack, attributed to Shadwell.

15. Gould, *To the Society of the Beaux Esprits*, p. 11.

16. It is not easy to say of what any Restoration person died. In the plague year the compilers of lists included as the causes of death beyond the plague: age, ague, cancer, childbed, canker, consumption, convulsion, distraction, dropsy, fever, flux, fright, gangrene, gout, griping in guts, small pox, French pox, grief, jaundice, King's Evil, lethargy, pleurisy, rickets, sciatica, scouring, scurvy, spotted fever, stone, surfeit, ulcer and worms.

17. Ward, *The London Spy*, pp. 119–20.

18. The present stone reads 'Mrs Aphra Behn Dyed April 16 A.D. 1689'. The original stone read 'Mrs. APHARA Behn'.

19. Sam Briscoe at least must have scented something derogatory in the lines, since, in his dedicatory epistle to *Familiar Letters of Love, Gallantry* (1718), he complains of the taste of the Restoration, claiming that, if it had the same taste as now, Milton and Tom Brown would not have been neglected nor Dryden relieved of his pension nor 'Mrs. *Behn* ever had but *two Lines* upon her *Grave-stone*'. At some point, however, the two lines were four with the addition: 'Great Poetess! Thy stupendous Lays / The World admires, and the Muses praise.' See Bodleian MS Eng. Poet.e.40, fo. 38; Top. gen.e. 32, fo. 13. The extra two were removed, perhaps in the recutting of the stone recorded by Joseph Chester in *The Marriage, Baptismal, and Burial Registers of the Collegiate Church or Abbey of St. Peter Westminster*, Harleian Society, 10, 1876. The 'Memoirs' declares the 'wretched Verses' made by 'a very Ingenious Gentleman, tho' no Poet, the very Person whom the Envious of our Sex, and the Malicious of the other, wou'd needs have the Author of most of hers'. This sounds like Hoyle, but, since Ravenscroft was also said to have helped Behn with her plays, the reference could conceivably be to him; the remark on his being no poet would then have been occasioned solely by the lines themselves.

20. Behn had said as much of Rochester. See also 'To the Memory of the Incomparable Orinda', *Poems and Songs*, 4th edn (London, 1686): 'Thou, / Whose happy Verse made others live, / And certain Immortality could give; / Blasted are all thy blooming Glories now' and 'Upon these and other Excellent Works of the Incomparable *Astrea* in *Poems on Several Occasions*: 'even *Astrea* with all her sacred store, / Be wreckt on Death's inevitable Shore,' though this writer declares she has left examples of her 'immortal Wit' behind.

21. The stone was most recently recut in April 1986.

APPENDIX

Chronological List of Behn's Original Works, Ascribed Works, Edited Works and Translations

1671   *The Forc'd Marriage*

1671   *The Amorous Prince*

1671   'To the Author of the *New Utopia*', *The Six days Adventure, or The New Utopia*

1672   *Covent Garden Drolery*
       including   'I led my Silvia to a Grove'
                 'Come my Phillis, let us improve'
                 'When Jemmy first began to love'
                 'Damon being asked a reason for loveing'

1673   *The Dutch Lover*

1677   *Abdelazer*, including the song 'Love Arm'd'

1677   *The Town-Fopp*

1677   *The Rover*

[1677   *The Debauchee*]

1678   *Sir Patient Fancy*

1679   *The Feign'd Curtizans*

1680   'A Paraphrase on Oenone to Paris', *Ovid's Epistles, Translated by Several Hands*

1680   *The Revenge*

1681   *The Second Part of The Rover*

1681   *Song. To a New Scotch Tune*

1682   *The False Count*

1682   *The Roundheads*

1682   *The City-Heiress*

1682   Prologue to *Like Father, Like Son*

1682   Prologue and epilogue to *Romulus*

1683   'To the Unknown Daphnis', in *T. Lucretius Carus. The Epicurean Philosopher*

1683 *The Young King*
1684 Prologue to *Valentinian*
1684 *Love-Letters Between a Nobleman and his Sister Part I*
1684 *Poems upon Several Occasions*
      including 'The Golden Age'
                'A Farewell to Celladon'
                'On a Juniper-Tree, cut down to make Busks'
                'On the Death of Mr. Grinhil'
                'A Ballad on Mr J. H. to Amoret'
                'Song. The Complaint'
                'Our Cabal'
                'To Mrs. W. On her Excellent Verses'
                'The Sence of a Letter Sent Me'
                'On a Copy of Verses Made in a Dream'
                'The Return'
                'To my Lady Morland at Tunbridge'
                'The Disappointment'
                'The Dream, A Song'
                'A Letter to a Brother of the Pen in Tribulation'
                'Song. To Pesibles Tune'
                'Silvio's Complaint'
                'To Lysander, who made some Verses on a Discourse of Love's Fire'
                'To Lysander, on some Verses he writ, and asking more for his Heart than 'twas worth'
                'To Lysander at the Musick-Meeting'
                The Voyage to the Island of Love
1685 *Pindarick on the Death of Charles II*
1685 *Poem to Catherine Queen Dowager*
1685 *A Pindarick on the Happy Coronation of...James II*
1685 *Love-Letters Part II*
1685 'On the Author of that Excellent and Learned Book, entituled *Way to Health, Long Life, and Happiness*'
1685 *Miscellany*
      including 'A Letter to Mr. Creech at Oxford'
                'On the Death of the late Earl of Rochester'
                'Cease, cease, Aminta to complain'
                'Paraphrase on the Lords Prayer'
                'A Pindaric to Mr. P. who sings finely'
                'Epitaph on the Tombstone of a Child'

'Ovid to Julia'

'Pastoral to Mr. Stafford'

Reflections on Morality or Seneca Unmasqued

1686   *La Montre*

1687   *The Luckey Chance*

1687   *The Emperor of the Moon*

1687   *To the Most Illustrious Prince Christopher Duke of Albemarle*

1687   *Love-Letters Part III*

1687   'To the Honourable Sir Francis Fane, On his Excellent Play, *The Sacrifice*'

1687   To Henry Higden, Esq; On his Translation of... *Juvenal*

1687   *Aesop's Fables*

1688   *Lycidus... Together with a Miscellany of New Poems*

     including   'To Damon, to inquire of him'

                'To Alexis in Answer to his Poem against Fruition'

                'To Alexis, On his saying, I lov'd a Man that talk'd much'

                'Pastoral Pindarick On the Marriage of... Dorset'

                'On Desire A Pindarick'

                'To Amintas, Upon reading the Lives'

                'On the first discovery of falseness in Amintas'

                'To the fair Clarinda'

1688   *A Congratulatory Poem... On the Universal Hopes... for a Prince of Wales*

1688   *Congratulatory Poem... On the Happy Birth of the Prince of Wales*

1688   *The Fair Jilt*

1688   *Poem to Sir Roger L'Estrange*

1688   *Oroonoko*

1688   *Agnes de Castro*

1688   *A Discovery of New Worlds*

1688   *The History of Oracles*

     including   'Essay on Translated Prose'

1688   *To Poet Bavius Occasioned by his Satyr*

1688   'On the Death of E. Waller, Esq', *Poems to the Memory of... Waller*

1689   *The History of the Nun*

1689   *A Pindaric Poem to the Reverend Doctor Burnet*

1689   'Of Plants', *The Second and Third Parts of the Works of Mr Abraham Cowley*

APPENDIX

1689   *A Congratulatory Poem to Queen Mary*
1689   *The Lucky Mistake*
1690   *The Widdow Ranter*
1692   *Miscellany Poems*
         including   'Verses... to be sent to a fair lady'
1696   *The Younger Brother*
1696   *The Histories and Novels*
         including   'Love-Letters'
1698   *All the Histories and Novels*
         including   'Memoirs of the Court of the King of Bantam'
                          'The Nun, or the Perjured Beauty'
                          'The Adventure of the Black Lady'
1700   *Histories, Novels, and Translations*
         including   'The Unfortunate Bride or the Blind Lady'
                          'The Dumb Virgin'
                          'The Unfortunate Happy Lady'
                          'The Wandring Beauty'
                          'The Unhappy Mistake'
1701   *The Muses Mercury*
         including   'Complaint of the poor Cavaliers'
1718   *Familiar Letters of Love and Gallantry* together with T. Brown's
        Remains
         including   'To Mrs. Price'
                          'A Song. 'Tis not your Saying'
                          'A Letter to the Earl of Kildare'

BIBLIOGRAPHY

Works Written before 1800

An Account of the Proceedings at the guild-hall of the City of London on Saturday, September 13, 1679.

An Account of what happened at the Execution of the Late Duke of Monmouth. London, 1685.

Adis, Henry. *A Letter Sent from Syrranam, to His Excellency, the Lord Willoughby of Parham, General of the Western Islands, and of the Continent of Guianah, &c. Then residing at the Barbados.* London, 1664.

Alcock, Thomas. *The Famous Pathologist, or the Noble Mountebank.*

————. *An Exact Survey of the Affaires Of the United Netherlands.*

An Alphabetical Account of the Nobility and Gentrey, Which are (or lately were) related unto the several Counties of England and Wales. London, 1665.

Apology: Or, the Genuine Memoirs of Madam Maria Mancini. London, 1679.

Astell, Mary. *A Serious Proposal to the Ladies.* London, 1694 (Part 2, 1697).

The Banish'd Duke: Or, the Tragedy of Infortunatus. London, 1690.

Behn, Aphra. *The Works of Aphra Behn.* Ed. Janet Todd. London, 1992–6.

————. *The Works of Aphra Behn.* Ed. Montague Summers. London, 1915.

Benskins Domestic Intelligence. 1682.

Biet, Antoine. *Voyage de la France equinoxiale en l'isle de Cayenne.* 1654.

Blome, Richard. *Britannia: or, a Geographical Description of the Kingdoms of England, Scotland, and Ireland.* London, 1673.

————. *A Description Of the Island of Jamaica; With the other Isles and Territories in America, to which the English are Related.* London, 1678.

————. *The Present State of his Majesties Isles and Territories in America.* London, 1687.

Boileau, Nicolas. *Oeuvres Complètes.* Paris, 1966.

Boothby, Frances. *Marcelia.* London, 1670.

Boscobel Tracts. Ed. J. Hughes. London, 1830.

Boyle, Roger, Earl of Orrery. *Poems.* 1667.

Brémond, Gabriel de. *Hattigé ou les Amours du roy de Tamaran*. Cologne, 1676 (transl. 1676).

Brome, Alexander. *A Description of Mr. D...s Funeral*. London, 1700.

———. *Rump, or an Exact Collection of the Choycest Poems 1639–61*. London, 1662.

Brown, T., ed. *Familiar Letters of Love and Gallantry*. London, 1718.

———. *The Late Converts Exposed: Or, the Reasons of Mr. Bays changing his Religion*. 1688.

———. *Letters from the Dead to the Living*. London, 1702.

———. *The Whole Comical Works of Monsr. Scarron*. London, 1703.

———. *The Works of Mr. Thomas Brown*. London, 1715.

Bruce, Thomas, Earl of Ailesbury and Elgin. *Memoirs, Written by Himself*. London, 1890.

Burnet, Gilbert. *Bishop Burnet's History of His Own Time*. Oxford, 1833.

———. *An Enquiry into the Measures of Submission to the Supream Authority*.

———. *A Second Collection of Several Tracts and Discourses Written in the Years 1686, 1687, 1689*. London, 1689.

———. *Some Passages of the Life and Death of the right honourable John Earl of Rochester who died 26 July, 1680*. London, 1680.

Byam, William, 'The Description of Guiana', BL Sloane 3662.

———. *An Exact Relation of The Most Execrable Attempts of John Allin, Committed on the Person of His Excellency Francis Lord Willoughby of Parham, Captain General of the Continent of Guiana, and of all the Caribby-Island, and our Lord Proprietor*. London, 1665.

Calendars of State Papers Domestic, Colonial and *Venice*.

Calendar of Treasury Books.

Carte, Thomas. *An History of the Life of James, Duke of Ormond*. 1736. Oxford, 1851.

A Catalogue of the Damages for which the English demand Reparation from the United Netherlands. London, 1664.

Cavendish, Margaret, Duchess of Newcastle. *Philosophical and Physical Opinions*. 1655.

———. *Sociable Letters*. 1664.

———. 'A True Relation of my Birth, Breeding and Life', *Nature's Picture's drawn by Fancies Pencil to the Life*. London, 1666.

Cellier, Elizabeth. *Malice Defeated*. London, 1680.

Child, Sir Josiah. *A New Discourse of Trade*. London, 1694.

Cibber, Colley. *An Apology for the Life of Mr. Colley Cibber, Comedian*. Ed. Robert W. Lowe. New York, 1889.

[Cibber, Theophilus]. *Lives of the Poets of Great Britain and Ireland, to the Time of Dean Swift*. London, 1753.

A Comparison Between the Two Stages. London, 1702.

Confessions and Manner of the Execution of the Three Notorious, Outlandish Ruffians. London, 1682.

Cowley, Abraham. *The Essays and Other Prose Writings*. Ed. Alfred B. Gough. Oxford, 1915.

———. *Poems: Miscellanies, The Mistress, Pindarique Odes*. Ed. A. R. Waller. Cambridge, 1905.

Creech, Thomas. *T. Lucretius Carus, the Epicurean Philosopher, his six books De Natura Rerum Done into English Verse*. Oxford, 1682.

Crocker, Edward. *England's Pen-Man: Crocker's New Copy-Book*. London, 1671.

Crowne, John. *The English Friar*. London, 1690.

Dangerfield, Thomas. *Don Tomazo*. London, 1680.

D'Aulnoy, Marie Catherine. *Memoirs of the Court of England in 1675*. Trans. Mrs. William Henry Arthur. London, 1913.

Davenant, Sir William. *The Dramatic Works of Sir William Davenant*. Eds James Maidment and W. H. Logan. London, 1872–4.

Davies, John, trans. *The History of the Caribby-Islands*. London, 1666.

Dennis, John. *Works*. London, 1718.

De Witt, Johan. *Brievan aan Johan de Witt 1660–72*. Eds R. Fruin and N. Japikse. Historich Genootschap, 1922.

Digby, Kenelm, and George Sibscota. *The Deaf and Dumb Man's Discourse including the Method they use, to manifest the sentiments of their Mind*. London, 1670.

Dillon, Wentworth, Earl of Roscommon. *Essay On Translated Verse*. London, 1685.

Downes, John. *Roscius Anglicanus*. Eds Judith Milhous and Robert D. Hume. London, The Society for Theatre Research, 1987.

Dryden, John. *Works of John Dryden*. Eds Edward Niles Hooker, H. T. Swedenberg, *et al.* Berkeley, 1955

———. *Letters*. Ed. Charles Ward. Durham, N.C., 1942.

Dunn, Richard S. *Sugar and Slaves: The Rise of the Planter Class in the English West Indies, 1624–1713*. Chapel Hill, 1972.

D'Urfey, Thomas. *Sir Barnaby Whigg*. London, 1682.

Du Tertre, Jean Baptiste. *Histoire générale des Antilles habitées par les François*. Paris, 1667–71.

Eachard, John. *The Grounds and Occasions of the Contempt of the Clergy and Religion Enquired into*. London, 1670.

'Ephelia'. *Female Poems on Several Occasions*. London, 1679.

Etherege, Sir George. *Plays*. Ed. Michael Cordner. Cambridge, 1982.

———. *The Poems of Sir George Etherege*. Ed. James Thorpe. Princeton, 1963.

Evelyn, John. *The Diary of John Evelyn*. Ed. E. S. de Beer. Oxford, 1955.

———. *The Diary and Correspondence of John Evelyn*. Ed. William Bray. London, 1906.

———. *Sylva, or A Discourse of Forest-Trees*. London, 1664.

An Exact Survey of the Affaires Of the United Netherlands. London, 1665.

Familiar Letters: Written by the Right Honourable John Late Earl of Rochester with Letters Written by the Most Ingenious Mr. Thomas Otway. London, 1697.

The Female Tatler. Ed. Fidelis Morgan. London, 1992.

Filmer, Sir Robert. *Patriarcha*. London, 1680.

Finch, Anne, Countess of Winchilsea. *Selected Poems of Anne Finch Countess of Winchilsea*. Ed. Katharine M. Rogers. New York, 1979.

Gheradi, Evariste. *Le Théâtre Italien*. Paris, 1695.

Gibson, Thomas. *The Anatomy of Human Bodies Epitomis'd*, 1682.

Gildon, Charles. *The Life of Mr. Thomas Betterton*. London, 1710.

———. *The Post-Boy rob'd of his Mail*. 2nd edn, London, 1706.

———. *The Golden Spy: Or a political Journal of the British Nights Entertainment*. London, 1679.

———. (Rev.) *Lives and Characters of the English Dramatick Poets*. London, 1699.

———. *Miscellaneous Letters and Essays*. London, 1694.

Godwin, Francis. *The Man in the Moon*. London, 1629.

Gould, Robert. *Satires against Women*. Los Angeles, 1976.

———. *The Play-House. A Satire*. London, 1689.

Granger, James. *Letters between the Rev. J. G. and many of the most eminent literary men of his time*. Ed. J. P. Malcolm. London, 1805.

Granville, George. *The Genuine Works in Verse and Prose, of the Right Honourable George Granville*. London, 1732.

Graunt, John. *Natural and Political Observations on the Bills of Mortality*. London, 1662.

Great News from the Barbadoes. London, 1676.

Grey, Ford, Lord. *The Secret History of the Rye-House Plot; and of Monmouth's Rebellion. Written by Ford, Lord Grey in 1685. Now first published from a manuscript, sign'd by himself*. London, 1754.

Halkett, Anne. *The Memoirs of Anne, Lady Halkett and Ann, Lady Fanshawe*. Ed. John Loftis. Oxford, 1979.

Hamilton, Anthony. *Memoirs of the Court of Charles II by Count Grammont.* Bickers, 1906.

Head, Richard. *The English Rogue described, in the Life of Meriton Latroon, a Witty Extravagant.* London, 1666.

[Hickeringill, Edmund.] *The Mushroom: or, A Satyr In Answer to a Satyre against Sedition. Called The Medal.* London, 1682.

Higden, Henry. *A Modern Essay on the Thirteenth Satyr of Juvenal.* London, 1986.

Historical Manuscript Commission Reports: De Lisle and Dudley MS, Ormonde MS, Hastings MS.

Hobbes, Thomas. *Leviathan.* Ed. R. Tuck. Cambridge, 1991.

Howard, Edward. *The Six Days Adventure or the New Utopia.* London, 1671.

Howell, James. *Epistolae Ho-Elianae. Familiar Letters, domestic and forren.* London, 1655.

Hoyle, John. *Bibliotheca Hoyleana.* 1692.

Hutchinson, Lucy. *Memoirs of the Life of Colonel Hutchinson.* London, 1965.

Hyde, Edward, Earl of Clarendon. *The History of the Great Rebellion and Civil Wars in England.* Ed. W. Dunn Macray. Oxford, 1887.

———. *Clarendon State Papers.*

James II. 'Life of James II 1660–98, written by Himself', *Original Papers.* Ed. J. MacPherson. London, 1775.

Johnson, Samuel. *Lives and Characters of the English Poets.* London, 1779–81.

Johnston, Nathaniel. *The Excellency of Monarchical Government, Especially of the English Monarchy.* London, 1686.

Jones, Eldred. *Othello's Countrymen.* London, 1965.

Jonson, Ben. *Ben Jonson.* Eds C. H. Herford and Percy and Evelyn Simpson. Oxford, 1925–52.

Juvenalis Redivivus. London, 1683.

Killigrew, Thomas. *Comedies and Tragedies.* London, 1664.

Kirkman, Francis. *The Counterfeit Lady Unveiled.* London, 1673.

———. *The Unlucky Citizen.* London, 1673.

La Calprenède, Gauthier de. *Cassandra: The Fam'd Romance.* London, 1661.

———. *Cléopâtre.* Paris, 1647–56.

Lacy, John. *The Dumb Lady: Or, The Farriar Made Physician.* London, 1672.

Langbaine, Gerard. *An Account of the English Dramatic Poets.* Oxford, 1691.

Lee, Nathaniel. *On the Death of Mrs. Behn.* London, 1689.

———. *Works.* Eds Thomas B. Stroup and Arthur L. Cooke. New Brunswick, 1954.

L'Estrange, Sir Roger. *Five Love-Letters from a Nun to a Cavalier.* London, 1678.

———. *The Observator.* London, 1681–7.

A Letter from Amsterdam to a Friend in England. London, 1684.

A Letter from a Person of Quality to his Friend in the Country, c. 1675.

A Letter to Ferguson. London, 1684.

The Life and Death of Mistress Rump. London, 1660.

Ligon, Richard. *A True and Exact History of the Island of Barbados.* London, 1657.

The London Mercury. 1682.

Lovelace, Robert. *Poems.* Ed. C. H. Wilkinson. Oxford, 1930.

The Loyal Protestant and true Domestick Intelligence. London, 1682.

Ludlow, Edmund. *A Voyage from The Watch Tower.* Ed. A. B. Worden, Camden 4th series, vol. 21. London, Royal Historical Society, 1978.

Luttrell, Narcissus. *A Brief Relation of State Affairs from September 1678 to April 1714.* Farnborough, Hants, 1969.

Makin, Bathsua. *An Essay to Revive the Antient Education of Gentlewomen.* London, 1673.

Manley, Delarivier. *The New Atalantis.* Ed. Ros Ballaster. London, 1991.

Mansell, R. *An Exact and True Narrative of the Late Popish Intrigue to Form a Plot and Then to cast the Guilt and Odium Thereof Upon the Protestants.* London, 1680.

Marvell, Andrew. *The Growth of Popery and Arbitrary Government.* Amsterdam, 1677.

———. *The Poems and Letters of Andrew Marvell.* Ed. H. M. Margoliouth. Oxford, 1970.

Massinger, Philip. *The Guardian* in *Three New Playes.* London, 1655.

Mercurius Politicus. 1659.

Middleton, Thomas. *A Mad World, My Masters.* London, 1608.

Mistress Rump brought to bed of a Monster. London, 1660.

Molière (Jean-Baptiste Poquelin). *The Plays of Molière in French and English.* Ed. A. R. Waller. Edinburgh, 1907.

Monmouth Routed, and Taken Prisoner, with his Pimp the Lord Gray. London, 1685.

Montaigne, Michel de. 'On the Cannibals', *The Complete Essays.* Trans. M. A. Screech. Harmondsworth, 1993.

Morrice, Roger. 'Entring Book', Dr Williams's Library, Morrice MSS.Q. London.

Natural and Political Observations on the Bills of Mortality. London, 1662.

Neville, Henry. *Newes from the New-Exchange, Or, The Common-wealth of Ladies, Drawn to the Life, in their severall Characters and Concernments*. London, 1650.

A New Dictionary of the Canting Crew. c. 1690.

Newdigate Newsletter. London, 1683.

The Observator. London, 1682.

Osborne, Dorothy. *The Letters from Dorothy Osborne to Sir William Temple*. London, 1942.

Otway, Thomas. *Plays*. London, 1713.

The Parliament of Ladies. London, 1647.

Payne, Henry Nevil. *The Siege of Constantinople*. London, 1675.

Pepys, Samuel. *The Diary of Samuel Pepys*. Eds Robert Latham and William Matthews. London, 1983.

'A Pindarick To Mrs. Behn on her Poem on the Coronation. Written by a Lady', *Lycidus*. London, 1688.

A Plain and Easie Method: Shewing How the Office of Overseer of the Poor may be managed. London, 1686.

Playford's History of Music. 4th edn, 1687.

Poems on Affairs of State. Eds G. de F. Lord, W. J. Cameron, G. M. Crump, E. H. Ellis, E. F. Mengel and H. H. Schloss. New Haven, 1963–71.

Poems on Affairs of State for the Year 1620 to the Year 1707. London, 1716.

Polwhele, E. *The Frolicks*. Eds J. Milhous and R. Hume. Ithaca, 1977.

Pope, Alexander. *Poetical Works*. Ed. Herbert Davis. Oxford, 1978.

Powell, George. *The Treacherous Brother*. London, 1690.

Prior, Matthew. *The Literary Works*. Oxford, 1971.

Radcliffe, Alexander. *The Ramble*. London, 1692.

Ralegh, Sir Walter. *Discoverie of the large, rich and beautiful Empyre of Guiana, with a Relation of the great and Golden Citie of Manoa (which the Spanyards call El Dorado). Performed in the yeare 1595*. London, 1596.

———. *Sir Walter Ralegh's apology for his last voyage to Guiana*.

Ravenscroft, Edward, *The Careless Lovers*. London, 1673.

———. *Dame Dobson, the Cunning Woman*. London, 1684.

———. *The London Cuckolds*. London, 1682.

———. *Scaramouche a Philosopher, Harlequin a School-boy*. London, 1677.

Reresby, Sir John. *Memoirs of Sir John Reresby*. Ed. Andrew Browning. Glasgow, 1936.

Riddle of the Roundhead. An Excellent New Ballad.

Ringrose, Basil. *The dangerous Voyage and bold attempts of Captain B. Sharp and others upon the coasts of the South Seas. From the original Journal of the Voyage, written by B. Ringrose*. London, 1684.

————. *The History of the Bucaniers of America; From their First Original down to this Time*. London, 1699.

Roxburghe Ballads. Eds William Chappell and Joseph Woodfall. Hertford, 1871–99.

Rules of Civility. London, 1673.

Sackville, Charles, Earl of Dorset. *Poems*. Ed. Brice Harris. New York, 1979.

Sanford, R. *Surinam Justice. In the Case Of several persons proscribed by certain Usurpers of Power in that Colony*. London, 1662.

Savile, George, Marquis of Halifax. *The Lady's New-Year's Gift, Or, Advice to a Daughter*. London, 1688.

Savile, Henry. *The Savile Correspondence*. Ed. W. D. Cooper. London, 1858.

Scot, Thomas. 'Confessions and Transactions in the service of Parliament 1660', Stowe MS. 189.

Scudéry, Madeleine de. *Clelia: An Excellent New Romance*. Trans. J. Davies and G. Havers. London, 1678.

Settle, Elkanah. *The Female Prelate. The Life and Death of Pope Joan*. London, 1680.

————. *The Empress of Morocco*. London, 1673.

Shadwell, Thomas. *The Works of Thomas Shadwell*. Ed. Montague Summers. London, 1927.

Sheffield, John, Earl of Mulgrave. *An Essay upon Poetry*. London, 1682.

Southerne, Thomas. *Oroonoko*. London, 1696.

————. *Sir Anthony Love*. London, 1690.

The Speeches and Prayers of Major General Harrison, Mr. J. Carew, Mr Justice Cooke, Mr. H. Peters, Mr. T. Scott. Together with Severall Occasionall Speeches and Passages in their Imprisonment til they came to the Place of Execution. London, 1660.

Stevenson, Matthew. *Wits Paraphras'd: Or, Paraphrase upon Paraphrase. In Burlesque on the Several Late Translators of Ovid's Epistles*. London, 1680.

Strada, Famians. *The History of the Low-Country Warres: Relating The Battles, Sieges, and Sea-Fights*. Transl. Sir Robert Stapleton. London, 1667.

Strange News from Virginia; being a Full and True Account of the Life and Death of Nathaniel Bacon Esquire. London, 1677.

Tales and Jests of Mr Hugh Peters. London, 1660.

Tatham, John. *The Rump*. London, 1660.

Thurloe, John. *Collection of State Papers*. Ed. T. Birch, 7 vols. 1742.

The Tixall Letters; or, the Correspondence of the Aston family, and their friends, during the Seventeenth Century. Ed. A. Clifford. Edinburgh, 1815.

Tonson, Jacob. *Jacob Tonson in Ten Letters by and about him*. Eds Sarah Lewis and Carol Clapp. Austin, Texas, 1948.

A True and Perfect Narrative of the Great and Signal Success of a Part of His Majesties Fleet...within the Ulie. London, 1666.

A True Description of the Bull-Feast. London, 1683.

A True Narrative of the Rise, Progresse and Cessation of the Late Rebellion in Virginia. 1676. London, 1676.

True Protestant Mercury. London, 1683.

The Tryal and Sentence of Elizabeth Cellier. London, 1680.

The Tryal of William, Viscount Stafford, for High Treason. London, 1681.

Trye, Mary. *Medicatrix, or the Woman Physician*. London, 1675.

Tryon, Thomas. *Friendly Advice to the Gentlemen-Planters of the East and West Indies*. London, 1684.

van Berbel, Adriaan. *Travels in south America, between the Berbice and Essequito Rivers and in Suriname (1670–1689)*. Trans. Walter E. Roth. Georgetown, Guyana, 1925.

Villiers, George, Duke of Buckingham. *The Rehearsal*. Ed. D. E. L. Crane. Durham, 1976.

Waller, Edmund. *Poems* and *Second Part*. London, 1690.

Ward, Ned. *The London Spy*. London, 1703.

Warren, George. *An Impartial Description of Surinam upon The Continent of Guiana in America. With a History of several strange Beasts, Birds, Fishes, Serpents, Insects, and Customs of that Colony etc*. London, 1667.

Whitelock, Bulstrode. *Memorials of the English Affairs*. Oxford, 1853.

Wilkes, John. *A General View of the Stage*. London, 1762.

Wilmot, John. *Letters of John Wilmot, Earl of Rochester*. Ed. Jeremy Treglown. Oxford, 1980.

———. *Poems of John Wilmot, Earl of Rochester*. Ed. Keith Walker. Oxford, 1984.

Wilson, John. *The Cheats*. London, 1664.

Wolseley, Robert. *Preface to Valentinian*. London, 1684.

Wood, Anthony à. *Athenae Oxonienses*. 1691–92.

———. *The Life and Times of Anthony à Wood, antiquary of Oxford 1632–1695 described by Himself*. Collected by Andrew Clark. Oxford, 1891.

Woolley, Hannah. *Gentlewoman's Companion*. London, 1675.

Wright, James. *Historia Histrionica: An historical account of the English stage shewing the ancient use, improvement, and perfection of dramatick representations in this nation*. London, 1699.

————. *Humours and Conversations of the Town*. London, 1693.

Wroth, Lady Mary. *The Countess of Montgomerie's Urania*. 1621.

————. *The Poems of Lady Mary Wroth*. Ed. Josephine A. Roberts. Baton Rouge, Louisiana, 1983.

Wycherley, William. *Miscellany Poems*. London, 1704.

————. *Plays*. Ed. Arthur Friedman. Oxford, 1979.

Selected Works Published after 1800

Anderson, P. B. 'Buckingham's chemist', *Times Literary Supplement*, 1935, p. 612.

Anselment, A. *Loyalist Resolve: Patient Fortitude in the English Civil War*. London, 1988.

Aughterson, Kate. *Aphra Behn: The Comedies*. Basingstoke, 2003

Ballaster, Ros. *Seductive Forms: Women's Amatory Fiction from 1684 to 1740*. Oxford, 1992.

Barash, Carol. *English Women's Poetry 1649–1714: Politics, Community and Linguistic Authority*. Oxford, 1996.

Beckles, Hilary. *White Servitude and Black Slavery in Barbados, 1627–1715*. Knoxville, Tennessee, 1989.

Bernbaum, Ernest. 'Mrs. Behn's *Oroonoko*', *George Lyman Kittredge Papers*. Boston, 1913, pp. 419–35.

Bowditch, Claire and Elaine Hobby eds. *Aphra Behn: New Questions and Contexts. Women's Writing*, 22, 1, 2015.

Bridenbaugh, Carl and Roberta. *No Peace Beyond the Line: The English in the Caribbean 1624–1690*. New York, 1972.

Brown, Laura. 'The romance of empire: *Oroonoko* and the trade in slaves', *The New 18th Century*. Eds Felicity Nussbaum and Laura Brown. London, 1987.

Cameron, W. J. 'George Granville and the "Remaines" of Aphra Behn', *Notes and Queries*, 204, 1959, pp. 88–92.

————. *New Light on Aphra Behn*. Auckland, 1961.

Cartwright, Julia. *Sacharissa*. London, 1901.

Carver, Larry. 'Rochester's Valentinian', *Restoration and Eighteenth-Century Theatre Review*, IV, 1, Summer 1989, pp. 25–38.

Causton, S. F. K. *Howard Papers*. London, 1862.

Chalmers, Hero. *Royalist Women Writers 1650–1689*. Oxford, 2004.

Chester, Joseph. *The Marriage, Baptismal, and Burial Registers of the Collegiate Church or Abbey of Saint Peter Westminster*. Harleian Society, 1876.

Copeland, Nancy. *Staging Gender in Behn and Centlivre: Women's Comedy and the Theatre*. Aldershot, 2004.

Corman, Brian. *Genre and Generic Change in English Comedy 1660–1710*. Toronto, 1993.

Crawford, Patricia. 'The Sucking Child: Adult Attitudes to Child Care in the First Year of Life in Seventeenth-century England', *Continuity and Change*, 1, 1986.

———. 'Women's Published Writings, 1600–1700', *Women in English Society, 1500–1800*. Ed. Mary Prior. London, 1985.

Cressey, David. *Bonfires and Bells: National Memory and the Protestant Calendar in Elizabethan England*. London, 1989.

Crompton, Virginia, '"Forced to write for bread and not ashamed to owne it": Aphra Behn, Court Poetry and Professional Writing in the 1680s'. Diss., UEA, Norwich, 1994.

Crum, Margaret. *First-Line Index of English Poetry, 1500–1800, in Manuscripts in the Bodleian Library*. Oxford, 1969.

Cuder-Dominguez, Pilar. '"That dead commodity, a wife": Sexual and Domestic Economy in Aphra Behn's Comedies'. *Domestic Arrangements in Early Modern England*. Ed. Kari Boyd McBride. Pittsburgh, 2002, 103–23.

Curwen, Henry. *History of Booksellers*. London, 1873.

Danchin, Pierre. *The Prologues and Epilogues of the Restoration, 1660–1700*. Nancy, 1981–8.

Day, R. A. 'Aphra Behn's First Biographer', *Studies in Bibliography*, 22, 1969, pp. 227–40.

Dhuicq, Bernard. 'Further Evidence on Aphra Behn's Stay in Surinam', *Notes and Queries*, new ser., no. 6 (December 1979), pp. 524–6.

Duchovnay, G. 'Aphra Behn's Religion', *Notes and Queries*, 221 (1976), pp. 235–7.

Duffy, Maureen. *The Passionate Shepherdess: Aphra Behn 1640–1689*. London, 1977, rev. 1989.

Dugaw, Diane. *Warrior Women and Popular Balladry, 1650–1850*. Cambridge, 1990.

Everitt, A. *The Community of Kent in the Great Rebellion*. Leicester, 1973.

Ezell, Margaret. *The Patriarch's Wife: Literary Evidence and the History of the Family*. Chapel Hill, N.C., 1987.

Ferguson, Margaret 'The authorial ciphers of Aphra Behn', *Cambridge Companion to English Literature 1650–1740*. Ed. S. Zwicker. Cambridge, 2004.

———. 'Juggling the Categories of Race, Class, and Gender: Aphra Behn's *Oroonoko*', *Women's Studies*, 19, 1991.

Fitzmaurice, James. 'Aphra Behn and the Abrahams Sacrifice Case'. *Huntington Library Quarterly*. 56, no. 3, 1993, pp. 319–27.

Fraser, Antonia. *King Charles II*. London, 1979.

———. *The Weaker Vessel*. London, 1984.

Fraser, Peter. *The Intelligence of the Secretaries of State and their Monopoly of Licensed News 1660–1688*. Cambridge, 1956.

Freud, Sigmund. 'On Narcissism', *Metapsychology: The Theory of Psychoanalysis*. Harmondsworth, 1985.

Frohock, Richard. *Heroes of Empire: The British Imperial Protaganist in America 1596–1764*. Newark, NJ, 2004.

Gallagher, Catherine. 'Embracing the absolute: the politics of the female subject in seventeenth-century England', *Genders* I, 1988, pp. 24–39.

Gallagher, Catherine, with Simon Stern, ed. *Oroonoko*. Boston, 2000.

Goldie, Mark. 'The Roots of True Whiggism 1688–94', *History of Political Thought*, 1, 1980.

Goldie, Mark, Tim Harris and Paul Seaward, eds. *The Politics of Religion in Restoration England*. Oxford, 1990.

Goreau, Angeline. *Reconstructing Aphra: A Social Biography of Aphra Behn*. New York, 1980.

Gorges, Raymond. *The Story of a Family through Eleven Centuries, being a History of the Family of Gorges*. Boston, 1944.

Gray, G. J. 'The Diary of Jeffrey Boys of Gray's Inn, 1671', *Notes and Queries*, 159, 1930, pp. 452–6.

Greene, Graham. *Lord Rochester's Monkey*. London, 1974.

Greer, Germaine. 'Honest Sam Briscoe', *A Genius for Letters: Booksellers and Bookselling from the 16th to the 20th Century*. Eds Robin Myers and Michael Harris. Winchester, 1995.

———. *Slip-Shod Sybils: Recognition, Rejection and the Woman Poet*. London, 1995.

Greer, Germaine, Susan Hastings, Jeslyn Medoff and Melinda Sansone, eds. *Kissing the Rod: An Anthology of Seventeenth-century Women's Verse*. London, 1988.

Grew, Marion. *William Bentinck and William III*. London, 1924.

Guffey, George. 'Aphra Behn's *Oroonoko*: occasion and accomplishment', *Two English Novelists*. Los Angeles, 1975.

Haley, K. H. D. *The First Earl of Shaftesbury*. Oxford, 1968.

Ham, Roswell Gray. *Otway and Lee: Biography from a Baroque Age*. New Haven, 1931.

Hammond, Paul. 'The Prologue and Epilogue to Dryden's *Marriage A-la-Mode*', *PBSA*, 81, no. 8, 1987.

Harbage, Alfred. *Thomas Killigrew Cavalier Dramatist 1612–83*. Philadelphia, 1930.

————. *Annals of English Drama 975–1700*. Ed. S. Schoenbaum. London, 1964.

Hargreaves, H. A. 'New Evidence of the Realism of Mrs. Behn's "Oroonoko"', *Bulletin of the New York Public Library*, 74, pp. 437–44.

Harlow, V. T., ed. *Colonising Expeditions to the West Indies and Guiana*. Hakluyt Society, 2nd ser., 56. London, 1925.

Harris, Brice. 'Aphra Behn's "Bajazet to Gloriana"', *Times Literary Supplement*, 9 Feb. 1933, p. 92.

————. 'Robert Julian, Secretary to the Muses', *Journal of English Literary History*, 10, 1943, pp. 294–309.

Harris, Tim. *London Crowds in the Reign of Charles II*. Cambridge, 1987.

Heal, F. *Hospitality in Early Modern England*. Oxford, 1990.

Henderson, K. U. and B. F. McManus, eds. *Half Humankind: Contexts and Texts of the Controversy about Women in England 1540–1640*. Urbana, 1985.

Hensbergen, Claudine van. '"Why I Write Them, I Can Give No Account": Aphra Behn and "Love Letters to a Gentleman"'. *Eighteenth-Century Life*, 35. 1 (Winter 2011), 65–82.

Highfill, Philip H., Kalman A. Burnim and Edward A. Langhans, eds. *A Biographical Dictionary of Actors, Actresses, Musicians, Dancers, Managers and Other Stage Personnel in London, 1600–1800*. Carbondale, 1973–87.

Hill, Christopher. *The World Turned Upside Down*. Harmondsworth, 1975.

————. *Writing and Revolution in 17th Century England*. Brighton, 1985.

Hobby, Elaine. *Virtue of Necessity: English Women's Writing 1649–88*. London, 1988.

Holmesland, Oddvar. *Utopian Negotiations: Aphra Behn & Margaret Cavendish*. Syracuse, 2013.

Hopkins, Paul. 'Aphra Behn and John Hoyle: A Contemporary Mention, and Sir Charles Sedley's Poem on his Death', *Notes and Queries*, 239 (June 1994), pp. 176–85.

Hoppe, Harry R. 'English Actors at Ghent in the Seventeenth Century', *Review of English Studies*, 25, 1949, pp. 305–21.

Howe, Elizabeth. *The First English Actresses*. Cambridge, 1992.

Hughes, Derek. 'The Masked Woman Revealed; or, the Prostitute and the Playwright in Aphra Behn Criticism'. *Women's Writing*, 7, 2, 2000, 149–64.

————. *The Theatre of Aphra Behn*. Basingstoke, 2001.

————. Ed. *Versions of Blackness: Oroonoko, Race and Slavery*. Cambridge, 2007.

Hume, R. 'The Dorset Garden Theatre', *Theatre Notebook*, 33, 1979, pp. 12–13.

Hunt, Leigh. 'Poetry of British Ladies', *The Companion*, 14 May 1828.

Huttner, Heidi, ed. *Rereading Aphra Behn: History, Theory, and Criticism*. Charlottesville, 1993.

Hutton, Ronald. *The Restoration*. Oxford, 1986.

Jacobsen, Gertrude Ann. *William Blathwayt: A Late Seventeenth-Century English Administrator*. New Haven, 1932.

James, M. 'English Politics and the Concept of Honour', *Past and Present* Supplement 3, 1978.

Jones, George Hilton. *Convergent Forces: Immediate Causes of the Revolution of 1688 in England*. Ames, Iowa, 1990.

Jones, Jane. 'New Light on the Background and Early Life of Aphra Behn', *Notes and Queries*, repr. *Aphra Behn Studies*, ed. Janet Todd. Cambridge, 1996.

Jones, J. R. *Country and Court: England, 1658–1714*. London, 1978.

Kenyon, J. P. *The Popish Plot*. Harmondsworth, 1974.

———. *Robert Spencer, Earl of Sunderland 1641–1702*. Cambridge, 1958.

Kitchin, George. *Sir Roger L'Estrange: A Contribution to the History of the Press in the Seventeenth Century*. London, 1913.

Knight, Stephen. *The Killing of Justice Godfrey*. London, 1984.

Kofman, Sarah. *The Enigma of Woman*. Ithaca, 1985.

Kunzel, David. *The Early Comic Strip*. Berkeley, 1973.

Lachs, Phyllis S. *The Diplomatic Corps under Charles II and James II*. New Brunswick, 1965.

Langhans, Edward. *Eighteenth-century British and Irish Promptbooks: A Descriptive Bibliography*. New York, 1987. *Restoration Promptbooks*. Carbondale, 1981.

Laqueur, Thomas. *Making Sex: Body and Gender from the Greeks to Freud*. Cambridge, Mass., 1990.

Lewcock, Dawn. 'More for seeing than hearing: Behn and the use of theatre', *Aphra Behn Studies*. Ed. Janet Todd. Cambridge, 1996.

Lewis, B. *British Contributions to Arabic Studies*. London, 1941.

Lipking, Joanna, ed. *Oroonoko*. New York, 1997.

The Lismore Papers, 2nd Series, ed. A. B. Grosart. Private Circulation, 1888.

Lougee, Carolyn. *Le Paradis des femmes: Women, Salons and Social Stratification in Seventeenth-century France*. Princeton, 1976.

Love, Harold. *Scribal Publication in Seventeenth-Century England*. Oxford, 1993.

Luhring, Alan. 'The Music of John Banister'. Diss., Stanford, 1966.

Lynch, Kathleen M. *Jacob Tonson, Kit-Cat Publisher*. Knoxville, 1971.

Macfarlane, Allen. *The Family Life of Ralph Joscelyn*. Cambridge, 1970.

Marshall, Alan, '"Memorialls for Mrs Affora": Aphra Behn and the Restoration Intelligence World'. *Women's Writing*, 221, 2015.

McCartney, Martha W. 'Cockacoeske, Queen of Pamunkey: Diplomat and Suzeraine', *Powhatan's Mantle: Indians in the Colonial Southeast*. Eds Peter H. Wood, Gregory Waselkov and Thomas A. Hatley. Lincoln, Nebraska, 1990, pp. 173–95.

Mendelson, Sara Heller. 'Stuart Women's Diaries and Occasional Memoirs', *Women in English Society 1500–1800*. Ed. M. Prior. London, 1985.

The Mental World of Stuart Women, Three Studies. Brighton, 1987.

Mermin, Dorothy, 'Women becoming poets: Katherine Philips, Aphra Behn, Anne Finch', *English Literary History*, 57, 1990.

Milhous, Judith. 'The Duke's Company's Profits, 1675–1677', *Theatre Notebook*, 32, 1978, pp. 76–88.

Milhous, Judith and Robert Hume. 'Attribution Problems in English Drama, 1660–1700', *Harvard Library Bulletin*, 31, 1983, 5–39.

———. 'Dating Play Premières from Publication Data, 1660–1700', *Harvard Library Bulletin*, 22, 1974, pp. 374–405.

Miller, J. *Popery and Politics in England 1660–1688*. Cambridge, 1973.

Munns, Jessica. *Restoration Politics and Drama: The Plays of Thomas Otway*. Newark, Del., 1995.

———. '"But to the touch were soft": pleasure, power, and impotence in "The Disappointment" and "The Golden Age"', *Aphra Behn Studies*. Ed. Janet Todd. Cambridge, 1996.

Nicoll, Allardyce. *A History of English Drama, 1660–1900*. Cambridge, 1952–9.

North, Roger. *The Lives of the Norths*. Ed. Augustus Jessopp. London, 1890.

O'Donnell, Mary Ann. *Aphra Behn: An Annotated Bibliography of Primary and Secondary Sources*. New York, 1986; 2nd edn Aldershot, 2004.

———. 'Private Jottings, Public Utterances: Aphra Behn's published writings and her commonplace book', *Aphra Behn Studies*. Ed. Janet Todd. Cambridge, 1996.

———. 'A Verse Miscellany of Aphra Behn: Bodleian Library MS Firth c.16', *English Manuscript Studies 1100–1700*, vol. 2. Eds Peter Beal and Jeremy Griffiths. Oxford, 1990.

O'Donnell, Mary Ann, Bernard Dhuiq and Guyonne Leduc, eds. *Aphra Behn (1640–1689) Identity, Alterity, Ambiguity*. Paris, 2000.

BIBLIOGRAPHY

Ogg, D. *England in the Reign of Charles II*. Oxford, 1955.

Oldys, William. 'Choice Notes', *Notes & Queries*, 2nd series, 2. London, 1861, pp. 201–2.

Oman, Carola. *Mary of Modena*. Bungay, Suffolk, 1962.

Orr, Leah. 'Attribution Problems in the Fiction of Aphra Behn'. *Modern Language Review*, 108, 1, 2013, 30–51.

Owen, Susan J. *Perspectives on Restoration Drama*, Manchester, 2002.

Pacheco, Anita. 'Reading Toryism in Aphra Behn's Cit-Cuckolding Comedies'. *Review of English Studies*, 55, 2004, 690–708.

Pacheco, Nancy, ed. *Early Women Writers: 1660–1720*. London, 1998.

Payne, Deborah C. '"And Poets shall by Patron-Princes live": Aphra Behn and Patronage', *Curtain Calls: British and American Women Writers and the Theater, 1688–1820*. Eds Mary Anne Schofield and Cecilia Macheski. Athens, Ohio, 1991.

Pearson, Jacqueline. *The Prostituted Muse: Images of Women and Women Dramatists 1642–1737*. Brighton, 1988.

Plomer, Henry R. *A Dictionary of Printers and Booksellers who were at work in England, Scotland and Ireland from 1668 to 1725*. Ed. Arundell Esdaile. Oxford, 1922.

Pocock, J. G. A. *Virtue, Commerce, and History: Essays on Political Thought and History*. Cambridge, 1985.

Pollock, L. A. 'Teach her to Live under Obedience: The Making of Women in the Upper Ranks of Early Modern England', *Continuity and Change*, 4, 1989.

Pontbriant, Comte de. *Histoire de la Principauté d'Orange*. Avignon, 1891.

Postma, Johannes Nenne. *The Dutch in the Atlantic Slave Trade 1660–1815*. Cambridge, 1990.

Pratt, Mary Louise. *Imperial Eyes: Travel Writing and Transculturation*. London, 1992.

Price, Cecil. *Cold Caleb: The Scandalous Life of Ford Grey First Earl of Tankerville 1655–1701*. London, 1956.

Publications of the Catholic Record Society.

Quaintance, Richard. 'French Sources of the Imperfect Enjoyment Poems', *Philological Quarterly*, 42, 1963, pp. 190–9.

Ramsaran, J. A. '"Oroonoko": A Study of the Factual Elements', *Notes and Queries*, ccv, 1960, p. 144.

Robinson, John Martin. *The Dukes of Norfolk: A Quincentennial History*. Oxford, 1982.

Rogers, Katharine M. 'Fact and fiction in Aphra Behn's *Oroonoko*', *Studies in the Novel*, 20, 1988.

Rosvall, Toivo David. *The Mazarine Legacy: The Life of Hortense Mancini, Duchess Mazarine*. New York, 1969.

Rowen, H. H. *John de Witt: Statesman of the True Freedom*. Cambridge, 1986.

Rubik, Margarete. 'Love's Merchandize: Metaphors of Trade and Commerce in the Plays of Aphra Behn'. *Women's Writing*, 19, 2, 2012, 222–37.

Salzman, Paul. *English Prose Fiction 1558–1700*. Oxford. 1985.

Schwoerer, Lois. 'Propaganda in the Revolution of 1688–89', *American Historical Review*, 82, 1977, pp. 843–74.

Scott, Jonathan. *Algernon Sidney and the English Republic, 1623–1677*. Cambridge, 1988.

———. *Algernon Sidney and the Restoration Crisis, 1677–1683*. Cambridge, 1991.

Sedgwick, Eve Kosofsky. *Between Men: English Literature and Male Homosocial Desire*. New York, 1985.

Sharpe, K. and Steven M. Zwicker, eds. *Politics and Discourse: The Literature and History of Seventeenth-Century England*. Berkeley, 1987.

Spence, Joseph. *Observations, Anecdotes, and Characters*. Ed. E. Malone. London, 1820.

Spufford, Margaret. *Small Books and Pleasant Histories: Popular Fiction and its Readership in Seventeenth-Century England*. London, 1981.

Stapleton, M. L. *Admired and Understood: The Poetry of Aphra Behn*. Newark, Del., 2004.

Staves, Susan. *Players' Sceptres: Fictions of Authority in the Restoration*. Lincoln, Nebraska, 1979.

Stone, L. *The Family, Sex and Marriage in England, 1500–1800*. London, 1977.

Summers, Montague. *The Restoration Theatre*. London, 1934.

Taylor, Charles. *Sources of the Self: The Making of the Modern Identity*. Cambridge, 1989.

Thickstun, Margaret Olofson. *Fictions of the Feminine: Puritan Doctrine and the Representation of Women*. Ithaca, 1988.

Thomas, Patrick. Introduction to *Collected Works of Katherine Philips, The Matchless Orinda*. Stump Cross, Essex, 1990.

Thompson, Roger. *Unfit for Modest Ears: A Study of Pornographic, Obscene and Bawdy Works Written or Published in England in the Second Half of the Seventeenth Century*. London, 1979.

Thorn-Drury, G., ed. *Covent Garden Drollery*. London, 1928.

Thorp, Willard. 'Henry Nevil Payne, Dramatist and Jacobite Conspirator', *The Parrott Presentation Volume*, ed. Hardin Craig. Princeton, 1935.

Todd, Janet. *The Critical Fortunes of Aphra Behn*. Rochester, N.Y., 1998.

———. *Gender, Art and Death*. Cambridge, 1993.

———. Ed. *Aphra Behn Studies*. Cambridge 1996.

Todd, Janet and Elizabeth Spearing, eds. *Counterfeit Ladies*. London, 1994.

Todd, Janet and Derek Hughes eds. *The Cambridge Companion to Aphra Behn*. Cambridge, 2004.

Treadwell, Michael. 'London Trade Publishers 1675–1750', *The Library*. 6th ser., 4, 1982, pp. 99–134.

Trumbach, R., 'Sodomitical Assaults, Gender Role, and Sexual Development in Eighteenth-Century London', *The Pursuit of Sodomy*. Eds K. Gerard and G. Hokma. New York, 1989, pp. 408–9.

Tuck, R. *Natural Rights Theories*. Cambridge, 1979.

Underwood, D. *Etherege and the Seventeenth-Century Comedy of Manners*. New Haven, 1957.

Van Lennep, William, ed. *The London Stage 1660–1800*. Carbondale, 1965.

Vander Motten, J. P. 'Unpublished Letters of Charles II', *Restoration*, Spring 1994, 18, 1, pp. 17–26.

———. 'Thomas Killigrew: A Biographical Note', *Revue belge de philologie et d'histoire*, LIII, 1975, 3, pp. 769–75.

Vander Motten J. P. and René Vermeir, '"Reality, and Matter of Fact": Text and Context in Aphra Behn's *The Fair Jilt*'. *Review of English Studies*, n.s, 66, 274, 2015, 280–99.

Verney, F. P. and M. M., eds. *Memoirs of the Verney Family during the Seventeenth Century*. London, 1925.

Vieth, David M. *Attributions in Restoration Poetry: A Study of Rochester's 'Poems' of 1680*. New Haven, 1963.

Virginia Magazine of History and Biography. 2:1, 1894, and 4:1, 1898.

Wallbank, M.V. 'Eighteenth-century Public Schools and the Education of the Governing Elite', *History of Education*, 8, 1979.

Walsh, Elizabeth and Richard Jeffries. 'The Excellent Mrs. Mary Beale'. Inner London Education Authority, 1975.

Ward, Estelle. *Christopher, Duke of Albemarle*. London, 1915.

Wiley, Autrey Neil, ed. *Rare Prologues and Epilogues 1642–1700*. London, 1940.

Williamson, James A. *English in Guiana 1604–68*. Oxford, 1923.

Wilson, John Harold. *Court Satires of the Restoration*. Columbus, Ohio, 1976.

Winn, James Anderson. *John Dryden and His World*. New Haven, 1987.

———. *'When Beauty Fires the Blood': Love and the Arts in the Age of Dryden*. Ann Arbor, 1992.

Wiseman, S. J. *Aphra Behn*. British Council, 1996.

Woodbridge, Linda. *Women and the English Renaissance: Literature and the Nature of Womankind, 1540–1620*. Urbana, 1986.

Woodcock, G. *The Incomparable Aphra*. London, 1948.

Woolf, Virginia. *A Room of One's Own*. Harmondsworth, 1992.

Zwicker, Steven M. *Politics and Language in Dryden's Poetry: The Arts of Disguise*. Princeton, 1984.

INDEX

Actresses, 129–30, 131, 132, 142–3, 156, 184, 358, 503n.28

Adams, John, 355

Adis, Henry, 31, 44

Alemán, Mateo, 311

Allin, Thomas, 49, 431

Amazons, 60, 153, 236, 295, 396, 409, 505n.25

Amboyna, massacre of, 74

Amery, John, 216, 225–6, 503n.30

Androgyny, androgynes, hermaphrodites, 162, 205, 374, 395–7, 507n.18

Angel, Edward, 137, 142, 150, 169

Anne, Princess, 247, 297, 333, 396, 419, 440, 447

Anti-clericalism, 299–300, 303, 333

Apollonius, 172

'Ariadne', xxvii

Aristocracy, aristocratic culture, xxvi, 6, 22, 60, 106, 156, 196, 197, 199, 208, 209, 236, 280, 314, 337, 350, 375; *see also* monarchy

Arlington, *see* Bennet

Armstrong, Thomas, 256, 309

Astell, Mary, 15

Aston, Walter, 134

Atoms, atomic theory, 172, 193, 198, 298, 300, 332, 452

Attwood, William, 270

Austen, Jane, 172

Baber, John, 420–3, 445

Bacon, Nathaniel, 429–30, 431–2, 435, 436

Baggs, Zachary, 364, 365, 371, 375

Bampfield, Joseph, Colonel, 25, 36, 77–8, 79, 80, 83, 89, 93–4, 97, 98, 101–5 passim, 112, 361, 404, 476n.11, 501n.19

Banister, James, 32, 44, 46, 48, 115, 435

Banister, John, 175, 179

Barbados, 29–30, 33, 34, 39, 43, 44, 45, 48, 62, 63, 65, 470n.9

Barker, Jane, 528n.35

Barlow, Francis, 388, 441

Barry, Elizabeth, 162, 177, 192, 194–5, 215, 217, 224, 247, 251, 260, 265, 266, 276, 283, 290, 344, 371, 498n.40, 521n.10

Barry, Esther, 195

Basso Anthony, 119–20

Beale, Mary, 204–5

Beaumont, Francis and John Fletcher, 126, 138, 326, 373, 471n.22

Bedingfeild, Edward, 161, 163

Behn, Aphra, birth and early life, 6–17, 284; character, personality, 76–7, 352, 402–3; child-bearing, 67, 294; copying, 14, 192, 255, 345, 365, 383; death, 450–2; desire for fame, xxx, 374, 427, 438, 446, 454; education, 16–17, 21–2, 27, 127, 155, 171–2, 262, 490n.15; friends, 204–6, 210–11, 395–7, 402; health, 266, 269, 302, 312, 330, 375–6, 399, 401, 404, 412, 434, 449, 450–1; love,

176–86, 191–2, for Hoyle, 312, 319, 352, 387, for women, 124, 177, 192–3, 396–7, 409; marriage, 63–7; payment/money, 71, 81–107 passim, 113, 117–18, 129, 146, 159, 163, 280–1, 295, 334–5, 353, 358, 360, 364–5, 367, 399, 407, 443, 451; playwriting, 126–7, 172, 236, 239, 245, 261, 287–8, 353; poetry, 157–8, 261, 300–1, 444; politics, 60–1, 139–40, 149–50, 157, 161, 185, 189, 229–30, 237, 250, 264, 274, 278, 281, 283–93, 295, 299–300, 310, 315–16, 319, 332, 337–9, 355, 365–7, 389–90, 398, 401–7, 421, 422–3, 428–9, 447–8, 493n.19; portraits of, 204–6, 293; prison, 104, 117–18; as professional, 158–9, 195, 239, 268, 337, 402, 421–3, 449; as propagandist, 281, 293, 296, 327–8, 329, 355; prose, 310–11, 347; relations with Colepepers and Sidneys, 18–25; religion, 11–13, 53, 172, 198–9, 272–3, 299–300, 382, 385, 401, 416, 452, 459n.35; satires and attacks on, 213–14, 237, 258, 264, 269–70, 293–7, 322–4, 336, 348–9, 376, 393, 434, 449; sexuality, 176–7, 183–4, 194, 200, 311–14, 323–4, 343; Surinam, 29–62; as Tory, 261, 274, 281, 355, 367, 403; translation, 262–4, 330–1, 410, 412–16, 424–7; and adaptation and borrowed plots, 148, 166, 188, 237, 265, 274, 282, 284, 288, 376–7; and Samuel Briscoe, 325, 326, 328, 521n.15; and Thomas Brown, 322–8, 543n.19; and Dryden, 335–6, 382–3; and fictive world, 371, 387, 390, 391, 394; and Gildon, 326, 328; Works: *Abdelazer*, 186–92, 193, 195, 214, 215, 251, 312, 372, 503n.30; 'Adventure of the Black Lady', 326–7, 522n.22; *Aesop's Fables*, 388–9; *Agnes de Castro*, 410–11, 412, 420, 424; *The Amorous Prince*, 119, 138, 148–53, 166, 190, 232, 235, 492n.12, 493n.21, 503n.30; 'Astrea's Booke', 365–6, 375, 382, 392, 420, 525n.6, 527n.18, 537n.3; 'A Ballad on Mr. J.H. To Amoret', 177, 492n.12; 'Cease, cease, *Aminta* to complain', 394; *The City-Heiress*, 281, 289–91, 293, 294, 312, 327, 357, 540n.11; 'Complaint of the poor Cavaliers', 522n.25; *Congratulatory Poem . . .On the Happy Birth of the Prince of Wales*, 419–20, 434, 436, 439; *Congratulatory Poem . . .On the Universal Hopes*, 418, 419, 421; *Congratulatory Poem to Queen Mary*, 447–8, 449; *Covent Garden Drolery*, 156–8, 164, 494n.23, 523n.37; 'Damon being asked a reason for Loveing', 313; *The Debauchee*, 216–17, 235, 266, 350, 389, 503nn.30 and 31, 505n.20; 'Dialogue for an Entertainment' 496n.7; 'The Disappointment', 201–3, 206, 208, 300, 332, 491n.5, 531n.27; *A Discovery of New Worlds*, 412–16, 417; 'The Dream', 484n.38; 'The Dumb Virgin', 118–19, 257, 451, 467n.4, 521n.19, 541n.5; *The Dutch Lover*, 9, 24, 166, 178, 181, 184, 187, 191, 215, 217, 219, 220, 236, 238, 239, 247, 280, 300, 327, 341, 353, 373, 416, 467n.1, 502n.22, 530n.22; *The Emperor of the Moon*, 12–13, 353, 376–9, 381, 413; 'Epitaph On the Tombstone of a Child', 339; 'Essay on Translated Prose', 412–15; *The Fair Jilt*, xxx,

108–11, 347, 382, 408, 423, 451, 463n.27, 482n.17; *The False Count*, 281–4, 286, 288, 303, 368, 369, 370, 387, 465n.4, 507n.19, 513n.15, 540n.10; 'A Farewell to Celladon', 209–10, 398, 443; *The Feign'd Curtizans*, 12, 119, 247–51, 253–4, 258, 265, 285, 295, 458n.30, 488n.8, 501n.13, 507n.11, 510nn.23 and 30, 512nn.54 and 1; *The Forc'd Marriage*, 64, 138–43, 147, 148, 151–2, 169, 190, 191, 214–15, 232, 311; *The History of the Nun*, 26, 27, 107, 119, 408–9, 428, 451, 519n.13, 521n.18; *The Hostory of Oracles*, 415–16; 'I led my Silvia to a Grove', 157–8; 'In Imitation of Horace', 496n.7; *Lady Grey's Ghost*, 519n.10; *La Montre*, 390–3, 394, 412; 'A Letter to a Brother of the Pen in Tribulation', 173, 200; 'A Letter to Mr. Creech at Oxford', 329; 'Letter to the Earl of Kildare', 521n.13; 'Love Arm'd', xxx, 186, 276, 393; 'Love-Letter', 178–83, 185, 326, 352; *Love-Letters between a Nobleman and his Sister* Part I, xxvi, xxx, 27, 107, 314–20, 321, 331, 337, 345, 346, 347, 348, 350, 353, 354, 372, 383, 391, 401, 402, 403, 404, 406, 521n.15; *Love-Letters* Part II, 347–50, 353, 364, 402, 403, 404; *Love-Letters* Part III, 349–52, 354, 363, 401–8, 435, 440; *The Luckey Chance*, xxx, 64, 95, 333–4, 367–75, 379, 381, 386, 417, 420, 432, 501n.13, 525n.51, 532n.46, 540n.10; *The Luckey Mistake*, 21, 443; *Lycidus*, 390, 393–7, 412, 417; 'Memoirs of the Court of the King of Bantam', 325–6, 522n.22; *Miscellany* 271, 323,

337–8, 339, 358; 'The Nun, or the Perjured Beauty', 522n.22; 'Oenone to Paris', 263–4, 337, 345; 'Of Plants', 424–6, 451; 'On Desire A Pindarick', xxx, 312–13, 317, 397; 'On a Copy of Verses made in a Dream', 176; 'On a Juniper-Tree, cut down to make Busks', 203–4, 425; 'On the Author of that Excellent Book . . .', 266; 'On the Death of Mr. Grinhil', 206; 'On the Death of E. Waller', 398–9; 'On the Death of the late Earl of Rochester', 267–8, 277, 452; 'On the first discovery of falseness in Amintas', 125; *Oroonoko* xxvii, 4–5, 9, 11, 31–58 passim, 62, 65, 76, 95, 142, 324, 325, 347, 408, 428, 434, 435, 436–9, 446, 482n.17; 'Our Cabal', 125, 161–3, 175, 176, 186, 264, 397, 499n.40, 522n.25; 'Ovid to Julia', 297; 'Paraphrase on the Lords Prayer', 339, 414; 'Pastoral Pindarick. On . . . Dorset', 197, 366; 'Pastoral to Mr. Stafford', 340, 533n.1; 'Pindaric to Mr. P. who sings finely', 175; *Pindaric Poem to the Reverend Doctor Burnet*, 425–8, 444–6, 448, 449; *Pindarick on the Death of Charles II*, 355–6, 358; *Pindarick on the Happy Coronation of . . . James II*, 72, 356–9, 366–7, 411, 418, 420, 432, 436; *Poem to Catherine Queen Dowager*, 356; *Poem to Sir Roger L'Estrange*, 242, 244, 246, 272–3, 424; *Poems upon Several Occasions*, 170, 334–6, 388, 508n.1; Prologue and epilogue to *Romulus*, 296, 333; Prologue to *Like Father, Like Son*, 281, 288–9, 294; Prologue to *Valentinian*, 344–5; 'The Return', 176; *The Revenge*, 266, 325–6, 458n.30; *The*

Roundheads, 281, 284–8, 285, 286, 289, 293, 310, 370, 429, 432, 433, 450, 458n.25, 468n.19, 514n.20, 537n.16, 539n.4; *The Rover*, xxx, 185, 217–26, 231, 235, 236, 247–50 passim, 274–8 passim, 281, 283, 286, 288, 289, 290, 291, 312, 319, 327, 346, 350, 353, 360, 367, 368, 369, 372, 377, 379, 426, 453, 503n.30, 519n.10; ['A Satyr on Dr. Dryden'], 381–3, 443, 524n.41; *The Second Part of the Rover*, xxx, 274–8, 283, 288–91 passim, 350, 353, 368, 369, 427, 532n.46; 'Sence of a Letter sent me', 489n.6; *Seneca Unmasqued*, 385–9, 390, 394, 451; 'Silvio's Complaint', 280; *Sir Patient Fancy*, xxx, 67, 155, 231–9, 246, 250, 289, 301, 303, 325, 346, 351, 367, 368, 370, 374, 451; 'Song. The Complaint', 144, 152; 'Song: 'Tis not your saying that you love', 192, 494n.28; 'Song. To a New *Scotch* Tune', 280; 'Song. To Pesibles Tune', 198, 409; 'Song; While, *Iris*, I at distance gaze', 535n.14; Songs . . . in the *Wavering Nymph*, 495n.7; 'To Mrs. Price', 192–3; 'To the Author of the *New Utopia*', 154; 'To Damon, to inquire of him . . .', 312; 'To Lysander, at the Musick-Meeting', 175–6; 'To Lysander, on some Verses he writ', 163–4; *To the Most Illustrious Prince Christopher Duke of Albemarle*, 398, 443; *To Poet Bavius*, 421–3, 438; 'To the Honourable Sir Francis Fane', 191; 'To Alexis in Answer to his Poem against Fruition', 340–1; 'To Alexis, On his saying, I lov'd a Man that talk'd much', 341–2, 391; 'To Amintas, Upon reading the lives

. . .', 178; 'To Henry Higden', 384; 'To Mrs. W. On her Excellent Verses', 269, 301; 'To my Lady Morland at Tunbridge', 124, 483n.32; 'To the fair Clarinda', 395–7; 'To the Unknown Daphnis', 298–302, 304, 385–6; *The Town-Fopp*, 214, 215, 216, 217, 222, 232, 250, 311, 367, 503n.30; 'A Translation: *Lydia, Lovely Maid*', 510n.25; 'The Unfortunate Happy Lady', 327, 467n.4; 'Verses . . . to be sent to a fair Lady', 192; *The Voyage to the Island of Love*, 330–3, 334–5, 347, 354, 382, 386, 388, 390, 391, 392, 393, 524n.48; *The Widdow Ranter*, 33, 42, 47, 53, 397, 428, 429–34, 435, 438, 488n.8, 530n.13, 534n.18; *The Young King*, 4, 35, 59, 61, 63, 69, 138, 143, 149, 152, 153, 167, 181, 190, 258, 259, 295, 488n.6; *The Younger Brother*, 33, 145, 345–6, 347, 351, 369, 395, 428, 453, 521n.14

Behn, Mr, 63–8, 71, 84, 91, 106, 108, 119, 120

Bellon, Dr, 375

Bennet, Henry, Earl of Arlington, 78–88 passim, 197–8, 99, 104–6, 112, 117, 118, 128–9, 140, 161, 226, 296, 302, 462n.22

Bennet, Isabella, later Duchess of Grafton, 288, 296

Bentley, Richard, 147, 215, 238, 311, 450, 503n.30

Berkeley, Lady Henrietta, 307–11, 314, 315, 316, 348, 361, 363, 403, 404, 526n.18

Betterton, Mary, 137–8, 141

Betterton, Thomas, 136, 137, 138, 141, 146, 164, 168, 169, 170, 188, 191, 205, 214, 215, 224, 231, 235, 237, 251, 265, 274, 290, 302, 334, 371, 453, 501n.14,

503n.28, 512n.2; *The Amorous Widow*, 486n.13

Biet, Antoine, 468n.15

Blathwayt, William, 66, 119–20, 467n.9

Blome, Richard, 8, 471n.19, 489n.6, 540n.7

Blount, Charles, 198, 415, 496n.14, 517n.25, 537n.2

Blow, John, 368

Boileau, Nicolas, 303

Bonnecorse, Balthazar de, 303, 390, 393

Booth, Sir George; Booth's uprising, 23, 25–6, 37, 410

Boothby, Frances, 134, 455n.6, 485n.3, 486n.15

Boscobel Oak, 3

Bourne, Benjamin, 176, 178, 352

Bowman, John, 368, 371, 501n.16

Boyle, Roger, first Earl of Orrery, 195

Boys, Jeffrey, 124–5, 141, 151, 162, 163, 176, 177, 331, 462n.15, 484n.38, 522n.25

Bracegirdle, Anne, 191, 323, 326, 540n.16

Brathwait, Richard, 487n.18

Brémond, Gabriel de, 311, 488n.5

Bridgeport, Battle of, 362

Briscoe, Samuel, 4, 203, 325, 326, 328, 494n.28, 495n.30, 516n.2, 521n.15, 543n.19

Brome, Richard, 216, 225, 389

Brothels, 2, 166, 197, 247, 251, 327, 500n.5

Brown, Daniel, 292, 515n.38

Brown, Thomas, 130, 322–5, 326, 327, 328, 335, 336, 339, 365, 366, 369, 383, 453, 485n.5, 491n.5, 494n.28, 495nn.1 and 2, 522n.19, 543nn.14 and 19; *Letters from the Dead*, 322–3, 365

Buckingham, *see* Villiers

Bunyan, John, 12

Burnet, Gilbert, 1, 2, 128, 163, 214, 241, 243, 253, 256, 266–7, 269, 270, 271, 276, 277, 290, 301, 339, 344, 360, 381, 424, 435, 439, 442–50 passim, 452, 476n.9, 506n.1, 508n.6, 518n.35

Butler, Charlotte, 265, 292

Butler, Edward, 112, 116, 118, 119, 161

Butler, James, Duke of Ormonde, 209

Byam, William, 30, 32, 34, 36, 37, 39, 43, 44–6, 48, 49, 50, 52, 60, 61–2, 67, 77, 80, 82, 95, 114, 435

Calderôn de la Barca, Pedro de, 59

Campbell, Archibald, Earl of Argyll, 439

Canning, William, 392, 450

Carleton, Mary, 16–17, 20, 71, 169, 241, 283, 392, 526n.18

Cary, Elizabeth, Viscountess Falkland, 455n.6

Castel Rodrigo, Marquis of, 81–2, 85, 109, 111

Castlemaine, *see* Palmer

Catherine of Braganza, 228, 242, 243, 244, 245, 279, 356, 419, 448, 499n.41

Catullus, 208

Cavendish, Jane and Elizabeth, 455n.6, 462n.15

Cavendish, Margaret, Duchess of Newcastle, 15, 126–7, 135, 146, 218, 413, 455n.6, 462n.15, 474n.15, 485nn.50, 3 and 7, 488n.9, 504n.11, 515n.29

Cavendish, William, Duke of Newcastle, 69, 485n.3

Cecil, James, Earl of Salisbury, 336, 337

Cellier, Elizabeth, 256–8, 270, 273, 296, 459n.35, 528n.26, 542n.6

Censorship, 147, 279

Centlivre, Susannah, xxvi

Cervantes, Miguel de, 148, 532n.44
Charles I, 9, 20, 138, 149, 151, 163, 241, 253, 278, 435, 436, 437, 475n.4, 529n.6
Charles II, 1–3, 9, 11, 25, 39, 55–6, 73, 79, 96–101 passim, 123, 130, 217–18, 258, 260, 276, 362, 425, 430, 436–7, 450, 533n.50; and Behn, 67–8, 96, 101, 209, 329, 355, 379, 448; death, 354–6, 451; and monarchy, 149, 358, 429; and Monmouth, 296; sexuality, 128, 214, 227, 228, 315, 343–4; and Oxford Parliament, 278–9; and Popish Plot, 242–4, 245, 253, 274
Cheney ?, 82
Churchill, John, later Duke of Marlborough, 260, 362
Cibber, Colley, 137, 494n.26, 503n.35
Cibber, Theophilus, 523n.35
Cixous, Hélène, xxvi
Cleland, John, 349
Cleveland, see Palmer
Clifton, Sir William, 380, 410, 542n.9
Cockacoeske, Queen of the Pamunkeys, 430–1
Codrington, Christopher, Colonel, 33
Coffee houses, 121, 123, 136, 183, 365, 371–2, 376
Coleman, Edward, 242, 245, 255, 256
Colepeper, Barbara (formerly Lady Strangford, née Sidney), 6, 19
Colepeper, Sir Thomas, 6, 18–19, 81, 82, 100, 125, 476n.16
Colepeper, Sir Thomas, of Preston Hall, 210, 368
Colepeper, Colonel Thomas, 5–9, 18–20, 22–3, 24, 37, 54, 121, 124, 205, 250, 299, 410, 439, 453; 'Adversaria', 5, 18, 22, 55, 63, 67, 100

Collier, Jeremy, 490n.15
Columbus, Christopher, 51, 55, 60
Comedy, 153, 166, 172, 181, 215, 217, 221, 226, 227, 230, 261, 280, 283, 292, 374, 378
Commedia dell'arte, 164, 353, 532n.39
Comparison between the Two Stages, 145, 159, 279, 510n.32
Congreve, William, 521n.12
Constant Nymph, The, 192
Convents, 26–7, 234, 247, 249, 409
Cooke, Sarah, 344, 378
Cooper, Anthony Ashley, Earl of Shaftesbury, 228–30, 245, 250, 259, 279–80, 287, 289, 295, 302, 308, 309, 356, 401, 500n.2
Cooper, John, 161, 264, 336, 522n.25
Copernicus, 414
Corneille, Pierre de, 126, 127, 139, 188, 303, 486n.13
Corney, William, 78–80, 85, 87–8, 89, 94, 95–9, 100, 103–4, 105, 108, 112, 116, 196, 479n.7
Cottington, Elizabeth, 134
Cotton, Charles, 470n.7, 510n.24
Counterfeit Bridegroom, The, 216, 265
Cowley, Abraham, 3, 126, 205, 210, 301, 330, 360, 398, 427, 448, 449, 451; pindarics, 154–5, 445; translation, 262; Of Plants, 424–6
Creech, Thomas, 298–301, 304, 321, 322, 325, 329–30, 335–6, 340, 414, 447; Lucretius, 322, 330, 336
Crisp, Henry, 340, 524n.49
Crocker, Edward, 459n.42
Cromwell, Lady Elizabeth, 285
Cromwell, Oliver, 1, 3, 10, 11, 21, 23, 24, 37, 46, 72, 82, 116, 156, 284, 285, 367
Cromwell, Richard, 284
Cross-dressing, see transvestism
Crowne, John, 288, 373, 500n.7, 540n.11

Curll, Edward, 162
Currer, Elizabeth (Betty), 215, 237, 252, 283, 292, 434
Cutpurse, Mal, 122
Cyrano de Bergerac, Savinien, 513n.15

Dangerfield, Thomas, 255, 256–8, 402, 438, 451, 508n.6 and 10, 509n.11
D'Aulnoy, Marie, 520n.22
Davenant, Charles, 191
Davenant, Lady Mary, 136, 162
Davenant, Sir William, 125, 136, 152, 162, 205, 374, 411
Davies, Moll, 137–8
Defoe, Daniel, xxvi, 9, 527n.21
Denham, George, 7, 15, 457n.18
Dering, Charles, 461n.7
Dering, Sir Edward, 461n.7
Desborough, John, 284
Descartes, René, 413, 415
Desire, 144, 155, 190, 198, 215; sexual, xxvii, 12, 163, 168, 178, 181, 182–3, 186, 194, 201–2, 207, 215, 223, 248, 263, 269, 289–91, 300, 312–13, 316–18, 324, 333, 343, 348, 349, 350–1, 401
Desmarches, Sir Antony, 85–7, 90–1
de Witt, Cornelius, 73
de Witt, John, 73, 77–9, 80, 90, 98, 107, 115, 165
Dillon, Wentworth, Earl of Roscommon, 330, 413
Donne, John, 154
Dorset Garden, 164, 168, 205, 288, 305, 452, 497n.26
Douglas, James, Earl of Drumlangrig, 417, 441
Dover, Treaty of, 128, 235, 245
Downes, John, 137, 144, 145, 251
Downing, Sir George, 482n.9
Draghi, Giovanni, 292
Dring, Thomas, 151, 503n.30

Drummond, John, Earl of Melfort, 417, 439, 441
Dryden, John, xxv, xxx, 3, 8, 69, 129, 132, 135, 137, 138, 141, 151, 156, 164, 166, 169, 170, 171, 172–3, 189, 192, 197, 205, 207, 213, 228, 230, 237, 238, 247, 274, 279, 294, 297, 298, 299, 300, 302, 304, 317, 353, 354, 355, 356, 359, 360, 373, 379, 382, 384, 413, 427, 429, 436, 439, 443, 450, 488nn.12 and 18, 508n.27, 509n.22, 521n.12, 543n.19; *Absalom and Achitophel*, 259, 280, 436, 539n.4; *Aesop's Fables*, 335; *All for Love*, 222, 520n.18; *Amboyna*, 75, 165, 502n.25; *Annus Mirabilis*, 114; *Astrea Redux*, 3, 436, 498n.31; *Aulus Persius Flaccus*, 467n.3; *Conquest of Granada*, 150, 152, 153, 187; *Don Sebastian*, 509n.22; *Duke of Guise* (with Davenant), 310, 516n.10; *Evening's Love*, 135, 492n.15, 501n.17; *Hind and Panther*, 445; *Indian Queen* (with R. Howard), 69; 'Life of Lucian,' xxiii; *Marriage A-la-Mode* 156, 165, 168, 199; *Oedipus*, 237; *Ovid's Epistles*, 262–4, 345, 382, 424; Prologue and epilogue to *Widdow Ranter*, 428, 540n.17; Prologue to Jonson's *Silent Woman*, 172–3; *Religio Laici*, 299; *Sir Martin Mar-all*, 486n.10; *Spanish Friar*, 487n.1, 513n.9; *State of Innocence*, 528n.33; *The Tempest* (with Davenant), 257; *Threnodia Augustalis*, 355–6, 359, 538n.22; *Troilus and Cressida*, 246, 253; *Tyrannick Love*, 502n.25; *Wild Gallant*, 334, 530n.22; and Behn, 8, 156, 261–4, 323, 335–6, 366, 372; and payment, 145–6, 333; and plagiarism, 188; and *The*

Rehearsal, 151; as professional, 158–9, 199; conversion, 381–3, 443

Duke's Company, 125–6, 136–7, 143, 164, 169, 192, 214, 215, 217, 224, 251, 262, 265, 305, 368, 491n.21, 495n.29

Du Moulin, Peter, 479n.5

Dunton, John, 325

d'Urfée, Honoré, 45

D'Urfey, Thomas, 508n.27, 513n.13

Dutch War, First, 72

Dutch War, Second, 72–5, 114, 117, 120, 128, 408

Dutch War, Third, 75, 165, 218

Eachard, John, 171

Education, of boys, 14, 15, 171, 233, 258–9, 300–1, 377; of girls, 14–17, 172, 236, 258–9, 298, 300–1

Elizabeth I, 8, 379; Accession Day, 240, 250, 260, 271, 278, 308, 424, 512n.54

Enys, Renatus, 39, 49

Ephelia, 210–11, 304, 507n.12, 513n.12

Epicurus, 198

Esquemelin, 53

Etherege, Sir George, 132, 164, 166, 197, 201, 202, 211, 213, 276, 373, 494n.27, 524n.49, 533n.47; *Man of Mode*, 199, 214, 218; *She Wou'd if She Cou'd*, 130, 137, 158

Evelyn, John, 2, 52, 87, 114, 127, 129, 151, 160, 270, 271, 302, 308, 325, 354, 381, 425, 442, 447, 481n.25, 527n.18

Evelyn, Mary, 172

Everest, Ezekiel, 310

Exclusion, Exclusion Crisis, exclusionists, 228, 229, 278, 290, 292, 302, 338, 367, 404, 405, 515n.33

Fane, Francis, 191

Farce, 153–4, 189, 247, 274, 277, 281, 287, 353, 378, 379, 407, 438.

Farmer, Thomas, 237

Female body, 126, 129, 142–3, 200, 202, 204, 283, 312, 317, 343, 348, 448, 507n.17

Female Tatler, 142

Femininity, 12, 132, 140, 167, 197, 232, 239, 305, 318, 371, 493n.21

Feminism, xxvi, xxvii, 197, 236, 286, 301, 371

Ferguson, Robert, 309, 361, 529n.3, 536n.9

Ferrar, Richard, 393

Fielding, Henry, xxv

Filmer, Sir Robert, 218

Finch, Anne, Countess of Winchilsea, 5, 330, 528n.35

Fire of London, 96, 103, 114, 160, 234, 241, 362, 367, 388, 484n.35, 493n.19

Fitzroy, Anne, later Countess of Sussex, 245, 465n.11, 500n.2

Fitzroy, Henry, Duke of Grafton, 288, 296, 450

Flatman, Thomas, 204, 511n.39

Fleetwood, Charles, 284

Fletcher, John, 132, 379; *Love's Cure*, 59; *Philaster*, 176, 326, 333, 334–5

Fontenelle, Bernard de, 303, 412–15

Foxe's *Book of Martyrs*, 240

Frecheville, Anne, 396

Furley, Benjamin, 98, 101, 112

Galileo Galilei, 377

Gascoigne, Sir Bernard, 112, 118, 270, 304, 517n.32, 532n.41

Gibbons, Grinling, 392

Gildon, Charles, 4, 33, 145, 170, 324–5, 326, 328, 347, 412, 435, 491n.5, 494n.28, 495n.30, 510n.32

Gloucester, Henry, Duke of, 20, 24, 304

Godfrey, Sir Edmund Bury, 17, 241–2, 244, 272, 404

Godwin, Francis, 532n.42

Golden Age, 13, 45, 53, 55, 206–9, 223, 261, 266, 312, 331–2, 357, 432

Good Old Cause, 9, 11, 284, 293

Gorges, Ferdinando, 62

Gould, Robert, 209, 211–12, 294, 298, 301, 302, 336, 355, 365, 375, 376, 378, 427, 450

Granville, George, later Lord Lansdowne, 304, 342, 398, 409, 439, 443, 522n.22

Greenhill, John, 205–6, 293

Grey, Ford, Lord, 256, 278–80, 307–10, 314, 315, 316, 320, 361, 362, 363, 401–6 passim, 436, 440, 526n.18

Grey, Lady Mary, 307, 315

Gwyn, Nell, 2, 128, 130, 137, 150, 191, 195, 205, 215, 227, 243, 252–3, 253–4, 279, 288, 409–10, 448, 518n.32

Hall, Constance, 70

Halsall, Major James, 82, 83, 88–98 passim, 100, 102, 103, 104

Hamilton, Anthony, 123

Harley, Sir Robert, 43, 44, 45, 46, 51, 61, 62, 77, 80, 82, 114

Harris, Henry, 136, 164

Head, Richard, 466n.17

Henrietta Maria, 126, 140, 194, 455n.6, 476n.9

Herbert, George, 12

Hesiod, 207

Higden, Henry, 335, 383–4, 413

Hill, Joseph, 94, 101

Hobbes, Thomas, Hobbism, 172, 198–9, 207, 217, 218, 280, 299, 300, 316, 385, 415, 416, 496n.14

Holmes, Sir Robert, 91; Holmes's Bonfire, 91, 115, 479n.5

Holt, R., 366, 392

Homosexuality, 148, 156, 162, 163, 175, 176–7, 197, 203, 241, 320, 326, 344, 489n.5, 507n.18

Horace, 329, 357, 425, 445

Howard, Edward, 18, 135, 138, 141, 145, 151, 153–5, 165, 170, 172, 295, 384

Howard family, 18, 135

Howard, Henry, 6th Duke of Norfolk, 292

Howard, Henry, Earl of Arundel, later 7th Duke of Norfolk, 18, 119, 271, 292, 325, 355, 357, 366, 379, 441

Howard, James, 500n.4

Howard, John, 86, 447

Howard, Lady Mary, 24

Howard, Mary, Duchess of Norfolk, 357, 366, 527n.18

Howard, Moll, 325, 366

Howard, Robert, 69, 500n.4, 502n.22

Howard, Thomas, Earl of Berkshire, 29

Howard, William, Viscount Stafford, 18, 87, 89, 90, 94, 107, 112, 242, 256, 340, 447; trial and death, 270–3, 292, 294, 302, 309, 360, 406, 451

Howe, John Grubham, 345

Hoyle, John, 161, 198, 276, 298, 299–300, 319, 329, 331, 402, 453–4, 505n.18; character, 163; homosexuality, 163, 203, 320, 352; relationship with Behn, 175–86, 191–2, 195, 214, 223, 226, 264–5, 275, 312, 313, 314, 326, 387, 388

Hutchinson, John, 466n.26

Hutchinson, Lucy, 467n.26, 517n.19

Hyde, Anne, later Duchess of York, 141, 247, 476n.9

Hyde, Edward, Earl of Clarendon, 12, 25, 26, 39, 140, 196, 375, 476n.9

Hyde, Laurence, later Earl of Rochester, 39, 374–5, 417, 465n.4

Impotence, premature ejaculation, 156, 165, 177, 200–1, 202–3, 207, 217, 220, 232, 275, 283, 319, 368, 372
Incest, 118, 166, 167, 259, 308, 320, 331
Indentured servants, 47, 56, 58
Islam, 187–8

Jacobitism, 441, 443
Jamaica, 34, 398, 470n.9
James, Duke of York, later James II, 1, 25, 26, 72, 73, 149, 160, 205, 218, 228, 230, 247, 256, 273, 289, 308–9, 320, 321, 337, 476n.9; and Behn, 140, 226, 258, 274, 315, 355–9, 379, 380, 392, 431, 436–8, 439–40, 482n.7; and Catholicism, 186, 227–8, 240, 374, 375, 381, 515n.33; and Popish Plot, 242, 261; as king, 254–9, 361–4, 366, 376, 405–11 passim, 416–24 passim, 426, 429, 435–41 passim, 442–50 passim; Exclusion, 278
James I, 19, 29, 56, 149, 311
James Francis Edward, Prince of Wales, 418, 419, 421, 439, 445
Jeffreys, George, Judge, 308, 363–4, 416, 441
Jenkins, George, 393, 540n.17
Jenkins, Sir Leoline, 310, 536n.6
Jennings, Mrs, 141
Jesuits, 111, 229, 240–1, 248, 252, 265, 417
Jevon, Thomas, 224, 265, 371, 378, 490n.14
Johnson, ?, Aphra's brother, 6, 39, 54, 71, 82, 90, 93, 97, 100, 115, 145

Johnson, Bartholomew (or father), 7–8, 10, 11, 31–2, 33–4, 39, 459n.35
Johnson, Elizabeth née Denham (or mother), 5, 7, 8, 10, 39, 100, 116, 145, 266, 457n.17
Johnson, Frances, 5, 6, 39, 64
Johnson, George, 7
Johnson, Dr Samuel, 253, 288, 503n.34
Jonson, Ben, 19, 125, 132, 135–6, 153–4, 156, 170, 171, 172, 231, 274, 285, 287, 378–9, 486n.7, 487n.28; The Alchemist, 19, 285; Every Man in His Humour, 485n.6; Volpone, xxviii, 276, 277, 379, 504n.8
Julian, Robert, 345, 365, 366, 421
Juvenal, 383, 384

Keats, John, 454
Kendrick, Daniel, 539n.32
Kepler, Johann, 377
Kérouaille, Louise de, later Duchess of Portsmouth, 128, 237, 243, 252, 262, 274, 279, 302, 354, 518n.32
Killigrew, Anne, 336, 528n.35, 539n.32
Killigrew, Charles, 372
Killigrew, Henry, 197
Killigrew, Thomas, 24–5, 26, 68, 69, 75, 79, 80–1, 85, 218, 304–5; and Behn, 24, 75, 79, 81, 82, 96, 97, 100, 102, 104, 116–17, 117, 118, 136, 138, 156, 196, 217–20, 225, 276, 304; Parson's Wedding, 156; Thomaso, 26, 68, 69, 167–8, 217–21, 225, 226, 238, 274–5, 404, 486n.13
Kingdon, Lemuel, 364
King's Company, 68, 69, 125, 137, 155, 156, 305, 344, 485n.3, 494n.29

Kirkman, Francis, 15–16, 492n.16, 527n.18
Knatchbull, Mary, 26, 106

La Calprenède, Gauthier de, 13, 20, 51, 53, 56, 236, 259, 303, 310, 311; *Cassandra*, 13, 56, 68, 108; *Cleopatra*, 13, 59
Lacy, John, 457n.15
Lambert, Frances, 285, 286
Lambert, John, 284, 285
Langbaine, Gerard, 148, 188, 226, 292, 492n.16, 495n.30, 510n.32, 536n.3
Language, 61, 218, 222–3, 227, 234, 235, 246–7, 251, 285, 290, 295, 347, 357, 394, 413, 426, 430, 432, 436, 445, 505n.19
La Rochefoucauld, François, Duke of, 385–7, 391
Law, 9, 45, 93, 157, 175, 190, 199, 245, 251, 286, 328, 363, 424, 430, 433
Lazarillo, 311
Lee, Mary, later Lady Slingsby, 137, 142, 191, 251, 296
Lee, Nathaniel, 127, 145, 186–7, 189, 200, 203, 205, 211, 213, 231, 237, 280, 291–2, 310, 333, 441, 521n.12; *Caesar Borgia*, 230; *Lucius Junius Brutus*, 230, 246; *Nero*, 187, 188; *Princess of Cleves*, 267; *Rival Queens*, 326
Leigh, Anthony, 237, 283, 292, 371, 372, 378
Lely, Sir Peter, 204–5, 293, 504n.10
Lesbianism, 215, 245, 283, 395–7
L'Estrange, Sir Roger, 246, 258, 270, 272, 279, 280, 295, 311, 360, 366, 367, 372, 424, 441, 445, 458n.31, 512n.54, 534n.12, 536n.7
Locke, John, 243
Locke, Matthew, 188
London, 114, 121–2, 160–1, 215, 227, 234, 304, 328–9, 367, 383, 428, 438
London Gazette, 108–9, 111, 115, 307, 309, 367, 403, 491n.1
Long, Jane, 169
Louis XIV, 72, 128, 227, 241, 242, 243, 245, 302, 407, 449
Love, 385–6; platonic, 126, 127, 194, 317, 498n.40; romantic, 223, 275, 317, 343, 349, 370, 393, 431, 437
Lowestoft, Battle of, 72, 426
Lucretius, 172, 198, 298–301, 317, 330, 332, 385, 415, 452, 496n.14
Ludlow, Edmund, 467n.28, 477n.17
Lusts Dominion, 188, 189, 190, 193
Luttrell, Narcissus, 241–2, 266, 297, 321, 423, 447

Magnes, James, 147, 151, 158, 215, 238, 311, 503n.30
Maitland, John, first Duke of Lauderdale, 438–9
Maitland, Richard, Lord, 435, 438–9, 441
Makin, Bathsua, 459n.45
Mancini, Hortense, Duchess of Mazarine, 199, 237, 239, 240, 242, 243, 245, 252, 311, 354, 366, 398, 409, 410, 411, 419, 428, 448, 465n.11
Mancini, Maria, 311
Manley, Delarivier, xxvi, 359–60, 517n.13
Marlowe, Christopher, 14, 492n.16
Marriage, 63–4, 144, 148, 165, 181, 184, 185, 216, 223, 233–4, 249, 275, 283, 291, 346, 352, 453, 507n.17, 511n.34; arranged and forced marriage, 65, 139, 232, 275, 328, 512n.1, 526n.10
Marston, John, 247, 265
Marten, George, 30, 32, 33, 46, 58, 61, 115, 127, 304, 346, 347, 402, 428, 432, 435, 521n.14

Marten, Henry, 30, 46, 60–1, 346

Marvell, Andrew, 3, 73, 129, 197, 240, 482n.7

Mary of Modena, 247, 256, 304, 336, 356, 357–9, 362, 407, 417–18, 434, 437, 438, 440, 444, 448, 450

Mary, Princess of Orange, later Mary II, 242, 247, 360, 366, 418, 442, 447–50, 452, 503n.35

Masks, masking, xxiv, 132, 145, 204, 276, 319, 324

Massinger, Philip, 289

Meal-Tub Plot, 256–7, 274

Medburne, Matthew, 224, 231, 244

Medway, assault on, 102, 115, 482n.12

'Memoirs', xxx, 4, 5, 31–2, 33, 35, 63, 107–8, 112, 113, 117, 200, 395, 397, 450, 475n.1, 476n.13, 479n.5, 522n.22, 526n.12

Mercurius Anglicanus, 514n.25

Mercurius Politicus, 24

Middleton, Thomas, 216, 289

Milton, John, xxvii, 3, 12, 213, 415, 485n.50, 488n.12, 543n.19

Molière, Jean-Baptiste Poquelin, known as, 164, 188, 451, 490n.16; *Georges Dandin*, 486n.13; *Les Femmes savantes*, 233, 303; *Les Fourberies de Scapin*, 513n.15; *Le Malade imaginaire*, 231, 234, 235, 238; *Les Précieuses ridicules*, 282, 303, 514n.19

Monarchy, kingship, divine, right, xxvii, 3, 60–1, 149, 185, 187, 190, 207, 209, 218, 229, 243, 246, 261, 280, 315–16, 358, 441, 446, 509n.15; and aristocrats, 337–8, 355, 385, 405, 411, 417, 439; and poets, 337, 379–80, 385, 426

Monck, George, first Duke of Albemarle, 2, 71, 82, 91, 115, 285, 287, 304, 398

Monck, Christopher, second Duke of Albemarle, 362, 398, 519n.9

Money, 81–106 passim, 113, 117, 129, 159, 163, 170, 171, 208, 232, 254, 283, 333, 335, 353, 358, 360, 364–5, 367, 374, 399, 443

Monmouth, James Scott, Duke of, 60, 228–9, 261, 274, 279, 302, 307, 355–6, 377, 401, 436; Behn's attitude, 264, 280, 284, 297, 310, 315, 316, 333, 403–8, 431; and plots, 256, 259, 309; as Protestant, 243, 389; Rebellion, 361–3, 364, 379, 398, 404–5, 439, 540n.9

Montagu, Lady Mary Wortley, 376

Montaigne, Michel de, 53, 57

More, Sir Thomas, 154

Morland, Carola (*née* Harsnett), 123–5, 177

Morland, Sir Samuel, 6, 36, 124, 392, 528n.34

Morrice, Roger, 184, 308, 519n.6

Mountfort, William, 363, 371, 378, 503n.35

Murry, Anne, 25, 476n.11

Muses Mercury, 155, 158, 483n.32, 484n.38

Newton, Isaac, 415

Nipho, Hieronymus, 91, 96, 99, 102

Nokes, James, 137, 142, 150, 237, 251, 283, 292, 371

North, Mary, 13

Oates, Titus, 241–2, 244, 246, 251, 271, 279, 283, 360, 389, 406

Observator, 424

Ogniate, Sir Mark, 81–2, 86, 304, 481n.25

Old men, 64, 233, 283, 290, 328, 368–70, 389, 515n.37

Oosterlincx, Casper, 109–10
Osborne, Dorothy, 1, 13, 19, 146, 504n.11
Otway, Thomas, xxv, 189, 191, 193, 194, 195, 197, 205, 207, 213, 226, 227, 230, 231, 237, 246, 262, 280, 302, 333–5, 353, 506n.28, 516n.38, 533n.47; and Behn, 143–4, 145, 168, 190, 191, 235, 239, 252, 259–60, 291–2, 293–4, 323, 369, 372, 496n.11; death, 333–4; *Alcibiades*, 194; *Caius Marius*, 259; *Cheats of Scapin*, 513n.15; *Don Carlos*, 144, 191, 494nn.22 and 24; *Friendship in Fashion*, 506n.28; *Orphan*, 145, 265; *Souldiers Fortune*, 239, 501n.19, 506n.28; *Venice Preserv'd*, 145, 252, 289, 500n.5, 514n.20
Oudart, Nicholas, 78, 79, 80, 85, 94, 482n.9
Ovid, 202, 263, 264, 297, 424; *Amores*, 200; *Heroides*, 262, 311; *Metamorphoses*, 207

Pack, Simon, 224
Paisible, James, 198, 409
Palmer, Barbara, later Countess of Castlemaine and Duchess of Cleveland, 2, 70, 128, 243, 245, 260, 288, 294, 311, 354, 499n.2, 527n.22
Pastoral vision, Arcadia, 20, 52, 56, 139, 177, 197, 201, 202, 203–4, 206, 207, 210, 261, 267, 311, 318, 331, 385, 395, 396, 398, 445, 493n.21
Patrons, patronage, 59, 127, 148, 158, 197, 218, 226, 246, 252, 254, 261, 292, 320, 337, 357, 359, 367, 379, 381, 398, 411, 412, 419, 445, 447, 533n.50
Payne, Henry Nevil, 127, 218, 235, 244, 255–7, 381, 402, 423, 424, 438, 441, 450, 524n.49

Penshurst, 19, 20, 21, 22, 25, 86, 126, 302, 398
Pepys, Samuel, 2, 3, 17, 67, 69, 70, 75, 115, 116, 130, 131, 132, 135, 198, 320, 322, 485n.3, 487n.28
Percival, Susannah, later Mountfort and Verbruggen, 363, 371, 378
Perversity, 275, 289, 343, 350, 531n.25
Peters, Hugh, 285
Pett, Sir Peter, 483n.22
Philips, Edward, 213
Philips, Katherine (Orinda), 10, 14, 126–7, 134, 146, 152, 157, 194, 204, 210, 213, 262, 270, 336, 427, 455n.6, 461n.7, 462n.15, 471n.22, 485n.50, 498n.40
Phillipott, Thomas, 388–9
Piers, Mr, 83, 84, 93, 100, 106, 120
Pindar, 154–5, 262
Pix, Mary, 487n.21
Plagiarism, 188, 193, 219, 226, 237, 238, 247, 336, 495n.30, 503n.30
Plague, 69–71, 82, 86, 103, 114
Playford, Henry, 528n.31
Player, Sir Thomas, 289
Plutarch's *Lives*, 14, 49, 50, 178, 432
Polwhele, Elizabeth, 134
Pope, Alexander, xxv, 208, 497n.27
Popish Plot, 240–7, 252, 255, 256, 270, 272, 274, 278, 282, 285, 287, 292, 305, 321, 359, 374, 376, 380, 387, 389, 403–4, 424, 429, 433, 436, 445
Powell, George, 518n.37
Powis, Lady, 257
Price, Emily, 192–3, 237, 365
Price, Joseph, 494n.27
Prince of Wales, *see* James Francis Edward
Prior, Matthew, 264, 299, 348–9, 393
Professionalism, writing as profession, 199, 239, 386

Propaganda, xxix, 231, 246, 260, 280, 288, 289, 292, 310, 332, 366, 381, 417, 418, 428, 429, 439, 443, 445, 446

Prostitutes prostitution, 173, 215, 220, 249, 275, 294–5, 370, 500n.8; male gigolos, 216, 222, 327, 369, 432, 507n.18

Puleston, Sir Roger, 410

Purcell, Henry, 175, 494n.26

Puritans and Dissenters, xxvi, 9, 11, 60, 62, 70, 74, 75, 77, 155, 163, 171, 187, 221, 234, 235, 250, 279, 286–9 passim

Quin, Ann, 236

Quinault, Philippe, 188

Quintana, Francisco de, 166

Rabble, mob, crowd, xxvii, 21, 61, 154, 187, 229, 230, 243–4, 246, 250, 259–60, 273, 274, 278, 285–6, 287, 292, 303, 333, 364, 371, 390, 505n.14

Race, xxiv, 57–8, 189

Radcliffe, Alexander, 264

Rake, libertine, 149, 164, 165, 168, 172, 186, 214, 216, 217, 218, 220, 222, 223, 227, 248, 268, 276, 290, 294, 305, 315, 319, 327, 351–2, 369, 374, 401, 432, 435; female rake, 233, 236, 248, 275, 290, 305, 346–52

Ralegh, Sir Walter, 55–6

Randolph, Thomas, 136

Rape, images of rape, 202, 203–4, 221, 224, 248, 287, 291, 319, 343, 515n.37, 526n.12

Ravenscroft, Edward, 127, 153, 165, 168, 170, 184, 213, 231, 235, 237, 238, 246, 294, 353, 365, 368, 373, 506n.28; and Behn, 135, 138, 141, 142, 166, 169, 170, 173–4, 191, 192, 197, 200, 215–17, 281, 291–2; *Careless*

Lovers, 164, 501n.17, 503n.27; *Citizen Turn'd Gentleman*, 164; *London Cuckolds*, 326, 506n.28, 516n.5; *Scaramouch*, 513n.15

Reeves, Mrs, 156

Reresby, Sir John, 524n.45

Restoration, xxv, 1, 4, 12, 287, 321, 375, 432, 453

Richardson, Samuel, xxv

Richelieu, Cardinal, Armand Jean du Plessis, 375

Riley, John, 293

Rochester, *see* Wilmot, John

Roman Catholicism, Roman Catholics; and Behn, 12, 27, 106, 109, 240, 247, 250, 256, 382, 416, 419–20; and James, 187, 227–8, 374, 381, 382, 407; fear of Catholics, anti-Catholicism, anti-popery, 165, 200, 228, 234, 235–6, 240–3, 245, 250–1, 255, 265, 272, 278, 367

Romance, romantic fiction, 12, 13, 32, 49, 52, 53, 55, 56, 59, 61, 87, 114, 138, 140, 178, 192, 236, 343, 350, 430–1, 437, 506n.25, 511n.36

Ross, Alexander, 188

Royal Society, 6, 68, 86, 171, 198

Rump Parliament, 11, 284, 287

Rupert, Prince, 25, 91

Russell, William, Lord, 309, 518n.35, 529n.7, 534n.6

Rye House, Plot, 308–9, 330, 362, 406

Sackville, Charles, Earl of Dorset, 153, 197, 352, 366–7, 488n.15

Saint-Évremond, Charles de Saint-Denis de, 199, 277, 398, 409

Salter, Thomas, 459n.38

Sanford, Robert, 36–7, 39, 43, 46, 466n.19

Sappho, 182, 262, 263, 264, 268, 294, 296, 336, 426, 427, 453, 506n.25

Saunders, Charles, 516n.1

Savile, George, Marquis of Halifax, xxv, 71

Savile, Henry, 173, 197–8, 227, 245, 363, 495n.3, 509n.22

Scandal, 129, 130, 196, 245, 307, 320, 391, 403

Scarron, Paul, 325, 326, 327

Scharf, Sir George, 497n.28

Scot, Thomas, 24, 25, 37, 38, 88–9, 284

Scot, William, 37–9, 45–6, 69, 75, 77–84, 85–99, 101–3, 104, 105, 107, 111–12, 113, 114, 127, 185, 209, 284, 304, 346, 361, 402, 438, 502n.19, 526n.12

Scots, 11, 280, 285, 378, 416–17, 438–9, 441

Scrope, Sir Car, 264, 500n.3

Scudéry, Madeleine de, 13, 146, 236, 303, 488n.12, 513n.16

Sealed Knot, 23, 24, 25

Sedgemoor, Battle of, 362, 398, 401, 402

Sedley, Sir Charles, 122, 197, 485n.48, 495n.30, 542n.11

Seneca, 385, 386, 451

Sequestrated lands, 10, 250

Settle, Elkanah, 127, 129, 187, 189, 191, 213, 230, 240, 278, 364, 383, 488n.4, 493n.21, 496n.11

Sévigné, Madame de, 447

Sex, Sexuality, xxvii, 94, 129, 149, 190–1, 200, 202, 205–6, 207–8, 223, 231, 232, 238–9, 259, 263, 276, 286, 290, 291, 300, 305–6, 312, 317–19, 331–2, 343, 391, 453

Shadwell, Thomas, 127, 132, 135, 170, 171, 172, 213, 224, 230, 240, 264, 274, 281, 293, 295, 304, 360, 384, 413, 446, 450, 496n.11, 507n.14; moral purpose and rules, 171, 172; *Humorists*, 141; *Lancashire-Witches*, 288, 524n.45; *Libertine*, 218, 518n.38; *Psyche*, 188; *Sullen Lovers*, 135, 172; *True Widow*, 237, 485n.45

Shaftesbury, *see* Cooper, Anthony

Shakespeare, William, xxv, 124, 126, 133, 136, 143, 170, 379, 432; *Hamlet*, 170, 190; *Henry IV*, 229; *King Lear*, 447; *Macbeth*, 190, 493n.21; *Measure for Measure*, 347; *Much Ado about Nothing*, 137, 496n.20; *Othello*, 32, 56, 65, 129, 138, 465n.11; *Richard III*, 487n.28; *Romeo and Juliet*, 246; *Tempest*, 145, 223, 378; *Titus Andronicus*, 246, 492n.16; *Troilus and Cressida*, 246; history plays, 486n.6

Sheffield, John, Earl of Mulgrave, 158, 198, 200, 210–11, 267, 268, 297, 333, 336, 344, 345, 366, 373, 386

Ships, *Abraham's Sacrifice*, 66, 119, 475n.23; *Castel Rodrigo*, 86; *King David*, 63, 66–7, 74, 475n.23; *Orange*, 426; *Royal Charles*, 1–2, 115; *Yarmouth*, 23

Shirley, James, 531n.22

Sidney, Algernon, 20, 21, 23, 24, 94, 98, 103, 124, 126, 190, 198, 227, 243, 308, 309

Sidney, Dorothy, later Countess of Sunderland, 19–20, 302

Sidney, Henry, 198, 439

Sidney, Isabella, later Lady Strangford, 22, 23, 24

Sidney, Mary, later Mary Herbert, Countess of Pembroke, 19, 455n.6

Sidney Philip, Lord L'Isle, later third Earl of Leicester, 20–2, 59, 180–1, 198, 509n.22

Sidney, Robert, first Earl of Leicester, 18

Sidney, Robert, second Earl of
  Leicester, 18, 19, 20, 23
Sidney, Sir Philip, 19
Sidneys, 302, 304, 336, 528n.36
Slaves, slavery, 51, 54, 56–9, 65, 435,
  437
Smith, William, 137, 224
Somerset, Charles, Marquis of
  Worcester, 379
Somerset, Henry, Duke of Beaufort,
  379
Somerton, John, 365, 366
Southerne, Thomas, *Oroonoko*, 347,
  469n.22, 500n.9; *Sir Anthony Love*,
  434
Spectator, 379
Spencer, Robert, Earl of Sunderland,
  19, 197, 253, 271, 302, 309, 310,
  338, 356, 361, 362, 363, 366,
  375, 403–7, 410, 416, 417, 419,
  436, 439, 440, 539n.5
Spencer, Robert, 407
Spenser, Edmund, 331
Spies, spying, espionage, xxvii,
  xxviii, 11, 25, 28, 29, 36–9, 72,
  74, 75, 77, 80, 82, 85, 87–90, 96,
  103, 107, 127, 132, 142, 165,
  196, 218, 245, 367, 404, 425,
  463n.23, 479n.3, 480n.16,
  518n.32
Spinoza, Baruch 415
Sprat, Thomas, 151, 171, 301, 304,
  417, 425, 446, 450, 453
Stafford, *see* Howard, William
Steele, Richard, 503n.32
Stevenson, Matthew, 345
Stewart, Frances, 149
Strangford, Philip, Lord, 19, 20,
  22–4, 25, 59, 81, 121, 410
Surinam, xxix, 23, 29–62, 63, 65,
  67, 68, 69, 71, 75, 77, 78, 80, 81,
  82, 83, 88, 94, 95, 107, 109,
  114–15, 118, 147, 165, 187, 346,
  375–6, 428, 431, 435, 437, 438
Swift, Jonathan, 155

Sydserff, Thomas, 136, 171
Sykes, William, 77, 78, 79

Tallemant, Abbé Paul, 303, 330–1,
  332, 354, 394
Tarquini, Francisco de, 109–11, 307
Tasso, Torquato, 207, 208, 359, 396
Tate, Nahum, 230, 262, 299, 304,
  358, 393, 424, 503n.25, 539n.32
Tatham, John, 284, 285, 286, 287,
  365
Taylor, Elizabeth, 210, 364, 368,
  397, 525n.49
Taylor, Randal, 319–20, 383,
  534n.12
Taylor, Sir Thomas, 210
Temple, Sands, 93–4
Theatre, 2, 68, 71, 72, 121–33, 158,
  164, 168, 173, 192, 194–7
  passim, 204, 217, 234, 245, 252,
  255, 261, 274, 279, 280, 377–8,
  452; and politics, 171, 230–1,
  240, 310
Thomas, Elizabeth, 8, 14
Thurloe, John, 24, 25, 34, 37, 124,
  284–5
Tillotson, John, 348
Tonge, Israel, 241
Tonson, Jacob and Richard, 238,
  254, 261, 262, 264, 292, 298,
  304, 328, 329, 330, 334–6, 337,
  364, 382, 383, 441, 516n.38
Tories, xxvi, 229, 243, 279, 281,
  288, 295, 310, 360, 367, 505n.19
Tragedy, 148–9, 186, 187, 188, 190,
  191, 231, 247, 407, 429, 432,
  494n.26
Tragicomedy, 59, 138, 139, 150,
  151, 152, 164, 165, 215, 217,
  265, 305, 429, 432, 500n.9
Translation, 262–4, 298, 330–1,
  384–5, 410, 412–13, 424
Transvestism, cross-dressing, 149,
  156, 167, 192, 223, 239, 311,
  323, 351, 374, 395, 433–4

Trefry, John, 32, 44, 45, 58, 435
Trotter, Catherine, xxvi, 487n.21
True Protestant Mercury, 296
Trye, Mary, 70, 517n.18
Tryon, Thomas, 43, 55, 57, 266, 451, 465n.7, 511n.36
Tunbridge Wells, 123, 124, 125, 279, 325, 397
Turner, William, 308, 310, 315, 361

Underhill, Cave, 137, 224, 251, 378
United Company, 305, 344, 368, 431
Unities, theatrical rules, 150–1, 170–3, 230, 274

Van Mechelen, Anna Louisa, 109–11
Van Mechelen, Maria Theresa, 109–11
Van Schurman, Anna Maria, 477n.5
Vaughan, Henry, 12
Venereal disease, 53, 70, 76, 169, 173, 194, 201, 227, 270, 302, 349, 376
Venice, 64, 118–19, 502n.21
Vernatty, Nick, 162
Vernattys, 462n.15
Verney, Sir Ralph, 459n.45
Verney, Tom, 41
Verrio, Antonio, 392
Vertue, George, 516n.2
Villiers, George, second Duke of Buckingham, 227; *Rehearsal*, 151–2, 166, 167, 170, 188, 189, 490n.13, 540n.17
Vincent, Samuel, 485n.45
Virgil, 225, 357, 425, 498n.31
Virginia, 30, 41, 42, 429–30, 432–3, 435
Voyeurs, voyeurism, 130, 163, 176, 203–4, 221, 291, 343, 350

Wakeman, Sir George, 242, 244
Waller, Abigail, 399

Waller, Edmund, 3, 19, 20, 154, 268–9, 293, 339, 398, 399–400, 425
Warcup, Captain, 192, 365
Ward, Mary, 26
Ward, Sir Patience, 234, 289, 376, 536n.9
Warner, Father John, 257, 258
Warren, George, 32, 51–2, 53, 58–9
Welldon, Madam, 397, 434
Wentworth, Lady Henrietta, 297, 309, 361, 362, 363
Wentworth, Thomas, Earl of Strafford, 9
Westminster Abbey, 125, 368, 450, 453
Weston, Peter, 392
Wet-nurse, 8–9
Wharton, Anne, 268–70, 301, 339, 344, 345, 447, 510n.24, 520n.20, 525n.49
Whigs, 229, 230, 234, 243, 246, 251, 260, 274, 278, 279, 281–2, 284, 285, 288, 289, 293, 295, 310, 366–7, 425–6, 505n.19, 515n.32, 536n.2
Whitelocke, Bulstrode, 352
Whores Rhetoric, 526n.15
Wilkins, George, 214
William, Prince of Orange, later William III, 72–3, 78, 89, 98, 166, 228, 242, 302, 357, 360, 361, 366, 367, 405, 418, 420, 426, 439, 440, 441, 442–52 passim
Williamson, Joseph, 83, 103, 116, 120
Willoughby, Francis, Lord of Parham, 23, 24, 29–30, 31, 34, 35, 38, 39, 44, 45, 48, 54, 55, 56, 61, 62, 410, 431, 507n.10
Wilmot, Henry, Viscount, 196, 276
Wilmot, John, Earl of Rochester, xxv, 2, 21, 122, 129, 153, 173, 216, 243, 252, 262, 290, 298, 302, 304, 329, 345, 366, 382,

385, 386, 400, 443, 452, 509n.22; 525n.49; 'Fair Cloris in a Piggsty', 202; 'Lais Junior', 528n.22; 'Letter from Artemiza', 211; 'Platonick Lady', 194; 'Ramble in Saint James's Park', 331; 'Signior Dildo', 247; 'Tunbridge Wells', 123; *Valentinian*, 343–5, 368; and Barry 195; and Behn 196–212 passim, 298, 301, 377, 447, 452, 519n.10; as fictional rake, 218, 222, 351; death, 266–9, 274, 276–7, 283, 381

Wilson, John, 326–7

Wolseley, Robert, 267, 345, 368, 496n.9

Woman Turn'd Bully, The, 491n.19

Wood, Anthony à, 1, 57, 128, 523n.35

Woolf, Virginia, xxv–xxvi, 453

Woolley, Hannah, 14, 455n.6

Worcester, Battle of, 3, 11, 196, 217, 276, 425

Wren, Sir Christopher, 160

Wright, James, 231, 262, 335

Wright or Write, John, 478n.13, 479n.20

Wright Thomas, 205, 504n.10

Wroth, Lady Mary, 19, 146, 311

Wycherley, William, xxv, xxix, 127, 131, 132, 158, 168, 197, 203, 207, 213, 231, 294–5, 324, 333, 488n.12, 533n.47; *Country Wife*, 132, 203, 217, 320, 368, 485n.45; *Plain-Dealer*, 35, 347

Wythens, Francis, Judge, 210, 364, 368